GEOGRAPHERS OF THE
ANCIENT GREEK WORLD

VOLUME II

Ancient Greek geographical writing is represented not just by the surviving works of the well-known authors Strabo, Pausanias, and Ptolemy, but also by many other texts dating from the Archaic to the Late Antique period. Most of these texts are, however, hard for non-specialists to find, and many have never been translated into English. The present volumes, the work of an international team of experts, present the most important thirty-six texts in new, accurate translations. In addition, there are explanatory notes and authoritative introductions to each text, which offer a new understanding of the individual writings and demonstrate their importance: no longer marginal, but in the mainstream of Greek literature and science. The book includes twenty-eight newly drawn maps, images of the medieval manuscripts in which most of these works survive, and a full Introduction providing a comprehensive survey of the field of Greek and Roman geography.

GRAHAM SHIPLEY is Professor of Ancient History at the University of Leicester, and the author of many studies of Greek history that bring together written sources, archaeology, and landscape, such as *The Greek World after Alexander* (2000) and *The Early Hellenistic Peloponnese* (Cambridge, 2018). In 2019, he was elected a member of the international association GAHIA, 'Geography & Historiography in Antiquity'.

About the Author

D. Graham J. Shipley, a native of Northumberland and alumnus of the Royal Grammar School, Newcastle upon Tyne, is Professor of Ancient History and a Public Orator at the University of Leicester, where he was a founding member of the highly regarded School of Archaeology & Ancient History. He is the author of many studies of Greek history that bring together written sources, archaeology, and landscape.

A Literae Humaniores graduate of Wadham College, Oxford, he held research fellowships at Wadham and Balliol, and then at St Catharine's College, Cambridge, before his appointment at Leicester. He has been Visiting Fellow at the British School at Athens, and has held a British Academy–Leverhulme Senior Research Fellowship. He is a fellow of the Royal Astronomical Society, the Royal Geographical Society, the Royal Historical Society, and the Society of Antiquaries of London, as well as a Senior Fellow of the Higher Education Academy. He holds a D.Phil. from Oxford, and was awarded a D.Litt. by examination in 2020. His interest in local identities led him to inaugurate the successful campaign for a registered flag for the historic county of Leicestershire.

A former Chair of the Council of University Classical Departments and member of the UK Education Honours Committee, he currently serves on the Oxford Classical Texts Committee of Oxford University Press. In 2019 he was elected a member of GAHIA, the Asociación Internacional 'Geography & Historiography in Antiquity'.

Selected works by the same author

A History of Samos 800–188 BC
(Clarendon Press, 1987; revised Modern Greek edition, 2021)

(edited with J. W. Rich)
War and Society in the Greek World and *War and Society in the Roman World*
(Routledge, 1993)

(edited with J. B. Salmon)
Human Landscapes in Classical Antiquity: Environment and Culture
(Routledge, 1996)

(with W. G. Cavanagh, J. H. Crouwel, R. W. V. Catling)
Continuity and Change in a Greek Rural Landscape: The Laconia Survey
(British School at Athens, 1996–2002)

The Greek World after Alexander: 323–30 BC
(Routledge, 2000; Spanish translation, 2001; Modern Greek edition, 2012)

(edited with J. Vanderspoel, D. J. Mattingly, L. Foxhall)
The Cambridge Dictionary of Classical Civilization
(Cambridge University Press, 2006)

Pseudo-Skylax's Periplous: The Circumnavigation of the Inhabited World
(Exeter University Press, 2011; 2nd edition, Liverpool University Press, 2019)

The Early Hellenistic Peloponnese, 338–197 BC: Politics, Economies, and Networks
(Cambridge University Press, 2018)

GEOGRAPHERS OF THE ANCIENT GREEK WORLD

Selected Texts in Translation
VOLUME II

BY

D. Graham J. Shipley

*Professor of Ancient History at the
University of Leicester*

with contributions by

Colin E. P. Adams	Daniela Dueck	Ralph Morley
David C. Braund	James W. Ermatinger	Oliver Nicholson
Stanley M. Burstein	Robert C. Helmer	Thomas Russell
J. Brian Campbell	Yumna Z. N. Khan	Richard J. A. Talbert
Katherine J. Clarke	Aidan Liddle	

Completed with the assistance of

Ancient World Mapping Center, University of North Carolina, Chapel Hill
Arts & Humanities Research Council
Loeb Classical Library Foundation

CAMBRIDGE
UNIVERSITY PRESS

Shaftesbury Road, Cambridge CB2 8EA, United Kingdom

One Liberty Plaza, 20th Floor, New York, NY 10006, USA

477 Williamstown Road, Port Melbourne, VIC 3207, Australia

314–321, 3rd Floor, Plot 3, Splendor Forum, Jasola District Centre, New Delhi – 110025, India

103 Penang Road, #05-06/07, Visioncrest Commercial, Singapore 238467

Cambridge University Press is part of Cambridge University Press & Assessment, a department of the University of Cambridge.

We share the University's mission to contribute to society through the pursuit of education, learning and research at the highest international levels of excellence.

www.cambridge.org
Information on this title: www.cambridge.org/9781009174893

DOI: 10.1017/9781009184236

© Cambridge University Press & Assessment 2024

This publication is in copyright. Subject to statutory exception and to the provisions of relevant collective licensing agreements, no reproduction of any part may take place without the written permission of Cambridge University Press & Assessment.

First published 2024

Printed in the United Kingdom by CPI Group Ltd, Croydon CR0 4YY

A catalogue record for this publication is available from the British Library.

Library of Congress Cataloging-in-Publication Data
NAMES: Shipley, D. Graham J., editor.
TITLE: Geographers of the ancient Greek world : selected texts in translation / [compiled] by D. Graham J. Shipley.
DESCRIPTION: Cambridge, United Kingdom ; New York, NY : Cambridge University Press, 2024. | Includes bibliographical references and index.
IDENTIFIERS: LCCN 2023052633 | ISBN 9781009174893 (set ; hardback) | ISBN 9781009194204 (v. 1 ; hardback) | ISBN 9781009184229 (v. 2 ; hardback) | ISBN 9781009174930 (set ; ebook)
SUBJECTS: LCSH: Geography, Ancient – Sources.
CLASSIFICATION: LCC G87.A1 G28 2024 | DDC 910.92/238–dc23/eng/20231220
LC record available at https://lccn.loc.gov/2023052633

ISBN – 2 volume set 978-1-009-17489-3 Hardback
ISBN – Volume I 978-1-009-19420-4 Hardback
ISBN – Volume II 978-1-009-18422-9 Hardback

Cambridge University Press & Assessment has no responsibility for the persistence or accuracy of URLs for external or third-party internet websites referred to in this publication and does not guarantee that any content on such websites is, or will remain, accurate or appropriate.

TO THE MEMORY OF
Yi-Fu Tuan, geographer
(1930–2022)

Κύπριδος οὗτος ὁ χῶρος, ἐπεὶ φίλον ἔπλετο τήνᾳ
    αἰὲν ἀπ' ἠπείρου λαμπρὸν ὁρῆν πέλαγος,
ὄφρα φίλον ναύτῃσι τελῇ πλόον· ἀμφὶ δὲ πόντος
    δειμαίνει λιπαρὸν δερκόμενος ξόανον.

Kypris' place is this, since it was her own joy ever
    to look from land at the shining open sea (*pelagos*)
and complete sailors' own journey for them. Around her
    the main (*pontos*) is fearful, beholding the bright carved statue.

> Anyte of Tegea (C3e),
> *Anthologia Graeca* 9. 144 (my translation)

Contents

VOLUME I

List of Figures	xiv
List of Maps	xv
List of Tables	xvi
Contributors	xvii
Preface	xxi
Glossary	xxv
Abbreviations	xxxii

Introduction: Greek Geography and Geographers *D. Graham J. Shipley*	1
I. Aims	1
II. What Is, and Was, Geography?	2
III. The Character of Ancient Geographical Writing	8
IV. Distance	26
V. Space and Cartography	30
VI. The Range of Ancient Geographical Writing	36
VII. Scope of the Volumes	57
VIII. Transmission	67
IX. Organization of the Volumes	73
X. The Translator's Art	74
XI. Selected Further Reading	79
Time-line *D. Graham J. Shipley*	86
Prologue: The Homeric Catalogue of Ships (*Iliad*, 2. 484–760)	
D. Graham J. Shipley	96
Introduction	96
Text	97

PART I: ARCHAIC PERIOD

1	**Aristeas of Prokonnesos** *David C. Braund*	109
	Introduction	109
	Texts	116
2	**Skylax of Karyanda** *D. Graham J. Shipley*	120
	Introduction	120
	Texts	122
3	**Hekataios of Miletos** *D. Graham J. Shipley*	127
	Introduction	127
	A. General Texts	130

B. *Histories* or *Genealogies* … 133
C. *Periegesis* (*Guided Tour*) or *Periodos ges* (*Circuit of the Earth*) … 136

PART II: CLASSICAL PERIOD

4 **Hanno of Carthage**   Richard J. A. Talbert and D. Graham J. Shipley … **149**
   Introduction … 149
   A. *Circumnavigation* (*Periplous*) … 151
   B. Other texts … 155
5 **Hippokrates of Kos (?), Airs, Waters, and Places**   D. Graham J. Shipley … **157**
   Introduction … 157
   Text … 159
6 **Eudoxos of Knidos**   D. Graham J. Shipley … **177**
   Introduction … 177
   Texts … 180
7 **Pseudo-Skylax**   D. Graham J. Shipley … **193**
   Introduction … 193
   A. *Periplous of the Inhabited World* … 198
   B. Other texts … 229
8 **Pytheas of Massalia**   D. Graham J. Shipley … **231**
   Introduction … 231
   Texts … 236

PART III: HELLENISTIC PERIOD

9 **Dikaiarchos of Messana**   D. Graham J. Shipley … **249**
   Introduction … 249
   Texts … 252
10 **Timosthenes of Rhodes**   D. Graham J. Shipley … **258**
   Introduction … 258
   Texts … 262
   Appendix: Aristotle, *Meteorologika*, 2. 6 … 271
11 **Herakleides Kritikos**   D. Graham J. Shipley … **275**
   Introduction … 275
   A. *On the Cities in Hellas* … 278
   B. Other Texts … 287
   Appendix: Anonymous Description of Piraeus (*BNJ* 369) … 288
12 **Eratosthenes of Kyrene**   D. Graham J. Shipley … **289**
   Introduction … 289
   Geographia or *Geographika* … 292
13 **Mnaseas of Patara**   Daniela Dueck … **360**
   Introduction … 360
   Periplous or *Periegesis* … 362
14 **Skymnos of Chios**   D. Graham J. Shipley … **370**
   Introduction … 370
   Periplous (*Circumnavigation*) … 371

15 Agatharchides of Knidos, *On the Erythraian Sea*   *Stanley M. Burstein*
    and *D. Graham J. Shipley*   **373**
    Introduction   373
    A. *On the Erythraian Sea*   378
    B. Other Texts   439
16 Hipparchos of Nikaia   *D. Graham J. Shipley*   **445**
    Introduction   445
    A. Testimonia   447
    B. *Against the Geography of Eratosthenes*   449
17 The *Nikomedean Periodos* ['Pseudo-Skymnos']   *D. Graham J. Shipley*   **466**
    Introduction   466
    A. Continuous Text   471
    B. Fragments   494
18 Artemidoros of Ephesos   *D. Graham J. Shipley*   **501**
    Introduction   501
    Text   510
    Appendix 1: The Artemidoros Papyrus   555
    Appendix 2: The 'Munich Fragment'   559
19 Poseidonios of Apameia   *Katherine J. Clarke*   **561**
    Introduction   561
    A. Principles and Practice of Geography   565
    B. Geology, etc.   582
    C. Hydrology, etc.   587
    D. Observed Geography   599
    E. From the *History*   603
    F. Other Historical Extracts   605
20 Dionysios son of Kalliphon   *D. Graham J. Shipley*   **612**
    Introduction   612
    Text   615
21 Menippos of Pergamon   *J. Brian Campbell*   **620**
    Introduction   620
    A. Markianos' *Epitome*   622
    B. Other Texts   627

VOLUME II

PART IV: ROMAN PERIOD

22 Juba II of Mauretania   *D. Graham J. Shipley*   **631**
    Introduction   631
    A. *On Assyria* (?)   634
    B. *Wanderings of Hanno*   634
    C. *Libyka*   634
    D. From *Libyka* or *On Arabia*   641
    E. *On Arabia*   642
    F. *On Euphorbion*   651

23 **Isidoros of Charax**   *Richard J. A. Talbert*   **653**
   Introduction   653
   A. *Stathmoi Parthikoi*   654
   B. Other Texts   660

24 **Pseudo-Aristotle, *On the Cosmos* (*De mundo*)**   *D. Graham J. Shipley*   **663**
   Introduction   663
   Text   666

25 **Pseudo-Arrian, *Circumnavigation of the Erythraian Sea***   *Colin E. P. Adams*   **684**
   Introduction   684
   Text   690

26 **Pseudo-Plutarch, *On the Names of Rivers and Mountains and the Things in Them***   *J. Brian Campbell*   **710**
   Introduction   710
   Text   717

27 **Arrian of Nikomedeia, *Circumnavigation of the Euxine***   *Aidan Liddle*   **740**
   Introduction   740
   Text   745

28 **Dionysios Periegetes**   *Yumna Z. N. Khan*   **760**
   Introduction   760
   Text   769

29 **Agathemeros son of Orthon**   *D. Graham J. Shipley*   **809**
   Introduction   809
   Text   811

30 **Dionysios of Byzantion**   *Oliver Nicholson and Thomas Russell*   **820**
   Introduction   820
   Text   825

31 **Pseudo-Hippolytos, *Stadiasmos* (*Stade Table* or *Circumnavigation of the Great Sea*)**   *James W. Ermatinger and Robert C. Helmer*   **853**
   Introduction   853
   Text   860

PART V: LATE ANTIQUE PERIOD

32 **Avienus (Avienius), *Ora maritima* (*The Sea Coast*)**   *Ralph Morley*   **889**
   Introduction   889
   Text   894

33 ***Expositio totius mundi et gentium* (*Account of the Whole World and its Peoples*) and Iunior Philosophus**   *Richard J. A. Talbert*   **921**
   Introduction   921
   Text   926

34 **Markianos of Herakleia**   *D. Graham J. Shipley*   **939**
   Introduction   939
   A. *Epitome of the Geographoumena of Artemidoros*   943
   B. *Periplous of the Outer Ocean*   943

C. Preface to the *Epitome of Menippos*	980
D. Preface to Pseudo-Skylax	983
E. *Distances from Rome to the Notable Cities of the Inhabited World* (?)	983
F. Other sources	984

35 *Hypotypōsis tēs geōgraphias en epitomēi* (*Outline of Geography in Summary*)   D. Graham J. Shipley   **985**

Introduction	985
Text	988

36 Pseudo-Arrian, *Circumnavigation of the Euxine* D. Graham J. Shipley   **1000**

Introduction	1000
Text	1004
Appendix: *Anametresis of the Oikoumene and Perimetros of the Pontos*	1025

Sources of Extracts (Selected)	1028
Works Cited	1038
Concordances	1095
I. Concordance of Extracts by Chapter	1096
II. Concordance of Extracts by Source Author	1132
Selective Index D. Graham J. Shipley	1167

PART FOUR
ROMAN PERIOD

∼

(C. 30 BC–AD 300)

The whole of the land inhabited by you—narrowed at the corners, broader at the sides—is something of a small island embraced by that sea which you people in these lands call the Atlantic, the Great Sea, the Ocean: yet you can see, for all its great name, how small it is.

Surely your name, or that of any of our people, has not succeeded in going from these very lands we cultivate and know, to transcend either this Caucasus that you observe, or swim across that Ganges over there? Who, in the rest of the distant places under the rising or setting sun, or in the parts belonging to the north or south wind, shall hear your name? Cut them off and you shall observe in what a tight space your glory would like to be broadcast.

Cicero, *De re publica*, 6. 21–2 (my translation)

22
JUBA II OF MAURETANIA
(ACTIVE C.27 BC–AD 23/4)

Selection of geographical testimonia and fragments

D. Graham J. Shipley

To the memory of
Simon J. W. Squires, classicist
(1944–2023)

INTRODUCTION

Juba II of Mauretania (c.47 BC–AD 23/4) is the only author in these volumes—apart from Hanno (Chapter 4), if that text be genuine—whose first language was probably neither Greek nor Latin.[1] He was, however, both a Roman citizen and steeped in the Greek culture of the hellenistic kingdoms ruled by Macedonian dynasties during the last three centuries BC. He may have been personally acquainted with the historian and geographer Strabo;[2] at the least, he must have been aware of him.[3] Juba's wide-ranging intellectual accomplishments include richly detailed accounts of the physical geography of North Africa and Arabia, including copious new observational data on hydrology, geology, and natural history which—as we are now learning from new research on the use of his work by Arabic and, via them, Latin scholars—were highly influential on the development of the natural sciences.

Juba (in Latin *Iuba*; in Greek *Iobas*) was the direct descendant of Numidian kings, including the Romans' enemy-turned-ally Masinissa (r. 202–148 BC) and their vanquished enemy Jugurtha (r. 118–105). He married Kleopatra Selene II, daughter of Kleopatra VII by Mark Antony; she was the last acknowledged descendant of the Ptolemaic dynasty until she and Juba had a son, significantly named Ptolemaios. After supporting Octavian, the future Augustus, at the battle of Actium (31) which ended the Roman civil wars, Juba, still a teenager, was made king of Numidia. When that was made into a Roman province he received as his kingdom Mauretania,[4] lying further west and corresponding to northern Morocco and northern Algeria today, and running from the area of the strait of Gibraltar up to the province of Africa Proconsularis, including Carthage, to the east. The royal couple had their capital at Iol, which they renamed

---

[1] For a general outline, see Dueck 2012, 45.
[2] Roller 2003, 69; Dueck 2000, 88, however, implies that they did not coincide at Rome. Strabo 17. 3. 7, C828, says that Juba has recently died.
[3] The point is discussed by Draycott 2010, 215–16.
[4] The modern state of Mauritania (*sic*) lies further S and W than ancient Mauretania.

Caesarea (mod. *Cherchel*). An effective client king of Rome, he and his queen fostered Greek culture and architecture and promoted Mauretania's international trade, including the luxury commodities that feature often in the extracts below.[5]

Juba's considerable literary output, likewise, can be seen as part of the attempt to integrate the kingdom into Roman culture at the highest level through royal patronage, and to add lustre to its reputation. He deserves to be remembered as one of the greatest scholars of his age. As well as early books on Roman culture and history, a study of the Greek and Latin languages, a probable autobiography, and histories of painting and the theatre—fragments of the last are a valuable source for ancient comedy and music—he ventured into geography with a study of the voyage of Hanno of Carthage (2 below; Chapter 4 above) and important researches into Mesopotamia, the Arabian peninsula, and his own homeland in the wider context of Libyē (North Africa) as a whole.[6] His late works *Libyka* (3-16, possibly 17-19) and *On Arabia*[7] (20-40, possibly 17-19) were drawn upon (but rarely cited) by Strabo and frequently cited by Pliny the Elder as well as later authors, though the geographical fragments in the present chapter are nearly all from Pliny (and probably do not exhaust the material on Arabia which Pliny took from Juba without continually naming him).[8] They were extensively based not only on expeditions that Juba commissioned but also on his own travels to Egypt and western Asia. He also relied extensively on earlier writers such as Agatharchides (Chapter 15 above) and Carthaginian authors to whom he had direct access, as well as eye-witness reports which allowed him to produce, among other things, the first detailed *periplous* of the Ocean coast of the Arabian peninsula (possibly in Latin). His most extended 'fragments' (20-3) are lengthy paraphrases by Pliny of parts of that work.

His conception of geography was a wide one—indeed, as with other writers in these volumes it is slightly misleading to call him a 'geographer' when his interests in these fragments embrace the origins of names (1, 8, 14, 16, 19, 21-3, 30, 38), geology and mineralogy (13-14, 18, 33-9), ethnography (6 §176, 20, 22-3), flora (2-3, 8, 12, 24-7, 29-30) including medicinal plants (31, 41-3), and fauna (4, 9-11, 15-17, 19, 32) including the now extinct North African elephant (9, 15).[9]

Unsurprisingly, his scholarly interests included the geography of North-West Africa, such as the Atlas mountains and the Nile (3-5, 16, 23, 41 §78); he was not alone in placing its source in that region.[10] He is particularly keen to note islands (3-8,

---

[5] On J., see Roller 2003; Roller 2008 (with English trans.); and generally Zucker 2008; Dueck 2012, 45; Roller 2015, 157-61.

[6] Roller 2003, 261-4, identifies ten works by J. and lists all known 'fragments' (in a commendably wide sense of the term).

[7] Its exact title is uncertain; possibly *Peri Arabias* (*On Arabia*), *Arabika* (*Arabian Matters*), *Peri Arabōn* (*On the Arabians*), or even *De Arabia* in Latin.

[8] A point made by Roller 2008b commenting on various 'fragments'.

[9] On the identity of the African elephant, see Charles 2020.

[10] Silberman 1988, 318-19, on Mela 3. 96, says the view went back to the early writer Promathos of Samos and to Hdt. 2. 32-4. Roller 2003, 193-6, finds that the idea that the Nile rose here made sense; he offers several possible rivers, including the Ziz in Morocco (*c*.32° 16' N, 4° 30' W). For the evolution of this tradition, see also Merrills 2017, 44-8.

11–12, 20, 22–4, 26, 34, 36, 38–9), important for traders, including those of the eastern Atlantic such as the Canaries (3 §15, 8), which he did not, of course, discover—they, or the clouds over them, are visible from the mainland—but on whose names and fauna he reported in detail, though he did not necessarily visit them. He may not have devised their collective name, derived from the species of dogs (*canes* in Latin) found there, but he is at least responsible for its transmission, as he is for the name of the plant family *Euphorbiaceae*, the spurges (3, 41–3).

Juba is praised by Avienus in a striking passage of the *Ora maritima* (Chapter 32 below, lines 273–83) for his power, his pride in the Roman connexion, and his devotion to literature. His influence on other writers, notably Pliny (see the many extracts below), Plutarch, and Aelian—especially for matters other than geography—extended into the Middle Ages: medieval Latin authors (some still unpublished) cite him often, both from Pliny and from an Arabic version, for information on an astonishing range of plants and animals.[11] The fact that most of those citations refer to species not attested in the fragments below will allow us to extend the range of Juba's interests with some confidence.[12]

The passages below follow Roller's edition of testimonia and fragments,[13] from which a selection has been re-translated. This is the first collection of extracts representing Juba's geographical work as such.

SELECTED FURTHER READING

Domínguez Monedero, A. J. (2017), 'Rex Iuba, monarca e intellectual helenistico, y la Hispania de Augusto', *Gerión*, 35: 61–85.

Draelants, I. M. C. (2000), 'Le dossier des livres sur les animaux et les plantes de Iorach: tradition occidentale et orientale', in I. M. C. Draelants (ed.), *Occident et Proche-Orient: contacts scientifiques au temps des Croisades* (Turnhout), 191–276.

Roller, D. W. (2003), *The World of Juba II and Kleopatra Selene: Royal Scholarship on Rome's African Frontier*. London.

*—— (2018), 'Juba II of Mauretania (275)', in *BNJ*².

Zucker, A. (2008), 'Iouba II of Mauretania, C. Iulius (ca 20 BCE–24 CE)', *Encyclopedia of Ancient Natural Scientists*, 441–2. [Fuller than most *EANS* entries on geographers.]

---

[11] Sometimes under the name Iorach, a modification of 'Iobas'; see esp. the revelatory work of Draelants 2000; pp. 230–76 catalogue citations of Iorach, principally by Arnoldus Saxo, *De floribus rerum naturalium* (c.1225–60); see nn. on 4, 8–9, 17, 27, 29, and 40 below. The identification of Iorach with J. was suggested, but not published, by H. Prell in 1946 (Draelants 2000, 192 n. 2; 231).

[12] To name only some of the more easily identified: (*plants, trees*) cedar, cypress, fig, mandragora, olive, plane, rose, vine; (*animals*) ant, antelope, bear, beaver, camel, crocodile, deer, dormouse, dragon, fox, hedgehog, horned serpent, hyena, ibex, lion, lizard, newt, panther, rhinoceros, salamander, scorpion, *seps* (a venomous snake), snake, tiger, viper, water-serpent, weasel, wolf; (*birds*) bee-eater, crane, crow, diver, eagle, kingfisher, kite (?), owl, partridge, peacock, pelican, quail, sparrow, swan, turtle-dove, vulture, plus the legendary phoenix; (*sea-creatures*) crab, dolphin, mullet, murena, ray, sea-monster, sea-serpent, whale; (*spices and perfumes*) balsam, cinnamon, nard. All from Draelants 2000, 234–75.

[13] Roller 2008b.

A. ON ASSYRIA (?)

1 Pliny, *Natural History*, 6. xxx. 124: *The navigable Euphrates*
Nearchus and Onesicritus record that one can sail on the Euphrates to Babylon from the Persian sea for 412 miles.[14] Those who wrote later, however, (*say it is*) 440 to Seleucia; Juba (*says that*) from Babylon to Charace (*i.e. Characene*) (*is*) 175½.

B. WANDERINGS OF HANNO

2 Athenaios 3. 25, 83a–c: *The citron fruit*
There is much investigation into this . . . as to whether there is mention of it among the old (*writers*). Aemilianus said that Iobas (*Juba*), king of the Maurousians, a very learned man, when mentioning the *kitrion* in his compositions *On Libyē*, stated that it was a Hesperic apple among the Libyans, from whom Herakles brought to Hellas the apples that are called golden on account of their appearance. . . . Looking at them, Demokritos said, 'if Iobas says any of these things, say farewell to his Libyan books and even his *Wanderings of Hanno*; but I say this name does not exist among the old (*writers*), though the fact that the thing is said by Theophrastos in his *History of Plants* compels me to hear his observations about *kitria*'.[15]

C. LIBYKA

3 Pliny, *Natural History*, 5. i. 14–16: *Forests of Mauretania*
(14) Suetonius Paulinus, whom we saw when he was consul (AD 66), is the first among Roman generals to have passed through the whole of (*Mt*) Atlas; he also went a number of miles beyond.[16] He has reported what others have about its height, and also that its roots were full of dense, tall forests of an unknown kind of tree, which was notable for its altitude and its shiny appearance, free of knots. It had leaves similar to the cypress, apart from the heaviness of their scent; they were covered in a fine down from which, with the application of skill, garments could be made like those from the silk-worm. The summit was covered in deep snow even in summer.
(15) . . . The people who inhabited the adjacent forests, which were packed with elephants, wild animals, and all kinds of serpents, were called the Canarii (*Dog-people*) because they had a common diet with the said animal, including portions of

---

[14] On these explorers, see Introduction, §VI. 2. h.
[15] This may be the first literary reference to the citron (*kitron* or *kitrion*) under the name familiar today (Roller 2008b, commentary on F6). Theophrastos, *HP* 1. 13. 4 and 4. 4. 2, mentions the citron (cf. Loeb trans.) but calls it 'Median apple', *mēlea Mēdikē*.
[16] Reading *emensus, transgressus quoque* with Desanges. This took place after J.'s lifetime, so 'what others have' (next sentence) is the key phrase (Roller 2008b).

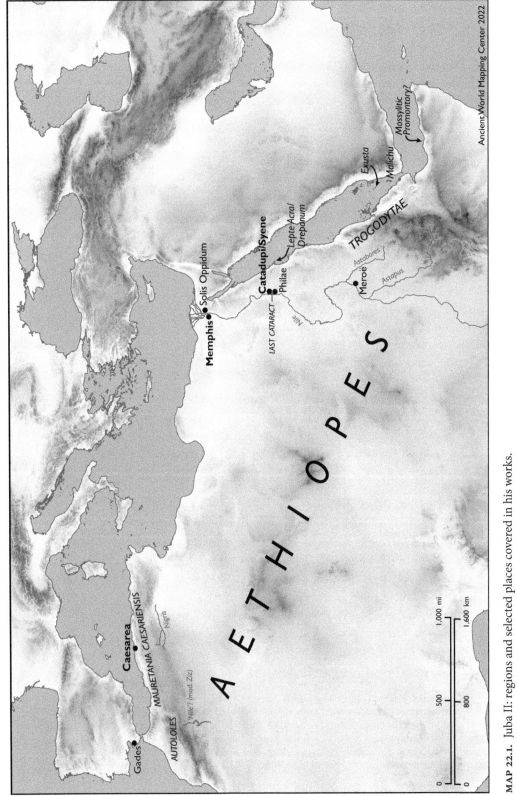

MAP 22.1. Juba II: regions and selected places covered in his works.

the innards of wild animals.[17] (16) It is agreed that the neighbouring nation (*gens*) is that of the Aethiopes whom they call the Perorsi. Juba, father of Ptolemy, who was the first to exercise command over both Mauretanias—more renowned for the distinction of his scholarship even than for his reign—has related similar things about the Atlas, as well as that there grows there a plant called Euphorbea, named after its finder, his physician.[18] He commends its milk-like juice with exceptional praise for (*bringing*) clarity to the vision and (*for its power*) against serpents and all poisons, and devotes a special book to it.

4 Pliny, *Natural History*, 5. x. 51–5: *Source and course of the Nile*

(51) The Nile—rising from unknown springs, for it travels through deserts and torrid places over the unmeasurable distance of its length, and has been searched for only by unarmed rumour without the wars that have revealed all other lands—has its origin, as King Juba was able to ascertain, in a mountain of lower Mauretania not far from the Ocean, at first in a stagnant lake which they call Nilis. Fish are found there: the *alabetae*, *coracini*, and *siluri*. To furnish a proof (*that the Nile rises here*), a crocodile from this place, donated by him, is on show today at the shrine of Isis in Caesarea.[19] Furthermore, it has been noted that in proportion as the snows and rains have filled up Mauretania, so the Nile rises.

(52) Pouring forth from this lake, it scorns flowing through sandy or rough places, and conceals itself for a journey of some days. Soon it bursts forth at a larger lake in (*the territory of*) the nation (*gens*) of the Masaesyles, who belong to Mauretania Caesariensis, and it surveys, as it were, the gathering of humans, using the same proofs in the form of animals (*as before*). Once more, embraced by the sands of the desert, it hides again for twenty days as far as the nearest Aethiopes and, when it once more becomes aware of a human it leaps out in a fountain, very probably the one they have named Nigris.

(53) From this point it divides Africa from Aethiopia, and even though it does not immediately support people it is stocked with wild animals and monsters. It cuts through the middle of the Aethiopes, and is here given the additional name of Astapus (*Sobat*), which in the language of those nations (*gentes*) signifies 'water flowing forth from darkness'. It strews countless islands about, some of such vast size that, however great its speed, it still flies past them in a run of not less than five days. Round the most famous of these, Meroë, it is called Astabores in the left channel, that is, 'branch of water coming from darkness', but Astosapes on the right, which gives the meaning

---

[17] So Rackham and Desanges; alternatively, with Winkler, they consume dogs as well as wild animals.

[18] See nn. on 41–3.

[19] The former Iol, J.'s capital of Mauretania. On the search for the source of the Nile, and the ancient belief that it arose in NW Africa, see chapter introduction, and Introduction, §III. 3. k. Draycott 2010 argues that by consecrating a crocodile at Caesarea Juba and his Ptolemaic queen were imitating sacred crocodiles at the temple of Sobek in Egypt. Kleopatra Selene may have used a crocodile as her symbol on coins (Draycott 2012). Arnoldus Saxo (see chapter introduction) cites Iorach (Juba) on crocodiles; see Draelants 2000, 267 no. 7 (comparing Pliny 8. xxxvii. 89).

'side'. Nor is it (*again*) the Nile before it reunites all of itself with the waters once more in harmony.

(54) Here, though, it is still named Giris as it was before, but also over its whole course it was the Aegyptus for Homer, for others the Triton. Presently it collides with islands. Hastened on by so many incitements, and finally enclosed by mountains, it is nowhere more furious and is carried along by the hurrying waters to the place in (*the territory of*) the Aethiopes which is named Catadupi. (*Here,*) at the last cataract,[20] between rocks that continually obstruct it, it is believed not (*merely*) to flow but to dash with a mighty crash.[21] After that it is smooth, its waters tamed and its violence subdued, and it is rather tired by the (*long*) distance. It spills itself into the Egyptian sea by a fair number of mouths, but for several days, with great expansion, it spreads over the whole of Egypt and with its fertility it floods over the earth.

5 Pliny, *Natural History*, 5. x. 59: *The Nile's course in Egypt*
It (*the Nile*) begins to be under Egyptian jurisdiction where Aethiopia ends, at Syene. This is the name of a peninsula which has a circuit of 1,000 (*double*) paces (*1 mile*), where there is a fort on the Arabian side (*of the Nile*); opposite are the four islands of Philae, 600 (*miles*) from the division of the Nile, from which point on, as we have said, the area is called the Delta. This distance is given by Artemidorus, who says there are 250 towns in it; Juba (*gives*) 400 miles; Aristocreon[22] 750 from Elephantis to the sea.

6 Pliny, *Natural History*, 6. xxxiv. 175–xxxv. 179: *The Erythraian sea (western Indian Ocean)*
(175) After the Mossylitic promontory,[23] Juba makes the Atlantic sea begin, to which one can sail, past his own Mauretania, as far as Gades with the Corus (*north-westerly wind*). One must not fail to mention the entirety of his opinion at this point.

From the promontory of the Indians that is to be called Lepte Acra ('*Narrow Cape*' *in Greek*), or by others Drepanum (*Sickle*), he proposes that by a direct course past Exusta (*Burnt I.*)[24] to the islands of Malichu is 1,500 miles; from there to the place they call Scenei[25] 225 miles; and from there to the Adanu islands 150.[26] Thus it is 1,875 miles to the open sea (*apertum mare*).

(176) The others have all believed that no sailing is possible because of the sun's heat. In fact, trade voyages themselves are also attacked from the islands by the Arabs called Ascitae ('*Wineskin Men*' *in Greek*) because they cover pairs of oxhide flasks with rafts and pursue piracy using poisoned arrows.

---

[20] i.e. the First Cataract in modern parlance (the most northerly), at *Aswan* (anc. Syene).
[21] *non fluere . . . sed ruere.* Cf. the rhyme in **16**.
[22] Aristokreon (*BNJ* 667) is assumed to have been despatched by Ptolemy II to explore the Nile.
[23] As this cape, near the trading-place of Mosylon, is in the Horn of Africa (in mod. Somalia), J. is here claiming that the Atlantic extends all the way round Libyē to Arabia.
[24] Probably *Jabal al-Tair* in the S part of the (mod.) *Red Sea*, Brodersen.
[25] Or Skeneos, Brodersen; unidentified.   [26] Unidentified.

The same Juba records the nations of Trogodytae called Therothoae (*'Hunt-runners' in Greek*), who are named from their hunting—and are marvellously fast, like the Ichthyophagi (*Fish-eaters*) who can swim like sea creatures—(*and*) the Bangeni, Zangenae, Thalibae, Saxinae, Sirechae, Deramae, and Domazenes. (177) Indeed, he says that the people living on the Nile from Syene onwards are not nations of Aethiopes but of Arabs, as far as Meroë. Furthermore, (*he says*) Solis Oppidum (*Sun's Town, i.e. Heliopolis*), which we said was not far from Memphis in the region of Egypt, has Arab founders. There are those who detach the further bank from Aethiopia and attach it to Africa. Leaving to each (*reader*) the judgement about how to understand this, we shall set out the towns on each side, in the order in which they are recorded, beginning from Syene.

xxxv. (178) First, on the side towards Arabia, is the nation of the Catadupi . . . (*list of places*) . . . So Bion relates.[27] (179) Juba says otherwise: the fortified town of Megatichos (*'Great Fort' in Greek*), between Egypt and Aethiopia, which the Arabs have called Mirsion. Then Tacompsos, Aramus, Sesamus, Pidema, Muda, Corambis beside a spring of bitumen, Amodata, Prosda, Parenta, Mania, Tessata, Gallae, Zoton, Grau Come (*'Old Woman's Hair' in Greek*), Emeum, the Pidibotae, the Endondacometae, the Nomads who live in tents, Cistaepe, Magadale, Parva (*Little*) Primis, Nups, Direlis, Patinga, Breves (*Short Men*), Magasneos, Egasmala, Cramda, Denna, Cadeum, Athena, Nabatta, Alana, Macua, Scammos, Gora on its island, from there Abale, Androcalis, Sere, Mallos, and Agoce.[28]

7   Pliny, *Natural History*, 6. xxxvi. 201: *Islands off Mauretania*
Nor is there any more reliable report concerning the islands of Mauretania; it is only agreed that a few were found opposite the Autololes by Juba, in which he had established dyeing with Gaetulic purple.[29]

8   Pliny, *Natural History*, 6. xxxvii. 202–5: *The Fortunate Islands*
(202) Some would believe that beyond these (*islands*) lie the Fortunatae (*Fortunate*) islands and certain others.[30] Together with their number, the same Sebosus has ascertained their distances: he records that Iunonia is 750 miles from Gades, and that at the same distance westwards from it lie Pluvialia (*Rainy I.*) and Capraria (*Goat I.*); and that in Pluvialia there is no water other than from the rain. At 250 miles from these, the Fortunatae lie against the left hand of Mauretania towards the eighth hour by the

---

[27] Bion is perhaps another explorer under the early Ptolemies.

[28] The spelling of names follows Desanges.

[29] These purple-processing stations may be those on *Mogador* I. at *Essaouira* in Morocco, rather than those in the Canaries (for which see 8). On purple-processing in this region, and on J.'s involvement, see among other studies López Pardo and Mederos Martín 2008; Álvarez Delgado, Mederos Martín, and Escribano Cobo 2015; Mederos Martín and Escribano Cobo 2015.

[30] Here identified with the *Canary Is.*, the Fortunate Islands or Blessed Isles were a *topos* of ancient legend. J. was the first writer to describe them. This passage may lie behind a citation of 'Iuba' by David de Dinant (C12/C13) for the Insulae Beatorum (Isles of the Blest); see Draelants 2000, 234 at 'B'.

sun. They are called, (*first*) Invallis for its roundness,³¹ (*second*) Planasia from its (*level*) appearance; and the tallness of the trees attains 140 feet.

(203) Juba discovered this about the Fortunates: they also lie towards the south and by the sunset: 625 miles from the Purpurarii (*Islands*), that is, if one were to sail 250 beyond (*i.e. north of*) west and then 375 eastwards. The first (*he says*) is called Ombrios (*Rainy*) and has no traces of buildings; it has a pool in the mountains, and trees like fennel from which liquid is expressed: from the black ones bitter, from the paler ones pleasant to drink.

(204) The second island is named Iunonia. On it is only a small shrine built of stone. Not far from it is a smaller (*island*) of the same name; then Capraria, packed with great lizards. Within sight of these is Ninguaria, which received this name from the endless snow; a cloudy island.

(205) Very close to it is Canaria, so called from the multitude of dogs (*canes*) of enormous size, two of which were brought to Juba. (*He says*) traces of buildings are seen there. While all (*the islands*) are well supplied with fruits and with birds of all kinds, this last is also supplied with palm-groves that produce *caryotae* (*nut-shaped dates*), and with pine cones; there is also plenty of honey; even papyrus and the *silurus* (*catfish*) grow in the rivers. They (*the islands*) are infested with sea-monsters that are continually washed up and go rotten.

9   Pliny, *Natural History*, 8. iv. 7: *North African elephants*
They themselves (*the elephants*) know that the prize for which they are sought is only in their weapons, which Juba called horns but Herodotus, so much earlier, as well as common custom, more accurately call teeth.³²

10   Pliny, *Natural History*, 8. xlv. 107: *The mantichora*
The *mantichora* in Aethiopia, too, imitates the speech of men; the authority for this is Juba.³³

11   Pliny, *Natural History*, 10. lxi. 126–7: *The Diomedean birds*
(126) Nor shall I fail to mention the Diomedean birds.³⁴ Juba calls them *cataractae* (*divers*), and records that they have teeth and eyes of a fiery colour while the rest of them is white. These birds always have two leaders: one leads the procession, the other drives it (*from behind*). (*He says*) they excavate trenches with their beak, strew twigs over them and cover them with the earth they previously removed, and in these they rear their young. Each trench has double openings: the eastward by which they are to go out to feed, the westward by which they are to return. To empty their bowels they

---

³¹ Possibly we should read Nivalis, 'snowy' (Brodersen ad loc.).
³² J. is the main written source for the now extinct North African elephant (Roller 2008b, commentary). Cf. **15**. Arnoldus Saxo (see chapter introduction) cites Iorach (Juba) on elephants; see Draelants 2000, 242–3 no. 13 (comparing Pliny 8. xii. 34).
³³ If not a creature of fantasy, the *mantichora* may be based on a tiger (Roller 2008b).
³⁴ Arnoldus Saxo (see chapter introduction) cites Iorach (Juba) on a bird called the *dyameda*; see Draelants 2000, 257 no. 11.

always fly up and into the wind. (127) These birds are seen only in one place in all the world: in the island which we called notable for Diomedes' tomb and shrine, facing the shore of Apulia. They are similar to *fulicae* (*coots*). They harry barbarian visitors with their cry but fawn upon Greeks alone with admirable judgement, as if paying tribute in this way to the nation of Diomedes. His temple they wash clean and purify each day with their throat full (*of water*) and with wetted wings;[35] whence comes the story that Diomedes' companions were turned into the likeness of these birds.

12   Pliny, *Natural History,* **13. lii. 142:** *Corals on the Trogodytic islands*
Juba records that around the islands of the Trogodytae there is a shrub in the depths that is called Isis' Hair, similar to coral without the leaves; and that when it is cut off, its colour changes to black and it turns hard; when it falls, it is broken. (*He records*) another which is called Chariton Blepharon (*Graces' Eyelid*), efficacious in matters of love; women (*he says*) make bracelets and necklaces out of it. (*He says*) it realizes when it is being caught and turns as hard as horn, even blunting a blade of iron; but if the attack has caught it by surprise, it is transformed into stone.

13   Pliny, *Natural History,* **37. xviii. 69:** *Emeralds from Aithiopia*
After these (*sc. emeralds from Cyprus*), the Aethiopic are praised; they are twenty-five days' journey from Coptus, for which Juba is the authority. They are intensely green but not commonly pure or consistent in colour.

14   Pliny, *Natural History,* **37. xxxv. 114:** *Green stones from Aithiopia*
India produces these (*green*) stones and also *nilios*, which is inferior (*to chrysoprase*) by reason of its limited brightness, deceptive when one looks at it. Sudines[36] says it also occurs in the river Siberus in Attica, but is the colour of smoky, or sometimes of honey-coloured, topaz. Juba records that it is produced in Aethiopia on the banks of the river which we call the Nile and takes its name from that.

15   Philostratos, *Life of Apollonios* **2. 13:** *Elephants' tusks*
This Iobas (*Juba*) thinks that (*elephants'*) teeth are horns, from the fact that they grow from the place where the temples are and are in no way sharpened one upon the other but stay as they grew and do not fall out and regrow as teeth do. But I do not accept this account.[37]

---

[35] Cf. the similar story of Achilles' Isle in Arrian 21. 4. Juba was surely aware of the importance of the Homeric hero Diomedes for Greek cults in colonial settings (cf. Ps.-Skylax §16; *Nik.* 432–3; Artemidoros 73; Poseidonios 40; Dion. Peri. 483), and seized an opportunity of extending Homeric geography to his own domains.
[36] Possibly the author cited several times by Pliny, incl. at 18 below, for the qualities of various pearls including those from Mauretania. The stone is identified as the blue sapphire by Roller 2008b ad loc., citing Healy 1999, 268.
[37] Cf. **9**.

16 Ammianus Marcellinus 22. 15. 8: *Source and course of the Nile; its mouths*
But King Juba, relying on the text of Punic books,[38] declares that it (*the Nile*) rises from a particular mountain which is located in Mauretania and looks over the Ocean. This, he says, is proclaimed by the following indications: that similar fish, plants, and water-monsters (*to those in the Nile*) grow in its marshes.   (9) But the Nile, wandering across parts of Aethiopia, and after the variety of names with which several nations have endowed it as it travels the world has been discarded,[39] swelling (?) with the richest flood, comes to the cataracts—that is, rugged crags—from which it throws itself rather than flows.[40] For this reason necessity compelled the neighbouring Ati, their sense of hearing reduced by the continuous crashing, to change their home for quieter parts.

(10) Wandering more smoothly from there, it is discharged through seven mouths, all of which individually present the utility and appearance of continuous rivers, aided by no outside waters within Egypt. Besides the numerous rivers deviating from the originating channel and falling into its nearly comparable (*channels*), seven are navigable with waves forming in them. The old (*writers*) endowed them with the appellations set out below: Heracleotic, Sebennytic, Bolbitic, Pathmitic, Mendesian, Tanitic, and Pelusiac.

D. FROM *LIBYKA* OR *ON ARABIA*

17 Pliny, *Natural History*, 8. xiii. 35: *Giant snakes in Aithiopia*
Aethiopia gives birth to ones (*sc. snakes*) that are the equal of the Indian ones,[41] each 20 cubits in length. This only is surprising: why Juba believed they were crested. The Aethiopes among whom most of them are born are called Asachaei. They tell that in the coastal parts (*of their land*) groups of four and five of them, weaving themselves together after the manner of hurdles, set sail by raising up their heads and are borne by the waves to the better pastures of Arabia.

18 Pliny, *Natural History*, 9. lvi. 115: *Varieties of pearls*
In our sea they (*pearls*) used to be found more often around the Thracian Bosporos: small red ones in shells that they call *myës* ('mice' in Greek). But in Acarnania grows the one that is called the *pina*, by which it is evident that they do not grow in just one variety of shell: for Juba also records that the Arabian ones have a shell that is like an

---

[38] A vital element in building a picture of J.'s intellectual achievement: the proof that he used books in Punic language, perhaps preserved from the destruction of Carthage in 146.
[39] Several words in this sentence are uncertain.
[40] *ruit potius quam fluit*. Cf. the rhyme in 4 §54. Ammianus, however, includes information not found in the Pliny passage.
[41] The information about crested snakes has become tangled with Pliny's discussion of elephants in the preceding passage (Roller 2008b ad loc.). Cf. **19** for other giant snakes. Arnoldus Saxo (see chapter introduction) cites Iorach (Juba) for many kinds of snakes; see Draelants 2000, 268–75 *passim* (comparing Pliny 8. viii. 25; xli. 99; etc.).

incised comb, that it is hairy like a hedgehog, and that there is a singleton within the flesh, similar to a hailstone. Shells of this variety are not brought to us. And neither are the ones I praised found in Acarnania, the giant ones, rough and marble-coloured. Better ones (*are found*) around Actium, but these too are small; also in the coastal parts of Mauretania. Alexander Polyhistor and Sudines believe that they age and that their colour is dissipated.

19 Pliny, *Natural History*, 31. xv. 18: *Strange waters in Aithiopia*
Juba (*says that*) among the Trogodytae lies Lacus Insanus (*Crazy Lake*), so named from its noxious power. Thrice daily (*he says*) it turns bitter and salty, then sweet again. It swarms with serpents, each 20 cubits long.[42] The same author (*says that*) in Arabia a spring bursts forth with such force that no heavy object, if thrust in, is not spat out again.

E. ON ARABIA

20 Pliny, *Natural History*, 6. xxvi. 96–100: *The voyage of Onesikritos and Nearchos, as told by Juba*[43]
(96) But before we pursue these matters one at a time, it is fitting that those things should be disclosed which Onesicritus related after sailing in Alexander's fleet from India into the inland parts of Persis, which have very recently been narrated by Juba; and then that sea-route journey (*navigatio*) that was discovered in those years and is used today. The sea journey 'route description' (*navigatio*) by Onesicritus and Nearchus contains neither the names of the stations nor the distances. First, it is not made sufficiently clear where Xylinepolis (*Wooden City*), founded by Alexander,[44] from which they made their start, was located or which river it adjoins.

(97) The following things worthy of remembering are, however, related. The town of Arbis (*Hab?*), which was founded by Nearchus during the sea journey to the river Arbis and capable of accommodating ships; opposite it, an island 70 stades away. Alexandria (*Khandawari?*), founded by Leonnatus by order of Alexander, in the confines of this nation. Argenuos, with a salubrious harbour. The river Tonberus (*Hingol?*), which is navigable; around it the Pasirae (*Ormara?*).[45] Then the Ichthyophagi, over so lengthy a stretch that they sailed past them for a duration of 20 days. An island named Solis (*Island of the Sun*), the same being (*called*) Nympharum Cubile (*Nymphs' Bed*;

---

[42] Cf. the 20-cubit snakes (?) at **17**.

[43] J. does not appear to have used Nearchos' account directly, unlike Arrian in his much fuller *Indike*, §§20–43, but to have relied on that of Onesikritos (André and Filliozat 1980, 126).

[44] Somewhere in the area of the mouths of the Indus. See Roller 2008b ad loc. for this and the other identifications in this passage.

[45] We are passing the coast of Pakistan here.

Astalu?), ⟨always⟩ coloured red, on which there is no creature that does not die, for unknown reasons.

(98) The nation of the Ori. The river Hyctanis river in Carmania, which has harbours and is productive of gold. From this place on, they observed that the Septentriones (*Ursa Major*) had first become visible, nor could Arcturus be spotted every night, or for the whole night. (*Juba says*) the Achaemenidae had possessed it all the way from that point; and that veins of copper, iron, arsenic, and cinnabar were worked. Next is the promontory of Carmania from which the crossing to the opposite shore and the nation of the Macae in Arabia is 50 miles wide. Three islands, among which only Oracta (*Tavilah?*)[46] is settled and has water; (*it is*) 25 miles from the mainland.

(99) Next four islands in the gulf, opposite Persis; in the area of these, sea-hydras, each 20 cubits long, swam up and terrified the fleet. The island of Athotadrus; also the Gauratae, in which (*lives*) the nation of the Gyani. The river Hyperis in the middle of the Persian gulf, capable of accommodating cargo ships.[47] The river Sitioganus, by which Pasargadae is reached in 7 days' sailing. The navigable river Phristimus. An island without a name. The river Granis, which accommodates ships of middling size, flows through Susiane; its right bank is inhabited by the Mountain Dexi, who process bitumen. The river Zarotis, with an entrance that is difficult except for the skilful. Two small islands, and from there one sails shallow water similar to a marsh, but one gets through via particular channels.

(100) The mouth of the Euphrates. The lake which the Eulaeus and the Tigris form near Charace (*Charax*). Then via the Tigris[48] to Susa; there they found Alexander keeping a holiday in the seventh month since he had diverted from them at Patale, and the third month of their voyage. Such was the voyage of Alexander's fleet.

21 Pliny, *Natural History*, 6. xxxi. 136–41: *Topography and history of Characene in Arabia*

(136) The part of it (*Elymaïs*) that is particularly inaccessible is called Characene after the town in Arabia that marks the end of those kingdoms. We shall speak of it after first setting out the opinion of Marcus Agrippa.[49]

(137) For he has related that Media, Parthia, and Persis are demarcated on the east by the Indus, on the west by the Tigris, on the north by the Caucasian Taurus, and on the south by the Rubrum Mare,[50] and have a length of 1,320 miles and a breadth of 840; furthermore, that Mesopotamia proper is enclosed on the east by the Tigris, on the

---

[46] On the Straits of *Hormuz*, the entrance to the Arabian gulf.
[47] This section reveals the influence of J.'s commercial awareness, modifying the original data of Alexander's captains (Roller 2008b, ad loc.).
[48] i.e. Pasitigris (*Karun?*), a different river.
[49] An indication that Pliny had consulted the map or gazetteer of the Roman empire prepared by Agrippa: see Introduction, §V. 4.
[50] Lit. 'red sea', equivalent to 'Erythraian sea', i.e. NW Indian Ocean plus modern Red Sea.

west by the Euphrates, on the north by the Taurus, and on the south by the Persian sea, and is 800 miles in length and 360 in breadth.

(138) Charax is the innermost town in the Persian gulf;[51] from it the Arabia named Eudaemon (*Fortunate*) extends. It is a settlement on a manmade hill of 2 miles' breadth, between the Tigris on the right and the Eulaeus on the left, where they flow into one another. It was first founded by Alexander the Great, its settlers brought from the royal city of Durine which ceased to exist at that time. Leaving invalided soldiers there, he had given orders that it be called Alexandria, and had created a Pellaean district, (*named*) after his fatherland, reserved for Macedonians.

(139) The rivers captured this town. Later Antiochus (*III*), the fifth of the (*Seleukid*) kings, restored it and called it by his own name. When it was again destroyed, Spaosines son of Sagdodonacus, king of the neighbouring Arabs, whom Juba mistakenly records as a satrap of Antiochus,[52] restored it with ramparts opposite one another and gave it his own name, the adjacent area being fortified[53] for 6 miles' length and slightly less in width. Formerly it was 10 stades from the shore—the Porticus Vipsania[54] actually makes it a coastal place, though Juba relates 50 miles.

(140) But envoys from the Arabs, and our traders coming from there, assert that it is now 120 (*miles*) from the shore. Nor is there any place where the lands have progressed, borne on by rivers, in greater quantity or more swiftly. More amazing is that they are not beaten back by the surge of the sea, though it advances well beyond this point.

(141) It does not escape me that it was in this place that Isidorus[55] was born, the latest authority on the territory of the Earth, whom the divine Augustus had sent ahead to the East to research everything fully when his elder son was due to go to Armenia to manage the business with the Parthians and the Arabians.[56] Nor have I forgotten that, at the opening of this work, it was my view that each author is most diligent regarding his own territory. In this passage, however, my resolve is to follow the Roman forces and King Juba in the books he wrote to the same Gaius Caesar concerning the same Arabian expedition.

22 Pliny, *Natural History*, 6. xxxii. 149–56: *The coasts of the Arabian peninsula*
(149) It is Juba who records that beyond this[57] the sea voyage (*of Arabia*) on that side is unknown because of reefs, though he omits to mention the town of the Omani called

---

[51] J. produced the first full account of the entire coast of the Arabian peninsula, including the Ocean-facing shore (Roller 2008b, ad loc.). Charax (now in SE Iraq) was the starting-point of his circuit, and home city of Isidoros (Ch. 23 above), probably named at §141 below.

[52] In fact, Hyspaosines (the correct form of his name) was a client ruler under Antiochos IV (r. 175–164), seceding later (Roller 2008b, F 1).

[53] Or perhaps 'built up'.

[54] i.e. Agrippa's survey, displayed at Rome in a colonnade named after him.

[55] The MSS have 'Dionysius' here; Brodersen prints 'Isidorus'.

[56] Gaius Caesar's expedition began in AD 1; he died in AD 4 (Brodersen 1996, 225).

[57] J.'s circuit—probably not an eye-witness account—has reached the vicinity of Tylos (*Bahrain*); but many of the place-names appear to have been rendered unidentifiable by being turned into Latin and in the course of MS transmission (Roller 2008b, F 30–3).

Batrasaves, as well as Omana, which earlier writers made a notable harbour in Carmania; also Homna and Attana, which our businessmen say are the most renowned towns in the Persian sea. Past the river Canis, Juba says, is a mountain that looks as if it is burned; the nations of the Epimaranitae; not far beyond are the Ichthyophagi; an uninhabited island; the nations of the Bathymi; the Eblythaei mountains; the island of Omoemus; the harbour of Mochorbae; the islands of Etaxalos and Inchobriche; (150) the nation of the Cadaei; many islands without names, but also the renowned ones of Isura and Rhinnea, and one very close by on which there are stone pillars with unknown scripts; the harbour of Coboea; the uninhabited Bragae islands; the nation of the Taludaei; the region of Dabanegoris; Mount Orsa with a harbour; the bay of Duatas; many islands; Mt Tricoryphus (*Three Heads*); the region of Chardaleon; the islands of Solanades and Cachina, and those of the Ichthyophagi; then the Clari; the shore of Mamaeum, where there are gold mines; the region of Canauna; the nations of the Apitami and Casani; the island of Devade, the spring of Coralis; the Carphati; the islands of Alaea and Amnamethus; the nation of the Darae;   (151) the islands of Chelonitis (*Turtle I.*), many others of the Ichthyophagi, the uninhabited Odanda, Basa, and many of the Sabaei; the rivers Thanar and Amnum; the Doric islands; the springs of Daulotos and Dora; the islands of Pteros, Labatanis, Coboris, and Sambrachate and a town of the same name on the mainland; to the south many islands, the greatest being Camari; the river of Musecros; the harbour of Laupas; the Sabaei (*called*) Scenitae (*Tent-dwellers*); many islands; their trading-place Acila, from which one sails to India;   (152) the region of Amithoscatta; Damnia; the greater and lesser Mizi; Drymatina; and the Macac, whose promontory is opposite Carmania at a distance of 50† miles.[58]

An amazing thing is reported there: that Numenius, put in charge of Mesena by King Antiochus,[59] won a battle with his fleet on the same day that, when the tide turned, he was fighting against the Persians again with his cavalry, and set up twin trophies in the same place to Jupiter and Neptune.

(153) Opposite on the open sea is the island of Ogyris, famous as the burial place of King Erythras;[60] it is 125 miles from the mainland and has a circuit of 112½.[61] The next one in the Azanian sea is no less famous: Dioscorides's (*Island; Socotra*), at a distance of 280 (*miles*) from the tip of the promontory of Syagros.

The other people on the mainland, continuing to the south, are the Autaridae, 8 days' journey into the mountains; the nations of the Larendani and Catabani; the Gebbanitae with numerous towns, though the largest are Nagia and Thomna with sixty-five temples; this is a mark of its size.

---

[58] We have reached the Straits of *Hormuz*.
[59] One of the four Seleukid kings of that name.
[60] The supposed eponym of the Erythraian sea; cf. Eratosthenes 87 §5; Agatharchides 4ab, 5a; Artem. 100.
[61] Cf. Erat. 87.

(154) (*Next is*) a promontory from which it is 50 (*miles*) to the mainland of the Trogodytae;[62] the Thoani, Actaei, Chatramotitae, Tonabaei, Antiadalaei, Lexianae, Agraei, Cerbani, and Sabaei, who are the most famous of the Arabs on account of frankincense; these nations extend to the sea on both sides. The towns on the Red coast are Merme, Marma, Corolia, and Sabbatha; inland are the towns of Nascus, Cardava, Carnus, and the one to which they bring down their cargoes of aromatics, Thomala. (155) One division of them is the Atramitae, whose chief town is Sabota (*Shabwa?*), which contains sixty temples within its walls; but the royal capital of them all is Marelibata (*Marib?*). They occupy 94 (*miles of the coast*),[63] packed with perfume-bearing islands. Adjoining the Atramitae in the interior are the Minaei. Also living on the sea are the Aelamitae with a town of the same name. Contiguous with them are the Chaculatae and the town of Sibi, which the Greeks called Apate (*Deceit*); the Arsi, Codani, and Vadaei with a large town; the Barasasaei and Lechieni; the island of Sygaros, which dogs are unable to alight upon and so, having disembarked around the shores, they die from wandering about.

(156) (*Next is*) a deep gulf in which (*live*) the Laeanitae, who have given their name to it. Their royal capital is Agra, and (*they have*) Laeana (*Aqaba*), or as others have it Aelana, in the bay; for our own writers have written the name of the gulf (*of Aqaba*) as Laeaniticus, others as Aelaniticus, Artemidorus as Alaeniticus, Juba as Leaniticus. The circuit of Arabia from Charax to Laeana is related as 4,765 miles;[64] Juba thinks it is not much less than 4,000. It is broadest at the north, between the towns of Heroönpolis (*Heroes' Town*) and Charace (*i.e. Charax*).

23   Pliny, *Natural History*, 6. xxxiii. 165–70: *From the gulf of Aqaba along the west coast of the Red Sea*

(165) After the Laeanitic gulf there is the other gulf that the Arabians call Aea, on which is the town of Heroön (*Hero Shrine*); there, too, was Kambyses' Town between the Neloi and the Marchadae, the sick men in his army being brought there. (*Then*) the nation of the Tyri; the harbour of the Danei. The plan to drive a navigable channel through from here to the Nile in the area where it runs into the aforementioned Delta, across the interval of 62½ miles lying between the river and the Red Sea, was first devised by Sesostris king of Egypt, later by Darius of the Persians,[65] next in sequence by Ptolemy (*II*), who also made a ditch with a breadth of 100 feet and a depth of 30 over a distance of 37½[66] miles up to Fontes Amari (*Bitter Springs*). (166) Beyond that, the fear of flooding discouraged (*him*), once it was understood that the Red Sea was 3 cubits higher than the land of Egypt. Some do not refer to this as the reason rather than the fear that the water of the Nile, which alone supplies drinkable water, would be corrupted by letting the sea in.

---

[62] J. has progressed rapidly to the general area of Yemen.

[63] 96 Loeb, probably a misprint.

[64] Presumably in Agrippa's survey. So Mayhoof, Brodersen; 4,665 Rackham.

[65] Necho tried to construct a canal to the Red Sea (Hdt. 2. 158); Darius succeeded (cf. 4. 39, 4. 42).

[66] Rackham adopts the variant reading 34½.

Nevertheless, the whole journey is often made by land from the Egyptian sea. It is threefold: one (*route*) from Pelusium through the sands, on which the way cannot be found unless the fixed reeds guide one, as the wind immediately obscures the tracks.   (167) The second is beyond Mt Casius, which after 60 miles returns to the Pelusiac Way; the Arabs called Antaei live beside it. The third is from Gerrhum, which they call Agipsus, via those same Arabs; it is 9 (?)[67] miles closer, but a rough way with mountains, and without water supplies.

All these routes lead to Arsinoë, founded under his sister's name by Ptolemy (*II*) Philadelphus on the gulf of Carandra. It was he that first opened up Trogodytice. He named the river that flows past Arsinoë the Ptolemaeus.

(168) Soon after lies the small town of Aenum; others write 'Philoterias' instead. Then there are the Asaraei, who are wild Arabs produced by intermarriage with the Trogodytae. Then the islands of Sapirine and Scytala; soon desert lands up to Myos Hormos (*Mussel Anchorage*), where the spring of Tatnos lies; Mount Aeas; the island of Iambe; many harbours; the town of Berenice, bearing the name of Philadelphus' mother, to which the journey from Coptos, mentioned above, leads; then the Arabs (*called*) Autaei and Gebadaei.

(169) Then Trogodytice, which ancient writers called Midoë and others Midioë; Mount Pentedactylos (*Five Fingers*); the islands of Stenae Thyrae (*Narrow Gates*), of which there are several;[68] the Halonesi (*Salt Is.*), at least as many; Cardamine; Topazos, which gave its name to the gemstone.[69] Then a bay packed with islands; of these, those called Maraeos' (*Islands*) are well-watered while those called Eraton's (*Islands*) arc thirsty; the prefects of the kings were once here. Inland are the Candaei, whom they call Ophiophagi (*Snake-eaters*) and who are used to feeding on serpents; for no other region is so productive of those.[70]

(170) In this district Juba, who appears to have gone into these matters most diligently, omitted—unless it is a fault in the copies (*of his work*)—the other Berenice which is surnamed Panchrysos (*All-golden*), and a third which (*is surnamed*) Epi Dirēs (*On the Neck; Ras Siyyan?*), notable for its situation, for it is located on a long neck (*of land*) that runs far out where the jaws of the Red Sea are 7½ miles from Arabia.[71]

24   Pliny, *Natural History*, 12. xxi. 38–xxii. 39: *Silk from Bahrain*

(38) ... On a rather lofty height of the same island (*Tylos; Bahrain*) are trees that bear wool in a different way from those of the Seres. These have infertile leaves, which, but for the fact of being smaller, might have been thought to belong to vines. They bear gourds about as big as an apple which, at the point of ripeness, break to reveal balls

---

[67] Desanges 2008, 3 and 50–1, prints IX for the LX of the MSS (which would only make sense if translated as 'shorter than 60 miles').
[68] Desanges emends *Deirae* to *Thyrae*.   [69] Cf. **34, 36**, and **38** below; Agatharch. 84abc.
[70] Names in this passage follow the spelling in Desanges 2008.
[71] At *Djibouti*; the mouth of the Red Sea is in fact c.16 mi (c.26 km) wide today. The figure of 7½ miles is from Timosthenes 15 (cf. Erat. 104; Artem. 113).

of wool from which people make garments of costly linen.⁷² (39) They call the tree *gossypinus*, and the island of Tylus Minor (*Lesser Tylos*), which is 10 miles away, is more productive of them. xxii. Juba (*says*) that around the fruit are quantities of wool, and that these linen fabrics are more excellent than the Indian kind. There is (*he says*), however, a tree in Arabia called the *cynas* from which they make garments, with a leaf similar to a palm-tree.⁷³

25 Pliny, *Natural History*, 12. xxxi. 56: *Frankincense from Arabia*
King Juba, in those volumes which he wrote to Gaius Caesar, son of Augustus, who was passionate about the reputation of Arabia, recorded that it (*the frankincense tree*) had a twisted stem with branches very much those of the Pontic maple, and discharged juice in the manner of the almond; and that such trees were present in Carmania, and had been cultivated in Egypt by the efforts of the ruling Ptolemies.⁷⁴

26 Pliny, *Natural History*, 12. xxxii. 60: *Frankincense from Arabian islands*
Certain people think that a better sort (*of frankincense tree*) is produced in the islands. Juba denies that it is produced in the islands.

27 Pliny, *Natural History*, 12. xxxiv. 67: *Myrrh*
Others say that the bark (*of the myrrh tree*), which is smooth and similar to the arbutus, is rough and thorny, its leaf like that of the olive-tree but more wrinkled and prickly; Juba (*says it is like*) the *olusatrum* (*black cabbage*).⁷⁵

28 Pliny, *Natural History*, 12. xxxviii. 78–xl. 80: *The perfume trade*
(78) Arabia itself, amazingly, searches for perfumes from abroad and goes to people elsewhere for them. . . . (80) They have opened Carra (*Carrhae*) for these trades, because there is a market-day there. They all used to make for Gabba from there, by a journey of twenty days, and for Syria Palaestina. Afterwards it began to be Charace (*i.e. Charax*) that they made for and the kingdom of the Parthians, for this purpose; Juba is the authority for this.

29 Pliny, *Natural History*, 13. vii. 34: *Palm-trees*
In Arabia, too, palm-trees are recorded as being mildly sweet, although Juba esteems above all others the one in the land of the Scenitae (*Tent-dwelling*) Arabs that they call *dabla*.⁷⁶

---

⁷² Probably a variety of silk, now unknown (Roller 2008b, F 62).   ⁷³ Unidentified.
⁷⁴ J.'s emphasis on frankincense and other luxury products (cf. **24, 26–8**) reflects his interest in commerce, though his own kingdom was at the other end of Africa. Arnoldus Saxo (see chapter introduction) cites Iorach (Juba) on myrrh; see Draelants 2000, 240–1 no. 9.
⁷⁵ The myrrh tree grows over a wider area than Arabia (Roller 2008b, F 27).
⁷⁶ Unidentified. Arnoldus Saxo (see chapter introduction) cites Iorach (Juba) on palm-trees; see Draelants 2000, 237–8 no. 4.

30 Pliny, *Natural History*, 15. xxviii. 99: *The arbutus*
The fruit (*of the wild strawberry, 'unedo'*)[77] is unregarded, given that its name comes from the evidence that only one can be eaten (*unum edendi*). The Greeks, however, call it by the two following names: *comaron* and *memaecylon*. By this it appears that there is also that number of varieties. Among ourselves it is called by another name, *arbutus*. Juba is the authority (*for the information*) that in Arabia they have a height of 50 cubits each.[78]

31 Pliny, *Natural History*, 25. v. 14: *A magical plant*
And Juba records that in Arabia a man was brought back to life by a herb.[79]

32 Pliny, *Natural History*, 32. iv. 10: *Creatures of Arabia*
Juba, in those volumes about Arabia which he wrote to Gaius Caesar, son of Augustus, records that its mussels have a capacity of three *heminai*;[80] that a sea-monster with a length of 600 feet and a breadth of 360 entered a river in Arabia, and that traders did business in its fat;[81] and that camels in that location are anointed with the grease of every fish in order to drive gadflies away from them by the smell.

33 Pliny, *Natural History*, 33. xl. 118: *Cinnabar from Karmania*
Juba records that *minium* (*cinnabar*)[82] is produced in Carmania too; Timagenes (*says*) in Aethiopia too.

34 Pliny, *Natural History*, 35. xxii. 39: *Minerals from Topazos I.*
Juba records that *sandaraca* (*realgar*)[83] and ochre are produced on the island of Topazos in the Red Sea.

35 Pliny, *Natural History*, 36. xlvi. 163: *Translucent stone from Arabia*
In Arabia, too, there is a strong stone, translucent after the manner of glass, which they use in place of 'mirror-stones';[84] Juba is the authority for this.

36 Pliny, *Natural History*, 37. ix. 24: *Rock-crystal stones from Red Sea islands*
Juba is the authority (*for the information*) that in a certain island in the Red Sea, lying off Arabia, a type (*of rock crystal*) is produced which is called Necron (*Dead*),[85] as well as on the neighbouring one that bears the gemstone topaz. A cubit-sized piece was excavated by Pythagoras, Ptolemy's prefect.

---

[77] It is, however, unrelated to the cultivated strawberry (König 1981, 310).
[78] An error, or an exaggeration (Roller 2008b, F 68).
[79] Once again, J. is no doubt relying on second-hand information about Arabia.
[80] Nearly a litre, and unlikely (Roller 2008b, F 3).
[81] Possibly a reference to whaling, though the size is impossible (Roller 2008b, F3).
[82] A red pigment.   [83] Another red dye, also medicinal.
[84] Probably translucent onyx-marble, thin slabs of which created light within a building. Which stone from Arabia was the substitute for these is uncertain (König 2007, 196–7).
[85] Unidentified.

37 Pliny, *Natural History*, 37. xviii. 73: *Emeralds*
Juba is the authority (*for the information*) that the *smaragdus* they call *chlora* (*green*) is inserted into the decoration of buildings in Arabia, and likewise the stone which the Egyptians call *alabastritēs*; but several (*authors*) close to our own day (*say that*) Laconian ones are dug up in (*Mount*) Taÿgetos, similar to those of Media; and others in Sicily.[86]

38 Pliny, *Natural History*, 37. xxxii. 107–8: *Topaz (peridotite) from a Red Sea island*
(107) Even now, exceptional fame attaches to topaz; it is one of the green variety (*of stones*).[87] When it was first found, it was preferred to all other (*stones*). It occurs on an island in Arabia which used to be called Cytis (*St John's I.?*), to which Trogodyte pirates had put in, tired out by hunger and the weather; while excavating for plants and roots, they dug up topaz. This is the opinion of Archelaus. (108) Juba records that the island of Topazus in the Red Sea is 300 stades from the mainland, and that it is cloud-covered and accordingly has been the object of searches by sailors on many occasions. (*He says*) it gained its name for that reason, for *topazin* in the tongue of the Trogodytae has the sense of 'seeking'.[88] From this (*he says*) it was first brought to Queen Berenice—who was the mother of the Ptolemy who succeeded (*the first one*)—by the king's prefect, Philo, and pleased the king wonderfully; wherefore a statue of Arsinoë, Ptolemy's wife, 4 cubits high, was made (*from it*) and dedicated in the sanctuary that was surnamed the Arsinoëum.

39 Aelian, *On the Nature of Animals*, 15. 8: *Pearls from different seas*
Now the best (*pearl*) is the Indic and that from the Erythraian sea.[89] It is also found in the western Ocean, where the island of Brettanike lies, and appears to be somewhat more gold-like, also with a duller and darker shine.[90] Iobas (*Juba*) says it is also found in the strait by the Bosporos and this one is outclassed by the Bretannic (*sic*) and in no way compares to the Indian or Erythraian in its origin. The inland sort is not said to have its own nature but to be a progeny of crystal, since it is constituted not from the frosts but by mining.

40 Hesychios s.v. Terebinthos: *A city (or a plant?)*
Terebinthos: a city. Iobas (*Juba*).[91]

---

[86] *alabastritēs* may be a type of onyx (Roller 2008b, F74). *Smaragdus*, usually 'emerald', also refers to semi-precious stones such as the variegated green Laconian marble mentioned here, known by the Latin name *lapis Lacedaemonius*, which was used to decorate Roman buildings. It was (and is) found not in Mt Taÿgetos but at Krokeai in the foothills of Mt Parnon, across the Eurotas valley to the E (see e.g. Warren 1992).

[87] Probably peridot (Eichholz 1962, 250 n.; 'a green semi-precious variety of forsterite (olivine)', *COD*[12]), which occurs on St John's I. What we call topaz today is '1 a precious stone, typically colourless, yellow, or pale blue, consisting of a fluorine containing aluminium silicate. 2 a dark yellow colour' (*COD*[12]).

[88] In fact, *topazein* is simply the infinitive of the Greek verb 'seek', 'guess'.

[89] *PME* §59.   [90] Tacitus, *Agricola* (from after Juba's time), 12.

[91] Roller 2008b, F 45, suggests that this may have been a reference not to a place but to the 'Indian terebinth' or pistachio, which would reflect J.'s interest in luxury trade. Arnoldus Saxo (see chapter introduction) cites Iorach (Juba) on the terebinth; see Draelants 2000, 238 no. 5.

F. ON EUPHORBION

41 Pliny, *Natural History,* 25. xxxviii. 77–9: *Discovery of euphorbia*
(77) In the days of our fathers, King Juba found (*a plant*) which he named Euphorbea after the name of his doctor.[92] That man was the brother of Musa, by whom, as we have noted, the divine Augustus was saved. These brothers introduced the practice of constricting the body with plenty of cold (*water*) on leaving the bath; earlier it was not the custom to wash except in warm, just as we likewise find in Homer. (78) But Juba's book on this plant is also extant and is an enthusiastic celebration. He found it on Mount Atlas, having the appearance of a thyrsus and leaves like an acanthus. Its power is so great that the juice is removed at a distance after it is cut with a pike; it is received in receptacles made from the stomach of a young goat. What flows down has the appearance of milk; when it dries and has congealed, it looks like frankincense. Those that collect it see more clearly. It is efficacious against serpents, a cut being made on the crown of the head irrespective of where the bite is, and the medication applied there. (79) The Gaetuli who collect it adulterate it with milk because of its unpleasant taste, but it can be identified by applying fire: for by the fact of being impure it has a smell that is found disgusting. Far inferior to this juice is the one that is produced in Gallia from the *chamelaea* plant, which bears a seed (*like that*) of the kermes oak (*Quercus coccifera*). When broken, it is like gum resin, and after even a slight taste it keeps the mouth feeling burnt, more so after an interval, until the throat goes dry as well.[93]

42 Pedanios Dioskorides, *On Medical Material,* 3. 82. 1–2: *Processing of euphorbia*
Euphorbion:[94] this is a Libyan tree similar to fennel, growing in Autololia by Mauretania. It is full of the most bitter juice, which the people here collect fearfully because of the intense inflammation. At any rate, they tie round the tree the washed bellies of sheep, and split the stem with javelins from a distance. Straightaway, as if from a vessel, a large quantity of juice pours out into the bellies and also squirts out in a spray onto the ground. (2) There are two kinds of juice. The first is translucent like *sarkokolla*[95] and about the size of vetch (*seeds*); the other is full of particles and compacted. It is adulterated with *sarkokolla* and gum mixed together. Choose the translucent, bitter sort; but it is difficult to test by being tasted, because as soon as the tongue is caught[96] the inflammation persists for quite a long time, so that everything

---

[92] In 3 §15 Pliny credits Euphorbos himself with the discovery. Roller 2008b, F 7, cites a suggestion that the particular plant in question was the Canary Island spurge (*Euphorbia canariensis*), now a symbol of *Gran Canaria*; it is toxic, like other Euphorbiaceae.
[93] Cf. 3 §15.
[94] Beck 2005, 220, translates the name as 'spurge' and identifies it as *Euphorbia resinifera* Berg.
[95] A Persian gum. Arnoldus Saxo (see chapter introduction) cites Iorach (Juba) on gum (*gummi*); see Draelants 2000, 240–1 no. 9.
[96] Lit. 'bitten'.

brought into contact with it seems to be *euphorbion*. But its discovery was attested by Iobas (*Juba*) king of Libyē.

43 **Galen,** *On Compound Drugs according to Places, 9, p. 271: Nature of euphorbia juice*

It (*euphorbion*) is the juice of a certain acanthus-like plant that grows in the land of the Maurousioi, very hot in its action. A small booklet has been written about it by Iobas (*Juba*) who held the kingship of the Maurousioi.

23

ISIDOROS OF CHARAX

(ACTIVE C. AD 1–14)

Richard J. A. Talbert

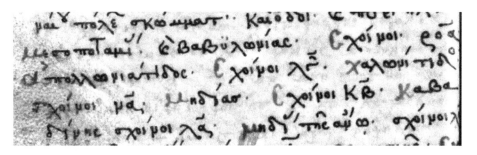

FIG. 23.1. Opening of the text of Isidoros, p. 106 (detail).

INTRODUCTION

Isidoros from Charax in the Tigris delta is an elusive figure to us. According to Pliny the Elder writing in the 70s AD, our sole informant,[1] he was the most recent author to describe the world, and was sent (Pliny does not say from where) to the East by Augustus 'to make a complete record' when Gaius Caesar was dispatched there on a diplomatic mission in 1 BC. To judge by Pliny's numerous citations of distance figures drawn from Isidoros, it is plain that the coverage of his works did indeed extend far beyond the East, but altogether their scope, character, and relation to one another are irrecoverable. Only one work is named by a reader of Isidoros (Athenaios, around AD 200; 20 below), a *Guided Tour of Parthia* (*Parthias periegetikon*)—the Parthian empire, that is, not just the region so named. He is included in a list of authors of *periploi* by Markianos (21), but this evidence is not precise enough to permit us to credit him with a work of that name.

Most of our citations of Isidoros are indeed by Pliny (2–18), who lists him among his foreign (non-Roman) sources in books 2 to 6 (2), citing him repeatedly for distances (9–10, 17) and perimeters (6–7, 12–16), and once for peoples in Asia (11).

Nothing by Isidoros himself survives except a terse itinerary in Greek entitled *Parthian Stopping-points* (1),[2] in the course of which (after §1) the information offered

---

[1] **18** below. In the MSS the name here is Dionysium, but editors are surely justified in taking this to be a copyists' slip for Isidorum.

[2] In the late C13 manuscript 'D' (Parisinus supplément grec 443, pp. 106. 13–111. 10) and the contemporary or later manuscript 'E' (Parisinus graecus 571, pp. 417ʳ–418ʳ); see Introduction, §VIII. 2. b; also introduction to Ch. 11 above. According to Diller 1952, 30, the copies are almost identical though E remedies three omissions and avoids some of the errors in D.

becomes notably (and inexplicably) less detailed. The route proceeds in eighteen long stages from the Roman–Parthian frontier at Zeugma on the Euphrates through to the Parthians' easternmost region, Arachosia (now in southern Afghanistan), a distance of over two thousand miles spanning some thirty degrees of longitude. Isidoros seems often to match Artemidoros, though sometimes adding slightly to his predecessor's distances (cf. **9, 15**). If this itinerary was compiled with one or more particular concerns in mind, these are not readily apparent: they could be military operations, for example, or trade, or communications. Distances are given in *schoinoi*, a flexible unit (30–120 stades, roughly 3¾–15 miles, see Introduction, §IV. 1, but here probably closer to the shorter value), which leaves them inexact; some names of places and regions defy identification and may have been garbled by copyists.[3] Even so, this overland itinerary is of marked interest as the only surviving example in Greek of a type of record commonly found in Latin.[4]

SELECTED FURTHER READING

Hartmann, U. (2017), 'Die Parthischen Stationen des Isidor von Charax: eine Handelsroute, eine Militärkarte oder ein Werk geographischer Gelehrsamkeit?', in Wiesehöfer–Müller (below), 87–125.

Hauser, S. R. (2017), 'Isidor von Charax Σταθμοὶ Παρθικοί: Annäherungen an den Autor, den Routenverlauf und die Bedeutung des Werkes', in Wiesehöfer–Müller (below), 127–87.

Kramer, N. (2003), 'Das Itinerar Stathmoi Parthikoi des Isidor von Charax: Beschreibung eines Handelsweges?', *Klio*, 85. 1: 120–30.

*Roller, D. W. (2019), 'Isidoros of Charax (781)', in *BNJ*².

Schmitt, R. (2012), 'Isidorus of Charax', *Encyclopaedia Iranica* xiv. 2. 125–7.

—— (2017), 'Isidors "Stathmoi Parthikoi" aus Sicht der iranischen Toponomastik', in Wiesehöfer–Müller (below), 189–220.

Schuol, M. (2017), 'Isidor von Charax und die literarische Gattung der Stathmoí', in Wiesehöfer–Müller (below), 71–85.

Wiesehöfer, J., and Müller, S. (eds 2017), *Parthika: Greek and Roman Authors' Views of the Arsacid Empire*. Wiesbaden.

A. *STATHMOI PARTHIKOI*

1 Codex Parisinus supplément grec 443, pp. 106. 13–111. 10
Summary (in the manuscript)
(*Through*) Mesopotamia and Babylonia, 171 *schoinoi*.

Apolloniatis, 33 *schoinoi*.

Chalonitis, 21 *schoinoi*.

---

[3] For all names and distance figures, with outline maps, see Hauser 2017, 166–82.
[4] On Roman *itineraria*, cf. Dueck 2012, 60–1.

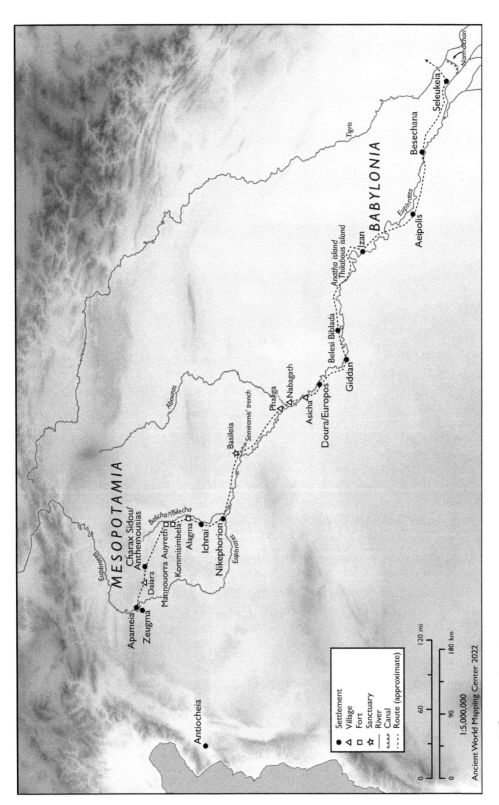

MAP 23.1. Isidoros: western stages.

Media, 22 *schoinoi*.

Kambadene, 31 *schoinoi*.

Upper Media, 38 *schoinoi*.

Rhagiane Media, 58 *schoinoi*.

Choarene, 19 *schoinoi*.

Komisene, 58 *schoinoi*.

Hyrkania, 60 *schoinoi*.

Astauene, 60 *schoinoi*.

Parthyene, 25 *schoinoi*.

Apauarktikene, 27 *schoinoi*.

Margiane, 30 *schoinoi*.

Areia, 30 *schoinoi*.

Anaue, 55 *schoinoi*.

Zarangiane, 21 *schoinoi*.

Sakastane, 63 *schoinoi*.

Arachosia, 36 *schoinoi*.

Total, **858** *schoinoi*.

Main text

1. Mesopotamia and Babylon, 171 *schoinoi*.

Opposite Zeugma, for those crossing the Euphrates, there is a city Apameia.

Next a village Daiara. Its distance from Apameia and the river Euphrates is 3 *schoinoi*.

Next Charax Sidou city, ⟨called⟩ Anthemousias by Greeks, 5 *schoinoi*.

After it, Koraia in Batane, stronghold, 3 *schoinoi*.

To its right, Mannouorrha Auÿreth stronghold and spring from which the locals draw water, 5 *schoinoi*.

Next Kommisimbela stronghold which river Bilecha skirts, 4 *schoinoi*.

Next fortress Alagma, royal stopping-place, 3 *schoinoi*.

After it, Ichnai, Greek city founded by Macedonians, situated on Balicha river, 3 *schoinoi*.

Next Nikephorion on Euphrates, Greek city founded by king Alexander, 5 *schoinoi*.

From there, on the riverbank Galabatha, deserted village, 4 *schoinoi*.

Next Choumbane village, 1 *schoinos*.

From there Thillada Mirrhada, royal stopping-place, 4 *schoinoi*.

Next Basileia, temple of Artemis founded by Darius, village-city; Semiramis' trench is here, and the Euphrates has been blocked by boulders so that its confinement should cause the plains to be flooded, although in summer boats are wrecked as a result, ⟨7 *schoinoi*⟩.

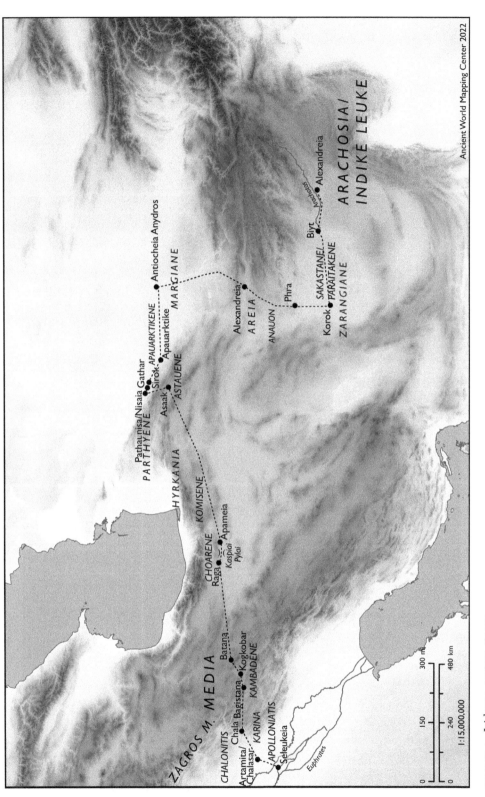

MAP 23.2. Isidoros: eastern stages.

Next Allan, village-city, 4 *schoinoi*.

From there, Beonan, shrine of Artemis, 4 *schoinoi*.

Next Phaliga, village on the Euphrates—said to mean 'halfway point' in Greek—6 *schoinoi*.

From Antiocheia to here, 120 *schoinoi*.

From here to Seleukeia on the Tigris, 100 *schoinoi*.

Situated by Phaliga is village-city Nabagath, skirted by river Abouras, which empties into the Euphrates. From here armies cross to the limit of Roman control.

Next Asicha village, 4 *schoinoi*.

From there, Doura, Nicanor's city founded by Macedonians—called Europos by Greeks—6 *schoinoi*.

Next stronghold Merran, village-city, 5 *schoinoi*.

Next Giddan city, 5 *schoinoi*.

Next Belesi Biblada, 7 *schoinoi*.

From here an island in the Euphrates, 6 *schoinoi*; here used to be treasure of the Phraates who slaughtered his concubines when attacked by the fugitive Tiridates.

Next Anathō island in the Euphrates, 4 stades (*in size*), with a city on it, 4 *schoinoi*.

After it, Thilabous island on the Euphrates, with Parthians' treasure here, 2 *schoinoi*.

Next Izan island-city, 12 *schoinoi*.

Next Aëipolis with streams of bitumen here, 16 *schoinoi*.

From here Besechana city with a temple of Atargatis there, 12 *schoinoi*.

Next Neapolis on the Euphrates, 22 *schoinoi*.

From there, proceeding across the Euphrates and Narmalchan to Seleukeia on the Tigris, 9 *schoinoi*.

Here Mesopotamia and Babylonia end, and from Zeugma to Seleukeia is 171 *schoinoi*.

2. From there begins Apolloniatis, which extends for 33 *schoinoi*. It has [— (*number lost*)] villages in which there is a stopping-place, and a Greek city, Artamita; through its middle flows river Silla.

From Seleukeia to it is 15 *schoinoi*. However, nowadays the city is called Chalasar.

3. From there, Chalonitis, 21 *schoinoi*, with 5 villages in it and a stopping-place in them, Chala a Greek city 15 *schoinoi* from Apolloniatis.

Next, 5 *schoinoi* on, a mountain called Zagros, which divides the Chalonitis region and that of the Medes.

4. From there, Media which extends for 22 *schoinoi*. It starts at [— (*name missing?*)] and Karina region, with 5 villages in it and a stopping-place in them, but no city.

5. From there, Kambadene which extends for 31 *schoinoi*, with 5 villages in it and a stopping-place in them, and a city Bagistana situated on a mountain with Semiramis' statue and pillar there.

6. From there, Upper Media, 38 *schoinoi*. Right at the start of it is Konkobar city with a temple of Artemis, 3 *schoinoi*. Next Bazigraban, which is a customs-post, 3 *schoinoi*.

Next to Adrapana the establishment of Batana's royalty, which the Armenian Tigranes destroyed, 4 *schoinoi*.

Next, Batana, metropolis of Media and a treasury and temple of Anaitis where sacrifices are made regularly, 12 *schoinoi*.

Next three villages in succession and a stopping-place in them.

7. From there, ⟨Rhagiane⟩ Media, ⟨58⟩ *schoinoi*, with 10 villages in it, 5 cities. Seven *schoinoi* further, Rhaga and Charax, Rhaga the largest of Media's (*cities*). At Charax the first king Phraates settled the Mardoi; it is below the mountain called Kaspios, with the Kaspiai Pylai (*Caspian Gates*) beyond.

8. From there, after proceeding beyond the Kaspiai Pylai, there is a valley and Choarene, ⟨19 *schoinoi*⟩, with a city in it, Apameia, 4 *schoinoi* further on.

Four villages and a stopping-point in them.

9. From there, Komisene, 58 *schoinoi*, with 8 villages in it and a stopping-point in them. There is no city.

10. From there, Hyrkania, 60 *schoinoi*, with 11 villages in it and a stopping-point in them.

11. From there, Astauene, 60 *schoinoi*, with 12 villages in it and a stopping-point in them.

A city, Asaak, where Arsakes was first proclaimed king, and a perpetual fire is maintained here.

12. From there, Parthyene, 25 *schoinoi*, with a valley.

Six *schoinoi* further, the city Parthaunisa, with royal tombs here; Greeks call it Nisaia.

Next Gathar city, 6 *schoinoi* further.

Next Sirōk city, 5 *schoinoi* further. It has only a single village, by the name of Saphri.

13. From there, Apauarktikene, 27 *schoinoi*, with a city in it, Apauarktike.

Next Rhagau city and 2 villages.

14. From there, Margiane, 30 *schoinoi*, with the Antiocheia called Anydros (*Waterless*) here, but there are no villages.

15. From there, Areia, 30 *schoinoi*, with Kandak city here and Artakauan city and Alexandreia among the Areioi. Four villages.

16. From there, Anauōn, a region of Areia, 55 *schoinoi*; in it Phra city, the largest, and Bis city and Gari city and Niē city. There is no village.

17. From there, Zarangiane, 21 *schoinoi*, with Parin city and Korok city here.

18. From there, Sakastane of (*the*) Skythian Sakai which is also Paraitakene, 63 *schoinoi*, with Barda city and Min city and Palakenti city, and Sigal city with a royal establishment of (*the*) Sakai here; and nearby, Alexandropolis city.

Six villages.

19. From there, Arachosia, 36 *schoinoi*; the Parthians call it Indike Leuke (*White India*).

Biyt city here and Pharsana city and Chorochoad city and Demetrias city.

Next Alexandreia, metropolis of Arachosia; it is Greek, and Arachotos river skirts it. This is as far as the Parthians' rule extends.

B. OTHER TEXTS

In date order.

2 Pliny, *Natural History*, 1. 2–6: *Pliny's sources*
In the 2nd book are contained ... the measurement of the entire Earth ... from these authors: ... foreign (*i.e. non-Roman*): ... Isidorus of Charax ...

In the 3rd book are contained places, peoples, seas, towns, harbours, mountains, rivers, measurements, and peoples who exist or who existed ... from these authors: ... foreign (*i.e. non-Roman*): ... Isidorus ...

In the 4th book ... (*the same*).
In the 5th book ... (*the same*).
In the 6th book ... (*the same*).

3 Pliny, *Natural History*, 2. cxii. 242: *Earth's west–east extent*
As was stated (*earlier*), our part of the Earth, which I am discussing—swimming, as it were, in the surrounding Ocean—extends furthest from sunrise to sunset: that is to say, from India to the Pillars of Hercules dedicated at Gades (*Cádiz*) it is 8,578 miles in the judgement of Artemidorus, but 9,818 in that of Isidorus.[5]

4 Pliny, *Natural History*, 2. cxii. 245: *Earth's south–north extent*
But the width of the Earth from the southern position to the north is roughly one-half less: for Isidorus it amounts to 5,462 (*miles*).

5 Pliny, *Natural History*, 2. cxii. 246: *Distance from the Tanaïs (Don) to Thule*
From the entrance of the Tanaïs, the most careful authors have perpetrated no exaggerations. ... Isidorus added 1,250 (*miles*) up to Thyle (*Thoule*), which is an interpretation based on divine foresight.

6 Pliny, *Natural History*, 4. iv. 9: *Circumference of the Peloponnese*
The Peloponnese ... because of its angular bays amounts to 563 miles in circumference, according to Isidorus.

7 Pliny, *Natural History*, 4. xvi. 102: *Circumference of Britannia*
Pytheas and Isidorus report that in its circuit it (*Britannia*) extends 4,875 (*miles*).

8 Pliny, *Natural History*, 4. xxiii. 121: *Distance from the Tanaïs to Gades*
With the tour of Europe complete, a reckoning must now be given, so that nothing may be inconvenient for those who desire knowledge. Artemidorus and Isidorus have presented (*the distance of*) 8,714 (*miles*) from the Tanaïs to Gades.

---

[5] See nn. on Artemidoros 4.

9 Pliny, *Natural History*, 5. vi. 40: *Tingi to Canopus*
Isidorus (*has given the distance as*) 3,697[6] (*miles*) from Tingis to Canopus, Artemidorus 40 miles less than Isidorus.[7]

10 Pliny, *Natural History*, 5. ix. 47: *Egypt to Tanaïs river*
Asia joins it (*Libyē*) . . . Eratosthenes and Isidorus (*record*) the whole of it, including Egypt, as far as the Tanaïs, as 5,013 miles and 750 paces (*i.e. ¾ mile*).

11 Pliny, *Natural History*, 5. xxxiii. 127: *Former peoples of Asia*
From Asia various nations have perished: . . . Isidorus (*names*) Arienei and Capreatae, where Apamea was founded by King Seleucus between Cilicia, Cappadocia, Cataonia, and Armenia, and (*records that?*) since it had subdued very fierce races (*gentes*) it was at first called Damea.[8]

12 Pliny, *Natural History*, 5. xxxv. 129: *Cyprus*
Timosthenes offers the figure of 427½ miles for its (*Cyprus's*) circuit; Isidorus gives 375.

13 Pliny, *Natural History*, 5. xxxvi. 132: *Rhodos and its distance from Alexandria*
Rhodes, with a circumference of 125 (*miles*) or, if we rather believe Isidorus, 103. . . . It is 583 (*miles*) from Alexandria in Egypt, as Isidorus records; 469 as Eratosthenes (*says*); as Mucianus, 500; from Cyprus, 176.

14 Pliny, *Natural History*, 5. xxxvii. 135: *Samos*
Samos, with a circumference of 87½ (*miles*) or, as Isidorus says, 100.

15 Pliny, *Natural History*, 5. xxxviii. 136: *Chios*
Chius . . . amounts to 125 (*miles*) in circumference, as older writers recorded; Isidorus adds 9.

16 Pliny, *Natural History*, 5. xxxix. 140: *Lesbos*
The circumference of the whole island (*Lesbos*) is, as Isidorus (*says*), 168 (*miles*); as older writers (*say*), 195.

17 Pliny, *Natural History*, 5. xliii. 150: *Kalchedon to Sigeion*
Isidorus records 322½ (*miles*) from Calchadon to Sigeum.

18 Pliny, *Natural History*, 6. xxxi. 141: *Isidoros' work superseded by that of Juba*
It does not escape me that it was in this place that Isidorus was born, the latest authority on the territory of the Earth. The divine Augustus had sent him ahead to the East to research everything fully when his elder son was due to go to Armenia to manage the business with the Parthians and the Arabians. Nor have I forgotten that, at the opening of this work, it was my view that each author is most diligent regarding his own territory. In this passage, however, my resolve is to follow the Roman forces and King Juba in the books he wrote to the same Gaius Caesar concerning the same Arabian expedition.[9]

---

[6] 3,519 Rackham.   [7] Cf. **8**.
[8] Roller (whose translation differs) notes that the last comment is not necessarily by Isidoros.
[9] See nn. on this passage at Juba 21 §141 above.

19 Pseudo-Lucian, *Makrobioi* ('*The Long-lived*'), 15–17: *Historical information from Isidoros*

(15) Another Persian king, Artaxerxes—who reigned, according to the Charakene historian Isidoros, in the time of his forefathers—was murdered at the age of 93 as a result of a plot by his brother Gosithras. . . . (17) According to Isidoros of Charakene, the king of Omana—known for its spices—in his youth was Goaisos, who died from an illness at the age of 115.

20 Athenaios 3. 46, 93d–94b: *Pearl-fishing*

Isidoros of Charakene in his *Guided Tour of Parthia* says that there is some island in the Persian open-sea (*pelagos*) where great quantities of pearls are found. Consequently the island is encircled by reed rafts from which men dive 20 *orguiai* (fathoms) down into the sea to bring up bivalve shellfish.

It is said that the oysters mostly conceive during bouts of thunder and pouring rain, and that this is when the pearls are most numerous and of good size. The oysters typically go down to recesses on the seabed during the winter, but in summer they swim around open at night though closed by day. Those that attach to rocks or cliffs put down roots and produce pearls there. They give birth and are fed through the part attached to their flesh. This is a growth at the shell's mouth which has claws and draws in food; really it is like a small crab and is called *pinophylax* (*oyster-guard*). From here, flesh extends to the centre of the shell like a root; next to it a pearl, after being generated, grows thanks to the shell's toughness, and it is fed for as long as it stays attached. But in the course of this growth the flesh worms under it and by gently cutting in separates the pearl from the shell, so that with this embrace it no longer feeds it, but makes it smoother, more translucent and less flawed. Oysters from the seabed produce pearls that are the most translucent and large, whereas those that rise to the surface are discoloured and smaller because of their exposure to the sun's rays.

Men who hunt for pearls take a risk whenever they put their hand into an open shell, because then it closes and often their fingers are sliced off; some even die there and then. But if they can successfully put a hand underneath from the side, then it is easy for them to prise shells from the rock.

21 Markianos of Herakleia, *Epitome of the Periplous of Menippos of Pergamon* 2: *Isidoros as a source*

I write this having encountered many *periploi* and having spent a lot of time acquiring knowledge of these topics. . . . Those who in my view have investigated these matters intelligently are: Timosthenes of Rhodes . . . and after him Eratosthenes . . . in addition to these Pytheas of Massilia, Isidoros of Charax . . .

22 Hesychios s.v. Dousaren: *A Nabataean name for Dionysos*

Dousares: Dionysos to the Nabataeans, according to Isidoros.[10]

---

[10] It is plausible, though not certain, that the reference is to Isidoros Charakenos.

24

PSEUDO-ARISTOTLE, *ON THE COSMOS* (*DE MUNDO*)

(1ST C. AD?)

D. Graham J. Shipley

To the memory of
Michael D. J. Easton, traveller
(1955–2012)

INTRODUCTION

This elegant philosophical–theological disquisition—relatively neglected in modern scholarship—is more literary than most works in these volumes, characterized as it is by polished periods and a rich vocabulary including a notable number of *hapax legomena* (words 'said once', found nowhere else). Written in Greek and apparently entitled *Peri kosmou* (*On the Universe*), it is usually known by the Latin title *De mundo* (*On the World*).[1] Although not a work of detailed geographical exposition, it draws upon the Greek and specifically Peripatetic (Aristotelian) tradition of geographical science and deploys it in the service of philosophical and theological debate.

The treatise is preserved among the works of Aristotle, and presents itself as an address to his sometime pupil Alexander the Great, but among other features it uses certain items of vocabulary not attested in Aristotle's day and probably drawn from philosophical compendia of hellenistic times.[2] It is generally believed to have been written long after both Alexander and Aristotle's lifetimes: current consensus favours the 1st century BC or the Julio-Claudian period (reigns of Augustus to Nero, 27 BC–AD 69), and certainly it can be no later than the third quarter of the 2nd century if it was adapted by Apuleius (below).[3]

---

[1] Not to be confused with Aristotle's genuine work *Peri ouranou* (*On the Heavens*), known as *De caelo* in Latin.

[2] Gregorić and Karamanolis 2020a, 6; Baksa 2020, 124, 137, 141, 146, 148.

[3] Geus and Dan 2018, 415, prefer Wilamowitz's Julio-Claudian dating to that proposed by Mansfeld 1992 (not pre-C1). Furley 1955, 339–41, argues for 'before or not long after' (p. 341) Andronikos' edition of Aristotle appeared (C1l), and at the outside between *c.*50 BC and *c.* AD 180–90. (Apuleius was born *c.* AD 125 and died by *c.*190, *BNP* s.v.) Among recent commentators, Keyser 2008b adopts 80–20 BC (and is less precise about the work's relationship to Aristotelianism than are the chapters in Gregorić and Karamanolis 2020b); Thom 2014b, 7, identifies a dependence upon Eratosthenes (d. *c.*200 BC) and suggests a date around 'the turn of the era' (i.e. *c.* AD 1) at the latest. Gregorić and Karamanolis 2020a, 8, while preferring not to debate the chronology, prefer a wide window of 250 BC–AD 50, though Pajón Leyra and Bartoš 2020, 120, in the same volume, suggest that Ps.-Arist. knew

The author's primary aim is philosophical and theological rather than scientific; he offers a 'protreptic' work: that is, one designed to encourage the reader to learn more about the field—in this case, philosophy. Accordingly, he does not indulge in polemic against particular schools, but maintains a positive tone and implicitly approves of certain features of different philosophies. The work stands close to the fountain-head of a broad current of reworked Platonism and Aristotelianism that stretches forward through the centuries into the medieval period, when the *De mundo* was much read; but as well as drawing largely upon Eratosthenes (Chapter 12 above) for its geography,[4] it carefully positions itself in the Peripatetic tradition of cosmology, albeit with modifications.[5] Some scholars have seen echoes of Jewish writers of the hellenistic period, such as Aristoboulos of Alexandria (2nd century);[6] one might add Ecclesiasticus or Sirach (written in Hebrew and translated into Greek in the same century),[7] though again there are philosophical differences.[8] It is also firmly, albeit implicitly, opposed to Stoic cosmology:[9] the chief difference being that God is not immanent in the world, only his power is, he himself standing at the highest level of the concentric spheres and making the world move.[10]

Conventionally divided into seven chapters of uneven length, which seem to correspond to an original programme, the text begins by urging 'Alexander' to cultivate the study of the universe (*kosmos*). The author develops his theme by describing the geocentric universe, then moves downwards and inwards via the celestial bodies to the form of the Earth, its seas, and the placement of the inhabited portion of the globe (*oikoumenē*)—or, rather, portions, for he supposes that other inhabited areas exist (an idea with a precedent in Aristotle, *Meteorologika*, 2. 5)[11]—and a range of meteorological and geological phenomena.

In the long chapter 6 he begins to build upwards and outwards again to his cosmological climax, using a series of twelve similes and analogies about the divine power ('a god' or 'the god') who maintains the balance and smooth running of the universe. These comparisons are not randomly juxtaposed, but form a careful developmental

---

the work of Artemidoros (fl. 104–100 BC) and therefore favour 100 BC–AD 50. Exceptionally, Bos 2020, reviewing Gregorić and Karamanolis, still attributes it to Aristotle (as do Reale and Bos 1995); while Sider 2015, reviewing Thom, likewise upholds a date before 323 but sees 'this patently unAristotelian' work as by a pupil of Arist.

[4] Geus and Dan 2018, 402.   [5] Gregorić and Karamanolis 2020a, 6–9.
[6] On Aristoboulos, see J. Cook 2008.
[7] Cf. Ecclus. 43: 11–26, a paean to the panorama of Nature, with ch. 4 of *De mundo*. On the date of Ecclus., see McKechnie 2000.
[8] Tzvetkova-Glaser 2014, 135–7.
[9] In particular, it cannot be proved that *De mundo* drew directly upon Poseidonios: Pajón Leyra and Bartoš 2020, 81–2.
[10] For the work's relation to Stoicism and Aristotle, see now the chapters in Gregorić and Karamanolis 2020b, especially the introduction (Gregorić and Karamanolis 2020a).
[11] See Jirsa 2020, 77–9, also noting *De caelo* 2. 2 and 2. 13 as well as Strabo's discussion of Eratosthenes at 1. 4. 6, C65 (Erat. 26 above), but only as a hypothesis.

sequence, each refining the message of the one before.¹² (i) The god is like leaders of men, who need to rule from a distance, not administer in detail (6. 3–4). (ii) Instrument-makers and (iii) puppeteers may, by a single movement, create many movements (6. 5). (iv) Objects and (v) animals of different form can be impelled or released into movements that bear their individual character (6. 6). (vi) A chorus leader directs his chorus to sing in harmony (6. 8). (vii) The cosmos is like an army at war, each member fulfilling his role in accordance with signals that he understands (6. 9). (viii) The soul is an instance of an unseen mover that produces ordered effects (6. 10). (ix) The keystone in an arch creates an instantaneous and unchanging harmony which is broken if the stone is removed, while (x) Pheidias' portrait was built into Athena's statue in such a way that its removal would cause the whole to collapse (6. 11). The last two examples are inanimate, but (xi) humans, too, can direct other animate beings or inanimate or objects (6. 12). (xii) Finally, and most memorably, the cosmos is compared to a *polis* or city-state run by the unchanging law that enables each of its members to play his part (6. 13). Short-term change is continually contrasted with the essential constancy of everything. The author seems to engage in a debate among Aristotelians, in which he may be taking the position that the deity not only exercises power remotely but can be credited with the material effects of that power in both the sublunary world and the wider cosmos.

Finally, in the short but almost ecstatic chapter 7, 'the god' is equated with Zeus. Previously named only at 2. 4 and 6. 7 in reference to the planet Jupiter, then in his own person at 6. 11—with a quotation from the *Iliad* showing that he occupies the loftiest place in the world—Zeus is now praised with a catalogue of titles to illustrate his many roles, and then an enumeration of the ways in which he embodies fate and justice (7. 3). One can hardly read this final chapter without taking it as a passionate expression of devotion. It is no coincidence, perhaps, that the 2nd-century AD author Apuleius—whose most famous work, *The Golden Ass*, presents itself as a work of personal allegiance to a deity, in his case the Mother Goddess—probably adapted the *De mundo* for a Latin readership.¹³ The work ends with an invocation of Plato in support of the author's theology.

The author demonstrates his broad learning by a wide-ranging appeal to the knowledge accumulated by his hellenistic predecessors and the cosmological and geographical theories they developed. He also makes frequent use of etymologies to explain the workings of the universe. Astronomy, meteorology, and geography are deployed in the service of theology with the aim of inspiring the reader to further study of philosophy. The enumeration of islands, gulfs, continental boundaries, climatic and geological phenomena in chapters 3–4 seems designed to pique the reader's interest

---

¹² See Betegh and Gregorić 2020, 181–201.
¹³ Brodersen 2019; on its adaptation to a new cultural context, see Harrison 2000. Furley 1955, 340, comments that 'it is not quite certain' that Apuleius was the adapter.

with fascinating details, and adds up to an important overview of late hellenistic geographical understanding.

This translation follows the Greek of Furley's Loeb edition,[14] with one change necessitated by a recent comparison with the Armenian version of the text.[15]

SELECTED FURTHER READING

Federspiel, M., and Levet, J.-P. (eds 2018) with A. Cohen-Skalli and M. Cronier, *Pseudo-Aristote, Du monde; Positions et dénominations des vents; Des plantes*. Paris. [Translation; pp. 55–82 (nn., 130–64).]

*Furley, D. J. (1955), 'Aristotle, On the Cosmos', in E. S. Forster and D. J. Furley, *Aristotle, On Sophistical Refutations; On Coming-to-be and Passing Away; On the Cosmos* [Loeb edition], 333–409. ['Introduction' at pp. 333–43; useful notes.]

Gregorić, P., and Karamanolis, G. (eds 2020), *Pseudo-Aristotle, De Mundo (On the Cosmos): A Commentary*. Cambridge. [Includes detailed chapter on the geography by Pajón Leyra and Bartoš, cited in the notes below.]

Kraye, J. (1990), 'Aristotle's god and the authenticity of "De mundo": an early modern controversy', *Journal of the History of Philosophy*, 28. 3: 339–58.

*Reale, G., and Bos, A. P. (1995), *Il trattato Sul cosmo per Alessandro attribuito ad Aristotele*, 2nd edn. Milan.

*Thom, J. C. (2014a), *Cosmic Order and Divine Power: Pseudo-Aristotle, On the Cosmos*. Tübingen.

TEXT

The chapter divisions (1–7) are traditional; section numbers have been added for the present edition.

1. (1) (391a 1) On many occasions, Alexander,[16] philosophy has seemed, to me at least, an essentially godlike and divine thing; especially when, raising itself independently to a view of the wholes,[17] it has endeavoured to learn the truth in them. While other pursuits had stood aside from this viewpoint by reason of its lofty and grand character, this one neither feared the undertaking nor considered itself unfit to contemplate the most beautiful things, but deemed such learning most akin and especially fitting to itself.

(2) (391a 8) For—since it was not possible to arrive at the heavenly location, or to leave the Earth and observe that heavenly space, as the unintelligent Aloadai[18] once

---

[14] In Forster and Furley 1955, 333–409. The Greek text of Thom 2014c differs only occasionally.

[15] Reading πολυμερεστάτοις ὕδασι in ch. 3, with Geus and Dan 2018, 403–10.

[16] The work purports to be addressed to Alexander the Great. On the subject matter of ch. 1, see Karamanolis 2020.

[17] Perhaps 'the massive structures of the universe', as argued by Karamanolis 2020, 17. Cf. the beginning of ch. 2, two contexts in ch. 5, and two in ch. 6.

[18] The giants who attempted to pile Mt Pelion on top of Mt Ossa in order to get to heaven.

did—at any rate through philosophy the soul, taking intelligence as guide, has passed over and ventured abroad to find some unwearying road; and has comprehended in understanding the things that are most distant from one another in location. It has, in my view, easily recognized kindred things and with the divine eye of the soul has grasped equally divine things and proclaimed them to the human race. It had this experience, in so far as it was able, because it wished to share ungrudgingly with all people the treasures it possessed. Therefore those who have earnestly depicted for us the nature of a single place, the form of one city, the size of a river, or the beauty of a mountain, as some in the past have done—some telling of Ossa, others of Nyssa, others again of the Korykian cave,[19] others of whatever detail of an area it happened to be—these might be pitied for their small-mindedness, fascinated as they are by chance encounters with things and thinking great thoughts about small objects of reflection. This is their experience because they are unobservant of greater matters—I mean the cosmos and the greatest things in the cosmos; for if they genuinely knew about these things they would never be amazed by the others, but these other things would appear of no value compared with the pre-eminence of the former.

(3) (391b 3) Let us speak and, in so far as it is attainable, theologize about all these things: what nature each has, what position, and what movement. Actually I consider it fitting even for you, best of leaders, to pursue an inquiry into the greatest things; and (*fitting*) for philosophy to conceive of nothing mean but to shake hands with the best men and present them with these kinds of gifts.

2. (1) (391b 9) *Kosmos*, then, is the combination of heaven, Earth, and the natures[20] contained within them. *Kosmos* can be otherwise expressed as the appointment and adornment of the wholes,[21] which is preserved by the god and because of the god. The middle of this, being unmoved and fixed, has been taken by the 'life-bearing Earth'[22] which is the hearth and mother of all kinds of creatures. The place above it, whose extremity is entirely and everywhere in the highest, is the dwelling-place of the gods and has been named heaven. It is full of divine bodies which we are accustomed to call stars. Moving with an eternal motion, it performs a continual dance in circular revolution with all these (*bodies*), never ceasing through the ages.

(2) (391b 19) Since the entire heaven or *kosmos*[23] is spherical and, as I have said, moves continuously, there are of necessity two unmoved points directly opposite one another, as in a revolving sphere on the lathe; they remain stationary and hold together the sphere, and around them the whole mass turns in a circle. They are called poles; and if we were to conceive of a straight line, which some call an axle, it shall be the diameter of the cosmos, having the Earth in its centre and the two poles as the

---

[19] On Mt Parnassos: Pausanias 10. 32. 2.
[20] *physeis*, a metonymy for 'things with a nature'. On the polysemy of the term *physis*, see Jirsa 2020, 63–4. On the content and organization of ch. 2, see Thein 2020; on its later part, Jirsa 2020.
[21] For this expression, cf. n. on ch. 1.   [22] A quotation from Hesiod, *Theogony*, 693.
[23] A sense of *kosmos* distinct from those in the previous paragraph (Furley ad loc.).

extremities. Of these unmoving poles one is always visible overhead, in the northern latitude, and is called the Arctic; the other is always hidden below the Earth in the southern, and called Antarctic.

(3) (392a 5) The aether (*aithēr*) is what we call the substance (*ousia*)[24] of the heaven and the stars; not, as some say, because being made of fire it *aithetai*, 'burns'—they are mistaken about its (*the aithēr's*) power, quite removed from that of fire—but because it *aëi thei*, 'always runs', being carried round in a circle. It is a different element from the other four;[25] it is pure and divine. Of the stars contained in it, some do not wander but revolve with the entirety of heaven, keeping the same positions; in the middle of them is the so-called *zōöphoros*, 'animal-bearing', circle (*Zodiac*), formed as a girdle obliquely between the tropics and divided section by section into the twelve spaces for the animals. Others, being *planēta*, 'wanderers', do not by nature move at the same speed as the above, or as each other, but in one or another circle so that one of them will be closer to the Earth, another higher.   (4) (392a 16) The multitude of the unwandering, fixed ones is undiscoverable by humans, even though they move upon a single surface of the entirety of heaven. That of the planets, appointed in seven sections, exists in as many circles lying in succession so that the upper is always greater than the lower and the seven are contained within one another; all of them, nevertheless, are embraced by the sphere of the unwandering ones. The circle called that of the shining one (*phainōn*) or Kronos (*Saturn*) has its position permanently contiguous with this (*outermost*) one; next is the one called the (*circle*) of the radiant one (*phaëthōn*) or Zeus (*Jupiter*); next the fiery one (*pyroëis*), designated the circle of Herakles and Ares (*Mars*); next the gleamer (*stilbōn*), which some call the sacred circle of Hermes (*Mercury*) but others that of Apollo; after which is that of the light-bringer (*phosphoros*) which they designate as that of Aphrodite (*Venus*), though others of Hera. Next is the circle of the Sun; the last is that of the Moon whose limit extends to the Earth. The aether contains the divine bodies and their appointed movement.

(5) (392a 31) After the aetherial and divine nature—which, as we have demonstrated, is so appointed, is unalterable, unchangeable, and unaffected by anything—the next adjacent nature is in all respects able to be affected and altered and, to tell the entire tale, capable of being destroyed and of perishing. Of this the first substance is the fine-grained and inflammable one, set on fire by the aetherial nature on account of the latter's size and the rapidity of its motion. In this fiery and disorganized one the meteors dart through, flames are shot, beam-meteors and cavity-meteors and so-called comets are set and often extinguished.

(6) (392b 5) Next after this flows the *aēr* (*air*), which is by its nature opaque and ice-cold, but when in motion becomes illuminated as well as burning, both radiant and heated. In this, as it belongs to the (*sphere*) capable of being affected and is itself associated with power and is altered in every way, clouds are produced and rains

---

[24] On the translation of *ousia*, see Jirsa 2020, 64–5.   [25] Earth, air, fire, and water (Furley ad loc.).

tumble down, with snow, hoar-frost, hail, and breaths of winds and whirlwinds (*typhōnes*),[26] plus thunder, lightning, thunderbolts, and ten thousand collisions of dark clouds.

3. (1) (392b 14) Next after the aerial nature are fixed the Earth and sea, teeming with plants and animals, springs and rivers, some winding across the Earth, others disgorged into the sea.[27] It is variegated with ten thousand kinds of greenery, high mountains, thick-set forests, and cities which the wise creature, the human, has founded; and with sea-girt islands and continents. The majority of accounts have divided the inhabited world into islands and continents, not realizing that the whole is one island surrounded by the so-called Atlantic sea (*thalassa*). It is probable that many other (*inhabited worlds*) lie far away across the water from this one, some larger than it, others smaller; but all except this one are invisible to us.[28] The islands in our part bear the same relationship towards these open seas (*pelagē*) here as does this inhabited world in relation to the Atlantic sea (*thalassa*), and many others in relation to the entire sea; for these are like great islands with great open seas (*pelagē*) beating upon them. The entire nature of the moist is on the surface, but in some parts of the Earth it reveals the so-called cliffs, which are the inhabited areas and might be said to belong to the aerial nature. After this, in the depths at the very centre of the cosmos, stands the Earth, firmly set and compressed, unmoved and undisturbed; and this is the whole lower part, as we call it, of the cosmos.

(2) (392b 35) These five elements, lying in five spaces in a spherical relationship, the lesser always being enclosed by the greater—I mean the Earth in the water, the water in the air, the air in the fire, the fire in the aether—have constituted the whole cosmos and appointed all the upper part as the dwelling-place of gods, the lower that of short-lived creatures. Of the latter part, some is moist, which we are accustomed to call rivers, streams, and seas; and some dry, which we name land, continents, and islands.

(3) (393a 9) Of the islands some are large, as is this entire inhabited world, as has been said, and many others surrounded by great open seas (*pelagē*); others smaller, being visible to us and within (*our sea*). Of the latter some are noteworthy, (*namely*) Sicily, Sardo (*Sardinia*), Kyrnos (*Corsica*), also Crete, Euboia, Cyprus, and Lesbos; others less substantial, among which some are named Sporades, others Cyclades, and others differently.[29]

---

[26] See ch. 4 for a possibly different use of this term.
[27] On the first part of ch. 3, see Jirsa 2020; on the geographical content, see Burri 2014, and the comprehensive discussion by Pajón Leyra and Bartoš 2020.
[28] Cf. Erat. 26 §6.
[29] On lists of islands in the geographers, see Pajón Leyra and Bartoš 2020, 82–5, noting (83) that the only identical list is in the C4f–C3e comic poet Alexis, fr. 260 in Arnott 1996 (268 in Kock 1880–8) = Steph. Byz. σ 155a Sikelia (from Constantine Porphyrogennetos): 'of the seven greatest islands which Nature has shown to mortals Sikelia, it is said, is the greatest, second Sardo, third Kyrnos, fourth Crete the nurse of Zeus, narrow-formed Euboia fifth, sixth Cyprus; Lesbos has received the seventh rank'.

(4) (393a 16) The open sea (*pelagos*) outside the inhabited world is called the Atlantic and Okeanos, and it surrounds us; and opening out from a narrow passage in the west (*of our inhabited world*) it forms, at the so-called Pillars of Herakles, its inflow into the inner sea as if it were a harbour; broadening out little by little, it flows along and incorporates great bays connected to one another: here given a mouth at a narrow neck, there broadening again. The first gulf that is formed on the right as one sails in at the Pillars of Herakles is in two parts: the so-called Syrteis, one of which they call Great (*gulf of Sidra*), the other Small (*gulf of Gabès*). On the other side it is not similarly formed into a gulf but makes three open seas (*pelagē*), the Sardinian, the so-called Galatic (*Gallic*), and the Adriatic; and next after these at an oblique angle the Sicilian; after this the Cretan; contiguous with this in one direction the Egyptian, the Pamphylian, and Syrian, in the other the Aegean and the Myrtoan. Running beside and opposite the aforementioned (*seas*) with their many parts[30] is the Pontos, of which the innermost (*part*) is called Maiotis and the outer, towards the Hellespont, is connected by a mouth to the so-called Propontis.

(5) (393b 2) In the direction of the Sun's uprisings (*anascheseis*),[31] the Ocean flows in again, opening up the Indian and Persian gulfs, and reveals the contiguous Erythraian sea, dividing it off. Towards the other horn (*of Asia*),[32] running through a long, narrow neck, it widens out again and defines the Hyrkanian or Caspian (*land*);[33] beyond this, it has a deep place beyond Lake Maiotis. Next, beyond the Skythians and Keltike, it constricts the inhabited world towards the Galatic gulf and the aforementioned Pillars of Herakles, outside which Okeanos flows round the land. In this part there turn out to be two very large islands, called the Brettanic: Albion (*Great Britain*) and Ierne (*Ireland*), lying beyond the Keltoi. No smaller than these are Taprobane beyond the Indians, at an angle to the inhabited world; and the so-called Phebol (*Socotra?*), which lies by the Arabian gulf (*Red Sea*).[34] A good number of small ones in the area of the Brettanic islands and Iberia form a crown round this inhabited world, which of course is an island, as we have said, whose breadth at the deepest point of the continent wants little of 40,000 stades—as those who have practised geography well assert—and whose length is roughly about 70,000.[35] It is divided into Europe, Asia, and Libyē.

(6) (393b 23) Europe is the (*part*) whose boundary markers in a circle are the Pillars of Herakles, the head of the Pontos, and the Hyrkanian sea at the point where a very narrow isthmus runs through into the Pontos; though some have said it is the

---

[30] Reading πολυμερεστάτοις δ' οὖσι with Geus and Dan.
[31] Rare word, nowhere else used thus.   [32] 'Horn' (*keras*) in the sense of headland; see Glossary.
[33] On the identity of this region, and the question whether the Caspian was a gulf of Ocean, see Pajón Leyra and Bartoš 2020, 96–102.
[34] Altomare 2014 identifies Phebol as Madagascar, which suits some evidence, but somewhere further N is implied here. Pajón Leyra and Bartoš 2020, 84–5, suggest (at 84) a corruption of 'Phoibos' in reference to the Island of the Sun (mentioned e.g. by Iamboulos as reported by Diod. 2. 55. 1–60. 3), which they tentatively identify as either *Socotra* or Sri Lanka.
[35] Pajón Leyra and Bartoš 2020, 112–18, prefer 'around 70,000 stades at most'.

river Tanaïs (*Don*) rather than the isthmus. Asia is the (*part*) from the isthmus previously mentioned, the Pontos, and the Hyrkanian sea up to the other isthmus that lies between the Arabian gulf and the outer sea, enclosed by this and Okeanos on the outside; though some make the boundary of Asia run from the Tanaïs up to the mouths of the Nile. Libyē is the (*part*) from the Arabian isthmus as far as the Pillars of Herakles; though some say (*it runs*) from the Nile to the latter. Some attach Egypt, surrounded (*sc. at its seaward end*) by the mouths of the Nile, to Asia, others to Libyē. Some make the islands independent, others assign them to their various neighbouring sections.   (394a 4) Now we have inquired after the nature and position of the Earth and of the sea, what we are accustomed to call the inhabited world, and found it to be of the above character.

4.   (1) (394a 7) Let us now speak of the most noteworthy phenomena within and around it, summarizing the essentials.[36]   (394a 9) For two particular exhalations are continuously carried out of it into the air above us; they are fine-grained and wholly invisible unless they are sometimes observed around the dawn (*hours*) being carried up along rivers and streams. The first of these is dry and smoky, flowing out of the Earth; the second is damp and vaporous, being exhaled by the moist nature. From the latter arise mists, dews, and forms of frost, also clouds, rain, snow, and hail; from the dry one winds, varieties of breeze, thunder and lightning, firestorms, lightning bolts, and other things that are akin to these.

(2) (394a 19) Mist is a vaporous exhalation unproductive of water, thicker than air and thinner than cloud; it arises from the initial stage of a cloud or from its remnant. The opposite of this is said to be a clear sky, as indeed is the case, for it is nothing except cloudless and mistless air. Dew is moisture that is carried out of a clear sky and has a fine consistency. Ice is compacted water solidified in a clear sky. Hoar-frost is solidified dew. Dew-frost is half-frozen dew. Cloud is a thick, vaporous concentration productive of water. Rain arises from the squeezing out of well-thickened cloud, and has as many varieties as does the compression of cloud; for when the latter is mild it sprinkles soft raindrops, but if intense they are solider; we call this a rainstorm, greater than rain and carried to the ground as continuous concentrations. Snow arises at the breaking up of thickened clouds which are cut up before they are turned into water; the cutting produces foaminess and extreme whiteness, while the consolidation inside produces the coldness of the moisture which is not yet liquefied or thinned out. When this is strongly and thickly deposited, it is named a blizzard. Hail arises from a blizzard that has been concentrated and has gained weight from compression (*lit. 'felting'*) so that its descent is swifter; according to the sizes of the fragments broken off, the masses are greater and their courses become more violent. These, therefore, are the things that occur as a result of moist exhalation.

---

[36] On ch. 4, see Baksa 2020; and cf. Aristotle, *Meteorologika* 2. 6 (appendix to Ch. 10 above).

(3) (394b 7) From the dry (*exhalation*), pressured into flowing by cold, wind has arisen; for this is nothing other than a lot of air flowing as a mass, which at the same time is called a breath. 'Breath' is a term used in another sense for the substance in plants and animals that runs through all things and is animate and fertile; it is not necessary to talk of this now. The 'breaths' that blow in air we call winds; the exhalations carried from moisture we call breezes. Of the winds, those blowing from soaked earth are called land winds; those darting out from gulfs are called gulf winds. Winds from rivers and lakes have a certain similarity to these. Those arising from the break-up of cloud and the dissolution of its density towards themselves, are called cloud winds; if they break up massively with water they are called water winds.

(4) (394b 19) And the continuous winds from the east (*i.e. eastern quarter*) are called Euroi, but those from the north (*i.e. northern quarter*) are called Boreai, those from the west (*i.e. western quarter*) Zephyroi, and those from the south (*i.e. southern quarter*) Notoi.[37] Of the Euroi, moreover, Kaikias is the name of the wind blowing from the area around the summer sunrises (*north-east*), but Apeliotes (*is the name*) of that from the area around the equinoctial[38] ones (*due east*), and Euros of that from the area around the winter ones (*south-east*). And of the contrary Zephyroi the Argestes, which some call Olympias and others Iapyx, is that from the summer sunset (*northwest*), but Zephyros is that from the equinoctial one (*due west*), and Lips that from the winter one (*south-west*). And of the Boreai the one next to the Kaikias is specifically called Boreas (*NNE*), but the next one Aparktias (*north*), blowing from the pole onto the south point, and the next one Thraskias (*NNW*), which some call Kirkias, blowing next to the Argestes. And of the Notoi the one running contrary to the Aparktias from the invisible pole (*i.e. the South Pole*) is called Notos, but the one between Notos and Euros Euronotos (*SSE*), and the one on the other side, between Lips and Notos, some call Libonotos (*SSW*), others Libophoinix.

(5) (394b 34) Some of the winds are 'straight-blowing', those that blow forwards in a straight line; others are 'curve-blowing', such as the so-called Kaikias. Some predominate in winter, like the Notoi; others in summer, like the so-called Etesiai, which contain a mixture of those carried from the north and of the Zephyroi; the so-called Ornithiai (*'bird-winds'*), which are among the spring winds, are of the Boreas category.

(6) (395a 5) Among the violent winds, a squall is a wind that strikes suddenly from above; a hurricane is a violent wind that springs up suddenly. A storm or tornado is a wind twisting upwards from below. An up-draught is a wind carried upwards during emission from some depth or fracture. When it has a tightly twisting movement, it is a 'land firestorm'. When wind is twisted within a thick, damp cloud and forced out through it, violently breaking the compressed layers (*lit. 'feltings'*) of the cloud, it has developed a great crashing and banging which is called thunder, like wind forcefully driven through water. During the break-up of the cloud the wind is set on fire and

---

[37] For the wind rose, see Timosthenes 18 and nn.
[38] Lit. 'equidiurnal'. See Introduction, §X. 3. b fin.

becomes luminous, and is called lightning, which has fallen (*upon us*) earlier than the thunder despite happening later: for in the nature of things what is heard is overtaken by what is seen. The latter is seen from afar, the former only when it approaches the hearing; particularly when the latter is the swiftest of essences—I mean the fiery one— but the former is less swift because it is made of air and arrives at one's hearing by an impact. Once aflame, the hurled lightning that hastens violently to the ground is called a thunderbolt; if it is half on fire but otherwise substantial and dense, a firestorm; if wholly without fire a whirlwind (*typhōn*).[39] Each of these, striking the ground, is named a lightning strike. Some thunderbolts are called 'sooty' if they are dark; others that dart rapidly, 'brilliant'; 'forked' if carried along a line; 'lightning strikes' if they strike something.

(7) (395a 28) In short, some appearances in the air are by reflection, others by substance. Those by reflection are rainbows, staves, and such things; those by substance are darting meteors, comets, and things similar to those. A rainbow is a reflection, as in a mirror, of a section of the Sun or Moon in damp, hollow cloud of continuous appearance, observed to resemble the circumference of a circle. A stave is a straight reflection of a rainbow. A halo is a very bright reflection of the illumination of a star; it differs from a rainbow in that the rainbow appears opposite the Sun or Moon, while the halo is seen in a circle round the whole star. A meteor is the ignition of dense fire in the air. Among meteors some are cast like javelins, others are stationary. The javelin throw is the generation of fire by rubbing; the fire is carried swiftly in air and presents the appearance of length because of its speed; the stationary position is an elongated extension without movement, like the motion of a star; when broadened at the end, it is called a comet. Often it happens that some of the meteors persist for a considerable time while others are extinguished immediately. Many other forms of appearances are observed, called torches, bars, jars, and pits, having been so designated in accordance with their resemblance to these things. Some of these are observed in the west, some in the east, others everywhere; rarely in the north and south. All are unstable; for none of these has been described as always visible and fixed in position. So aerial matters have the above character.

(8) (395b 18) But just as the Earth contains in itself many springs of water, similarly there are springs of wind and fire. Of these, some are invisible under the ground, but many have places where they inhale and exhale, such as Lipara, Aitna (*Etna*), and those in the Aeolian islands. They often flow in the manner of a river, and throw up fiery anvils. Some, being underground near spring-waters, warm these and send up warm streams, boiling ones, or those with a good mixture. Similarly, many mouths have opened for winds in many parts of the Earth; some cause people who come near them to be divinely inspired, others to lose appetite, others to prophesy, like those at

---

[39] At ch. 2 *typhōn* appears to mean a variety of wind, but here it seems to be a form of lightning without fire.

Delphi and Lebadeia;[40] others kill outright, as is the case in Phrygia. Often a related breath of moderate quality within the Earth has been forced into the inner ends of caves, being displaced from its usual region, and has severely rocked many parts. Often a large quantity from outside has been cooped up in the cavities of the Earth and, being confined with no way out, has agitated the Earth very violently, seeking its exit, and has created this effect, which we are accustomed to call an earthquake. (9) 395b 36. Among earthquakes, some move the Earth obliquely at sharp angles; these are called 'leaners'. Those that throw the Earth up and down at right angles are 'boilers';[41] those causing subsidence into cavities, 'sinkers'; those opening chasms and shattering the Earth are called 'breakers'. Some of these additionally project wind, some rocks, some mud; others reveal springs that previously did not exist. Some overturn things at one push; they are called 'thrusters'. Others, which make the shaken ground sway back and forth and, by inclining and swaying back, continually correct the movement, are called 'swingers'; they induce an effect similar to trembling. There are also 'bellower' earthquakes, shaking the ground with a loud noise; often, too, a roaring of the ground takes place without an earthquake, when the wind is insufficient to shake it, but being cooped up in it is beaten about with a roaring force. The penetrating winds are also corporealized (*i.e. condensed*) by the moisture hidden in the Earth.

(10) (396a 17) Analogous things to these also occur in the sea. For sea chasms appear, and often there are retreats and assaults by waves; sometimes with a reverse strike, sometimes with only a forward thrust, as is reported about Helike and Boura.[42] Up-draughts of fire often occur in the sea, springs gush forth, rivers discharge, trees grow up; there are currents and whirlpools analogous to those of winds, some in the middle of open seas (*pelagē*), others at narrows and straits. Many ebb-tides and receding waves are said to occur in time with the Moon, at particular defined times.

(11) (396a 27) In sum, since the elements are mixed with one another, it makes sense that in the air, Earth, and sea similarities of effects are produced. Some bring about the destruction and generation of particular parts (*of the whole*) while protecting the entirety from ruin and generation.

5. (1) (396a 33) All the same, it seems amazing to some persons how, if the cosmos is composed of contrary principles—I mean those of dry and moist, cold and hot—it has not been destroyed and annihilated long since; as if one were amazed by how a city survives when it is composed of the most contrary nations—I mean poor and rich, young and old, weak and strong, wicked and noble.[43] They do not know that the most amazing thing about civic concord has been this: I mean the fact that out of

---

[40] For exhalations from the ground at Delphi, see Etiope, Papatheodorou *et al.* 2006; inconclusive as to possible psychological effects.

[41] Cf. Pos. 39 above; also Arist. *Meteorologika* 2. 8 (368b).

[42] Towns in Achaia (N. Peloponnese) destroyed by a geological or tectonic event in 373. See Introduction, §III. 4. b.

[43] On the content and organization of ch. 5, see Gregorić 2020.

many things it accomplishes one organization that is uniform yet made of dissimilar things, and accommodates every nature and fortune. Perhaps, however, nature clings to contraries and accomplishes unison out of these and not out of similar things: for example, it has combined male with female and not combined either with the object of the same sex; it has conjoined them into the first concord through contraries, not through similar things. Art, too, appears to do this by imitating nature. For by mixing together the natures of white and black colours, ochres and reds, it effected images that conform to the objects that precede them. Music, on the other hand, by mixing high and low sounds, long and short, effected harmony among different voices. Grammar, again, by making a blend of vowels and consonants composed its whole art from them.

(2) (396b 19) This very same thing was said by Herakleitos, known as the Dark Man: 'conjunctions are wholes and non-wholes, combination and separation, unison and dissonance; and from all, one; yet from one, all'.[44] Thus, therefore, the composite of the wholes[45]—I mean the heaven, the Earth, and the entire cosmos—has been appointed by a single harmony through the blending of the most contrary principles. For the single power that runs through everything has mixed the dry with the moist, the hot with the cold, with the light the heavy, the straight with the round; it has coordinated all the Earth, sea, and air; Sun, Moon, and the whole of heaven. It has crafted the entire cosmos from things unmixed and alien—air, earth, fire, and water—and has taken each within the single surface of a sphere; has compelled the most hostile natures within it to make agreements; and from them has contrived the safe keeping of the whole.

(3) (396b 34) The cause of this security is the agreement of the elements. The cause of the agreement is equality of shares and the fact that none of them is more powerful than another: for heavy things have the same equilibrium with light as do hot things with their contrary. Nature teaches that equality has some power to maintain concord, and concord to maintain the ancestor of all: that most beautiful of beauteous things, the cosmos. For what (*particular*) nature could be mightier than the cosmos? For whatever one might name is a part of the cosmos.

(4) (397a 6) All that is beautiful, all that is appointed, is named after this: it is said *kekosmēsthai*, 'to have been well ordered', from *kosmos*, the 'good order' (*of everything*). What, among the parts, could be equated with the appointment and motion in heaven of the stars, Sun, and Moon, which move in the most precise measures from one age to another age? What honesty could be like that which is preserved by the beautiful and generative seasons of all things, which bring around summers and winters at the appointed time, and days and nights to the accomplishment of the month and the year? Moreover, in size this (*cosmos*) is supreme, in movement swiftest, in brightness most radiant, in power ageless and indestructible. This is what has separated the natures of marine creatures, those on foot, and those of the air, and has measured their lives by its own movements. From it, all creatures inhale and hold onto life. Even its

---

[44] This is probably not from Herakleitos but from Neo-Pythagorean sources (Furley ad loc.).
[45] I follow Betegh and Gregorić 2020, 177, in translating τὰ ὅλα as 'the wholes'.

unexpected novelties are accomplished in the appointed manner: the various winds that clash, the thunderbolts that fall from heaven, the exceptional storms that break out. Through these things the moist that is forced out, and the fiery that is transpired, bring everything into concord and establish it. The Earth also, shaggy with all kinds of plants, bursting with springs, crossed in all directions by creatures, putting forth everything in season, nourishing it and receiving it, bringing about ten thousand forms and effects, likewise conserves its ageless nature despite being agitated by earthquakes, awash with high tides, and in places aflame with conflagrations.

(5) (397a 30) All these things seem to happen to the Earth for good ends and to give it safe keeping through the ages. For when it is shaken, the influxes of the winds dart through it and make their exhalation at the breaches, as has been said above. When it is cleaned by rains, all harmful things are washed away. When it is blown by breezes, the things under it and over it are purified. Moreover, the flames soften the icy material and the frosts moderate the flames. And of the particular things some arise, some reach their prime, and others are destroyed. Generation resists destruction, destruction reduces the weight of generation. One (*power of*) safe keeping—passing through all things that surround and oppose one another and now dominate, now are dominated—protects the entirety from destruction through the ages.

6. (1) (397b 9) The remaining task is to tell of the sustaining cause of the wholes,[46] at least in outline, in the way we have treated other matters; for it is outrageous, if we are speaking of the cosmos—if not in a precise manner, at least for the purpose of summary learning—to leave out the highest power in the cosmos.[47] It is an ancient account, inherited by all humans, that all things are constituted by the god and through the god, but that no kind of nature exists by itself and independently if it is deserted by the power of safe keeping that comes from him. Therefore certain ancient (*writers*) were induced to say that all the things that appear to us through the eyes, hearing, or any other sense are full of gods. They let fall an account befitting the divine power but not its substance (*ousia*).

(2) (397b 20) For the keeper of all things and progenitor of the things in this cosmos, however they be accomplished, is truly the god; truly he does not undergo the hard labour of a self-employed, hard-working creature, but employs an unwearied power through which he prevails even over things that seem to be far away. He himself possesses the highest and first seat and for this reason is named Highest. According to the poet, he is installed 'upon the topmost peak' of the whole of heaven. The body close to him has the greatest benefit of his power; next the one after it, and so in succession as far as our regions. (397b 30) For this reason, the Earth and the things on the Earth, being at the greatest distance from the god, are naturally weak and incongruous and filled with great confusion. All the same, in so far as it is natural for the divine to reach everything, both the things in our world and those above us turn out similarly,

---

[46] For this expression, see n. on ch. 1 above. [47] On this section, see Betegh and Gregorić 2020.

partaking of the benefit of the god to a larger or smaller degree according to whether they are nearer or further from him.

(3) (398a 1) It is therefore stronger to suppose—as is also befitting and especially appropriate for the god—that the power established in heaven is also the cause of safe keeping both for the things most distant, to put it briefly, and for all things, rather than that it does its work by running around and roaming where it is neither good nor elegant (*that it should be*).

(i)[48] For this is not appropriate even for the leaders of men: to stand over every task that happens to arise, such as the governor of an army, city, or house—supposing it were necessary to tie up a sack of bedding or accomplish some even more trivial task that any random slave might do—but rather only what is recorded under the Great King.[49] For the outward show of Kambyses, Xerxes, and Darius was ordered magnificently, to the height of solemnity and eminence. For he himself, the story goes, was established in Sousa or Ekbatana, invisible to everyone, occupying a marvellous royal palace, its outer wall glittering with gold, electrum, and ivory. The long line of gateposts, the porches separated from one another by distances of many stades, were fortified by bronze doors and great walls. Outside these, the first and most trusted men were placed in order, some as spear-bearers and servants around the king himself; others, called gatekeepers and eavesdroppers, as guards of each outer wall; so that the king himself, who was named master and god, might see all things and hear all things.   (4) (398a 23) As well as these, others were installed as revenue stewards, generals for wars and hunts, and receivers of gifts, and for other tasks; while others were superintendents of the remaining tasks, according to need. The whole empire of Asia, whose extremities were the Hellespont in the parts towards the west and the Indos in those towards the east, had been divided, nation by nation, between generals, satraps, and kings—the Great King's slaves—with day-runners, scouts, message-carriers, and watchmen for beacon-towers. Such was the good order—particularly of the beacon-towers, which would light up one after the other from the extremities of the empire to Sousa and Ekbatana—that the king knew within one day of everything that was developing in Asia. It is to be supposed that the king's pre-eminence was as inferior to that of the god who holds the cosmos as the (*status of the*) most trivial and weakest creature fell short of that of the king. Thus, if it was undignified for Xerxes to be seen to be performing his own labour, accomplishing what he wanted, and directing things by supervising them, it would be much more unbefitting for the god.   (5) (398b 6) It is more solemn and befitting for him to be established upon the highest place, but for his power, running through the entire universe, to move the Sun and Moon and turn round the whole of heaven, and be responsible for the safe keeping of the things upon the Earth. He does

---

[48] I assign roman numerals to the series of analogies that begins here, in accordance with the discussion in Betegh and Gregorić 2020, 183–201.

[49] Cf. Deiokes' luxurious surroundings at Ekbatana (Hdt. 1. 98) (Furley ad loc.).

not need the ingenuity and service of others, in the way that rulers in our world need a host of hands because of their weakness.

This has been the most divine thing: to bring into being all kinds of forms with ease and with a single movement; (ii) as do, for example, the makers of instruments,[50] who accomplish many and various actions with one trigger on a device.

(iii) Similarly, puppeteers by pulling one cord cause the creature's neck to move, or its hand, shoulder, or eye, and sometimes all the parts, in a rhythmical sequence.   (6) (398b 25) Thus, therefore, the divine nature, from a simple movement of the first (*body*), passes his power to the succeeding one and again from these to the ones further off, until it has come through the whole. For one thing, being moved by another, then itself moves another in due order; all of them act in the manner suited to their own make-up. The road is not the same for all, but different and alien and, for some, contrary. The first keynote for the process, as it were, is a single one.

(iv) Likewise, if one were to throw from a vessel[51] a sphere, a cube, a cone, and a cylinder at the same moment, each of them will be set in motion according to its own form.

(v) Or if one were to hold a water-creature, a land-creature, and a winged creature in one's cloak and throw them out at the same moment, it is clear that the swimmer will jump into its own dwelling-place and swim away, but the land animal will move away to its own normal behaviour and feeding-place, and the aerial creature will rise from the ground and be gone, flying high in the air. A single cause, the first, will have given each of them its own opportunity.   (7) (398b 35) It is the same with the cosmos: for with a single revolution of the entirety of heaven, terminated in a day and a night, the differing trajectories of them all are produced; and, though contained in a single sphere, some move more rapidly, others more tardily in relationship with the lengths of their distances and each one's specific make-up. For the Moon passes through its own circle in a month, increasing, decreasing, and perishing; the Sun does so in a year, as do its running partners Phosphoros (*Venus*) and Hermes (*Mercury*); the Fiery One (*Mars*) in double its time; Zeus (*Jupiter*) in six times longer than the latter; and last of all the one called Kronos (*Saturn*) in two and a half times (*the period of*) the one beneath it. From all of them, singing together and dancing across the heavens, one harmony starts from a single place and ends at a single place, giving the totality the accurate name of *kosmos*, 'order', not *akosmia*, 'disorder'.

(8) (399a 14) (vi) As, in a chorus, when the leader starts off, the whole chorus of men and sometimes of women takes up the sound, blending a well-tuned harmony with their different voices, some high and some low: so it is, too, with the god who manages everything. For in accordance with the keynote (*sounded*) by him who would appropriately be designated leader, the stars and all the heaven move continuously

---

[50] Or military catapults (Furley ad loc.).
[51] i.e. a pot (not a ship). Furley emends ἄγγους to αἴπους 'height', but the text makes sense.

and the resplendent Sun travels its double course: by one (*movement*) dividing day and night by its rising and setting; by the other bringing the four seasons of the year by moving away forwards when in the north and backwards when in the south. Rains occur in season, and winds, dew, and the effects that arise in the enclosing (*substance*) through the first, originating cause. Upon these follow the emergence of rivers, up-swellings of the sea, the sprouting of trees, the ripening of fruits, the reproduction of animals, the upbringing, prime, and decline of all things. The make-up of each has an input to these events, as I have said. (9) (399a 30) When, therefore, the leader and progenitor of all, invisible other than to reason, signals to every nature that is present between heaven and Earth, it is all moved continuously in its own circles and extremities, now disappearing, now revealed, revealing ten thousand forms and hiding them again, from one principle.

(vii) It closely resembles what is done at times that occur most in war, when the trumpet signals to the camp. For after each hears the sound, one lifts up his shield, but another gets into his breastplate; another puts on greaves, helmet, or belt; one sets a bridle on a horse, one mounts a chariot, another communicates the password; the captain quickly gets into position in his company, the commander in his contingent, the cavalryman runs to his squadron, the light-armed solider to his own place: everything is in commotion under one signaller, in line with the specification of the leader who wields the power. (10) (399b 10) One must conceive of the entirety (*of things*) in the same way. By one displacement, the particular tasks of all things are brought about as they are spurred on; yet it is invisible and unrevealed, which in no way hinders it from acting or us from believing.

(viii) For the soul, through which we live and have houses and cities, though it is invisible, is seen in its works. All the ordering of life has been discovered, arranged, and sustained by it: the ploughing and planting of the ground, the devices of art, laws' application, a constitution's good order, international affairs, external war and peace. This also must one conceive about the god, who is most strong in power, most conspicuous in beauty, immortal in life, mightiest in virtue: for, while he has been unobserved by any mortal nature, he is observed through his very deeds. All the effects in the air, on the land, and in the water could rightly be said to be the works of him that holds the cosmos. (399b 25) From him, according to the natural philosopher Empedokles,[52] come

> all things that were, and are, and shall come after,
> the trees that have grown up, the men and women,
> animals, birds, the water-nourished fish.

---

[52] Fr. B 21 in Diels and Kranz 1959–60, i. 319–20.

(ix) It truly resembles, if one may compare a minor thing, the so-called navel-stones of vaults, which lying in the middle are so connected to each side as to keep in harmony and proper arrangement the whole form of the arch, and make it immovable.

(x) They say, again, that the statue-maker Pheidias, while constructing the Athena on the Acropolis, carved his own face in the centre of her shield and connected it to the statue by some unrevealed craft, so that if someone should wish to take it off he would necessarily cause the whole statue to be dismantled and collapse.   (11) (400a 3) This, then, is the rationale that the god has in the cosmos, holding together the harmony and safe keeping of everything; except that he is not in the middle, where the Earth and this unclean region are found, but upward, a clean one set in a clean place which we correctly called *ouranos*, 'heaven', because it is the *horos anō*, the 'boundary above', or 'Olympos' in that it is *hololampes*, 'all-shining', and separated from all the dark region and uncoordinated movement such as occurs in our world because of the force of a storm or winds, as the poet has said:

> to Olympos, where they say the gods' steadfast seat
> lies ever: not shaken by winds, nor ever soaked
> by rain, nor neared by snow, but fresh air spreads out
> cloudless, and gleaming white light overruns it.[53]

All of life testifies to this, assigning the upper space to the god. As humans, we all extend our hands to heaven as we make our prayers. On this basis the following utterance, too, is not inappropriate:

> Zeus hath wide heaven in aether and the clouds.[54]

(12) (400a 20) Wherefore also the most distinguished of sensory things hold place: the stars, Sun, and Moon. On this account the heavenly bodies alone are always ordered so as to preserve the same arrangement, are never altered, never relocated as are the things upon the Earth, which being easily turned entertain many mutations and effects. For violent earthquakes have broken up many parts of the Earth in the past; exceptional rains have broken out and inundated them; assaults and retreats by waves have often made continents into seas and seas into continents; the force of winds and whirlwinds (*typhōnes*) has sometimes uprooted cities; and in former times conflagrations and flames from heaven, they say, burned the eastern parts in the time of Phaëthon,[55] while in the west they boiled up out of the Earth and were blown out, for example when the craters on Aitna (*Etna*) broke up and were carried over the ground like a torrent. There the divine power particularly honoured the race of pious men when they were caught and surrounded by the stream, for they lifted up their aged parents onto their shoulders and saved them: and when the river of fire came close it was split apart and

---

[53] Hom. *Od.* 6. 42–5.   [54] Hom. *Il.* 15. 192.
[55] The son of Helios (the Sun), while rashly driving his father's chariot which he could not control.

turned one of its parts to this side, one to the other, thus keeping unharmed not only the parents but also the young men.

(13) (400b 6) (xi) All in all, what the steersman is to the ship, the charioteer to the chariot, the leader to the chorus, the lawgiver to the city, and the governor to the camp, so the god is to the cosmos; except in so far as for the former the task of ruling is full of toil, movement, and cares while for the latter it is without pain and effort, and separated from all corporeal weakness. For being established in the unmoved he moves and brings around all, where and how he wishes, in different forms and natures; (xii) just as, for example, the law of the city, being unmoved, manages the affairs of the constitution in the souls of those who employ it. For it is evident that by attending to it the rulers go out to their offices, the judges to their own courts, the councillors and assembly members to the meeting-rooms assigned to them; one man walks to the *prytaneion* to enjoy a meal, one to the jurors to speak in his defence, another to the prison to die. There are public meals instituted by law, annual festivals, sacrifices to the gods, worship of heroes, and libations to the deceased; while other things practised in other ways, according to one injunction or legal power, truly confirm that, as the poet said:

> The city at one time is laden with incense,
> at the same time with paeans and with groans.[56]

(14) (400b 27) We must understand the same of the greater city—I mean the cosmos. The god is an evenly balanced law for us, undergoing no correction or alteration. He is, I believe, more powerful and more reliable than those written upon *kyrbeis*.[57] While he gives unmoving and well-tuned leadership, the whole good order of heaven and Earth is managed, distributed over all natures—plants and animals—through their own seeds, according to their race and form. For vines, date-palms, and perseas, 'both sweet fig-trees and olives',[58] as the poet says; those without fruit but meeting other needs, (*such as*) planes, pines, box-trees, 'the alder, the poplar, and the well-scented cypress';[59] those bearing autumn fruit, sweet but hard to preserve, (*such as*) 'pear-trees, pomegranates, shiny-fruited apple-trees';[60] and among animals the wild and the tame, those feeding in the air, upon the ground, and in the water—all these arise, reach their prime, and are destroyed in obedience to the ordinances of the god. 'For all that walks is driven to the fields with blows'; so says Herakleitos.[61]

7. (1) (401a 12) Being one, he is many-named, being so named from the effects that he inaugurates himself.[62] We call him Zena and Dia,[63] employing the names in parallel, as if we said 'the one *dia hon*, "through whom", we *zēn*, "live"'. He is said to be the child

---

[56] Sophokles, *Oedipus the King*, 4–5. [57] Early law-tablets of the Athenians.
[58] Hom. *Od.* 11. 590.   [59] Hom. *Od.* 5. 64.   [60] Hom. *Od.* 11. 589.
[61] Fr. B 11 in Diels and Kranz 1959–60, i. 153.
[62] On ch. 7, see Hladký 2020, though at p. 229 he overstates the closeness of the text's relationship to Stoic authorities, cf. Thein 2020, 37, 42; Jirsa 2020, 67, 72.
[63] Alternative forms of the name 'Zeus' in the accusative (grammatical object) case.

of Kronos (*Cronus*) and of *chronos* (*time*), since he runs through from one boundless age to another age. He is called the god of lightning and thunder, of the clear sky and the *aithēr*, of the thunderbolt and the rain, after the rains, thunderbolts, and the rest.

(2) (401a 19) He is indeed called Epikarpios after the harvest; Polieus after cities; Genethlios (*of Kindred*), Herkeios (*of the Courtyard*), Homognios (*of Siblings*), and Patroös (*of the Family*) from his association with these things; Hetaireios (*of Companionship*), Philios (*of Friendship*), Xenios (*of Guests*), Stratios (*of Armies*), Tropaiouchos (*Trophy-holder*); also Katharsios (*of Purification*), Palamnaios (*of Blood-guilt*), Hikesios (*of Suppliants*), Meilichios (*of Mildness*), as the poets say. Truly he is Soter (*Saviour*) and Eleutherios (*of Freedom*). In short, he is a god of heaven and Earth, named after every nature and every degree of fortune; since he himself is the cause of all things. (3) (401a 27) Wherefore in the Orphic books it is written, not inappropriately:[64]

> Zeus was born first, Zeus last, the lord of thunderbolts.
> Zeus is head, Zeus centre, from Zeus all is made.
> Zeus is foundation of Earth and starry heaven.
> Zeus was born man, Zeus became immortal bride.
> Zeus is breath of all, Zeus the thrust of untiring fire.
> Zeus the root of the main (*pontos*), Zeus Sun and Moon.
> Zeus is king, Zeus chief of all, lord of thunderbolts.
> Hiding all men, he brought them up again into joyous
> light from his sacred heart, dealing out mischief.

(4) (401b 8) I believe, too, that Ananke, 'necessity', refers to none other than him, since he is a cause that is *anikētos*, 'unconquerable'; likewise Heimarmene, 'destiny', because he *eirei*, 'strings together', and goes unhindered; and Pepromene, 'fate', because everything *peperatōsthai*, 'is limited', and nothing that exists is without limit; and Moira, one's 'lot', because things *memeristhai*, 'are allotted' (*by him*); Nemesis, 'retribution', from the *dianemēsis*, 'distribution' to each; and Adrasteia, 'ineluctability', because he is the inescapable (*anapodrastos*) cause by his nature; and Aisa, 'dispensation', because (*this cause*) is *aëi ousa*, 'always existing'.

(5) (401b 14) The matters concerning the Moirai (*Allotters, i.e. Fates*) and the spindle inclines in the same direction. For the Moirai are three in number, and are allotted to different times. The thread on the spindle is in one part fully made, another is about to be made, and the other is being spun. To the past is assigned one of the Moirai, Atropos, since all past things are *atrepta*, 'unalterable'; to the future Lachesis, for a *lēxis*, 'chance outcome', awaits all things according to their nature; and to the present Klotho, who brings about and 'spins', *klōthei*, each creature's particular end. And the myth, too, ends; and in no irregular way.

---

[64] On this hymn, see Hladký 2020, 218–25; at p. 219, Hladký notes that the hymn's origins go back before C5l.

(6) (401b 23) All these things are nothing other than the god, as the noble Plato says:⁶⁵

> The god, as the ancient tale goes, holds the beginning, end, and middle of all things that exist. He draws them to an end, travelling straight as is his nature. Always he is followed by justice, which punishes those who depart from divine law. He who is to become happy and blessed, let him partake of this from the very start. (401b 29)

---

⁶⁵ A combination of *Laws* 715e–716a and 730c (Furley ad loc.).

25

PSEUDO-ARRIAN, *CIRCUMNAVIGATION OF THE ERYTHRAIAN SEA*

(*PERIPLUS MARIS ERYTHRAEI*; *PME*)

(1ST C. AD)

Colin E. P. Adams*

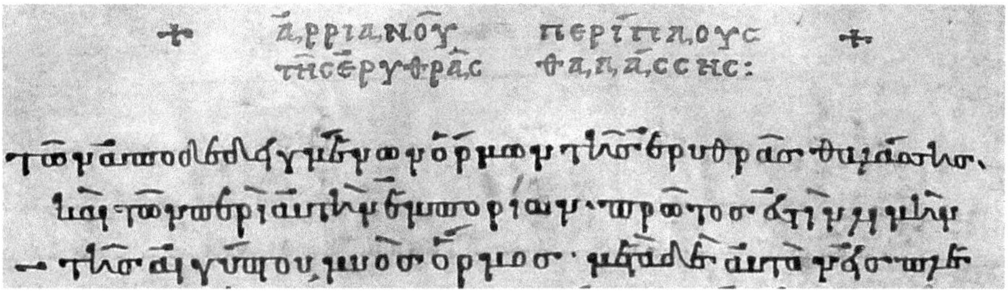

FIG. 25.1. Opening of the *PME*, fo. 40ʳ (detail).

INTRODUCTION

The Greek *Periplous tēs Erythras thalassēs* (*Circumnavigation of the Erythraian Sea*), often known by its Latin title *Periplus maris Erythraei*, or *PME* for short, is preserved in the 9th-century *Codex Palatinus Graecus* 398 (fols. 40ᵛ-54ᵛ) in the Universitätsbibliothek, Heidelberg—one of the two main geographical manuscripts discussed in the Introduction to the present book.[1] The work is quite unique. It does not really correspond in style and content to other known *periploi*. The identity, even the background, of the author is debated.[2] Although it is attributed to Arrian of Nikomedeia in the manuscript, this is almost certainly nothing more than wishful thinking.[3] It was written before his time, around the mid- to late 1st century AD (at the end of §26, it refers to the annexation of Egypt in 30 BC as 'not long before our own time'), and the

---

* The late Alan Astin introduced me to this wonderful text many years ago. I would like to thank Graham Shipley for his invitation to contribute and for his insightful comments on drafts, and Ben Cartlidge for his advice on etymology. Over the years I benefited greatly from discussions of the Red Sea with Steven Sidebotham, Dario Nappo, and Federico de Romanis.

[1] There is a later apograph in codex B, dated C15 (see Introduction, §VIII. 2. a).
[2] On authorship, see Casson 1989, 7–10; Belfiore 2013, 2–3. Brodersen 2021 presents a text with German trans.   [3] Marcotte 2012.

mentioning of the Nabataean king Malichas (§19) suggests a date between 40 and 70.[4] It was undoubtedly written by one man, who, although he says nothing of himself, was most probably from Egypt and of Greek descent.[5] Internal evidence suggests that he had personal experience of the regions he describes, due to his direct reporting, detailed account, and occasional use of the first person plural. It is written in *koine* Greek by a man who was most probably an experienced merchant.[6] Thus, the text is replete with lexicographical and orthographical problems, compounded by errors in copying and careless emendation by the medieval scribes responsible for the transmission of the original. The Greek is quirky and difficult, and not a little graceless at times, even if there is the occasional literary touch. It is not the Greek of Arrian, and the consistency of composition prohibits any notion that it is his work, developed and augmented by others after him.[7] One hint at the identity of the author is contained in the later work of Markianos of Herakleia in his *Epitome of Menippos* (Chapter 21 below), in which it is clear he has read the work of Sosandros, a ship's captain (*kybernētēs*), styled *The Places in Indike* (*Ta kata tēn Indikēn*).[8] That this is our author is an attractive possibility, although its title suggests a work more narrow in focus.

While we should accept some personal experience on the part of the author, we should not see *PME* merely as a travelogue. Its ambition is to be a comprehensive guide to the topography, political geography, and commercial characteristics of the African, Arabian, and Indian coasts.[9] As such it falls partly within the genre of *historia periodikē* described by Ptolemy as a synthesis of information set out by a larger literary tradition.[10] A curious feature of *PME* is its clear periplographic organization, despite the fact that Egyptian sailors *en route* to southern Arabia or India would sail directly and continuously across water (by a *diaplous*, sea crossing, rather than a coastal *periplous* or *paraplous*), not stop at all ports and stations along the way.[11] Their *modus operandi* was not cabotage.[12] It seems clear that our author has gathered information preserved in a range of different accounts and organized his material. This is apparent in the author's account of the discovery of the monsoon winds (§57). He describes how 'people previously sailed . . . by coasting' in small ships, until the captain Hippalos 'discovered the route across the open sea'. In other passages a linear sequence is evident,

---

[4] *PME* §19, with Casson 1989, 7. Josephus, *BJ* 3. 4. 2, states that a King Malichas sent troops to support Titus in the Jewish war in AD 70.

[5] On the date, see literature cited by Raschke 1978, 979–81 nn. 1342–6; Casson 1989, 6–7; Robin 1997; Belfiore 2013, 3–6.

[6] Casson 1989, 10.   [7] As argued by Marcotte 2012, 9.

[8] Markianos, *Epitome of Menippos*, 2.

[9] See Marcotte 2016, 174–83, on the contribution of the text to knowledge of the Indian Ocean.

[10] Ptolemy, *Geog.* 1. 2. 2.

[11] The practice of using *diaploi* was, for example, well known to Pliny, e.g. at 6. xxvi. 100–6, where he describes three such routes.

[12] De Romanis 2020, esp. 59–83, argues that two patterns of trade existed: the first, the coastal trade depicted in the *PME*; second, that from C2 AD larger ships sailed directly to and from India from the Red Sea ports, largely carrying pepper. Thus, the commercial activity recorded in the *PME* is very different in character from that of the Muziris Papyrus.

places described as being 'one after the other'.[13] This points towards a range of different sources used by the author. It has been pointed out that distances in *PME* are recorded either in multiples of 400 and 600 *stadioi* or in *dromoi* ('days' running'). The differences in *stadioi* can be put down to the different speeds of ships used for coasting and direct navigation, which could be accurately assessed, and in *dromoi*, where it could not.[14] This again suggests different sources.

But the genre to which this work can be attached is not at all clear, for it is specific in its focus on trade.[15] Thus it is a handbook for merchants, not a work of geographical research in the tradition of other so-called *periploi* such as that of Ps.-Skylax (Chapter 7) and in part that of Arrian (Chapter 27)—if that is indeed what they are. It is not a work of ethnography, *paradoxa,* or history. The author is concerned with recording details that would not only be useful to merchants, but to sailors—indeed there is a focus on navigational matters, wind direction, dangerous reefs, shoals, and currents. However, that the author has an interest in *paradoxa* is clear, and although perhaps a little rough round the edges, this points to some education, whether through reading or experience, or both. This, perhaps, goes some way to making him a more reliable reporter than other writers in the related genres. How might such works be related to geographical scholarship? There is a hint in our sources that such handbooks may indeed have been carried by ships—for Ptolemy III Euergetes is said have issued an order to seize books found on those entering the harbour of Alexandria and for them to be copied, the originals being deposited in the Library of Alexandria.[16] Captains are perhaps unlikely to have been interested in written copies of Homer. Did, then, the information from these works before *PME* find its way into the work of Agatharchides of Knidos (Chapter 15) or Artemidoros of Ephesos (Chapter 18), who were both resident in Egypt at times, not to speak of Poseidonios (Chapter 19) and eventually Strabo?[17] It is clear from Diodoros that he was aware of, and made use of, accounts of journeys made by merchants in the Red Sea region, when he states that they agree in their accounts of the region up to the land of the Ichthyophagoi.[18] Agatharchides, though, like Strabo, was sceptical of merchants and their like as sources of evidence.[19] The importance, however, of such information is noted by a number of authors, and is surprisingly well encapsulated by Cicero (*Pro Murena*, 4) in a simile where he states that sailors exchanged information on weather, pirates, and ports.[20]

---

[13] e.g. §7 κείμενα μὲν κατὰ τὸ ἑξῆς.   [14] De Romanis 2016.

[15] For general discussion of 'genre' in ancient geographical writing, see the Introduction to the book, §III. 2. a.

[16] See Galen's commentary on Hippokrates, *Epidemics*, 3, in Wenkebach 1936, 79: 'eager concerning books, Ptolemy the king of Egypt at that time ordered all books to be collected in this way, that the books of all who sailed there were brought to him and were copied into new manuscripts, the new copies being given back to those whose books had been brought to him after they had sailed there, and the original books were put into the library with the inscription 'from the ships'.

[17] On both writers in Egypt, see Diod. 3. 11. 1.   [18] Diod. 3. 18. 3.   [19] Strabo 15. 1. 4, C686.

[20] *praecipere summo studio solent et tempestatum rationem et praedonum et locorum*. Cited by De Romanis 2016, 104. Note also Caesar's hope for similar information from merchants on Britain, cf. *BG* 5. 1.

All this points to the author of *PME* being an individual who was a merchant, a member of Egypt's metropolitan class, and thus most likely associated with people of considerable influence and wealth. Modern scholars tend to focus on Roman traders, but the identity of the author of the *periplous* is to be sought in the Egyptian evidence. The 1st-century 'Archive of Nikanor' preserves the names of a number of the Alexandrian metropolite class who received deliveries of produce in the Egyptian ports of Myos Hormos and Berenike, including one Marcus Julius Alexander, a wealthy man and brother of the *praefectus Aegypti* Tiberius Julius Alexander.[21] A more likely background is that similar to two women of metropolite class described as *nauklēroi* and *emporoi Erythraïkai* ('shipowners' and 'traders in the Erythraian sea').[22]

Greeks and Egyptian had sailed in the Red Sea and beyond for a considerable time, and this increased with the discovery of how to use the monsoon winds, this attributed by Strabo to Eudoxos of Kyzikos in *c*.116 BC.[23] The author of *PME* credits a captain named Hippalos (§57) but assigns no date to his journey.[24] Whatever the case, the increase in traffic noted by Strabo may have prompted the production of a handbook to assist merchants.[25] The author begins his description at the Egyptian Red Sea ports of Myos Hormos and Berenike. Sixty-six short sections follow, which make their progress through the Red Sea and western Indian Ocean past the shores of Ethiopia, describing ports on these shores and the opposite Arabian peninsula, before turning east into the Arabian sea as far as the gulf of Oman, then east to the coast of India, and south-south-east to the tip of India and Sri Lanka.[26] It is significant that the Persian gulf is not included; it is possible that this was due to Parthian hostility to Rome, but equally it may be that Palmyrene trading interests through Spasinou Charax provided an easier overland route, obviating the need for the much longer maritime route.

Most of the chapters contain information on the ports of trade that merchants would find along the route, with details of what was regularly imported and exported, often with information on the quantities and qualities generally traded. But there is a good deal of other information, including the nature and identity of the rulers, the names of the principal cities, snippets of ethnographical information, some historical reference, and importantly, a good deal of navigational information. This covers the best times of year to sail (from Egypt), the distances and duration of different

---

[21] C. E. P. Adams 2007a, 223–4; Kruse 2018. On notable traders and their links with Roman authorities, see De Romanis 2020, 298–324.

[22] *SB* 5. 7, 539 = *SEG* 8. 703 from Medamud.

[23] Strabo 2. 3. 4–5, C98–102; see Habicht 2013; Roller 2015, 141–2, 146–7, for Eudoxos of Kyzikos; *contra*, Dueck 2012, 57; and Roller 2015, 99, on the use of Nearchos' and Onesikritos' route until the discovery of the monsoon. On Eudoxos, see also Introduction, §VI. 4. c; Poseidonios 2 §§34–5.

[24] De Romanis 1997 points out that the character of Hippalos is fictional; the name given to the south-westerly monsoon in Greek was *hypalos* (ὕπαλος). Casson 1989, 224, discounts this. Mooren 1972 suggests a connection between Eudoxos of Kyzikos and Hippalos, perhaps being shipmates; pure speculation, of course. Pliny 6. xxvi. 100 and 104 simply calls the wind *hippalus*; see Mazzarino 1997.

[25] Strabo 2. 5. 12, C117–18; 17. 1. 13, C798.

[26] See Roller 2015, 174–8, on Chryse and lands E of India.

components of the routes, direction, information on reefs and shoals, currents and tides—all pointing towards the author's particular interest in navigating safely to ports of trade. Occasionally, *paradoxa*, observations on levels of civilization, and other curiosities are mentioned. Strangely, there is no information on local taxation, but only of the *tetartē*, the tax of 25 per cent charged on goods entering Egypt and at Leuke Kome.[27] This tax was focused on luxury goods, and this too is the main interest of the author. The African shores traded principally in ivory, tortoiseshell, aromatics, frankincense, cassia, and some slaves; the Arabian coast in myrrh, frankincense, and aloe; and India in spices, pepper, nard, silk, cotton, pearls, gems, and clothes, among other things. We know from other evidence that these were items of particular interest to traders in Roman Egypt. Most goods were easily transported in bulk, and cargoes were of considerable value. There was risk, but the rewards in terms of profit were spectacular. The so-called Muziris Papyrus gives a notion of scale and value and is supported by increasing archaeological and textual evidence from the port of Berenike especially.[28]

PME departs from other *periploi* in another important way. The journeys it either envisages or records indirectly were entirely private in nature; there is no sign of state involvement, implied clearly in Hanno's journey (if genuine) or in Arrian's *periplous*. The value of trade, however, suggests, as noted above, that the traders were, or at least represented, wealthy individuals. Evidence suggests that traders employed agents in the Red Sea ports of Egypt, and it is quite possible they had them in foreign ports as well.[29] A papyrus of AD 72/3 notes that a certain Gaion is 'away in India', quite possibly acting as such an agent.[30] The Archive of Nikanor clearly shows that non-luxury staple items were transported to Red Sea ports, no doubt to feed the communities there.[31] Ports in India, too, no doubt had their complement of Roman agents, who may have wanted some goods 'from home', but the evidence is ambiguous.[32] In *PME* §56, the author notes that grain is imported into Muziris 'for those involved in shipping there', suggesting Romans.[33] The 'Muziris Papyrus' was a contract clearly drawn up by individuals in both Egypt and Muziris. It is clear too that foreigners were involved in trade—we know of Palmyrenes, a man from Aden, and Indians in Alexandria.[34]

The question of state involvement remains an important one, however.[35] There is evidence to suggest the presence of a Roman fleet in the Red Sea, perhaps as early as the Augustan period; Roman navy officers are mentioned in the Archive of Nikanor receiving supplies; and it is possible that under Trajan the canal re-excavated between Klysma and the Nile offered increased naval access to the sea. Additionally, inscriptions recently found on the *Farasan* islands, at the southern end of the Red Sea, attest

---

[27] §19. See De Romanis 2020, 277–94.
[28] De Romanis 2020; Sidebotham 2011 for an overview; Nappo 2018a.
[29] On agency, see Ruffing 2013.   [30] *P. Lond.* 2. 260 = *Stud. Pal.* 4. p. 74, l. 549.
[31] C. E. P. Adams 2007a, 224–5.   [32] Sidebotham 2011, 191.
[33] Casson 1989, 24.   [34] Discussed by Casson 1989, 34 with n. 53.
[35] Most recently Nappo 2015; A. I. Wilson 2015a.

to the presence of a Roman military unit in the 2nd century AD.[36] Perhaps this is how we must also understand *PME* §19, which mentions a centurion and detachment at Leuke Kome on the Arabian coast.[37] State involvement is also suggested by the military presence in the eastern desert of Egypt, where there were garrisons at strategic points along desert routes and where watering-stations (*hydreumata*) were maintained. Roman fiscal administration came under the remit of the *Praefectus Montis Berenicidis*, and 'arabarchs' supervised tax collection.[38] It is clear also that the state possessed warehouses at Koptos and Alexandria in which to receive the *portoria* collected from the eastern trade.[39] It seems likely that they were redistributed by the state for further profit, perhaps from imperial warehouses in Rome.[40] A further indication of state involvement was the dual role played by the *stratēgoi* (state officials in charge of nomes) of the Koptite and Ombite nomes, who were also *paralemptai* (receivers of tax) of the Red Sea.[41]

The evidence provided by *PME* adds weight to the statements of Pliny the Elder that India absorbed (*exhauriente*) 50 million sesterces, and that India, the Seres, and 'all their peninsula' absorbed 100 million sesterces 'every year' from the Roman empire.[42] Until the discovery of the 'Muziris Papyrus' this was usually thought to be an exaggeration. It is clear it was not. *PME* records the importation of bullion and Roman coin into the ports of India. That there was onward trade with China is also clear, Indians no doubt serving as middlemen.

PME offers a wealth of information on the political geography of the regions concerned. It complements information preserved in other geographical works such as Agatharchides (Chapter 15 above) and Strabo on economic matters, geographical features, indigenous peoples, rulers, local climates, and fauna. It also offers the opportunity for comparison with non-Greek and Roman sources, especially those on India.[43] Strabo yields important information on trade between Rome and the east, and especially on matters of taxation, where it is possible to infer, for example, that import taxes were not a Roman innovation. His stress on the 'heavy' nature of the taxes is not misplaced.

What use was made of *PME*, and the contribution it made to general knowledge of the regions covered, is hard to gauge. It is worth noting Pliny the Elder's observation, in his discussion of routes to India (relating to AD 48–52), that it was only recently that

---

[36] *AE* 2005, 1638 and 1639, with corrections at *AE* 2010, 1761. See Speidel 2016.

[37] ἑκατοντάρχης μετὰ στρατεύματος ἀποστέλλεται, 'a *hekatontarchēs*' ('commander of a hundred', sc. men) 'is sent off with an army'. See Casson 1989, 145. De Romanis 2020, 318, assumes a Roman officer. It seems unnecessary to run with the suggestion that it was a Nabataean 'centurion', cf. Bowersock 1983, 71.

[38] On 'arabarchs', see De Romanis 2020, s.v.   [39] Rathbone 2000; De Romanis 2020, 277–97.

[40] Dio 72. 24. 1.   [41] Ast and Bagnall 2015, 182.

[42] Pliny 6. xxvi. 101 (India 50 million sesterces); 12. xl. 84 (India, the Seres, and 'all their peninsula' 100 million).

[43] See generally Karttunen 1997; Whittaker 2004; Parker 2008 on India; Pitts and Versluys 2015 on Rome and globalization.

reliable information had become available.⁴⁴ This goes nicely with a date between 40 and 70 for the writing of *PME*. Perhaps Pliny read it, among other material? Marcotte has argued that it was used directly by Markianos.⁴⁵ There is no satisfactory answer as to why, out of all the similar literature which must have formed the evidence base for the work of Ptolemy and others, *PME* is the sole survivor.

The Greek text translated is that of Belfiore.

SELECTED FURTHER READING

*Belfiore, S. (2013), 'Periplus maris Erythraei (2036)', in *FGrH* v.
Bowersock, G. (1983), *Roman Arabia*. Cambridge, Mass.
*Brodersen, K. (2021), *Periplus Maris Erythraei: zweisprachige Ausgabe*. Speyer.
*Casson, L. (1989), *The Periplus Maris Erythraei: Text with Introduction, Translation, and Commentary*. Princeton.
De Romanis, F. (2020), *The Indo-Roman Pepper Trade and the Muziris Papyrus*. Oxford.
Nappo, D. (2015), 'Roman policy on the Red Sea in the second century', in F. De Romanis and M. Maiuro (eds), *Across the Ocean: Nine Essays in Indo-Roman Trade* (Leiden), 55–72.
Sidebotham, S. E. (2011), *Berenike and the Ancient Maritime Spice Route*. Berkeley.

TEXT

1. Of the anchorages for departure found in the Erythraian sea and the trading-places around it,⁴⁶ the first is the Egyptian harbour of Myos Hormos (*Mussel Anchorage*). For those sailing on from it, after 1,800 stades, on the right, there is Berenike.⁴⁷ The harbours of each of them are inlets of the Erythraian sea, on the edge of Egypt.

2. On the right of these, continuing on from Berenike, is the Land of the Barbaroi (*Barbarians*). Those parts beside the sea are inhabited by the Ichthyophagoi (*Fish-eaters*) living in scattered enclosures they have built in narrow passes,⁴⁸ while inland live the Barbaroi, and those beyond them, the Agriophagoi (*Wild-animal-eaters*) and Moschophagoi,⁴⁹ living under chieftains (*tyrannoi*). Behind them, further inland towards the West, there is a ⟨mother-city called Meroë⟩.

---

⁴⁴ Pliny 6. xxvi. 101, cited by De Romanis 2016, 105.   ⁴⁵ Marcotte 2012, 19.

⁴⁶ Over-interpretation of the participle ἀποδεδειγμένους has led to the translation 'designated harbours' (Casson 1989, 272–4), which in turn has found its way into scholarly discussion. The use of the participle suggests 'pointing away from', i.e. 'points of departure'. *Hormos* was used to denote an 'anchorage', not a port or *emporion*, so the term can have nothing to do with trading status. In the texts cited by Casson, 'designated' harbours are merely those harbours to which individuals were instructed to go. There seems to me to be no good reason to adopt a technical sense.

⁴⁷ The locations of Myos Hormos and Berenike are now well established. In the following, modern place-names of locations outside Egypt are added in parentheses (when plausibly known) at first appearance. I have omitted those for which there are difficulties of identification or disputed attribution. Regions and nations are not included in this.

⁴⁸ μάνδρα–*mandra*: huts or pens; 'enclosures' seems a better description.

⁴⁹ Either Calf-eaters or Twig-eaters.

3. Beyond the Moschophagoi there is a small trading-place upon the sea, at a distance †the end of the return† about 4,000 stades, called Ptolemaïs Theron (*Ptolemaïs of the Hunts*); under the Ptolemaic kings, hunters left it for the interior. This trading-place has small quantities of true land-tortoise, white and smaller in the shell. Here is also found a little ivory, similar to that of Adoulis.[50] But this place has no harbour, and shelters only small craft.

4. Beyond Ptolemaïs Theron about 3,000 stades, there is Adoulis, a legally limited trading-place,[51] lying in a deep bay running due south. In front of this is an island called Oreine (*Mountainous*), situated about 200 stades towards the open sea from the innermost part of the bay, and, on both sides, the shores of the mainland lie close by. Ships now arriving at this port anchor because of attacks from the mainland. Before now they used to anchor at the innermost point of the bay, at an island called Didoros (*i.e. Diodoros*), close by the mainland, which has a crossing on foot by which the barbarians attacked the island.[52] Opposite Oreine, on the mainland, 20 stades from the sea, lies Adoulis, a village of moderate size. From here it is three days' journey to Koloë (*Kohaito*), an inland town, the first trading-place for ivory; and from that place another five days to the mother-city called Axomites (*Axum*).[53] Into that place is brought all the ivory from beyond the Nile through what is called Kyeneion, and from there to Adoulis.[54] The whole multitude of the elephants and rhinoceroses inhabit the upland areas, although occasionally they are observed on the coast near to Adoulis. Lying in front of the trading-place, towards the open sea, to the right, lie several small, sandy islands, called the Alalaiou; these provide the tortoiseshell which is carried to the trading-placc by the Ichthyophagoi.

5. And about 800 stades beyond there is another very deep bay, near the entrance of which there is a great sandbank spreading out on the right; deeply buried under this is obsidian stone, the only place where it occurs.[55] The king of these regions, from the Moschophagoi to the other Barbaria, is Zoskales,[56] miserly in his ways and holding out for more, but for the rest a good person and versed in Greek literature.

---

[50] Ivory from Adoulis was held to be a standard of quality against which other ivory was compared; cf. Pliny, *NH* 8. iv. 7 and *PME* §§6 and 16–17, with De Romanis 2020, 105 n. 93, and 273.

[51] *emporion nomimon*: the meaning of this term is debated. Casson 1989, 274–6, summarizes this, and his suggestion that a legally limited port was one with no free market, but one in which all trade passed through an authorized office, seems the best solution.

[52] *ēpeiros*, 'mainland', sometimes shore.

[53] The village, town, and city are distinguished from each other as *kōmē, polis, and mētropolis* respectively.

[54] *kynēgion* or *kynēgesion*, 'hunting-ground'.   [55] *Baia di Oucachil*.

[56] Perhaps the first *known* king of Axum, but other possibilities exist, cf. the exhaustive commentary of Casson 1989, 109–10.

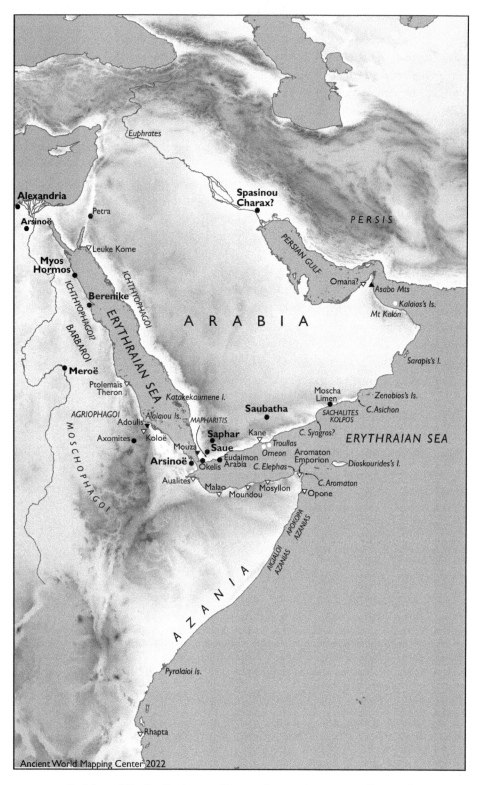

MAP 25.1. *Periplous* of the Erythraian sea. ▼ *emporion nomimon*. ▽ small *emporion*.

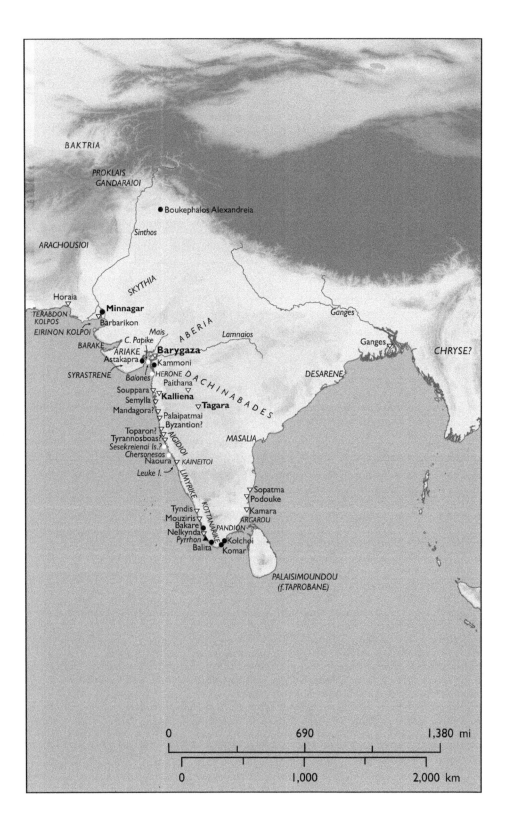

6. Imported into this area are undyed cloaks made in Egypt for the Barbaroi;[57] robes from Arsinoë;[58] second-rate coloured cloaks;[59] linens, and double-fringed clothes; several kinds of coloured stones, others of *myrrhinē*[60] made in Diospolis; and brass, which they use for ornaments and cut up as a substitute for coinage; and copper honey-jars for cooking and for cutting up as bracelets and anklets for women; and iron, which is employed for spearheads used against elephants and other wild animals, and for their wars. Among other things, axes are imported, along with adzes and large knives; copper drinking-vessels, round and large; a small amount of *denarii* for those living among the people there;[61] Laodikeian and Italic wine, a little;[62] olive oil, a little. For the king, gold and silver plate manufactured in local style, and among clothing military cloaks and heavy cloaks, these of modest quality. Among other things, from the interior of Ariake across the sea, there is imported Indian iron and steel, and Indian cotton of broad cut, the so-called *monachē* and *sagmatogēnai*,[63] girdles, heavy cloaks, some muslins, and coloured *lakkos*.[64] Exported from this region are ivory, tortoiseshell, and rhinoceros (*horn*). Most of these are exported from Egypt in the months of January to September, that is, from Tybi to Thoth; the best time to leave Egypt is around the month of September.

7. The gulf of Arabia now stretches eastward and reaches its narrowest point at Aualites. After about 4,000 stades' sailing along the mainland to the east, there are other trading-places of the barbarians, called 'The Far Side';[65] they are located one after the other, and have anchorages with places to drop anchor (*ankyrobolia*) and roadsteads (*saloi*) as seasons allow. The first is called Aualites; from this point the crossing to the coast of Arabia is the shortest. At this place lies the small trading-place called Aualites, which is reached by rafts and small boats. You find a market in this place for assorted glass stones; ⟨juice⟩ of unripe olives[66] from Diospolis;[67] assorted clothing for

---

[57] *P. Oxy.* 14. 1684 (C4 AD) mentions a *barbarikon* in a list of clothing. See van Minnen 1986 on textile production in Oxyrhynchus, based on *P. Oxy. Hels.* 40 (AD 275), which, allowing for variation in interpretation due to textual uncertainties, still suggests production on a significant scale.

[58] On textiles from Roman Egypt and the *PME*, see Vivero 2013 and Droß-Krüpe 2013. The main study of the Egyptian textile industry remains Wipszycka 1965.

[59] 'Crude': the adjective defining *abollai* is *nothos* (normally 'illegitimate child'), which often carries the meanings 'spurious', 'counterfeit'. I wonder in this case if we see an equivalent to imitation luxury goods, available the world over.

[60] Myrtle-coloured (Pliny 37. lxiii. 174).

[61] Perhaps traders living abroad. On the flow of money to the East, see Nappo 2018b.

[62] Egypt being the conduit, see Rathbone 1983; evidence for its transport in the Nikanor archive, see C. E. P. Adams 2007b, 220–8, and Kruse 2018. Ruffing 1993, 24, rejects the notion that the wine so carried was for export; it is difficult to explain its presence in the *PME* if at least a proportion of it was not, and ostraca from Berenike show wine going through the customs process and being loaded onto ships, see *O. Ber.* 1. pp. 16–21.

[63] Cotton garments?   [64] A red dye, resin.   [65] τὰ πέρα⟨ν⟩—perhaps 'The Other Side'.

[66] Müller argues for the insertion of *chylos* (juice) in a small lacuna before Diospolis. *Omphax* can be unripe grapes or olives; Casson B 7. 3 argues for the latter.

[67] Thebes in Egypt, see www.trismegistos.org/place/576.

the barbarians, cleaned by fulling;[68] wheat, wine, and a little tin. Exported from this place, and sometimes by the *barbaroi* themselves crossing to Okelis and Mouza on the opposite shore on rafts, are aromatics, a little ivory, tortoiseshell, and a very small amount of myrrh that is better than others. The barbarians living in this place are rather unruly.

8. About 800 stades' sailing beyond Aualites there is another, better trading-place called Malaō (*Berbera*). Its anchorage is a rough roadstead (*episalos*)[69] sheltered by a promontory extending from the east. The natives here are more peaceful. You find a market in this place for the aforementioned items as well as various tunics,[70] cloaks (*sagoi*) from Arsinoë cleaned by fulling and dyed,[71] drinking-cups, honey-jars in small numbers, iron, and Roman money, both gold and silver, but not much. Exported from this place are myrrh, a small amount of Far Side frankincense, hard cassia, *douaka*,[72] *kankamon*,[73] and *makeir*,[74] which are exported to Arabia, and, rarely, slaves.

9. Two days' running beyond Malaō is the trading-place of Moundou (*Heis*), where ships anchor quite safely at the island very close to the shore. Imported into this place are the aforementioned items; exported from this place are the aforementioned cargoes ⟨as well as⟩ the incense called *mokrotou*.[75] The merchants who dwell around here are harsh (*bargainers*).

10. From Moundou, on an eastward heading, similarly after two days' running, perhaps three, near ⟨a promontory?⟩, lies Mosyllon, on a beach and with a poor anchorage. Imported into this place are the aforementioned categories, also silverware, ironware to a lesser extent, and precious stones.[76] Exported from this place are cassia, in large quantity—for this reason larger ships are required at this trading-place—and other perfumes and aromatics, poor-quality tortoiseshell in small quantity, *mokrotou* of lesser quality than from Moundou, Far Side frankincense, and rarely ivory and myrrh.

11. From Mosyllon †after two days' running beside† the so-called Neiloptolemaiou, Tapatege†, and a small laurel-grove, is Elephas promontory [—] it has a river, the so-called Elephas, and a large laurel grove called Akannai, the only place which produces Far Side frankincense, in great quantity and of good quality.

12. And beyond this, with the land now going back towards the south, is the Trading-place of the Aromatics (*Damo*) and a precipitous promontory (*Ras Asir*), the last in the land of the Barbaroi towards the east. Its anchorage is a rough roadstead,

---

[68] Perhaps previously owned clothes? If so, this is interesting in terms of both economics and charity.
[69] For this term, cf. *Stadiasmos* §55 (in Ch. 31 below).
[70] προχωρέω. LSJ has 'to be imported' (citing *PME* §6), or to 'find a market' cf. *P. Amh.* 2. 133, l. 18.
[71] A square woollen cloak, fastened on the right shoulder with a pin, somewhat similar to an *abolla*, and often red in colour.
[72] Either an inferior form of cinnamon imported from India, or a local incense. Unattested elsewhere.
[73] A gum resin, mentioned by Dioskorides 1. 24 and Pliny 12. xliv. 98.
[74] Possibly a medicine derived from bark imported from India, cf. Pliny 12. xvi. 32.
[75] Probably an incense, unattested elsewhere.
[76] *lithia*; others translate it as 'glass', but see Casson B 10. 4. 9.

dangerous in some seasons as the place is exposed to the north wind. A local sign of an imminent storm is when the deep water becomes turbid and changes colour. When this happens, everyone flees to the large promontory for shelter, the so-called Tabai. Imported into this trading-place are the aforementioned items. It produces cassia, *gizeir*, *asyphē*, aromatics, *magla*, *motō*, and frankincense.[77]

13. From Tabai after sailing 400 stades along a peninsula towards which the current draws you, there is another trading-place, Opone (*Hafun*), into which are imported the aforementioned items. In it is produced the greatest amount of cassia, aromatics, *motō*, better-quality slaves,[78] most of whom are imported into Egypt, and the greatest amount of tortoiseshell, finer than any other.

14. One sails to all these Far Side trading-places from Egypt around the month of July, that is Epeiph. It is customary to fit out from the inner parts of Ariake and Barygaza with goods exported from those places to the trading-places on the Far Side: wheat, rice, ghee, sesame oil and cotton, the *monachē*, the *sagmatogēnē*,[79] girdles, and the cane honey called *sakchari*. Some ships sail directly to these trading-places, others sail ⟨along⟩ the coast taking on cargo when they fall upon them. The region is not ruled by a king, but each trading-place is managed by its own chieftain (*tyrannos*).

15. From Opone, with the coast veering more to the south, there are first the so-called Small and Great Bluffs of Azania—†for places to drop anchor there are rivers†—six days' running directly towards the Lips (*south-west wind*). Then there are the Small and Great Seashores for another six days' running; and after that, by turn, the runs of Azania, first the so-called Sarapion, then the Nikōn. Beyond that, several rivers and harbours come at once, separated by stations and days' running, seven in all, up to the Pyralaoi islands (*Lamu archipelago*) and the so-called Dioryx (*Canal*); from here, a little round from the Lips (*i.e. to the WSW*), after two nights' and days' running due west comes Menouthias island (*Madagascar*), about 300 stades from land, low and wooded. On it there are rivers and a great number of birds of many types, and mountain tortoise. There are no wild animals, except crocodiles, but not at all harmful to humans. On it there are sewn boats and others made of a single piece of wood[80] used for fishing and for catching turtles. On this island they have their own way of catching them in baskets instead of nets, placing them across the mouths †of inlets†.

16. Two days' running beyond this comes the final trading-place on the mainland of Azania, called Rhapta (*Dar es Salaam*), a name derived from the sewn (*rhapta*) boats already mentioned, where there are great quantities of ivory and tortoiseshell. Large-bodied people inhabit the land, the Rha⟨p⟩toi, administered from place to place by men acting like chieftains (*tyrannoi*). The region is held by the chieftain of Mapharitis, for by some ancient right it is subject to the kingdom of Arabia from when it first came into being. Those from Mouza have charge of it through the king subject to taxes,

---

[77] These are terms to denote the best, second best, and cheaper grades of cassia.
[78] Poorer- and better-quality slaves.   [79] Probably different grades of cotton cloth or clothing.
[80] *monoxylae*: see De Romanis 2020, 89, cf. Pliny 6. xxvi. 105.

and send out to it small barges,⁸¹ mostly under the charge of Arab captains and crew, who, being familiar with the natives and intermarried with them, know the place and its language.

17. Imported into these markets are principally spearheads from Mouza manufactured locally, axes, knives, small awls, and various types of glass. And to some places, wine and wheat in no small quantity, not however for trade, but to use to ensure the favour of the Barbaroi. Exports from this place are ivory in great quantity, but inferior to that of Adoulis, rhinoceros (*horn*), and tortoiseshell, superior to others except the Indian,⁸² and nautilus shell in small quantity.

18. These are more or less the last trading-places on the coast of Azania to the right of Berenike. For beyond these regions lies the unexplored Ocean that bends back to the west, and extending south to the remote parts of Aithiopia and Libyē and Africa (*Aphrikē*), mingles with the western sea.

19. To the left of Berenike, after two or three days' running eastward from Myos Hormos, after one has sailed across the adjoining bay, there is another anchorage with a fort, called Leuke Kome ('*White Village*'; '*Aynûnah*), from which there is ⟨a road⟩ to Petra and Malichas, the king of the Nabataeans.⁸³ This trading-place also regularly serves for fitting out⁸⁴ Arabian ships, not large ones. Therefore, for the sake of safeguarding, a collector of the 25 per cent tax on incoming goods is sent there, as well as a centurion with a detachment of soldiers.⁸⁵

20. Straight after this it (*the gulf*) joins the coast of Arabia, stretching far down the Erythraian sea. It is inhabited by different peoples speaking different languages, some (*different*) to a limited extent, others completely. Similarly, the areas by the sea are interspersed with the enclosures of the Ichthyophagoi, while inland there are villages and pastures inhabited by roguish, bilingual people. Any people who fall among them while voyaging away from the middle course are plundered, and any who are shipwrecked and saved are enslaved. For this they are continually taken prisoner by the chieftains (*tyrannoi*) and kings of Arabia. They are called Kanraitai. On the whole, the coastal sailing along the mainland of Arabia is dangerous, for the territory has no harbours and poor anchorages, and is plagued by rocky shores,⁸⁶ unapproachable because of cliffs, and is in all manners threatening. For this reason, when sailing we follow ⟨the⟩ course in the middle, and make exceeding haste to Katakekaumene (*Burnt*)

---

⁸¹ *epholkia*: LSJ gives 'small boat towed after a ship'.

⁸² *nauplios*. Casson translates as 'nautilus shell', but states at B 17. 6. 20 that the reading ναύπλιος is clear in the MS. Discussion at Casson 1980, 496–7.

⁸³ On the location, see Nappo 2010.

⁸⁴ *exartismos*, the equipment of a ship. Fitting out is suggested by ostraca from Berenike, where the phrase εἰς ἐξαρτισμόν (or -μοῦ followed by a name in the genitive) appears, e.g. *O. Ber.* 1. 68–79, orders for outfitting ships.

⁸⁵ *paralēmptēs*, a tax-collector. De Romanis 2020, 318, properly assumes a Roman officer is meant by 'centurion'. On the Roman military presence in the Red Sea regions, see Speidel 2016.

⁸⁶ Possibly tidal flows in the rocky inlets?

Island (*Jabal at Ta'ir*), for straight after this there are continuous shores with peaceful peoples, pasture animals, and camels.

21. And beyond these places, in the last bay on the left-hand shore of this open sea, on the coast, is the legally limited trading-place of Mouza (*al Mukha*), about 12,000 stades distance in all from Berenike along a course due south. Truly the whole place abounds with Arabs—shipowners and sailors—and is busy with matters of commerce. For they have dealings with the Far Side and Barygaza using their own outfittings.

22. Three days' journey ⟨inland⟩ beyond there is Sauē (*Sawwâ*), the city of the country around it, called Mapharitis. It is there that the chief (*tyrannos*) Cholaibos himself dwells.

23. And in another nine days ⟨inland⟩ is ⟨S⟩aphar (*Zufar*), the mother-city, where Charibaël, the rightful king of the two peoples—the Homerite and the adjacent one called the Sabaite—resides, a friend of the emperors through successive embassies and gifts.

24. The trading-place of Mouza, although harbourless, offers a good roadstead and anchorage because of the sandy seabed all around where one can drop anchor. Cargoes which it imports are: purple cloth, excellent and lower quality; sleeved Arabian cloaks, some plain and some regular, some chequered, some embroidered with gold; saffron; *cyperus*;[87] cloth; cloaks; blankets, but not many, plain and of local type; dark girdles; a reasonable amount of unguent; money, in considerable amounts; wine and grain in limited quantities, for the country produces a reasonable amount of wheat and even more wine. To the king and chief are offered horses and pack-mules;[88] gold vessels; turned silver; expensive cloaks; and copper vessels. Exported from here are local products, choice myrrh and *staktē*,[89] Abeir⟨ian and⟩ Minaean myrrh, white marble, and all of the aforementioned cargoes from around Adoulis on the Far Side. The best time to sail to them is around September, that is Thoth, although nothing prevents a quicker departure.

25. Beyond this, after you sail about 300 stades, at this point the Arabian mainland and the Far Side land of the barbarians below the Aualites, come together. There is a narrow passage, not long, which confines and shuts in the open sea (*pelagos*). Diodoros' Island (*Perim*) blocks the middle of the passage, (*which is*) 60 stades wide. Hence, strong currents, blown along by winds from the adjacent mountains, affect the passage through it. Beside this isthmus, on the coast, is the Arab village of Okelis (*Shykh Sa'îd*), belonging to the same chiefdom (*tyrannis*); it is less of a trading-place than an anchorage and watering-station, and the first place to hold up for those sailing on.

26. Beyond Okelis, the sea opening out once more towards the east the open sea is gradually revealed. After as much as 1,200 stades is Eudaimon Arabia, (*and*) a village on the coast, in the said kingdom of Charibaël. It has convenient anchorages and

---

[87] A leek-like medicinal plant.
[88] The sense seems to be that this is separate from trade, so probably gifts.
[89] Oil produced from myrrh of high quality.

watering-stations with much fresher water than is found at Okelis. It lies immediately at the head of a gulf receding from the coast. Eudaimon Arabia, being formerly a city called Eudaimon, at the time when vessels from India did not dare come to Egypt and those from Egypt did not dare to cross further into the places beyond, but (*only*) reached this place. In the same way, Alexandria received cargoes brought from Egypt and beyond. Now, not long before our own time, Caesar (*Augustus*) overthrew it.[90]

27. Next after Eudaimon Arabia comes at once a long seashore and a bay stretching 2,000 stades or more, settled with villages of Nomads and Ichthyophagoi, where after the projecting cape there is another trading-place on the coast, Kanē (*Husn al Ghurab*), of the kingdom of Eleazos, a frankincense-bearing land. Beside it are two uninhabited islands, one called Orneōn (*Bird Island; Sikha*), the other Troullas (*Barraqah*), about 120 stades from Kanē. Above it inland is the mother-city of Saubatha (*Shabwa*), which is also where the king dwells. All of the frankincense produced in the country is brought in for storage as it were, by camels and on leather rafts of a local type made of hide bags, and by ships. It also carries out trade with trading-places on the Far Side, Barygaza (*Broach*), Skythia, Omana, and neighbouring Persis.[91]

28. Imported into it from Egypt are indeed as usual: wheat in small quantities, wine, as it is to Mouza, Arabian cloaks, some plain and some regular and much of it fake, copper, tin, coral, *storax*, and the other items that go to Mouza. Further, large quantities of worked silverware and money for the king, also horses and statues and plain cloaks of superior quality. Exported from it are local cargoes, that is, frankincense and aloe; the remainder are down to its connections to other trading-places. The time to set sail is around the same as for Mouza, but earlier.

29. Beyond Kanē, the ⟨land⟩ receding further, there comes next another deep bay called Sachalites, stretching out a great way, and a frankincense-bearing land; both mountainous and impassable, having dense haze and mist, with frankincense produced by the trees. The frankincense-bearing trees are neither large nor tall; they produce frankincense solidified upon their bark, just as some of the trees we have in Egypt exude gum. The frankincense is collected by royal slaves and others sent for punishment. The region is terribly disease-ridden, pestilent to those sailing by, and always deadly to those working there, and besides, they die more readily through lack of food.

30. On this bay there is a massive promontory, facing east, called Syagros (*Ras Fartak*), on which is a fort for ⟨the defence of⟩ the land, a harbour, and a storehouse for gathering frankincense. In the open sea beside it is an island called Dioskourides' Island (*Socotra*), between it and the Cape of Aromata (*Spices*) opposite, but much closer to Syagros; it is very large but desolate and very damp, and contains rivers, crocodiles, very many snakes, and lizards exceedingly large, whose flesh is eaten; their fat is

[90] This refers to Augustus' ill-fated expedition into Arabia Eudaimon, led by Aelius Gallus in 26/5 BC, cf. *RGDA* 26. 2; Strabo 16. 4. 22–4, C780–2; Cassius Dio 53. 29. 3; Pliny 6. xxxii. 160, with Jameson 1968; Marek 1993; Nicolet 1991, 21, on Roman knowledge of the region.
[91] Skythia here is NW India.

melted down and used instead of olive oil. The island produces no crops, either vine or wheat. Those few dwelling there live only on one side of the island, towards the north wind, facing towards part of the mainland. They are immigrant foreigners, a mixture of Arabs and Indians and even some Greeks, who sail out there to trade. The island produces tortoiseshell, the genuine thing found there, the land tortoise, and white coloured, in great quantity and excellent in quality by reason of its larger shell,[92] and produces mountain tortoiseshell, exceedingly thick, of which the parts over the belly which are needed do not admit cutting, and are quite hard. What can be used is made into caskets, tablets, and plates,[93] and any such small pieces are cut up. Also found there is the so-called Indian cinnabar, collected as sap from trees.

31. Actually, this island falls under the king of the frankincense-bearing land, just as Azania does to Charibaēl and the chieftain (*tyrannos*) of Mapharitis. Some of the (*shippers*) from Mouza dealt with it, and those sailing out of Limyrike and Barygaza, as several of them by chance put in there. They exchanged rice, wheat, Indian cloth, and female slaves, finding a market for importing in their absence there, in return for large quantities of tortoiseshell. At present the island is leased out by the kings, and it is guarded closely.

32. Beyond Syagros there is an adjoining bay, cutting deeply into the land, Omana, with a strait 600 stades in width, and beyond it high mountains, rocky and precipitous, with men living in caves, for another 500 stades. And beyond them an anchorage was found for loading Sachalite frankincense, called Moscha Limen ('*Moscha Harbour*'; *Khôr Rûri*). Customarily some ships are sent to it from Kanē; and those sailing by from Limyrike or Barygaza winter there in late season, and through the authority of the king take as a return cargo cloth, wheat, and oil in exchange for Sachalite frankincense at a jetty placed there and unguarded, for the power of gods is watching over that place. For neither secretly nor openly can ships be loaded without the authority of the king. Even if a granule was to be taken, a ship would not dare to sail against the will of the god.

33. Next after Moscha Limen for about another 1,500 stades as far as Asichōn (*Ras Hasik*), a mountain extends along the shore and off the furthest tip of this lie seven islands in succession one after another, called Zenobios' Islands (*Kuria Muria Is.*). Beyond these lies another barbarian land, no longer of the same kingdom but now in Persis. After sailing over open water for about 2,000 stades from Zenobios' Islands, you encounter the so-called Sarapis' Island (*Masirah*), about 120 stades from the coast. It is some 200 stades across and 600 long, inhabited by three villages, and the holy men of the Ichthyophagoi. They speak the Arabic language and wear loincloths of palm leaf. The island is rich in superior tortoiseshell. Those from Kanē customarily fit out ships and small barges to go to it.[94]

---

[92] I think the author is trying to stress that these shells are different in size and quality.

[93] *magidion*: LSJ says it is a diminutive of *magis*, also scholion on Aristophanes, *Clouds* 1250.

[94] *epholkia*, cf. n. 80. Oddly, Casson does nothing with this, but it clearly should be taken in the pl. with σκάφας–*skaphas*, and 'trade', though implied, is not specifically stated. On barges, see Strabo 2. 3. 4, C99, rowed barges' used by pirates.

34. After cutting closely along the following coast due north, around the entrance to the Persian gulf there lie several islands, called Kalaios' Islands (*Jazair Daymaniyat Is.*), stretched out beside the coast for almost 2,000 stades. The men who dwell there are roguish and do not look out much during the day.[95]

35. Around the furthest point of Kalaios' Islands and of the so-called Kalon (*Good*) Mountain, a little beyond is the mouth of the Persian gulf, and there are the greatest fisheries for pearl oysters. On the left side of this mouth there are great mountains called the Asabō (*Ruus al Jibal*); on the right side, visible opposite, is another, round and high, called Semiramis' Mountain. The sailing in between them across the mouth is about 600 stades; through this is the Persian gulf, vast and broad, flowing into its innermost parts. At the edge of it is a legally limited trading-place called Apologou (*Apologos' Trading-place; Ubulla*), lying near Spasinou Charax and the River Euphrates.

36. After sailing by the mouth of the gulf, after six days' running there is another trading-place in Persis, called Omana. Customarily those from Barygaza fit out great ships to go to both trading-places in Persis with copper and teak-wood, and beams,[96] sailyards,[97] logs of sissoo and ebony; frankincense from Kanē is imported into Omana, and from Omana to Arabia are sent local sewn boats,[98] called *madarate*. Each of these trading-places exports to Barygaza and Arabia pearls in great quantity but lesser quality than Indian; and purple, local clothing, wine, dates in great quantity, gold, and slaves.

37. Beyond the land of Omana in like manner lies that of the Parsidai, another kingdom, and the bay called the Bay of the Terabdoi, where in the middle into the bay [—] stretches alongside. And by this there is a river, into which boats can set a course; at the mouth of which there is a small trading-place called Horaia (*Seasonable*), and behind it there is an inland city, being seven days' road from the sea, where there is a palace, called [—]. The country bears grain in great quantity and wine and rice and dates, but along the coast there is nothing except bdellium.[99]

38. Beyond that land, now with the land curving like a horn from the east because of the depth of the bay, next comes the coastal parts of Skythia, lying due north, exceedingly low-lying, from which flows the river Sinthos, the greatest of the rivers of

---

[95] Casson has 'who do not do much looking during the daytime'; it might be better understood as 'they aren't seen much during the day', a different version of the same metaphor.

[96] See N. Lewis 1960 on timber and Nile shipping. Judging by the Coptos Tariff Inscription (*OGIS* 674), detailing charges for road use in the eastern desert of Egypt, such wood also found its way into the Nile Valley, notoriously short of good timber.

[97] Literally 'horns': Casson B36. 12. 6a, citing Casson 1986, 232.

[98] Cf. Strabo 7. 4. 1, C308.

[99] I translate ἤπειρος–*ēpeiros* as 'coast' instead of the usual 'mainland'. Bdellium: resin of *Commiphora*, see §§48–9, Dioskorides 1. 67; Pliny 12. xix. 35–6.

the Erythraian sea region, discharging vast quantities of water into the sea, up to a long way out, and before you reach land, this white-coloured water meets you in open sea. A sign to those coming from the open sea that they are approaching land is that serpents come out of the depths to meet them; for there is such a sign also in the places above and around Persis, which are called *graai*.[100] This river has seven mouths, these narrow and formed of shoals, and indeed none of these have passage, but only the middle one, where, by the coast there is the trading-place Barbarikon. A small islet lies before it, and behind it the mother-city of Skythia itself, Minnagar. It is ruled by the Parthians, who drive out each other continuously.

39. Therefore, ships anchor at Barbarikon, but all cargoes are carried up the river to the king at the mother-city. Imported into this trading-place are: cloaks, plain but of sufficient quality and not often second-rate,[101] multi-coloured fabrics,[102] goldstone,[103] coral, storax, frankincense, glass vessels, silverware, money, and wine, but not much. Exported are: *costus*,[104] bdellium, *lykion*,[105] nard, turquoise, lapis lazuli; and Sirikan hides, cloth, and yarn; and Indian Black.[106] Those who set out sailing with the Indian (*winds*) leave around the month of July, that is Epeiph; the voyage is hard going, but quicker if they are favourable.

40. Beyond the Sinthos river there is another bay, hidden, to the north. It is named Eirinon, with the epithets Small and Great. Both open bodies of water (*pelagē*) are formed of shoals and continuous shallow eddies far from the land; thus frequently, with the land out of sight, ships run aground, and being taken further in are destroyed utterly. Above this bay a promontory, curving around Eirinon, first east and south, then west, surrounds another bay called Barake (*gulf of Kutch*), (itself) surrounding[107] seven islands. Here vessels which happen upon the beginning of this bay and pull back a little to the open sea escape, but those drawn into the bowels of Barake are destroyed utterly. For the waves there are large and very strong, with a rough and turbid sea which has shoals and violent whirlpools.[108] The bottom here has in some places

---

[100] Karttunen 1997, 227 on Indian sea-snakes.   [101] Or 'counterfeit' Cf. §6.
[102] Pliny 8. lxxiv. 196, a speciality of Alexandria.
[103] *chrysolithon* is peridot according to Casson 1989, 190 and B39. 13. 8a. Casson connects this with a highly prized peridot from *St John's I.* in the Red Sea serving as 'gifts to royalty', see Pliny 37. xxxii. 107–8 (who calls it topaz; he mentions *chrysolithon* by name at 37. xxiv. 90–1; xxviii. 101; xlii. 126–xliii. 127; xlvi. 154; xlviii. 127; lxii. 172). If this is the case, it is odd indeed that it is merely contained within a list of much more common items. Translating as 'goldstone' leaves open a more mundane interpretation.
[104] A fragrant root, possibly from Kashmir. Papyri show its use in medicine.
[105] Possibly an extract from acacia trees.
[106] Casson has 'Chinese hides'; more likely 'seric' cloth, or silk, which was 'combed' from trees, cf. Pliny 21. viii. 11 (thus could be seen as a hide or bark; it was not known to be an animal product until C2 AD), cf. Karttunen 1997, 219. Ben Cartlidge suggests to me that there may be a link with σέος–*seos*, possibly derived from the Semitic for 'moth'. I am not convinced by Casson B 39:13. 11, for although he agrees that this is Chinese silk, he does nothing with the noun *sirikon*. Indian Black is thought to be indigo of a very deep colour.
[107] ἐμπεριειλημμένον, a correction to the MS, which is corrupt at this point.
[108] Whirlpools, from εἴλω–*eilō*, 'whirl', leading to a vortex. This area near the *gulf of Kutch* is known to be treacherous, with shoals and strong rip tides.

precipitous drops, in others rocky and sheer, such that anchors set beside each other to hold against the treacherous water are cut, and some are smashed together in the deep. A sign of these for ships approaching from the open sea are the huge black snakes that come out to meet them. For in the regions beyond this, and around Barygaza, those (*snakes*) encountered are smaller and yellow and golden.

41. Immediately beyond Barake there is the bay of Barygaza and the coastline of the land of Ariâke, which is the beginning of the kingdom of Manbanos and in fact of the whole of India. This part inland bordering on Skythia is called Aberia, that part on the coast Syrastrene (*Kathiawar peninsula*). The country bears much grain, rice, sesame oil, ghee, cotton,[109] and the ordinary Indian cloths made from it. But there is the greatest number of herds of cattle and the men are of great size with skin dark in colour. The mother-city of the land is Minnagara, from which great quantities of cloth are brought down to Barygaza. Even now in the region signs of Alexander's expedition are preserved: ancient shrines, foundations of encampments, and great wells. The coastal sailing along this land from Barbarikon as far as the promontory at Astakapra, opposite Barygaza, called Papike (*Kuda Point*), is 3,000 stades.

42. Beyond it there is another bay, outside the waves, which goes in northwards. Near its mouth there is an island called Baiones (*Piram I.*), and at the innermost places there is a very great river called the Mais (*R. Mahi*). Those sailing to Barygaza cross this bay, which is about 300 stades wide, leaving on their left the island, so that its highest point is visible, and (*head*) due east, straight towards the mouth of the river at Barygaza. The river is called the Lamnaios.

43. The narrow bay which leads down to Barygaza is risky for those coming from the open sea to undertake. For they fall either to the right or to the left-hand side, but the latter approach is better than the former. For on the right, by the mouth of the bay itself, lies a jagged and rocky strip of land, called Herone, beside the village of Kammoni. Opposite this, on the left side, is the promontory in front of Astakapra, called Papike. Anchoring here ⟨is difficult⟩ because of the current around it, and because ship's tackle and anchors are cut by the jagged, rocky bottom. Even if you attempt the bay itself, the mouth of the river itself at Barygaza is hard to find, for the land is low-lying and nothing of it can be observed safely from closer in. Even if you find it, it is hard to enter because of the shoals of the river around it.

44. Right around the entrance, because of this, local fishermen in the king's service[110] show goodwill to those sailing in with crews and long ships called *trappaga* and *kotymba*, and come out as far as Syrastrene to meet them and to guide the ships up to Barygaza. For they (*the fishermen*) steer using the crews (*sc. by rowing?*) directly from the mouth of the bay through the shoals they tow them to stations already appointed,

---

[109] κάρπασος–*karpasos*, from the Sanskrit, should be distinguished from ὀθόνιον–*othonion*, which many translators take to be cotton but is linen cloth made from flax, or simply 'cloth' here.

[110] Lit. 'royal local fishermen', essentially local pilots in the king's service.

beginning when the tide rises and establishing them at anchorages and potholes[111] when it stops. These potholes are deeper points along the river up to Barygaza. For this lies upstream at about 300 stades from the mouth of the river.

45. All over the land of India there are many rivers, with strong ebb and flow tides, which at the rising (*i.e. at new moon*) and at the full moon last for three days, lessening in the intervening phases of the moon.[112] They are more frequent and stronger down to Barygaza, in as much as the bottom suddenly becomes visible and some parts of the land, which shortly before were navigable, are now dry land, the rivers with incoming tides from the open sea are completely pushed back violently against the flow of their natural stream for many stades.

46. Thus it is dangerous for ships to put in and draw out for those unacquainted and setting into this trading-place for the first time. As, by the time of the impulse of the flood tide nothing can hold fast and ⟨the⟩ anchors cannot hold, and thus the ships are taken by its force, thrust sideways under the quickness of the stream, and run aground on the shoals and break up, and smaller ⟨ships⟩ even capsize. In the case of some channels, some (*ships*) are broached on their sides during the ebb tide, if not propped, and when suddenly high tide occurs they pitch head-first and are swamped with the flow.[113] There is so much strength produced in the surge of the sea that, under the new moon,[114] if the flood-tide arrives at night, inasmuch as when it first begins to flow in, and the sea is calm, it carries to the people at the mouth (*of the river*) a noise resembling an army heard from afar, and after a short pause the sea rushes over the shoals with a hiss.

47. Lying behind Barygaza there are several inland nations: those of the Aratrioi, Arachousioi, Gandaraioi, and the Proklaïs, where Boukephalos Alexandreia is found. And beyond these is a warlike nation, *that of* the Baktrians under a king, †in its own place†. And Alexander setting out from these parts passed as far as the Ganges but failed to reach Limyrike or the south of India. Even now, from the region of Barygaza old drachmas are in circulation,[115] inscribed with Greek characters the devices of Apollodotos and Menandros, who ruled after Alexander.

48. To the east of this region there is a city called Ozene (*Ujjain*), the former seat of the kingdom, from which all the good produce of the country is brought down to Barygaza and that which is traded with us: onyx, agate, Indian cotton, and *molochinon*, and great quantities of clothing of ordinary quality. Things also brought down through this region are nard, which is brought through Proklaïs (the Kattybourine,

---

[111] χυτρῖνος–*chytrinos* (κυθρῖνος–*kythrinos* in Ionic and later Greek) is a deep hole or basin. For χύτροι in the same sense, see Thphr. *HP* 4. 11. 8.

[112] Referring to high 'spring' tides at full and new moon, and lower 'neap' tides in between.

[113] I have inserted terms here which are more nautical in sense.

[114] *symmēnia*: LSJ gives 'period when the moon does not shine'. The period of new moon is when the Moon is on the same side of Earth as the Sun, and is neither illuminated nor visible.

[115] προχωροῦσιν: LSJ gives 'pass current', i.e. be regarded as legitimate tender, 'be expended', etc.

Patropapige, and Kabalite), and that coming through the neighbouring Skythia, and costos, and bdellium.

49. Finding a market in this trading-place are wine, principally Italian and Laodikeian and Arabian, copper, tin, and lead; coral and goldstone; plain clothing, and counterfeits of all sorts; multi-coloured girdles a cubit in width, storax, yellow sweet clover,[116] unfinished glass, realgar, sulphide of antimony; gold and silver denarii, exchanged with the local currency with interest, unguent of low value, but not much of it. For the king at that time there was imported valuable silverware, slave musicians, beautiful girls as concubines, fine wines, plain but expensive clothing, and excellent unguent. Exported from this region are: nard, costos, bdellium, ivory, onyx, agate, *lykion*, all sorts of cotton clothing, silk, *molochinon*, yarn, long pepper, and that brought from the trading-places. They sail to this trading-place from Egypt in season, around the month of July, that is Epeiph.

50. Just beyond Barygaza the succeeding coast extends directly from north to south. Therefore, the country is called Dachinabades, for Dachanos is what the south wind is called in their tongue. That inland ⟨region⟩ which lies above to the east has much desolate land and great mountains and wild animals of several kinds: leopards, tigers, elephants, enormous dragons, *krokottai* (*hyenas*), many kinds of 'dog-heads' (*monkeys*), and many populous nations as far as the Ganges.

51. Of those in Dachinabades itself, two trading-places are important: Paithana (*Paithan*), twenty days' road south from Barygaza, and from there about ten days to the east the other city, a large one, Tagara (*Têr*). From these are brought down to Barygaza, by wagon through great roadless tracts, from Paithana onyx in large quantities; from Tagara, many clothes of ordinary quality, all kinds of cotton, and *molochina*, and any other wares from the coastal parts that find a market there. The whole coastal sailing as far as Limyrike is 7,000 stades; most people go on to Aigialos (*'The Shore'*).[117]

52. The local trading-places located one after the other are Akabarou, Souppara, and the city of Kalliena (*Kalyân*), which became an authorized trading-place in the time of the Elder Saraganos, but no longer is, for after Sandanes seized it it was much held back. And for those Greek ships that by chance come to these places they are led into Barygaza under guard.

53. Beyond Kalliena other local trading-places are Semylla (*Chaul*), Mandagora (*Bânkot*), Palaipatmai (*Dâbhol*), Melizeigara (*Jaigarh*), Byzantion (*Vijayadurg*), Toparon†, and Tyrannosboas†. Next come the so-called Sesekreienai Islands (*Vengurla Rocks*), that of the Aigidioi (*Goa*), and that of the Kaineitoi by the so-called Chersonese (*Oyster Rocks*), around which places there are pirates, and beyond these Leuke (*White*) Island (*Pigeon Island*). Next are Naoura (*Mangalore*) and Tyndis (*Ponnâni*),

---

[116] μελίλωτον–*melilōton*: Casson has 'yellow sweet clover'. Some sort of mustard?
[117] Casson has 'The Strand', an unusual English synonym for beach or sea-shore (cf. *COD*[12] s.v. 1). Belfiore has 'Spiaggia'.

the first trading-places of Limyrike (*Malabar coast*), and beyond these Mouziris (*Cranganore*) and Nelkynda (*Niranom*); these are now busy.

54. In the kingdom of Keprobotos is Tyndis, an important village on the coast. In the same kingdom is Mouziris, flourishing because of ships that come there from Ariake and those of the Greeks. It lies by a river and is 500 stades from Tyndis by river or by sea, and from [—] it is 20. Nelkynda is almost 500 stades from Mouziris, similarly by river, on foot, and by sea, and is in another kingdom, that of Pandion. It also lies beside a river, about 120 stades from the sea.

55. Another village lies before the mouth of the river: Bakare (*Pirakkâd*), to which ships arrive coming upstream from Nelkynda. One anchors in a roadstead in order to take up cargoes because the river has reefs and shallow channels. Themselves, the kings of both trading-places dwell inland. A sign of these for those approaching this region from the open sea are the snakes that come out to meet them; these, too, are black in colour, but shorter and with dragon-shaped heads and blood-red eyes.

56. Ships sailing to these trading-places are of great size and burden for the pepper and *malabathron*.[118] Imported into them are principally large amounts of money, goldstone, plain clothing in limited quantity, multi-coloured ⟨clothing⟩, sulphide of antimony, coral, unfinished glass, copper, tin, lead, wine in limited quantity, as much as to Barygaza, realgar, orpiment, grain, as much as is necessary for shippers as the traders there do not furnish it. Exported are pepper, which grows only in one place for these trading-places, in large quantity, called Kottanarike (*Kuṭṭanâḍu*). Also exported: pearls of fine quality in reasonable amounts, ivory, and silk cloth, Gangetic nard, *malabathron*, brought here from the interior places, all sorts of transparent stones, diamonds, sapphires, tortoiseshell, both from Chrysonetikōn (*'Golden Island', Lakkadive Is.*) and from the sort hunted in the islands around Limyrike itself. They sail here from Egypt in season, setting off, the time to set out to sea is around the month of July, that is Epeiph.

57. People ⟨previously⟩ sailed all the aforementioned circumnavigation from Kanē and Eudaimon Arabia in small ships by coasting, before Hippalos the sea-captain,[119] after observing the position of trading-places and the form of the sea, discovered the route across the open sea. In this part the winds we call etesian blow seasonally from the Ocean, (*and thus*) the Libonotos (*south-south-westerly*) appears in the Indian open-sea. It is also called after the name of the man who first discovered the crossing. Because of this, until now, some set forth directly from Kanē, and some from the trading-place of the Aromata. Those making for Limyrike mostly sail with the wind on the (*starboard*) quarter,[120] while those setting for Barygaza and those for Skythia

---

[118] See De Romanis 2020, 138–9.   [119] See introduction.

[120] This is difficult. Casson has 'on the quarter for most of the way'. LSJ defines τράχηλος–*trachēlos* as usually the neck, etc., but the 'middle part of a mast'. The quarterdeck is the deck behind the mast. It could mean 'at a broad reach', 'running before the wind', or the like. For discussion, see De Romanis 2020, 64–6.

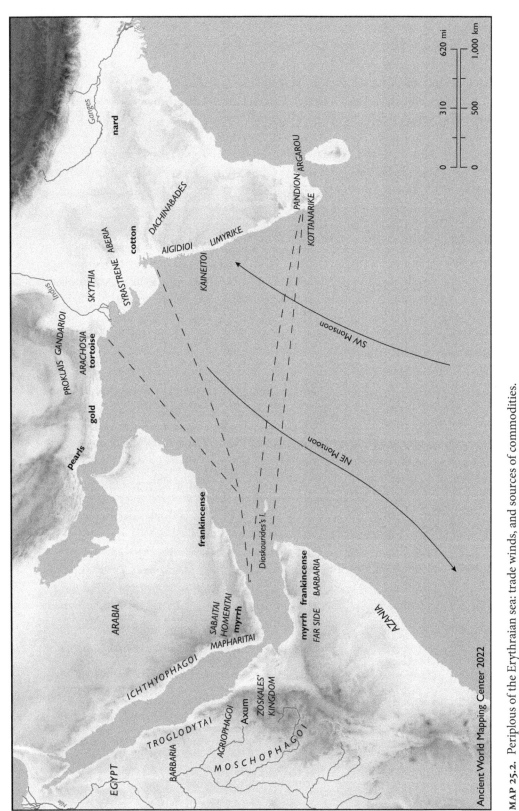

MAP 25.2. Periplous of the Erythraian sea: trade winds, and sources of commodities.

hold this course for not more than three days, and then for the rest †are borne along† on their own course away from the land, on the high ⟨seas⟩ and through the outer (*Ocean*), and sail past the aforementioned gulfs.

58. After Bakare is the so-called Pyrrhon (*Red*) Mountain ⟨and⟩ another land extends [—] called Paralia (*The Coast*), directly to the south. The first place is called Balita, with a village on the coast, and has a good anchorage. After this comes another place called Komar (*Cape Comorin*), where there is a settlement (?) and harbour.[121] To it those wishing to become holy in their future life come there and perform ablutions and remain celibate. Women do likewise. For it is recorded that the goddess at one time stayed and performed ablutions.

59. After Komar the land extends as far as Kolchoi, where pearl fishing is carried out by convicts; it is under King Pandion. Beyond Kolchoi is first Aigialos† (*The Shore*), lying in a bay and with territory inland, called Argarou. In one place ⟨along it bountiful⟩ pearls are collected.[122] Exported are the cotton clothes called Argaritides.

60. Of the trading-places and anchorages here, where those sailing both from Limyrike and the north come to land, the significant ones, lying one after another, are the trading-places of Kamara, Podouke (*Pondicherry*), and Sopatma, at which there are local boats sailing along the coast as far as Limyrike, and other kinds of very large boats, called *sangara*, made from a single piece of wood and held together by yokes. The ships that set out for Chryse and the Ganges are the very large *kolandiophonta*.[123] Imported into these places are all of the merchandises imported into Limyrike, and, in general, money coming from Egypt is brought down to them at all times and all of the many things brought to Limyrike and furnished abundantly along this coast.

61. Around the lands beyond it, with the course turning away to the east, an island projects into the open sea to the west, now called Palaisimoundou, but by the ancients Taprobane (*Sri Lanka*).[124] Those parts that are to the north are civilized and they sail through there [—] and it extends almost up to the coast of Azania opposite to it. It produces pearls, transparent stones, fine cloth, and tortoiseshell.

62. Around those regions, extending far inland, lies the adjacent country of Masalia. Much fine quality cloth is produced there. Due east from this, after you cross a bay that lies alongside, is the country of Desarene, producing ivory called *bōsarē*, and beyond it, the course turning to the north, are many barbarian nations, among

---

[121] βριάριον–*briarion*: Belfiore suggests 'un centro di commercio'. The MS is unclear, and φρούριον–*phrourion* has been suggested as a restoration, for 'fortress' or 'citadel'.

[122] This part of the MS is corrupt, and a number of restorations and explanations have been suggested. Belfiore has 'lungo la costa della regione sono soggette ai diritti di dogana', suggesting τελωνεῖται.

[123] Large ocean-going ships from SE Asia.

[124] From Παλαισιμούνδου to ⟨Τα⟩προβάνη, see Casson 1989, 230–1; Belfiore 2013, nn. 611–14, for references. *PME* here contradicts Ptolemy 7. 4. 1, who says its ancient name was *palai* ('long ago') Simoundou, but no easy resolution is possible. Pliny 6. xxiv. 85–6 has *Palaesimundus* as a mother city and a river. The MS of *PME* is clear in these readings, despite Casson's note that it is defective. πάλαι Σιμούνδου, 'Simoundou of old', is suggested by the early edition of Stuckius 1577, but not followed by Frisk 1927.

which are the Kirrhadai, a race of people with flat noses, and wild, and another nation, that of the Bargysoi, and that of the Hippoprosopoi (*Horsefaces*), who, it is said, are man-eaters (*anthrōpophagoi*).[125]

63. Beyond this to the east, keeping the Ocean on the right and sailing outside the other outer parts on the left, you meet the Ganges, and around it the furthest point of the mainland to the east, Chryse (*Golden Land*). There is a river near it, itself called the Ganges, the greatest of the rivers of India, which has a rise and fall just like the Nile, and on it there is a trading-place with the same name as the river, Ganges, through which are carried *malabathron*, Gangetic nard, pearls, the finest cloths, called Gangetic. It is said there are gold mines in the area, and gold coin called *kaltis*. By this river there is an island in the Ocean, the furthest extremity to the east of the inhabited world, under the rising sun itself, called Chryse. It has the finest tortoiseshell of all the regions of the Erythraian sea.

64. Beyond this country, now to the north, the sea ends at a place on the outside, where lies a great inland city called Thina, from which silken thread, yarn, and cloth are carried overland through Baktria to Barygaza and via the river Ganges back to Limyrike. It is not easy to get to Thina, for rarely does anyone come from it, and (*then*) not many. The place lies under the Little Bear (*Ursa Minor*), and it is said that it joins with the remote parts of Pontos and the Caspian sea, near where the adjacent Lake Maiotis discharges into the Ocean like them.

65. Every year there appears at the borderland of Thina a certain people, circumcised,[126] and very flat-faced, †notable in the end, themselves† called Sesatai. They come with their wives and children carrying large loads resembling mats of fresh vine leaves, and stay at a certain place on the borderland between them and those at Thina. They hold a festival for several days setting out the mats beneath them, and then set off for their own homes in the interior regions. Expecting this, the locals (?) come to that place and gather up what the Sesatai have laid out. They separate the fibres from reeds, which they call *petroi*, lay the leaves out in layers, and roll them into globe shapes, stringing them on the fibres from the reeds. There are three types: from the bigger leaf what is called large-globular *malabathron*; from the smaller, medium-globular; and from the smallest, small-globular. Thus three types of *malabathron* are produced, and they are often carried to India by those that made them.

66. That which lies beyond these parts, through fierce storms, harsh cold, and impassable terrain, as though through some divine power of the gods, has not been investigated.

---

[125] Cf. 'man-eaters' or 'man-eating' cf. *Nik.* fr. 15 = *Eux.* §78 and Markianos, *Periplous* 1. 13, both on the Black Sea; *Hypotyposis* §18 on the E coast of Africa further S.
[126] Lit. 'mutilated', see Strabo 16. 4. 9, C771.

26

PSEUDO-PLUTARCH, *ON THE NAMES OF RIVERS AND MOUNTAINS AND THE THINGS IN THEM*

('*DE FLUVIIS*')

(1ST C. AD, OR FIRST HALF OF 2ND C.)

J. Brian Campbell

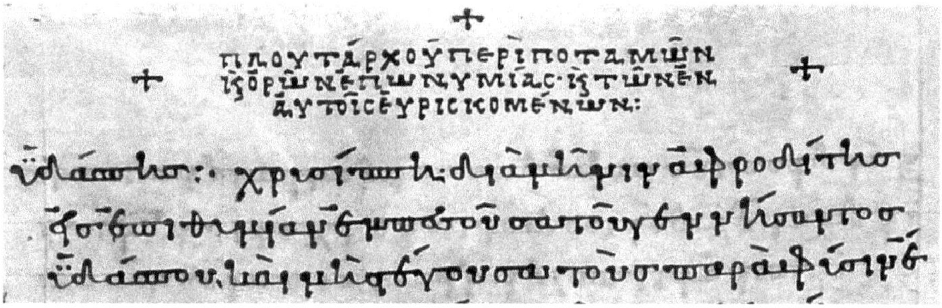

FIG. 26.1. Opening of the text of Ps.-Plutarch, fo. 157ʳ (detail).

INTRODUCTION

THE TEXT

A Greek text is preserved in manuscript A (the 9th-century AD Heidelberg Codex 398; see Introduction, §VIII. 2. a) as one of a collection of eighteen works. The manuscript's contents, mainly non-geographical—and by no means all genuine—are worth listing in order to appreciate the context and nature of the present text (the geographical ones are marked *):

*Ps.-Arrian, *Periplous of the Euxine* (*Eux.*)
Arrian, *Kynegetikos* (Huntsman)
*Arrian, *Periplous of the Euxine*
*Ps.-Arrian, *Periplous of the Erythraian sea* (*PME*)
*Hanno
Philon of Byzantion, *On the Seven Wonders of the World*
Chrestomatheiai (extracts from Strabo)
*Plutarch, *On the Names of Rivers and Mountains* (the present text)
Parthenios, *Love Stories*

Antonius Liberalis, *Collection of Metamorphoses*
Hesychios, *Byzantine History*
Phlegon, *Marvels*
Apollonios, *Miraculous Stories*
(Pseudo-)Antigonos, *Collection of Miraculous Stories*
Hippokrates, *Letters*
Themistokles, *Letters*
Diogenes, *Letters*
Brutus, *Letters*

This is a curious grouping; besides the geographical works, the contents comprise accounts of miraculous events, historical snippets, and erotic stories. The text *On the Names of Rivers and Mountains*, which appears under the name of Plutarch, between Strabo and Parthenios, more or less fits into all these categories.

THE AUTHOR

There is general agreement that the author of the treatise on the names of rivers and mountains is not Plutarch of Chaironeia.[1] Indeed, on the manuscript there is an anonymous marginal comment: 'This is falsely ascribed. The thought and diction are far from the grandeur of Plutarch; unless he might be some other Plutarch'. Therefore the author is now referred to as Pseudo-Plutarch. There are some grounds for thinking that he may be identical with the person responsible for *A Collection of Parallel Greek and Roman Histories*, which the codices of Plutarch place among his real works (at *Moralia* 306–16). The reasons for making the identification are subjective but reasonably convincing, in that both works exhibit similar failings with a self-important, cumbersome presentation, tedious repetition of words and phrases, and the frequent citation of other writers to support the contentions of the author. One advantage of making the identification is that the work on parallel histories is vaguely datable. The author refers to a Juba (*Parallel Histories* 23 = *Mor*. 311b 9–c 4); this was Juba II, king of Mauretania (Chapter 22 above), who wrote about Libya and Rome and died c. AD 23. Furthermore, Clement of Alexandria (end of 2nd century AD) knew of these *Parallel Histories*. Therefore Pseudo-Plutarch (if we accept that the authors of the names of rivers and mountains and of the parallel histories are identical) lived in the 1st century AD or the first half of the 2nd.[2] Beyond that there is no clear date, and no evidence on the author's origins or domicile.

---

[1] As observed in the earliest printed edition, that of Gelenius 1533, p. [iii] (preface), who had read the Heidelberg MS.

[2] Bollansée, Haegemans, and Schepens 2008 prefer a date around AD 300. But if, as is generally believed, our text was included in his geographical corpus by Arrian (see Introduction, §VIII. 2. a), it must date from before c.150 BC.

How did Pseudo-Plutarch come to be confused with Plutarch of Chaironeia? If we accept the idea that our author simply shares a name with Plutarch, we have to accept the coincidence that, like his homonym, he wrote a series of parallel histories. However, it is possible that Pseudo-Plutarch's parallel histories were originally written by an anonymous author and included along with the real Plutarch's *Parallel Lives*; by this association the anonymous author acquired the name Plutarch, which then came to be given to the other work of the same author on the names of rivers and mountains.[3] Anonymous works often acquire the name of an author with whom they happen to be joined in a codex. This seems a more plausible explanation, though no certainty is possible.

NATURE OF THE WORK

The treatise explains the origins of the names of rivers, and of mountains situated nearby. The author usually gives an older name with its explanation, and then the more recent with an explanation for the change. He proceeds to describe plants and rocks found in the rivers and on the mountains, and their often miraculous qualities. At the end of every section an authority is cited for the information given. All this material is presented in a very formulaic way, as each section follows a regular plan with little variation and a limited number of phrases frequently repeated.

The work names twenty-five rivers, with a strong bias towards Greece and the east: Greece (6), Asia (6), Thrace (2), Skythia (3), Egypt (1), India (3), Armenia (1), Mesopotamia (2), and Gaul (1). There are no Italian rivers, only one from the western part of the empire, and no mention of the Rhine or Danube. This, of course, does not mean that the author came from the Greek east. In compiling or choosing the rivers he may have been at the mercy of his sources. It is possible that the surviving text was excerpted from a longer work, or perhaps another section dealing with additional rivers has been lost.

On the Names of Rivers and Mountains is not really geographical in character, though it does in very general terms give the location of rivers and mountains. The author is more interested in nomenclature, mythological story-telling, often with a strong erotic content, and the miraculous qualities of plants and stones. Given the limited connection with geography, and in some cases the author's geographical ignorance (see below), it is worth asking about his choice of this topic and the cultural context in which it was written. Are rivers merely incidental to his purpose or integral in some way? The work may to some extent be part of the tradition of paradoxography, often enhanced by illicit sexual activity, and it is true that some of the other works in the Heidelberg codex deal with marvels and the trials of love. In the treatise there is a recurrent theme of just retribution, the punishment of the wrongdoer, and vindication of those who suffered injustice through the memorial of riverine or mountain

[3] *GGM* ii, p. lii.

nomenclature. Rivers and mountains are the locations on which are played out the mythological or quasi-mythological dramas. This may, perhaps, suggest that there was a lot of interest in natural phenomena and that it served the author's purpose to attach his stories to rivers and mountains. Rivers, personified as lusty men, had always had a strong association with erotic adventures and were no strangers to the abduction and rape of women. The author presumably knew his audience. Such stories, as well as being a good read, may have contributed to a process of establishing local identity for communities in the riverine vicinity and may reflect the cultural and psychological importance of locality and local traditions. It is worth noting that the genre of literature on rivers can be traced back to Homer and especially Hesiod, and this tradition may have inspired Kallimachos to write on rivers, along with winds and marvels. Furthermore, Suetonius dealt with rivers, seas, and winds.

Pseudo-Plutarch makes mistakes in basic geography and seems not to have studied any geographical writers. For example, he claims that the Hydaspes was once called the Indus (1. 1), and manages to conflate the Inachos and the Haliakmon (18. 1) although the first is in the Argolid in the Peloponnese, the second is near Argos in Macedonia. In claiming that the Indus was previously called Mausolos (25. 1), the author seems to be confusing the river with the one flowing in Lycia. He is also in error in claiming that Euphrates was previously called Medos (20. 1), and conflates the Araxes with the Baltros in Baktria (23. 1). Furthermore, mountains are sometimes inaccurately identified in relation to rivers: Mt Sipylos is located next to the Maeander (9. 4), whereas it is near the Hermos in Lydia. Mt Pangaios is adjacent to the Strymon not the Hebros (3. 2). He locates Mt Kokkygion next to the Inachos (18. 1 and 4), whereas it is adjacent to Hermion in the Argolid.

While some of Pseudo-Plutarch's material is reliably confirmed by other writers, in many cases we have no other evidence for his assertions about rivers (Arar, Brigoulos, Kaikos, Astraios, Euphrates, Xaranda) and mountains (Elephas, Anatole, Athenaion, Drimylon, Argillon). It is difficult to trust our author's information and much is likely to be fictitious or based on imaginative fantasy. In respect of stones and plants, we have information from elsewhere about certain stones (*aëtites*, *antipathes*, *lychnis*) and plants (*leukoion*, *prometheios*; the Thracian plant at 3. 3). There is no other information on any of the other stones and plants he mentions.

NOMENCLATURE

Our author's explanations of riverine names are very similar. With a few exceptions rivers are named because people throw themselves into them as a result of grief, pain, insanity, or fear. The background to this is often sexual, including forbidden liaisons, often incestuous. In some cases a man sees gods naked, or making love, or is caught committing theft or murder, or spurns divine mysteries, or a stepmother lusts after her stepson. The same type of story appears in other authors: for example, Livy describes how the Indus was allegedly named because one Indos had fallen off an elephant into it (38. 14). And some stories are known elsewhere: for example, Apollodoros (1. 7. 8) has the same story on the naming of the river Euenos, adding the detail that Euenos slaughtered his horses before throwing himself in the river. But in other cases we have no confirmation. In other cases, The Tigris was so-named because Dionysos was carried across the river on a tiger (24. 1), while the Marsyas is connected to the legend of the famous piper (10. 1). The Tanaïs was formerly called the Amazonios because the Amazons bathed there (14. 1), while the Eurotas was formerly the Himeros after Eurotas' amorous exploits (17. 1). The Ismenos was formerly called the Foot of Kadmos, based on an old fable (2. 1).

In the author's presentation, events and the fate of humans in individual regions occasionally match the plants in the vicinity. Marsyas, having lost his musical contest with Apollo, was flayed and from his blood the river flowed; the indigenous plant was the *aulos* (pipe) and the local stone was the *machaira* (knife). (10). At the river Phasis we have the story of an adulterous woman that is linked to a stone that protects the purity of marriage (5. 2). At the river Paktolos the story concerns a virgin who is raped, and the local stone protects virgins from assault (7. 5–6). Another story attached to the same river concerns a thief and the related stone wards off thieves (7. 1). When Palaistinos threw himself in the Strymon because of grief at the death of his son, the stone is called *pausilypon* ('grief-stopping'; 9. 1–2). At the Kaikos a man is afflicted with leprosy and the local stone is a remedy for skin infections and leprosy (21. 4–5). In another case the name of a mountain (Mykenai) is derived from the sound of the Greek word describing an incident in the related story (18. 6). The author's method neatly combines local history and the supernatural, and in some regions events, the fate of men and women, and the qualities of plants and stones found there, are inextricably linked.

It is an interesting point that some of the explanations for the earlier names of rivers are based on characteristics of the river or the surrounding environment. The Maeander was formerly called the Anabainon ('ascender') since it seemed to flow back on itself (9. 1). The Phasis was formerly the Arktouros because of its position in cold regions (5. 1), while the Thermodon was formerly called the Krystallos since it froze over (15. 1). The Hebros was previously the Rhombos, getting the name from its violently swirling water (3. 1). The Sagaris was formerly the Xerobates because in the summer season it was often seen to be dry (*xeros*; 12. 1). The Acheloös was previously called Axenos because it was situated in an inhospitable region (22. 1). This form of nomenclature is likely to be fictitious, but that may not be as important as a story based on local characteristics and connections.

SOURCES

Pseudo-Plutarch is meticulous about citing his sources. Forty-five names of authors are adduced, most of whom also appear in the *Parallel Histories*, and he refers to 14 works about rivers, 8 about stones, 2 about mountains, and 1 about trees. Others deal with the history of regions and other topics, for example, foundations (of cities), hunting, and collections of mythological stories. However, our author does not refer to Kallimachos, who wrote on winds, marvels, and rivers. In the case of the story of Marsyas, the satyrs who spring from his blood, and the naming of the river, which is attributed to Alexander Polyhistor's work on Phrygia, the author, his work, and the story are well known. This may inspire some confidence in Pseudo-Plutarch's reliability. But even this is not certain since the Marsyas story may not fit in its position and was perhaps added by a later author.[4] Furthermore, since this is the only instance where the name of author, the work and the story are known, perhaps we should not place much emphasis on it. Elsewhere (5. 3) Pseudo-Plutarch refers to Kleanthes and his work the *Battle of the Gods*; he was probably thinking of the Stoic philosopher, who did write about gods and giants. Timagenes (6. 3) seems to be the Greek scholar from Alexandria (no other writer claims that he came from Syria) who was captured and brought to Rome in 55 BC. He was set free and later became a friend of Augustus, though after a quarrel he was barred from the emperor's house. He produced a universal history and wrote extensively about Gaul.[5]

In some cases it may be that Pseudo-Plutarch has confused the name of a genuine author or that the name has been corrupted in the manuscript tradition. For example, Kallisthenes, cited as author of a work *Galatika* (6. 3), might be a mistake for Eratosthenes, whose work was used by Stephanos of Byzantion. 'Plesimachos' (18. 13) is probably the well-known Lysimachos, while Ktesias of Ephesos (18. 6) may well be Mousaios of Ephesos (3rd century BC) who wrote an epic poem, *Perseis*. The scholiast on Apollonios of Rhodes, *Argonautika*, 2. 401 and 1017, cites information about mountains taken from the work of one Ktesias, who may be identical with Ktesias of Knidos (21. 5), writing on Mt Teuthras. Kleitophon on *Foundations* (6. 4) may be the same man who wrote about the origins of Miletos, as cited by the scholiast on *Iliad* 20. 404. Thrasyllos, who is cited as the author of a work on stones (11. 4), also appears as the author of a work on Egypt (16. 2), where he describes the building of a wall to prevent flooding by the Nile, a story that also appears in the Elder Pliny (10. xlix. 94).

Other writers whose works Pseudo-Plutarch claims to be using are completely unknown to us. It is difficult to say how many of these authors are fictitious, and we might compare the late antique *Historia Augusta* (written in Latin), which is assiduous in its invention of authorities. Even when an author is known from other sources, we cannot be sure that they wrote the works cited, since many ancient writers tend to attribute to famous authors works they never wrote. Therefore we may incline to agree with Carl Müller that even when Pseudo-Plutarch cites material from well-known authors we must suspect that he has invented it, unless there are strong arguments to the contrary. Hercher argued bizarrely that Pseudo-Plutarch cited his authorities on the basis of a kind of word game, in that in some instances the first syllable in the name of an author is identical with the first syllable of another name which occurs in the preceding

---

[4] Suggested by Müller, *GGM* ii, p. lvi.   [5] *BNJ* 88.

section.[6] He apparently meant that, for example at 1. 1 the name of the protagonist, Chrysippe, starts with the same letters as the authority cited just below, Chrysermos (1. 4). At 21 Timandros is killed and the authority cited later is Timagoras. These and other similar suggestions, such as Agathokles (9. 1) followed by Agenor (9. 4) and Agatharchides (9. 5), seem entirely fanciful, but if true would further undermine the credibility of Pseudo-Plutarch's citation of sources.

EDITIONS

After early printed editions, the text was well served by several 19th-century editors.[7] The text used in this edition is mainly that of Müller, with changes indicated in the notes.

SELECTED FURTHER READING

In Greek myth there are connections between love-madness and leaping into water and engulfment. See (in date order):

Nagy, G. (1973), 'Phaethon, Sappho's Phaon, and the white rock of Leukas: "reading" the symbols of Greek lyric', *Harvard Studies in Classical Philology*, 77: 137–77. Reprinted with revisions in G. Nagy, *Greek Mythology and Poetics* (Ithaca, NY, 1990), 223–62 (ch. 9). [Esp. pp. 141–54 (226–40).]

Segal, C. (1974), 'Death by water: a narrative pattern in Theocritus', *Hermes*, 102: 20–38.

Calame, C. (1992), 'Espaces limineaux et voix discursives dans *l'Idylle* 1 de Théocrite', in C. Calame (ed.), *Figures grecques de l'intermédiaire* (Lausanne), 58–85.

Other References

Bonneau, D. (1993), *Le Régime administratif de l'eau du Nil dans l'Égypte grecque, romaine et byzantine*. Leiden.

Braund, D. C. (1994), *Georgia in Antiquity: A History of Colchis and Transcaucasian Iberia 550 BC–AD 562*. Oxford.

Broadhead, H. D. (1960), *The Persae of Aeschylus*. Cambridge.

Hercher, R. (1855-6), 'Über die Glaubwürdigkeit der Neuen Geschichte des Ptolemaeus Chennus', in A. Fleckeisen (ed.), *Jahrbücher für classische Philologie, 1. Supplementband* (Leipzig), 269–93.

Hunter, R. L. (1989), *Apollonius of Rhodes, Argonautica, Book III*. Cambridge.

Lightfoot, Jane L. (1999), *Parthenius of Nicaea*. Oxford.

Magie, D. (1950), *Roman Rule in Asia Minor: To the End of the Third Century after Christ*. 2 vols. Princeton.

*Müller, *GGM* ii, pp. lii–lvii, 637–55.

Thonemann, P. J. (2011), *The Maeander Valley: A Historical Geography from Antiquity to Byzantium*. Cambridge.

---

[6] Hercher 1851, 22–3; Hercher 1855-6, 279–80.

[7] Hercher 1851; Dübner 1856; Müller, *GGM* ii, pp. lii–lvii, 637–55; and Bernardakis 1896, 282–328, who makes few changes to the text.

TEXT

Treatise of Plutarch concerning the Naming of Rivers and Mountains and Those Things Found in Them[8]

1. HYDASPES[9]

(1) Chrysippe, as a result of Aphrodite's anger, was infatuated with her father Hydaspes and, unable to master this unnatural passion, at dead of night had intercourse with him with the connivance of her old nurse.[10] When the king discovered what had happened, he buried alive the old woman who had ensnared him. His daughter, however, he crucified, and in an extremity of grief threw himself into the river Indos, which was renamed Hydaspes after him. This river is in India and flows with great force into the Saronike Syrtis.[11]

(2) A stone called *lychnis* originates in it. It is olive-coloured and exceedingly fiery (*zestos*) in nature. When the moon waxes, it is found at the sound of pipes. The chief men use it.[12]

(3) A plant similar to heliotrope is found there near the so-called *Pylai* (*Gates*).[13] They (*the locals*) rub it and with (*the resulting*) liquid anoint themselves against burning heat, and can endure without danger the vapour arising from excessive temperatures.

(4) The local inhabitants attach to stakes virgins who have behaved indecently and throw them into this river, singing a hymn to Aphrodite in their own language. As well as this, every year, they bury alive at the hill named Therogonos (*Beast-bearer*) an old woman who has been condemned. Simultaneously with the burial of the woman,

---

[8] This is the title, Πλουτάρχου περὶ ποταμῶν καὶ ὀρῶν ἐπωνυμίας καὶ τῶν ἐν αὐτοῖς εὑρισκομένων, that stands in the manuscript.

[9] The Hydaspes (*Jhelum*), according to Pliny 6. xxiii. 71, is a tributary of the Indus and brings the waters of four other distinguished rivers with it. Indeed, the Hydaspes merges with the Akesinos (*Chenab*) before both join the Indus. Ps.-Plut., along with some other writers, possibly believes that the Hydaspes flows all the way to the coast. He does not think that the name Hydaspes was given to the whole course of the Indus, since at §25 he has a separate entry for the Indus.

[10] Hercher 1851 wishes to add a sentence at the beginning to make it conform to other introductions, which announce the river and its geographical location. The only exception is §17, where material also seems to have been omitted. It is possible that since the work lacks a prologue the whole opening section has been lost. We should expect an introduction such as 'The Hydaspes is a river in India that was previously called the Indus. It was renamed for the following reason'.

[11] The Saronic gulf is actually in Greece, the greater and lesser Syrteis in N. Africa. Ps.-Plutarch is confused: he seems to mean the bay of the E mouth of the Indus, Lonibarai (?) Stoma.

[12] *Lychnis*: Pliny 37. xxviii. 102–xxix. 103 refers to a gemstone particularly found in India often with a fiery colour like burning lamps (*lucernae*), though sometimes it was purple and sometimes yellow. It also allegedly had a magnetic effect when heated. It was associated with a gem *sandastros*, olive-green in colour. The word *zestos* is surely meant to convey the impression of heat from the colour, and there is no need for Müller's suggested reading of *nastos* ('dense'). John Lydus, *On Months*, 3. 11, understands *pros melōdian aulōn* to mean that the stone emitted a sound like that of pipes at the full moon.

[13] Philostratos, *Life of Apollonios*, 2. 42, refers to two sets of Gates two days' journey from Taxila, erected as a trophy to Alexander's victory over Poros. Heliotrope is a strongly scented plant with purple blossoms.

reptiles in huge numbers come from the summit and eat all the dumb creatures flying round (*the body*), as Chrysermos relates in book 80 of the *Indika*.[14] Archelaos has a more precise account of these matters in book 13 of *Concerning Rivers*.

(5) Adjacent to it is situated the mountain called Elephas (*Elephant*) for the following reason. When Alexander of Macedonia arrived in India with his army and the local people were discussing whether to fight against him, an elephant belonging to Poros, the king of the region, was suddenly driven wild, charged up the hill of Helios (*the Sun*), and speaking with a human voice said 'My lord king, who are descended from Gegasios, do not do anything to oppose Alexander. For he is the son of Zeus, ⟨not of⟩ Gegasios'.[15] When it had said this it dropped dead. When Poros heard this he was terrified and fell at Alexander's knees begging for peace. Having received what he wanted he changed the name of the mountain to 'Elephas', as Derkyllos relates in book 3 of *Concerning Mountains*.

2. ISMENOS

(1) The river Ismenos is in Boiotia near the city of Thebes.[16] Formerly it was called the Foot of Kadmos for the following reason. When Kadmos shot with an arrow the serpent guarding the spring and discovered that the water was, so to speak, poisoned with its blood, he roamed round the country looking for a source of water. Having arrived in the vicinity of the cave Korykion thanks to the providence of Athena, he planted his right foot more deeply into the mud. From this spot a river flowed out, and the hero after sacrificing a bull named it the Foot of Kadmos. A little later Ismenos, son of Amphion and Niobe, struck by an arrow fired by Apollo and afflicted by pain, threw himself headlong into this river, which was named Ismenos after him, as Sostratos relates in book 2 of *Concerning Rivers*.

(2) Adjacent to it is situated Mount Kithairon, which was formerly named Asterion (*Little Star*) for the following reason. When Boiotos son of Poseidon wished, of two distinguished ladies, to marry the one who would be most valuable to him, and was waiting for both of them one night on the heights of an unnamed hill, suddenly a star drawn down from the heavens fell onto the shoulders of Eurythemiste before immediately vanishing. Boiotos understood the meaning of the sign, married the girl, and named the mountain Asterion because of this occurrence. Later it was called Kithairon for the following reason.[17] Tisiphone, one of the Furies, fell in love with a handsome boy called Kithairon and, unable to subdue the intensity of her passion, sent him

---

[14] The MS reading is π′ (80). This seems improbable and suggested emendations are β′ (2) and η′ (8).

[15] The text is meaningless as it stands, and something seems to have been omitted. I accept Müller's supplement (οὐ) and emendation *Gegasiou*.

[16] Ps.-Plut. apparently refers to a river flowing N of Thebes into L. Hylike; Pausanias 9. 10. 2–5 says that it was previously called Ladon; in mythology Ismenos was the son of Okeanos and Tethys, but for other versions see Pindar, *Pythian* 11. 3–7; Ovid, *Metamorphoses* 6. 224–9.

[17] Mt Kithairon and Mt Helikon (2. 3 below) are in Boiotia in central Greece.

a message about an encounter. But he was terrified by the horrifying appearance of the Fury and did not even deign to give her a reply. When the Fury did not get what she wanted she plucked one of the serpents from her curls and threw it onto the arrogant youth. The snake tightly coiled round his middle and killed him while he was looking after his flocks on the heights of Asterion. By decision of the gods the mountain was renamed Kithairon after him, as Leon of Byzantion relates in *The History of Boiotia*.

(3) However, Hermesianax of Cyprus mentions the following story. Helikon and Kithairon were brothers with distinctly different characteristics. Helikon was gentle and kind, and compassionately looked after his elderly parents. But Kithairon was greedy and wanted to get all the property for himself; first he killed his father and then ambushed his brother and threw him down a precipice, but was dragged down with him. By decision of the gods both were changed into mountains named after them, but Kithairon because of his impiety became the cave of the Furies, while Helikon because of his love of his parents became the dwelling-place of the Muses.

3. HEBROS

(1) The Hebros is a river in Thrace.[18] ⟨It was previously called Rhombos⟩,[19] getting the name from the swirling of the water as it plunged down. Kasandros, the king of this region, married Krotonike and from her sired a son, Hebros. Then, breaking off his relationship with his first wife, he took Damasippe, daughter of Atrax, as a second wife and stepmother for his son. She fell in love with her stepson and sent him a message about an encounter. But Hebros fled from his stepmother as if she were a Fury and spent his leisure time hunting. Since she did not get what she wanted this lascivious woman falsely accused the virtuous youth, saying that he had wanted to rape her. Carried away with jealousy Kasandros charged into the wood and drawing his sword pursued his son, believing him to be a violator of his marriage. His son when trapped hurled himself into the river Rhombos, which was renamed Hebros after him, as Timotheos relates in book 11 of *Concerning Rivers*.

(2) Adjacent to it is situated Mount Pangaios, which gets its name for the following reason.[20] Pangaios, son of Ares and Kritoboule, unknowingly had intercourse with his daughter and overcome with despair fled to Mount Karmanion, where because of an

---

[18] The Hebros (*Evros*, *Martisa*) flows through E. Thrace for c.335 mi (c.540 km), passing Hadrianoupolis (*Edirne*) and entering the sea at Ainos; important tributaries are the Harpessos (*Ardhas*) and Tonzos (*Tundja*); Strabo 7, fragments 51, 51a.

[19] The supplement is necessary to maintain the sense. Müller speculated (based on Parthenios, *Erot.* 19) that for Kasandros we should read 'Kassamenos', who was notorious as a rapist of Thessalian women. But Jane L. Lightfoot 1999, 344 and 491–3, accepts a reading of 'Agassamenos' at *Erot.* 19.

[20] Hercher unnecessarily places §2 after §3; Ps.-Plut. describes the adjacent Mt Pangaios and then discusses plants growing in the river and on the mountain. There is a geographical error: Mt Pangaion is adjacent to the R. Strymon, not the Hebros. At 7. 5 Ps.-Plut. gives Karmanorion as the previous name of Mt Tmolos in Asia; possibly 'Karmanorion' should be read here.

extremity of grief he drew his sword and killed himself. By decision of the gods the place was renamed Pangaios.

(3) A plant similar to oregano grows in this river. The Thracians harvest the top of it and place it on a fire after they have had their fill of nourishment from corn, and then inhaling the rising vapour they are stupefied and plunge into a deep sleep.[21]

(4) There also grows on Mount Pangaios a plant called *kithara* (*lyre*) for the following reason. Women who tore apart Orpheus threw his limbs into the river Hebros. The dead man's head by decision of the gods changed into the physical shape of a serpent.[22] But his lyre was conveyed to the stars according to Apollo's decision. From his flowing blood a plant sprang up called *kithara*. During the ceremonies of Dionysos it emits the sound of a lyre. The local people don fawn-skins, shake the thyrsus and sing a hymn: 'Do not display wisdom whenever you will be wise in vain'. Kleitonymos relates this in book 3 of *The History of Thrace*.

4. GANGES

(1) The Ganges, a river in India, obtained its name for the following reason.[23] A nymph called Kalauria bore to Indos an outstandingly handsome son whose name was Ganges. This youth when drunk unknowingly had intercourse with his mother. On the following day he learnt the truth from his nurse and in an excess of grief hurled himself into the river called Chliaros, which was renamed Ganges after him.

(2) A plant similar to *bouglossos* (*ox-tongue*) grows in it, which they grind down and carefully keep the juice; then in the dead of night they sprinkle it round the lairs of tigers. The tigers because of the power of the liquid spread around are unable to come out, and then die, as Kallisthenes relates in book 3 of *Concerning Hunting*.

(3) Adjacent to it is situated a mountain called Anatole for the following reason. Helios (*the Sun*), when he saw the nymph Anaxibia enjoying herself dancing, was consumed with a passion for her, and unable to subdue his lust chased her, intending to rape her.[24] But, being trapped, she fled into the sanctuary of Artemis Orthia, which was on the mountain called Koryphe (*summit*), and vanished.[25] The god, following on behind and finding his beloved nowhere in sight, in an extremity of grief ascended

---

[21] Herodotos 4. 75 mentions *kannabis* (hemp-seed) which the Skythians throw onto hot stones, enjoying the resulting vapour bath so much that they howl with delight.

[22] The phrase *tēn morphēn tou sōmatos* (lit. 'the shape of the body') is difficult. But we may compare the similar phrase at 24. 1 and interpret 'in respect of its bodily shape'. Müller wishes to read *tou schēmatos* for *tou sōmatos*, 'in respect of its appearance'.

[23] The Ganges flows eastwards for 1,568 mi (2,525 km) from the Himalayas to the *Bay of Bengal*.

[24] The words *ton erōtōn* as they stand do not make sense. The easiest change is to read *ton erōta*, or perhaps *epistasin tōn erōtōn*, 'the onset of his lust'.

[25] Artemis Orthia: cf. 21. 4, where the MS has Orthosia. There is a Mt Koryphos in Greece in the Argolid.

from there. The local people changed the name of the mountain to Anatole (*Ascending*) because of this occurrence, as Kaimaron relates in book 10 of *Indian History*.[26]

5. PHASIS

(1) The Phasis (*Rioni*) is a river in Skythia flowing past a city.[27] It was formerly called Arktouros, getting that name from its location in cold regions. It was renamed for the following reason. Phasis, son of Helios and Okyrrhoë daughter of Okeanos, catching his mother in the act of committing adultery killed her. Driven mad by the appearance of the Furies he flung himself into the Arktouros, which was renamed Phasis after him.

(2) A shoot named *leukophyllos* (*white foliage*) grows in this river. In the celebration of the mysteries of Hekate it is found around dawn during the divinely inspired hymn of praise, at the beginning of spring. Jealous men pick the plant, spread it around the bridal chamber, and so ensure that the marriage is kept irreproachable. If some unprincipled man[28] approaches aggressively while drunk and comes to this place (*the bridal chamber*), he is deprived of his proper wits and immediately confesses to everyone whatever improper thing he has done or is intending to do. The bystanders seize him and sewing him up in skins hurl him into the place called 'Mouth of the Wicked'. This is circular in shape, resembling a well, and thirty days later spits out into Lake Maiotis what has been thrown into it, now full of worms. Vultures suddenly appear and thronging round tear to pieces the body lying there, as Ktesippos relates in book 2 of *Skythian History*.

(3) Adjacent to it (*the river*) is situated Mount Kaukasos (*the Caucasus*). It was formerly called the 'Bed of Boreas' (*the North Wind*) for the following reason. Boreas in the throes of passion seized Chione, daughter of Arktouros, brought her to a hill called Niphante, and from her sired a son, Hyrpax, who became king in succession to Heniochos. So, the mountain was renamed 'Bed of Boreas'. Later it was named Kaukasos in the following circumstances. After the battle of the giants, Kronos avoiding the threats of Zeus, fled to the summit of the 'Bed of Boreas'. Changing himself into a crocodile ⟨he escaped detection. But Prometheus⟩ cut up one of the local people, a shepherd called Kaukasos, and inspecting the disposition of his entrails said that the

---

[26] Kaimaron is suspect. Müller, *GGM* ii, p. lvi, thinks that it was corrupted from Daimachos, who is known to have written about Indian affairs.

[27] The Phasis, in Georgia, flows W for 203 mi (327 km) from the Caucasus to the Black Sea; see Braund 1994, 25. The name of the city adjacent to the river may have fallen out of the text; it was possibly Phasis. In one legend the Phasis was the son of Okeanos and Tethys (Hesiod, *Theog.* 337–40). For the character of the river see Hdt. 4. 37–8; Ap. Rhod. 2. 1261 (a broad estuary where the Black Sea ends); Virgil, *Georgics* 4. 367 (one of the great rivers); Strabo 11. 2. 17, C498 (its sources and current); 11. 3. 4, C500 (its many bridges and eventual navigability); Pomponius Mela 1. 108; Arr. §§8–9 (its water); Paus. 4. 34. 2 (its large fish).

[28] For the meaningless *ti*, Gilenius restored *tis*, as translated in the text.

enemy were not far away.²⁹ When Zeus appeared he bound his father with plaited wool and threw him down into Tartaros. He (*Zeus*) changed the name of the mountain to Kaukasos in honour of the shepherd, and binding Prometheus to it, forced him to endure torture by an entrail-devouring eagle, because he had committed an atrocity on entrails, as Kleanthes narrates in book 3 of *The Battle of the Gods*.

(4) A plant called *prometheios* grows on it, which Medea collected, ground down and used against the enmity of her father, as the same writer relates.³⁰

6. ARAR

(1) The Arar is a river in Keltike (*Gaul*), and it got its name from the fact that it joins with the Rhodanos (*Rhône*), for it flows into this river in the land of the Allobroges.³¹ It was formerly called Brigoulos and was renamed for the following reason. Arar entered a wood while hunting and finding his brother Keltiberos torn apart by wild beasts, fatally stabbed himself in an extremity of grief and threw himself into the Brigoulos, which was renamed Arar after him.

(2) A large fish is nourished in it, named *skolopias* by local people.³² This is white at the time of the waxing of the moon but becomes entirely black when it is waning. However, if it gets too big it is pierced by its own spines.

(3) At the head (*of the river*) a stone is found which resembles a lump of salt, which, if attached to the left side of the body when the moon is waning, is particularly effective against quartan fevers, as Kallisthenes of Sybaris relates in book 13 of *The History of the Gauls*, from whom Timagenes of Syria took the subject.

(4) Adjacent to it is situated a mountain called Lougdounos, which was renamed for the following reason. Momoros and Atepomaros were ejected by Seseroneus from his kingdom and ⟨came⟩ to this mountain according to a command ⟨of an oracle⟩, wishing to found a city.³³ When they were digging the foundations, crows suddenly appeared and flitted about, filling the neighbouring trees. Momoros was skilled in augury and named the city Lougdounon (*Lyon*). For in their language they call a crow *lougos*, and a high place *dounon*, as Kleitophon relates in book 13 of *Foundations*.

---

²⁹ Prometheus needs to be added to the text to establish the context for the rest of the section. For Prometheus, see Lucian, *Dialogues of Gods, Zeus and Prometheus* 5. 1; *Zeus Catechized*, 8. For the story of how Saturn was tied up with woollen bands, see Macrobius, *Sat*. 1. 8. 5.

³⁰ For the qualities of the plant see Apollonios of Rhodes 3. 845–57; it allegedly protected a man against sword and fire and gave him exceptional strength. Apollonios may have been referring to mandrake, or possibly a poisonous plant called *kolchikon*. See also Hunter 1989, 187–8.

³¹ The Arar (*Saône*) flows for *c*.300 mi (480 km) from the E side of the *Rhône* to join the river at *Lyon*. Ps.-Plut.'s opening sentence is inaccurate since the explanation of the name Arar emerges subsequently.

³² For the name of the fish we may accept the MS reading *skolopias* (*skolopes* are spines or spikes), although John Lydus, *On Months*, 3. 11, with reference to this river mentions *klopias*, a fish that whitens as the moon waxes. This should not be confused with *clupea pisces* in Pliny 9. xvii. 44, a small fish which kills larger fish.

³³ The supplements suggested by Wyttenbach are necessary to complete the sense. In Ps.-Plut. *Parallel Histories*, 30, Atepomaros appears as king of the Gauls.

7. PAKTOLOS

(1) The Paktolos is a river in Lydia near the city of Sardis.[34] It was formerly called Chrysorrhoas ⟨for the following reason. Chrysorrhoas⟩, son of Apollo and Apathippe,[35] practised an engineering trade, and, being afflicted with dire poverty, in dead of night opened up the treasure houses of king Kroisos (*Croesus*), and taking away the gold distributed it among his household. But he was pursued by the guards and when trapped hurled himself into the river, which was renamed to Chrysorrhoas (*golden flowing*) after him.

It was changed to Paktolos in the following circumstances. Paktolos, son of ⟨Zeus⟩ and Leukothea, during the mysteries of Aphrodite unknowingly raped his sister Demodike and, discovering what had happened, in an extremity of grief hurled himself into the river Chrysorrhoas, which was named Paktolos after him.

(2) There originates in it the dust of Darius' gold, which is carried down to Eudaimon (*Happy*) gulf.[36]

(3) There originates in it a stone called *argyrophylax* (*money-guard*), which resembles silver.[37] It is difficult to find mixed up with the gold dust that has been carried down. It has the following property. The chief men among the Lydians buy it up and, putting it in front of the entrance to the treasuries, safely guard the gold placed inside. For whenever thieves come the stone emits the sound of a trumpet. The thieves, as if closely pursued by spearmen, are swept over precipices. The place where they meet this violent death is called the Guard Post of Paktolos.

(4) A plant also grows ⟨there⟩ with purple flowers called *chrysopolē*. With its help the inhabitants of the neighbouring cities test if gold is uncontaminated. For as soon as they liquefy gold they dip this plant in it. If the gold is unadulterated the leaves become coated in gold. But if the gold is impure they reject the moisture spread over them and keep the property of a plant, as Chrysermos relates in book 3 of *Concerning Rivers*.

(5) Adjacent to it is situated Mount Tmolos, which is full of all kinds of wild animals. It was formerly called Karmanorion after Karmanor, son of Dionysos and Alexirrhoia, who died while out hunting after being wounded by a boar. Later it was renamed Tmolos for the following reason. Tmolos, son of Ares and Theogone, was king

---

[34] Paktolos (*Sart Çay*), with its source on Mt Tmolos in Lydia, flows past Sardis. Pliny notes the two names of the river and also observes that Tmolos was previously called Timolos (5. xxx. 110).

[35] The MS has the meaningless *Chios . . . Pais*. Hercher plausibly suggests *ho huios* for *Chios*, arguing that *huios* 'son' is a variant of *pais* 'child' employed elsewhere. Apathippe has not found acceptance among scholars, but there is no consensus on an alternative reading. The MS's *oeiolios* is meaningless, and again it may be a corruption of *huios Dios* 'son of Zeus'.

[36] *Dareikon* is suggested for *Dareion*, see Pollux, *Omonastikon*, 7. 98; but 'Dareion' might stand for the better-known word. The Happy Bay in Müller's view does not refer to the sea but to the valley of the Hermos and the plain round Sardis.

[37] The MS has *arouraphylax*, which is inappropriate in the context of protecting treasure. Of various suggestions, *argyrophylax* (Herscher) is translated here; but note *thesaurophylax* (Müller), 'treasury-guard'. Strabo 13. 1. 56, C610, describes a stone found near Andeira in Mysia which, when heated, produces 'mock-silver', that is, zinc.

of Lydia, and while hunting on Mount Karmanorion caught sight of Arsippe, a virgin who accompanied Artemis, and lusted after her. Overcome with his passion he pursued her, intending to rape her. She becoming trapped fled to the shrine of Artemis. The tyrant, disdaining any respect for religious sanctity, raped the virgin in the shrine. Overcome with despair she ended her life with a noose. The goddess was furious at what had been done and sent against Tmolos a bull that had been goaded to madness. He was tossed up in the air by the bull and crashing down onto sharp stakes died in agony. Theoklymenos, son of this Tmolos, buried his father and renamed the mountain after him.

(6) A stone similar to pumice originates on it, but is rarely found: for four times a day it changes its colour. It is observed by virgins who because of their youth have not attained awareness. But if those who have attained marriageable age see it, they suffer no outrage from those wanting to molest them, as Kleitophon relates [—].

8. LYKORMAS

(1) The Lykormas is a river in Aitolia.[38] It was renamed Euenos for the following reason. Idas son of Aphareus because of sexual passion seized Marpessa and took her away to Pleuron. Euenos, when he was informed about what had happened, pursued the man who had corrupted his daughter. But when he got to the Lykormas he gave up hope of catching (*the culprit*) and threw himself into the river, which was renamed Euenos after him.

(2) A plant ⟨named *sarisa*⟩ similar to a spearhead grows in it, which is exceptionally valuable in treating dim-sightedness, ⟨as Archelaos relates in book 1 of *Concerning Rivers*⟩.[39]

(3) Adjacent to it is situated Mount Myenon, called after Myenos, son of Telestor and Alphesiboia. This man was loved by his stepmother, and unwilling to defile his father's bed, retired to Mount Alphion.[40] But Telestor, responding to the jealousy of his wife, pursued his son with his spearmen into that desolate spot with the intention of capturing him. But Myenos escaped his father's threats by throwing himself off a precipice. By decision of the gods the mountain was renamed Myenon after him.

(4) There grows on it a flower, the white violet (*leukoion*), which withers whenever the name of a stepmother is mentioned, as Derkyllos relates in book 3 of *Concerning Mountains*.

---

[38] For the change of name see also Strabo 7. 7. 8, C327; 10. 2. 5, C451.

[39] The supplement *sarisa* is taken from Stobaeus, *Florilegium* 110, as is the reference to Archelaos. Stobaeus (C5 AD) assembled a collection of excerpts from a wide range of authors, and is often valuable as a check on textual problems in the MS tradition of those authors.

[40] Müller makes the plausible suggestion that we should read *Taphion* for *Alphion*, arguing that the reference is to Mt Taphiassos, adjacent to the Euenos.

9. MAEANDER

(1) The Maeander is a river in Asia formerly called Anabainon (*Flowing Back*).[41] For it alone of all rivers rises from its own source and then flows back on itself. It was named Maeander after Maiandros, son of Kerkaphos and Anaxibia, who, while fighting a war against the people of Pessinous, made a vow to the Mother of the Gods that if he gained a victory he would sacrifice the first person who congratulated him as he brought back trophies for his valiant deeds. However when he returned, the first to meet and congratulate him was his son Archelaos, followed by his mother and his sister. Maiandros, remembering this religious vow, had to lead his own kin to the altar. In despair at what he had done he hurled himself into the river Anabainon, which was named Maeander after him, as Timolaos relates in book 1 of *The History of Phrygia*. Agathokles of Samos also recounts these events in *The Constitution of the Pessinountians*.

(2) But Demostratos of Apameia relates the following story. Maiandros, having just been chosen as commander in the war against the people of Pessinous,[42] won a victory contrary to expectation and distributed to the soldiers offerings belonging to the Mother of the Gods. By decision of the goddess he was suddenly deprived of his proper wits and killed his wife and son. Soon after, he regained his senses and coming to repent of what he had done threw himself into the river, which was given the name Maeander after him.

(3) A stone originates in it called in the contrary sense *sophron* (*wise*), and if you throw it into someone's lap he becomes possessed and murders one of his relatives. However, if he propitiates the Mother of the Gods he will escape from the affliction, as Demaratos relates in book 3 of *Concerning Rivers*. Archelaos refers to these matters in book 1 of *Concerning Stones*.

(4) Adjacent to it is situated Mount Sipylon, which gets its name from Sipylos, son of Agenor and Dioxippe.[43] For this man unknowingly killed his mother, and having been driven mad by the Furies came to Mount Keraunion and in an extremity of grief ended his life with a noose. By decision of the gods the mountain was named Sipylon after him.

(5) A stone similar to a cylinder originates on it, and when pious sons find it they place it in the shrine of the Mother of the Gods and never incur any sin of impiety, but love their fathers and are tender towards their relatives, as Agatharchides of Samos relates in book 4 of *Concerning Stones*. Demaratos refers to these matters in more detail in book 4 of *Phrygia*.

---

[41] The Maeander (Çine Çay) flows from the W part of central Turkey westwards for 340 mi (548 km) into the Aegean near Miletos; Thonemann 2011. In Hesiod, *Theog.* 339 Maeander was the son of Okeanos and Tethys.

[42] For *akmestratēgos* of the MS editors have suggested *akmēn*, 'just then'. Müller doubts this meaning and suggests that the text may originally have read *archistratēgos*, 'chief general'.

[43] For the geographical error with Mt Sipylos see introduction to the chapter.

10. MARSYAS

(1) The Marsyas is a river in Phrygia situated near the city of Kelainai.[44] It formerly had the name the spring of Midas for the following reason. Midas, the king of the Phrygians, while journeying round the more remote areas of his country and suffering from a lack of water, touched the earth and it sent out a golden stream, with the water itself turning into gold. Since he was very thirsty and his subjects were also afflicted, he called upon Dionysos. The god heard him and provided a generous supply of water. When the Phrygians had had their fill of water, Midas called the river flowing from the spring the Spring of Midas.

It was renamed Marsyas for the following reason. When Marsyas had been defeated by Apollo and flayed, from the stream of his blood Satyrs grew up, and also the river of the same name, called Marsyas, as Alexander Kornelios relates in book 3 of *The History of Phrygia*.

(2) But Euemeridas of Knidos relates the following story. When the skin of Marsyas had been eaten away by the passage of time, it slipped down and fell from the land into the Spring of Midas. Being carried gradually downstream it came up to a fisherman. In accordance with the command of an oracle, Peisistratos the Lakedaimonian founded a city near the remains of the satyr, and named it Norikon because of this occurrence.[45] For the Phrygians in their language call a wineskin *norikon*.

(3) A plant named *aulos* (pipe) grows in this river, and if someone shakes it in the wind it produces a musical melody, as Derkyllos relates in book 1 of *Concerning Satyrs*.

(4) Adjacent to it is situated the mountain called Berekynthion, which gets its name from Berekynthos, who became the first priest of the Mother of the Gods.

(5) A stone originates on it called *machaira* (knife), for it is similar to iron. If anyone finds it while the celebration of the mysteries of the goddess is taking place, he goes mad, as Agatharchides relates in *The History of Phrygia*.[46]

---

[44] The Marsyas (Çine Çay) was a tributary of the Maeander. Marsyas was the inventor of the pipes and the rules of playing them; he challenged Apollo to a contest, lost, and was flayed alive: Ovid, *Metamorphoses* 6. 382–91. Müller suggests that material in §2 about the fate of Marsyas' skin should be transposed to §1, which goes on to describe the birth of Satyrs from his flowing blood; but this is unnecessary since §2 simply builds on the details of the story set out in §1.

[45] Norikon in Phrygia is not otherwise known. There is no plausible emendation of the text.

[46] In Ps.-Aristotle, *On Miraculous Things Heard* (dated C3?), §173, 847a 5–7 = Eudoxos 8 (in Chapter 6 above), Eudoxos rather than Agatharchides is cited as the authority for the qualities of this stone. Müller thinks that the full text of Ps.-Plut. was excerpted, and that the excerptor in places has substituted the name of a well-known author in place of the more obscure writer that occurred in the fuller version of the text that is occasionally preserved by Stobaeus.

11. STRYMON

(1) The Strymon is a river in Thrace near the city of Edonis.[47] It was formerly named Palaistinos after Palaistinos son of Poseidon.[48] For he was engaged in war with the neighbouring peoples and, when he became seriously ill, sent his son Haliakmon as commander. He fought too recklessly and was killed. When Palaistinos heard what had happened he slipped away from his spearmen and in an extremity of grief hurled himself into the river Konozos, which was named Palaistinos after him.

⟨However, it was called Strymon for the following reason.⟩[49] Strymon, son of Ares and Helike, hearing about the death of Rhesos[50] and, overcome with despair, hurled himself into the river Palaistinos, which was renamed Strymon after him.

(2) A stone called *pausilypon* (*grief-ending*) originates in it. If anyone who is grieving finds it he is immediately set free from the affliction enveloping him, as Iason of Byzantion relates in *The History of Thrace*.

(3) Adjacent to it are situated the mountains Rhodope and Haimos. These were sister and brother and fell in love with one another; he named her Hera, and she named her beloved Zeus. But the gods, being dishonoured, took what had been done very badly and changed the two into mountains of the same names.[51]

(4) Stones originate on them called *philadelphoi* (*brother-sister-loving*), black in colour like crows and with human shape. If these are placed apart and their name called, they immediately ⟨leap across the space⟩,[52] as Thrasyllos of Mende relates in book 3 of *Concerning Stones*. He refers to these matters in more detail in *The History of Thrace*.

12. SAGARIS

(1) The Sagaris (*Sangarios*) is a river in Phrygia.[53] It was formerly named Xerobates because of the following occurrence. In the summer season it is often seen to be dry (*xeros*).

---

[47] The Strymon (*Strúma, Strymónas*) flows 258 mi (415 km) from the mountains of Bulgaria, entering the Aegean sea at Amphipolis. Edonis is not known; if not simply in error, Ps.-Plut. may refer to Eion, the port of Amphipolis at the mouth of the Strymon. In Hesiod, *Theog.* 339, Strymon is the son of Okeanos and Tethys.

[48] The original name Palaistinos for the river may be the origin of the incredible story that the Odomantes (they were allegedly circumcised: Aristophanes, *Acharnians* 157–8) who lived round the Strymon were Jewish. But note John Lydus, *De magistratibus populi Romani*, 3. 46, who relates the view that the people of Epeiros (who allegedly had a city called Palaiste) were colonists from Syria, and so Epeiros was once called Palaistina.

[49] The supplement is necessary to explain the transition to Strymon.
[50] Leader of the Thracian force in the Trojan war.   [51] See Ovid, *Metamorphoses* 6. 87–9.
[52] The text *dialuontai parachrēma kai idias* makes no sense as it stands. The context seems to require that stones do something brotherly (*philadelphoi*). I therefore accept Müller's plausible suggestion (and his emended text) that they immediately leap across the distance (between them), *diallontai parachrēma to diastēma*.

[53] Sangarios (*Sakarya*): a river in Phrygia flowing for 512 mi (824 km) from the *Bayat* plateau to the Black Sea; Magie 1950, 38–9, 302–3. According to Hesiod, *Theog.* 344 Sangarios was the son of

It was called Sagaris for the following reason. Sagaris, son of Mygdon and Alexirrhoë, mocked the mysteries of the Mother of the Gods and insulted her priests, the Galloi.[54] She took this behaviour very badly and inflicted madness on him. He, being out of his proper wits, threw himself into the river Xerobates, which was renamed Sagaris after him.

(2) A stone originates in it called *autoglyphos* (*self-engraved*). It is found with an image of the Mother of the Gods engraved on it. This stone can rarely be found and if one ⟨of those⟩ who have been castrated finds it,[55] he is not astonished but courageously bears the sight of what was done contrary to nature, as Aretades relates in *The History of Phrygia*.

(3) Adjacent to it is situated the mountain called Ballenaion, which is interpreted as indicating royalty, getting its name from Ballenaios, son of Ganymede and Medesigiste.[56] For this man when he saw his father wasting away [—] to the neighbouring peoples, and established the 'feast of Ballenaios', which even now still has this name.

(4) A stone called *aster* (*star*) originates on it. From the start of autumn this normally burns like a fire at dead of night. In the language of the local people it is named *ballēn*, which is interpreted as 'king', as Hermesianax of Cyprus relates in book 2 of *The History of Phrygia*.

13. SKAMANDROS

(1) The Skamandros is a river in the Troad.[57] It was formerly called the Xanthos and was renamed for the following reason. Skamandros, son of Korybas and Demodike, during the celebration of the mysteries of Rhea suddenly caught sight of ⟨the goddess⟩, went mad, and swept along in an impulsive rush to the Xanthos threw himself into this river, which was renamed Skamandros after him.

(2) A plant called *seistros* (*shaker*), similar to the chickpea, grows in it; this has seeds moving to and fro in it, from which it gets its name. People who have this do not fear phantoms or the manifestation of a god, as Demostratos relates in book 2 of *Concerning Rivers*.

(3) Adjacent to it is situated Mount Ida, which formerly was called Gargaron and on which are situated the altars of Zeus and the Mother of the Gods.[58] It was renamed

---

Okeanos and Tethys. As a river god he was venerated in Pessinous, Juliopolis, and Nimaia. Sagaris is probably a variant of Sangarios.

[54] Galloi were the priests of Kybele, the mother goddess of Anatolia, a spirit of fertility who also acted as protector of her followers. She was brought to Rome in 205/4 BC and her worship was celebrated in public games, the Megalesia. Some of the Galloi were self-castrates.

[55] This translation follows Hercher's rearrangement of the disturbed word order of the MS.

[56] For the name Ballenaios and *balēn* as a possibly Phrygian word for king, see Aeschylus, *Persians* 657–9, and commentary by Broadhead 1960, 170. Some words seem to have fallen out of this section explaining how the mountain got the name Ballenaion.

[57] Skamandros (*Menderes Çay*) is a river in the Troad, in NW Turkey, rising on Mt Ida. According to Hesiod, *Theog.* 345, Skamandros was the son of Okeanos and Tethys; he was said to be the father of Teukros (Diodorus Siculus, 4. 75).

[58] I accept the emendation *Gargaron* for *Tartaron* of the MS.

Ida for the following reason. Aigesthios son of Zeus[59] fell in love with the girl Ida, who carried the sacred basket, had intercourse with her, and sired from her the children known as the Idaean Daktyloi. But when Ida lost her wits in the temple of Rhea, Aigesthios renamed the mountain Ida in her honour.

(4) A stone originates on it (*called*) *kryphios* (*secret*) which appears only during the mysteries of the gods, as Herakleitos of Sikyon relates in book 2 of *Concerning Stones*.

14. TANAÏS

(1) The Tanaïs is a river in Skythia.[60] Formerly it was called Amazonios because the Amazons bathed in it, but was renamed for the following reason. Tanaïs, son of Berossos and Lysippe, one of the Amazons, was exceptionally temperate, hated the entire race of women, worshipped only Ares, and had no respect for marriage. But Aphrodite instilled in him a passion for his mother. To start with he fought against his feelings, but was overcome by a goading compulsion, and wanting to remain virtuous, hurled himself into the river Amazonios, which was renamed Tanaïs after him.

(2) A plant called *halinda* grows in it and has foliage resembling a cabbage.[61] The inhabitants of the country grind this down and anoint themselves with the juice, as a result of which they become warm and can stoutly endure the cold. In their language they call this 'oil of Berossos'.

(3) A stone similar to crystal originates in it, which resembles a man wearing a garland. Whenever a king dies they hold the meeting close to the river to choose his successor, and whoever is found in possession of this stone immediately becomes king and takes the sceptre of the dead king, as Ktesiphon narrates in book 3 of *Concerning Plants*. Aristoboulos also refers to these matters in book 1 of *Concerning Stones*.

(4) Adjacent to it is situated a mountain, which, in the language of the inhabitants, is named Brixaba, which is interpreted to mean Kriou Metopon (*Ram's Brow*). It was named for the following reason. Phrixos, having lost his sister Helle in the Euxine sea, was naturally very upset and lodged on the heights of a hill. Some barbarians saw him and climbed up fully armed. The ram with the Golden Fleece peering out and seeing the mass of men approaching, adopted a human voice, aroused Phrixos from his sleep, and then lifted him up and carried him to the Kolchoi. As a result of this occurrence the hill was named Kriou Metopon.

---

[59] The MS *ek tou dios phorou korēs* is difficult to explain. I follow the emendation of Wyttenbach: *kanēphorou korēs*. W. also suggests that for *aphronos* ('lost her wits') we should read *aphanous* ('disappeared'); cf. 4. 3.

[60] The Tanaïs (*Don*) flows for c.1,210 mi (1,950 km) into the Sea of Azov. In the explanation of the name change, *Aphrodite*, omitted by the MS, was added by another hand in the margin.

[61] 14. 2 Herscher prefers to read *alinda* as the name of the plant, thinking that it was repeated from the name of a town, but none is known in this vicinity. Müller notes that Ptolemy, 3. 5. 10 refers to the Borouskoi who dwell at the Rhipaian Mts from which the Tanaïs flows; perhaps Berossos is associated with this.

(5) There grows on it a plant called *phrixa* in the language of the barbarians, which can be interpreted to mean 'hating the wicked'. It resembles rue, and if stepchildren get hold of it they suffer no harm from stepmothers. It grows particularly abundantly round the place named 'Cave of Boreas'. When picked it is colder than snow, but whenever a stepmother plots harm against someone it emits flames. Taking this sign, those who fear wives from a second marriage avoid the compulsion of fear hanging over them, as Agathon of Samos relates in book 2 of *The History of Skythia*.

15. THERMODON

(1) Thermodon is a river in Skythia which gets its name from an occurrence.[62] It was formerly called Krystallos, since even in summer it froze over, a characteristic caused by its particular location. It was renamed for the following reason. [—]

16. NILE

(1) The Neilos (*Nile*) is a river in Egypt near the city of Alexandria.[63] It was formerly called Melas after Melas son of Poseidon. Later it was called Aigyptos for the following reason. Aigyptos, son of Hephaistos and Leukippe, was king of the region. Because of a civil war the Nile did not rise and the inhabitants were afflicted by famine. The oracle of Pythian Apollo prophesied that there would be plenty if the king sacrificed his daughter to the gods as an averter of evil.[64] Crushed by his troubles, the tyrant led Aganippe to the altar. When she had been slaughtered, Aigyptos in an extremity of grief hurled himself into the river Melas, which was renamed Aigyptos after him.

It was named Nile for the following reason. Garmathone, queen of the land of Egypt, lost her son Chrysochoas in the bloom of his youth, and along with her household servants deeply mourned him. But when Isis suddenly appeared she put aside her grief for a time and, putting on an appearance of happiness, received the goddess kindly. But Isis wished to change this state of affairs because of her piety and gave instructions to Osiris to bring Garmathone's son back from the underworld. Osiris indulged her plea, but Kerberos, whom some call Phoberos, barked. Consequently Neilos, husband of Garmathone, suddenly became divinely possessed and hurled himself into the river called Aigyptos, which was renamed Nile after him.

(2) A stone resembling a bean originates in it, and if dogs see it they do not bark. It is most helpful for those who are possessed by an evil spirit. For as soon as it is placed

---

[62] Thermodon (*Terme Çay*): a river in N. Turkey flowing into the Black Sea. Part of the text has been lost at the end of the section.

[63] The Blue Nile originating in L. *Tana*, and the White Nile originating in L. *Victoria*, join at *Khartoum* to form the Nile; its total length is c.4,132 mi (6,650 km); Bonneau 1993. The Nile as a divinity was invented by the Greeks and was thought to be the son of Okeanos and Tethys.

[64] Herscher, on the basis of 23. 1 and 3, prefers *apotropaiois* ('(the gods who) avert evil') to the MS *apotropaion*, which must otherwise refer to the about-to-be sacrificed daughter.

against the nostrils, the evil spirit departs. Other stones originate there, called *kollotes*. Swallows collect these during the ⟨rising⟩ of the Nile⁶⁵ and make what is named the 'Swallows' Wall', which holds back the surge of water and does not allow the land to be destroyed by a flood, as Thrasyllos relates in *The History of Egypt*.⁶⁶

(3) Adjacent to it is situated a mountain called Argillon for the following reason. Zeus in the throes of passion seized the maiden Arge from the city of Lyktos in Crete and carried her away to the mountain in Egypt called Argillon.⁶⁷ He sired a son from her called Dionysos. When he grew up he changed the name of the mountain to Argillon in honour of his mother. Enlisting an army comprising Pans and the Satyrs he brought the Indians under his own rule. When he had conquered Iberia he left Pan behind to run the place, and he changed its name to Pania after himself. Subsequent people, making a slight change, named it Spania, as Sosthenes relates in book 13 of the *History* of *Iberia*.

17. EUROTAS

(1) The Eurotas ⟨is a river in Lakedaimon, which was formerly called Himeros for the following reason⟩.⁶⁸ Himeros, son of the nymph Taÿgete and Lakedaimon, because of Aphrodite's anger, in ignorance forced himself on and raped his sister Kleodike during an all-night festival. The following day he was overcome with despair when he realized what had happened and in an extremity of grief hurled himself into the river Marathon, which was renamed Himeros after him.

Later it was called Eurotas for the following reason. When the Lakedaimonians were at war with the Athenians and were waiting for the full moon, Eurotas, their commander, despising all religious feeling, drew up his army and committed it to battle, although thunder and lightning were against him. He lost his army and overcome with grief hurled himself into the river, which was renamed Eurotas after him.

(2) A stone resembling a helmet originates in it and is named *thrasydeilos* (*brave-coward*). As soon as it hears the sound of a trumpet it advances to the bank. But when the Athenians are mentioned it slips down into the depths. Many of these stones lie consecrated in the temple of Athena Chalkioikos (*of the Bronze House*), as Nikanor of Samos relates in book 2 of *Concerning Rivers*.

---

⁶⁵ The MS *asebeian* (wickedness) is inappropriate. I translate *anabasin*, originally conjectured by Wyttenbach, referring to the rising of the river. Another possibility is *astheneian* ('weakness', i.e. when the river had low water).

⁶⁶ On the wall built by swallows, see Pliny 10. xlix. 94.

⁶⁷ This name is incorrect since the existing name of the mountain is required. Also, instead of its new name Argillon we might expect Argennon or Arginnon, if the name of the nymph is correct.

⁶⁸ Eurotas (*Evrótas*): a river in Lakonia flowing past Sparta for 51 mi (82 km) into the Laconian gulf. See Pausanias 3. 1. 1 for Eurotas, son of Myles, cutting a channel to drain away marsh water and naming Eurotas the river left running there; Strabo 6. 2. 9, C275. There is a conjectural restoration at the start of §1, where some words are missing.

(3) Adjacent to it is situated the mountain named Taÿgetos, which gets its name from the nymph Taÿgete whom Zeus forced himself on and raped. She was overcome with grief and ended her life with a noose on the heights of Mount Amyklaios, which was named Taÿgetos after her.

(4) A plant called *charisia* grows on it, which women at the beginning of spring attach to their neck with the result that they are loved more passionately by their men, as Kleanthes relates in book 1 of *Concerning Mountains*.[69] Sosthenes of Knidos deals with these matters in more detail, from whose work Hermogenes took the subject.

18. INACHOS

(1) The Inachos is a river in the territory of Argos.[70] It was formerly called Karmanor. Haliakmon, a Tirynthian by family, was shepherding his flock on mount Kokkygion when he accidentally saw Zeus and Hera making love. He became mad and swept along in an impulsive rush threw himself into the river Karmanor, which was renamed Haliakmon after him.

It was named Inachos for the following reason. Inachos son of Okeanos (*Ocean*), after his daughter Io had been raped by Zeus, followed along behind bombarding the god with profane abuse. Zeus was furious at this insulting treatment and sent one of the Furies, Tisiphone, against him. Driven mad by her he threw himself into the river Haliakmon, which was renamed Inachos after him.

(2) A plant called *kynoura* resembling rue grows in it. Whenever women want to abort a child without risk, they soak it in wine and place it in their navel.

(3) A stone similar to beryl is found in it, which, if held by those intending to bear false witness, turns black.[71] Many of these stones lie in the sanctuary of Hera Prosymnaia, as Timotheos relates in *The History of Argos*. Agathon of Samos mentions them in book 2 of *Concerning Rivers*. Agathokles of Miletos in his work *Concerning Rivers* says that Inachos was struck by a thunderbolt from Zeus because of his wickedness and dried up.

(4) Adjacent to it are situated the mountains Mykenai, Apesantos, Kokkygion, and Athenaion, which got their names for the following reasons.[72] Apesantos was formerly

---

[69] The MS has *charision* and the plant name *charisia* is taken from Ps.-Aristotle, *On Miraculous Things Heard*, §163, 846b 7–9, quoting this passage.

[70] The Inachos (mod. *Inachos*) rises in the Peloponnese in Mt Lyrkeion and flows past Argos into the Argolic gulf. The etymology is unclear, and is perhaps pre-Greek. In mythology Inachos was the son of Okeanos and Tethys: Pausanias 2. 15. 5; 2. 18. 3; Strabo 6. 2. 4, C271. Ps.-Plut. confuses the Argive Inachos with the Haliakmon in Macedonia (possibly because of a town named Argos in N. Macedonia). See introduction to this chapter.

[71] The last sentence in the section should perhaps come at the end of §1. Hercher thinks that the story about the stone changing colour in hands of those bearing false witness is accommodated to the legend that Inachos bore false witness against Poseidon when it was decided that the Argolid belonged to Hera. Ps.-Plut. may have left out this story deliberately, or our text may have been excerpted from a longer work. For the story see Pausanias 2. 15. 5.

[72] It is possible that §9, which offers an alternative story about the naming of Mt Apesantos, should be placed at the end of §4. These mountains are not known.

called Selenaion. For Hera, wishing to punish Herakles, enlisted Selene (*the moon*) as an accomplice. Selene using magic spells filled a chest with froth, from which a huge lion was born; Iris bound the lion with her own belt and took it to mount Opheltion. The lion ripped apart and killed a local shepherd called Apesantos, and by decision of the gods the place was renamed Apesantos after him, as Demodokos relates in book 1 of *Herakleia*.

(5) A plant called *selene* ('moon') grows on it and the shepherds collect the froth that comes from it at the beginning of summer and anoint their feet with it; as a result they suffer no harm from reptiles.

(6) Mount Mykenai was formerly called Argion after Argos the all-seeing. It was renamed Mykenai for the following reason. When Perseus killed Medusa, Stheno and Euryale, sisters of the murdered woman, pursued the treacherous killer. When they got to this mountain, giving up hope of catching him, in their distress they emitted a bellow (*mykēthmos*). The local inhabitants because of this occurrence changed the name of the mountain to Mykenai,[73] as Ktesias of Ephesos relates in book 1 of *Perseid*.

(7) But Chrysermos of Corinth mentions the following story in book 1 of the *History of the Peloponnese*. Perseus was carried aloft and when he arrived at this mountain the cap of his sword's scabbard accidently fell. But Gorgophonos, king of the Epidaurians, who had been thrown out of his kingdom, obtained an oracle that he should go round the cities of the Argolid and found a city where he discovered the scabbard-cap of a sword. When he came to Mount Argion and found the ivory scabbard cap he founded a city, which he named Mykenai because of this occurrence.

(8) A stone called *korybas*, raven black in colour, originates on it. If anyone finds it and keeps it next to his body he will not fear monstrous visions.

(9) The mountain ⟨Apesantos was named after⟩ Apesantos son of Akrisios.[74] For when he was hunting in that place he trod on a poisonous snake and perished. The king buried his son and changed the name of the mountain, then called Selinountion, to Apesantos.

(10) Mount Kokkygion was so named for the following reason. Zeus fell in love with his sister Hera and feeling ashamed about his beloved, ⟨changed into the form of a cuckoo and⟩ from her sired Ares.[75] Therefore the mountain called Lyrkeion was named Kokkygion (*Cuckoo*) as a result of this occurrence, as Agathonymos relates in *Perseid*.

(11) A tree called *palinouros* grows on it. If any of the dumb animals sits on the tree it is held fast as if by bird-lime, except for the cuckoo. For it spares this bird, as Ktesiphon ⟨relates⟩ in book 1 of *Concerning Trees*.

---

[73] Here there is a play on the sound of the Greek word 'to roar' (*mykēsasthai*). Furthermore, in §7 there is another play on sound with *mykēs*, the scabbard-cap; see Steph. Byz. μ 231 Mykenai.

[74] Editors have accepted the supplement necessary to complete the sense.

[75] After *agapomenēn* some words have fallen out; the context suggests a reference to Zeus changing into a cuckoo; cf. Pausanias 2. 36. 2.

(12) Mount Athenaion got its name from Athena.[76] For after the sack of Ilion (*Troy*) Diomedes returned to Argos, went up Mount Keraunion, and established a sanctuary of Athena; he renamed the mountain Athenaion after the goddess.

(13) On the summit of the mountain grows a root resembling rue. If a woman accidentally eats it she becomes mad. It is called Adrasteia, as Plesimachos relates in book 2 of *Returns*.[77]

19. ALPHEIOS

(1) The Alpheios is a river in Arkadia near Pisa at Olympia.[78] It was formerly called Stymphelos after Stymphelos, son of Ares and Dormothea. For when this man lost his son, the horse-loving Alkmaion, he was overcome by despair and hurled himself into the river Nyktimon, which was renamed Stymphelos after him.

But it was called Alpheios for the following reason. Alpheios, one of those who traced their descent from Helios, fought with his brother Kerkaphos over the kingship, killed him, and driven on by the *Poinai* (*goddesses of vengeance*) threw himself into the river Nyktimon, which was renamed Alpheios after him.

(2) A plant named *kenchritis* resembling honeycomb grows in this river. If doctors boil this down and give it as a drink to those who have lost their wits, they free them from their madness, as Ktesias relates in book 1 of *Concerning Rivers*.

(3) Adjacent to it is situated a mountain which is named for the following reason. After the battle of the giants, Kronos, avoiding the threats of Zeus, came to the mountain called Ktouron, which he renamed Kronion after himself. He hid here for a short time, then seizing an opportunity moved over to Mount Caucasus in Skythia.

(4) There originates on this mountain a stone called *kylindros* because of the following occurrence. Whenever Zeus sends lightning or thunder, it rolls down from the summit in fright, as Derkyllos relates in book 1 of *Concerning Stones*.

20. EUPHRATES

(1) The Euphrates is a river in Parthia near the city of Babylon.[79] It was formerly called Medos after Medos son of Artaxerxes. For this man in the grip of passion forced himself

---

[76] There is no evidence for this mountain in the Argolid.

[77] 'Plesimachos' is perhaps a mistake for Lysimachos, who was known as a writer of *Nostoi*; for the problem of the authorities cited by Ps.-Plut., see introduction to this chapter.

[78] The Alpheios (mod. *Alpheios*) in the Peloponnese flows past Olympia. Alpheios was the son of Okeanos and Tethys (Hesiod, *Theog.* 338), or a descendant of Helios. In one story he fell in love with Arethousa or Artemis, Pausanias 4. 30. 2; 5. 7. 2; 6. 22. 9–10; 7. 23. 2; 8. 20. 3 (Leukippos grows his hair long in honour of the river); Ovid, *Metamorphoses* 5. 572–641. In the context perhaps we should read 'Stymphelon' for Nyktimon in the last sentence; but Müller thinks that Nyktimon may refer to the subterranean course of the Alpheios.

[79] The Euphrates (*Firat*) from its source in E. Turkey flows for 1,740 mi (2,800 km) through Syria and Iraq into the *Shatt al-Arab* and the Persian gulf. Various legends are associated with the river, which was allegedly the son of the priestess of Aphrodite and brother of the Tigris.

on and raped Rhoxane, the daughter of Kordyos. Next day when he was sought out by the king for punishment, in terror he threw himself into the river Xaranda, which was then named Medos after him.

It was named Euphrates for the following reason. Euphrates son of Arandakos found his son Axourtas asleep with his mother and thinking that he was one of the citizens, in a spate of wicked jealousy drew his sword and cut his throat. When he saw that he was responsible for this unimaginable deed, in an extremity of grief he threw himself into the river Medos, which was renamed Euphrates after him.

(2) A stone called *aëtites* originates in it. Midwives place it on the stomachs of those women who have difficulty in giving birth, and they immediately give birth without pain.

(3) A plant grows in it called *axalla*, which is interpreted to mean 'hot'. Whenever people suffering from quartan fever place it on their chest they are immediately freed from the symptoms, as Chrysermos of Corinth relates in book 13 of *Concerning Rivers*.

(4) Adjacent to it is situated a mountain called Drimylon, on which originates a stone resembling sardonyx, which kings use in their crowns. When thrown into hot water it is an excellent remedy for dim-sightedness, as Nikias of Mallos relates in his work *Concerning Stones*.

21. KAIKOS

(1) The Kaikos is a river in Mysia that was formerly called Astraios after Astraios son of Poseidon.[80] This man during the all-night festival in honour of Athena unknowingly forced himself on and raped his sister Alkippe and took her ring. Next day when he recognized his sister's seal, in an extremity of grief he threw himself into the river Adouros, which was renamed Astraios after him.

But it was named Kaikos for the following reason. Kaikos, son of Hermes and the nymph Okyrrhoë, killed Timandros one of the nobles, and in fear of his kinsfolk hurled himself into the Astraios, which was renamed Kaikos after him.

(2) A poppy grows in the river and instead of flowers bears ⟨a number of⟩ pebbles.[81] From these come certain black things resembling wheat, which the Mysians hurl onto ploughed earth. If the land is destined to be barren the pebbles lie in the place where they were thrown, but if fertile, they jump about like locusts.

(3) A plant called *helipharmakos* also grows in it, which doctors place on those suffering from a haemorrhage and cut off the flow of blood from the veins, as Timagoras relates in book 1 of *Concerning Rivers*.[82]

---

[80] The Kaikos (*Bakir Çay*) in Asia flows through Mysia and Lydia. According to Hesiod, *Theog.* 343, Kaikos was the son of Okeanos and Tethys; Pomponius Mela 1. 90.
[81] I follow Müller's simple solution of adding *plēthos* to make sense of the problematic text.
[82] On the basis of Stobaeus, *Florilegium*, 100. 17, *en autōi* 'in it' has been added (probably by oversight, the phrase is not bracketed as a supplement in Müller's text, whereas it is at 22. 3); also *helipharmakos* for the MS's *pharmakos*. Hercher suggests *elelisphakos* (salvia).

(4) Adjacent to it is situated the mountain called Teuthras after Teuthras, king of the Mysians, who climbed Mount Thrasyllos to go hunting, and catching sight of an enormous boar chased it with his spearmen. But the boar got away and fled as a suppliant to the temple of Artemis Orthosia. When they all tried to force their way into the temple the boar shouted out in a human voice loud enough to be heard: 'King, spare the nursling of the goddess'. But Teuthras buoyed up by his emotions killed the animal. Artemis was furious at what he had done, revived the boar, and inflicted leprosy and madness on the perpetrator. He was ashamed of this affliction and spent his time in the heights. However Lysippe, his mother, when she was informed about what had happened, ran into the wood, bringing with her the seer Polyidos son of Koiranos. By careful enquiry she got the entire truth out of him and placated the anger of the goddess by the sacrifice of oxen. Having rescued her son, whose sanity now returned, she set up an altar to Artemis Orthosia. She also had a golden boar manufactured, fashioned with a man's face. Even now, when hunters enter the temple, this statue, just as if it is being pursued, emits a voice: 'Spare me!' Teuthras, having unexpectedly got his normal countenance back, renamed the mountain Teuthras.

(5) A stone called *antipathes* originates on it, which is an excellent remedy for skin infections and leprosy when ground down with wine and applied to those who are afflicted, as Ktesias of Knidos relates in book 2 of *Concerning Mountains*.[83]

22. ACHELOÖS

(1) The Acheloös is a river in Aitolia.[84] It was formerly called Thestios for the following reason. Thestios, son of Ares and Peisidike, because of family circumstances went to live abroad in Sikyon, and when he had spent a sufficient time there he returned to his ancestral land. Finding his son Kalydon asleep with his mother and thinking that he was an adulterer, he killed him in ignorance. When he saw that he had committed this unimaginable act he hurled himself into the river Axenos, which was renamed Thestios after him.

But it was named Acheloös for the following reason. Acheloös, son of Okeanos (*Ocean*) and the nymph Naïs, unknowingly had intercourse with his daughter Kletoria, and overcome with despair threw himself into the river Thestios, which was renamed Acheloös after him.

---

[83] For the stone see Dioscorides, *De materia medica*, 5. 140; it resembled *corallium*, useful for treating diseases of the eye, the bringing up of blood, and urinary problems.

[84] The Acheloös (mod. *Achéloös*) flows for 135 mi (217 km) through Aetolia and Akarnania into the Ionian sea (Adriatic); in mythology he was son of Okeanos and Tethys. The name Acheloös is perhaps pre-Greek, and smaller rivers also have the name. Acheloös was seen as the father of other springs: Kastalia at Delphi, Peirene in Corinth, and Dirke in Thebes. It was the scene of the battle between Herakles and Acheloös (in the form of a bull) when Herakles ripped off his horn which became the horn of plenty. See Homer, *Il.* 21. 194–7; Strabo 10. 2. 2, C450; Paus. 1. 34. 2; 8. 38. 9–10; 10. 8. 5; Ovid *Metam.* 9. 8–88.

(2) A plant called *zaklon* resembling wool grows in this river. If you rub this and throw it into wine it turns into water and retains the bouquet but not the potency.

(3) There is found in it a stone of livid colour called *linourgos* because of the following occurrence. If you throw it onto linen cloth, through mutual attraction it takes its shape and becomes white (?),[85] as Antisthenes relates in book 3 of his *Meleagrid*. Diokles of Rhodes refers to these matters in more detail in *The History of Aitolia*.

(4) Adjacent to it is situated the mountain called Kalydon, which got its name from Kalydon, son of Ares and Astynome.[86] For this man unintentionally saw Artemis washing herself and had the shape of his body changed into a rock. By decision of the gods the mountain previously called Gyron was renamed Kalydon after him.

(5) A plant named *myops* grows on it, and if someone throws it into water and washes his face he loses his sight, but if he propitiates Artemis he regains the light, as Derkyllos relates in book 3 of *The History of Aitolia*.

23. ARAXES

(1) The Araxes is a river in Armenia and gets its name from Araxes son of Pylos.[87] For this man being in dispute with Arbelos his grandfather over the kingship, shot him with an arrow. Pursued in vengeance by the Furies he hurled himself into the river Baktron, which was renamed Araxes after him, as Ktesiphon relates in book 1 of *The History of Persia*.

Araxes, king of Armenia, when he was marshalling the army during his war with the neighbouring Persians, received an oracle that he would gain a victory if he sacrificed two of the most nobly born virgins to the gods who avert evil. He spared his own daughters because of his fatherly feelings, but led two of the most admired girls of one of his subjects to the altar and killed them. Mnesalkes, the father of the slain girls, was furious at what had been done, but for a time concealed his feeling of outrage. Then seizing his opportunity he ambushed the tyrant's daughters and killed them; leaving his ancestral land he sailed to Skythia. Araxes when he found out what had happened was overcome with despair and hurled himself into the river Halmos, which was renamed Araxes after him.

(2) A plant called *araxa* in the language of the local inhabitants grows in it, which is interpreted to mean 'hater of virgins'. As soon as this plant is found by virgins it pours out blood and withers away.

(3) A stone called *sikyonos*, which is black in colour, originates in it. Whenever any oracle involving the killing of a man is issued, this stone is placed by two virgins on

---

[85] *argion* seems meaningless in the context; the most plausible conjecture, taking account of the name of the stone (*linourgos*) is one propounded by Müller, *kai othonion araion ginetai*, 'and becomes linen of loose texture'.

[86] There is a town in Aitolia called Kalydon.

[87] The Araxes (*Aras, Arax*) flows E from mountains S of *Erzurum* in Turkey for 665 mi (1,070 km) through the Caucasus.

the altars of the gods who avert evil. When the priest touches it with a knife there is a copious flow of blood. When they have performed the religious ceremonies in this way they withdraw uttering lamentations, and move the stone to the temple, as Dorotheos of Chaldaea relates in book 2 of *Concerning Stones*.

(4) Adjacent to it is situated the mountain called Diorphon after Diorphos the earthborn, about whom the following story is told. Mithras wishing to have a son but hating the race of women, masturbated onto a stone.[88] The stone became pregnant and after the appropriate time gave birth to a child named Diorphos. When he grew up he was killed by Ares whom he had challenged to a contest of valour. By decision of the gods he was changed into a mountain of the same name.

(5) A tree resembling a mulberry grows on it; it produces a generous crop of fruit similar to grapes but with a taste of apples. If someone plucks ripe fruit from this tree and calls on Ares by name, it turns pale as it is plucked, as Ktesiphon relates in book 13 of *Concerning Trees*.

24. TIGRIS

(1) The Tigris is a river in Armenia and flows into the Araxes and the Arsakis marsh.[89] It was formerly called Sollax, which is interpreted to mean 'sloping downwards'. It was named Tigris for the following reason. Dionysos became mad by decision of Hera and roamed the land and sea wanting to escape his affliction. When he came to the area round Armenia, being unable to cross this river, he called upon Zeus. The god came to Dionysos' assistance by sending him a tiger on which he was carried across without any danger. In honour of what had happened he renamed the river Tigris, as Theophilos relates in book 1 of *Concerning Stones*.

But Hermesianax of Cyprus records the following story. Dionysos fell in love with the nymph Alphesiboia and, being unable to seduce her either with gifts or entreaties, changed the shape of his body to that of a tiger. He therefore terrorized his beloved into acceptance, swept her up, carried her across the river, and sired a son, Medos. When he grew up, in honour of this occurrence he renamed the river Tigris, as Aristonymos relates in book 3 of [—].

(2) There originates in it a stone called *myndan*, which is entirely white in colour. If someone holds it he suffers no harm from wild beasts, as Leon of Byzantion relates in book 3 of *Concerning Rivers*.

---

[88] *Diorphon*: Hercher suggests *Dimorphon* as the earthborn are sometimes referred to as *dimorphoi*, but it is probably best to follow Müller's warning and avoid conjecture.

[89] The Tigris (*Tigris*) from its source in L. *Hazar* flows for 1,150 mi (1,850 km) through Turkey, Syria, and Iraq to the *Shatt Al-Arab* (Persian gulf). For L. Arsakis cf. Ptolemy 5. 2, L. Arsissa; Strabo 11. 14. 8, C529, refers to L. Arsene. Tigris in legend was the brother of Euphrates. Sollas perhaps stands for Silla, supposed to be a tributary of the Tigris.

(3) Adjacent to it is situated the mountain called Gauranon after Gauranos the satrap, son of Rhoxanes.[90] He was pious towards the gods and received good fortune in return. For alone of all the Persians he lived for 300 years, died without suffering any illness, and was thought worthy of an elaborate tomb on the heights of Mount Mausoron. By decision of the gods the mountain was renamed Gauranon after him.

(4) A plant resembling wild barley grows on it. The local inhabitants heat this in olive oil and having anointed themselves with it never suffer any illness until the compulsion of death, as Sostratos relates in book 1 of the *Collection of Mythical Tales*.

25. INDOS

(1) The Indos is a river in India, flowing with a rapid current down to the land of the Ichthyophagoi (*Fish-eaters*).[91] It was formerly called Mausolos after Mausolos son of Helios. It was renamed for the following reason. When the mysteries of Dionysos were being carried on and the local inhabitants were intent on observing the religious rites, Indos, an aristocratic young man, forced himself on and raped king Oxyalkos' daughter, Damasalkida, who carried a sacred basket. Pursued by the tyrant for punishment, Indos in a panic threw himself into the river Mausolos, which was renamed Indos after him.

(2) A stone named [—] originates in it.[92] Whenever virgins carry it they do not in any way fear seducers.

(3) A plant called *karpyle* resembling ox-tongue grows in it. If given with tepid water to those suffering from jaundice, it is an excellent remedy, as Kleitophon of Rhodes relates in book 1 of *Indian History*.

(4) Adjacent to it is situated a mountain named Lilaion after the shepherd Lilaios. For this man was very god-fearing, and, worshipping only Selene (*the Moon*), carried on her religious ceremonies at dead of night. The other gods took this insult badly and sent two huge lions against him. He was ripped apart by them and lost his life. Selene changed her devotee into a mountain of the same name.

(5) A stone named *kleitoris*, which is very dark in colour, originates on it. The local inhabitants wear it on their earlobes as a decoration, as Aristotle relates in book 4 of *Concerning Rivers*.

---

[90] Gauranon or Gaurus is a mountain in Campania near Cumae, perhaps mistakenly transferred to the vicinity of the Tigris by Ps.-Plut. Note that Pliny 6. xxxi. 133 refers to a Mt Carbantus near the Tigris.

[91] The Indos (*Indus*) from its source in Tibet flows for c.1,990 mi (3,200 km) through China, Pakistan, and India before discharging into the Arabian sea. For the problem with the name Mausolos, see the introduction to the chapter.

[92] The name of the stone has fallen out of the text.

27

ARRIAN OF NIKOMEDEIA, *CIRCUMNAVIGATION OF THE EUXINE*

(WRITTEN C. AD 131–5)

*Aidan Liddle**

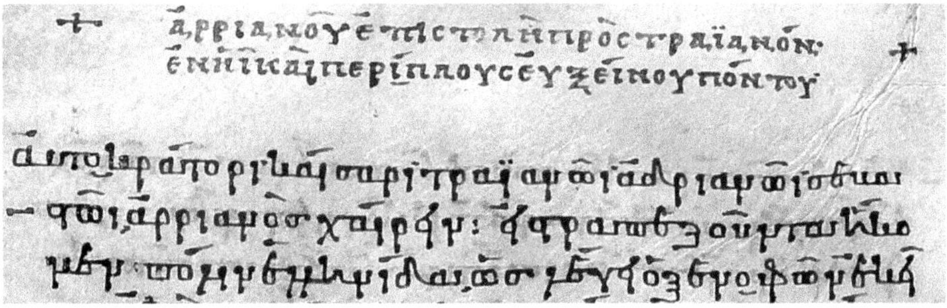

FIG. 27.1. Opening of Arrian's *Periplous*, 398, fo. 30ᵛ (detail).

INTRODUCTION

Arrian (Lucius Flavius Arrianos Xenophon, *c.* AD 86–*c.*150), a native of the Greek city of Nikomedeia on the southern shore of the Black Sea, is the writer among those in these volumes about whom we know the most. A Roman citizen, as his forenames show, he was the first member of his ancient family to attain the consulship at Rome (in 129 or 130), and probably the first to reach senatorial rank. He returned to Asia Minor as a statesman and soldier at the peak of his public career under the emperor Hadrian (r. 117–38) to govern its most important province, Cappadocia, whose capital was his home city.

The work in Greek that this return to the Black Sea inspired, the *Periplous tou Euxeinou Pontou* or *Circumnavigation of the Black Sea* (often known by its Latin title, *Periplus Ponti Euxini*), was written between the death of Kotys II, ruler of the Bosporan kingdom, in 131/2 (*Periplous*, 17. 3) and Arrian's expedition against the Alani in 135 (below).[1] It is a strange and disparate work—part military and diplomatic report,

---

* I would like to thank all those who have offered helpful comments on my 2003 translation and commentary, particularly Stephanie West, Owen Hodkinson, Torben Retboll, and especially the originator of the present volumes, Graham Shipley. Nicholas Purcell sparked my original interest in Arrian's Periplous and the world it describes, for which I am ever grateful.

[1] Liddle 2003 (hereinafter 'Liddle'), 5 n. 12 (on p. 35) and p. 11.

part fantastic mythological guidebook, part friendly private correspondence (covering an accompanying report in Latin, which does not survive: see 6. 2; 10. 1)—but sheds much light upon a vital corner of the Roman frontier; it illuminates the contemporary image of Hadrian, one of the most elusive men ever to have ascended to the purple; and it stands almost alone as a record of the activity of the governor of this important province. Above all, it is a product of its times, and its author, as revealed in its pages, supremely representative of them.[2]

Part of Arrian's responsibility as provincial governor was to quell the threat to Roman control from piracy, especially emanating from the area of Kolchis (approximately the western part of modern Georgia). The voyage he narrates in the present work focuses most of its attention, accordingly, on the eastern half of the Black Sea, an area that had been less well known to Greeks and Romans than the western half, where Greek colonies were more numerous. The area was vital to shore up Roman control of the Black Sea as a whole, and to prevent any unrest that might spark a civil war in the empire. The many navigable rivers of the eastern Black Sea needed to be monitored, as they gave access to, and from, the interior of the Caucasus lands from which not only trade but also potential trouble might come. Arrian's repeated mentions of living rulers in the area whose allegiance to Rome needed to be kept firm (e.g. in ch. 11) reflects these strategic and economic interests. The Caucasus also represented a military avenue to the regions of Iberia and Armenia, and thus north-eastern Asia Minor, which Hadrian's predecessor, Trajan, had exploited a few years earlier and which Arrian himself would defend from the invading Alani in 135 from the Roman base at Apsaros (mentioned in the *Periplous* at ch. 6). Arrian's responsibilities also extended to oversight of the Roman fleet based at Trapezous, the *classis Pontica*, and his reports on the condition of the ships, during his anti-clockwise tour of the Black Sea, form an important part of the present text.

After a six-year tenure in Cappadocia, Arrian held the archonship at Athens in the year 145/6; the date of his death is unknown. Such was his prodigious literary output that it seems difficult to suppose he had not begun to publish before attaining provincial command. He is best known today for his *Anabasis of Alexander*, the best account we have of Alexander the Great along with Plutarch's *Life*, even though both were composed several centuries after Alexander's death in 323 BC. His works also included surviving treatises on hunting and military tactics, though it was as a philosopher that he was chiefly honoured in his lifetime. Much has been made of his close association with the philhellene emperor Hadrian, and the two of them embody the complex world of the early 2nd century, in which Greek culture and the old families of the East were raised from the doldrums of the previous two hundred years of Roman occupation.

That great flowering of Greek letters and rhetoric, looking back to the golden age of Hellenic culture, is the cultural movement known as the Second Sophistic, best seen in

---

[2] Important points are covered by Braund and Kakhidze 2022, of which it has not been possible to take full account.

the works of such orators as Dio Chrysostom and Aelius Aristeides, as well as those of the biographer and essayist Plutarch (who, like Arrian, wrote a *Dion* and a *Timoleon*, in his celebrated *Parallel Lives*). Important elements of this movement were a renewed interest in the classical Greek past, especially in what we would call 'local history', and a corresponding new generation of tourists, who formed the audience for Pausanias' guide to the sights of old Greece.

The most obvious manifestation of this great respect for classical Greek culture in Arrian is clearly visible in his deliberate echoes of the Athenian soldier-philosopher Xenophon. Arrian took his hero's name as part of his own: whether this was a nickname bestowed by his literary milieu or the emperor himself, or even a given name from birth, is unclear, though he does use it to refer to himself in his writings, especially in connection with 'the elder Xenophon' (as he is referred to, for instance, at ch. 12. 5 of the *Periplous*). It was not only a name that they shared: Xenophon, like Arrian, was a soldier as well as an historian, philosopher, and essayist; both enjoyed, and wrote treatises on, hunting; both composed instructive memoirs of their youthful studies with great philosophers. Throughout Arrian's oeuvre there is a deliberate reflection of his respect for the Athenian, and thus an affinity for the world of classical Greek culture. More than his near-contemporary Plutarch, however, Arrian expresses the standpoint of the Roman elite as well as the Greek. That standpoint included an interest in supporting the traditional cultural life of the Greek *poleis* (cities, formerly city-states) in the various provinces, as we see from Hadrian's patronage of Athens and his foundation of the Panhellenion, a cultic association spanning many of the oldest and most admired Greek cities.

The *Periplous* is addressed to Hadrian in person; the emperor, though originally from Roman Spain, had spoken Greek before he knew Latin. The relationship between the two men was a close one, and Arrian has no hesitation in writing frankly about conditions in the Black Sea, expressing the assumption that Hadrian has a genuine concern for the region (which he himself visited twice in the 120s), not only from the strategic point of view but also because of his interest in Greek *polis* culture, antiquities, and mythology (e.g. the anchor of the *Argo*, 9. 2; the lengthy discussion of Achilles' presence on Leuke Island, chs 21–3). Like other geographical writers, Arrian evinces an interest in the origins of city names (see the brief aside concerning the village of Athenai, 5. 3). But strategic realities also impinge, as when Arrian suggests the need for information following a potential change in the balance of power in the area (17. 3).

At the same time, the *Periplous*, as its name suggests, consciously places itself in the tradition of 'circumnavigation' texts of which several earlier examples occur in the present volumes; though this is, perhaps, the first prose *periplous* that we can call 'literary' (see discussion in the Introduction, §III. 1. b), with the possible exception of Arrian's own *Indike*, appended to the seven books of his *Anabasis*. The model of the *periplous* provided a framework which would easily accommodate the narrative of a voyage of inspection—the pretext for writing the letter to Hadrian in the first place—as well as plenty of scope, given the development of the genre, for the inclusion of material of more general interest to the reader.[3] Thus Arrian—again demonstrating the ease with which he could work in an idiom deriving elements from both Greece and Rome—could incorporate his letter, concerned as it was with contemporary issues facing the Roman empire and its *princeps*, within a form that was both a successor to a long-established tradition of Greek scholarship and a suggestion of the power of military exploration in the sophisticated imagery of the Roman emperors.

So, the *Periplous* is cast at once as both revealing private correspondence and a new take on the traditional Greek scholarly geographical treatise, mixed with the Roman military report.[4]

The odd structure of the *Periplous* will be apparent to the reader, though it need not occasion any doubts as to the authenticity of the work, which is perfectly consistent with the style of Arrian as witnessed in his other extant works.[5] The tour of the Black Sea begins at Trapezous on the southern shore, and moves eastwards as far as Dioskourias–Sebastopolis, the last Roman town on the east coast. Then, at chapter 12, we have a 'flashback' (which runs to the end of 17. 1) describing the coastline from Byzantion eastwards as far as Trapezous. The third and last part of the work (18–25) resumes the description of the coast from Dioskourias, continuing anticlockwise to Byzantion, thus completing the description of the Black Sea coasts. This time, though, there is a bridge paragraph (17. 2–3), summing up the journey from Byzantion to Dioskourias and supplying the reason for continuing the description—namely, that, following the death of the ruler of the Bosporan kingdom, the emperor would need information concerning the region upon which to decide Roman policy. The description thus continues without a break, all the way round to Byzantion, completing the *Periplous*, like its predecessors, at the customary point rather than at Trapezous. The partly literary nature of the work is reinforced by the use of the rivers Phasis and Istros as complementary landmarks, as well as the blend of references to sources (e.g. 'they also report these things', 22. 1) with personal observations and literary references. The latter include frequent allusions to Xenophon, to whom Arrian looked for much of his inspiration, and whose visit to the southern shore of the Black Sea with the Ten Thousand is echoed so strongly in Arrian's treatment of that part of his work. The elegant, implicit reference to Hadrian and his beloved companion Antinoös, who had died as recently as 130—paralleled by the acrostic in the contemporary poem of Dionysios Periegetes (Chapter 28 below)—removes any doubt about the authenticity of the work; a forger would have had to be exceptionally skilled to devise so convincing a deceit; and to what purpose? No other antique forgery so far recognized is as inventive and learned

---

[3] On A.'s possible use of the Augustan geographer Menippos' account of the Black Sea, see introduction to Ch. 21.
[4] On the *Periplous* as evoking the Black Sea as a 'storied landscape', see Rood 2011 (phrase quoted from p. 138).
[5] For fuller discussion of this and other points regarding the *Periplous*, see Liddle 1–38.

as this one would be;[6] least of all the Pseudo-Arrianic *Periplous of the Black Sea* (*Eux.*) from the 6th century AD, though that work deserves rehabilitation (Chapter 36 below) and explicitly offers new names for over thirty places mentioned by Arrian.

The *Periplous* gives us a vital glimpse of the dynamics of a remarkable, yet obscure, part of the Roman world, and some idea of how such a place could be governed and controlled within the flexibility of the Roman system. Written by a man standing astride two worlds, and addressed to the master of both, it offers us an insight into the workings of the elusive Hadrian through his friend and servant who, though born at the opposite end of the Roman dominions, shared (or at least understood) the convictions and aims of his emperor. Written by a man who grew up in the traditions of the classical Greek authors, it demonstrates how a conventional, scholarly form could be adapted by a literary craftsman to incorporate interesting local legend, useful strategic information, and subtle encomium of Rome's Princeps. Above all, written by a man who was perhaps the most representative of the culture of his age, it affords us an epitome of that culture in a tightly packed nutshell. It is a nutshell well worth opening.

We are fortunate that Arrian's *Periplous* has survived at all. Like many Greek and Roman works, it has come down to us in only one manuscript, in this case the 9th-century Heidelberg codex described in the Introduction (known as 'P' in scholarship on the *Periplous*, but as 'A' to scholars of Greek geography). The Pseudo-Arrianic *Periplous* is partly preserved in the same manuscript; together these two works formed the nucleus of a corpus of Greek geographical writings compiled, in all likelihood, by Arrian himself (see Introduction, §VIII. 2. a).

The present translation follows the standard Teubner edition of Arrian's works.[7] It follows the chapter divisions established by Müller,[8] rather than those in his *GGM*.[9] The translation is adapted from my Bristol Classical Press edition, used by permission of Bloomsbury Publishing plc. Modern names of important places are in parentheses; others in footnotes. [The 1st edition (2022) of Brodersen 2023a appeared too late to be taken into account.]

SELECTED FURTHER READING

*Belfiore, S. (2009), *Il Periplo del Ponto Eusino di Arriano e altri testi sul Mar Nero e il Bosforo: spazio geografico, mito e dominio ai confini dell'impero romano*. Venice.
Braund, D. C., and Kakhidze, E. (2022), 'Reflections on the southeastern coast of the Black Sea in the Roman period', in D. C. Braund, A. Chaniotis, and E. K. Petropoulos (eds), *The Black Sea Region in the Context of the Roman Empire* (Athens), 59–73.
*Liddle, A. (2003), *Arrian, Periplus Ponti Euxini*. London.
*Marenghi, G. (1958), *Arriano, Periplo del Ponto Eusino*. Naples.

---

[6] The consensus that the work is genuine is exemplified by Silberman 1993.
[7] Roos and Wirth 1968. The edition of Marenghi 1958 (with Italian trans.), and the Budé of Silberman 1995 (with French trans.), have also been consulted.
[8] C. W. L. Müller 1846.   [9] *GGM* i. 370–401.

Rood, T. (2011), 'Black Sea variations: Arrian's Periplus', *Cambridge Classical Journal*, 57: 137–63.

Silberman, A. (1978), 'Quelques remarques sur la composition du Périple d'Arrien', *Revue des études grecques*, 91: 158–64.

—— (1993), 'Arrien, "Périple du Pont-Euxin": essai d'interprétation et d'évaluation des données historiques et géographiques', in *Aufstieg und Niedergang der römischen Welt*, ii. 34. 1, 276–311.

*—— (1995), *Arrien, Périple du Pont-Euxin*. ['Budé' edition.] Paris.

TEXT

ANTI-CLOCKWISE FROM TRAPEZOUS TO DIOSKOURIAS–SEBASTOPOLIS

To the Emperor Caesar Trajan Hadrian Sebastos (*Augustus*), Arrian (*sends*) greetings.

1. We came to Trapezous, a Hellenic city, as the other Xenophon says,[10] founded on the sea, a colony of the Sinopeans; and gladly we looked down on the sea of the Euxine from the very same spot as both Xenophon and you.[11] (2) The altars are already set up, though in rather rough stone, and as such the inscribed letters are not particularly clear; the Greek inscription is also inaccurately carved, as it was written by barbarians. I therefore decided to rebuild the altars in white stone, and to carve the inscriptions in clear letters.[12] (3) And though your statue has been erected in a pleasing pose—it points out to the sea—in its workmanship it neither resembles you nor is beautiful in any other way. (4) So send for a statue worthy to bear your name, in the same pose; for that spot is very well suited to an everlasting monument.[13]

2. The temple[14] has also been built in squared stone, not without care; but the image of Hermes is worthy neither of the temple nor of the place itself. If you approve, send me a statue of Hermes about five feet tall—for it seems to me that that will be proportionate to the temple—and another, four feet tall, of Philesios; (2) for it is not

---

[10] i.e. the famous historian of the *Anabasis*, as opposed to Arrian himself; see introduction to this chapter.

[11] Xenophon and the Greek army reached Trapezous in the spring of 400 BC (*Anabasis* 4. 8. 22); Hadrian visited in AD 123/4 or 129. A. places himself and Hadrian in an historical continuum with Xenophon, emphasizing the roots of Hadrian's new imperial culture in Cl Greece.

[12] For this passage as an example of rulers' names being added to renovated structures, as well as expressing A.'s own claim to power, see Zadorojnyi 2013, 373. On the possible site of Hadrian's shrine, see Mitford 2000, 129.

[13] A. reports on progress on two public works projects commissioned by Hadrian, as was his habit, during his visit. 'The altars' refers to the construction of a sanctuary dedicated to Hadrian, and possibly to Rome as well.

[14] The second project is a temple to Hermes and Philesios, probably a local hero or the legendary founder of the city, descended from the former. The double cult echoes that of Achilles and Patroklos at Leuke I. (see ch. 21 below).

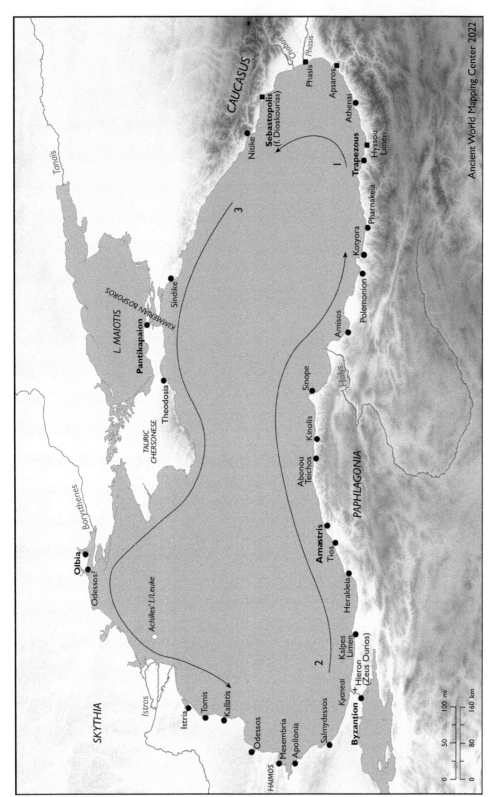

MAP 27.1. Arrian, *Euxine*: the three stages, and principal places. ■ military fort.

against the custom, I think, for him to share a temple and an altar with his ancestor, and what one passer-by will sacrifice to Hermes, another will to Philesios, and still another to both. All of these will gratify both Hermes and Philesios; Hermes, because they will be honouring his descendant, and Philesios, his ancestor. (3) I also sacrificed an ox there—not like the other Xenophon in Kalpes Limen (who, lacking animals for sacrifice, took an ox from a chariot),[15] as I had been provided with an ox of not ignoble stock by the Trapezountines themselves—and we examined the entrails on the spot, and poured a libation on them. (4) We do not forget that you, for whose well-being we first offered prayers, are aware of our custom, and that you know yourself to be worthy of prayers from all, including those who have benefited less from you than we have, for your prosperity.

3. Having set off from Trapezous, on the first day we put into Hyssou Limen[16] and exercised the infantry who were there.[17] That cohort, as you know, is made up of infantry and also has 20 cavalry, which is sufficient; but we also made the latter throw their javelins. (2) From there at first we sailed with the winds that blow from the rivers in the morning and at the same time used the oars; for the winds were cold, as Homer too says,[18] but were not strong enough for those who want to sail quickly. Soon a calm took hold, so we too just proceeded by rowing. (3) Then suddenly clouds rose up and broke out from the east, and an extraordinary wind came upon us from exactly the opposite direction, which was the only thing that helped us, as for a short while it made a hollow in the sea, without which we would have been swamped with plenty of water from both sides, not only over the oars but even over the decks too. (4) Just as in that tragic verse,

We baled it out, but it still rushèd in;[19]

but the surf did not come over the sides. So we made our way with difficulty by rowing: but at last, having suffered much, we arrived at Athenai.

4. For there is in the Euxeinos Pontos a place so named,[20] and there, there is a Hellenic sanctuary of Athena from which I imagine the place got that name, and also an abandoned fort. (2) The anchorage at the right time of year can accommodate only a few ships and shelters them from the Notos (*south wind*), and even the Euros (*SE wind*); it may also save ships that are anchoring from the Boreas (*NNE wind*), but not from the Aparktias (*north wind*), nor from the wind called the Thraskias (*NNW wind*) in the Pontos, and the Skiron in Hellas. (3) Towards night came violent thunder, and lightning too; the wind was not constant, but had turned into a Notos, and for

---

[15] Xen. *Anab.* 6. 4. 22.   [16] Hyssos's Harbour; *Araklıçarşışı/Sürmene*.
[17] An auxiliary cohort garrisoning a small fort, possibly ('as you know') visited by Hadrian on his tour in 129.
[18] *Od.* 5. 469.   [19] A line in tragic metre; author unknown.
[20] A. enjoys the coincidence of finding a spot in such a remote location that shares a name with the cosmopolitan centre of culture and learning both he and Hadrian knew so well, seeming to put the storm that forced them to put in there down to Providence. The name may in fact derive from a local word meaning a shady place, rather than have any connection to Athena.

a while from the Notos to the Lips (*SW wind*), and the anchorage (*hormos*) was no longer safe for the ships.   (4) Therefore, before the sea turned completely savage, we beached all the ships that that place Athenai could hold, except the trireme; for that, anchored (*hyphormousa*)[21] by a rock, safely rode at anchor (*esaleuen*).

5. I decided to send the large ships to the neighbouring coast to be beached. They were beached so that they all came through unscathed except one, which, its side having turned side-on too early while anchoring, was taken up by a wave and dashed against the shore, and broken up.   (2) Everything was rescued, though; not only the sail, the rigging, and the men, but also the nails and sealing-wax were stripped off, so that nothing of the fittings was lost but the ship's timber, of which, as you know,[22] there is a great abundance in the Pontos.   (3) The storm lasted two days, and forced us to stay there. And thus we could not sail past Athenai in the Pontos like some deserted and nameless anchorage.

6. Having started from there towards morning we did battle with the waves coming over the sides, but as the day went by a light Boreas (*NNE wind*) blew down and steadied the sea and made it thoroughly calm. And before midday we came more than ⟨2⟩50 stades to Apsaros (*Gonio*), where the five cohorts are stationed.   (2) I gave the army its pay and inspected its weapons, the fort,[23] the trench, the sick, and the food supplies that were there. My opinion about this latter point I have written to you in the Latin (*lit. 'Roman'*) report.[24]   (3) It is said that Apsaros was once, long ago, called Apsyrtos; for it was there that Apsyrtos was killed by Medea,[25] and the tomb of Apsyrtos is pointed out. The name was subsequently corrupted by the barbarians who live around there, just as many others were corrupted too;   (4) since they say that Tyana in Kappadokia was named Thoana after Thoas, king of the Tauroi, who, while pursuing Orestes and Pylades, is claimed to have come as far as this region and to have died here of a disease.

7. The rivers we passed on our coastal sailing from Trapezous were the Hyssos, after which the Hyssou Limen (*The Harbour of Hyssos*) is named, and which is 180 stades from Trapezous, and the Ophis ('*Snake*'; *mod. Of*), which is about 90 stades from

---

[21] The term *hyphormos* does not occur in A.; only this compound here.

[22] Another nod to Hadrian's tour, and his personal knowledge of his empire. Xen. *Anab.* 6. 4. 4 and Strabo 12. 3. 12, C546, also talk about the abundance of good shipbuilding timber in this area.

[23] Apsaros was a significant military installation (mentioned also by Pliny 6. iv. 12) guarding the frontier between the Roman-controlled coastal strip and the Iberian kingdom of the hostile King Pharasmanes. Its importance can be seen from the size of its garrison mentioned by A. and of its fortifications, later used by the Byzantine and Ottoman empires, which are still impressive today. A. may have launched his campaign against the Alanoi from here in 135.

[24] The *Periplous* is presented as a learned and discursive personal letter in Greek, accompanying an official report in Latin, of A.'s tour of inspection of this important and sensitive sector of the Roman frontier. Hadrian's interest in this part of the world is therefore suggested to be at once historical and cultural, and military and political.

[25] In the legend of the Argonauts, Apsyrtos was the brother of Medea, who either killed him and scattered his body to slow her father down as he pursued her and Jason in their escape from Kolchis, or set him up for an ambush to be killed by Jason.

Hyssos harbour and separates the territory of the Kolchoi from Thiannike. (2) Then the river called Psychros ('*Cold*'; *Baltacı Dere*), about 30 stades from the Ophis. Then the Kalos (*Good*) river (*İyi Dere/Kalopotamos*); this one too is 30 stades distant from the Psychros. Coming next after the Psychros is the Rhizios (*Rize*) river, 120 stades distant from the Kalos. (3) And 30 after this comes another river, the Askouros (*Taşlı Dere*), and one called Adienos (*Kanlü Dere/Kıbledağı Dere*) 60 after the Askouros; then it is 180 to Athenai. The river Zagatis (*Pazar Dere/Susa Dere*) lies near Athenai, about 7 stades distant from it. Setting off from Athenai we passed by the Prytanis ('*Chief*'; *Büyük Dere/Furtuna Dere*), where Anchialos' palace is.[26] And that is 40 stades distant from Athenai. (4) The Pyxites river (*Piskala Dere?*) is the Prytanis' neighbour; there are 90 stades between the two. And from the Pyxites to the Archabis (*Arhavi*) is another 90, and from the Archabis to Apsaros,[27] 60.

Starting from Apsaros we passed the Akampsis (*Çoruh*) by night, 15 stades distant from Apsaros. (5) The river Bathys (*Qorolistsqali*) is 75 distant from there, and the Akinases (*Kintrish*) 90 from the Bathys, and the Isis (*Natanebi*) 90 from the Akinases. Both the Akampsis and the Isis are navigable, and send out strong winds in the morning. From the Isis we passed the Mogros (*Supsa*); there are 90 stades between the Mogros and the Isis. It too is navigable.

8. From there, we sailed into the Phasis (*Rioni*),[28] 90 stades distant from the Mogros, which supplies the lightest and the strangest-coloured water of any of the rivers I know. (2) One may judge its lightness by means of a balance, and, more immediately, by the fact that it floats on the sea, not mixing with it, just as Homer said of the Titarcsos, that it floats 'on top of the Peneios 'like olive oil'.[29] (3) Indeed, if one should dip just beneath the surface, it was possible to draw out fresh water, but then, if one sinks the cup deeper, to draw out salty water. Moreover, the whole Pontos has much fresher water than the sea outside it; the reason for this is its rivers, being so many and so great in volume. (4) The proof of this freshness—if proof of

---

[26] Anchialos was an important Roman client king, who ruled over the Machelones and Heniochoi, and had been received by Trajan at Satala on his way to Mesopotamia in 114 (Cassius Dio 68. 19).

[27] Mentioned earlier, at 1. 6.

[28] The significance of the Phasis in A.'s narrative was both mythological and strategic. The river was the means by which Jason and the Argonauts came to Kolchis on their quest for the Golden Fleece, and by extension had acquired metaphorical status for the limit of the navigable seas (Ap. Rhod. 2. 1261; Strabo 11. 2. 16, C497); that the river was now an integrated part of the Roman world was a symbol of the uniting of Cl Greek myth and contemporary Roman power as personified by Hadrian. Xenophon had also travelled in this region, following the route of the Argonauts (*Anab*. 6. 2. 1). Strategically, the river controlled access to the interior of this sensitive part of the Roman frontier. The identification of A.'s Phasis with the modern *Rioni* appears safe, though see Dan 2016 for a discussion of other rivers in the region that may have shared its name.

[29] *Il*. 2. 754, quoted in the Prologue to these volumes. The R. Peneios was the boundary between Thessaly and Macedonia, and for some the limit of continuous Hellas (see Introduction, §VI. 4. b). The relative freshness of the Black Sea, owing to the large number of rivers emptying into it and the small volume of water leaving it at the Bosporos, is commented on by Aristotle, *Problems* 23. 6; Polybios 4. 42; and Strabo 1. 3. 4, C50. In fact, the Black Sea as a whole has two distinct layers of water, an upper one of lighter, fresher water and a lower one of denser, salt water.

perceptible phenomena be necessary—is that those who live around the sea lead all their cattle down to the sea and water them from it; they seem to drink happily, and the opinion is that this drink is more beneficial to them than fresh water is. (5) The colour of the Phasis is that of water that has been tainted with lead or tin; but, being left to stand, it becomes extremely clear. Furthermore, those who sail in[30] are traditionally forbidden from importing water into the Phasis, and as soon as they enter its stream they are ordered to pour out all water that is on the ships. Those neglecting to do so, it is said, will not otherwise sail on favourably. And the water of the Phasis does not stagnate, but remains unchanged for upwards of ten years—if anything, it becomes fresher.

9. On the left-hand side for those entering the Phasis has been erected (*an image of*) the Phasian goddess. Judging by her pose, she is Rhea;[31] for she has a cymbal in her hands and lions beneath her throne, and sits just like the one by Phidias in the Metroön at Athens.   (2) Here too is displayed the anchor from the *Argo*. This object, made of iron, does not look old to me—although it is not the size of modern anchors, and the shape has been altered in some way—but appeared to me of more recent date. But also pointed out were some old fragments of a stone one, and it is rather these, one would guess, which are the remains of the anchor of the *Argo*. But there was no other monument there to the legends about Jason.   (3) In any case, the fort itself, in which 400 select troops are quartered,[32] seemed to me, owing to the nature of its site, to be very secure, and to lie in the most convenient spot for the safety of those who sail this way. In addition, a double ditch has been put round the wall, each ditch as broad as the other.   (4) The wall used to be of earth, and wooden towers were set up above it; now both it and the towers are made of baked brick. And its foundations are firm, and war engines are installed—and in short, it is fully equipped to prevent any of the barbarians from even approaching it, let alone to place those garrisoning it at any risk of a siege.[33]   (5) But since the anchorage for the ships must also be secure, as well as the whole area outside the fort settled by veterans of the army, various merchants and others, I decided to throw out another ditch from the double ditch that surrounds the wall as far as the river, which will enclose both the harbour and the houses outside the walls.

10. From the Phasis, we passed the navigable river Charieis (*Khobi*); there are 90 stades between the two. From the Charieis, we sailed on another 90 stades to the river Chobos (*Inguri*), and there we anchored. The reason for this, and what we did there, my

---

[30] The Phasis was navigable even by large vessels for 38½ miles: Pliny 6. iv. 13.

[31] Rhea was the wife and sister of Kronos and the mother of the gods, and often identified with the Phrygian earth-goddess Kybele, who was assimilated into the official cult of the Roman empire by Claudius.

[32] 'Select troops' could denote auxiliaries (e.g. Xen. *Anab.* 3. 4. 3; Polyb. 6. 26. 6–8), but probably here refers to the governor's *singulares* or personal guard.

[33] The fortifications described here are unusually strong, and the presence of artillery is unexpected in a frontier fort. It is unclear what threat these measures were designed to counter; the Iberian king Pharasmenes (see 11. 2 below) has been suggested by Speidel 2016.

letter in Latin will explain to you.³⁴ (2) From the Chobos, we passed the navigable river Sigames (*Galizga*); it is approximately 210 stades from the Chobos. After the Sigames is the river Tarsouras (*Tanoush*); there are 120 stades between the two. The river Hippos (*Horse*) is 150 stades beyond the Tarsouras, and the Astelephos 30 beyond the Hippos.³⁵ (3) Leaving behind the Astelephos, we came to Sebastopolis (*Sukhumi*) before midday, having set out from the Chobos and having done 120 stades since the Astelephos, so that we could give the soldiers their pay on the same day, and inspect the horses and weapons, the horsemen leaping on to their mounts,³⁶ the sick and the supplies, and also make a tour of the fort and the ditch. (4) It is 630 stades from the Chobos to Sebastopolis; from Trapezous to Sebastopolis it is 2,260. Sebastopolis used to be called Dioskourias, and is a colony of the Milesians.³⁷

11. We passed the following nations. The Kolchoi border on the Trapezountines, just as Xenophon says.³⁸ And the people he records as being most warlike and hostile towards the Trapezountines, he calls Drillai, but I think they are actually the Sannoi.³⁹ For they too are very warlike, even to this day, (2) and are extremely hostile to the Trapezountines, live in fortified places, and are a nation (*ethnos*) without a king. They were also formerly liable for tribute to the Romans, although, being pirates, they are not anxious to pay their tribute. But nowadays, God willing, they will be, or we will crush them. After them come the Machelones and the Heniochoi; their king is Anchialos.⁴⁰ Coming after the Machelones and the Heniochoi are the Zydreitai; they are subject to Pharasmanes. After the Zydreitai are the Lazoi; the king of the Lazoi is Malassas, who holds his kingdom from you. (3) After the Lazoi come the Apsilai; their king is Ioulianos (*Julian*), and he holds his kingdom from your father.⁴¹ The Abaskoi⁴² border on the Apsilai; the king of the Abaskoi is Rhesmagas, and this man,

---

³⁴ A.'s activity, presumably diplomatic, was clearly too sensitive for a general readership, and is left to the confidential official report of his tour. Vespasian's forces had cornered Aniketos, who had fomented a rebellion in Pontos on behalf of Vitellius and had sought the protection of a local king, at the river Chobos in 68/9 (Tacitus, *Hist.* 3. 47–8).

³⁵ The Astelephos and the Hippos may be the two mouths of the *Kodor*, separated by a low island.

³⁶ Horsemen leaping onto their mounts as they galloped by was the climax of the series of drills described by A. in his *Taktika* (43. 3), and must have been immensely difficult, particularly before the invention of stirrups. Under the name of *kelēs*, racing with dismounts was a well-established part of Greek cavalry training: see Christesen 2019 for its importance in C4 BC and later Sparta.

³⁷ The colony of Dioskourias was still a flourishing town in Strabo's time (11. 2. 16, C497–8), but a generation later Pliny 6. v. 15 describes it as abandoned, and places the fort of Sebastopolis 30 miles further N along the coast. The town of *Sukhumi* now stands on the site.

³⁸ The Kolchoi, according to Hdt. 2. 104–5, were of Egyptian origin, being the remnants of the army of the legendary pharaoh Sesostris. Though the term is sometimes used as a blanket name for all the tribes of the region, A. distinguishes a separate tribe of that name.

³⁹ Another reference to Xenophon's expedition, this time the battle of Feb. 400 BC, in which the Ten Thousand fought with the Trapezountines against the Drillai (*Anab.* 5. 2). Strabo 12. 3. 18, C548, and Pliny 6. iv. 12 and 14, also record the Sannoi, but the former equates them with the Makrones, and the latter with the Heniochoi, recorded by A. as a distinct group here.

⁴⁰ See n. 25 above.

⁴¹ Nothing is known of King Ioulianos, though his name suggests he was a Roman citizen, and perhaps that he had received his crown from Trajan at Satala in 114.

⁴² The name of the Abaskoi lives on in that of Abkhazia, the troubled NW extremity of mod. Georgia; this is their first appearance in recorded history.

too, holds his kingdom from you. After the Abaskoi come the Sanigai, where Sebastopolis was founded: the king of the Sanigai is Spadagas, who holds his kingdom from you.[43]   (4) As far as Apsaros we were sailing towards the east, in the right-hand part of the Pontos, and Apsaros seemed to me to be the limit of the length of the Pontos; for from there our voyage was northwards as far as the river Chobos, and beyond the Chobos to the Sigames. From the Sigames we veered towards the left-hand flank of the Pontos as far as the river Hippos.   (5) From the Hippos to the Astelephos and Dioskourias, we clearly sailed directly towards the left of the Pontos, and our voyage was into the setting sun; then, turning from the Astelephos towards Dioskourias, we saw the Caucasus mountain, which is just as high as the Keltic Alps. And one summit of the Caucasus—the summit called Strobilos—was pointed out, where, legend has it, Prometheus was hung up by Hephaistos, as instructed by Zeus.[44]

ANTI-CLOCKWISE 'FLASHBACK' FROM BYZANTION TO TRAPEZOUS

12. The coast from the Thracian Bosporos as far as Trapezous is like this.   (2) The sanctuary (*Hieron*) of Zeus Ourios[45] is 120 stades from Byzantium, and it is here that the so-called mouth of the Pontos is narrowest, where it enters the Propontis. These things that I tell you, you already know.[46]   (3) But on sailing from Hieron to the right,[47] there is the river Rhebas (*Riva Kalesi*); it is 90 stades from the sanctuary of Zeus. Thereafter, Cape Melaina (*Dark*; *Kara Burunu*), as it is called, is 150 stades away. From Cape Melaina to the river Artane (*Kuzgun*), where there is an anchorage for small vessels near the sanctuary of Aphrodite, it is another 150.   (4) From the Artane to the river Psilis (*Gök Su*) it is 150; small boats might be anchored near the rock that emerges not far from the outlet of the river. From there to Kalpes Limen (*Kerpe Limani*) it is 210 stades.   (5) Of Kalpes Limen, of the nature of the place and of its anchorage, of the spring there of cold, pure water, and of the forest, infested with wild beasts, of shipbuilding wood near the sea, Xenophon the Elder spoke.[48]

---

[43] This phrase offers an insight into the fluid dynamics between the tribes of the region. Writing a century before A., Strabo puts Dioskourias in the territory of the Kolchoi (11. 2. 14, C497); Pomponius Mela, in about AD 43, locates it in the territory of the Heniochoi (1. 111); Pliny places it under the control of the Melanchlaeni and Coraxi (6. iv. 15); and here A. has it in Sanigai country.

[44] The name of the peak is not attested in any other ancient author, but the location of Prometheus' punishment in the Caucasus, at the extremity of the known world, goes back to Aeschylus' *Prometheus Unbound*.

[45] Mentioned again at 25. 4 below.

[46] Hadrian knew Bithynia from his travels, but there is no evidence that he visited this shore of the Black Sea. This part of the coast though was very well documented, having been part of the Graeco-Roman world for centuries.

[47] 'Sailing to the right', or anticlockwise, had been predominant in the *periplous* tradition since Artemidoros in C1l–C1e.

[48] Xen. *Anab*. 6. 4. 3–6.

13. From Kalpes Limen to the Rhoë (*'Stream'*; *Kumkagız Dere*), where there is an anchorage for small ships, 20 stades. From Rhoë to the small island of Apollonia (*Kefken Adası*),[49] a short distance from the mainland, is another 20. There is a harbour at the bottom of the islet. From there to Chelai is also 20 stades. 180 from Chelai is where the river Sangarios (*Sakarya*) flows into the Pontos. (2) From there to the mouth of the Hypios (*Büyuk Melen Çayı*) is another 180. To the trading-place of Lilaion (*Akçakoca*) from the Hypios is 100 stades, and from Lilaion to (*the?*) Elaion (*Aftun Deresı?*) is 60. From there to Kalēs (*Alaplı*), (3) another trading-place, is 120. From Kalēs to the river Lykos (*Gülüç Çay?*) is 80, and from the Lykos to the city of Herakleia (*Ereğli*), a Hellenic, Dorian one and a colony of the Megarians, is 100 stades. In Herakleia there is an anchorage for ships. From Herakleia to the so-called Metroön is 80 stades. (4) From there to the Posideion is 40, and from there to Tyndaridai 45, and 15 from there to the Nymphaion.[50] From the Nymphaion to the river Oxinas (*Ilık Su*) is 30. And from the Oxinas to Sandarake (*Zonguldak*), 90. (5) Sandarake is an anchorage for small ships. From there to Krenides (*Kilimli*), 60. From Krenides to the trading-place of Psylla (*Çatal Ağzi*), 30. From there to Tios (*Filyos/Hisarönü*), a Hellenic, Ionian city built on the sea, another colony of the Milesians, 90. From Tios to the river Billaios (*Filyos Çayı/Yenice Ç.*), 20 stades. From the Billaios to the river Parthenios (*Bartin Çayı*) is 100 stades. Up to here live the Bithynian Thracians, of whom Xenophon also made mention in his writings,[51] to the effect that they were the most warlike people in Asia, and that it was in their territory that the Hellenic army suffered most of their hardships after the Arkadians had been separated from the portion of Cheirisophos and Xenophon.

14. From here onwards is Paphlagonia. From the Parthenios to the Hellenic city of Amastris (*Amasra*) is 90 stades; it is an anchorage for ships. From there to Erythinoi, 60. And from Erythinoi (*by Çakraz Burunu*) to Kromna (*Korç Şile/Tekeönü*), another 60. (2) From there to Kytoros (*Kidros*), 90; there is an anchorage for ships in Kytoros. And from Kytoros to Aigialoi (*Karaagaç Limanı*), 60. (3) To Thymena (*Timne*), 90. And to Karambis (*C. Kerempe*), 120. From there to Zephyrion (*near Doganyurt*), 60. From Zephyrion to Abonou Teichos (*Inebolu*), a little city, 150. The anchorage is not secure for ships; though they could ride at anchor (*saleuoien*) without harm, unless a large storm occurred. From Abonou Teichos to Aiginetes (*Hacıveli Burunu*), another 150. From there to the trading-place of Kinolis (*Ginoğlu*), another 60; and at Kinolis ships could ride at anchor (*saleuoien*) in the season of the year. (4) From Kinolis to Stephane (*Usta Burunu*), 180; there is a safe anchorage for ships. From Stephane to Potamoi (*by Cebelit Burunu*), 150. From there to Cape Lepte (*İnce Burunu*), 120. From

---

[49] Known as Thynias in Pliny (5. xliv. 151), Ps.-Skylax (§92) and Ap. Rhod. (2. 672), who tells of an encounter there between the Argonauts and Apollo; hence, presumably, the name used by Arrian. Also, it seems, known in ancient times as Daphnousia, the contemporary names being given in the margin of MS P and in *Eux.* §6.

[50] The four places just named were probably local sanctuaries.   [51] Xen. *Anab.* 6. 4. 1.

Cape Lepte to Armene (*Ak Limanı*), 60; there is a harbour there. Xenophon also mentions Armene.⁵² (5) And from there to Sinope (*Sinop*) is 40 stades; the Sinopeans are colonists of the Milesians. From Sinope to Karousa (*Gerze*), 150; there is a roadstead (*salos*) for ships. From there to Zagara (*Çayağzi*) is again another 150; from there to the river Halys (*Kızıl Irmak*) is 300.⁵³

15. This river was of old the boundary between the kingdoms of Kroisos (*Croesus*) and of the Persians, and now flows under Roman rule—not from the south, as Herodotos says, but from the rising sun. And there, where it flows into the Pontos, it separates the territories of the Sinopeans and the Amisenians. (2) From the river Halys to Naustathmos, where there is a lagoon, is 90 stades. From there to Konopeion (*Mosquito Place*),⁵⁴ another lake (or 'harbour'), again 50. From Konopeion to Eusene, 120. (3) From there to Amisos (*Samsun*), 160. Amisos, a Hellenic city and a colony of the Athenians, is built on the sea. From Amisos to the harbour at Ankon, where the Iris (*Yeşil Irmak*) flows into the Pontos, is 160 stades. From the outflow of the Iris to Herakleion (*at Caltı Burunu*), 360; it is an anchorage for ships. From there to the river Thermodon (*Terme Suyu*), 40. This Thermodon is where, they say, the Amazons lived.

16. From the Thermodon to the river Beris (*Miliç Suyu*) is 90 stades. From there to the river Thoaris (*Zindan Dere*), 60. From the Thoaris to the Oinoë (*Ünye Dere*), 30. From the Oinoë to the river Phigamous (*Yevis Dere?*) 40. From there to the fort of Phadisane (*Fatsa*), 150. From there to the city of Polemonion⁵⁵ is 10 stades. From Polemonion to the so-called Cape Iasonion (*Yasun Burunu*) is 130 stades. From there (3) to the Island of the Kilikians (*Hoynat Kale*) is 15 stades. From the Island of the Kilikians to Boön (*Persembe/Vona*), 75. In Boön there is an anchorage for ships. From there to Kotyora (*Ordu*), 90. Xenophon mentions this town, and says that it was a colony of the Sinopeans; now it is a village, and not a large one. From Kotyora to the river Melanthios (*Melet Irmak*), is about 60 stades. From there to the Pharmatenos (*Bazar Suyu*), another river, 150. (4) And from there to Pharnakeia (*Giresun*), 120. This Pharnakeia used to be called Kerasous,⁵⁶ and was another colony of the Sinopeans. From there to the island of Aretias,⁵⁷ 30. From there to Zephyrion (*Çam Burunu*), 120; there is an anchorage (*Zefre Liman*) for ships. From Zephyrion to Tripolis (*Tirebolu*) is 90 stades. From there to the Argyria ('*Silver Mines*')⁵⁸ is 20 stades.

---

⁵² Xen. *Anab*. 6. 1. 15.

⁵³ A. highlights another resonant landmark of Cl Greece now incorporated into the Roman world: the Halys was the river King Kroisos (*Croesus*) of Lydia crossed to invade Persia, in his misinterpretation of the famous oracle that foretold the destruction of a great empire (Hdt. 1. 53, 72–5).

⁵⁴ This, like Naustathmos and Eusene, is not definitely identified, though the mosquitoes fit the marshy area E of the Halys.

⁵⁵ Earlier Sidē (Strabo 12. 3. 16, C548); renamed after either Polemon I (r. 38–8 BC) or Polemon II (AD 38–64) of Kappadokia.

⁵⁶ It was renamed Pharnakeia after the king of that name in or after 183 BC, and again Kerasous from AD 64. For discussion of the changing toponyms and sites, see Liddle 117.

⁵⁷ Unlocated.   ⁵⁸ At *Halkavala*.

(5) From the Argyria to Philokaleia, 90. From there to Koralla, 100. From Koralla to the Sacred Mountain (*Yoros Burunu*), 150. From the Sacred Mount to Kordyle (*near Akçakale*), 40; there is an anchorage for ships. (6) From Kordyle to Hermonassa (*Akçaabat*), 45; here too is an anchorage. From Hermonassa to Trapezous is 60 stades. There you are building a harbour;[59] for of old there was an anchorage where one could ride at anchor (*aposaleuein*) only in the season of the year.

17. The distances from Trapezous as far as Dioskourias are already given by the measurements between the rivers. They amount collectively, from Trapezous to Dioskourias, now called Sebastopolis, to 2,260 stades.

ANTI-CLOCKWISE FROM DIOSKOURIAS–SEBASTOPOLIS TO BYZANTION

(2) Thus, then, is the voyage sailing to the right[60] from Byzantion to Dioskourias, the camp which is the limit of Roman control when one sails to the right of the Pontos. (3) But when I heard that Kotys, king of the so-called Kimmerian Bosporos, had died,[61] I decided that it was my duty to explain the voyage as far as the Bosporos[62] to you, so that, if you were planning something with regard to the Bosporos, you would be able to plan it without being ignorant of the voyage.

18. For those who have set out from Dioskourias, then, the first anchorage would be at Pityous (*Pitzunda*); it is 350 stades. From there it is 150 stades to Nitike (*Gagra?*), where a Skythian tribe used to live of old, of whom the writer Herodotos makes mention.[63] (2) He says that they are the eaters of fir-cones (*or 'lice'*); and still people hold that opinion concerning them. From Nitike to the river Abaskos is 90 stades. And the Borgys[64] is 120 stades distant from the Abaskos, and the Nesis 60 from the Borgys, which also has Cape Herakleion (*C. Adler?*). (3) From the Nesis to Masaitike (*Matsesta*) is 90 stades. From there to the Achaious (*R. Sochi*) is 60 stades, which river separates the Zilchoi and the Sanigai. King of the Zilchoi is Stachemphax; and he holds his kingdom from you. From the Achaious to Herakleia Point (*Mys Kodosh?*)

---

[59] The remains of an ancient harbour wall, now largely submerged, known as the Molos, are associated with Hadrian's harbour, another legacy of the emperor's visit (see ch. 1 above).
[60] See n. 36 above.
[61] Kotys II was client ruler of the Bosporan kingdom in what is now Crimea from 123/4 until his death in the year 131/2. As Kotys, or Tiberius Julius Cotys, was a Roman citizen who called himself 'friend of Caesar and friend of Rome', A. was well aware of the importance of his kingdom for control of both the Bosporan corn supply and the barbarian tribes between Crimea and the Danube. In the event, Kotys' successor, (Ti. Julius) Rhoimetalkes I, dedicated a statue to Hadrian on his accession and was also an assiduous friend of Rome until his own death in 153/4.
[62] The first phrase refers to both the sections of the anti-clockwise circuit—the first from Trapezous to Dioskourias (1–11), the second the 'flashback' from Byzantion to Trapezous (12–16). We now resume the anti-clockwise circuit from Dioskourias–Sebastopolis round the N and W Black Sea as far as Byzantion; but this time the voyage is not an eye-witness account of A.'s own travel, but a second-hand 'journey' based on oral and written sources (cf. 19. 3, 23. 3 below).
[63] Hdt. 4. 109. [64] Unlocated.

is 150 stades.⁶⁵ From there to the cape (*Mys Gryaznova?*) which is a shelter from the Thraskias (*NNW wind*) and Boreas (*NNE wind*), 180. (4) From there to Palaia (*Old*) Lazike, as it is called, is 120 stades. From there to Palaia (*Old*) Achaia, 150;⁶⁶ and from there to Pagra Limen (*Gelendzhik?*), 350. From Pagra Limen to the Sacred Harbour (*Novorossisk*), 180. From there to Sindike, 300.⁶⁷

19. From Sindike to the so-called Kimmerian Bosporos and city of Pantikapaion (*Kerch'*) on the Bosporos, 540. From there to the river Tanaïs (*Don*), which is said to divide Europe from Asia, 60.⁶⁸ And it starts from the Maiotis lake (*Sea of Azov*), and flows into the sea of the Euxeinos Pontos. (2) Aeschylus, however, in *Prometheus Unbound*, makes the Phasis the boundary of Europe and Asia. In his play the Titans, at any rate, tell Prometheus:

> We have come, Prometheus, to witness
> Your struggle, and your torment in chains.⁶⁹

Then they recount the lands they have come through:

> Where the soils of Europe and Asia
> have a twin limit in the great Phasis.

(3) It is said that the circumnavigation round the Maiotis lake is about 9,000 stades.⁷⁰ From Pantikapaion to the village of Kazeka (*Katschik*), which is built on the sea, is 420 stades. From there to Theodosia (*Feodosiya*), a deserted city,⁷¹ is 280 stades. (4) It used to be a Hellenic, Ionian city, a colony of the Milesians, and there is a mention of it in many works. From there to the deserted harbour (*Sudak*) of the Skythotauroi is 200 stades; and from there to Lampas (*Biyuk Lambat*) in Taurike is 600 stades. (5) From Lampas to the harbour of the Symbola⁷² (*in the bay of Balaklava*), also in Tauris, is 520 stades. And from there to the Taurike Cherronesos,⁷³ 180. From Cherronesos to Kerkinitis (*near Evpatoria*)⁷⁴ is 600 stades, and from Kerkinitis to Kalos Limen (*Good Harbour; Chernomorskoye*), also in Skythia, another 700.

---

⁶⁵ For the possible identification of this and the next cape, see Liddle 121–2.
⁶⁶ Palaia Lazike and P. Achaia are in the area of the anchorages at *Tenginskaya* and *Gelendzhik*.
⁶⁷ Sindike is a region rather than a city; cf. Strabo 11. 2. 10, C495, who situates its main settlement at Gorgippia, 'near the sea'.
⁶⁸ A. does not commit to either the Phasis (8. 1–5) or the Tanaïs as the beginning of Asia.
⁶⁹ Aeschylus' *Promethus Unbound* is lost; these lines appear to come at the very beginning of the play.
⁷⁰ An indication of the second-hand sources A. is using for this part of the *Periplous*. Strabo 2. 5. 23, C125, uses the same figure; Polybios 4. 39 is closer with 8,000 st. Pliny 4. xii. 78 gives the circumference as 1,406 miles, almost double the real size of the Sea of Azov.
⁷¹ Theodosia was founded in C6e. There is no other evidence that it was deserted when A. was writing, and plenty, literary and archaeological, to indicate that it was flourishing. A. could be referring to a temporary abandonment after a barbarian raid, or relying on an old source going back to the destruction of the city by Polemon I of Pontos in C1.
⁷² Reading Συμβόλων λιμήν with Radt. *Symbola* are usually tokens, sometimes treaties.
⁷³ Or Chersonesos; the *Crimea* in mod. Ukraine. ⁷⁴ For the identification, see Liddle 125.

20. From Kalos Limen to Tamyrake,⁷⁵ 300; within Tamyrake there is a lake, which is not large. From there to the outflow of the lake, another 300. From the outflow of the lake to Eïones⁷⁶ (*'Beaches'; Tendrovskiy Point*) is 380 stades. From there to the river Borysthenes (*Dnieper*), 150.   (2) On the Borysthenes, as one sails upstream, a Hellenic city called Olbia (*Parutino*) has been created. From the Borysthenes to a small island, deserted and nameless (*Berezan*), is 60 stades. And from there to Odessos,⁷⁷ 80. In Odessos there is an anchorage for ships. After Odessos comes the harbour of the Istrianoi (*Luzanovka?*).   (3) It is 250 stades to there. After there comes the harbour of the Isiakoi (*Odessa*). It is 150 stades to there. And from there to the mouth of the Istros (*Danube*) called Psilon, 1,200. The places between are deserted and nameless.⁷⁸

21. Just about opposite this mouth—straight across the open sea (*pelagos*), especially when you sail with the Aparktias wind—lies an island beside it, which some call Achilles' Island (*Zmiinyi*), others Dromos Achilleos (*Achilles' Racetrack*),⁷⁹ and others still Leuke (*White*) because of its colour. Thetis is said to have set it up for her son, and that Achilles lived there. And there is a temple of Achilles there, and a wooden image (*xoanon*) of ancient workmanship.⁸⁰   (2) The island is deserted of humans, but a few goats live there—they say that those who put in there dedicate one to Achilles—and there are many other votive offerings set up in the temple—bowls and rings and rather costly stones. All these thank-offerings are laid up for Achilles, as well as inscriptions, some made in the Roman way (*i.e. in Latin*), some in the Greek way, in one metre or in another, praising Achilles;⁸¹   (3) and there are some for Patroklos too, for those who wish to please Achilles also honour Patroklos along with him.⁸² Many birds also nest on the island—gulls, great and small shearwaters,⁸³ and cormorants in an innumerable

---

[75] Tamyrake corresponds to the long strip of land known in antiquity as Dromos Achilleos, 'Achilles' Racetrack'. At 21. 1, A. mistakenly gives that as an alternative name for Achilles' Island, or Leuke; cf. *Eux.* §87, where it is correctly a beach or shore, but also §93 where Arr.'s error is repeated.

[76] On *Tendra* island.

[77] Unlocated, though clearly E of the large mod. city of *Odesa* to which it has given its name; not to be confused with the Odessos at 24. 4.

[78] Arr. is wrong again: this stretch of coast includes the mouth of the major river Tyras (*Dniester*), and the city of the same name (Strabo 7. 3. 16, C305–6), in the Roman province of Lower Moesia. See Liddle 127–8.

[79] See n. on 20. 1 Tamyrake. It is clear that several locations in the NW corner of the Black Sea had a strong association with Achilles, including *Berezan* (the 'deserted and nameless' island mentioned by A. at 20. 2) and the city of Olbia, which housed the cult of Achilles Pontarchos, 'lord of the Pontos'.

[80] The temple is first mentioned in Euripides' *Andromache* (1259–62), and attested to by several authors including Dio Chrysostom in C1 AD (*Orat.* 36. 21–3) and Pausanias in C2 AD (3. 19. 11–13). The remains of a temple on *Zmiinyi* were investigated by a Russian sea-captain in 1823 but obliterated shortly after by the construction of a lighthouse, and its identification with the temple of Achilles is uncertain.

[81] See Robert 1960, 274, for the few (Greek) inscriptions found on *Zmiinyi*.

[82] The double cult echoes that of Hermes and Philesios at Trapezous (2. 2 above).

[83] On Achilles' afterlife in the Black Sea, see S. R. West 2003, esp. 162–4 on Leuke I. and Achilles' cult there. On the possible identification of these two bird species, *aithuia* and *korōnis thalassia*, see Thompson 1936, 27–9, 172–3, to which Prof. West drew my attention. On birds washing temples, cf. Juba 11.

quantity. (4) These birds attend to the temple of Achilles. Each morning they fly down to the sea; then, having wetted their wings in the sea, they quickly fly up again to the temple, and sprinkle the temple. When this has been done thoroughly, they beautify the pavement, again with their wings.

22. There are also those who report this: that of those who have put in to the island, the ones who deliberately sail there bring offerings on board their ships, and sacrifice some of them and set the rest free for Achilles; (2) whereas others are forced to put in by a storm, and ask for a victim from the god himself, whom they consult regarding the sacrifices—whether it is better and preferable for them to sacrifice whatever grazing animal they have taken, according to their liking—while depositing the value which seems appropriate to them. (3) And if the oracle—for oracles are given at the temple—should refuse, they add to that sum; if it should still refuse, still they add; and when it agrees, they know that that sum is sufficient. (4) The victim then stands there of its own accord, and no longer tries to escape. And this is why there is so much money laid up to the hero as payment for the victims.

23. It is also said that Achilles appears in dreams to those who put in to the island, and to those who sail by when they are not far from it, and shows them where the best place on the island to put in is, and where to anchor. And others say that Achilles has appeared to them when awake, on their sail or on the tip of the prow, like the Dioskouroi; (2) they say that Achilles is only inferior to the Dioskouroi in that the Dioskouroi appear visibly to sailors everywhere, and having appeared they behave as saviours, whereas he appears only to those already approaching the island. (3) They also say that they have seen Patroklos in dreams. These things that I have recorded about Achilles' Island are reports from those who have either put in there, or have learned it from others, and they do not seem incredible to me. (4) For I myself believe that Achilles was a hero second to none, on the evidence of his nobility, beauty, and strength of soul; his early departure from mankind; Homer's poem to him; and the love and friendship because of which he wanted to die after his beloved.[84]

24. From the mouth of the Istros called Psilon to the second mouth is 60 stades.[85] From there to the mouth called Kalon (*Good*) is 40 stades, and from Kalon to Narakon, as the fourth mouth of the Istros is called, it is 60 stades. (2) From there to the fifth, 120; and from there to the city of Istria (*or Istros*), 500 stades. From there to the city of Tomis (*Costanţa*) is 300 stades. (3) From Tomis to the city of Kallatis (*Mangalia*) is another 300; there is an anchorage for ships. From there to Karōn Limen[86] (*Nos Shabla*), 180; and the land in a circle around the harbour is called Karia. From Karōn Limen to Tetrisias (*Nos Kaliakra*) is 120 stades. (4) From there to Bizone, a

---

[84] The relationship between Achilles and Patroklos recalls that between Hadrian and Antinoös, the emperor's favourite, who had drowned in the Nile in 130, only a year or two before the composition of the *Periplous*. Arrian subtly reinforces the comparison, elevating Patroklos by making him appear with Achilles in visions to sailors (a detail not attested elsewhere), and emphasizing the nobility of Achilles' grief.

[85] For these multiple mouths of the *Danube*, see Liddle 127, 131.   [86] Lit. 'Karians' Harbour'.

deserted spot,[87] is 60 stades. From Bizone to Dionysopolis (*Balchik*) is 80 stades. From there to Odessos (*Varna*) is 200;[88] there is an anchorage for ships. From Odessos to the foothills of Haimos,[89] which falls right down to the Pontos, is 360 stades; and here there is an anchorage for ships. (5) From Haimos to the city of Mesembria (*Nesebur*), 90; there is an anchorage for ships. And from Mesembria to the city of Anchialos is 70 stades; and from Anchialos to Apollonia (*Sozopol*), 180. (6) This is all of the Hellenic cities founded in Skythia, on the left-hand side as one sails into the Pontos. From Apollonia to Cherronesos[90] is 60 stades; there is an anchorage for ships. And from Cherronesos to Aulaiou Teichos (*Akhtopol*), 250. From there to the headland of Thynias (*Tunny*; mod. *Koru Burunu*), 120.

25. From Thynias to Salmydessos (*Midye*) is 200 stades. Xenophon the Elder makes mention of this place:[91] it was to here, he says, that the army of the Hellenes came which he led when he campaigned for the last time with Seuthes the Thracian. (2) And he wrote much concerning the lack of harbours in that place, how ships are wrecked there when hit by storms, and how the neighbouring Thracians fight among themselves over the wreckage. (3) From Salmydessos to Phrygia (*Kara Burunu*)[92] is 330 stades. From there to the Kyaneai, 320. These Kyaneai are those that the poets say once used to wander, and through which the first ship to pass was the *Argo* when it carried Jason to Kolchis.[93] (4) From the Kyaneai to the Sanctuary (*Hieron*) of Zeus Ourios, where the mouth of the Pontos lies,[94] is 40 stades. From there to the harbour of Daphne, called Mainomene (*The Mad*), is 40 stades. From Daphne to Byzantion, 80. These, then, are the things from the so-called Kimmerian Bosporos to Thrace and the city of Byzantion.

---

[87] For details of its successive locations, see Liddle 132.   [88] Distinct from the Odessos at 20. 2.
[89] The vast range of *Stara Planina* or Great Balkan.
[90] Not certainly located; the place-name, meaning 'peninsula', is common.
[91] Xen. *Anab.* 7. 5. 12–13.   [92] A headland, not the region of central N. Turkey.
[93] The Kyaneai ('dark') rocks, also known as the Symplegades, guarded the passage from the Bosporos into the Black Sea. In mythology they clashed together, crushing passing ships between them. The *Argo*, however, passed through them safely, with the help of Athena, and the rocks were thereafter fixed in place (Ap. Rhod. 2. 317–40, 549–606).
[94] Already mentioned at 12. 2 in the description of the outward journey from Byzantion. Both the sanctuary of Zeus Ourios (*Anadolu Kavağı*) and the harbour of Daphne are on the Asian side of the Bosporos.

28

DIONYSIOS PERIEGETES

(DIONYSIOS OF ALEXANDRIA)

(WRITTEN AD 130–8)

Yumna Z. N. Khan*

INTRODUCTION

THE AUTHOR

The *Oikoumenes periegesis* (*Guided Tour of the Inhabited World*) attributed to Dionysios of Alexandria was probably more popular, among the educated classes of late antiquity and the medieval period, than any other work in this volume, judging by the number of copies that survive. It was probably the first work of ancient geography to be printed in the original Greek (at Ferrara in 1512) rather than in a Latin translation.[1] It comprises nearly 1,200 hexameters in Homeric dialect, outlining the geography of the world as known to the Greeks and Romans in the first half of the 2nd century AD. In accordance with the title of the work, the author has received the sobriquet Periegetes, 'guide'.

He is named in an acrostic in lines 109–34 that also identifies him as Alexandrian ('My (*book?*), by Dionysios, (*one*) of those within Pharos'). The acrostic is one of two discovered within the poem in the late 19th century by Leue,[2] though the author had always been known as Dionysios. The second, in lines 513–32 ('The god Hermes in the reign of Hadrian'), identifies the work as a product of Hadrian's reign (117–38). The reference to Hermes has been variously explained as, among other things, a proclamation

---

* I would like to offer my sincere and deepest thanks to Graham Shipley for his encouragement and support, his invaluable insights, comments, and suggestions, and his assistance in reworking the lines containing acrostics to reproduce them in English.

[1] Macochius 1512; Greaves 1994, 5. Latin editions had appeared a generation earlier, the first known being Beccaria 1477 (information from 'Incunabula Short Title Catalogue', British Library, last accessed 26 January 2022).

[2] Leue 1884. Leue originally held that the acrostic of ll. 109–34 began ἐμή ('my'), but he later emended μακρὸν to πολλὸν in 110 in order to read the beginning of the acrostic as ἔπη ('epic verses') (Leue 1925). This emendation was first proposed by Nauck 1889, 325. There is no evidence, however, to support altering the text. Indeed, the only reason for adopting any such emendation lies in the difficulty of reading ἐμή as part of the acrostic. C. Wachsmuth 1889 argues that the initial letters of 109–11 were not, in fact, intended to form part of the acrostic. On the acrostics, see further the 'Supplementary note' at the end of this chapter; and Introduction, §X. 4.

of faith in the deified Antinoös (Hadrian's late companion, also alluded to in Arrian's contemporary account of the Black Sea, Chapter 27 above), with a date-stamp intended by Dionysios to place the *Periegesis* at, or not long after, the time of Antinoös' death in 130;[3] a declaration by Dionysios of his own role as a guide to the inhabited world;[4] and an allusion to Hermes' role as creator of, and guide to, the *oikoumenē*.[5]

Little is known about the author beyond what is communicated in the acrostics. A biography transmitted in the 15th-century manuscript Vaticanus Chisianus R. IV. 20, and hence known as the *Vita Chisiana*, provides the fullest extant account.[6] The *Vita Chisiana* tells us that Dionysios was also the name of the poet's father, whom Klotz identified with the Dionysios of Alexandria described in the *Suda* as having lived in the second half of the 1st century AD and as having served as a librarian and imperial secretary.[7] The *Vita Chisiana* also makes Dionysios author of several other works including *Lithiaka* (*On Stones*), *Gigantias* (*Tale of the Giants*), *Bassarika* (*Bacchic Matters*), and *Ornithiaka* (*On Birds*). The *Suda*, however, expresses uncertainty as to whether the author of the *Guided Tour of the Oikoumene in Epic Verses*, whom he makes a Corinthian, is the Dionysios who wrote the *Lithiaka*.[8] No text of a *Lithiaka* ascribed to a Dionysios has survived and, although an interest in stones is certainly shown by the Periegete, it is impossible to say with any certainty that he was in fact the author of a work on the subject. In 1973 Livrea published an edition of the fragments of a *Gigantias* and a *Bassarika* which had previously been ascribed to the Periegete, and convincingly refuted earlier claims that these works were by the same Dionysios on the grounds that the language and style of the poems are quite distinct.[9] As for the *Ornithiaka*, there has survived a prose paraphrase of a poem on birds that is said to have been composed by a certain Dionysios.[10] The nature of the paraphrase makes it difficult, however, to identify the author of the original poem, and this poem is variously identified with the *Ornithiaka* ascribed to the Periegete and with the *Ixeutika* (*On Fowling*) ascribed to Oppian of Apameia.

DIONYSIOS AND THE GEOGRAPHICAL TRADITION

There is no clear indication in the poem as to which geographical sources Dionysios used in composing the *Periegesis*. Similarly, to what extent he relied on earlier geographical texts and to what extent, if any, he innovated upon previous descriptions of the *oikoumenē* is largely difficult to gauge. He appears to have taken his material from more than one source, so that the resulting picture is in some respects original to him.

---

[3] Tsavari 1990, 30–1.   [4] Brodersen 1994a, 10; Jacob 1981, 31–2.   [5] Khan 2002, pp. 10–11.
[6] Two shorter biographies have also survived: one transmitted with the text of the scholia, the other with Eustathios' commentary, on which see p. 767 below.
[7] *Suda* s.v. Dionysios of Alexandria, son of Glaukos (δ 1173). Three bearers of the name are identified in *Suda* as authors of *Oikoumenes periegeseis*: D. of Corinth (δ 1177); D. of Miletos (δ 1180); and D. of Rhodes (δ 1181); but only in the first case does *Suda* specify that the work was a poem in epic Greek.
[8] *Suda* δ 1177 s.v. Dionysios of Corinth.   [9] Livrea 1973, 10.   [10] Garzya 1963.

In the opening verses of the poem Dionysios describes the inhabited world as not quite circular, but wider from east to west[11] than from north to south, like a sling (lines 5–6). The background to this way of characterizing the shape of the inhabited world is somewhat obscure. Poseidonios (15–16 in Chapter 19 above) is cited as having drawn this same comparison,[12] and it may be that Dionysios used him as a source for his geography. However, there is little else in the poem to indicate that this representation of the world was based specifically on Poseidonios, and Dionysios' depiction of the *oikoumenē* later in the poem (271–8) as divided into two cones (*kōnoi*)—their bases joined, one apex pointing east, the other west—finds no parallel in the earlier author.

Berger traced the division of the *oikoumenē* into two *kōnoi* back to the 3rd century BC and Eratosthenes of Kyrene.[13] There are, however, essential differences between Eratosthenes' depiction of the *oikoumenē* and Dionysios', which make it impossible to assert that the former was a source used directly by the latter. Berger also notes that there is some correspondence between Dionysios' representation of Europe and that of Eratosthenes, in that both describe the continent as having three south-facing peninsulas;[14] but again the distinction between Dionysios' definition of these three peninsulas and that of Eratosthenes makes it difficult to tie the two conclusively together.

There are various parallels between the geographies of Dionysios and Strabo, and it has been suggested that Dionysios depended on Strabo to a significant extent.[15] It is in the descriptions of specific regions that these parallels are obvious. The outlines of the Black Sea (146–57), Libyē (174–7), Iberia (287), the Peloponnese (404), and India (1130–1) are each similar to the descriptions of these regions by Strabo. In Strabo there can be found the same comparisons, made by Dionysios, of the Euxine to a Skythian bow (2. 5. 22), of Libyē to a leopard-skin and to a trapezium (2. 5. 33), of Iberia to an oxhide (2. 1. 30), of the Peloponnese to a plane-leaf (ibid.), and of India to a rhombus (2. 1. 22). Strabo, however, does not claim that these comparisons are his own. In fact, he states specifically in the case of India that it was Eratosthenes who drew the country as a rhombus. It is also possible, if not likely, that such comparisons held greater currency at a time when maps were less easily accessible. Thus, with Strabo, as with Poseidonios and Eratosthenes, it is difficult to show direct influence upon Dionysios.

---

[11] D. actually says 'towards the sun's paths', which strictly should mean the ecliptic but here more vaguely connotes the notion of a westward progress across the *oikoumenē*.

[12] Eustathios (Poseidonios 15–16 in Ch. 19 above) notes the parallel between D. and P. See also Agathemeros i. 2.

[13] H. Berger 1903, 432–3.

[14] See the discussion of Eratosthenes fr. III B, 97 = Strabo 2. 4. 8, C108–9, in H. Berger 1964, 342–3.

[15] See Greaves 1994, 61–75. See also Jane L. Lightfoot 2014, 29–33. It is worth remembering, however, that Strabo's *Geography* is not cited before C6 AD, and widespread interest in the work is attested really only from C9 on (Aujac 2000, esp. 134–5).

CONTENTS AND STRUCTURE

Dionysios' *oikoumenē* has a neat and symmetrical structure, which is reflected in the order of the poem itself:

General prologue (1–9): Ocean and continents

Division of continents (10–26)

Ocean (27–169): division into seas (27–57); the Mediterranean (58–168)

Prologue to continents (170–3)

Libyē (174–269): overall form (174–83); Pillars of Herakles to Kyrene (184–210); the interior (211–21); the Nile and Egypt (222–64); summary of remaining peoples (265–9)

Europe (270–446): overall form (270–80): Pillars of Herakles to Rhine (281–97); Danube, north (298–319); Danube, south (319–29); Pillars of Herakles to Greece (330–446)

Islands (447–619): invocation (447–9): Mediterranean islands, Pillars of Herakles to Hellespont (450–537); Hellespont to Maiotis (538–53); islands in the Ocean, clockwise from Pillars of Herakles (555–611); summary of remaining islands (612–19)

Asia (620–1165): overall form (620–51); the north, Tanaïs to Kolchis (652–94); Kolchis to Caspian (695–761); Kolchis to Hellespont (762–98); Hellespont to Syria (799–880); prologue to southern Asia (881–6); the south, its form (887–96); Syria to Arabia (897–961); west of Erythraian sea (962–9); Syria to Persia (970–1079); Persia to Pillars of Dionysos (1080–165)

Epilogue (1166–86)

Virtually all the first half of the poem is dedicated to the two continents that make up the western hemisphere, while the second half is devoted to the eastern, comprising Asia. For almost every subdivision of the *oikoumenē* Dionysios begins his description in the north and then proceeds to describe the south. He makes an exception of the western hemisphere, where he begins in the south with Libyē, his native continent. There is also linear movement from west to east, discernible at various levels within the *Periegesis*. The west–east progression is present both in his description of the two hemispheres and, for example, within the description of Libyē. Dionysios begins by tracing the overall shape of the continent and proceeds to divide it into northern and southern zones. He then describes each in turn in an eastward movement. This same pattern of description is seen in the section on Europe. A west-to-east movement is, of course, typical of geographical texts and seems to go back to the early Ionian *periploi*.[16]

LITERARY MODELS

Dionysios makes no claim to be giving an empirical or scientific account of the inhabited world and its peoples. On the contrary, in a passage just over halfway through the poem he disclaims physical travel, and thereby autopsy and empiricism, asserting that

[16] On spatial orientation in DP, see Ilyushechkina *et al.* 2014.

his knowledge comes directly from the Muses (707–17). Here he highlights the literariness of his work by the very language of his claim, recalling a passage from Hesiod's *Works and Days* (646–53), also imitated in the hellenistic period by Kallimachos (fr. 178. 33 Pfeiffer). By alluding to the Hesiodic passage as he does here, Dionysios is not simply distancing himself from merchants but describing himself first and foremost as a poet. He is also asserting his literary affiliations.

Hesiod's didactic epic is an obvious model for Dionysios' poem as a whole. He borrows language, motifs, and subject matter from both *Works and Days* and *Theogony*. Sometimes he recalls a passage from one or other of these poems in a deliberate allusion to the Hesiodic context, as at 186–94 (cf. *WD* 529–35). More often he echoes the language and rhythm of a particular verse without any obvious direct appeal to its context. On one occasion he cites the name of a river only otherwise attested in Hesiod, the Aldeskos (line 314).

Dionysios' language is largely Homeric. Parallels between the *Periegesis* and the Homeric poems vary widely in form and significance. Dionysios frequently recalls Homeric *clausulae* (end-of-line rhythms recalling those of Homer), at times drawing on the Homeric context, as at 189 (cf. *Od.* 24. 250). Occasionally he echoes longer Homeric passages and can be seen to be drawing on these passages similarly as a means of heightening the significance of his words, as at 341–2 (cf. *Il.* 15. 410–12). Another way in which he points explicitly to the literariness of the *Periegesis* is by alluding to problems perceived in the interpretation of the Homeric texts, as in his reference to the Aithiopes at 179–80 (cf. *Od.* 1. 23–4). Similarly, Dionysios' frequent use of Homeric *hapax legomena* also indicates the literary nature of the *Periegesis*. Rarely he uses a Homeric *hapax* which is not earlier attested elsewhere, such as *auchmēëssa* (182, meaning 'parched'; cf. *Od.* 24. 250 *auchmeis*). More often, however, the *hapax legomena* which are found in Dionysios are also to be found in hellenistic poetry.

Dionysios' debt to the hellenistic poets Kallimachos, Theokritos, Apollonios of Rhodes, Nicander, and Aratos in particular is significant. The imitation of the beginning of Apollonios' *Argonautika* (1. 1–2) in the opening verses of the *Periegesis* (1–3) seems to be indicative of the hellenistic poet's importance for Dionysios, and, as Bowie has pointed out, Apollonios' books on the travels of the Argonauts were an obvious source of material for Dionysios.[17] Dionysios sometimes recalls Apollonios' descriptions of particular places, as at 315 (the Rhipaian mountains, cf. Ap. Rhod. 4. 287), and from time to time imitates Apollonian phrases for places and peoples, as at 185 ('peoples of the Maurousian land', cf. 'customs of the Kianian land', Ap. Rhod. 1. 1177 and elsewhere). More surprisingly, perhaps, some of Dionysios' descriptions of geographical features appear to be modelled upon Nicander's descriptions of snakes, as at 23 and elsewhere with 'creeps' (*herpei*, cf. Nicander, *Theriaka*, 159 etc.) and 286 with 'massifs' (*oronkoi*, cf. Nicander, *Alexipharmaka*, 42). He imitates the didactic language

---

[17] Bowie 2000, 7–8.

of Nicander's epics on snakes and poisons at 238 and elsewhere (*audēsaimi*, 'may I voice', cf. Nicander, *Theriaka*, 770); and of course the acrostic of 112–34 recalls that of *Theriaka* 345–53 ('*Nikandros*').[18] Of all the hellenistic poets Dionysios owes most, however, to Aratos, whose didactic poem on the stars and constellations, like Hesiod's *Works and Days*, provides a model for the *Periegesis* as a whole. Aratos' *Phainomena* (1,154 lines) is of almost the same length as the *Periegesis* and, as Dionysios maps the inhabited world, so Aratos maps the skies. Dionysios' language contains numerous echoes of the *Phainomena*. In some cases similarities between the two poets may stem from a common dependence on the Homeric poems, as at 202 (cf. Aratos 425-6, cf. Homer, *Od.* 5. 331–2). But at times Dionysios seems to have had in mind a specific Aratean imitation of Homer, as at 235 (cf. Aratos 44, cf. Homer, *Il.* 18. 508), and the closing verses of the *Periegesis* are a clear evocation of the opening of Aratos' *Phainomena* specifically.

Moreover, a third acrostic was found in the *Periegesis* recently by Counillon, which seems to affirm the importance of Aratos for Dionysios.[19] The acrostic reads *stenē*, 'slender' (307–11). The initial letter of the acrostic introduces another form of the same word (*steinon*) on the horizontal, suggesting that the acrostic was intentional. Furthermore, the gamma (Γ) pattern thus created is also visible at Aratos, *Phaen.* 783–7, where the word *leptē* ('slim') is found vertically and horizontally. Aratos' acrostic seems to offer something of a programmatic statement, serving to link him with Kallimachos, who claims to have pursued *leptotēs*, 'slimness', in his own poetry (see esp. *Aitia* fr. 1. 23–8), and indeed praises Aratos for his *leptai rhēseis*, 'slim expressions'.[20] In Kallimachos' *Reply to the Telchines* (fr. 1. 1 Pfeiffer) Apollo's address begins with an explicit demand for *leptotēs* and ends with an exhortation to the poet to follow the unworn path, even though it may be *steinoterē*, 'narrower'. It is surely more than coincidental that Dionysios chooses to highlight through his acrostic a word that, like *leptē*, carries echoes of Kallimachos' work. Dionysios seems here to claim for his poem an affiliation with that of Aratos.

It is here proposed to identify a fourth acrostic, and a second of the 'gamma' form, at lines 681–5, which evokes the acrostic at 307–11 and similarly highlights the literary nature of this didactic poem (see 'Supplementary note' following the translation).

The densely allusive and highly literary nature of the poem appears to suggest that it was intended to appeal to a learned adult readership. Thus, although the *Periegesis* was to become popular as a school text, it is unlikely to have been intended as such, as certain scholars have recently tried to suggest it was.[21]

---

[18] For a fuller treatment of Dionysos' debt to Nicander, see Jane L. Lightfoot 2014, esp. 88–9, 108–9.
[19] Counillon 1981.
[20] *Anth. Pal.* 9. 507 = fr. 27. 3-4 in Pfeiffer 1949–53 = Gow and Page 1965, Callimachus 56. On λεπτότης as a literary term see Hutchinson 1988, 77–84, 278–354; Pfeiffer 1968, 136–8.
[21] Jacob 1981, 57–62.

THE MANUSCRIPT TRADITION

The *Oikoumenes periegesis* survives in more than 140 known manuscripts.[22] The earliest of these, Parisinus suppl. gr. 388 (A), is dated to the 10th century. The most recent critical edition of the text, by Brodersen, is based almost entirely on the readings of A, which he describes as the 'oldest preserved manuscript and likewise the most valuable'.[23]

Tsavari collated 134 manuscripts in preparing her edition of the text. She, like Brodersen, trusts heavily in A, and shows a tendency to privilege chronological priority over other criteria in determining the value of the manuscripts, which is reflected also in her decision to report readings from only those 44 that antedate the 15th century.[24] Tsavari claims to have used as a basis for her edition of the text the 1861 edition by Müller,[25] the first to report the readings of A.[26] Where Tsavari differs from Müller it is almost always to follow A.

Tsavari's trust in A rests largely on the argument that it was copied from a Roman archetype and was not subject to the contamination suffered by the vast majority of the surviving manuscripts which, she argues, belong to a separate tradition, descended from one lost source in Constantinople.[27] According to Tsavari the only extant manuscript to have descended from A is Vaticanus gr. 910 (V⁹), which she dates to the beginning of the 14th century. Counillon, however, has pointed out that the double readings which Tsavari herself admits are transmitted by A[28] indicate that A also shows signs of contamination;[29] he goes on to reject the idea of an early Roman edition altogether,[30] and concludes by rightly questioning Tsavari's assumption of the superiority of the testimony of A in establishing the text.[31] The stemma constructed by Tsavari has also been criticized by Reeve, who has shown that Tsavari has inadequately defined the relationships between a number of manuscripts.[32] Therefore, although I have used

---

[22] See Amato 2005, 176–8.

[23] 'ältesten erhaltenen und zugleich wertvollsten Handschrift', Brodersen 1994a, 147. (Jane L. Lightfoot 2014 includes a selective *apparatus criticus* but does not claim to offer a full critical edition; see her p. 197.)

[24] See also Nicolai 1992, esp. 481: 'non sembra aver tenuto presente il principio pasqualiano dei *recentiores non deteriores* (per i manoscritti dei secc. XV e XVI esamina soltanto dei campioni di testo e dichiara di non tenerne conto nell'edizione: cosi a p. 443)'.

[25] Müller, *GGM* ii. 103–76.   [26] Tsavari 1990, 22.

[27] Tsavari 1990, esp. 43–7, 212–17.   [28] Tsavari 1990, 45.

[29] Counillon 1991, esp. 368: 'en admettant l'existence de ces doubles leçons, elle renonce à la "pureté remarquable" de sa tradition romaine, et reconnaît que l'ancêtre de toute la tradition lui-meme était déjà fortement contaminé, ce qui entache terriblement ses conclusions'.

[30] 'Il faut donc renoncer au mythe inutile de la "Recension Romaine" et chercher l'ancêtre commun de toute la tradition à Constantinople' (Counillon 1991, 371).

[31] Counillon 1991, 371: 'Quant à l'etablissement du texte, on ne peut se contenter de s'en remettre à A [...] Il serait sans doute beaucoup plus profitable d'analyser de plus près le Vaticanus 910 et sa constitution. Tant que cela ne sera pas fait on n'aura pas des meilleures raisons de choisir l'une ou l'autre leçon que celles qu'avaient nos prédécesseurs, depuis le premier copiste jusqu'à K. Müller'.

[32] See Reeve 1992; Reeve 1994.

Tsavari's edition as the basis for my commentary and translation, I also list (in n. 41 below) those variant readings I have preferred.

SCHOLIA, COMMENTARIES, TRANSLATIONS, ETC.

Two Latin verse translations provide some suggestion of the early popularity of the *Periegesis*, the one by Avienus (or Avienius) in the 4th century (the *Descriptio orbis terrae* or *terrarum*) and the other by Priscianus (Priscian) Caesariensis (called *Periegesis*) in the 6th.[33] Tsavari argues that Avienus and Priscian based their translations on different manuscripts, which indeed seems to be borne out by differences in their translations, such as at Avienus 319, where *urbs procera arces* suggests that εὔπυργος (*eupyrgos*) stood in Dionysios' line 213, whereas at Priscian 197 *clarorum mater equorum* translates εὔιππος (*euippos*).[34] However, whether, as Tsavari suggests, Avienus had before him the archetype from which A was copied is a matter for debate, given that the very existence of such an archetype has been questioned (see above).

Avienus' translation is relatively free. It seems unwise, then, to rely on his readings in attempting to establish the text of the *Periegesis*, even though Tsavari argues that his access to the 'Roman' archetype from which A was copied makes his translation particularly valuable as testimony to the original text of the poem.[35] Priscian seems to be more faithful to Dionysios' Greek than does Avienus, and his translation may often, therefore, prove the more useful in helping to assess the relative weight of different readings.

Scholia to the poem, which formed the basis for Eustathios' 12th-century commentary, may have been in circulation as early as the 4th century, if, as Gualandri suggests, the freedom with which Avienus often translates Dionysios' words is indeed due to the fact that a set of scholia already accompanied his text of the *Periegesis*.[36] According to Tsavari, scholia in fact accompanied the archetypes of both the 'Roman' and 'Constantinopolitan' traditions and, therefore, also the 2nd-century 'prearchetype' from which these two archetypes were copied.[37]

Eustathios' commentary is transmitted in over fifty known manuscripts, the majority of which also preserve the text of the poem itself.[38] Tsavari argues that of the many manuscripts to which Eustathios had access one was an early descendant of A, the now lost ancestor of V⁹.[39]

There is also an anonymous paraphrase of the poem in Greek prose that accompanies the text in around fifty of the extant manuscripts. It has so far proved impossible to date this paraphrase with any certainty, but Tsavari tentatively assigns it to the 9th or

---

[33] For Avienus' text, see Müller, *GGM* ii. 177–89; van de Woestijne 1961. For Priscian's, see Müller, *GGM* 190–9. These poems are not included in the present work, as they would largely duplicate Dionysios Periegetes and form part of the Latin geographical tradition rather than the Greek; but Avienus' *Ora maritima* is included as Ch. 32 below, since it preserves material from lost Greek sources.
[34] Tsavari 1990, 43–5, 212–14.   [35] Tsavari 1990, 41–7.   [36] Gualandri 1982.
[37] Tsavari 1990, 41.   [38] See Diller 1975b, appendix.   [39] Tsavari 1990, 61–5.

10th century on the evidence of similarities between the paraphrase itself and the MSS she classifies as belonging to family e.[40] (Another Greek paraphrase of the *Periegesis* purports to be by the 13th-century writer Nikephoros Blemmydes, but is a later invention.)[41] The paraphrases are of less help as a tool for establishing the text of the *Periegesis*, but provide a useful testimony to interpretations of Dionysios (see below on lines 348 and 350).

I follow Tsavari's Greek text, with the exceptions noted in this footnote.[42]

SELECTED FURTHER READING

Bowie, E. L. (1990), 'Greek poetry in the Antonine age', in D. A. Russell (ed.), *Antonine Literature* (Oxford), pp. 53–90.

—— (2004), 'Denys d'Alexandrie: un poète grec dans l'empire romain', *Revue des études anciennes*, 106: 177–86.

*Brodersen, K. (1994), *Dionysios von Alexandria, Das Lied von der Welt (zweisprachige Ausgabe)*. Hildesheim–Zürich–New York. [Includes translation into German hexameters.]

Counillon, P. (2001), 'Dionysos dans la Description de la terre habitée de Denys d'Alexandrie', in I. Zinguer (ed.), *Dionysos: origines et resurgences* (Paris), 105–14.

—— (2004), 'La Périégèse de la terre habitée et l'Hymne à Délos de Callimaque', *Revue des études anciennes*, 106: 187–202.

Cusset, C. (2004), 'Denys lecteur d'Apollonios de Rhodes? L'exemple de la description des fleuves', *Revue des études anciennes*, 106: 203–16.

Hunter, R. (2004), 'The Periegesis of Dionysius and the traditions of hellenistic poetry', *Revue des études anciennes*, 106: 217–32.

Ilyushechkina, E. (2010), 'Studien zu Dionysios von Alexandria'. Ph.D. thesis. Universiteit van Groningen.

—— (2011) 'Die sakrale Geographie: zu einigen Passagen des Apollonios Rhodios in der Bearbeitung des Dionysios Periegetes', in M. A. Harder *et al.* (eds), *Gods and Religion in Hellenistic Poetry* (Leuven), 165–79.

Jacob, C. (1990), *La Description de la terre habitée de Denys d'Alexandrie: ou la leçon de géographie*. Paris.

*Khan, Y. Z. N. (2002), 'A commentary on Dionysius of Alexandria's Guide to the Inhabited World, 174–382'. Ph.D. thesis. University College London.

---

[40] Tsavari 1990, 58–61.

[41] This text (Müller, *GGM* ii. 458–68) has been shown to be a C16 forgery by Antonios Episkopoulos (Diller 1936). Tsavari suggests that Episkopoulos used a number of MSS, in particular Vaticanus gr. 121 (V^{22}), dated C13, and a lost MS (d^{12}) whose earliest surviving descendant, Parisinus gr. 2708 (L), is dated C15/C16 (Tsavari 1990, 69–70). Reeve, however, has cast doubt on Tsavari's classification of V^{22}, and shown that there are problems with her definition and classification of the MSS of family d (Reeve 1994, esp. 214, 216–20).

[42] Readings differ from Tsavari as follows: 6 ὀξυτέρη, 35 αἰεί, 128 ἐπὶ, 267 εὐρείης Τριτωνίδος ὕδατι, 268 πόντον, 299 αὐτός, 321 ἐρεμνά, 333 αὐτῶν, 339 ἄκρη, 430 ἐστεφάνωται, 444 μεγάλῳ, 485 τηλίστων, 509 αἶα, 548 ἐπήρατον, 549 ἀνὰ, 555 ἄλλας . . . περὶ ῥόος ἐστεφάνωται, 564 παῖδες, 569 οὐ κέ . . . ἰσοφαρίζοι, 583 ἀγκέχυται, 642 ὀρθόκραιρον, 660 μεσά, 760 κεκλειμένη, 792 αὐτόθι, 822 παῖδες, 835 ἔτι, 861 περιτέλλεται, 934 γαιάων, 940 αὐτός, 941 γείνατο πέζαν, 943 αὐτόματοι, 948 δ' ἀνεδήσατο, 1080 λεπτόν, 1118 προμολῇσιν, 1142 ἄσπετα, 1160 κισσῷ, 1164 ἐρύσας, 1165 μέγα, 1177 ὑπὸ μορφῇ, 1178 ἐναλιγκίου.

—— (2004), 'Denys lecteur des Phénomènes d'Aratos', *Revue des études anciennes*, 106: 233–46.
*Lightfoot, Jane L. (2014), *Dionysius Periegetes, Description of the Known World*. Oxford.
Oudot, E. (2004), 'Athènes dans la Périégèse de Denys d'Alexandrie ou la mutation d'une image', *Revue des études anciennes*, 106: 247–61.
*Schneider, P. (forthcoming), 'Denys le Périégète (2019)', in *FGrH* v.

TEXT

To begin my song of the Earth and the broad main,
and the rivers and cities and countless tribes of men,
I shall recall the deep-flowing Ocean. For therein
the whole world is crowned, like an immense island,
not wholly circular all round, but on either side,
towards the sun's paths, becoming narrower,
like a sling. And, although it is one,
men have divided it into three lands:
first Libyē, and then Europe and Asia.

10   Well, then, Libyē has an oblique division from Europe
and, on this line, are Gadeira[43] and the mouth of the Nile,
where lies the northernmost corner of Egypt
and the well-known precinct of Amyklaian Kanobos.[44]
The Tanaïs divides Europe from Asia, through the middle.
This river, winding through the land of the Sauromatai,[45]
sweeps forth to Skythia and Lake Maiotis
in the north. In the south the boundary is the Hellespont,
and the line stretches further south to the mouth of the Nile.
        But others divide the land by continents.
20   A certain isthmus stretches above, uppermost in the
Asian land, in between the Caspian and Euxine seas.
This they have called the boundary of Europe and Asia.
Another again, unutterably long, creeps towards the south,
In between the Arabian gulf and Egypt,
and this divides Libyē from the Asian land.
        Such have mortals broadcast about the boundaries,

---

[43] *Cádiz.*

[44] Kanobos or Kanopos was the Greek name for the westernmost mouth of the Nile and the settlement beside it, famous for its sanctuary of Sarapis. According to one tradition, Kanobos took its name from Menelaos' helmsman, buried there after being bitten by a snake. Amyklai, S of Sparta, fell within the realm of Menelaos, according to the Homeric *Catalogue* (see Prologue to these volumes); D. uses 'Amyklaian' as a poeticism for 'Spartan' throughout the poem.

[45] D., like his contemporary Ptolemy, has the Sauromatai or Sarmatai occupying areas of E Europe and central Asia either side of the R. Tanaïs (*Don*) (Ptolemy, *Geography* 3. 5; 5. 10).

> but on all sides flows the might of the tireless Ocean,
> one, yet endowed with many appellations.
> Indeed by the furthest recess of Lokrian Zephyros[46]
> it is called the western Atlas, but beyond, to the north,
> where dwell the children of the war-mad Arimaspoi,[47]
> they call it the Frozen (*pepēgos*) main and Kronian.
> Others again call it the Dead one (*nekros*), because of the
> weakness of the sun, for it shines over that salt-sea
> with a dim light; always it is dulled by dark clouds.
> But there, where it first shines upon men,
> they call the swell of the sea Eastern or Indian.
> Nearby they call it Erythraian and Ethiopian,
> to the south, that is, where a great curve of uninhabited
> land lies stretched, burned by the sun's fierce rays.
>   Thus does the Ocean run round the whole Earth,
> in such a form and bearing such names among men.
> Here and there it churns out gulfs, casting itself inward
> into a salt-sea. There are many small gulfs, but four large ones.
> So, then, first of all, it begets the Western salt-sea,
> sweeping from Libyē to the Pamphylian land.
> The second is small, but far surpassing others,
> which, spreading from the Kronian salt-sea in the north
> sends forth a lofty stream into the Caspian sea,
> which others have called the Hyrkanian sea.
> Of the others, which are both from the southern salt-sea,
> one reaches higher, pouring forth the Persian wave,
> turned to face the Caspian Amphitrite,[48]
> and the other, the Arabian gulf,[49] swells within,
> winding its channel south of the Euxine main.
>   So many are the gulfs of the deep-waved Ocean,
> the greater ones, but there are countless others.
>   Now I will tell of the path of the western salt-sea, which
> wanders to and from all the lands with its oblique open seas (*pelagē*),
> sometimes encircling islands, and sometimes in turn
> brushing below the feet of mountains or cities.
> But you, O Muses, tell of its winding paths,

---

[46] The west wind.

[47] The storied Arimaspoi were commonly located in the extreme N of Europe (see e.g. Hdt. 4. 13. 1–2).

[48] The Nereid Amphitrite was the wife of Poseidon. Her (tetrasyllabic) name is used a dozen times in the poem as a synonym for 'sea' (cf. 'the waves of Amphitrite' at Odyssey 3. 91).

[49] Mod. *Red Sea*.

beginning in order from the western Ocean.
   Here, by the boundaries the Pillars of Herakles
stand, a great marvel, beside outermost Gadeira,[50]
beneath the high peak of the far-flung Atlas mountains,
where too a bronze column reaches to heaven,
tall, and enveloped within dense clouds.
   First of all, as one begins, the Iberian main
70 flows forth, which is the beginning of Europe
and of Libyē, for it winds in the midst of the two.
The Pillars stand on its shores, on this side and that,
the one looking at Europe, the other at Libyē.
After this comes the Gallic stream, where the land
of Massalia lies stretched, with its curved harbour.
Next after these flows the Ligurian salt-sea,
where the sons of the Italians dwell on the land,
descendants of Ausonian Zeus, ever mighty rulers.
Beginning from the north the sea stretches as far as the White Rock,[51]
80 which is rooted in the Sicilian strait.
Next the briny water bellows at Kyrnos.
After this the Sardinian main roars within,
and after this the swell of the Tyrrhenian[52] sea howls
towards the south. But then towards the rays of the sun[53]
the curved Sicilian stream runs back and forth, bringing waters
up from its depths between wave-beaten Pachynos
and the headland of Crete, which juts far into the salt-sea,
beside holy Gortyn and mainland Phaiston,
stretched forth, in the image of the head of a ram.
90 Because of this they call it the Ram's Brow.[54]
indeed it also stretches towards the Iapygian land.
   From there the swell of the Adriatic salt-sea grows wide and
stretches to the north, creeping again to the western corner,
and those dwelling nearby also call it the Ionian sea.
It pours forth onto two lands. As one travels,
on the right there appears the Illyrian land,
and Dalmatia above, province of warlike men.
On the left extends the immense isthmus of the Ausonians,

---

[50] D.'s location of the Pillars of Herakles is somewhat vague.
[51] This promontory is now *Capo dell'Armi* at the toe of Italy.
[52] i.e. Etruscan.   [53] i.e. eastwards.
[54] 'Kriou Metopon', the SW tip of Crete (as distinct from Kriou Metopon in the Black Sea, ll. 153, 312).

	far-reaching, and surrounded by three Amphitrites,
100	the Tyrrhenian, the Sicilian, and the brimming Adriatic.
	Each one stretches its channel in the direction of a wind,
	the Tyrrhenian to Zephyros, the Sicilian to Notos, the Adriatic to Euros.[55]
	But beyond the soil of Sicily the main flows towards Libyē
	raising crested waves, winding about the southern Syrtis,[56]
	the one which they also name the Wider Syrtis.
	The other one,[57] which has a lesser path, being an inlet,
	receives the flood of the main making its way from afar.
	So do the two bays thunder as they twist and turn,
	Even as the wave of Crete stretches from the
110	Mountains of Sicily far to the east, as far as the headland, the
	Eastern cape of Crete, as they say, Salmonis.
	Double seas next further ahead tremble,
	Ismaric Boreas' blasts driving them
	Onward, blowing straight at them, for they lie opposite.
	Navigators call the first the Pharian salt-sea[58]
	Up to the furthest cape of Kasion stretching;
117	Sidonian the other,[59] where stretching into the land's recess
119	Issos' boundless main does northward drive,[60]
120	Outstretching not far in this direction; for it halts directly
	Under the dark bend of the Kilikians' land.
	Then it disgorges its crooked salt-water to the west (*zephyros*).
	On, as a grim-looking serpent winds, coiled and creeping,
	Now sluggish, and beneath it the summit of a mountain is crushed
	Entirely as it moves—so that gulf winds in the salt-sea, full-flowing,
	Now and again weighed down by the flooding waters.
	The Pamphylians dwell around its flood-waters,
	Over to where it reaches the Chelidonian islands.
	So it has as its boundary far in the west the summit of Patara.
130	Figure[61] now, turning from there again to the north,
	A broad path of the Aegean main, where the waves

---

[55] Notos is the south wind; Euros here, it seems, is the east wind.

[56] The Great Syrtis (*Gulf of Sidra*).   [57] The Lesser Syrtis (*Gulf of Gabès*).

[58] The Egyptian sea, called 'Pharian' after the island of Pharos at Alexandria. The co-occurrence of 'Pharian' here and 'Pharou' as part of the acrostic (130–4) is hardly coincidental.

[59] D. again uses metonymy to refer to the Phoenician sea by way of the Phoenician city of Sidon.

[60] I have here excluded the preceding line, included in my 2002 trans. (Khan 2002, 200–44) and in Lightfoot's trans.: 'To Issos city, going along the Kilikians' land'. In Greek it begins with an iota, which would make the name in the acrostic *Dionysiiou*. For arguments in favour of excluding it rather than the present line, see Amato 2004, 1–4; Jane L. Lightfoot 2014, 289.

[61] For 'F' understand 'PH'. It has so far proved impossible to find a suitable word beginning with *ph* with which to begin this line.

>   Round the Sporades islands thunder as they break.
>   Other paths of the Amphitrite, roaring
>   Up high, do not raise waves like this one.
>   It sets its limit at furthest Tenedos,
>   with Imbros on the other side, whence there goes a narrow strait,
>   sweeping northward within all Propontis.
>   Above this the countless tribes of the land of Asia extend
>   towards the south, for it reaches a wide isthmus of land.
> 140   After this is the mouth of the Thracian Bosporos,
>   which Io, as a young heifer, once swam at Hera's
>   prompting. That is the narrowest strait of all
>   the others, which the stormy sea holds,
>   where the story goes that the pitiless Dark Rocks[62]
>   range in the salt-sea and clash against one another with a resounding din.
>   From here opens up and spreads the nearby Pontos.
>   It is vast, and vast is its creeping span into the heart
>   of the east. Its paths run on obliquely,
>   always looking to the north and to the east.
> 150   In the middle, on this side and that, rise two peaks,
>   one to the far south, which they call Karambis,
>   the other further north, above the European land,
>   which those who dwell round about call the Ram's Brow.[63]
>   These two meet face to face, although they are not
>   close, but as far apart as a ship might reach on the third day.
>   From here you could also see that the Pontos is two seas,
>   and resembles the cord of a rounded bow in its curvature.
>   Now the right-hand side of the Pontos would be the bow-string,
>   drawn straight, but Karambis is alone,
> 160   standing outside the line, and looking to the north.
>   The left-hand path has the shape of horns. It is bent
>   in a double curve, like the horns of a bow.
>   To its north the waters of Lake Maiotis
>   spread. Around this dwell the Skythians,
>   men of countless number, and they call it the Mother of the Pontos.
>   For from this flows the measureless water of the Pontos
>   straight through the Kimmerian Bosporos, on which
>   many Kimmerians dwell beneath the cold foot of the Tauros.
>   Such, then, is the shape of the dark-shining Amphitrite.
> 170   Now I shall recall the form of the whole Earth,

---

[62] The Symplegades rocks are within the Thracian Bosporos.
[63] 'Kriou Metopon' (cf. 312), as opposed to the one in Crete (90).

so that, even without seeing it, still you should have a distinct view,
and as a result of this you should be honoured and well respected,
as you explain the details to the man of ignorance.
    Well, then, Libyē goes creeping to the south,
to the south and east, like a trapezium in form.
Beginning first from Gadeira, where the point
is sharp and reaches into the heart of the Ocean.
A wider boundary is marked near the Arabian sea,
where lies the land of the dark Aithiopes,

180   the other ones,[64] close to whom stretches the soil of the Eremboi.[65]
Men say that the continent is like a leopard-skin,
for indeed it is dry and parched,
and dotted here and there with dark spots.
    So, then, below the outermost point there dwell
near the Pillars the peoples of the Maurousian land.[66]
After them there stretch the countless nations of Nomads,
where the Masaisylioi and country-dwelling Masyleës[67]
go to pasture with their children through plain and forest
chasing a grim and wretched hunt for sustenance.

190   For they do not know the cleft of the earth-parting plough
and they never hear the sweet sound of the carriage's course,
nor the lowing of cattle, returning to their pens.
But they just herd through the thickets, like wild animals,
ignorant of corn and unaware of the harvest.
After them Carthage embraces her lovely harbour,[68]
Carthage, now Libyan, but once Phoenician,
Carthage, which the story says was measured with an ox-hide.
Next the Syrtis rolls its strong-flowing course,
the Lesser Syrtis. After this towards the sunlight the other flows,

---

[64] D. seems to allude here to Homer *Od.* 1. 23–4, which lines were a subject of debate among Homeric scholars (Strabo 1. 2. 24–8, C31–5). Pliny asserts that Homer was right to distinguish two *Aethiopiae*, one in the E and one in the W (5. viii. 43).

[65] The Eremboi are first attested at Homer *Od.* 4. 84. Their identification was another subject of concern for Homeric scholars (see Strabo 1. 1. 3, C2; 1. 2. 34–5, C41–2). According to Strabo, their name was derived from the fact that they lived in caves, and they were therefore probably to be identified with the Trogodytai, whom he situates on the W coast of the Erythraian sea (mod. *Red Sea*), on the borders of Egypt and Aithiopia.

[66] For the Maurousioi occupying NW Libyē, see e.g. Strabo 17. 3. 2, C825–6; Pliny 5. i. 17.

[67] On the Masaisylioi and Masyleës, see Strabo 2. 5. 33, C131; 17. 3. 7–9, C828–30; and Pliny 5. i. 17, who indicates that the former became extinct and their land occupied by the Gaitouloi.

[68] Carthage is the first of four places to receive special emphasis in the poem. After Carthage, D. highlights the Tiber and Rome (350–6), then the Rhebas (794–6), and finally Ilion or Troy (815–19) using the same device of epanalepsis and repeating the place-name three times in each case but the last, where Ilion is repeated four times.

200 immense, burdened as it is by fuller floods.
   Here, when the Tyrrhenian Amphitrite raises its crested waves,
   sometimes the flood rises high, and sometimes, in turn,
   the ebb-tide runs over the dry sands.
   In the middle of these two is set a city,
   which they call Neapolis. Inland of this
   the Lotus-eaters dwell, a people who welcome strangers.[69]
   Here the wily Odysseus once came in his wanderings.
   In that region you might view the deserted homes
   of the Nasamones[70] who have perished,
210 for the Ausonian spear destroyed this people who paid no heed to Zeus.[71]
   After them are the Asbystai, inland,[72]
   and the precinct of the Libyan god,[73] beneath thick sand,
   and Kyrene of the fine horses, seat of the Amyklaians.[74]
   Nearby are the Marmaridai who extend before Egypt,
   and the Gaitouloi beyond them and the neighbouring Nigretes.[75]
   Next after these are the Phaurousioi,[76] and beyond them the land
   is inhabited by the innumerable Garamantes.[77]
                              The remote corners
   of the continent feed the furthermost Aithiopes,[78]
   by the Ocean itself, beside the vales of farthest Kerne.[79]

---

[69] For the Lotus-eaters as a historical people situated near the Syrtes, see also e.g. Hdt. 4. 177, Strabo 17. 3. 17, C834; Pliny 5. iv. 28, Ps.-Skylax §110.

[70] Commonly situated E and S of the Greater Syrtis (see e.g. Hdt. 2. 32–3; Ps.-Skyl. §109; Strabo 2. 5. 33, C131; Pliny 5. v. 33–4).

[71] The only Roman defeat of the Nasamones which the surviving sources relate is that under Domitian in AD 86 (see e.g. Dio 67. 4. 6).

[72] On this people in Cyrenaica, see e.g. Hdt. 4. 170; Pliny 5. v. 34; Strabo 2. 5. 33, C131.

[73] The temple of Zeus Ammon at *Siwa*, once famous for its oracle (Hdt. 1. 46, 2. 55; Strabo 1. 3. 4, C50; etc.).

[74] For 'Amyklaian', see n. on l. 13. On Kyrene and the neighbouring Marmaridai (below), see Pliny 5. v. 33; Strabo 2. 5. 33, C131; 17. 3. 23, C838.

[75] The Gaitouloi lived inland from the Lesser Syrtis. The Nigretes or Nigritai were further W but possibly in proximity to the Melanogaitouloi.

[76] This people are similarly mentioned in connection with the Nigretes by Strabo 17. 3. 7, C828. Pha(ou)rousioi was another name for the Gymnetes, according to Pliny (5. viii. 43).

[77] The Garamantes may have been further N, inland from the Greater Syrtis.

[78] D. here presumably refers to the western Aithiopes. Cf. Strabo 17. 3. 7, C828, for the Phaurousioi and Nigretes as dwelling near them.

[79] D. here appears to situate Kerne on the mainland, and indeed he does not mention it in his discussion of the islands. Most other ancient writers, however, refer to it as an island, although they differ as to its position. For example, Pliny tells us that Polybios and others situate it off the W coast of Libyē, in the Atlantic ocean, while he himself describes it as lying in the Aithiopian sea, S of Libyē (6. xxxvi. 98; cf. Ps.-Skyl. §112. 5–6 for earlier evidence of the view supported by Pliny). Diodoros does relate an account by Dionysios Skytobrachion (*BNJ* 32 F 7), who, like the Periegete, appears to place Kerne on the mainland. It seems clear that there was no consensus as to its whereabouts. Indeed, Strabo 1. 3. 2, C47–8, questions its existence altogether.

220   Above them there rise the peaks of the smoky Blemyes,[80]
    Down from which flow the waters of the most fertile Nile,
    which, as it creeps from Libyē towards the east,
    is called Siris[81] by the Aithiopes. But the inhabitants of Syene,
    once it has turned, change its name to Nile.
    From there stretching towards the north, this way and that,
    it winds through seven mouths and falls into the salt-sea,
    enriching with its waters the fertile plain of Egypt.
    For of all the rivers none is like the Nile,
    not in depositing silt, nor in increasing the wealth of the land.
230   This river also divides Libyē from the land of Asia,
    to the Lips[82] Libyē, and to the sunlight the Asian land.
    Beside it dwells a race of most illustrious men,
    who were the first to distinguish the ways of life,
    the first to put the beloved plough to the test,
    and scatter seed over the straightest furrow,
    and the first to divide the heavenly pole with lines,
    considering at heart the oblique course of the sun.
    May I voice the limits and form of their land itself,
    for it has been allotted no small share of honour,
240   and it is of no small size, but beyond others
    it abounds in pasture and meadows, and yields every glory.
    Its shape, then, rests on three sides.
        It is broad around the northern shores, but pointed towards the east,[83]
    and stretches as far as high-peaked Syene,
    fenced on both sides by sheltering mountains,
    through the middle of which pour the waters of the fair-flowing Nile.
    And many prosperous men occupy this land,
    as many as inhabit glorious Thebes,
    ancient Thebes, with a hundred gates, where, with a loud cry,
250   Memnon welcomes his mother, Dawn, as she rises.[84]

---

[80] The ancient sources differ somewhat as to the precise location of this people. According to Strabo 17. 1. 2, C786 = Eratosthenes 89, they lived either side of the Nile, between the island of Meroë and the Red Sea. Strabo later mentions them among the nomadic Aithiopian peoples inhabiting S Egypt (17. 1. 53). Mela too makes them nomadic (1. 4), but, like Pliny (5. viii. 44), locates them in the interior of the continent.

[81] Or Giris, Pliny 5. x. 53.   [82] The south-west wind.

[83] According to Eustathios, and consistent with D.'s use of similar phrases in ll. 332, 421, and 437, he uses 'dawn' here to refer to the south and Thebes.

[84] The Greeks identified the colossus of Amenophis III in front of the Memnoneion near Thebes with Memnon, the son of Eos. After the colossus was damaged by an earthquake, it would reportedly give out a sound at sunrise (Strabo 17. 1. 46, C816).

>   As many too as inhabit the midmost land of the Seven Cities,[85]
>   and as many as there are on the moist shores of the sea
>   occupying the coast as far as lake Serbonis.[86]
>   To the west of this is the Macedonian city,[87]
>   where stands the home of mighty Zeus of Sinope,[88]
>   adorned with precious gold. You could not see
>   another temple more divine than that among men,
>   nor another city as wealthy, where high up
>   there appear the summits of Pallenian Eidothea.[89]
> 260 Next, towards the east, by the rock of Kasios
>   the city named after Peleus[90] is occupied by a people
>   exceptionally skilled in seafaring. Those men are not
>   numbered among the Libyans, for the city allotted them
>   is situated towards the sunlight[91] from the seven-mouthed Nile.
>   But a great many others inhabit this land,
>   some by the Ocean, some in the centre of the mainland,
>   and others around the wide water of Lake Tritonis,[92]
>   which embraces a wide gulf in the middle of Libyē.
>   Such, then, is the shape and form of Libyē.
> 270 But if you want an outline of Europe too, I shall not hide it from you.
>   The shape is the same as that of Libyē, but it is turned
>   towards the north, and it creeps back towards the east
>   just as that of the southerly Libyē leans towards the boundary.
>   Both alike have their furthest track on the border with Asia,
>   the one to the north, and the other to the south. But if you made
>   the two of them one land, then altogether
>   it would be the shape of a cone with two equal sides,
>   pointed in the west, but broad in the east at the middle.
>   So, having seen that this is the course of the two
> 280 continents, you will easily grasp the bounds of Europe.

---

[85] D. coins this term for the Heptanomid, the Roman district of middle Egypt. Cf. Ptolemy 4. 5. 25.
[86] *Bardawil*. See n. on Agathem. i. 3.   [87] Alexandria.
[88] The Serapeion at Alexandria, originally built under Ptolemy III Euergetes (r. 241–221 BC) and reconstructed in the imperial period, is described by Ammianus Marcellinus as the most magnificent monument in the world after Rome's Capitol (22. 16. 2).
[89] Probably the lighthouse of Alexandria situated on the island of Pharos, which was said to have been the home of Proteus and his daughter Eidothea by Torone of Pallene (for which see l. 327 below). The scholiast and Eustathios, however, suggest that the reference may be to the Antipharos in Taphosiris.
[90] Pelousion.   [91] i.e. the east.
[92] The precise location of this lake was disputed in antiquity, although it was commonly situated near the Mediterranean coast (see e.g. Hdt. 4. 178; Strabo 17. 3. 20, C836). It may have been near the Greater Syrtis.

At its furthest borders there dwell,
near the Pillars, the nation of brave-hearted Iberians,
reaching across the length of the land, where lies the cold
stream of the northern Ocean, where the Britons
and the white tribes of the war-mad Germans dwell,
running beside the massifs of the Hercynian forest.[93]
They say that that land is like an ox-hide.
After the Iberians are Mount Pyrene and the homes of the Keltoi,
near the springs of the fair-flowing Eridanos,[94]
290   beside the streams of which once in the solitary night
the Heliades cried, lamenting Phaëthon.
There the children of the Keltoi, seated beneath the poplars,
milk the tears of gold-gleaming amber.
Next after this are the haunts of the Tyrrhenian land.[95]
To the east of this appears the start of the Alp,
through the middle of which flow down the waters of the Rhine,
towards the furthermost tide of the northern Amphitrite.
Next after the Rhine there rises the sacred Istros[96]
itself, turned to the east as far as the Euxine
300   sea, where it emits all the foam of its water,
winding around Peuke with its mouth of five channels.[97]
    To its north dwell very many scattered tribes
which succeed one another as far as the mouth of Lake Maiotis:
Germans and Samatai[98] and Getai together with Bastarnai,[99]
and the boundless land of the Dakai and the mighty Alans,[100]

---

[93] In antiquity this forest was situated as far S as the Pyrenees by some (see the scholia ad loc.) and as far N as the N coast of Germany by others (see e.g. Diod. Sic. 5. 21). Its exact location remains unclear.

[94] The river was identified variously with the Rhodanos (*Rhône*) and Padus (*Po*), singly and together. 'Eridanos' is an alternative name for the *Po*.

[95] D. is unusual in omitting Liguria (cf. e.g. Ap. Rhod. 4. 647, Ps.-Skyl. §§3–4, Strabo 2. 5. 28, C128). It is possible he uses 'Tyrrhenia' here for Italy as opposed to the administrative region of Tyrrhenia or Etruria. However, see ll. 347–50, where the Tyrrhenians or Etruscans are distinguished from other peoples of Italy.

[96] The Danube.

[97] Peuke was the name given to a southern promontory and an 'island' within the delta. D.'s description suggests that he, like Apollonios of Rhodes (4. 309–13), may apply the name to the entire delta.

[98] Probably the Sarmatai, as the scholia here suggest.

[99] For the Getai as occupying the lower stretch of the Istros, see e.g. Strabo 7. 3. 13–14, C305. For the Bastarnai as occupying Peuke and an area NW of the delta, see e.g. Strabo 7. 2. 4, C294.

[100] For this area (a shore or promontory), see n. to Arrian 21. 1; *Eux.* §§87, 93–5. For the Dacians, who occupied a vast area, as probably a Thracian people like the Getai, see Strabo 7. 3. 12–13, C304–5. The Alans were a Skythian people sometimes identified with the Massagetai (see e.g. Amm. Marc. 23. 5. 16, Dio 69. 15, and Ptolemy 3. 5. 7).

and the Tauroi, who inhabit the lofty Racetrack of Achilles,[101]
Slender both and long, as far as the mouth of the lake itself.
The Agauoi[102] tribe extends above them, rich in horses.
Even the Melanchlainoi[103] and the Hippemolgoi,
310 Neuroi, Hippopodes,[104] Gelonoi,[105] and Agathyrsoi.[106] Here
Extends the far-reaching stream of the Borysthenes river,[107]
mixing with the Euxine before the Ram's Brow,[108]
directly in a line opposite the Kyaneai.
Here the waters of the Aldeskos[109] and Pantikapes[110]
roar each in their own corner of the Rhipaian mountains.[111]
Beside them, near the waters of the Frozen Sea[112]
sweet-gleaming amber swells, like a beam
of the waxing moon, and nearby you might see
diamonds all-a-glitter beside the cold Agathyrsoi.
320 So many, then, are the peoples north of the Istros,
while to the south are the Gerrhai[113] and the obscure towns of the Norikoi,[114]
and Pannonians and Mysians,[115] north of the Thracians,
and the Thracians themselves, who inhabit a limitless land,[116]
some on the shores of the Amphitrite of the Propontis,

---

[101] On the Tauroi as once occupying the greater part of the Chersonesos and continuing to occupy pockets of the peninsula and neighbouring regions on the Euxine, see Hdt. 4. 11; Strabo 7. 4. 2–5, C308–11; Ptolemy 3. 6 Stückelberger-Graßhoff; Mela 2. 1. The 'Racetrack' (Dromos) of Achilles was an elongated peninsula NW of the Chersonesos, though sometimes confused with Achilles' Island (cf. Arr. §§20. 1 and 21. 2 with nn.; *Eux.* 87 and 93). The following five lines describing the peninsula and the surrounding peoples include a 'gamma' acrostic (στενή–*stenē*), which D. appears to use not only as a nod to Homer (see Counillon 1981), but also as a programmatic statement by way of a reference to Aratos' *Phainomena*, on which connection see Khan 2004.

[102] In referring to the Agauoi and Hippemolgoi (below) as two separate peoples D. is alluding to Homer, *Il.* 13. 1–6, and the debate over which of these two forms is to be taken as an adjective and which a proper noun. An alternative reading here is Alanoi.

[103] This people, like the Neuroi below, are situated by Herodotos on the N borders of Skythia (4. 17–20).

[104] This people is treated as historical and also grouped with the Melanchlainoi, Gelonoi, and Agathyrsoi as occupying the same region of Skythia by Ptolemy (3. 5. 10).

[105] Herodotos appears to locate this people further E (4. 108–9).

[106] This people is situated N of Skythia.   [107] The *Dnieper*.   [108] Cf. l. 153.

[109] The only earlier extant reference to this river is in Hesiod's catalogue (*Theog.* 345).

[110] Herodotos (4. 54), Pliny (4. xii. 83), and Mela (2. 1) describe this river as joining the Borysthenes near the Racetrack of Achilles.

[111] These mountains were widely associated with the mythical Hyperboreans (see e.g. Mela 3. 5), and located to the far north of the inhabited world. The mountains themselves are treated as mythical by Strabo 7. 3. 1, C295.

[112] Cf. l. 32.

[113] There is no other surviving reference to these Gerrhai. Some editors have therefore been tempted to emend the text (see Bernhardy ad loc.).

[114] According to Pliny, the Norikoi were previously known as the Tauriskoi (3. xx. 133; see also 3. xxiv. 146), located in the Roman province of Noricum.

[115] Mysia is here the Roman province of Moesia, not the region in NW Asia Minor.

[116] The exact boundaries of the province of Thrace, particularly in the W, seem to have been unclear.

some beside the strong-flowing Hellespont, and others
beside the deep wave of the loud-roaring Aegean sea itself.
Here on the summits of bee-feeding Pallene,[117]
springs the beautiful *asterios* stone, which glows
like a star, and the *lychnis*, just like a flame of fire.

330 So many are the peoples who dwell round the river Istros.
Consider now the remaining path of Europe,
which extends towards the east on three foundations, the Iberians',
the Panhellenes', and that of the very Ausonians.
    Well, then, the outermost is that of the illustrious Iberians,
neighbours of the Ocean to the west. On it stands
the summit of Alybe,[118] one of the Pillars. Below this
is lovely Tartesos,[119] land of affluent men,
and the Kempsoi,[120] who dwell by the foot of Pyrene.
    In the middle of the other two extends the Ausonian cape,

340 far-reaching. A mountain cuts it in two down the middle,
straight, as though it had been aligned with a ruler. No
skilled servant of artful Athene would find fault with it.
This they call the Apennine, and beginning from the
Alp in the north it ends at the Strait of Sicily.
Many tribes dwell around it, and I shall easily tell you of them all,
beginning on the west (*zephyritis*) side from the north.
The Tyrrhenians[121] are first, and after them are the tribes of the Pelasgians,[122]
who once came from Kyllene[123] to the western salt-sea,

---

[117] Pallene, the westernmost of the three peninsulas to project into the Aegean from Chalkidike, was also known as Phlegra.

[118] Although the scholia on l. 64 indicate that Charax of Pergamon gave this as the name for the European Pillar of Herakles, the pillar was commonly called Kalpe, while the African Pillar was known by the name Abyla. D. may have had in mind Homer, *Il.* 2. 856–7, where Alybe is the 'birthplace of silver', given that S. Spain was associated with silver-mining (see e.g. Strabo 3. 2. 8, C146; Pliny 3. iii. 30). The Homeric lines were the source of some discussion. For D.'s allusions to such Homeric problems see above on ll. 308 and 333.

[119] The name of a river near *Cádiz*, and also a city which stood between its mouths according to Strabo 3. 2. 11, C149; Pausanias 6. 19. 3; *Nikomedean Periodos* 162–6; Avienus, *OM* 283–5; *et al*. Certain ancient authors identified the city of Tartessos with the site at *Cádiz* (Pliny 4. xxii. 120; Avien. *Descriptio orbis* 610–16, *OM* 265–72). Others attributed the name to a town known also as Karteia (Pliny 3. i. 7; Mela 2. 6), Karpe(i)a (Strabo 3. 2. 14, C151; Pausanias 6. 19. 3) or Karpessos (Appian, *Iberike* 2 and 63), situated beside Mt Kalpe, the Pillar of Herakles, with which it was sometimes apparently assimilated (*Itin. Anton.* 406. 3; Strabo 3. 1. 7, C145; Nik. Dam. *BNJ* 90 F127. 23).

[120] The only other surviving references to this people are by Avienus, who describes them as inhabiting Ophioussa in NW Iberia: *OM* 195–201, 255–9, 301–2.

[121] The Etruscans.

[122] This Greek people was sometimes identified with the Tyrrhenians (see e.g. Dion. Hal. 1. 28) and sometimes said to have displaced the Tyrrhenians (see e.g. Pliny 3. v. 71, Strabo 5. 2. 3, C220).

[123] Probably Mt Kyllene in Arkadia. See Strabo 5. 2. 4, C220–1, for the tradition that the Pelasgians originated in Arkadia.

    where they settled with the Tyrrhenian men.
350   After them comes the dread nation of the noble Latins,
    who inhabit a lovely land, through the middle of which
    the Thymbris[124] winds, casting its pure stream into the salt-sea,
    the fair-flowing Thymbris, most regal of all rivers,
    the Thymbris which divides in two beloved Rome,
    Honoured Rome, the great home of my lords,
    the mother of all cities, rich abode.
        After this is the fertile plain of the Campanians, where
    stands the home of chaste Parthenope,[125] laden with sheaves of corn,
    Parthenope, whom the sea welcomed in its embrace.
360   To the south, some way beyond the Siren's Rock,[126]
    appear the streams of the Pikentine Silaros.[127]
    Nearby are the men of the Leukanoi and the Brentioi,
    who inhabit the land as far as the White Rock.[128]
    From there to the north appears the cape of Zephyros,[129]
    below it are the Lokroi,[130] all those who in years gone by,
    came to Ausonia, after coupling with their ladies.
    Even now their people dwell by the streams of the Alēx.[131]
    Next after them are the Metapontioi, and near them
    the beloved city of well-crowned Kroton,
370 situated by the waters of the charming Aisaros,
    where you might see the lofty home of Lakinian Hera.[132]
    There too, at the anger of mighty Zeus
    is wretched Sybaris, mourning her fallen inhabitants,
    who were overly mad for Alpheios' honours.[133]

---

[124] The R. Tiber.   [125] A poetic name for *Naples*.
[126] The Sirens were sometimes associated with the Cape of Minerva (see e.g. Strabo 1. 2. 13, C22–3), so that the rock mentioned may be the Cape of Minerva itself (as Pliny 3. v. 62) or the Kapreai just off the cape (as Servius *ad Aen.* 5. 684). The cape is *Punta Campanella* at the tip of the *Sorrento* peninsula, where there is a temple of Minerva–Athena.
[127] The river formed the N border of Lucania (see e.g. Strabo 5. 4. 13, C251; Pliny 3. v. 38). Between the Silaros and the Cape of Minerva was the Ager Picentinus (Pliny 3. v. 70), to which D. presumably alludes here.
[128] Leukopetra was the name of a promontory on the outermost tip of the Bruttian peninsula.
[129] Zephyrion was the name of the promontory lying across from Leukopetra in the bay of Bruttium.
[130] A reference to Lokroi Ephizephyrioi, which lay N of Zephyrion on the Bruttian coast.
[131] The precise identification of the R. Alex or Halex, first mentioned by Thucydides (3. 99), is uncertain. Strabo 6. 1. 9, C260, tells us that it divided Lokroi from Rhegion. It was at the tip of the Bruttian peninsula.
[132] A temple to Hera was situated on C. Lakinion, SE of Kroton. According to Livy the temple was more famous than Kroton itself (24. 3).
[133] There are various accounts of the hubris of the inhabitants of Sybaris and it is not entirely clear to which of these accounts D. is alluding here. The scholia and Eustathios *ad loc.* suggest that the allusion is to the story that the Sybarites stole offerings made to the R. Alpheios of Olympia. In another account

The Saunitai[134] after them inhabit the middle territory,
and the nimble tribes of the Marsoi.[135] Taras[136] lies near the salt-sea,
which strong Amyklaian Ares once built.[137]
Next after these are the haunts of the Calabrian land
and the tribes of the Iapyges reaching as far as Hyrion,[138]
380 by the salt-sea, Hyrion, where the flood of the Adriatic flows
to the neighbouring sea of Aquileia where stands
the city of the Tegestraioi, on the edges of the innermost sea.[139]
    So many are the nations who inhabit the Ausonian land.
From there to the sunlight[140] the winding salt-sea flows,
brushing at the Libyrnian shores,[141] and around all the
fortified country of the Hylloi,[142] all that lies beside the isthmus,
and the coasts of the Boulimeis.[143] Onward it drives its immense course,
winding to the Illyrian land as far as the peak
and the steep mountains, which they call the Keraunians.[144]
390 Moreover in that region you might see the famous tomb,
the tomb which rumour has it belongs to Kadmos and Harmonia.
For it was there that they were changed into coiled snakes,[145]
when they came from Ismenos in their rich old age.
Here the gods brought about another miracle for them.
For in that region, on either side two rocks stand firmly fixed,
which both tremble and come together, whenever any
ill begins to threaten those who dwell there.[146]
    To the south, quite far below[147] fertile Thrace

---

attributed to Herakleides of Pontos the Sybarites are described as having established a festival to compete with that at Olympia (12. 522c–d = Timaios, *BNJ* 566 F45). D.'s reference to Zeus may suggest that it is this tradition to which he alludes.

---

[134] i.e. Samnites.
[135] For the Samnites and Marsi, near L. Fucinus (as Livy 26. 11. 11; Strabo 5. 3. 13, C240; etc.).
[136] Tarentum.   [137] Taras was a Spartan colony.
[138] Probably Hyria, Uria, or Urion in Apulia, on the N shores of the Garganum promontory.
[139] Also called Tergeste and Trieste.   [140] i.e. the east.
[141] The coastal region between Histria and Dalmatia.
[142] Ptolemy lists the Hyllaioi among the peoples occupying the Illyrian coast (2. 16. 5). The Hylloi are similarly listed among the peoples of Illyria by Ps.-Skyl. §22 and *Nik*. 405–12, who make them inhabitants of a peninsula almost as large as the Peloponnese. The promontory of Hyllis is below Liburnia on the Dalmatian coast, occupied by the Hylloi and Boulinoi (see on the Boulimeis below).
[143] See again Ptolemy 2. 16. 5, Ps.-Skyl. §22, and *Nik*. 404 for the Boulimeis or Boulinoi as neighbours of the Hyllaioi or Hylloi.   [144] Coastal mountain range, just N of Epeiros.
[145] For the Illyrian metamorphosis of Kadmos and Harmonia into snakes, see Apollodoros 3. 5. 4; Eurip. *Bacch*. 1330–2; Nicander, *Ther*. 607–9; *et al*. For the descendants of K. and H. ruling over the Illyrian Encheleis, see Hdt. 5. 61, 9. 43; Strabo 7. 7. 8, C326 (Encheleioi). On them and their relationship to similarly names peoples, see Proeva 2021.
[146] Cf. Ps.-Skyl. §24 for the rocks of Kadmos and Harmonia in Illyria. The precise location is unclear.
[147] This surely suggests a cartographic perspective.

	and beyond the land of Orikia,[148] is the beginning of Hellas,
400	stretching far, girded by twin seas,
	the Aegean and the Sicilian. Each has been allotted a wind:
	the Sicilian sea the western, which they also call Zephyros,
	the Aegean the Euros.
	The island of Pelops follows next,
	like the tapering leaf of a plane-tree.
	For the narrow Isthmus to the north is pinched
	like the stem, and is attached to Hellas by a common path.
	The land is like a wind-tossed leaf in outline,
	wreathed with coastal bays on this side and that.
	To its west are the haunts of the Triphylian land,[149]
410	where the loveliest of rivers, the Alpheios, makes its way
	separating itself from the waters of the Messenian Eurotas.[150]
	Both these rivers churn forth their streams from Asea,[151]
	but the one divides the land of the Eleians, and the other that of the Amyklaians.
	In the middle of the island the Apidanian Arkadians
	inhabit a hollow country below the peak of Erymanthos,[152]
	where Melas, where Krathis, where the moist Iaon flows,[153]
	where too ancient Ladon stretches with its waters.[154]
	Nearby is the soil of the Argives and the land of the Lakones,
	the one looking to the east, the other to the south.
420	Two seas thunder around the shores of the Isthmus,
	one flowing opposite Ephyre[155] towards the darkness,
	the other towards the dawn. This they call the Saronic.

---

[148] The town of Orikos was located in the bay formed by the Keraunian mountains. It is not clear what, beyond this town, D. intends as the 'land of Orikia'.

[149] Triphylia was a small region on the W coast of the Peloponnese, S of Elis.

[150] Although the Eurotas flowed through Laconia and Sparta, E of Messenia, Strabo, in discussing Homeric geography, suggests that Messenia and Laconia were once considered as one (8. 3. 29, C352–3; 8. 4. 1, C358–9). This was certainly the case during the period of Spartan rule over Messenia, when the political name for the combined territory was Lakonike.

[151] An Arkadian town near Megalopolis, where the Alpheios and Eurotas were said to have flowed as one (Strabo 8. 3. 12, C343; Pausanias 8. 44. 4 and 54. 2).

[152] The name was shared by a river and mountain range in N. Arkadia.

[153] All three rivers are named in Kallimachos, *Hymn* 1. His reference to the Iaon in verse 22 of the hymn is the earliest extant reference and the river's identification remains obscure. Similarly the Arkadian Melas is first attested in l. 123 of the same hymn, and has proved difficult to identify with any certainty. The R. Krathis, however, is first attested by Herodotos, who locates it in Aigai in Achaia (1. 145).

[154] The Ladon is the first of the rivers named in Kallimachos' catalogue of Arkadian rivers (*H.* 1. 18). It is first attested at Hesiod, *Theog.* 344. According to Strabo it flowed into the Alpheios (8. 3. 12, C343).

[155] Corinth.

> Beyond the Isthmus to the sunlight lies the Attic land,
> through which flows the stream of the divine Ilissos.
> It was from here too that Boreas once snatched Oreithyia.
> After this there is the plain of the Boiotians and the Lokrian soil,
> and Thessaly is after these and the cities of Macedonia.
> After this there appear the summits of snowy Haimos[156]
> in Thrace. Facing this towards the blast of the Zephyros
> 430 the immense land of Dodona[157] is crowned.
> Beyond this, below the peak of Arakynthos, the great
> plain of the Aitolians goes towards the south.[158] Through
> the middle sweeps the silver-eddied Acheloös,[159] driving its course,
> winding to the sea of Trinakria[160] through the midst
> of the islands, which they call the Echinades.[161] There
> follow here and there the cities of the neighbouring Kephallenians.[162]
> After this there is the soil of Phokis, towards the east and the dawn,
> coursing northwards to the mouth of Thermopylai,
> below the cleft of snowy Parnassos. Through the middle
> 440 of this the great wave of Kephisos descends with a murmur.
> Beside this is the fragrant plain of Python,[163] where the coil
> of the serpent Delphyne lies next to the tripods of the god,
> the coil, rough with countless scales,
> in the great temple, where often Apollo himself
> stops and loosens the cord of his golden quiver,
> just back from Miletos or from Klaros.
>   So, then, may he be gracious. But you, Muse of Zeus, tell
> me of the sacred path of all the islands, which appear in
> the sea before men's eyes, facing this way and that.
> 450 Well, then, in the middle beneath the western Pillars
> furthest Gadeira appears before men,
> on a sea-bound island, beside the limits of Ocean.
> Here dwells a race of Phoenician men

---

[156] Mt Haimos (i.e. the Balkan range) is NE Macedonia.

[157] Renowned for its ancient oracle (see e.g. Strabo 7. 7. 9–12, C327–9; Pausanias 10. 12. 10), Dodona is in central Epeiros.

[158] Mt Arakynthos is in the SW corner of Aitolia (mod. *Zygos*).

[159] The Acheloös flows through W. Aitolia and exits into the Ionian sea.

[160] 'Three-cape', i.e. Sicily.

[161] These islands off the Aitolian coast are described as gradually becoming assimilated by mainland Greece as the mouth of the Acheloös became silted up (Hdt. 2. 10; Thuc. 2. 102; Ps.-Skyl. §34; Strabo 10. 2. 19, C458–9).

[162] The Kephallenians were held to have occupied various islands in the Ionian sea, including Kephallenia itself, and mainland Akarnania also (see Hom. *Il.* 2. 634).

[163] Delphi.

who worship mighty Zeus' son, Herakles.
This island too, which among men of old
was called Kotinoussa, the inhabitants call Gadeira.
Next are the Gymnesian islands.[164] Nearby there is Bousos,[165]
and broadest Sardo, and Kyrnos lovely in the salt-sea,
which the people who live there call Korsis.[166]

460 There is no forest which is as vast as that.
After this the islands of Aiolos form a circle in the salt-sea,
Aiolos, son of Hippotas, the king who welcomes strangers,
Aiolos, who was allotted gifts wondrous among men,
the command of the winds as they rage and as they rest.
He has seven, named by men the Plotai,[167]
because in their midst they have a winding path that may be sailed around.
After these Trinakria[168] extends beyond the land
of the Ausonians, standing on three sides.
its headlands are Pachynos, Peloris, and Lilybe.

470 So, then, Lilybe rises up into the blast of the Zephyros,
Pachynos is towards the sunlight, and towards the north
lies windy Peloris, looking at Ausonia.
To its north the passage is deadly for sailors,
narrow and winding and unruly, where the sea
as it flows thunders about the high rocks,
the sea pierced by the many-barbed Aonian iron.[169]
To the south is the path of Libyē and the beginning of the Syrtis,
the one. The other you might see as you made your way further,
the western one. Before this there are two islands,

480 Meninx and Kerkinna, occupying the Libyan anchorage.
But whenever you sail the left-hand path of the Adriatic
Amphitrite in your ship, to the Iapygian land,
you will immediately find the island of mighty Diomedes,[170]
where the hero came, after enraging Aphrodite,
when he sought the nation of the furthest Iberes,
at the advice of his wife, ill-minded Aigialeia.

---

[164] The *Balearic* islands.   [165] Bousos or Ebousos is *Ibiza*.   [166] Sardinia and Corsica.
[167] 'Navigable Isles'. The Aiolian or Liparaian Is. seem to have been known by various names (Pliny 3. viii. 92).
[168] Lit. 'Three-capes', i.e. Sicily.
[169] The reference appears to be to Poseidon's trident via the poeticism for Boiotian, 'Aonian' (cf. Kallimachos, *Hymns* 4. 75). For Boiotian Onchestos as site of a famous sanctuary of Poseidon, see e.g. Pausanias 9. 26. 5.
[170] The islands of Diomedes are off the S coast of Italy in the Adriatic. For the connection of the Homeric hero with these islands, cf. *Nik.* 425; Strabo 5. 1. 9, C215; 6. 3. 9, C283–4.

> Next after this passage towards the rays of the sun,
> there appears the immense course of the islands of Apsyrtes,[171]
> which the sons of the Kolchoi once invaded, when they took pains
> 490 in searching after the traces of the errant daughter of Aietes.
> Next after these the Libyrnian islands stand rooted.
> To the south, after the Keraunian forests, before the passing ship,
> there would appear on the far side the islands of the Amprakians,
> and fertile Kerkyra,[172] beloved land of Alkinoös.
> After this is fixed the seat of Nerikian Ithaca,[173]
> and of all the other islands that Acheloös flowing
> from Chalkis creeps about with silver eddies.
> Many can be seen to the north of Amnisos:[174]
> Aigila, and Kythera and rugged Kalauria.[175]
> 500 Karpathos is on the other side. Towards the darkness, nearby,
> is Crete full of honour, mighty Zeus' nurse-maid,
> great and fertile and abounding in pastures, above which is Ida,
> Ida, lush under its fair-tressed oaks.
> Its size too is indeed immense. Opposite the foot
> of Egypt is Rhodes, land of the Ialysian men.[176]
> After this to the east are the Chelidoniai,[177]
> three islands inside the great promontory of Patara.[178]
> To the sunlight, in the Pamphylian gulf, Cyprus
> is washed by the sea, the lovely land of Dionaian Aphrodite.[179]
> 510 Near Phoenicia Arados sits in the great gulf.[180]
> before the peak of Sounion, beyond the Abantes,[181]
> there appear Salamis and the city of Aigina.
>
>   The deep path of the Aegean is a wonder,[182]

---

[171] Islands N of the Liburnian Is. in the Adriatic.   [172] *Corfù*.

[173] Nerikos seems to have been the name of a town on the neighbouring island of Leukas said to have been captured by Laërtes (Homer, *Od*. 24. 375–82; Thucydides 3. 7; Strabo 10. 2. 8, C452; *et al*.).

[174] Amnisos was the name of a river on the N shores of Crete, renowned for the nearby sanctuary of Eileithyia (Homer, *Od*. 19. 188; Strabo 10. 4. 8, C476; *et al*.).

[175] Aigila and Kythera are in the waters NW of Crete; Kalauria further N, off the shores of Argolis near Troizen.

[176] Ialysos was a *polis* on the N tip of Rhodes.

[177] On the Chelidoniai Is. (*Beş Adalar*) off SW Lykia, see e.g. Ps.-Skyl. §83, Pliny 5. xxxv. 131, Mela 2. 102.

[178] Patara was renowned for its temple of Apollo (Hdt. 1. 182; Strabo 14. 3. 6, C666; *et al*.), and was the homeland of the geographer Mnaseas (Ch. 13 above).

[179] Cyprus.

[180] On this island and city of the same name off the coast of Phoenicia, see Ps.-Skyl. §87, Pliny 5. xvii. 78, *et al*.

[181] The Abantes were a people in Euboia, as D. indicates in l. 520 below.

[182] With this line D. introduces the extended acrostic θεὸς Ἑρμῆς ἐπὶ Ἀδριανοῦ ('the god Hermes in the time of Hadrian') which he uses to sign and date his poem (see Introduction on the acrostic of ll. 513–32).

Endless the islands lined on either side in it,
Over to the narrow water of Helle, Athamas' child, where
Sestos and Abydos each have a harbour facing the other.[183]
Europe's islands beneath the left-hand quarter of heaven
Run in order, and those of Asia lie to the right,
Making lengthways for the Bears' north.
520 Europe also holds Abantian Makris,[184]
Skyros the windy, and lofty Peparethos.[185]
Elsewhere Lemnos, the rugged land of Hephaistos,[186]
Projects, and ancient Thasos, Demeter's headland (*aktē*),
Imbros, and Thracian Samos, the city of the Korybantes.[187]
Asia's islands that took the first place by lot have encircled
Delos round about, and are called the Cyclades.
Round they all go in their dances, their offerings to Apollo,
In the sweet new spring as it begins, when in the mountains,
Away from people, the clear-voiced nightingale conceives.
530 Next the Sporades islands beam brightly all around,
On a time when stars are seen through cloudless air
Upon swift Boreas' dispersal of damp mists.
After these are the Ionian islands. Here are Kaunos
and lovely Samos, the abode of Pelasgian Hera,[188]
and Chios at the foot of steep Pelinnaion.[189]
From there the mountains of the Aiolian isles appear,
spacious Lesbos, and beloved Tenedos.
From there too the gulf of Melas flows towards the Hellespont,
churning foam. As one goes far to the north,
540 there extends on this side and that the swell of the Propontic sea.
There is also, above the left-hand path of the Euxine,
opposite the Borysthenes, a well-known island in the salt-sea,
the Island of Heroes. They call it by the name of Leuke,[190]
because the serpents there are white.
There rumour has it the spirits of Achilles and other
heroes roam this way and that through the deserted glens.
This is the gift from Zeus which attends the most noble

---

[183] Sestos and Abydos are on opposite sides of the Hellespont.
[184] Makris = 'Long One'. This poeticism for Euboia is borrowed from Kallimachos, *Hymn* 4. 20. The Abantes were said to have occupied the island in antiquity (Homer, *Il* 2. 536–45; Hdt. 1. 146; Strabo 10. 1. 3, C445, *et al.*).
[185] Skyros and Peparethos are N of Euboia.   [186] Lemnos was sacred to Hephaistos.
[187] For Samothrake as centre of a mystery cult see Hdt. 2. 51, Dion Hal. 1. 68. 1, Tacitus *Ann.* 2. 54, *et al.*
[188] Kaunos is on the coast of Lykia. Hera was the patron goddess of the island of Samos.
[189] Pelinnaion is the principal mountain on Chios.   [190] 'White' I. Cf. Ps.-Skyl. §68. 4.

in reward for their virtue. For virtue is allotted a lovely honour.[191]
As one goes straight up along the Kimmerian Bosporos
550 there is another immense island, which is situated
within Lake Maiotis on the right-hand side,
and on which stand Phainagora and well-built Hermonassa.[192]
Here dwell the children of the Ionian land.
  These are the islands in the salt-sea famous among men,
but there are others the Ocean's stream garlands all around.
I would tell of the notable position of these,
and at the foot of which wind each of them lies.
  So, then, there dwell about cattle-rearing Erytheia,[193]
by the wave of the Atlantic, the god-fearing Aithiopes,
560 noble sons of the Makrobioi,[194] who once came here
after the death of proud Geryon. Below the Sacred
cape, which they say is the head of Europe,[195]
the islands of the Hesperides, the birthplace of tin,[196]
are inhabited by the rich children of the illustrious Iberians.
There are other islands by the northern shores
of Ocean, twin Bretanides, opposite the Rhine.
For there the river pours forth its last eddy into the salt-sea.
The size of these islands is immense and no other
among all the islands could equal the Bretanides isles.
570 Nearby there is another path of islets, where the wives
of the noble Amnitian[197] men on the opposite shores
excitedly perform the sacred rites for Bakchos according to custom,
wreathed with clusters of black-leaved ivy
by night; and the clear sound of the tumult rises.
Not so on the banks of the Thracian Apsynthos
do the Bistonides[198] call upon loud-roaring Eiraphiotes;

---

[191] For Leuke as inhabited by the spirit of Achilles see Euripides, *Andromache*, 1259–62; Pliny 4. xiii. 93; Arrian §21; etc.

[192] Phanagoria and Hermonassa are on the Asian side of the Thracian Bosporos.

[193] For Erytheia as located near Gadeira see Hdt. 4. 8; *Nik.* 137; *et al.* Herakles was said to have killed Geryon here, after being sent by Eurystheus to steal the monster's cattle (Hesiod, *Theog.* 270 and 979; Eurip. *Her.* 420; *et al.*)

[194] 'Long-lived'. This people were identified with the Aithiopes by Herodotos (see e.g. Hdt. 3. 21).

[195] Cape Hieron (*Sacred*), the SW tip of Portugal.

[196] D. alludes to the alternative name for these islands, the Kassiterides, apparently situating them in or near Tartessos (cf. above on l. 337).

[197] There is no other extant reference to this people. However, cf. the Namnetai at Strabo 4. 2. 1, C190; Caesar *BG* 3. 9. 9; Pliny 4. xviii. 107; and the Samnitai at Strabo 4. 4. 6, C198, who occupy an island at the mouth of the Loire and perform Bacchic rites.

[198] For the possible location of this Thracian people and the region of Apsinthis, to which D. presumably refers, see *Barr.* 51.

>   not so beside the black-eddying Ganges do the Indians,
>   with their children, lead the revelry for loud-thundering Dionysos,
>   not as the women in that spot raise their cries of 'Euoi'.
> 580 Cutting further along Ocean's long path
>   in your well-built ship you would reach the island of Thoule.[199]
>   Here, when the sun reaches the pole of the Bears,
>   the ever-blazing fire pours forth days and nights alike.
>   For then it revolves in a more oblique orbit
>   its rays travelling in a straight descent,
>   until it moves along its southern path again towards the dark peoples.
>   But whenever you cleave the deep stream of the Skythian
>   ocean in your ship, and you turn further towards the eastern salt-sea,
>   your path leads you to the island of Chryseia,[200] where the
> 590 rising of the bright sun itself is even visible.
>   Turning from there before the southern headland,
>   you would immediately come to the island of mighty Kolias,
>   Taprobane,[201] mother of the Asian-born elephants,
>   beyond which, raised high in the revolution of the heavens,
>   the fiery Crab spins in a circle in the ether.
>   This island is very broad in size, and all around
>   sea-creatures inhabit the shores, beasts of the Erythraian sea,
>   like lofty mountains. On the ridges
>   of their backs there rises a long track of spines.
> 600 May the children of our enemies, as they wander over the sea,
>   meet these creatures in their travels! For there is no escape
>   inside their wretched jaws, since it is a gaping chasm.
>   Often these monsters even gulp down the ship along with the
>   ship's very men. For the god (*daimōn*) has placed myriad ills
>   on the salt-sea and on land for those who are wicked.
>   There is further on, outside the Karmanian headland
>   Ogyris, where lies the tomb of king Erythraios.[202]
>   From there you would make your way to the mouth of the Persian salt-sea,
>   if you set out northwards, and you would come to Ikaros,[203]

---

[199] For discussion of the existence and location of this island, first recorded by Pytheas and synonymous with the extreme north, see e.g. Strabo 2. 5. 8, C115; Pliny 4. xvi. 104; Mela 3. 57.

[200] For Chryse(ia) as an island in the Indian Ocean (to which mythical qualities may have been ascribed), see e.g. Pliny 6. xxiii. 80.

[201] The Koliakon promontory is situated across from Taprobane (Sri Lanka).

[202] For the island of Ogyris (*Hormuz*) as site of the tomb of Erythras (as he is usually spelled), see e.g. Strabo 16. 3. 5, C766; Pliny 6. xxxii. 153.

[203] The island of *Failaka* in the Persian gulf, near the mouth of the Euphrates.

610   Ikaros on the sea, where the altars of the goddess Tauropolos,[204]
        full of the steam of burnt sacrifices, bear bitter smoke.
             So many are the islands which Ocean's stream meets,
        the larger islands. But there are countless others,
        some in the waters of the Libyan Amphitrite,
        some Asian, and some again around the latitude of Europe.
        The other islands elsewhere are innumerable. There are
        some which are inhabited by men and have a lovely anchorage for ships,
        and some which have high cliffs and are not suitable for sailors.
        The names of all these it is not easy for me to relate.
620   The shape of Asia is the same as the form of the two
        continents, facing in the other direction, like the outline of a cone,
        heading little by little towards the furthest nooks of all the east,
        where too stand the Pillars of Theban-born Dionysos,
        beside the stream of the outermost Ocean,
        in the most distant mountains of the Indians, where
        the Ganges winds its white water to the Nysaian plain.[205]
        But the size of the Asian land is not so great,
        nor is its shape entirely alike. For there is one sea
        which guides its stream into those continents,
630   but in Asia there is the great Ocean. For it winds
        and pours forth three seething gulfs, casting them inwards:
        the Persian, the Arabian, and the Hyrkanian with its deep eddies.
        Two in the south, and one looking towards Boreas,[206]
        looking towards Boreas and the Lips,[207] neighbour to the
        Euxine sea, where countless men dwell all around.
        An immense isthmus of land marks the boundary between the two,
        stretching here and there in vast plains.
        At the centre of all Asia a mountain range extends,
        beginning from the Pamphylian land as far as even the Indians,
640   at times at an angle and winding, and at times in turn
        completely straight in its tracks. They call it Tauros,
        because it looks like a bull and makes its way with upright horns,
        divided here and there into outstretched mountains.

---

[204] Tauropolos was an epithet of Artemis. On this island, like the homonymous island in the Aegean, as the site of a temple of Apollo and oracle of (Artemis) Tauropolos, see Strabo 16. 3. 2, C766; temple of Artemis, Arrian, *Anab.* 7. 20. 3–4.

[205] On the tradition that Nysa(ea), where Dionysos was said to have been born (*Hom. Hymn* 1; Hom. *Il.* 6. 130–7; etc.), was an area of N. India see e.g. Strabo 15. 1. 7–8, C687–8; Arrian, *Anab.* 8. 1. 4–5. On the Pillars of Dionysos in this same region see e.g. Strabo 3. 5. 6, C171. See also l. 1159 for the 'Nysaian path'.

[206] The north wind.   [207] The SW wind.

From there countless rivers flow with a loud din,
some to the north, some to the south, and some towards
the blasts of the Euros and Zephyros. Who could tell the names of them all?
It has not been allotted one name, but in each
valley it has a name. These names might concern those
men who have their homes in the neighbouring country.
650   Now, then, I will go through all the renowned nations
who dwell there. May the Muses lead a most straight path.
    Well, then, near lake Maiotis there dwell
the Maiotai themselves and the nation of the Sauromatai,
noble race of warlike Ares.[208] For they are sprung
from that powerful love of the Amazons,
in which they once joined with the men of the Sauromatai,
when they had wandered from their homeland far from the Thermodon.[209]
Because of this great-hearted children were born too,
who inhabit an immense forest, through the middle of
660 which the Tanaïs sweeps, falling into the middle of the Maiotis.
The river also divides Europe from the Asian land,
to the west Europe, and to the sunlight the land of Asia.
Its springs roar in the Caucasian mountains
far away. Broad, it rushes here and there
running over the Skythian plains.
And, when it seethes in immense waves from the north,
you would see ice freezing in the frost.
Wretched are those who have their homes around that place.
Constantly they suffer the cold snow and excessive frost.
670 Indeed, when the winds bring the fiercest frost,
you could see horses dying before your eyes,
or even mules, or the tribe of field-dwelling sheep.
Not even the men themselves would stay unharmed,
those who remained exposed to those blasts.
So they harness up their carts and roam
to another place, leaving the land to the wintry
gales, which rage against them in cruel storms,
and shake the land and the pine-covered mountains.
    So many dwell around the Tanaïs river,
680 while beside the Sauromatai one after another are[210]

---

[208] These peoples lived E of L. Maiotis.
[209] See Hdt. 4. 110–14 for this story of the union of the Amazons and Sarmatai. The Thermodon joins the Euxine in the region of Pontos.
[210] The following lines (681–5), listing the peoples neighbouring the Sarmatai to the S, appear to contain another acrostic, σκοπέ. See Note at end of chapter.

Sindoi and Kimmerioi[211] and, bordering on the Euxine,[212]
Kerketioi, Toretai, and the valiant Achaioi[213] whom,
Once on a time, the gusts of the Notos and the Zephyros
Parted from Xanthos and Idaian Simoëis,
Escorting as they were Ares' son, the king, after the battle.
After them there dwell, inhabitants of the neighbouring land,
the Heniochoi and Zygioi, descendants of the Pelasgian land.[214]
Beside the furthest nook of the Pontos, after the country of the Tyndaridai,[215]
there dwell the Kolchoi, settlers from Egypt,

690 near the Caucasus, which rises in lofty mountains
around the Hyrkanian sea.[216] Here the Phasis
winds across the flat of the Kirkaian plain,[217]
and churns its swift foam towards the wave of the Euxine,
beginning first from the Armenian mountain.[218]
To the east and north of this there lies an isthmus,
the isthmus of the Caspian and Euxine seas.
Here dwells the eastern nation of the Iberians,[219]
who once came from Pyrene to the east,
when they engaged in a hostile war with the Hyrkanians,

700 and the great tribe of the Kamaritai, who once
received and welcomed Bakchos after his war with the Indians,
and, together with the Lenai, established a sacred dance,
placing loin-cloths and fawn-skins around their middles,
crying 'Euoi, Bakchos!' And the god cherished in his
heart the race of those men and their haunts on the land.[220]

---

[211] D. is referring to the Kimmerian Bosporos and to Sindike on its SE shore.

[212] This and the following four lines contain another acrostic, σκοπέ–skope. See Supplementary Note below (following the translation).

[213] For these peoples on the NE shores of the Euxine, see e.g. Strabo 11. 2. 1, C492, and 11. 2. 11–12, C495–6 (Strabo here offers one of various accounts as to the origins of these Achaians; cf. e.g. Amm. Marc. 22. 8. 25; Strabo 9. 2. 42, C416).

[214] These peoples were E and S of the Euxine. See Strabo 11. 2. 12, C495–6; Pliny 6. v. 16, for the tradition that the Heniochoi were Spartan in origin, descendants of the 'charioteers' of Castor and Pollux.

[215] D. appears here to refer to the city of Dioskourias, named after Castor and Pollux, the twin sons of Tyndareus (Appian *Mith*. 2. 101, Hyginus *Fab*. 275, *et al*.).

[216] The tradition that the Kolchians were originally from Egypt can be traced back to Herodotos (2. 104–5).

[217] Both the R. Phasis on the E shore of the Euxine and the Kirkaian plain recall the voyage of the Argonauts (see esp. Ap. Rhod 2. 400–1).

[218] For the location of the source of the Kolchian Phasis in Armenia, see Strabo 11. 2. 17, C498.

[219] On the eastern Iberians as descended from those in the W. Mediterranean, see Strabo 11. 2. 18–19, C499.

[220] On the Kamaritai and the establishment of the rites of Dionysos near the R. Kallichoros in the same region, see Amm. Marc. 22. 8. 23–4. Cf. Ap. Rhod. 2. 904 for a similar description of the establishment of a Bacchic festival beside the R. Kallichoros. See Ps.-Skyl. §73 for the location of this river in Paphlagonia.

After them the Caspian Amphitrite swells with waves.
I would easily draw you this sea, without having seen
its faraway paths, without having travelled in a ship.
For my livelihood is not on black ships,
710 and my family is not in commerce, nor do I sail to
the Ganges, like others do, through the Erythraian sea,
without a care for their lives, in order to win immense wealth,
and I do not mix with the Hyrkanians, nor search for
the Caucasian peaks of the Erythraian Arianoi.[221]
But I am carried by the mind of the Muses, who,
without wandering, can measure vast tracts of salt-sea,
the mountains, the mainland, the course of the heavenly stars.

    So, then, the shape of the great Caspian salt-sea as a whole
would be round, circular. You would not cross it
720 in a ship before the circling of the third moon.
For so great is its relentless course. Flowing sharply
towards the north, it mixes with the waters of Ocean.
Indeed it nurtures many other marvels for men.
It produces crystal and cloudy jasper,
hateful to spectres and other phantoms.
I shall tell you of all those tribes who dwell around it,
beginning on the western side from the north.

    First are the Skythians, as many as inhabit the coast
near the sea of Kronos along the mouth of the Caspian salt-sea.[222]
730 Next are the Thynoi,[223] and after them are the Caspians,
and the warlike Albanoi after them, and the Kadousioi[224]
who dwell beyond the rugged land. Nearby are the Mardoi,
the Hyrkanians,[225] and the Tapyroi.[226] After them the Mardos[227] winds

---

[221] See e.g. Strabo 11. 8. 2, C511; 11. 10. 1, C516; 15. 2. 1, C720; Arrian, *Anab.* 3. 25. 1, and Amm. Marc. 23. 6. 69 for the Arianoi as inhabiting a region in the extreme NE bounded by the Caucasus and the Erythraian sea. They took their name from the plain of Ar(e)ia in western Asia.

[222] For the name 'Skythian' as attached to a large number of peoples in the N of Europe and Asia, see e.g. Strabo 11. 6. 2, C507.

[223] This people is typically said to have originated in Thrace, before settling in Bithynia (see e.g. Strabo 12. 3. 3, C541).

[224] See e.g. Strabo 11. 7. 1, C508, for the location of this people on the W shores of the Caspian.

[225] For the Mardi and Hyrkanians following the Albanians and Kadusians on the coast of the Caspian as one travels S, see Strabo 11. 6. 1, C507.

[226] See e.g. Strabo 11. 8. 8, C514, Pliny 6. xviii. 46, for the Tapyroi as situated on the S shore of the Caspian.

[227] Presumably the R. Amardos.

its course, the draught of the Derkebioi[228] and the rich Baktrians.[229]
For between the two it descends into the Hyrkanian salt-sea.
So, then, the Baktrians inhabit a wider region
inland beneath the ridges of Parnasos,[230]
and the Derkebians dwell on the other side by the Caspian waters.
After them to the east, beyond the resounding Araxes,[231]
740 dwell the Massagetai,[232] drawers of swift arrows.
May neither I myself nor any companion go near
these men, for they are far more hostile to strangers than others.
For they do not have the food of sweet grain,
nor even native wine. But by mixing white milk
with the blood of horses, they prepare their meals.
After them to the north are the Chorasmioi,[233] beyond whom lies the land
of Sougdia,[234] through the middle of which winds the sacred Oxos,
which leaves the Emodos mountain[235] and descends into the Caspian.
After this there dwell beside the waters of the Iaxartes[236]
750 the Sakai,[237] bearing bows which no other archer
could put to shame. For it is not customary for them to cast arrows in vain.
Also Tocharoi, Phrouroi,[238] and barbarous nations of the Seres,
who renounce cattle and fat sheep
and comb the shimmering blossoms of their desolate land
and weave finely wrought garments, prized garments,
resembling in colour the flowers of the grassy meadow.[239]
No work of spiders would rival them.
There are other Skythians in dense numbers, who inhabit
the furthest regions. Beside them there lies stretched a stormy land,
760 confined by the wintry winds and hail.
So many are the peoples around the Caspian waves.

[228] Probably the Derbekes, situated in proximity to the Hyrkanians by Strabo 11. 8. 8, C514, and Pliny 6. xviii. 48 'Dribyces'.
[229] NE Afghanistan.
[230] Probably the Paropamisos (cf. e.g. Strabo 11. 8. 1, C511; 11. 8. 8, C513), a range S of Baktria.
[231] An Armenian river.
[232] On the location and customs of the Massagetai, see e.g. Hdt. 1. 201, Strabo 11. 8. 6–8, C512–13.
[233] For this people among a list of those belonging to the Massagetai and Sakai (l. 750 below) see Strabo 11. 8. 8, C513.
[234] Sogdiane, NW of Baktria.
[235] Probably the Himalayas. Cf. Pliny 5. xxvii. 98 for Emodos, like Paropamisos (l. 737 above), among the list of names given to the Tauros Mts in different parts.
[236] *Syr Darya*.
[237] On this large Skythian people, see e.g. Strabo 11. 8. 4–5, C511–12; Pliny 6. xix. 50.
[238] For the Tocharoi see Strabo 11. 8. 2, C511; for the Tocharoi and Phrouroi together, Pliny 6. xx. 55. Strabo seems to call the latter Phaunoi, mentioning them in connection with the Seres (below) at 11. 11. 1, C516.
[239] On the customs of the Seres see e.g. Pliny 6. xx. 54; Amm. Marc. 23. 6. 64–8.

But consider now from the Kolchoi and the Phasis to the west,
by the edge of the Euxine, the abundant nations of the Pontos
as far as the Thracian mouth, where lies the land of Chalkis.[240]
First there are the Byzeres and nearby the tribes of the Becheiroi,
the Makrones and the Philyres[241] and those who have
wooden houses (*mosynai*).[242] Near them are the Tibarenoi rich in lambs.
After them there are also the Chalybes, inhabiting a cruel
and harsh land,[243] experts in the working of toilsome iron,
770   who, standing over their loud-thundering anvils,
never cease from their labour and terrible misery.[244]
After them the alluvial soil of the Assyrian land extends,
where, from the Armenian mountain to the Amazons,
the furious Thermodon sends forth its white water,[245]
Thermodon, who once received Sinope, the wandering daughter of Asopos,
and, as she grieved, consoled her in his own land
at Zeus's bidding. For Zeus, desiring sweet love,
sent her from her fatherland, unwilling as she was.[246]
Men also inhabit a city named after her.[247]
780   Around the frozen banks of that river,
you could cut the pure stone of crystal, like ice
in winter. You will also find watery jasper.
Next the Iris casts its pure stream into the salt-sea.[248]
After this there roar the streams of the river Halys,
coursing towards the north near the peak of Karambis,[249]
beginning first from the Armenian mountain.
Next on the shores there reside the Paphlagonians
and the sacred plain of the Maryandinoi.[250] Here they say

---

[240] i.e. Chalkedon, opposite Byzantion across the Hellespont.

[241] Cf. Ap. Rhod 2. 392–7, 1242–5, for the Argonauts as travelling past these same four peoples. Here and in the following description of the Pontos, D. traces their journey in reverse.

[242] See Strabo 12. 3. 18, C548–9, on the 'Mosynoikoi' of this region, so called because they lived in trees or in towers which they called *mosynoi*. Cf. Ap. Rhod. 2. 1016–17 for an allusion to the same derivation for 'Mossynoikoi'.

[243] On the Chalybes, see Olshausen 2012.

[244] Cf. Ap. Rhod. 2. 377–8, 1000–8, for similar descriptions of the Tibarenoi and Chalybes. See Strabo 12. 3. 19, C549, on the Chaldaioi or Chalybes and the iron-mines of Pharnakia.

[245] See above on l. 657 for the Thermodon as associated with the Amazons. See also Ap. Rhod. 2. 966–1000. Bekker-Nielsen and Jensen 2015 show that D.'s description fits the R. Iris, not the Thermodon.

[246] Sinope's abduction by Zeus is related at Ap. Rhod. 2. 946–54.

[247] The settlement sat on the S shores of the Euxine.

[248] For D.'s confusion between Iris and Thermodon, see n. to 774 above.

[249] See Ap. Rhod. 2. 365–72 for the Halys, Iris, and Thermodon as rivers the Argonauts were to pass after rounding the promontory of Karambis.

[250] Cf. Ap. Rhod. 2. 351–2, 357–9, 720–4 for the territory of the Maryandinoi and Paphlagonians as passed by the Argonauts.

infernal Zeus' great dog with its voice of brass,
790 when dragged up by the hands of great-hearted Herakles,
cast from its mouth a terrible slavering humour,
which the Earth received and bore as a bane on the spot.[251]
Nearby the Bithynians inhabit a fertile land.
The Rhebas here sends forth a lovely stream,
the Rhebas, which courses beside the mouth of the Pontos,
the Rhebas, whose water is the fairest to sweep over the land.[252]
    So many are the men who dwell around the Pontos.
Let the Skythian tribes, then, be those that I have mentioned.
    Now, I would tell in turn of the path of the Asian coast,
800 which goes to the south at the Hellespont coursing
even to the southern stream of the most vast Aegean,
as far as Syria itself and lovely Arabia.
The Chalkidians first of all inhabit the land near the mouth,
looking at the soil of Byzantion on the opposite coast.
After these are the Bebrykes and the mountains of the Mysian land,[253]
where Kios sends forth its beloved streams,
at the waters of which a nymph once stole Hylas,
the ready servant of giant Herakles.[254]
From here to the Hellespont runs the immense curve
810 of Lesser Phrygia. The other Phrygia lies inland,
greater in extent, by the waters of the Sangarios.
So, then, it is vast and stretches to the east,
A fertile land grazed by horses. To the west you would see the other,
which lies beneath the foot of sacred Ida,
Ilion, wind-blown, held along its borders,[255]
Ilion, glorious city of heroes of old,
Ilion, which Poseidon and Apollo founded,
Ilion, which Athene and Hera destroyed,
beside the broad-flowing Xanthos and Idaian Simoeis.
820 After this there extend the haunts of the Aiolian land,
by the edge of the Aegean, beyond the great Hellespont.
After this there dwell the children of the noble Ionians,

---

[251] For a path to Hades as situated in the territory of the Maryandinoi near the promontory of Acherousia and the *polis* of Herakleia on the Euxine, cf. Ap. Rhod. 2. 351–6, 734–42.

[252] Cf. Ap. Rhod. 2. 650 for the Bithynian river Rhebas, situated N of Chalkedon, as passed by the Argonauts.

[253] The Bebrykes and Mysia both again have roles in the *Argonautica* (see e.g. Ap. Rhod. 2. 1–4; and 1. 1114–15 respectively).

[254] See Ap. Rhod. 1. 1177–272 for the Mysian river Kios and the story of Hylas and the nymph.

[255] Ilion was the *polis* near the site of Troy.

near the sea, in that country through the middle of which
the Maeander descends into the salt-sea with fertile eddies,
between Miletos and spacious Priene.
To the north of both these two you will see
Ephesos on the coast, the great city of the arrow-shooter,[256]
where the Amazons once built a temple to the goddess
in the trunk of an elm, an extraordinary wonder to men.[257]

830   After these Maionia extends to the east
beneath windy Tmolos, whence the Paktolos makes its way,
bringing gold in its eddies and murmuring.[258]
Sitting on its banks in the season of Spring
you would hear the clear voices of the swans, which beside the water
graze here and there on the grass still[259] growing.
For many meadows flourish in Asia,
especially on the plain of Maeander, where the gleaming
water of the gently splashing Kaÿstros flows.[260]
You certainly would not fault the women, who around

840   that divine spot, wearing a belt of gold at their waists,
dance, turning in a wondrous circle,
when the dances of Dionysos take place.
With them maidens skip, like young fawns,
and round about them the sounding winds
stir the lovely tunics on their breasts.
But this is the concern of the Lydian people.
By the salt-sea the Lykians inhabit a land
on the waters of the Xanthos, the fair-flowing river.
Here the mountains of the high-cliffed Tauros appear,

850   as far as Pamphylia. They call it Kragos.[261]
There you would see a city on the sea,
Aspendos, by the stream of the river Eurymedon,[262]
where they appease the daughter of Dione with the slaughter of swine.
Other Pamphylian cities follow in sequence,

---

[256] Artemis.

[257] See e.g. Kallim. *Hymn* 3 (*To Artemis*), 237–46, for the myth of the founding of the temple to Artemis at Ephesos by Amazons.

[258] Maionia, Mt Tmolos, and the R. Paktolos are E of Ionia. For the tradition that the river carried gold, see e.g. Hdt. 5. 101.

[259] For the swans of the Paktolos see Kallim. *Hymn* 4 (*To Delos*), 249–54; Ap. Rhod. 4. 1300–2.

[260] The Kaÿstros lies N of the Maeander. The reference to this river is an allusion to Homer *Il.* 2. 459–65, to which Ap. Rhod. also alludes in the passage cited above.

[261] For Kragos as a name for the Tauros, see also Pliny 5. xxvii. 98.

[262] On the Pamphylian town of Aspe(n)dos and the R. Eurymedon, see e.g. Ps.-Skyl. §84; Diod. Sic. 14. 99. 1; Strabo 14. 4. 2, C668.

Korykos, and Perge, and wind-blown Phaselis.²⁶³
To the east of these, inhabiting an inland region,
are the Lykaones with their crooked bows, experts in war.
After them there is the fertile plain of the Pisidians, where stand the cities
of Telmessos and Lyrbe and that city which the people
860   of Amyklai once built in times past, Selge, renowned in the land.²⁶⁴
From there to the sunlight a curved Amphitrite winds
A twisted path reaching far inland,
neighbour to the stormy Euxine sea.
That gulf sweeps around the nations of the Kilikians
A long way to the east. They call it the Strait of Asia.
The waters of many rivers which come from afar
mix with this, the waters of the Pyramos and the Pinaros,
and the winding Kydnos, which flows through the middle of Tarsos,
well-built Tarsos, where the horse Pegasus once,
870   lost a hoof and left his name to that place, when the hero
Bellerophon fell from the horse on his way to the home of Zeus.
There too is the Aleian plain, on the flat of which,
as he wandered far from men, Bellerophon rested.²⁶⁵
Next are the many cities of the Kilikians in sequence,
Lyrnessos and Mallos and Anchialeia and Soli,²⁶⁶
some inland, and others near the sea itself.
After these are the seat of Kommagenos and the cities of Syria
stretching along the winding shore.²⁶⁷ For the course of the
grey salt-sea turns around to the west, as far as the peak
880   of the mountain near the sea, high-cliffed Kasios.²⁶⁸
    I would easily tell of the remaining path
of the lands of Asia. Keep these words in your heart,

---

²⁶³ On Korykos see e.g. Strabo 14. 3. 8, C666. On Phaselis and Perge see e.g. Ps.-Skyl. §§83–4, Strabo 14. 3. 9–10, C666–7.

²⁶⁴ On Termessos, and on Selge as a Spartan settlement, see e.g. Strabo 12. 7. 1–3, C569–71; Arrian, *Anab.* 1. 28. 1. There is no earlier reference to Lyrbe, although it is listed among the cities of Kilikia by Ptolemy (5. 5. 8).

²⁶⁵ See e.g. Homer *Il.* 6. 200 for Bellerophon as left to wander the Kilikian plain of Aleia after being caused to fall from Pegasos by a gadfly, sent by Zeus.

²⁶⁶ On the Kilikian towns of Mallos and Sol(o)i see e.g., Ps.-Skyl. §85, Strabo 14. 5. 16–17, C675–6; Pliny 5. xxii. 91–2. For Anchiale(ia) see e.g. Strabo 14. 5. 9–10, C671–2; Pliny 5. xxii. 91. Lyrnessos is best known as the town from which Achilles took Briseis (Hom. *Il.* 2. 690, *et al.*) in the Mysian Kilikia, SW of Troy. Cf. Kallisthenes, *BNJ* 124 F 32 = Strabo 14. 4. 1, C667, on the 'Trojan Kilikians' founding a city by the same name in Pamphylia.

²⁶⁷ Kommagene is NW of Syria.

²⁶⁸ Probably not the Mt Kasios on the Phoenician coast (*Barr.* 68), but the Egyptian Mt Kasios (*Barr.* 70), also named as a landmark at ll. 116 and 260 above, and 901 below.

and do not let the grace of my hard work be carried away by the winds.
For if you were to observe this path clearly,
then you could soon tell others too in an expert fashion
of the rivers and of the location of the cities and of each land.
   So let there be a shape of four sides,
stretching towards the east in long plains.
Now you know, as you heard me say so in the first place,
890 that a mountain cuts all of Asia in two as far as the Indians.
That would form the more northerly of the sides,
and the Nile would be the western side. The eastern side
would be the Indian Ocean, and the southern would be formed by the waves
of the Erythraian salt-sea.
Consider how I shall now make my way to the sunlight along the coast,
beginning from Syria, where I left off, and no man
could accuse me of giving a false account.
   Well, then, Syria creeps beyond the salt-sea nearby
to the south and east, with a land that has many cities,
which they call 'Hollow', because it is in the middle
900 of mountain-peaks which render it low down,
the peaks of Kasios in the west and Libanos in the east.[269]
Many wealthy men inhabit this land,
though they do not dwell together under one name, but separately,
some inland, who are called Syrians,
and some near the salt-sea, named Phoenicians.
They are of the race of men who are Erythraians,
who first made an attempt on the sea in ships,
and were the first to turn their minds to trade by sea
and consider the far chorus of the heavenly stars.
910 These men inhabit Iope and Gaza and Elaïs,[270]
and ancient Tyre and the lovely land of Berytos,
and Byblos by the sea and flowery Sidon,
situated by the waters of the charming Bostrenos,
and fertile Tripolis, and Orthosis and Marathos
and Laodike, which lies on the shores of the sea,[271]
916 and the fields of Poseidon[272] and the sacred vales of Daphne.[273]

---

[269] Mt Libanos (Mt *Lebanon*) is on the Phoenician coast.
[270] Elaïs has proved difficult to identify with any certainty (see Counillon 1983 for a conjecture).
[271] On all these coastal cities, see e.g. Strabo 16. 2. 12, C753; Pliny 5. i. 17–18.
[272] Possibly a reference to Posideion S of the Phoenician Mt Kas(s)ios. Cf. Hdt. 3. 91, Strabo 16. 2. 8, C751; Pliny 5. xviii. 79 on the same.
[273] Daphne is immediately S of Antioch. The next line is excised by editors: 'Where lies Antioch, named after Antiochos'.

918	In the midst of these is the city of Apameia,
	to the east of which flows the moist Orontes,
920	immense, and dividing the land of Antiochos through the middle.[274]
	The whole region is fertile and abounds in pasture,
	to feed the sheep and cause the fruit on the trees to grow.
	Beyond this land you would see, as you made your way further south,
	the innermost path of the Arabian gulf, which winds
	between Syria and lovely Arabia,
	turning a little to the east as far as Elana.[275]
	From there the land of the most fortunate Arabs extends
	reaching far, and girded by twin seas,
	the Persian and the Arabian. Each has been allotted a wind,
930	The Arabian the Zephyros, the Persian the paths of the Euros.
	The southern coast facing the east
	is washed by the waves of the Erythraian ocean.
	And I shall tell you of its position. For exceptionally among
	lands it is inhabited by tribes who are very fortunate and noble.
	This land has been allotted another exceptionally great wonder.
	It always smells sweetly from the perfume of burnt offerings,
	either of incense, or myrrh, or fragrant grass
	or even divinely scented aged frankincense
	or cassia. For indeed it was in that very place that Zeus
940	himself freed Dionysos from his well-stitched thigh;
	and at his birth made the plain fragrant.
	The sheep too then became laden with shaggy fleeces
	in the pasture, and the lakes flowed with waters spontaneously.
	Birds from uninhabited islands elsewhere
	came bearing leaves of untouched cinnamon.
	Then the god stretched a fawn-skin over his shoulders
	and garlanded his fair hair with lovely ivy,
	slightly drunk with wine, and took up his wreathed thyrsi,
	smiling, and showered the men with great wealth.
950	For this reason even today the fields are thick with frankincense,
	the mountains with gold, and the rivers elsewhere with sacrificial offerings.
	The inhabitants themselves are a very wealthy people,
	glorying in soft robes of gold.
	So, then, first beyond the slope of Libanos
	dwell the rich people called the Nabataioi.
	Near them are the Chaulasioi and the Agreis, beyond whom

---

[274] The Orontes runs from Antioch S past Apameia.
[275] Presumably Ailana or Aila, described by e.g. Strabo at 16. 2. 30, C759.

is the land of Chatramis, opposite the Persian land.
Inhabiting the coast of the Erythraian sea
are the Minnaioi and Sabai and the neighbouring Kletabanoi.[276]
960 So many immense tribes inhabit Arabia,
but there are also many more, for it is extremely vast.
   Towards the opposite shore, under the blast of the Zephyros
appears the wretched land of the mountain-dwelling Eremboi,
who live their lives in dug-out rocks,
naked and without possessions. On their bodies
burning from the heat the parched skin grows black.[277]
Thus, like wild animals, they roam and suffer hardships,
unlike the people of the soft-living Arabs. For the deity
has not given to all men an equal share in wealth.
970 Beyond Libanos towards the rays of the sun
there lies stretched the extensive land of the other Syria,
reaching as far as sea-washed Sinope.[278]
In the middle of this deep land there dwell
the Kappadokians, experts in horsemanship,[279]
and the Assyrians near the salt-sea, by the mouth of the Thermodon.
   To the east, out from the rugged mountains
there appears the stream of the boundless Euphrates.
This starts first from the Armenian mountain
and goes far towards the south, and back, winding in curves,
980 facing the sun as it journeys through the middle of Babylon,
it pours forth its swift foam into the swell of the Persian salt-sea,
passing near Teredon with its furthermost waters.[280]
After this to the sunlight the most rapid of all rivers,
the fair-flowing Tigris bears its stream leading an even course,
As far as a strong, fast traveller could achieve
If he had travelled as much as seven days.
There is in the middle a certain lake encircled by its waters,
named Thonitis, into the corners of which the Tigris flows,

---

[276] For similar lists of peoples beyond Nabataea and on the coast of the Erythraian sea, cf. e.g. Strabo 16. 4. 2–3, C767–8; Pliny 6. xxxii. 144–56. (Both Strabo and Pliny have 'Kataban(o)i' rather than 'Cletabani', and neither author lists the Chaulasioi, although Strabo refers to 'Chaulotaioi' in connection with the Nabataioi and Agraioi.)

[277] D. describes the Trogodytai associated with E. Africa. Cf. Strabo 1. 1. 3, C2, alluding to Homer, Od. 4. 84 'Eremboi', whom S. takes to be the 'Trogodytai Arabes'.

[278] See above on ll. 775–9 for Assyrian Sinope on the S coast of the Euxine.

[279] On the Kappadokians as ('White') Syrians see e.g. Herodotos 1. 6. 72; Strabo 12. 3. 5, C542.

[280] Teredon remains difficult to identify; see e.g. Strabo 2. 1. 26, C80; Amm. Marc. 23. 6. 11. Ptolemy, however, situates it on the Tigris (5. 19), Pliny below the confluence of the Tigris and Euphrates (6. xxxii. 145).

sinking far below. On rising back up again,
990 it casts southward a swifter stream.²⁸¹ Among all the rivers
you would not see another more rapid.
All the land between the Euphrates and the Tigris
the people who live round about call 'amid the rivers'.²⁸²
No herdsman has faulted the pastures of that land,
nor anyone who honours horn-hoofed Pan on the syrinx
and follows the sheep of the field. No man who tends plants
has made light of the variety of fruits,
for such is the soil in that land, in fostering
the grass, the pastures full of flowers, and even the race
1000 of men, most handsome and similar to the immortals.
    To the north of this a fertile country is inhabited by
the Armenian men and the close-fighting Matienoi,
who live in the mountains, along the river Euphrates,
rich and wealthy and expert in war.²⁸³
To the south is the sacred city of Babylon, the whole of
which Semiramis crowned with impenetrable walls.²⁸⁴
Moreover on the acropolis she built a great temple to Belos,
and adorned it with gold and ivory and silver.
The plain of Babylon is immense, where many
1010 overhanging palms grow with leafy crowns.
Yes, it bears something else more beautiful than gold,
the sea-green stone of watery beryl, which forms
on the jutting rocks in that region within the stone of serpentine.
    Beyond Babylon towards the blast of Boreas
the Kissoi and Messabatai and Chalonitai dwell.²⁸⁵
But whenever you should journey beyond the Armenian mountains,
to the sunlight, then you will find the valleys of the Medes.
To the north of these a flourishing land is inhabited
by Geloi and Mardoi and Atropatenoi.²⁸⁶

---

[281] On the speed of the Tigris and its course through L. Tho(s)pitis, Arsene, or Arethusa, see e.g. Strabo 11. 14. 8, C529; Pliny 6. xxxi. 128 (Thospites and Arrhene), cf. 6. xxxii. 159 Arethusa.

[282] *Messē potamōn*, i.e. Mesopotamia.

[283] For the Matienoi as dwelling E of Phrygia, see Hdt. 1. 72; for Matiane as part of Media, see Strabo 11. 7. 2, C509.

[284] For Semiramis as building Babylon's walls and a temple to Belos, see Ktesias *BNJ* 688 F 1b, §8. 4–9. 4 = Diod Sic. 2. 8. 4–9. 4.

[285] For the Kissian country near Sousa, see Hdt. 3. 91. For the Kossiaioi (*sic*) as living E of Sousa, and the region of Mesabatene as N of this people, see Pliny 6. xii. 31. For Massabatike as in the S of Media, see Strabo 16. 1. 18, C744–5. For the Chalonitis as near Mt Zagron (mod. *Zagros*), see Strabo 16. 1. 1, C736, and for the same name as applying to a region near Ktesiphon, see Pliny 6. xii. 30.

[286] See on 732 above for the Mardoi, E of Media Atropatene near the Caspian. For the location of the Gel(a)i, S of the Albanians (on which cf. 731 above), see Strabo 11. 5. 1, C503–4.

1020   To the south there dwell the nations of the noble
            Medes, descendants of that glorious line
            of Aiëtes' daughter, blameless heroine.[287]
            For when, beside the stream of the Aktaian Ilissos,[288]
            she prepared the baneful drugs for the son of Pandion,
            she left that place in shame, and, as she wandered among men,
            she came to that rich land, which shares her name,
            not far from the Kolchoi. To the land of the Kolchoi
            she could not come, for she feared her father's anger.
            For this reason still now men expert in many drugs
1030   inhabit that immense land, some dwelling on the very
            rocks, which produce dark narcissite,
            and some also in the overgrown meadows,
            pasturing their fine flocks, which are utterly weighed down by their fleeces.
            These men reach towards the east, as far as the Caspian
            gates,[289] which lie below hollow rocks,
            keys to the Asian land, where a path
            lies stretched for those travelling both to the north and to the south,
            one to the Hyrkanians, another to the mountains of the Persian land.
                Well, then, below the foot of the Caspian Gates
1040   dwell the warlike Parthians,[290] who carry curved bows,
            experts in every form of combat. For they do not
            trace the furrow with the plough, cleaving the farm-lands,
            nor do they cut through the salt-sea with oars aboard ships,
            nor do they feed the race of cattle in the pastures. But from birth,
            as children, they concern themselves with bows and horses,
            and always over this echoing land there is the noise of
            javelins or arrows, and everywhere the running of storm-swift horses,
            racing. For it is not customary for them to take their
            supper before showering their heads with sweat from the strains of battle.
1050   They feed on the prey of a livelihood won by the spear.
            Nevertheless, though they are relentless in battle,
            the sword-point of the Ausonian king has tamed them.
                If sweet longing to learn of the Persians also grips you,
            with eloquent words I would tell you of their race too,
            and of the course of the ever-flowing rivers and of the paths of the mountains.

---

[287] See Hdt. 7. 62 for the tradition that the Medes were descended from Medea.
[288] For the Ilissos, see 424 above.
[289] See e.g. Arrian *Anab*. 3. 20 and Pliny 6. iv. 14–v. 15 on this narrow mountain pass, S of the Caspian.
[290] On the extent of Parthia, see e.g. Strabo 11. 9. 1, C514; Pliny 6. v. 17–vi. 18.

For they alone have the most kingly nation of Asia,
and they alone laid boundless wealth in their homes,
when they sacked Maionia and Sardis.²⁹¹
Golden is the armour worn on the flesh of those men,
1060 golden are the bits in the mouths of their horses,
and with gold they adorn the shoes on their feet.
For so immense is their wealth. Well, all
the land of Persia is surrounded by great mountains,
and its path reaches to the south of the Caspian Gates,
going even as far as the Amphitrite of the same name.
They inhabit it in three distinct areas, some in the north
situated near the shady mountains of the bow-carrying Medes,
some in the interior, and some to the south as far as the sea.²⁹²
First are the Sabai, after them are the Pasargadai, and nearby the Taskoi,²⁹³
1070 and others, who inhabit various parts of the Persian land.
Many rivers make this region very fertile,
turning this way and that with their winding waters.
On one side is the great Koros, on the other the Choaspes,²⁹⁴
drawing Indian water, and flowing beside the country of the Sousai.
On its banks you would see beautiful agate,
lying like a tree-trunk on the ground, which the torrents
of the stormy river sweep down from the rock.
What's more, ever rejoicing in the warm wind,
fruits flourish densely packed against one another.
1080   Now consider the small (*lepton*) path of Asia to the sunlight.
For nearby the coast of the land comes to an end.
So, then, by the Persian wave of the Ocean,
the Karmanoi dwell, beneath the rising sun.²⁹⁵
They occupy a land in two parts not far from Persia,
some as a coast-people, others mainlanders.
To the east of them extends the land of the Gedrosoi,²⁹⁶
neighbours of the Ocean with great monsters, to the sunlight from whom
dwell the southern Skythians beside the Indos river,²⁹⁷

---

²⁹¹ For Maionia (Lydia) see above on 830. Sardis was its capital.

²⁹² For a similar division of Persia into three, see e.g. Strabo 15. 3. 1, C727.

²⁹³ D. here seems to refer to three cities of Persia—Pasargadai and Taoke being two, Gabai a third—if we accept that 'Taskoi' is a corruption of Taoke, and 'Gabai' of Sabai. On the palaces at Pasargadai and Gabai and another near Taoke, see e.g. Strabo 15. 3. 3, C728.

²⁹⁴ See Strabo 15. 3. 6, C729, for the Choaspes and 'Kyros' rivers. (For the possible identification of the Choaspes, near Sousa, see *Barr.* 93; for the Koros (*Kor*) near Pasagardai see *Barr.* 94.

²⁹⁵ On Karmania as lying E of Persia and N of the Persian gulf, see also e.g. Strabo 2. 1. 22–3, C78.

²⁹⁶ See also below on 1096 (Gedrosoi).

²⁹⁷ See *Barr.* 5 for Indo-Skythia as E of Gedrosia and W of the Indus.

	which flows opposite the Erythraian sea,
1090	furiously driving its swift stream directly south,
	beginning first from the windy Caucasus.
	It has two mouths, and it runs past an island in the middle,
	an island which the inhabitants call Patalene.[298]
	That river divides the tribes of many nations:
	Towards the descent of the setting sun
	the Oreitai and the Aribai and the Arachotai in their tunics of linen,[299]
	and the Satraidai, and all those beside the valley of Parpanisos,[300]
	together with very well all those alike who are called Arianoi,[301]
	who do not inhabit a fair land, but one filled
1100	with fine sand and rough with thickets.
	But, nevertheless, the means are sufficient for those living there.
	For the land provides for them a pure wealth of a different kind.
	For everywhere there is the stone of red coral,
	and everywhere, moreover, beneath the rocks, the veins
	bear the fair stone of the golden and blue sapphire,
	from the mining of which they have the merchandise to live on.
	To the sunlight stretches the lovely land of the Indians,
	last of all, by the edges of Ocean.
	The sun as it rises over the workings of the blessed ones and mankind
1110	scorches this land with its first rays.
	For this reason the inhabitants of the land are dark-skinned,
	divinely sleek, and they bear on their heads
	the most luxuriant hair like hyacinths.
	Of these men, some mine the sources of gold,
	digging the sand with well-made picks,
	some weave webs of linen, and some polish
	the silvery sawn-off tusks of elephants.
	Others hunt at the approaches to mountain-torrents
	for the sea-green stone of beryl or sparkling
1120	diamond or green-glancing jasper
	or again the glittering stone of pure topaz
	and sweet softly flushing amethyst.

---

[298] See e.g. Strabo 15. 1. 32–3, C700–1; Pliny 6. viii. 23 on the course of the Indus and the island of Patalene at its mouth.

[299] For the 'Oreitai' and 'Arabiës' as separated by the R. Arabis on the Erythraian coast, see Arrian, *Indike* 21. 8–9. For the Arachotai (like the Gedrosoi) as an Indian people, see Pliny 6. vii. 23; for their location, 6. ix. 25. Cf. Strabo 11. 10. 1, C516, on Arachosia.

[300] Usually called Paropamisos; see above on 737 for the location. The Satraidai are not otherwise attested.

[301] For the Arianoi see above on 714.

For the land fosters wealth of every kind for the men,
watered here and there by ever-flowing rivers.
Yes, even the meadows are always thick with leaves.
For on one side millet grows, and on the other, in turn,
there flourish forests of the Erythraian reed.
   Consider how I am to describe to you the shape and the rivers,
and the windy mountains and the nations of the land itself.
1130 Well, then, it is fixed on four sides,
all of them at an angle, like the shape of a rhombus.
So Indos, neighbouring on the western waters,
cuts off the land, the Erythraian salt-sea's swell the south,
Ganges towards the sunlight, the Caucasus towards the pole of the Bears.
Many fortunate men inhabit this land,
Not all of them living under the same name, but
distinguished into separate groups. So, near the boundless river Indos,
are the Dardaneis,[302] where the Akesine, which flows in a crooked
course from the rocks, is received by the Hydaspes, navigable to ships.[303]
1140 After them there follows a third, the silver-eddying Kophes.[304]
Amidst these rivers there dwell the Sabai and the Toxiloi,[305]
and next the Skodroi.[306] And following on there are the boundless tribes,
of the Peukales.[307] After them the servers of Dionysos,
the Gargaridai,[308] dwell, there where the Hypanis and the
divine Magarsos,[309] most turbulent of rivers, bear the marvellous
progeny of gold. Starting from the mountain of Emodos,[310]
they flow towards the country of the Ganges,

---

[302] Possibly the same as the Dardai of Pliny 6. vii. 22, whose exact localization is not clear, and/or the Daradrai of Ptolemy 7. 1. 42 situated in the mountains NW of the Akesine(s), a tributary of the Indus.

[303] See e.g. Arrian, *Anab.* 6. 14, on the Akesine(s) and its confluence with the Hydaspes before joining the Indus.

[304] On the R. Kophe(s) see e.g. Strabo 15. 1. 26, C697; Pliny 6. viii. 23, who makes it the boundary of India.

[305] The Sabai are possibly the Sibai on the Akesine(s) (Arrian, *Ind.* 8. 5. 12; Strabo 15. 1. 8, C688; *et al.*). The Toxiloi are presumably to be identified with the Taxilai mentioned by Pliny (6. viii. 23) and Strabo (15. 1. 28, C698).

[306] These Skodroi are perhaps to be identified with the Oxydrakai or Soudrakai mentioned by Arrian (*Ind.* 8. 4. 9) and Strabo (15. 1. 33, C701) as situated near the confluence of the Akesine(s) and Hydaspes rivers. (Strabo here names them in connection with the Sibai.)

[307] See *Barr.* 6 for the possible location of Peukelaotis, along the R. Kophe(s), as indicated by Arrian (*Ind.* 8. 4. 11).

[308] Probably a reference to the people of Gandaris, the capital of the region of Peukolaïtis, rather than to the Gangaridai, typically situated near the mouth of the Ganges in NE India (see e.g. Strabo 15. 1. 27, C698; Pliny 6. vii. 22).

[309] For the Hypanis or Hyp(h)asis see e.g. Strabo 15. 1. 17, C391–2; Pliny 6. vii. 21. The Magarsos is perhaps to be identified with another river of the Punjab, but no such river is described in the surviving sources.

[310] See above on l. 748.

which reaches to the south along the borders of the Kolian land.[311]
This, indeed, juts out into the deep-eddying Ocean.
1150 It is steep, inaccessible to swift birds.
For this reason men call it Aornis, 'Land without Birds'.[312]
There is a certain spectacular place beside the fair-flowing Ganges,
a place which is revered and sacred, where Bakchos once
walked in anger, when the delicate fawn-skins
of the Lenai[313] were turned into shields, and their thyrsi
were changed into iron, and their belts and the tendrils
of the twisting vine into the coils of serpents,
then when in their folly they slighted the festival of the god.
For this reason they call it the Nysaian path,[314]
1160 and with ivy they established together with their sons all his rites.
He himself, when he destroyed the tribes of the dark Indians,
ascended the mountains of Emodos, below the foot of
which flows the mighty stream of the eastern Ocean.
Here he placed two pillars near the borders of the land,
and exultant he returned to the great wave of the Ismenos.

So many are the most eminent men on the Earth,
but others wander here and there over the lands
in their thousands, whom no-one could tell of clearly,
no mortal. Only the gods are able to do all with ease.
1170 For they rounded off the first foundations
and revealed the deep swell of the measureless sea.
They marked out all that is immutable in life,
distinguishing the stars, and allotting each
A share of the sea and the deep Earth.
For this reason each land has been allotted a nature of a different kind.
For one has been made white and shining,
another is darker, and another has the appearance of both.
One is red-hued like the blooms of Assyria,
others are otherwise. For mighty Zeus has conceived it thus.
1180 So is everything among men diverse.

Farewell, you countries and islands in the salt-sea,

---

[311] See above on ll. 593–4 for this promontory opposite Sri Lanka in the far S of India.
[312] Aornis or Aornos was a name given to various places. Cf. e.g. Arrian, *Anab*. 4. 28. 1–3 and Strabo 15. 1. 8, C688, for Aornos as a rocky summit in N. India, near the source of the Indus.
[313] Cf. 701 above for the Lenai as followers of Dionysos, who joined the Kamaritai in establishing the rites of the god near the R. Kallichoros.
[314] The mythical place of Dionysos' upbringing, Nysa, like Aornis or Aornos, was a name given to various locations. On the Indian Nysa, see e.g. Arrian *Ind*. 8. 1. 4–7 and Strabo 15. 1. 7–8, C687, who quotes a passage from Sophokles (fr. 959) connecting Nysa with Aornis or Aornos.

waters of Ocean and sacred waves of the deep,
rivers and springs and mountain glens.
Now I have run over the swell of the entire sea,
and the winding path of the lands. So may my hymns
receive from the Blessed Ones themselves a worthy answer.

NOTE ON THE ACROSTIC AT LINES 681–5

As noted above, the initial letters of lines 681–5 form an acrostic, σκοπέ–*skope*. If we exclude τε καί (*te kai*, 'both . . . and'), the initial letters of the remaining words in 681 (Σινδοὶ Κιμμέριοί τε καὶ οἱ πέλας Εὐξείνοιο, **Sindoi Kimmerioi te kai (h)oi pelas Euxeinoio**), also spell σκοπέ, thus offering a 'gamma' acrostic like that in lines 307–11. This suggests that this acrostic, like the others in the poem, is intentional.

In fact, the acrostic here evokes that at 307–11 in more than its form. In describing the peoples on the NE shores of the Black Sea, these lines—like 306–7, describing the Black Sea's NW coast—refer to the myths surrounding Agamemnon, Achilles, and the Trojan War (Khan 2002, 125). While σκοπός is widely used of mortals and immortals as observers or guardians (see e.g. Hom. *Il.* 23. 539 of Phoinix; Pindar, *Ol.* 1. 54 of the Olympian gods and 6. 59 of Apollo), the vocative form is found in the compound λιμενοσκόπε (*limenoskope*, 'harbour-watcher') in an address to Artemis by Kallimachos (*Hymn* 3. 259), which Dionysios may well have had in mind here, so that it is tempting to see in the acrostic an invocation to Artemis in her role as watcher over routes and harbours.

In the lines of his hymn that follow, Kallimachos goes on to allude to the myth of Agamemnon's sacrifice of Iphigeneia (*Hymn* 3. 262–3), consort of Achilles (cf. scholia on D. 306). He also refers to this myth in the preceding passage, in which he describes Artemis pursuing first Agamemnon (*Hymn* 3. 228–32) and then Lygdamis (251–8). He describes Lygdamis' Kimmerian troops as ἱππημολγοί–*hippēmolgoi* ('mare-milkers', 252), on which, as a proper name for a Skythian tribe at Dionysios line 309, see Khan 2002, 127.

Another indication that lines 681–5 are intended to evoke the passage containing the earlier acrostic may lie in Dionysios' reference to Sarmatai in 304 and Sauromatai in 680, both alternative names for the Sarmatians, on whom see Khan 2002, 122. This people, like the Tauroi whom Kallimachos has Artemis renounce in the same hymn (*Hymn* 3. 174), and whom Dionysios describes as occupying the area known as Achilles' Racetrack (306–7), were identified with the Skythians. (On the identification of the Tauroi, see Khan 2002, 125.) D. may have wished to suggest that the naming, identification, and location of such peoples were fluid, or to highlight symmetries between opposite shores of the Black Sea. For D.'s interest in drawing symmetries between peoples and places across continents, see Khan 2002, 19–21.

29
AGATHEMEROS SON OF ORTHON
(WRITTEN C. AD 125–50)

D. Graham J. Shipley

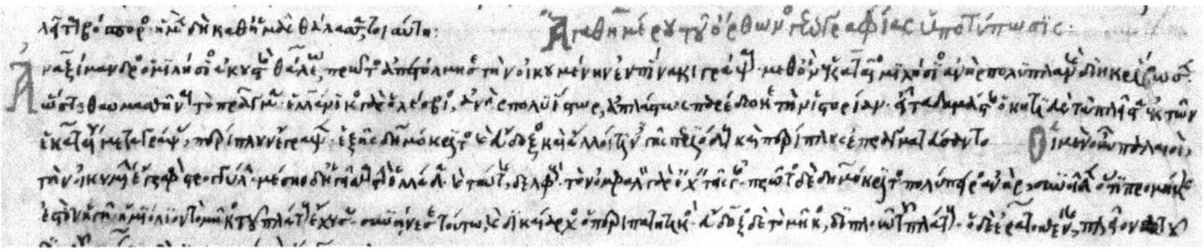

FIG. 29.1. Opening of the text of Agathemeros, fo. 3ʳ (detail).

INTRODUCTION

This Greek text—short but seemingly complete; strictly factual rather than literary—is contained within the detached London and Paris portions of the late medieval manuscript B (see Introduction, §VIII. 2. a).[1] The piece is entitled *Hypotypōsis geōgraphias*, meaning *Outline of Geography*.[2] Its author is named as Agathemeros son of Orthon, who is otherwise unknown. It falls naturally into five parts and is conventionally subdivided into 26 short sections, numbered continuously. Parts i–ii (§§1–7) make general observations about geography and the *oikoumenē*; parts iii–v (§§8–26) are more descriptive. It has no conclusion, and may have been designed as a preface to the corpus of geographical texts compiled by Arrian during or soon after the reign of Hadrian (AD 117–38; Arrian died around 150). Whether it was written at Arrian's instigation we can only surmise.

As regards the date of the work, strictly speaking we can only be sure that it postdates Menippos (cited at v. 20), and that it is unlikely to be later than the 3rd century AD because of the form in which Agathemeros' father's name is given in the title.[3] A date during or just after Arrian's lifetime, however, is a strong possibility if we consider that Agathemeros shows no knowledge of Ptolemy of Alexandria (*c*.100–70); that

---

[1] On the MSS see Guzmán Guerra 1977; González Ponce 2019a, 87–8. The second most important MS, a C16 copy of B, is Cambridge, University Library Gg. II. 33 (images at https://cudl.lib.cam.ac.uk/view/MS-GG-00002-00033/249 and next four pp.).

[2] Called *Geographiae informatio* by Müller in *GGM* ii. Not to be confused with the late antique *Hypotyposis* (Ch. 35 below); see below in the present chapter introduction.

[3] So González Ponce 2019a, 88.

Arrian, too, may have drawn upon the work of Menippos;[4] and that both writers comment on changing views of the division between Europe and Asia (formerly the river Phasis, now the Tanaïs: compare Arrian 19. 1–2, in Chapter 27 above, with i. 3 below).[5] Whether or not it was accompanied by a map, it is partly conceived in cartographic perspective, but it is no less dependent upon the hodological perspective that gives the reader a sense of movement and of connexions between places.[6]

A date around the second quarter of the 2nd century, and a relationship to Arrian's corpus (which apart from Arrian's own *Periplous* of the Black Sea contained only Hanno, *PME*, and Ps.-Plutarch), go some way towards explaining why Agathemeros presents a retrospective, essentially hellenistic picture of geography that takes no account of recent work.[7] Much of §§1–20 also appears in earlier chapters of the present volume, since it quotes several earlier authors.[8] Accordingly, his importance lies primarily in the material he preserves that is either unique or superior to similar information elsewhere. Apart from the authors he cites, part iv. 15–19, for example, is clearly based on Artemidoros, since Pliny repeatedly cites him by name for the same material (2. cxii. 242-6 = Artemidoros 4), though Agathemeros' version is the more detailed.[9]

The first part begins with a brief chronological catalogue of geographers, mapmakers (§1), and their changing views on the shape of the world or its inhabited portion (the *oikoumenē*; §2). The latest authority cited is Poseidonios (Chapter 19 above), who is probably the source for the rest of part i, covering the evolution of views of the continents (§3), the etymology of their names (§4), and a definition of Dikaiarchos' central parallel of latitude (§5).

The second part details the wind rose, initially (§6) in an eightfold scheme derived ultimately from Aristotle's *Meteorologika* (2. 6; see Chapter 10, introduction and appendix);[10] then (§7) in a twelvefold version, including an enumeration of which peoples live in the part of the world from which each wind blows. The originator of the latter version is named as Timosthenes (Chapter 10, no. 18), though the immediate source may have been Poseidonios.[11]

The third part lists some two dozen constituent bodies of water within the Mediterranean and Black Sea (§§8–9), the coastal lengths of the continents (§10), and the dimensions of four outer gulfs of the Ocean outside the Mediterranean (§§11–14). The whole of this part has been thought to derive ultimately from Artemidoros (though he is named only at v. 20).[12]

---

[4] Accepted by Leroy 2018, following Silberman 1995, xxix n. 104 and xxxiii, who notes that Diller 1952, 149, doubts it.
[5] Diller 1975a, 60; Leroy 2018, introduction, for these several dating arguments.
[6] González Ponce 2019a, e.g. 91–7, 99–102.   [7] González Ponce 2019a, esp. 89.
[8] See Hekataios 9, Eudoxos 1–2, Dikaiarchos 10–11, Timosthenes 18–19, Eratosthenes 37, Artemidoros 8, Poseidonios 12, Menippos 3.
[9] See Leroy 2018 (also citing Schiano 2010, 50–83, a wider discussion); Panichi 2013.
[10] On Arist. *Mete.*, see also Roller 2015, 76–7.
[11] For discussion of Agathemeros, I rely mainly on Leroy 2018; see also Diller 1975a.
[12] Leroy 2018, introduction.

The fourth part details the length of the *oikoumenē* from the Ganges to NW Iberia by adding up a sequence of shorter distances (§15–16), and then offers a second version extending only to Gadeira (§17). This exercise is repeated (§18) for the breadth of the *oikoumenē* from the coast south of Meroë to the Tanaïs, and then again in an alternative version starting at Alexandria but with the same endpoint (§19).

The fifth and final part (§§20–6) specifies its sources as Artemidoros (Chapter 18), Menippos (Chapter 21), 'other trustworthy writers', and (further on) Timosthenes. It is a collection of data about the 33 major islands and groups of islands in the Mediterranean, as well as Gadeira just outside the strait of Gibraltar. It proceeds from west to east, ending with Cyprus and the larger eastern Aegean islands. Along the way, the author dwells at some length on the Peloponnese (§24)—perhaps treated here as technically an island; its name means 'isle of Pelops'—and details its promontories and bays.

In the manuscript the treatise is preceded by a short, anonymous text from the late antique period with the same title, *Geōgraphias hypotypōsis* (Chapter 35 below), which was probably intended to remedy the lack of a perspective on recent work. Before both texts stands the jejune *Diagnōsis* of still later date (see Introduction, §VIII. 2. a).[13]

The translation follows the Greek text of Leroy.

SELECTED FURTHER READING

*Diller, A. (1975), 'Agathemerus, Sketch of Geography', *Greek, Roman and Byzantine Studies*, 16. 1: 59–76; repr. in A. Diller, *Studies in Greek Manuscript Tradition* (Amsterdam, 1983), 69–86.

González Ponce, F. J. (2019a), 'Agatémero y las reminiscencias de una literatura náutica', in S. Panichi (ed.), *Dall'Egeo all'Eufrate: dinasti, città e santuari in età ellenistica = Geographia antiqua*, 28: 87–104.

*Leroy, P.-O. (2018), 'Agathemeros (2102)', in *FGrH* v.

TEXT

The headings are in the manuscript, though perhaps added by Markianos rather than original to Agathemeros' work.

I. INTRODUCTION

On the Geography of the Old Writers

1. Anaximandros of Miletos, a pupil[14] of Thales, was the first man bold enough to draw the inhabited world (*oikoumenē*) in a map (*pinax*).[15] After him Hekataios of Miletos,[16]

---

[13] At one time, both these were also attributed to Agathemeros.   [14] *akoustēs*, lit. 'listener'.
[15] On Anaximandros and the cartographic issue, see Introduction, §V. 1–2. For the term *pinax*, see also the Glossary.
[16] *BNJ* 1; see Ch. 3 above, nos 5 and 9–10. It is difficult to avoid the inference that Hekat. is here credited with a map. See next n.

a much-travelled man, examined the matter thoroughly to the extent that it was a cause of wonder: for Hellanikos of Lesbos, a very knowledgeable man, transmitted his history without artistry.[17] Next Damastes of Kition, transcribing most of his writings from those of Hekataios, wrote a *Circumnavigation* (*Periplous*).[18] Then Demokritos,[19] Eudoxos,[20] and certain others created circuits of the Earth (*gēs periodoi*) and circumnavigations.

2. The old writers drew the inhabited world as round, and believed that Hellas lay in the middle, with Delphi in the middle of Hellas as it contained the navel of the Earth. But Demokritos, a man of great experience, was the first to perceive that the Earth (*i.e. the inhabited part*) is oblong, with a length one and a half times its breadth. Dikaiarchos the Peripatetic agreed with this; but Eudoxos (*made*) the length double the breadth, Eratosthenes more than double; Krates[21] made it a semicircle, Hipparchos[22] a trapezium, others the shape of a tail. Poseidonios the Stoic made it sling-shaped: broad in the middle from south to north, narrow to east and west, but broader towards the Euros (*south-east wind*), in the parts towards India.

Boundaries of the Continents

3. That of Europe and Libyē is the Pillars of Herakles, while that of Libyē and Asia is the Nile, though some say it is the isthmus running from Lake Serbonis[23] to the Arabian gulf (*Red Sea*). That of Asia and Europe, according to the old writers, is the river Phasis and the isthmus running as far as the Caspian, but according to later, more recent writers Lake Maiotis (*Sea of Azov*) and the river Tanaïs (*Don*).

4. The *ēpeiroi* (*continents*) were so called because some of them were *apeiroi*, 'boundless', though this was due to ignorance. Thus Asia was so called from its being *āsson*, 'nearer', to those departing from Europe whether on foot or by islands lying in a row including Euboia, Andros, Tenos, Mykonos, Ikaria, Samos, and (*Cape*) Mykale. Europe was named from its *euros*, 'breadth'. Libyē was altogether unknown to Hellenes, but the Phoenicians in their sailing voyages gave it its name, after a notable nation. The Ocean (*Ōkeanos*) was named from the fact that it *ōkeōs*, 'swiftly', *anuei*, 'finishes with', the Earth in a circle.

5. Dikaiarchos, however, divides the Earth not with waters but with a straight line in the temperate zone, from the Pillars (*of Herakles*) through Sardo (*Sardinia*), Sicily,

---

[17] Hellanikos (*BNJ* 4) was a C5s historian mentioned by Thucydides (1. 97). Depending on how this is translated, this may be a key passage in the debate about the place of cartography in antiquity before the Roman Imperial period. Leroy discusses alternative interpretations of the last phrase: the adverb *aplastōs* ('without affectation', 'without disguise') has been taken to mean that Hellanikos did not bother with a map.

[18] Rather, Damastes of Sigeion (see Introduction, §VI. 4. b); rather than this being a MS corruption, A. may indeed have written 'Kition' (Leroy ad loc.).

[19] Fr. B 15 in Diels and Kranz 1959–60, ii. 145.   [20] Eudoxos of Knidos.

[21] Krates of Mallos (*FGrH* v 2113 = Broggiato 2013).

[22] Hipparchos 15–16 (the present passage is extract 12).

[23] A lagoon on the Mediterranean coast E of the Nile Delta, on the N coast of the *Sinai* peninsula.

the Peloponnese, Ionia, Karia, Lykia, Pamphylia, Kilikia, and (*Mt*) Tauros as far as Mt Imaos (*Himalaya?*). Of the areas (*thus defined*) he names one the northern, the other the southern.

II. ON WINDS

6. The winds that blow are: from the equinoctial[24] sunrise (*due east*) Apeliotes; from the equinoctial sunset (*due west*), Zephyros; from the south, Notos; from the north, Aparktias.

⟨The easterly winds:⟩[25] from the summer turning-point (*solstice; approx. north-east*), Kaikias; next, from the equinoctial sunrise, Apeliotes; and from the winter one (*approx. south-east*), Euros.

The westerly winds: from the winter sunset (*approx. south-west*), Lips; from the equinoctial sunset, Zephyros again; from the summer sunset (*approx. north-west*), Argestes or Olympias, also known as Iapyx.

Next Notos and Aparktias, blowing opposite to one another.

Thus there are eight.[26]

7. But Timosthenes, the author of the *Periploi* (*Circumnavigations*), says there are twelve. Between Aparktias and Kaikias he adds the Boreas (*NNE*); between Euros and Notos, Phoinix (*SSE*), also called Euronotos; between Notos and Lips, Leukonotos or Libonotos (*SSW*); between Aparktias and Argestes, Thraskias (*NNW*), also ⟨named⟩ Kirkios by those living around that area.

He states that the nations living at the furthest points towards Apeliotes are the Baktrians; towards Euros, the Indians; towards Phoinix (*lie*) the Erythraian sea and Arabia; towards Notos, the Aithiopia that is beyond Egypt; towards Leukonotos, the Garamantes beyond the Syrteis; towards Lips, the western Aithiopes, ⟨those⟩ beyond the Mauroi; towards Zephyros, the Pillars (*of Herakles*) and the beginnings of Libyē and Europe; towards Argestes, Iberia, which is now Hispania; towards Thraskias, ⟨the Keltoi (*Celts*) and the neighbouring places; towards Aparktias⟩, those Skythians that are beyond the Thracians; towards Boreas, the Pontos, (*Lake*) Maiotis, and the Sarmatai; towards Kaikias, the Caspian sea and the Sakai.[27]

III. CIRCUMNAVIGATION OF THE SEAS

8. The Great Syrtis (*gulf of Sidra*) is 5,000 stades (*wide*), the Small (*gulf of Gabès*) 1,600 stades.

The mouth of the Adriatic, which some call the Ionian open-sea (*pelagos*), has a crossing of 700 stades from Cape Iapygia to the Keraunian mountains of Epeiros.

---

[24] Lit. 'equidiurnal'. See Introduction, §X. 3. b fin.   [25] Meyer's supplement.
[26] This 'wind rose' appears to be derived from that of Aristotle (see appendix to Ch. 10 above), probably via Poseidonios (Leroy on ii. 6 with full bibliography on wind roses).
[27] This passage is Tim. 18 (cf. 3); see nn. there as well as Fig. 10.1.

9. The Aegean open-sea (*pelagos*) is followed by the Hellespont, ending at Abydos and Sestos. Next the Propontis, ending at Chalkedon and Byzantion, where the narrows lie from which the Pontos begins. Next Lake Maiotis. Again from the beginning of Europe and Libyē: the Iberian (*open-sea*) from the Pillars to Mt Pyrene; the Ligurian as far as the limits of Tyrrhenia (*Tuscany*); the Sardoan (*Sardinian*) beyond Sardo, inclining down towards Libyē; the Tyrrhenic as far as Sicily, beginning from the points[28] of Ligystike (*Liguria*); next the Libyan, next the Cretan, the Sicilian, and the Ionian or Adriatic that spreads out from the Sicilian open-sea (*pelagos*), ⟨and the one⟩ which they call the Corinthian gulf or Halkyonid sea. The open-sea (*pelagos*) surrounding Sounion and (*Cape*) Skyllaion is the Saronic; next are the Myrtoan and the Ikarian, in which are the Cyclades; next the Karpathian, the Pamphylian, and the Egyptian. Beyond the Ikarian, the Aegean next spreads out.[29]

10. The circumnavigation of Europe, from the outflows of the river Tanaïs (*Don*) as far as the Pillars of Herakles, is **69,709 stades.**

That of Libyē from Tingis (*Tangier*) as far as the Canopic mouth (*of the Nile*), **29,252 stades.**

Of Asia from Kanobos to the river Tanaïs, with the gulfs, the coastal sailing is **40,111 stades.**

Altogether the ⟨coastal⟩ (*sailing*), with gulfs, of the inhabited world in our region is **139,072 stades,** including in the count Lake Maiotis, whose circumference is 9,000 stades. Its mouth, the Kimmerian Bosporos, is 20 stades (*wide*).[30]

11. The Pontos is 3,350 stades (*in breadth?*). The Thracian Bosporos, at the narrows where Darius connected (*the opposite banks*) with a raft against the Skythai,[31] is 6 stades (*wide*).

12. The Persian sea (*thalassa*),[32] being rounded and drawing together its mouth at the point (*akron*) of Karmania and Arabia, has a circumference of 20,000 stades. The mouth between Arabia and Karmania is of 400 stades.[33]

13. The Hyrkanian or Caspian sea, being crescent-shaped, but according to some elongated, is 20,000 stades (*in circumference*). Its mouth has a crossing of 1,000 stades.[34]

14. The Arabian gulf, being narrow and elongated, begins from the recess of Heroönpolis[35] (*and lies*) beside the Troglodytic land as far as Ptolemaïs of the Hunting (*Ptolemaïs Thērōn*), being 9,000 stades in length. From here there is next a

---

[28] *akra* (neuter plural), here meaning the extremity of a land mass or island.
[29] I take ἀναχέομαι to be metaphorical, not lit. 'is poured forth' *vel sim*.
[30] These distances are taken from Artemidoros, as also by Pliny: see Artem. 5–7 above.
[31] Hdt. 4. 83–8.   [32] i.e. Persian gulf.   [33] Actually *c.*30 mi (*c.*50 km) today, or *c.*240 st.
[34] This strange assertion may derive from Patrokles' information that it was possible to sail from India to the Caspian (Strabo 2. 1. 17, C74; 11. 11. 6, C518–19; Leroy on iii. 13).
[35] Possibly *Tell el-Maskhuta* in NE Egypt. The information in §14 derives from Eratosthenes (Leroy ad loc.).

voyage of 6,500 stades; and the narrows by Deira (*Ras Siyyan*) are of 60 stades.[36] Beside the Erythraian sea as far as the Ocean is (*a voyage*) of 5,000 stades; the remainder is not sailed. On the Arabian side, from the Ailanites recess (*gulf of Aqaba*) is 14,000 stades. Arabia itself extends into the Erythraian (*sea*) and is elongated to 12,000 stades.

IV. ON THE LENGTH AND BREADTH OF THE INHABITED WORLD

15. The length of the inhabited world (*oikoumenē*) from the Ganges to Gadeira (*Cádiz*) is **68,545 stades,** as follows:[37]

> From the river Ganges as far as Myriandros (*İskenderun*) in the gulf of Issos (*of Issos/of Alexandretta/of İskenderun*), **41,725 stades,** as follows:
>
> from the Ganges to the outflows of the river Indos, 16,000 stades;
>
> from the Indos to the Caspian Gates, 15,300;
>
> to the Euphrates, 10,050;
>
> to Myriandros, 375 stades.[38]

16. From Myriandros to Gadeira, **26,820 stades,**[39] as follows:

> from Myriandros to Kleïdes (*The Keys*) on Cyprus, 1,400 stades;
>
> to the promontory of Akamas, 1,300 stades;
>
> to the Chelidoniai (*islands; Beş Adalar*)[40] via the Pamphylian open-sea (*pelagos*), 1,900 stades;
>
> to Patara, 800 stades;
>
> to Rhodes, 700 stades;
>
> to Astypalaia via the Karpathian (*open-sea*), 140† stades;
>
> to Tainaron, 1,950 stades;
>
> to Pachynos in Sicily, 4,600 stades;
>
> to Lilybaion via the Libyan open-sea (*pelagos*), 1,520 stades;
>
> to Karalis in Sardo via the Tyrsenian (*Etruscan*) open-sea (*pelagos*), 1,800 stades;
>
> to Gadeira, sailing beyond the Gymnasiai (*Balearic*) islands, 10,000 stades.[41]

---

[36] Actually *c.*16 mi (*c.*25 km) today, which is approx. 144 st.
[37] Ch. 4 presents the same data as Artem. 4 = Pliny 2. cxii. 242–6, where they are in miles.
[38] The last four figures total 41,275.   [39] Which added to 41,725 gives 68,545, as above.
[40] The Turkish name means 'five islands'.   [41] The last eleven figures add up to 26,110, not 26,820.

From Gadeira via Hieron (*Sacred*) Promontory[42] to the harbour of Artabra (*Ortegal*), **7,932 stades.**[43]

Altogether these make **76,477.**[44]

17. Or in another manner:[45]

> from the Ganges as far as the river Euphrates, 41,350;[46]
>
> from the Euphrates to Mazaka (*Kayseri*) among the Kappadokians, 1,950 stades;
>
> from Mazaka via Phrygia Paroreia (*beside the Mountains*), Great (*Phrygia*),[47] and Karia as far as Ephesos, 3,990 stades.
>
> Altogether from the Ganges to Ephesos, **47,290 stades.**[48]
>
> From Ephesos to Delos via the Aegean, 1,600 stades;
>
> to the Isthmus, 1,700 stades;
>
> from the Isthmus via the Corinthian gulf to Patrai, 720 stades;
>
> to Leukas, 700 stades;
>
> to Kerkyra, 700 stades;
>
> to the Akrokeraunian mountains, 660 stades;
>
> to Brentesion (*Brindisi*), 700 stades;
>
> from Brentesion, for a man travelling on foot, as far as Rome, 2,880 stades;
>
> from Rome to the Alps as far as Skingomagos, located under the Alps, 4,152 stades;
>
> next via Keltike as far as the city of Illigyris, ⟨3,744 stades;
>
> from Illigyris⟩ via the inns as far as Gadeira, 6,654 stades;
>
> and the voyage across to Gadeira, 60 stades.[49]

Altogether from the Ganges to Gadeira, **71,560 stades.**

18. The breadth of the inhabited world from the Aithiopic sea to Meroë, 5,000 stades. From Meroë to Alexandria, 10,000 stades.

From Alexandria to the river Tanaïs (*Don*), 11,056†—for the parts above the mouths of the Tanaïs to the north are unknown—as follows:

> from Alexandria to Lindos on Rhodes, 4,500.
>
> to Thoanteion,[50] as you sail with Rhodes on your right, 400 stades;
>
> to Telos, 160 stades;

---

[42] Cape *St Vincent*, or possibly *Trafalgar*.
[43] At 8 st. to the mile, this exactly matches Pliny's 991½ miles at 2. cxii. 242: see Artem. 4.
[44] The sum of 68,545 and 7,932.   [45] This transect is mainly land-based (Leroy ad loc.).
[46] A much shorter journey than in §15.
[47] The former is part of the latter, Strabo 12. 8. 13, C576.
[48] The sum of the previous three figures.
[49] The last twelve figures (but one is restored) total 24,270, which being added to 47,290 makes 71,560.
[50] On the W side of Rhodes, opposite Chalke I.

to Lakter (*Andimáchi*) in Koan territory, 120 stades;

to Drepanon in Koan territory, 100 stades;

to Arkitis (*Arkoí*) island, 230 stades;

to (*the*) Korsiai (*islands; Phoúrnoi*), 100;

to (*Cape*) Ampelos in Samian territory, 30 stades;

to Argennon[51] †via the Aegean†, 500 stades;

to Korynaion in Erythraian territory, 270 stades;

to Phlion†, the tip of Chios, 50 stades;

to Melaneus, the tip of Lesbos, 450 stades;

to Sigrion on Lesbos, 500 stades;

to Tenedos island, 450 stades;

to Sigeion, 100 stades;

to the mouth of the Pontos, 2,500 stades;

to Karambis, 2,800 stades;

to the mouth of Maiotis, 2,500 stades;

to the Tanaïs, 2,200 stades.[52]

19. Or in another manner, from city to city:

From Alexandria to Rhodes, **4,670 stades:**

to Knidos, 700 stades;

to Kos, 200 stades;

to Samos, 800 stades;

to Chios, 750 stades;

to Mytilene, 520 stades;

to Tenedos, 950 stades;

to Sigeion, 100 stades;

to the mouth of the Pontos, 2,500 stades;

to Karambis, 2,800 stades;

to the mouth of Maiotis, 2,500 stades;

to the river Tanaïs, 2,200 stades.[53]

Altogether from Alexandria to the Tanaïs, **18,690 stades.**

---

[51] The mainland cape opposite Chios.
[52] The above nineteen figures add up to 17,960, close to the total in §19 below.
[53] These twelve figures correctly total 18,690.

V. MEASUREMENT OF THE ISLANDS

20. In what follows, we shall state the circumferences of the islands in our part of the world, taking them from Artemidoros, Menippos, and other reliable (*authorities*).

Gadeira is 120 stades in length, 16 in breadth. The crossing by the Pillars of Herakles is narrowest (*here*), at 80 stades.

In the Iberian open-sea (*pelagos*) are the islands called Pityoussai (*'Pine Is.'; Ibiza and Formentera*): the larger, inhabited one is 300 stades long, the lesser one 100 stades.

Of the Gymnasioi (*Balearic Is.*), which the Carthaginians called Baliariai—for their slingers are likewise called Baliareis—the larger (*Majorca*) is 1,200 stades in length and 400 stades in breadth; the lesser (*Minorca*) is 300 stades (*long*).

Those bearing the name Stoichades (*Îles d'Hyères*) lie in succession directly in front of the Massaliac cities; the greater are three in number, but two small ones are close to Massalia itself.

Sardo (*Sardinia*) has a form like that of a footprint, and is hollow in the middle; its length is 2,200. Kyrnos (*Corsica*) is close to Sardo but much more undistinguished; it is less than half the length of Sardo. The point of departure for Sardo and Kyrnos (*Corsica*) is Popoulonion (*Populonium*) in Tyrsenia (*Etruria*); the crossing is 1,200 stades.

The circumference of Sicily, according to Timosthenes, is 4,740 stades; its form is a triangle with unequal sides, and it has a crossing from Peloron Akron (*Monster Point*) to Italia of 12 stades. The side of the island from Peloron to Pachynos is 1,360 stades; from Pachynos to Lilybaion, 1,600 stades; according to Timosthenes, from Lilybaion to Pelorias (*Peloron*), 1,700 stades.[54] From Lilybaion, the voyage across to Aspis in Libyē is close to 1,500 stades.

21. Kerkina (*Grande Kerkenna/Chergui*) island is ⟨200⟩ (*stades*) in length, in breadth 70 stades, though where it is narrowest 40 stades. It lies beyond the mainland city of Theēnē, which lies in the Small Syrtis, at its beginning. Beside Kerkina lies the island of Karkinitis (*Petite Kerkenna/Gharbi*), joined to it by a bridge; in length 40 stades, in breadth 25 stades.

22. From Kerkina to the island of Meninx (*Djerba*) Lotophagitis (*the Lotus-eating*), the voyage across is 600 stades, as much as the mouth of the Small Syrtis is said to measure. Meninx is 200 stades in length, 180 stades in breadth. Around it are strong tides.

23. The island of Kephallenia, with four cities, has a length of 400 stades. There are also islands in the Adriatic beside Illyria, of which the more notable are Isse (*Vis*), Korkyra Melaina (*Black Corcyra*), Pharos (*Hvar*), and Melite (*Mljet*), whose circumferences I do not know.

24. The circumference of the Peloponnese, the gulfs also being reckoned in, is 5,627 stades; without following the gulfs the circumnavigation is 4,000 stades. Its length

---

[54] These three data do not total 4,740.

from Malea to Aigion is 1,400 stades. It has a form similar to a plane leaf, being dissected by great gulfs. It is drawn in at the isthmus of the Corinthians to 40 stades in breadth, between the Corinthian gulf and the Saronic. ⟨The Saronic gulf extends⟩ towards Sounion Point[55] on the left ⟨and towards Skyllaion Point on the right⟩, where the island of Kalauria, sacred to Poseidon, projects. Next is the Hermionic gulf.[56] Next is the Argolic gulf up to Cape Malea, which is set forward far into the open sea (*pelagos*). Next, after Malea, is the Laconic gulf as far as Tainaron on the right, which bounds the Messenian gulf on its left, on the right of which is Cape Akritas.[57] Next is set forward Ichthys (*Fish*) Point,[58] by which lies Zakynthos; and another (*point*), Chelonatas (*Tortoise Point*).[59] The last point (*of the Peloponnese*) is Araxos, confronting Akarnania; after this the Corinthian gulf spreads out,[60] closed by a mouth of 7 stades by Rhion Point, which is in the Peloponnese, while Antirrhion is in Lokris. From Tainaron to Phykous (*Ras Aamer*) in Libyē the crossing is 3,000 stades.

25. The oblong island of Aigina is 160 stades ⟨*in circumference*⟩; it lies opposite Attica. Salamis is 70 stades in length, Keia (*Keos*) 120.[61] Of the Cyclades the mightiest is Naxos, wherefore it is called Little Sicily. To the right are the Sporades. Euboia is joined to Boiotia by a bridge, and lies alongside Boiotis (*sic*), Phokis, the Lokrians, and on the other side to some extent by Attica: for it is long, for which reason it was named Makris (*Long Island*), 1,700 stades in length.

26. Crete approaches the Peloponnese opposite Malea. Its circumference is 4,100 stades, its length 2,300, for it is greatly elongated. Kythera is midway between Crete and Lakonike.

Cyprus is like an oxhide in form; its circumnavigation is 3,420 stades, its length 1,300. From Paphos to Alexandria is a passage of 3,800 stades with the north wind.

The circumference of Rhodes is 1,300 stades; the circumference of Kos 550 stades; that of Samos 630 stades. Ikaria is long, rough, and 300 stades in length. The circumference of Chios is 660 stades; the circumference of Lesbos 1,100.

---

[55] The S cape of Attica. [56] The last words stand after the following sentence in the MS.
[57] The writer seems to imagine sailing with the coast on one's right in this passage.
[58] In Eleia, in the NW Peloponnese. [59] Further N, also opposite Zakynthos.
[60] *anachei*, lit. 'pours out'. [61] In cases such as these, 'length' refers to coastal circumference.

30
DIONYSIOS OF BYZANTION
(C. MID-2ND C. AD)

Oliver Nicholson and Thomas Russell*

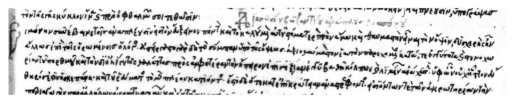

FIG. 30.1. Opening of the text of Dionysios of Byzantion, fo. 2ʳ (detail).

INTRODUCTION

The *Anaplous Bosporou* (*Upstream Voyage on the Bosporos*)[1] in Greek by Dionysios of Byzantion describes in detail the shores, currents, mythological associations, and fisheries of the Bosporos, the channel which connects the Black Sea to the Sea of Marmara and so separates Europe from Asia. After a brief ecphrasis of the northern end of the waterway, where it meets the Black Sea, the author takes his readers downstream to the city of Byzantion[2] at its southern end, and works his way up the Golden Horn and then the European bank of the Bosporos to the Clashing Rocks (Kyaneai, 'blue (*rocks*)') at the mouth of the Black Sea, where he turns round and takes them back down the eastern bank to the Asian cities of Chrysopolis and Chalkedon opposite Byzantion.

This is perhaps the most detailed description of a landscape to have survived from the ancient world. It is certainly the most detailed account of the physical, cultural, and sacred landscape of the Bosporos as it was before Constantine transformed the area completely by founding Constantinople and incorporating into it the ancient city of Byzantion. Dionysios appears to have been a local man, animated by local pride.[3]

---

* Oliver Nicholson acknowledges the award by the Graduate School of the University of Minnesota of a Faculty Summer Research Fellowship and McKnight Summer Fellowship in the Summer of 2002 which enabled him to make a start on Dionysios.

[1] The term *anaplous* (Latin *anaplus*) has a variety of meanings. In general terms, it refers to the 'sailing up' into the Black Sea through the Bosporos (e.g. Ps.-Skyl. §67), and more specifically to the European shore of the Bosporos.

[2] In accordance with a convention observed by some historians who study the eastern Roman Empire in late antiquity and the Middle Ages, the pre-Constantinian Greek city is referred to as Byzantion to differentiate it from the medieval empire known as Byzantium.

[3] As argued by T. Russell 2017, 4–5.

His work is more literary than the bald enumeration of distances typical of many a *periplous*. And it enters into more detail than the accounts of other classical authors who found so much to marvel at in Byzantion and the Bosporos: Herodotos (4. 83–9), for whom the Black Sea was 'the most marvellous of all open-seas'; Polybios (4. 38–52), who understood the currents in the Bosporos and much else; Strabo (7. 6. 1–2, C318–20); Tacitus (*Annals*, 4. 62–3), who was principally interested in Roman relations with so strategic a location; and Cassius Dio (75 [74]. 10–14) and Herodian of Antioch (3. 1. 5), both of them mightily impressed with the massive city walls of Byzantion destroyed in the late 2nd century AD.

Dionysios' purpose is to present readers with the experience they would have were they witnessing for themselves the spectacle offered by the Bosporos. He begins self-deprecatingly by comparing its beauties with the relatively disagreeable description he is going to provide; he finishes somewhat abruptly when he gets to Chalkedon and announces that this marks the end of the Bosporos and the end of his discourse. In between he has provided a portrait, *ut pictura poesis*, a description of the landscape in all its various detail, from the passage of the Argonauts on their way to Kolchis and the contrasting traditions of the foundations of Byzantion and Chalkedon, through the vicissitudes of the waterway during the classical and hellenistic periods, and the fish that are to be caught there, to the gods associated with each place along the shore. He shares with grammarians and Stoic philosophers a conviction that the name of a place is no arbitrary appellation but provides the key to understanding its quintessential character.

Much of what he says might be true of any period of classical or hellenistic history, but Dionysios clearly wrote in the Roman period, presumably in the 1st or 2nd century AD; he mentions the altar to Apollo set up 'by the Romans' on the Kyaneai (§86), but there is no sign in what he writes that he knew of the progress and destructive results of the siege of Byzantion laid by troops loyal to the emperor Septimius Severus in the years AD 193–5. The work which his *Anaplous* most closely resembles, not least in a shared engagement with Herodotos and Thucydides, is surely the large description of Greece by Pausanias, which comes from the middle years of the 2nd century AD.[4] For both men the landscape is punctuated by temples and understood in terms of classical mythology; they provide not just a catalogue of places but an interpretation of the entire terrain, seen not as wild but in terms of its relationship with both gods and men—and fish.

In this respect the landscape Dionysios describes is different from what could be seen in the centuries after Constantine had supplanted ancient Byzantion with Christian Constantinople. By the late 5th century the Bosporos was lined not with temples

---

[4] 'Perhaps Pausanias was [...] approaching seventy when he completed the work not later than A.D. 180': Bowie 2001, 23. For the details of Dionysios' debt to Herodotos and Thucydides, see Güngerich 1927, xxxix–xl.

but with monasteries and shrines of St Michael and other saints.[5] Its heroes were less Byzas and Keroëssa than the likes of St Alexander the Sleepless[6] and St Hypatios, who meeting one day on the road the goddess Artemis, ten times taller than a man, riding on wild boars, *potnia thērōn*, made the sign of the cross and so put the boars to flight.[7] When such men did seek out temples, it was to disinfect them of their demons, like those which, according to the disciple who wrote the *Life* of St Daniel the Stylite, 'often sank ships'.[8] Hieron, the greatest of the pagan temples, became notable as a customs post. That is not to say that Byzantine antiquarians had lost all interest in the Argonauts and the first founders of Byzantion. The learned Byzantine lawyer Hesychios Illustris (born c.505), whose *Chronike historia* survives in fragments and a summary, records the sites of former temples and embeds an account of the foundation of Constantinople in his world chronicle; he may indeed have used Dionysios of Byzantion, or the two writers may have drawn on a common source.[9] The chronicler John Malalas even tells a tale in which the Incarnation of Christ was prophesied to the Argonauts, who also founded the temple at Lasthenes (subsequently Sosthenion) which Constantine, so Malalas claims, turned into a church.[10] That an interest in the pre-Christian past of Byzantion and the Bosporos persisted among learned Byzantines is indicated by quotations from Dionysios' *Anaplous* in the 6th-century encyclopaedia of Stephanos of Byzantion, who cites Dionysios' description of Chrysopolis.[11] The 10th- or 11th-century encyclopaedia known as the *Suda* (or Suidas) notes Dionysios and his *Anaplous*, and adds that he also wrote a poem on lamentations, but may have been confusing him with the better-known Dionysios Periegetes, author of a lengthy didactic poem about world geography (Chapter 28 above).

The last person we can be sure read the whole of Dionysios, though, was French. Petrus Gyllius (Pierre Gilles, 1490–1555) was a man of large learning who lived an

---

[5] The urban planning and Christian sacred geography of Constantinople and the Bosporos have been a preoccupation of Byzantine scholars since C16, though ignored in Constable and Kazhdan 1982. Details of the churches, monasteries, and shrines on the European and Asiatic coasts of the Bosporos, respectively, are given by Janin 1969; Janin 1975. Details of the European coast, apart from the area inside the walls of the City (including details from the Cl period), are given by Külzer 2008 (hereinafter *TIB* 12). Belke 2020 (*TIB* 13) provides similar information for the Asiatic coast, but appeared too late to be considered in detail here. The secular gazetteer of the City and its suburbs by Janin 1964 is not always accurate.

[6] ed. de Stoop 1911, 605–704 (with French trans.).

[7] Kallinikos, *Life of Hypatios*, 45, ed. Bartelink 1971, 270–2 (with French trans.).

[8] *Life of Daniel the Stylite*, 14–16, ed. Delehaye 1923, 14–16.

[9] Summary in Photios, *Bibliotheca*, 69, ed. (with French trans.) Henry 1959, with index by Schamp 1991. Fragments in *Patria* i, 1–30, ed. A. Berger 2013 (with English trans.). For the context of the fragments, see Dagron 1984, 23–9. Kaldellis 2005 is inclined to consider this antiquarianism as in some way pagan.

[10] Malalas 4. 13. 78, trans. Jeffreys, Jeffreys, and Scott 1986, 38. A similar story appears among the fragments attributed to the C6 AD chronicler John of Antioch, ed. Roberto 2005, fr. 26. 2, pp. 62–5. On Malalas' antiquarianism, see R. D. Scott 1990.

[11] Steph. Byz. χ 59 Chrysopolis, quoting Dionysios of Byzantion 109. Stephanos wrote his *Ethnika* after AD 540.

exciting life.¹² He had already published copiously¹³ when in 1544 he was sent by Francis I, the scholarly king of France, to Constantinople to further his alliance with the Sultan Süleyman the Magnificent (Kanuni) and to collect manuscripts. On the death of Francis in 1547, Gyllius was left without money, so he joined the Ottoman army and in 1548 took part in a Turkish campaign against the Safavid rulers of Persia which carried him across Anatolia to Tabriz and back through Diyarbakir (Amida) and Urfa (Edessa) to Aleppo (Beroea) where he wrote a letter to a friend, detailing his experiences.¹⁴ Thence he went on to the Holy Land and Egypt, but was captured by Barbary pirates in 1550 who threatened to take his accumulated notes and throw them into the sea. He made it back to Constantinople where he was able to reconstitute his observations and then went back to France and on to Rome where he wrote up his two topographical accounts, *De topographia Constantinopoleos et de illius antiquitatibus libri IV* ('four books on the topography of Constantinople and its antiquities') and *De Bosporo Thracio libri III* ('three books on the Thracian Bosporos'). Both works are constructed around the framework of an ancient text: the book about Constantinople around the early 5th-century AD *Notitia urbis Constantinopolitanae*, and the book about the Bosporos around the *Anaplous Bosporou* of Dionysios of Byzantion.¹⁵ Gyllius died in 1555, and his nephew Antoine Gilles prepared the two books for publication in 1561. The whereabouts of the manuscript of Dionysios' original Greek, on which he drew, is unknown.¹⁶

Till the mid-19th century, all that was known of Dionysios, therefore, was the summary by Gyllius and the opening passage preserved in a number of Greek geographical manuscripts.¹⁷ Then a manuscript of the 13th or 14th century came to light at the monastery of Vatopedi on Mount Athos (Vatopedi 655; see also Introduction, §VIII. 2. a).¹⁸ A manuscript collector called Constantinos Minoides Menas (1788/9–1859), a former professor at Serres in Macedonia who had taken refuge in France in 1819, was sent to the Levant in 1840 by the French minister of public instruction to recover

---

¹² The most recent account of his life is in the French trans. of his topographical works by Grélois 2007.

¹³ Müller, *GGM* i, p. i n. 1, lists a Latin trans. of Demetrios of Constantinople (Pepagoumenos) on birds of prey, an edition of Aelian, *Historia animalium*, an edition of Theodoret of Cyrrhus' commentary on the Twelve Prophets, an edition of a historical work of Lorenzo Valla on Ferdinand of Aragon, and the speech he wrote asking the emperor Charles V to release Francis I from captivity in 1525, as well as contributions to a Greek–Latin dictionary, further work on Aelian and other ancient writers on animals, and a work on the French and Latin names of fish.

¹⁴ Conveniently available in the French trans. by Grélois (n. 12 above). Other autobiographical information is preserved in asides in his works on Constantinople and the Bosporos.

¹⁵ The text of the *Notitia urbis Constantinopolitanae* was published by Seeck 1876, 227–43.

¹⁶ Wescher 1874, xxii–xxiv, lists probable variations between the surviving MS and that used by Gyllius.

¹⁷ All, therefore, that is published by Müller, *GGM* i. 1–101, is the equivalent of Güngerich's first page, corresponding to Gungerich's §1 and the first part of §2, and the fragments, generously conceived, preserved by Gyllius.

¹⁸ What survives on Mt Athos of Vatopedi 655, principally Ptolemy and Strabo, is listed by Eustratiades and Arcadios 1924, 131.

manuscripts and bring them to Paris. Seven folios, the opening pages of Dionysios (containing §§1–56), were among the manuscripts found in his library after his death and they were subsequently acquired by the Bibliothèque Nationale (Paris, BN suppl. gr. 443a).[19] Then, in 1853, the notorious Constantinos Simonides (1824–67)[20] sold the folios which include the single page that provides the closing chapters of Dionysios' work (§§96–112) to the British Museum Library (now London, BL adds. gr. 19391, folio 4 recto).[21] The Greek text of the middle section (§§57–95), however, is still lost, and for it we are obliged to rely on Gyllius' Latin version.[22]

The present version follows the edition of Güngerich in giving only those passages from Gyllius where he specifically says he is quoting Dionysios.[23] The Vatopedi manuscript contained numerous geographical works besides this.[24] From what survives at Vatopedi itself, and in Paris and London, it is possible to infer what its complete contents were, and it appears that it is a descendant of ms. Palatinus Heidelbergensis 398 (codex A in the study of ancient geographers: see Introduction, §VIII. 2. a), a miscellany containing numerous geographical and paradoxographical works and written in the third quarter of the 9th century, from which unfortunately the leaves bearing the *Anaplous Bosporou* are missing.[25] It is likely therefore that the scholia in the margin of the surviving manuscript of the *Anaplous* derive from the manuscript now in Heidelberg when it was complete, and so date from the 9th century. These marginal notes mostly indicate the content of the passages to which they are appended. Where they provide further information, they have been translated in the notes to the present version.

In almost all particulars we translate the text of Güngerich.

SELECTED FURTHER READING

Belfiore, S. (2009), *Il Periplo del Ponto Eusino di Arriano e altri testi sul Mar Nero e il Bosforo: spazio geografico, mito e dominio ai confini dell'impero romano*. Venice.

---

[19] Minoides Menas's first stay in Greece lasted four years, from 1840 to 1843, He was at Vatopedi in mid-September 1841, returning in January 1843 to retrieve MSS he was to take away. He reported on the geographical MS containing the text of Dionysios in a letter to the minister of public instruction of 7 December 1841 (Omont 1916, 365–6), but does not appear to allude to it in his other reports.

[20] An account of the famous forger is given by Farrer 1907, 39–66. He spent time on Mt Athos between 1839 and 1841, just before Minoides Menas was there, and again in 1852.

[21] For a facsimile, see www.bl.uk/manuscripts/Viewer.aspx?ref=add_ms_19391_f004r.

[22] According to Wescher 1874, p. v n. 1, the leaf which would have contained §§57–95 was already missing when Minoides catalogued the manuscripts of Vatopedi in September 1841.

[23] Gyllius (Gilles) embeds such quotations in his own prose. Müller and Wescher both print more of the context in which each fragment occurs than Güngerich does. Fragments known only from Latin citations in Gyllius' *editio princeps* of 1561 (*De Bosporo Thracio*) are marked in this translation with the letters 'Gb' followed by his book, chapter, and page number.

[24] What is stated summarily here is argued in full in the introduction to the editions of both Wescher 1874, v–xix, and Güngerich 1927, vi–xiii.

[25] On this MS, its contents, and its context, see Eleftheriou 2015.

Belke, K. (2020), *Bithynien und Hellespont*, i (Tabula Imperii Byzantini, 13). Vienna. [Appeared too late to be taken fully into account.]

—— (2021), 'Gates to Asia Minor: the harbours of Chalcedon, Chrysopolis, Hiereia and Eutropiu Limen opposite Constantinople', in F. Daim and E. Kislinger (eds), *The Byzantine Harbours of Constantinople* (Heidelberg), 223–33.

Grélois, P. (2007), *Pierre Gilles, Itinéraires byzantins; Lettre à un ami; Du Bosphore de Thrace; De la topographie de Constantinople et de ses antiquités: introduction, traduction du latin et notes*. Paris.

*Güngerich, R. (1927), *Dionysii Byzantii Anaplus Bospori*. Berlin. (Reprinted with revisions, 1958.)

Kislinger, E. (2021), 'Neorion and Prosphorion: the old harbours on the Golden Horn', in F. Daim and E. Kislinger (eds), *The Byzantine Harbours of Constantinople* (Heidelberg), 133–9.

Külzer, A. (2008), *Ostthrakien* (Tabula Imperii Byzantini, 12). Vienna.

Mango, C. (2001), 'The shoreline of Constantinople in the fourth century', in N. Necipoğlu (ed.), *Byzantine Constantinople: Monuments, Topography and Everyday Life* (Leiden–Boston–Cologne: Brill), 17–28.

Russell, T. (2017), *Byzantium and the Bosporus: A Historical Study, from the Seventh Century BC until the Foundation of Constantinople*. Oxford.

TEXT

Section divisions follow Güngerich.

CODEX B, PARIS FOLIOS 2ʳ–3ᵛ

1. Although, for those who sail up into the Euxeinos Pontos along its so-called Mouth (*Stoma*), the sight of this place is both delightful and incredible, the description (*logos*) of the things which they have seen is on the other hand in itself disagreeable.[26] For everything is brought to perfection by looking at it; for it presents successively to the sight as worthy of wonder the narrows and straits of the channel, and the association through so small an expanse of sea of the two mainlands facing one another, together with the deep narrow outpourings of the gulfs and harbours beneath which the shelter and the abundance of fish is second to none.[27] The current for the most part flows

---

[26] D.'s preface raises questions about his intended audience. He claims that he is not writing only for those who have seen the strait, but also for those who have *not* seen it, and who have not appreciated its full wonder through personal autopsy. This is not merely a navigational treatise designed, like a modern 'pilot', with the aim of providing sailors with advice on passing through the strait by explaining how to overcome the currents at certain spots or avoid dangerous capes in the fog. Instead, D.'s purpose is to promote a 'full appreciation' of his homeland, encompassing both its natural and mythological landscapes.

[27] D. throughout the *Anaplous* tries to convey his own sense of wonder and amazement about the strait; he is a 'patriotic' geographer, perhaps more so even than Herakleides Kritikos (Ch. 11), Juba (Ch. 22), or Arrian (Ch. 27). Much of his wonder concentrates on the dangerous and deceptive

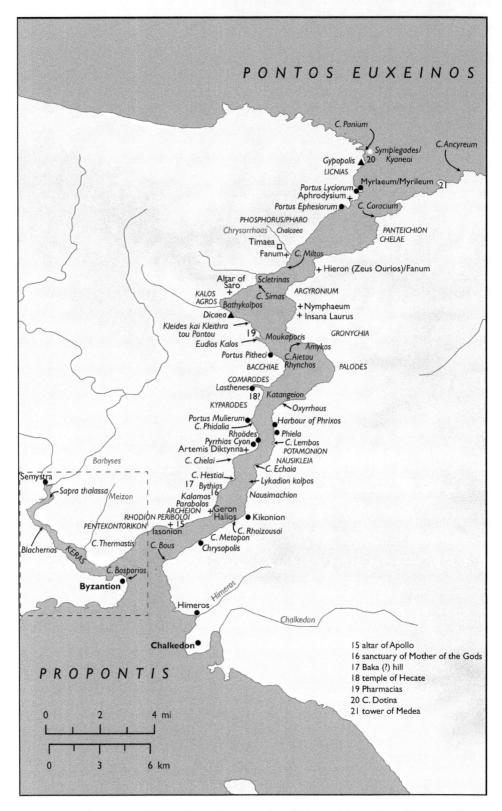

MAP 30.1. Dionysios of Byzantion: places mentioned. Around Byzantion, the map reflects the estimated shape of the coastline before late antique land reclamations (Mango 2001).

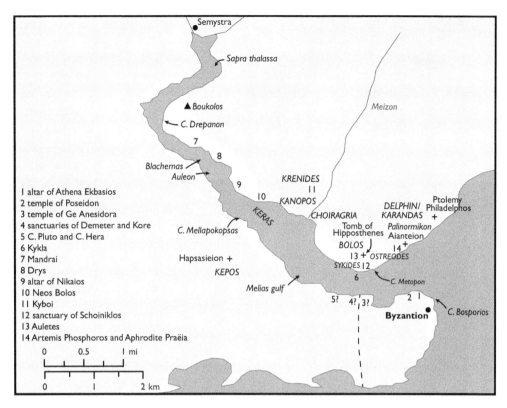

MAP 30.2. Dionysios of Byzantion: inset showing Byzantion area.

downwards, but it sometimes twists back on itself through being overcome, as the promontories enter it and unfold on either side as it goes round them, they divert the force of the current from its direct course. Since all this is apparent to the hearing not less than to the sight, it seemed necessary to me to write about these things, so that, for those who have seen them, there may be nothing wanting from a full and complete account (*historia*), while those who have not seen them may, at any rate, be able to learn at least something about them.[28]

currents of the strait, which in concert with the rolling, twisting capes of the Bosporos were infamous. Locals like D. understood the currents and could explain their apparently random violence, just as modern fishermen in Istanbul know what parts of the strait to avoid, or where to fish to exploit the currents better. D. provides the outsider with a taste of this local knowledge, but only a taste; a magician offering a glimpse into how the trick works. The emphasis on the importance of autopsy may be intended to encourage visitors.

---

[28] D. conceives of his task in Herodotean terms: his *Anaplous* is a display of inquiry, and he is endeavouring through *ekphrasis* to render in words the effect of what he sees: *ut pictura poiesis*. The dialect and style are consciously classicizing: the *Anaplous* should be viewed as part of the literary movement known as the Second Sophistic, in which Cl Greek texts, themes, and styles enjoyed a second renaissance under the Roman empire.

2. But the beginning, both of the account (*logos*) and of the nature of the places, is the open sea of the Pontos Euxeinos. In size it is the greatest in comparison to the other seas, apart from the Outer Ocean to which alone it is unequal. Only Lake Maiotis (*Sea of Azov*) pours in from beyond it, which the account (*logos*) passed down from ancient memory has agreed to be the mother and nurse of the Pontos. Its circumference is ⟨8,000 stades, the diameter⟩ 2,000,[29] and the river Tanaïs forms its limit, the boundary between two continents,[30] and springing up from an area, uninhabited on account of the icy cold.[31] There are narrow outflows along the so-called Kimmerian Bosporos, all of which the Pontos receives in a single mass and much of it flows back up into both sides of the mainland. Greek cities occupy the area around this sea, which some of the Greeks colonized after the birth of Byzantion, but beyond the sea are many great barbarian nations.[32] The sea shares with the Lake, and is altered by, the copious rivers coming down from each side of the continent, sweetening its harsh nature. The Pontos ends in the Thracian Bosporos and falls out through Stoma (*The Mouth*).[33]

3. This is a strait with a strong current; in length it is 120 stades, and in width, at its narrowest point, 4 stades.[34] Yet it is not productive of fish, either because Herakles had completely cleansed the Pontos, according to legend,[35] or because of the force of the sea, which is not straight, but broken by the continuous projections of the promontories parallel to one another, along which also are continuous whirlpools and checks to the sea. The current is stirred up at these spots, where the distance between the continents is most narrow and confined, and it is squeezed with spasm and confusion as it

---

[29] All the MSS read 'its circumference is 2,000 stades', but by any calculation the figure of 2,000 st. for the perimeter of the Black Sea is incorrect. This led Güngerich to suggest that some words had dropped out and that the clause should read 'Its circumference is ⟨8,000 stades, the diameter⟩ 2,000 stades', and his emendation is printed here.

[30] The various MSS which preserve only the beginning of the *Anaplous* (including Paris, BN 1405, 1406, 2554) break off here with the words 'two continents'. From this point onwards, the text survives only in the Vatopedi MS (see Introduction, §VIII. 2. a) and in the Latin epitome by Petrus Gyllius.

[31] On the divisions between continents, see Introduction.

[32] It is interesting to note that he imagines Byzantion to have been founded *before* the Greek cities of the Pontos, evidencing the ancient tendency to attribute foundational acts to discrete moments.

[33] *Stoma* means 'mouth', but became the proper name for the said channel. Detailed identification of sites in the Golden Horn is provided by Oberhummer 1921 (with map); along the Bosporos by Oberhummer 1897 (using Ottoman names), and by *TIB* 12. For a brief history of the waterway, see *TIB* 12, 295–7, s.v. Bosporos.

[34] D.'s description of the currents accords with reality. Digressions on the currents of the Bosporos have a long pedigree: they feature in Polyb. 4. 43, 3–44. 11 and Strabo 7. 6. 2, C320. D.'s account agrees generally with these authors, while the length and width of the Bosporos given by D. match the figures provided by Hdt. 4. 85. It is not clear what spot he measures the Bosporos from: the Kyaneai at the mouth of the Black Sea (as Strabo does), which mark the termination of his voyage N, or the sanctuary of Hieron, from where mariners measured the voyage in maritime loans (and which Polyb. uses as his terminus).

[35] The claim that the Black Sea is not productive in fish is difficult to digest. The Pontos is one of the few regions of the ancient world to preserve significant archaeological evidence of industrial-scale fishing and salting installations, and the ancients were well aware of the region's productive potential. It is possible that D.'s localist pride extends to the Bosporos fishing industries, and that he finds it difficult to acknowledge the Pontos as a rival exporter of fish.

issues down. The capes of the continents overlap each other, and they almost deceive navigators that the way forward is shut. This is why I think these rocks are called the Symplegades, since as people are sailing towards them they are separated, but on the voyage back they come close together—their appearance gives a false notion, for what seems to be the end is really just another beginning.[36]

4. The current is borne along a twisting course, and, at the point where the nature of the places first impels it, it is compacted and driven along, and is cloven in two at Cape Bosporios.[37] This is in Europe and juts out from the city, at a distance of 7 stades facing towards Asia.[38]

5. As the current is sharply rent asunder around it, the larger part pushes violently down into the Propontis, while the milder arm of the current, guiding in a harvest of fish, is received into the so-called Keras (*Horn*). This gulf, tucked in behind Cape Bosporios, is rather too deep for an anchorage—for it continues on for 60 stades (*northwest*)—but it is a safe harbour, enclosed by mountains and hills which protect it from the winds[39] but on the other hand they carry along in the rivers thick, soft mud down into the mouth under the cape upon which is the city.[40]

6. The whole of the city (*Byzantion*) is completely surrounded by sea, except for the isthmus which joins it to the mainland. The size of its entire circuit of walls is 35 stades, while at its neck, which alone prevents it (*Byzantion*) from being an island, it is 5 stades.[41] It all slopes towards the sea which washes it, except that it inclines on both sides gently and not abruptly away from the Thracian wall.[42] Through the middle it is

---

[36] This is the first reference to Argonautic traditions in the *Anaplous*. Allusions to the Argonauts form a leitmotif in the mythological tableau of D.'s Bosporos. Ancient inhabitants of the Bosporos shores derived a great deal of pride from identifying their local region and its individual places with Argonautic stories. D.'s explanation for the origin of the name of the 'clashing rocks' is elegant and rational, the myth deriving from the real phenomenon of the overlapping shores which seem to close the way ahead and behind. In poor weather or fog, the overlapping banks can be obscured, so causing shipwreck—a plausible explanation for the dangerous nature of the mythical rocks. On Argonautic traditions in the region, see Dewing 1924; Vian 1974.

[37] This promontory, mod. *Saray Burnu*, is the site of the acropolis of ancient Byzantion.

[38] Having contemplated the magnificence of the Black Sea, the reader is now carried down with the current to the S end of the Bosporos, to the site of the city of Byzantion. He is then taken up the European shore (beginning with the Golden Horn) to the Symplegades and then back down the Asian coast to finish at Chalkedon.

[39] Strabo 7. 6. 2, C319–20, also makes the Golden Horn 60 st. long. Procopius (*Buildings* 1. 5. 3) is closer to the truth in making it over 40 st.

[40] The Golden Horn (Turkish *Haliç*) provided the principal harbours of ancient Byzantion, including the Prosphorion and Neorion. Its advantages derive from the fact that it constitutes a sheltered, calm cul-de-sac hidden away from the violence of the currents in the strait itself.

[41] D.'s description of ancient Byzantion as connected to the mainland by a narrow isthmus only 5 st. in width does not accord with the topography of Byzantine Constantinople or modern Istanbul. It seems that in late antiquity considerable land was reclaimed from the shores of both the Golden Horn and the Sea of Marmara, in modern *Unkapanı* and *Aksaray*: Mango 1985, 16–18; Mango 2001, esp. 17–21.

[42] The walls of ancient Byzantion may have been called 'Thracian' because they enclose the W side of the city, which opens toward Thrace. Alternatively, they may have been called 'Thracian' because they were used for shelter each time the Thracians attacked Byzantion's hinterland: cf. Polyb. 4. 45. 5.

generally level, except on the heights, and on both sides there is level ground by the sea. The current flows round the whole city, deep and strong-flowing, driven by the Pontic open-sea and also by the narrowness of its strait, along which there are violent clashes each time it meets the blows and counterblows of the continents, before it gathers together and falls against the city. Thereupon the current is cloven in two at Cape Bosporios, and one part goes back into the gulf, where there is an abundance of fish, and it flows at its end into shallow shoals. This gulf is called Keras because of its resemblance to that shape. The size of the gulf provides, as I said before, the convenience of a harbour. It is surrounded by large mountains which protect it from the force of the winds, while the city and the mainland opposite shut off the sea at its mouth, as by running alongside and turning it away the narrowness caused by being turned sideways much diminishes the speed of the current. This is the overall account for those who do not wish to continue further, but now we must report point-by-point the things which follow.

7. Concerning the cape called Bosporios, the account is twofold.[43] Some say that a cow was driven to this place by a gadfly, and that it swam across the strait; while others, recollecting more in the vein of legend, say that Io the daughter of Inachos was driven by the jealousy of Hera and crossed into Asia from here. But let the more divine of these accounts be trusted. For the story would not, it seems to me, have prevailed to such an extent if it was only a local experience, nor would it have given the name to the Kimmerian Bosporos as well as the Thracian, unless there was something more than the local tale (*historia*). In any case the name seems to have taken some share from the memory of this event.

8. A little above this is the altar of Athena Ekbasios, where the leaders of the colonial expedition first disembarked, each of them forthwith competing for the land as if it was their own.[44]   9. There is also a temple of Poseidon, which is old, and also quite

---

Xenophon, who visited Cl Byzantion, mentions a square called the Thrakion, overlooked by the 'Thracian gates' (*Anab.* 7. 1. 15; *Hell.* 1. 3. 20). On Byzantion's relationship with its Greek neighbours, see Firath and Robert 1964, esp. 26–7, 37, 45, 133–5, 152; Loukopoulou 1989, 190–200. Herodian 3. 1. 7 suggests the extent of the damage to Byzantion's famous walls in the siege of AD 193–5 when he writes, 'even now the surviving ruins of this wall are enough to make the viewer marvel both at the technical skill of the original builders and the might of those who finally destroyed it'. Cassius Dio 75. 14. 4–5 also emphasizes the destruction of the walls in the siege.

---

[43] These stories must derive from local oral traditions, privileged information D. is sharing with the rest of the world.

[44] Ekbasios: 'of disembarkation'. The epithet is not otherwise known except for a reference to an Apollo Ekbasios in the *Argonautika* of Apollonios of Rhodes (1. 996 and 1186), which locates the altar near Kyzikos. The correspondence with the Argonautic story connects the European shores of the Bosporos with a story from that myth, transplanting it from a local rival. The mythological dispute may be mirrored in an actual territorial dispute between Byzantion and Kyzikos. In the Hl period, Byzantion possessed various territories along the S coast of the Propontis which neighboured the domains of Kyzikos, while Strabo 12. 8. 11, C576, claims that Byzantion possessed territory around Lake Daskylitis bordering the territory of Kyzikos. For bibliography on Byzantion's overseas possessions, see T. Russell 2017, ch. 3. 3 (pp. 104–12).

simple, and which overlooks the sea. They (*the Byzantines*) once contemplated moving this to a site above the running track, which was a very fine and spacious and, in a few similar respects, remarkable place, but he did not permit it.⁴⁵ For he advised them not to in an oracle: either because he was fond of his beloved place next to the sea, or to demonstrate what a small thing riches are in comparison to piety.   10. Under the temple of Poseidon, inside the circuit of the walls, are the stadiums, gymnasiums and running courses of the young men, all on level ground, while at sea the current flows gently and the voyage into the Keras is easy.

11. Three harbours follow in succession as one first rounds the cape;⁴⁶ of these the one in the middle is tolerably deep, and it is protected from other winds, though it is not entirely secure when the south-west wind dominates; it is closed off from both sides—for the onward motion of the sea is shut out by the construction of the walls.   12. After this, as one passes along its length there is a great tower, rounded in its appearance and particularly large, the wall joining on to the mainland. Then, in the first place, the flat terrain of the isthmus, which prevents the city from being an island, slopes down gently towards the shore. After this there is a sanctuary of Ge Anesidora (*Earth the Giftgiver*) overlooking the sea, not covered by any roof. These antiquities signify, I think, the self-determination of Earth.⁴⁷ This sanctuary is surrounded by a circuit-wall of polished stone.   13. A little above this are the sanctuaries of Demeter and Kore side by side; in them there are a number of paintings, surviving signs and remnants of an earlier prosperity, and the statues (*xoana*) are of an exact skill second to none of the highest.

14. There are two temples in the direction of the opening to the sea, of Hera and Pluto: nothing remains of them save their names. The first of these was burned down by the Persians who accompanied Darius on his expedition against Skythia, exacting vengeance for the King for the things which he accused the city of,⁴⁸ while that of Pluto was burned down by Philip of Macedonia, when he was besieging the city and in need of resources.⁴⁹ Memory endows the places with their names—for one is called Cape Pluto, the other Cape Hera. Here victims are sacrificed each year to the prophet Polyeides, and his children, as one year ceases and another begins. It is a Megarian custom.⁵⁰

---

⁴⁵ Poseidon was the father of Byzas (cf. §24), Byzantion's mythological eponymous founder.
⁴⁶ There are two medieval scholia here. One reads 'Concerning the harbours of the city below the Bosporian Heights'. The other says 'Concerning the harbour which still survives now in the so-called Neorion'. On the Neorion and Prosphorion, see Kislinger 2021.
⁴⁷ The cult may be a reflection of the fertility of this part of Byzantion's hinterland.
⁴⁸ See Hdt. 4. 85–7: Darius crossed the Bosporos on his Skythian expedition in 513 BC.
⁴⁹ Either Philip II of Macedonia in 340 BC, or possibly Philip V in 200/199 (Dumitru 2006; cf. n. 129).
⁵⁰ D. is alluding to the view that Megarians were involved in Byzantion's original foundation.

15. After this are the rocks called Skironides, so called by the Corinthians from their similarity to rough ground.[51] For Corinthians too took part in the colonization, and they wondered at the resemblance.[52]

16. After this there is a long beach, a place worse than none of the best for the hunting of fish thanks to its considerable depth—for it is, in a few words, precipitously profound—and for the mildness of the sea and the approach to the shore. It is named Kykla (*Circles*), because, I think, the Greeks here encircled the barbarians. Here is the altar of Athena Skedasia (*the Scatterer*), alluding to the scattering of this multitude by their encirclement.

17. Kykla is followed by the gulf of Melias, a rich hunting ground like no other, for it surpasses them all in every respect—it is shut in by lofty capes and on both sides by reefs under the sea. It is named after a certain local hero, and it never fails to provide large amounts of fish for hunting.[53]

18. After this is the place called Kepos (*Garden*), which takes its name from the land—for it is, in short, good for gardening, and its cultivation is aided by the sea. For it was not long ago discovered, and was before then idle and unexplored, but now offers access to migrating fish.[54]   19. Above this is the Hapsasieion: it was named thus by those from Arkadia and Zeus Hapsasios is honoured in this place.[55]

20. After this a great headland overshadows the others, and weathers the violence of both the current and the winds. From here the projecting part of the cape has collapsed into the sea, so that it runs over the deeps without support. Below the cape the rock is notched and cut through, so that it is joined to the mainland with only a small amount of rock, and it appears that it will be loosened and is likely ⟨to be cut off⟩. Its name was given to it for its similarity to the sight, for it is called Mellapokopsas (*About To Be Cut Off*).

21. After this there are two places which provide fishing all year long, on account both of their location below the capes and of the depths of gulfs and the sea pouring into them calm and undisturbed by the wind. One of these is called Ingenidas, named after a local hero; the other is Peraikos, named, according to the more popular account, after Peiraieus, which is near the city of Athens, though as others say a certain Peron, one of the ancient settlers named it after himself.[56] Kittos (*Ivy*) lies in the middle

---

[51] The Skironian rocks were located in the hilly country between Megara and Corinth. The word *skiros* means rough land covered with scrub.

[52] D. states here explicitly that the foundation of Byzantion was a mixed enterprise.

[53] Oberhummer (*RE* xi. 1. 258) places Melias at the foot of the hill now crowned by the *Süleymaniye Camii* and *Mahmudiye Camii*. Gyllius notes that the bay there was already filled in and built on by his time (ii. 2. 60).

[54] MS A places this sentence at the end of §19; Güngerich places it here.

[55] D. makes allusion to the possible involvement of Arkadians in Byzantion's early development. Oberhummer places the Apsasieion at *Unkapanı* (*RE* xi. 1. 258, s.v. Keras 1), but admits that the coastline has altered considerably since antiquity. Hapsasios is not otherwise attested.

[56] The reference to the Peiraieus may be an oblique allusion to the late tradition that Athenians were involved in the foundation of Byzantion (Amm. Marc. 12. 8. 8).

of both, named for the amount and luxuriance of ivy which it produces. 22. Beside Peraikos is Kamara (*Vault*), a steep shore positioned towards the winds, which weathers great impact from the sea.

23. Then comes the place called the Sapra Thalassa (*Foul Sea*), the very end of the entire gulf—for it lies at the base of the Keras—and is the beginning of the rivers which issue into it.[57] Why it is named so I do not know, either because of the proximity to these rivers which rise in this area—for by pressing forward they destroy the local character of the sea—or because the sea here is motionless and not affected by the wind. It might, however, be possible to explain the name from the silting up of the rivers, which carry down constant, soft sediment which makes the sea shallow and full of shoals. Fishing takes place here. The first of the places here is Polyrrhetion, named after the man called Polyrrhetos,[58] and after this comes Bathea Skopia (*Deep Watch*), named because of the depth of the water;[59] then third Blachernas, a barbarian name derived from one of the kings of the area,[60] and finally Palodes (*Marshy Place*), because of the fact that the sunken embankment of the rivers is marshy and mired in clay. For the depth is neither firm nor sandy, and because of the amount of mud being brought down it is not navigable for ships except for small ones. Here there is an estuary, raised and with shoals, which stretches as far as the outflow of the rivers, where they split in two from one another, but later come together at the outpouring as they fall out through one single mouth. In between the two rivers (*Kydaros and Barbyses*) the marshes are rich in animals, with meadows that give plentiful land for grazing beasts. The god spoke darkly of these (*the two rivers*) as whelps, when he was encouraging those who consulted the oracle about the colony. He spoke thus:

Where two whelps grasp the grey sea,
Where a fish and a deer feed on the same pasture.[61]

---

[57] The rivers are the Kydaros (mod. *Alibey Su*) and Barbyses (mod. *Kağithane Su*), the two rivers which flow together into the Golden Horn.

[58] Polyrrhetos is otherwise unknown.

[59] Given that D. has just mentioned the importance of fishing to this spot, it may be that the toponym relates to a fishing emplacement (madrague) with attached lookout tower, a *skopeia*. Over thirty madragues were located along the Bosporos in the 1920s: see T. Russell 2017, 152–3; Lytle 2006, 42–68.

[60] Site of the suburb of Blachernai (*Ayvansaray*), on the sixth hill and at the N end of the walls of late Roman and medieval Constantinople.

[61] Hesychios (2 = *BNJ* 390 F 1.3) quotes the same oracle and ascribes it to the Pythia. He adds two extra lines at the beginning: 'Blessed are those who will dwell in the sacred city | By the narrow Thracian shore at the mouth of the Pontos'. All four lines are also added in the margin of MS A of Dionysios (scholion 28), preceded by the words 'The oracle runs thus from beginning to end'. Steph. Byz. β 190 Byzantion cites similar lines, and there is yet another variant in the commentary by Eustathios on Dionysios Periegetes (l. 803). Gyllius (ii. 2. 65) prints a version of ll. 1, 2, and 4 but omits to mention the puppies. The riddle to which D. refers, which survives in longer versions, is imagined as an oracular pronouncement given to the future founders of Byzantion. In Hesychios' version, we are told that it was Argives who asked the oracle of Pythian Apollo. It was traditional to consult an oracle before embarking on a colonial enterprise, ideally the oracle of Apollo at Delphi.

He says these things because of an event which happens here: the deer come down from the woods during the winter and eat the reed which grows in the marsh, and those of the fish which lurk in the stillness of the Keras, mixed in with both the sea and the rivers, gorge themselves on the roots at the bottom of the sea, fat and lazy from their good eating.[62]

24. Of these rivers the Kydaros begins from the direction of sunset in the summer, the Barbyses on the other hand with the north wind. Some call this latter river after the nurse of Byzas, others after the helmsman of the boat of Jason and the Minyans who sailed with him, yet others after a local hero. Where the rivers join together and move forward, washing onto and over a massive headland facing them and going down into the sea there is the altar of Semystra, from which also comes the name of the place.[63] Semystra, a water nymph, was the nurse of Keroëssa. For when by the arts of Zeus on the one hand and the anger of Hera on the other, Io was let loose in the shape of a cow and, driven by fear of a winged gadfly, roamed over many lands, it was indeed at this spot that she endured the pangs of childbirth—for she was pregnant with a divine child—and she produced a female child. Semystra reared the child who bore a sign of her mother's transformation, for the form of horns with which she was marked projected on each side of her forehead. For this she was named Keroëssa.[64] From her and Poseidon the man Byzas was born, who is honoured equal to a god, and from whom Byzantion came to be. Semystra, in fact, nearly had the chance to become a city. For it was here that the leaders of the colonizers decided to found their city. But while the sacrifices were burning, a raven snatched some of the thigh bones from the middle of the flame, and raised them up in flight and bore them to Cape Bosporios. This the learned men of the Greeks thought to be a sign from Apollo. A herdsman, who had seen from a vantage point, indicated to them where the thing seized from the holy offerings had been set down. And so they followed the sign.[65]

25. After Semystra, a little beyond the outflow of the rivers, is the beginning of the circumambulation round the Keras on the other side, at the curved promontory of Drepanon (*Scythe*).[66] After this there is a sharp crest, inclining markedly downwards towards the sea. It is named Boukolos (*Cowherd*), in appropriate commemoration of

---

[62] A similar oracle suggesting that a city should be founded where land and sea meet was given to the founders of Ephesos who were told they should build 'wherever a fish shall show them and a boar shall lead the way': Rogers 2014, 106.

[63] This, the promontory between the two rivers flowing into the Golden Horn, is mod. *Sılahtarağa*. Cf. *TIB* 12, 643–44 s.v. Semystra. Hesychios (13) records a healing shrine of Castor and Pollux at the altar of Semestre.

[64] *Keras* is the Greek for 'horn'. Keroëssa, a maiden with horns, appears on Byzantine coins from the Roman period.

[65] The original location may have enjoyed fresh water from the Kydaros and Barbyses, but the Bosporios Akra could boast the ability to monitor shipping in the Bosporos. The provision of fresh water has always been a problem for Constantinople-Istanbul: Crow 2007; Crow, Bardill, and Bayliss 2008.

[66] Drepanon is modern *Sütlüce*, on the left bank of the Golden Horn. Foss 2000, 785–7, argues that *katopin* ('after') and *hyper* ('beyond') indicate that D. has crossed over to the other side of the water and is now proceeding down the left bank of the Horn.

the man who brought the information, for it was from here that he seems to have seen the founding bird.   26. After Boukolos are Mandrai (*Enclosures*)⁶⁷ and Drys (*Oak Tree*): the first is named from the still and sheltered character of the place—for it is washed by a windless sea—while Drys is named after a sacred grove: this is a sanctuary of Apollo.

27. Rounding the headland there is an oblong gulf, named Auleon.⁶⁸ ⟨After it there is a bridge⟩,⁶⁹ a work of Philip of Macedonia when he was extending a connection from both shores of the mainland. He threw down supports of stones into the depths, and a massive earthen mound was raised by many hands, so that with the Keras bridged for him by land he might be able to bring in plentiful supplies. For indeed this area was not conquerable with ships, since the Byzantines ruled the sea all around.⁷⁰

28. On this spot there is an altar of the hero Nikaios and it is a gently curving place. There is a reservoir of wild fish and so it is called, from what you find there, Neos Bolos (*New Cast*).⁷¹   29. Both the name and the nature of Aktina agree.⁷² ⟨After which is a gulf⟩ ... around it Kanopos, Kyboi (*Dice*), and Krenides (*Springs*).⁷³ These derive from the running streams that rise from springs, for the land is particularly damp and dewy here. Kyboi is an indication from Persian history—for certain people used to visit here and take part in its entertainments⁷⁴—while Kanopos took its name from Egypt as being most similar to the luxury in that place. Here the river Meizon (*Greater*) cuts into the depth, whence also comes the name of the gulf, which is big enough but not navigable.⁷⁵

30. From here there is a very deep mudflat, surrounded by undersea roots, which shuts off the gulf. In this area there is a lack of fish, because of the rock-pools met with in the sea about the entrances, except for the fish which glide through in error in the dimness of night.   31. After this mud is the so-called Choiragria (*Wild Hog*); it is called this for what happened there, since certain people used to seize by guile boars coming down from the mountains. For indeed the whole side of the Keras facing towards the south wind is covered with forests.⁷⁶

---

⁶⁷ The calm bay is that created by the bend of the Golden Horn near *Sütlüce*.

⁶⁸ This will be where the *Hasköy Çeşmesi* enters the Golden Horn, downstream from the present bridge at *Piri Paşa*.

⁶⁹ We follow Güngerich in inserting the words in angle brackets, basing them on Gyllius' statement that 'after Auleon, D. says there is a bridge, a work of Philip of Macedonia'.

⁷⁰ See note to §14.

⁷¹ Bolos relates to the modern Turkish *voli*, which denotes a fishing emplacement where fixed net traps can be deployed.

⁷² D.'s meaning is unclear.

⁷³ The brackets mark a lacuna in the MS. None of these three places is named elsewhere, but they appear to lie in the area of mod. *Kasımpaşa*.

⁷⁴ In C6l and C5e, before Byzantion entered the anti-Persian Delian league, the city was under Persian control with brief interludes, and may have become for Persians a gambling resort in Europe; the apolaustic tendency of Persians was proverbial: Hdt. 1. 135.

⁷⁵ The stream is that which flows down the *Kasımpaşa* valley into the Golden Horn.

⁷⁶ This area of mod. *Galata* is not otherwise referred to.

32. Along here the Keras terminates, and there begins the narrow channel that is laid out in front of the Pontos and is directed by this time towards the promontory which overlooks the broad and spread-out Propontis.[77] Upon it is the tomb of the hero Hipposthenes of Megara, after whom came the name of the land.[78]   33. Following Hipposthenes is Sykides (*Fig-trees*), named for the quantity and beauty of the plants. Some of the inquisitive say that here is where it (*the fig-tree*) took its general beginning.   34. Here there is a sanctuary of Schoiniklos, the honour and memory of which was brought by the Byzantines from Megara. They say that this man was the charioteer of Amphiaros the seer.[79]   35. The place connected to it is named Auletes, from the founder and piper Python. Memory honours his trade in the name.[80]   36. Then after this is Bolos, which is naturally suited in the winter for the hunting of fish.[81] At this place there is a sanctuary of Artemis Phosphoros (*Lightbearer*) and Aphrodite Praëia (*Gentle*), at which the Byzantines sacrifice annually. For indeed she seems to manage the good nature of the winds, making them gentle and causing them to settle from their considerable confusion.[82]

37. Then comes the place named Ostreodes (*Oystery*), named for a local event: for there is a reef under the sea, and the depth is whitened by the mass of oysters there; the depth is visible to observers at moments when the winds are silent and still. The place always reproduces what is consumed, so as someone might say, the provision is lavish, since their reproduction outstrips the speed at which they are caught.[83]

38. Next after Ostreodes comes the place called Metopon (*Brow*).[84] This lies before the face of the city—for it looks directly towards Cape Bosporios—and it is named after its shape: for it is level towards the mainland, with earthen hills, but abrupt and perpendicular where it rises from the sea. It is not, however, without a share in divine testimony, for Apollo is honoured at this place.

39. After Metopon comes Aianteion, named after Ajax son of Telamon, whom the Megarians honour according to a certain prophecy. For the customs of the founders gave laws to the colonists.[85]   40. From here, where the cliff falls away and turns into

---

[77] The narrow channel is the Bosporos itself. The cape is marked by the *Karaköy* end of the present *Galata* Bridge, where the Golden Horn meets the Bosporos.

[78] A further allusion to Megara's foundational role at Byzantion.

[79] Another reference is given to Megarian heroes. The temple was in Sykai, modern *Galata*. See further the note on §63.

[80] This is in the area of modern *Karaköy*: TIB 12, 275–76.

[81] This is in the area of modern *Karaköy* and *Kemankeş*.

[82] Phosphoros, 'light-bearer', was an important divine epithet at Byzantion, alluded to again at §78. The idea that the Byzantines honoured specific gods to seek help with the winds or currents is evidenced elsewhere: one inscription at Hieron records the dedication of cake offerings to Zeus Ourios in exchange for good winds: IKalch 14.

[83] This is in the area of modern *Kemankeş* and appears not to be otherwise attested: TIB 12, 554.

[84] lit. 'Forehead', but cf. the name Kriou Metopon for a cape in the Black Sea and another in Crete (trans. *Ram's Brow* in these volumes; and see the Index). This is the S part of *Tophane*.

[85] Modern *Tophane*. Here we have an explicit reference to Megarian involvement in the foundation. The Greek is rather abbreviated and laconic. This is the Greater Ajax of Iliadic fame: as for most other places in the Greek world, the Trojan war formed one mythological focal point on the shores of the Bosporos.

the sea, is Palinormikon, which is named for the second anchoring, since after they first put in here, having set off again they turned back; the experience of what happened here gave the place its name.[86]

41. A little above this comes the temple of Ptolemy Philadelphos: to this man the Byzantines gave honour equal to a god, since they have enjoyed both his great charity and his honour towards their city. For he gave them land in Asia, many myriads of grain, and arms, and money.

42. The next place is called Delphin and Karandas, and the reason for the names is the following. A man named Chalkis was settling here, a Byzantine by race, and by profession a lyre-player, second in skill to none of the best. At this place, wearing full apparel, he sang the Orthian Strain,[87] and a dolphin joined him from the open sea; moving down into earshot of the song and standing out by emerging from the sea, it rose from the water out into view, so that it might take its fill of all the melody, and so that it might not be hindered from a full appreciation by the depth of its movement. There was for the dolphin a measure of sweetness in the song of Chalkis, and when he had finished, it went back under the sea, and returned to its own recesses. Karandas was a shepherd who lived in the neighbouring area, and either out of envy and hatred of Chalkis, or maybe for personal gain as well, he lay in wait in the quiet as it slipped through the sea, and as it was gliding on the surface, enjoying the pleasure of the song, he killed it with a missile. But he did not make off with his prey. Chalkis buried his listener magnificently. Thus he gave this place the names Delphin and Karandas, the first in honour of its memory, the other for vengeance.[88]

43. After this there is a cape which unfolds for a short distance: its base and root, a rock along the depth, is named Thermastis (*Hot Springs?*).[89]   44. After this a beach spreads out facing the south wind. It is called, after those who came in their pentecounters and occupied it, Pentekontorikon.[90] For the founding of the city began at the same time as the names of each of its villages came into use. Next to it are Ta Skythou (*The Places of the Skythian*) for the following reason: 45. for they say that a Scythian migrant named Tauros had come from his own home to anchor here—they say that on his way to Crete that he ravaged Pasiphae, the daughter of Minos,[91] from which the story of his love and of his offspring (i.e. the Minotaur) arose.

---

[86] Presumably referring to the first arrival of Greek colonists.

[87] The Orthian Strain was the tune played by the bard Arion before he leapt into the sea and was carried away on a dolphin's back: Hdt. 1. 24.

[88] Dolphins held some amount of cultural significance in the lands surrounding the Bosporos. Byzantine coins carried an image of a cow on top of a dolphin. The image may relate to Io's famous passage of the Bosporos, and this spot, Delphin, stood opposite a place named Bous (*Cow*), on the Asiatic coast. See T. Russell 2012.

[89] The name is not otherwise attested. It was in the area of *Kabataş*.

[90] The coastline here has altered since antiquity, but this is in the neighbourhood of *Dolmabahçe*.

[91] The story serves to tie the shores of the Bosporos into a wider, popular Greek myth: Theseus and the Minotaur. Indeed, D.'s explanation allows for the claim that the myth of the Minotaur owed its origin to this Skythian immigrant, localizing it to the shores of the Bosporos.

46. One then comes immediately upon Iasonion where those who came with Jason anchored.⁹² There is a glade here of deep laurel, easy to traverse, as well as an altar of Apollo. The beach is elongated and is exposed to winds from the west and south. 47. After this there is the Rhodion Periboloi (*Enclosures of the Rhodians*)⁹³—here, having made fast their ships' cables, the Rhodians attacked those who disputed their command of the sea. There remain even to our own day some drilled stones used for tying up the ships, but most have been lost to time.⁹⁴

48. Following this is the place called Archeion.⁹⁵ Here there is a fairly fertile plain, rich in vineyards and shut in on either side by tall hills which fall away towards the sea. Through the middle of it a river flows to the soft and deep shore. Here there settled Archias of Thasos, son of Aristonymos, who resolved to found a city here. However he was prevented from this by the Chalkedonians, who feared that the place would be founded in opposition to them. Archias then removed himself and colonized Ainos, leaving behind his name to the place.⁹⁶

49. After Archeion there stands a large cliff, which is split right down to its base. It projects over the summit of the cape, and is the first place to receive the cumulative violence of the open sea and it has been cloven by the strong-running sea current. At its peak there is set up Gerōn Halios (*The Old Man of The Sea*). Some say that he was Nereus, others Phorkys, others Proteus, certain others the father of Semystra, still others that he was the guide for the voyage of Jason and his company, and that he became their pilot through the exit of the narrows. Lakiades, they say, a certain prophet of the ⟨Megarian?⟩⁹⁷ race, gave an oracle to those setting out at the birth of the colony, announcing a vision from a dream, that they should indeed sacrifice to Gerōn Halios; he is honoured by the community.⁹⁸

---

⁹² D. seems not to care that the number of disembarkations attributed to the Argonauts on their short passage through the strait is becoming excessive. Iasonion was in the area of modern Beşiktaş.

⁹³ In the neighbourhood of Çırağan Sarayı in Beşiktaş.

⁹⁴ This sea battle involving Rhodians may relate to early colonists; or it could relate to the siege of Byzantion by Rhodes in 220 BC during the short-lived Byzantine–Rhodian war: Polyb. 4. 47–52.

⁹⁵ At *Ortaköy*, N of Beşiktaş.

⁹⁶ For the Chalkedonians to be deterring would-be colonists from the European shores, Chalkedon would have to have existed before Byzantion, as the story of the famous 'riddle of the blind' claims. Ainos (mod. *Enez*) lies in Thrace.

⁹⁷ The reference to Megara is provided by Güngerich in order to make sense of the text (cf. his pp. lxii–lxiv).

⁹⁸ Nereus, Phorkys, and Proteus are all early sea-gods, mentioned in Homer as versions of the Old Man of the Sea. D.'s various explanations of the Old Man of the Sea reflect a particularly confused and muddled piece of local oral tradition, and each explanation serves to emphasize a slightly different feature of the site: Nereus, Phorkys, and Proteus relate the site to pan-Hellenic mythology and the Homeric myths; the relation to Semystra emphasizes his epichoric connection and relation to Byzas, the founder of the city of Byzantion; as the expounder for the Argonauts, the Old Man of the Sea fits in with the Argonautic cycle, while the version involving Lakiades links the site in to early Greek colonization of the area. These stories were fluid and malleable.

50. Neighbouring this is Parabolos (*Perilous*),⁹⁹ named because of the danger involved in hunting (*fish*) here due to the irregularity of the open sea. For as you pass down into this unprotected, naked and rocky shore of the sea, the current is deceptive as if to disguise its truth, which is that it gives forth good fishing to those who happen to come near it.¹⁰⁰   51. Then there is Kalamos (*Reed*) and Bythias (*Depth*).¹⁰¹ Kalamos is named from the number ⟨of reeds⟩, while Bythias, which ⟨lies in⟩ the shelter of the promontories, is named because of its depth at its turning point. There is laurel here, which was planted by Medea the daughter of Aietes, so the story goes.   52. Parallel to this there is a flat-crested hill, which inclines gently to the sea, and the sanctuary of the Mother of the Gods. It is called Baka (?) after those who colonized the area.

53. After this there is a cape which spreads out, and a completely enveloped harbour which is protected from the northern impact of the sea by a thick, protruding cliff. For along here it turns back towards the west, having fallen down into an immeasurable depth, and providing a big enough anchorage and protection from the winds.¹⁰² Since it stretches out here it receives the reckless force of the current, which is like that of a dragon. For sometimes a churning counter-surge of the open sea rushes against it, but at other times the rushing comes in the opposite direction and it thrusts the sea back. And I have seen many laden ships running with a fair wind in their sails be carried backwards on their course, the current fighting against the wind.¹⁰³ It is turned back on close contact with the rocks and, pushed back and forced into the direction opposite to that of the open sea, the sea itself runs back on its own course. Both fear and perplexity afflict ⟨sailors⟩, being unable to make a second attempt. It therefore comes about that often they take their ships in tow and drag them upstream from the land, forcing them against the current which is pressing upon them mightily. It is close to here that they give out the cables and loose themselves, using the momentum from their disembarkation to travel along the rocks and contend with the current, supporting their rowing towards the rocky shore and defeating the strength of the sea in alliance with the continent. There are certain marks and indentations of the feet of sea crabs which

---

⁹⁹ Parabolos is in the area of *Kuruçeşme*.

¹⁰⁰ Locations with *bolos* in their name relate to fishing spots from which nets could be thrown or coastal emplacements could be operated. Chaniotis and Mylonopoulos 2003, 280–2, stress the alternative meaning of Parabolos, 'deceitful' or 'dangerous', and it may be that the fishermen honoured Dionysos 'the deceiver' for his help dealing with the deceptive nature of the current at this spot.

¹⁰¹ These are in the area of *Kuruçeşme*.

¹⁰² The former harbour at *Arnavutköy* was sheltered by the promontory of *Akıntı Burnu* from the current coming down the Bosporos from the N.

¹⁰³ D.'s use of the first person is an important indication of his local knowledge. The dangerous current is nowadays called the 'Devil's Current' (*Şeytan Akıntısı*). Polybios (4. 43. 3–10) describes how it flows S from the Black Sea, is deflected by this promontory on the European shore, sweeps across to the Asian side and recoils to the European bank at Hestiai ('the Hearths'; cf. §§53–4) from which it passes over to a place on the Asian coast called Bous ('the Cow'; cf. §110) before dividing to go partly up the Golden Horn and partly S towards Chalkedon.

bypass the most forceful part of the current.[104] This place is called Hestiai (*Hearths*).[105] For the leaders of the colonizing expedition put in with their ships here, since when they had come past Cape Bosporios they saw that the landing sites were occupied by a massed barbarian army. They founded hearths according to the place where each city disembarked.[106] When they learned that the barbarians were coming by land against them, they waited until most of them had withdrawn a long way from these places, and launched their fleet into the current. Thus they landed on the now unguarded cape, emptied of men, having out-generalled the barbarians. For the voyage was short for them as they took shortcuts across the inlets, while the barbarians went round circuitously by land. Some say that Hestiai was founded not from cities, but from the seven best houses of Megara. Let each believe as he wishes.

54. Turning past Hestiai the voyage is largely peaceful and steady towards the curve of the promontory, and towards the force of the current of both open sea and air.[107] From here they say that before the Trojan War, Mysians with Teukrians passed through and reached right up to Thessaly, having overcome every land through which they passed; and that, around the time of the Iliac War (*Trojan war*), there was Asteropaios, King of those Paionians who lived at the river Axios.[108]   55. Chelai (*Claws or Hooves*)[109] comes after Hestiai, named for its resemblance to the image. For the name is similar to the sight: here are harbours on both sides, some bigger, others shorter.

56. After this is a sanctuary of Artemis Diktynna (*Thrower of Nets*). Here they dedicated to her the catches made at sea, as the only one of the gods that is capable in both types of hunting (i.e. on land and on sea). This goddess the Cyzicenes were instructed to honour when they were repressed by the barren nature of the sea. They secretly withdrew themselves, but the goddess became invisible—for a god has power over all things—and they drew no better experience from the sea. So the statue of the goddess was seated where she was before. But the Cyzicenes sailed openly bringing her back secured with golden chains, and from then the goddess let go of her anger for them.[110]

---

[104] Aelian, *Historia Animalium*, 7. 24, similarly describes how crabs crawl onto the shore of the Bosporos, as does Pliny 9. xx. 51.

[105] Mod. *Akıntı Burnu*. The name Hestiai appears in Pliny 5. xliii. 150 and elsewhere. Scholion 61 to the text of Dionysios (placed at the start of §53) alludes to 'the heights called Hestiai, where is now the Michaelion'.

[106] More evidence of a 'mixed' foundation, with a variety of *poleis* occupying the site.

[107] Scholion 63, placed at the start of this paragraph, reads 'Concerning the bay now called Philemporion and that in this place Mysoi and Teukroi came into Europe and Asteropaios crossed to Troy'.

[108] D. connects the shores of the Bosporos to mythology from the Trojan War: Asteropaios commanded the Paionians and was killed in single combat by Achilles: Homer *Iliad* 12. 123; 21. 159–230.

[109] Mod. *Bebek*.   [110] The command of the god presumably came through an oracle.

FROM THE LATIN OF PETRUS GYLLIUS (PIERRE GILLES)[111]

57. (ii. 12. 109–10) After the temple of Diana (*Artemis*) Dictynna, *says Dionysius*, navigation is turbulent and vehemently agitated because the current is held back. The place is called Pyrrhias Cyon (*Red Hound*), from the resemblance, it seems to me, which the sea here has to a dog. Indeed a story told by many people maintains that a shepherd's dog ran around the shore here and barked at those who were obliged by the violence of the current to navigate along the edge of the coast. There also the channel of the strait separating the two continents is narrowest.[112] In the same place also, it is said, was the crossing of Darius, for here Androcles of Samos joined together a bridge on the Bosporus.[113] This place offers other monuments of history, as well as a seat carved on the rock; for they say that Darius sat on it and looked out at the bridge and at the crossing over of the army.[114]

58. (ii. 15. 120) After Pyrrhias Cyon, *Dionysius locates* a sea coast with a cape raised up to a sheer height which is hard for sailors and difficult to pass on account of the violent collision caused by both continents resisting the Bosporus as it flows forward through the narrows. For the tide bursts out and foams with continuous whirlpools not less than a cauldron when a fire is placed under it is accustomed to boil and to bubble over with the emission of the flame and to rumble with a seething sound. Therefore on account of its nature this coast is called Rhoödes, that is to say turbulent.[115]

59. (ii. 13. 122) Then, *says Dionysius*, having gone beyond the promontory there appears a rock made by nature, not by the hand of men. It is white in colour, and bears in front of it the likeness of an eagle's wings and it stretches out like the sole of a foot, drawing back on the other side, like some plaything of nature imitating everything. It is called Phidalia,[116] and you would not know whether you ought to say it is an island or belongs to the mainland, being the one by nature and the other indeed by proximity.[117] Some say that it was called Phaidalia, from the fact that in it a fishery first appears.[118] Others say that it was named after the daughter of Barbyssa,[119] who when

---

[111] References in this section of the form 'ii. 12. 109–10' are to the book, chapter, and page numbers in Gyllius 1561.

[112] At its narrowest point, the Bosporos is less than ½ mi (*c.*800 m) wide. This is at the Ottoman castle called *Rumeli Hisar*. The narrowest point of the Mouth of the Black Sea is at Hieron.

[113] In 514 BC Darius king of the Persians, in preparation for his invasion of Skythia, ordered a bridge to be built over the Bosporos (Hdt. 4. 83).

[114] The seat of Darius known to Hdt. (4. 85) would seem (according to the MS reading) to have been at Hieron: Moreno 2008, 661–2.

[115] Gyllius prints Rhoödes in Greek. It is modern *Şeytan Burnu*.

[116] Gyllius prints this name in Greek.

[117] Phidalia is contiguous to Gynaikopolis (Portus Mulierum) which corresponds to modern *Balta Limanı*.

[118] T. Russell 2017, 147–51, relates D.'s references to fisheries to the actual operation of the coastal fisheries known as madragues.

[119] Barbyses, the eponym of one of the rivers which flows into the Golden Horn, was thought variously to be either the tutor of Byzas or the guide of Jason and the Argonauts: §24.

she had mixed herself in loving congress with Byzas was disturbed by the shame of her fornication and by fear of her father, so threw herself into the sea and perished. And Neptune her father, moved by mercy and by indulgence towards his own family, broke off a large part of the mainland and fixed and secured it in the deep, and the island was deemed to be the tomb of Phidalia by those who came after.[120]

60. (ii. 13. 123) A bay recedes inwards from the east, and is deep and fairly capacious, and enclosed by a short circuit of the mainland. Into the middle of the bay comes down a *cheimarrous*,[121] *that is a winter stream*, for it fails in the height of summer. In this bay is Portus Mulierum (*Harbour of the Women*), named either because it is in no way troubled either from the sea or from the mainland—for it is not less safe from the waves of the sea than it is protected from strong winds from the land—or it was named thus because men were absent when women caught a great multitude of fish which had come into this harbour.[122]

61. (ii. 13. 124–5) *Then the same Dionysius adds* a place called Kyparodes,[123] named after the cypress tree, follows immediately after Portus Mulierum.[124]

62. (ii. 13. 125) After Cyparodes, *Dionysius places* a Temple of Hecate on a rock which resounds loudly on being struck by waves when winds come, for around it waves whipped up together are broken apart. Indeed it gathers up the same quantity as it throws back under the overhang of the seashore.

63. (ii. 14. 127) After the Temple of Hecate, *he says*, follows ⟨a bay⟩ called Lasthenes, named after Lasthenes, a man of Megara.[125] It is similar to the inlet called Cornu (*Horn*) in its marshy inmost recess, in the loftiness of its headlands and in its profound depth, in so far as it is permissible to compare great things with small. At the entrance it is restricted, but going further it broadens greatly. It is tranquil and safe, surrounded by mountains, which protect like walls against winds. Into it also descends a certain river, perennial but inaccessible to ships. In this place Amphiaraus is worshipped in obedience to the divine command of an oracle.[126]

64. (ii. 15. 130–1) After Lasthenium, *he says*, is Comarodes, named from a forest of arbutus, beaten by the billowy sea.[127]   65. After Comarodes there succeeds a raised shore, harsh and with hollow crags rising up out of the sea, which the ancients named Bacchiae because around them the tide stirred into motion seems to rage and behave

---

[120] This legend recalls those in Ps.-Plutarch (Ch. 26 above).

[121] Gyllius prints this word in Greek.

[122] The river is now called *Baltalimanı*. Portus ... Mulierum is named in Pliny 4. xi. 46; Steph. Byz. γ 119 Gynaikospolis (Artemidoros 136).

[123] Gyllius prints this name in Greek.   [124] Mod. *Boyacıköy*, formerly Bapheochorion.

[125] The place Lasthenes is mentioned as such by Pliny 4. xi. 46, by John of Antioch (frag. 26. 3 = p. 64 Roberto) and by Steph. Byz. γ 119 Gynaikopolis as Leostheneion. It corresponds to modern İstinye, whose name derives from Byzantine Sosthenion, on which see John Malalas 4. 13. 78.

[126] Dionysios (§34) records a shrine of Schoiniklos, the charioteer of Amphiaraos the seer, which was honoured by the Megarians of Byzantion further S along the Bosporos shore.

[127] The Greek word *komaros* denotes the strawberry-tree (Linnaean *arbutus unedo*). Comarodes was within the bounds of mod. *Yeniköy* and Byzantine Neapolis.

bacchically. Here when the Byzantines had overcome Demetrius leader of the army of Philip they called the place Thermemeria (*Hot Day*)[128] from the event which had occurred, for they had fought the naval battle of that day with great care and the utmost ardour.[129]   66. Below the shore where it juts out there follows a bay in which is Portus Pitheci (*Harbour of the Ape*). They say that Asteropaeo, king of the barbarians living in this place, together with his sons, was the leader of the crossing over into Asia. The mainland here has a shore both rugged and precipitous.[130]   67. From there follows a shore sloping into a bay called Eudion Kalon (*Beautiful Calm*),[131] which is surrounded by a beach shrunk into such a small space by the sea that by nature it belongs to the mainland but seems by appearance to be an island.   68. Immediately thereafter succeeds a bay named Pharmacias after Medea of Colchis who stored in this place small boxes of drugs (*pharmaca*).[132] It is very beautiful and very suitable for fishing and most apt for running ships ashore. Up to the margin of the shore it is considered deep and extremely safe from winds. It attracts a multitude of fishes to it. Thick forests and deep woods of every kind and meadows overhang it, just as if, so I think, the earth was competing with the sea. Its circuit is overshadowed by a wood leaning down into the sea; down through the middle of it into the bay, there flows a river running without sound.

69. (ii. 16. 136–7) Rocky shores and cliffs follow Pharmacias. These overhang the sea looking, from the way that they present to the eyes a flexible appearance, like things bent by the vision.[133] For the Pontus which had been concealed by projecting promontories, is opened out, with nothing further impeding a proper view, for often what seems to be the end is found once more to be a new beginning, and afterwards the sight of the sea which had previously been hidden restores faith in the fact which was not previously believed. Those rocks and the crags of the coast are called (*the*) Kleides and Kleithra of the Pontos,[134] *that is, the Keys and Bars of the Pontus*.[135]   70. Now once one has gone past the Keys there is, rather than the sight of the Pontus, a rock raised up to a sharp peak, bearing a similarity to a pine cone. This is named Dicaea, *that is Just*, from the fact that some merchants sailing into the Pontus in triremes had deposited gold at this rock, having agreed between themselves that neither of them would take it away before both had come together to the rock at the same time. The talk of men has it that one of the two evaded the agreement but the gold concealed itself, because the

---

[128] Gyllius prints this name in Greek.
[129] The headland here is modern *Karaca Burnu*. Dumitru 2006 argues that the king whose forces were involved in this battle was Philip V of Macedonia in 200/199 BC. (Cf. n. 49.)
[130] This corresponds to mod. *Kalender Köy*.   [131] Gyllius prints this name in Greek.
[132] Modern *Tarabya*, Byzantine Therapia (*TIB* 12, 673–4). Medea will have deposited her potions at Pharmakias on the return voyage of the Argonauts from Kolchis, as indicated by Vian 1974, 103.
[133] §3 and Moreno 2008, 662 n. 18, indicate that actual experience of the visual effects produced by the promontories lining the Bosporos could inspire belief in the Clashing Rocks (Symplegades, Kyaneai) at the mouth of the Bosporos.
[134] These three names are printed in Greek by Gyllius.
[135] The point where travellers passing N up the Bosporos enjoy a first unimpeded view of the Black Sea corresponds to *Kireçburnu* in the *Sarıyer* district.

rock rejected the bad faith of the perfidious partner, until such time that both came together there and took the deposit. The name of the stone has remained as a reward for this righteousness.

71. (iii. 17. 140) Near the rock named Dicaea, *says Dionysius*, is the place called Bathykolpos,[136] *that is, the Deep Gulf*, not so much from the contour of its own very beautiful inner declivity which debouches onto a deep and broad beach as from the great depth of the sea, for there are steep and precipitous declivities right next to the sea shore. A river goes out into the bay, of which the name is the same as that of the bay. Here is the altar of Saron a hero of Megara, and a casting-place for fishes which, at a time suitable and appropriate for themselves, continually swim in close formation, first up and then down the Bosporus, deceived by the depth of the sea.[137]

72. (ii. 17. 141) A short way below the promontory of Saron is situated Kalos Agros[138] (*Good Field*); it has its name by nature from the pleasantness of both sea and land.[139]

73. (ii. 18. 144) After Kalos Agros, *says Dionysius*, is the promontory Simas and a statue of Venus Meretricia; for the word of men has it that a certain courtesan, Sima, beautiful and gifted and solicitous, inhabited this place and that she was accustomed to receive from those sailing past the payments of Venus.[140]

74. (ii. 18. 144) *To these things Dionysius adds that* for those who have passed the promontory called Simas there follows the bay (*named*) Scletrinas, I know not whether from the roughness of its wooded landscape or from the river flowing down into it. And after it follow also the Altars of Apollo and the Mother of the Gods and, after a brief interval, navigation into the Pontus.[141]

75. (ii. 19. 150) After Scletrina, *says Dionysius*, is the promontory Miltos (*Red Ochre*), named from its similarity to the colour.[142] There is also the house alongside of a certain naval commander, and a steep shore sloping directly and precipitately towards the sunrise. Around it the sea is broken up by reefs and there is Fanum (*Sanctuary*; '*Hieron*' *in Greek*), sited exactly opposite the frontage of the Asiatic Fanum.[143] They say that

---

[136] Gyllius prints this name in Greek.

[137] Saron was a mythical king of Troizen, who was drowned in a hunting accident and so gave his name to the Saronic gulf between Attica and the Argolid: Pausanias 2. 30. 7. On the seasonal migration of fish in the Black Sea and Bosporos, and the advantage taken of this phenomenon by coastal fisheries, both ancient and more recent, see T. Russell 2017, 143–4, 147–50, 152–9.

[138] Gyllius prints this name in Greek. [139] Kalos Agros corresponds to the valley of *Büyükdere*.

[140] The promontory of Simas is now called *Mesarburnu*.

[141] At anc. Skletrinas (from Greek *sklēros*, hard) are now the modern Istanbul suburbs of *Sarıyer* and *Yeni Mahalle*. The seasonal river flowing into the bay here is mod. *Gül Dere*. The statement that sailing into the Pontos begins just beyond Skletrinas reflects the way that ships gathered at Asiatic Hieron (roughly opposite *Sarıyer*) before passing into the Black Sea, so that Hieron was generally the point on the Bosporos from which distances were measured and was often deemed the mouth of the Black Sea (e.g. Arr. §25. 3–4; Ps-Skylax §§67, 92; see below, note on §92).

[142] The headland called Miltos corresponds to modern *Tellitabya*.

[143] There were two places on the shores of the Bosporos called Hieron (Temple, Latin *Fanum*); one, mentioned here, is on the European shore and the other, more celebrated, is on the Asiatic shore and is discussed in §93. On the latter, see Moreno 2008.

Jason sacrificed here to the twelve Gods.[144] These Fana are small towns placed next to the mouth of the Pontus;[145] there is also a temple of the Phrygian Goddess, a famous holy place publicly cultivated.

76. (ii. 20. 152–3) *Dionysius, after he has described the temple of the Phrygian Goddess, says this*: After these, the river Chrysorrhoas (*Golden Stream*) runs down with a mild flow through a narrow valley situated in its rear that is difficult of access. It carries down sand similar to gold. Around this are trenches cut in the earth and pits made to examine the veins of metal, works of men of old exploring the resources of the rich earth.[146] A little beyond the river are the so-called Chalcaea, a place neighbouring a choppy sea, but nonetheless full of fish; it is named after the metal bronze.   77. At the topmost peak of the hill down which the Chrysorrhoas runs, there is Timaea, a very high tower, visible and prominent across much of the sea, raised up for the safety of seafarers. For both parts of the Pontus lack harbours for receiving ships; for the long shore of the turbulent and unquiet sea has bends on neither mainland.[147] From this tower burning torches used to be carried all the way down at night, as guides to the right course to the gateway of the Pontus. But the barbarians destroyed trust in the true torches, by putting out fraudulent torches from the shores of Salmydessus so that mariners might be drawn into error and led on to shipwreck. The seaward shore has no harbour and the seabed is not firm for anchors because of the outflow of waters, so that for those who strayed from the right course, having confused the true signs with the false signals, a shipwreck was prepared.[148] Now indeed time devouring all things has extinguished the light and has in large part destroyed the tower.

78. (ii. 20. 154) Near to these places, *he says*, comes the place called Phosphorus, which has the further name of Pharo, either from Diana or from the former neighbouring lighthouse (*pharos*).[149]   79. Joined to this and continuous with it is a long

---

[144] Polybios 4. 39. 6 says that it was at Asiatic Hieron that Jason first sacrificed to the Twelve Gods on his way back from Kolchis, but Pindar refers to 'Thracian bulls' (*Pythian* 4. 204–6), an allusion which suggests the European shore as the site of this sacrifice, as emphasized by Vian 1974, 96. Similarly, in *Argonautica* 2. 531–2 Apollonios of Rhodes has the Argonauts raise an altar to the Twelve Gods on 'the foreshore opposite' and make offerings there on their outward voyage; the scholia to Ap. Rhod. take this to refer to the European shore opposite Asiatic Hieron. The scholia go on to say that Timosthenes (see Ch. 10 above, no. 22) ascribed the building of the altar of the Twelve Gods to the sons of Phrixos and that of the altar of Poseidon to the Argonauts, and also that Herodoros (a mythographer) says that the Argonauts sacrificed at the altar where Argos the son of Phrixos had sacrificed on his return. Pindar, *Pythian* 4. 204–5, says that the Argonauts established a shrine and altar to Poseidon.

[145] Much of this area is now occupied by the village of *Rumelikavağı*.

[146] The river called Chrysorroas is now the *İskender Dere*.

[147] This lighthouse is also marked on the Peutinger Map (VIII, 1).

[148] According to Strabo 7. 6. 1, C319, the Salmydessos coast, the stretch of Black Sea coastline NW of the mouth of the Bosporos, is an unsheltered, stony lee shore with no harbour, stretching 700 st. up from the Kyaneai, 'and all who are cast ashore on this beach are plundered by the Astai, a Thracian tribe' (cf. Artemidoros 129, from Steph. Byz.). Xenophon (*Anab.* 7. 5. 12–14) also accuses the Thracians of plundering wrecked ships (cf. Arr. §37).

[149] This light is to be distinguished from that further N at Phanarion (mod. *Rumelifener*): TIB 12, 591.

shore called Portus Ephesiorum, from the many ships of the Ephesians brought to land there.[150]

80. (ii. 20. 155) After the Portus Ephesiorum, *says Dionysius*, is Aphrodysium, sheltered by a formidable precipice.[151] 81. After this is the Portus Lyciorum; this has a somewhat sandy barren shore, in a small stretch extremely good and firm and safe.[152] 82. Above this is Myrlaeum, the home of those who on account of sedition were driven into exile from Myrlaea and headed hither to this land.[153]

83. (ii. 22. 160) After Myrileum (*sic*), *he says*, is Licnias (*Winnowing Fan*), perhaps named either from the fact that it is concave like a cradle or because it spreads out its raised height evenly from its lowest parts.[154]

84. (ii. 22. 160–1) At this place is a rocky hill called Gypopolis (*Vulture City*), a name it got either from Thracian savagery, both barbarian and uncouth—for they say that there lived here subjects of King Phineus very eminent for their cruelty—or indeed that it is called Gypopolis from the fact that vultures often rejoice to go about at this place.[155] *So, at least, says Dionysius.*

85. (ii. 23. 168) A little beyond Gypopolis, *says Dionysius*, is the rock called Dotina, not raised up to a great height above the sea nor standing out above the water. Ships run onto it; the name of the rock mocks with irony and dissimulation the ignorance of the sailors; the Dorians call *dōtinē* what is called *proix* (*gift*) by other Greeks.[156]

86. (ii. 24. 170) After the rock of Dotina, *says Dionysius*, is the promontory called Panium parallel to the Cyaneae—*that is to say, sited level with and contending against the Cyaneae*—the shore of the sea coming in between. For at the end of the promontory are small islands, the endpoints of the Pontic Sea, separated from the continent by a small intervening space of sea, for it is only possible for very light and extremely small ships to run through and go across on account of the very slight depth of the sea.[157] The Cyaneae are lofty and raised up above the sea; they bear an aspect like the blue cornflower (*cyanus*), either from being made from earth of many forms or from

---

[150] This is mod. *Büyük Liman*.

[151] The headland here corresponds to mod. *Çalı Burnu*, at the European end of the *Yavuz Selim* bridge over the Bosporos.

[152] The Harbour of the Lycians corresponds to modern *Garipçe*.

[153] The site of Myrileion probably lay about 200 yards inland from Limen Lykion. The city of Apameia Myrleia was on the Bithynian coast of the Sea of Marmara, NW of Prousa (mod. *Bursa*): Strabo 12. 4. 3, C563. But the original home of the exiles may rather have been Myra in Lycia.

[154] The etymology of Licnias is unclear; perhaps Gyllius associates it with *liknon*, which can mean a cradle or a winnowing fan, a broad shallow container from which threshed grain is thrown into the air to separate the corn from the chaff. It corresponds to mod. *Bağlaraltı Liman*.

[155] The 'rocky hill' of Gypopolis probably corresponds to the headland now called *Papazburnu*. Phineus was a mythical king ruling in Salmydessos who helped the Argonauts. On relations between Greek citizens and local Thracians (to whom Cl sources attribute an unwelcoming demeanour), T. Russell 2017, ch. 5.

[156] The two terms here are printed in Greek by Gyllius. *Dōtinē* is a word used to mean 'gift' in Homer and Herodotos. The irony is that this reef is an unwanted gift for those who run aground on it.

[157] The northernmost point of the European shore of the Bosporos is now occupied by the village and lighthouse of *Rumelifeneri* (Byzantine Phanarion).

the beating back of the sea.¹⁵⁸ An altar of Apollo has been set up by the Romans on the Cyaneae.¹⁵⁹

87. (iii. 2. 186) From the Cyaneae, *says Dionysius*, to the east the Pontus opens wide towards a limit not grasped by sight and a vastness not perceived by the eyes. I do not know whether the wonder or the pleasure of the spectacle is greater; for to the south is a promontory closing the beautiful mouth of the Pontus and a great and open sea draws together into a narrow strait.¹⁶⁰ For one going across into Asia from the European Cyaneae, indeed, the first promontory is called Ancyreum; for they say that those who sailed with Jason received a stone anchor on the advice of a prophet, so that they gave the same promontory the name Ancyreum.¹⁶¹

88. (iii. 3. 191) After the promontory Ancyreum, *says Dionysius*, is the Pyrgos (*Tower*) of Medea of Colchis, a round rock raised up on a steep mound.¹⁶² 89. Beyond the Pyrgos of Medea is an island, which is covered by the waves of a disturbed sea but appears openly in a calm sea. The uttermost parts and peaks of this they call Cyaneae, so that nature should not be devoid of islands on the Asian side nor the story lack credibility according to which the Cyaneae once clashed together and were called Symplegades from what had happened. Thus they have a firm position on both continents, resting by fate on the channel of the sea as to their own roots, and preserving confidence by their separation into two parts.¹⁶³ *So, at least, says Dionysius.*

90. (iii. 4. 196) *Dionysius says* that after the Cyaneae is the promontory of Coracium and a broad shore which has the name Panteichion (*Complete Wall*)¹⁶⁴ from the construction of ditches which go round this place.¹⁶⁵

---

¹⁵⁸ The Kyaneai ('Dark Blues') represent the European side of the famous Clashing Rocks, the mythical Symplegades through which the *Argo* was the first ship to sail. At §3 and §69 D. remarks on the optical illusions which appear to those sailing up the Bosporos.

¹⁵⁹ The drawing of the monument known as 'Pompey's Pillar' done by an anonymous German artist in 1574, now fig. 17 in the Freshfield Album at Trinity College, Cambridge, shows a round altar decorated with an inscription, garlands, and bulls' heads surmounted by a marble column with a composite capital. Discussion and black and white reproduction in Mango 1965, 313–15. It is illustrated also by Sandys 1621, 40. For the inscription, published already by Sandys, see *CIL* III, 1, 732 and *IByz*, inscr. 14. It reads *Caesari Augusto / f(e)c(i)t L. Annidius / L. f. Cla(udia) Fronto*. The column fell in 1680: de Bruijn 1700, 54. By the mid-C18 it was in three or four pieces: Pococke 1745, ii. 2. 138; little of the altar now survives.

¹⁶⁰ Arr. §25. 3-4 reckons 40 st. from the Kyaneai to Hieron (*stoma tou Pontou*). D. reiterates the admiration he expressed at the start of his treatise of the view from the Mouth of the Bosporos into the Black Sea. According to Herodotos (4. 85), King Darius admired the same view. The description now moves to the N end of the Asiatic shore of the Bosporos and works its way S.

¹⁶¹ The headland on the Asiatic shore at the NE end of the Bosporos is now called *Yum Burnu*.

¹⁶² The Tower of Medea is the most northerly of the places on the banks of the Bosporos which D. associates with Medea, as she accompanied the Argonauts on their return journey from Kolchis; the others are Pharmakias (§68) and Bythias (§§51–2).

¹⁶³ Apollonios of Rhodes has it that after the passage through them of the *Argo*, the Symplegades stopped clashing and were rooted fast (2. 604–6).

¹⁶⁴ Gyllius prints this name in Greek.

¹⁶⁵ *Corax* in Latin and Greek means 'raven'. *Teichos* in Greek means 'wall'. Coracium corresponds to mod. *Fil Burnu* (Elephant Headland).

91. (iii. 4. 199) The Chelae (*Claws or Breakwaters*), *he says*, follow on after Pantichium; some of them are named after their shape, the others are called after other things.[166]

92. (iii. 5. 199–200) *Then the Anaplus of Dionysius adds*: After Chelae is the so called Hieron, that is Fanum (*Temple*),[167] built by Phryxus son of Nephele and Athamas, when he sailed to the Colchians.[168] It is in fact a possession of the Byzantines but a common resort of all seafarers. Above the temple is a wall going about in a circle. On this is a fortified citadel which the Galatae laid waste like many others in Asia.[169] Ownership of Fanum has been disputed, many claiming it for themselves at the time when they controlled the sea, but above all the Chalkedonians used to attempt to assert this place as hereditary to themselves. However the ownership always remained of old with the Byzantines on account indeed of their hegemony and their native authority—for they possessed the sea with many ships—and again indeed when they bought (*it*) from Callimedes, the leader of the army of Seleucus.[170] *This, at least, is what Dionysius says about the Fanum.*

93. (iii. 5. 206–7) At Fanum, *says Dionysius*, is a bronze statue of ancient workmanship representing one of a boy's age holding his hands in front of him stretching them out.[171] Many reasons are brought forward why this statue was formed into this shape; certain people (*he says*) assert that it is a sign for the daring of sailors, deterring them from foolhardiness of navigation, replete as it is with dangers, and displaying dutifulness and good fortune in the safety of those who return home, for neither is lacking in terror. Others say that a boy wandering on the shore arrived some time after the ship had left the harbour and, being moved with despair for his safety, he stretched

---

[166] The primary meaning of Greek *chēlē* is 'hoof'. It comes to mean 'breakwater' because the outline of a breakwater may be considered hoof-shaped. Chelae corresponds to *Keçilik Liman* (Goat Harbour).

[167] Hieron, the temple on the Asiatic side of the Bosporos, overlooked what was generally considered to be the Mouth of the Bosporos, and it was in the harbour there that ships would wait for favourable sailing conditions into or out of the Black Sea. Moreno 2008, 656–66, shows that the temple occupied a position on the *Kavak* promontory now occupied by a Byzantine castle called *Yoros Kalesi*.

[168] Phrixos was the son of Nephele, a goddess of clouds and Athamas a king of Boiotia. He and his sister Helle fled from their wicked stepmother to Kolchis at the E end of the Black Sea on the back of a flying ram with a golden fleece. The four sons of Phrixos co-operated with Jason and the Argonauts in their voyage to Kolchis to recover the Golden Fleece. The circumstances of the founding of the temple at Hieron and of the god(s) to whom it was dedicated are variously recorded, and are confused by the existence of European Hieron. Only D. attributes the foundation to Phrixos; other accounts are conveniently collected by Moreno 2008. By the Roman period the temple was associated with Zeus Ourios (Jupiter of the Fair Airs): Cicero, *In Verrem* 4. 128–30; Arrian, *Periplous* 12. 2–3; 25. 4; Markianos, *Epitome of Menippos* (Ch. 21 above, A. 1), §§6–7; cf. *CIG* II, 3797 = *IKalch* 14. Catullus surely had this in mind in his poem about the boat which brought him back from Bithynia (4. 18–24).

[169] The Galatians destroyed Hieron probably soon after crossing over into Asia *c.*280 BC; on the importance of Hieron at this juncture, see T. Russell 2017, 95–8, 198.

[170] Strabo (7. 6. 1, C319) refers to Asiatic Hieron as Hieron of the Chalkedonians and European Hieron (on which see §75, with note) as Hieron of the Byzantines. In fact the city of Byzantion had purchased Asiatic Hieron from an official of the Seleukid kings in C3 (Polybios 4. 50, 2–3). On the wish of the citizens of Byzantion to establish a maritime 'zone of control', see T. Russell 2017, 108–13.

[171] A. B. Cook 1914–40, iii. 1. 149, provides extensive commentary on this statue, possibly by a pupil of Lysippos.

his hands to heaven and the god then hearing the prayers of the boy brought the ship back into the harbour. Others say that during a great calm at sea with all wind stilled a ship was held back for a long time and the sailors were suffering from lack of drink and that a vision came to the captain ordering that the captain should sacrifice his own son, for in no other way would he be able to procure progress and winds. The captain was compelled by necessity and made preparation to sacrifice his son, he had stretched out his hand to the boy when the god indeed moved by pity on account of the harsh execution of the boy and on account of the boy's age, raised the boy up and sent along a favourable wind. These things and those which contradict them as each man pleases, let them be considered credible.

94. (iii. 6. 212–13) Under the promontory of Fanum, *says Dionysius*, there succeeds and follows Argyronium, named from the fact that it had been bought with much money.

95. (iii. 6. 214–15) Afterwards, *says Dionysius*, there succeed and follow the places called Herculis Kline, *that is Bed (of Hercules)*,[172] and Nymphaeum, and then the so-called Insana Laurus (*Manic Laurel*),[173] at which they say Amycus Bebrycus the king used to live, the most outstanding man of his time in fighting with his fists, except that he was beaten by Pollux, the son of Jupiter and Leda.[174] For on the Colchian expedition, as the result of a challenge, he fought with Pollux and was killed by the same Pollux and paid the penalty for his cruelty to the foreigners, and as a sign of his insanity a plant was raised up divinely in a way which the human mind is able to comprehend: for if anyone should take this laurel to a banquet it will affect the guests with similar madness and will fill them with violence. From this indeed I have learned by experience that nature has passed down to immortal memory the iniquity of this king from this very laurel.

CODEX B, LONDON FOLIO 4ʳ

96. ⟨After this (*i.e. after Laurus Insana*) is Moukaporis, a very deep bay, named⟩[175] from a certain one of the kings of Bithynia.[176] There is an extremely fine harbour in it. Beyond this is the cape called Aietou Rhynchos (*Eagle's Beak*), the name being from its shape, being stony and deep inshore.

---

[172] Mod. *Yuşa Tepesi* (Mount Joshua). Gyllius prints Kline in Greek.

[173] Mod. *Umur Yeri*. It is the Daphne Mainomene (Greek for 'Manic Laurel'), mentioned by Arr. §25. 4; Steph. Byz. δ 35 Daphne. *Eux.* §119 (Ch. 36 below) erroneously identifies this with Sosthenion on the other side of the Bosporos.

[174] Apollonios of Rhodes 2. 1–177 places the fatal boxing match between Polydeukes and Amykos king of the Bebrykes on a beach visited by the Argonauts before they entered the Bosporos; Theokritos (*Idyll* 22. 27–134) places it after the Argonauts had safely passed through the Clashing Rocks. Vian 1974, 98–100, argues that D.'s version rather than those of the poets represents ancient local tradition.

[175] These words are restored from the Latin of Gyllius, iii. 5, pp. 215–16.

[176] Mod. *Hunkar İskelesi*.

97. From then on the bay they call Amykos and Gronychia, a level plain.[177] There is in it fishing for monstrous quantities of fish. Next is Palodes (*Marshy*), similar in shape to that which protrudes below Byzantion.

98. After this there is Katangeion, a bay alluring to fish like no other; if indeed one were restricted to telling the truth, it is the only part of the Chalkedonian shore rich in fish, for the other parts are as different from the European shore as sea is from land.[178] Beyond this is Cape Oxyrrhous.

99. After this there is a large level beach called Phrixos's Harbour.[179]

100. Beyond this another anchorage, Phiela of the Chalkedonians, men capable of doing great things.[180]

101. Above it is a low curved mound, whose base is circumscribed in the shape of a circle. One might compare it to a theatre in appearance, an unplanned work of Nature. And that indeed is what it is called.

102. Nearby is the cape called Lembos (*Skiff*). It is so called from its shape. There is also a beach alongside. Down from its mouth is a very low-lying island, beyond which the deep, foaming with submerged breakers, directs the run of fish away towards Europe. For indeed being alarmed at the current carried to their sight they cut off their passage.[181] The Chalkedonians call this Blabe (*Damage*), giving it an appropriate name and one fitting for the experience of those who pass by.

103. Then there is Potamonion and after that Nausikleia, off which, they say, the Chalkedonians defeated those sailing against them in a sea battle.[182]   104. Then Echaia, a cape with the sea flowing round it, and the reasonably deep bay of Lykadion. The former is named after a man of Megara, and Lukadion after one of the local people.[183]

105. Beyond this is Nausimachion, famous as the site of another naval battle.[184]   106. After this Kikonion, which is named from the overweening crudeness and depravity of the colonists there, for having been overcome in a revolution, they were cast out of their land.[185]

---

[177] The Bay is that of *Beyköz*, and *Çengelköy* occupies the plain.

[178] The medieval scholion reads: 'Concerning the so-called Katangion, now in accordance with corruption Katakios'. This is modern *Çubuklu*, opposite *Istinye* on the European shore, and the Oxyrrhous Cliffs are where the Asiatic coast briefly protrudes to the W. In this area was late Roman Irenaion (Place of Peace), the place where the important monastic community of the Akoimetoi finally settled, after their founder Alexander the Sleepless died at Gomon, at the N end of the Asiatic shore of the Bosporos, c. AD 430: Janin 1975, 13–15.

[179] This corresponds to *Kanlıca*.

[180] This corresponds to *Körfez* ('*Gulf*'), at the E end of the *Fatih Sultan Mehmet* bridge.

[181] Strabo (7. 6. 2, C320) and Pliny (9. xx. 50; cf. Tacitus, *Annals* 12. 6. 3) describe how when the shoals of *pelamydes* migrate from the Black Sea and down the Bosporos they are alarmed at 'a certain white rock' and are carried by the current across to the European bank.

[182] Potamion corresponds to *Anadoluhisarı*. Nausikleia corresponds to the mouth of the *Küçüksu*.

[183] These correspond to *Kandılı Burnu* and *Vanıköy*.

[184] Nausimachios corresponds to modern *Vanıköy*.

[185] The bay probably corresponds to modern *Çengelköy*.

107. After this is Cape Rhoizousai (*Rushing Ones*),¹⁸⁶ so called from the waves crashing and rushing round it and the Diskoi (*Quoits*), the former greater, the ⟨latter⟩ lesser by far, both named from their resemblance in form.   108. Next to these is Metopon (*Forehead*) opposite the one on the shore of Europe,¹⁸⁷ and next to it a harbour, very fine for its magnitude and peacefulness; a broad and soft beach circumscribes its great size.

109. Above the sea is a plain sloping onto the promontory. It is called Chrysopolis (*Golden City*).¹⁸⁸ Some say this is because in the time of Persian rule the accumulation of the gold coming in from the cities was put there, but as more people say, it is from the tomb of Chryses, the son of Chryseis and Agamemnon. For, fleeing from fear of Aigistheus and Klytaimnestra, he arrived there having it in mind to pass over to Tauris to his sister Iphigeneia, for Iphigeneia was now a priestess of Artemis. But falling ill of a disease what he left from himself to the place was his name. On the other hand it might also be that it is so called because of the convenience of the harbour, whose remarkable character can be compared to gold.

110. Thereafter a cape stands out, overrun by the blows of the sea; for a strong current pushing against it contends with what is called the Bous (*Ox*).¹⁸⁹ This is by way of being a setting-off point for sailing over into Europe; there is a column of white stone, on which is an ox, for there Boïdion, the concubine of Chares the general of the Athenians, perished and was mourned by him.¹⁹⁰ The inscription indicates the truth of the tale:¹⁹¹ for some, performing their investigation (*historia*) rashly and carelessly, suppose the image to be of the ancient swimming,¹⁹² wholly erring from the truth.

111. After the Bous there is the spring Heragora and the sacred enclosure of the hero Eurhostos,¹⁹³ after which is a flat beach watered by the river Himeros, and on it a sacred enclosure of Aphrodite,¹⁹⁴ and alongside it a small isthmus forms the limit of a large peninsula, on which is the city, slightly above the river Chalkedon.¹⁹⁵ There are

---

¹⁸⁶ Mod. *Kirazlıtepe* and *Nakkaştepe* respectively.   ¹⁸⁷ See §38.

¹⁸⁸ Mod. *Üsküdar* (formerly *Scutari*). Strabo calls Chrysopolis a village (12. 4. 2). Evidence for the harbour of Chrysopolis, now completely silted up, is summarized by Belke 2021, 227–9.

¹⁸⁹ The coastline here has altered considerably, but Bous, otherwise known as Damalis ('*Heifer*'), was the promontory which formerly closed off the S side of the harbour at Chrysopolis. Polybius (4. 44) explains in detail how the set of the currents favours Byzantion over Chalkedon.

¹⁹⁰ Chares (*c*.400–*c*.325 BC) was an Athenian general. In 340 he was sent to Byzantion to aid the city against Philip II of Macedonia. Boïdion, 'Little Calf', is a neuter name, but its bearer was evidently female since 'concubine' (*pallakē*) is grammatically feminine.

¹⁹¹ The medieval scholion in the MS provides the text of the inscription, which is also found in the *Anthologia Graeca* 7. 169, and other sources.

¹⁹² Reading νήξεως rather than the λήξεως ('termination'?) of the MS. (ON owes the suggestion to an annotation by the unknown earlier owner of his copy of Güngerich.) 'The swimming' will refer to the story of the ox swimming the Bosporos.

¹⁹³ Otherwise unknown: Frick 1865, viii.

¹⁹⁴ The Himeros river is the modern *Ayırlık Çeşme*.

¹⁹⁵ Chalkedon is modern *Kadıköy*. It was a colony of Megara, founded, according to Eusebios, in 685 BC, and known as the 'city of the blind' because its founders preferred it to the site of Byzantion (Hdt. 4. 144; cf. Strabo 7. 6, 2, C320; Hesychios 19). On the city of Chalkedon, the peninsula on which it stood and its ancient harbours, see Mango 2001, 22–3; Belke 2021, 224–7.

harbours on both sides, in accordance with the way the isthmus recedes: the one looking out towards the west being natural, that looking towards the east and Byzantion being manmade.[196] The city rises lower than the hill-crest but is more rugged than the plain. There are many things in it wonderful for the antiquity of the foundation and deeds, their destinies and their vicissitudes of both kinds, but especially for the sacred enclosure and oracle of Apollo, inferior to none of the most highly esteemed.

112. Let this be the conclusion of the exposition of my investigation, that and also of the traverse of the Bosporos.

---

[196] D. bizarrely refers to the more easterly harbour of Chalkedon as 'looking towards Byzantion'. Not only is it further from Byzantion than the other, but it opens to the S, not the W. Gyllius' Latin version does not render the words 'and Byzantion', whether because he sensed a problem or because they were not in the Greek text. If they are not the author's mistake, they may have been displaced from the previous clause, or may be a misplaced note deriving from an earlier copyist's marginal comment.

31

PSEUDO-HIPPOLYTOS, *STADIASMOS* (*STADE TABLE* OR *CIRCUMNAVIGATION OF THE GREAT SEA*)

(*STADIASMUS MARIS MAGNI*; *STADIASMUS MATRITENSIS*)

(3RD C. AD? EARLY 1ST C. AD?)

James W. Ermatinger and Robert C. Helmer

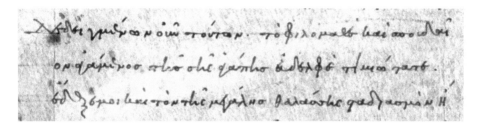

FIG. 31.1. Opening of the *Stadiasmos* (Madrid codex, fo. 63ʳ (detail)).

INTRODUCTION

The work commonly referred as the *Stadiasmus maris magni* (hereinafter *SMM*) is a gazetteer of short and summative navigational distances, whose surviving portions cover the coasts of North Africa (from Egypt to Tunisia), the Levant (from Alexandria to south-western Asia Minor), Cyprus, and Crete. It is uniquely detailed in ancient works of Greek geography in what it tells us about harbours and their facilities.

MANUSCRIPT

The surviving passages of the work are preserved at the end of a single Greek manuscript of around AD 950–75, written during or soon after the reign of the scholar–emperor Constantine VII Porphyrogennetos (r. 913–59) and now housed in the Biblioteca Nacional in Madrid.[1] The manuscript has 82 folios of variable size, approximately 8 by 6 inches (20 × 15 cm), the length of a line of text being 10 to 10.5 cm.[2] These contain, first,

---

[1] Originally catalogued as Matritensis Graecus 121, now 4701. Comparison with other MSS enables this close dating (Pérez Martín 2016, 81). Diktyon no. 40177. Images at http://bdh.bne.es/bnesearch/detalle/bdh0000253269 (last accessed 8 February 2023).

[2] Pérez Martín 2016, 80.

the *Chronikon* (*Chronicle* or *Chronology*) by the Christian author Hippolytos of Rome (fl. AD 234), an account of all the peoples of the world from Biblical times to his day. This is followed by the same author's *Diamerismos* (*Division*), a geographical extension of his Christian chronology; after the enumeration of the major mountains and rivers of the world, we encounter *SMM* on folios 63^r–82^v.[3] It has its own prologue, presumably by Hippolytos,[4] and is described in the first sentence as *Stadiasmos ētoi periplous tēs megalēs thalassēs*, 'stade table or circumnavigation of the Great Sea'.[5] Hippolytos' work in other manuscripts (but not the Madrid codex) then continues with an account of the kings of the Jews.

Debate has centred on its original author. Some argue for Hippolytos himself; others believe it is an appendage to his work. Diller argues for an earlier 1st-century AD date for *SMM*, while Müller and Cuntz view it as late 3rd-century.[6] Bunbury believes that the preface and title were added during the time of the manuscript's compilation and not during its original composition.[7] Arnaud follows Cuntz and Helm in suggesting that *SMM*—already lacking extensive passages—was incorporated into a second version of the *Diamerismos*.[8] Be that as it may, the latest date of which *SMM* shows awareness, that of the foundation of Caesarea Maritima by Augustus (§272), is AD 10.[9] Recent studies posit a core of Augustan or post-Augustan date with linguistic and factual modifications, some of them doubtless the result of Hippolytos' integration of the text into his *Chronikon*.[10] It may be a compilation from four or more sources, none later than Augustus and none attributable to a known author.[11] Whatever its 'original' date, *SMM* itself is agreed to be a compilation from various sources (see further below);[12] but, like other Roman-period itineraries, it may have undergone 'dynamic evolution' rather than being a fixed document.[13]

---

[3] The horizontal catchword at 82^v clearly indicates that the MS had a continuation. For full details of the physical character of the MS, see De Andres 1987, 264–5; and now Pérez Martín 2016, 79–84. We are grateful to Dr Joseph Werne (History Dept, Southeast Missouri State University, Cape Girardeau, Mo.) for helping translate the Spanish descriptions. According to Dr Solange Garcia Moll (Professor of Spanish, Bloomsburg University of Pennsylvania), who visited the library in June 2008 and who helped obtain information and images, the staff indicated that the MS is in fragile condition.

[4] Arnaud 2017b, 705, notes that its style reflects that of Christian exegetical works.

[5] Here the Mediterranean rather than the outer Ocean. The prologue to the *SMM* begins without any notification after the *Diamerismos*, where it ends with the Dead Sea. The title only occurs after the prologue.   [6] Diller 1952, 149–50; *GGM* i. 427–514; Cuntz 1905.

[7] Bunbury 1879, ii. 672–4.   [8] Arnaud 2017b, 707–8.

[9] The work does not contain any late Roman city names, and does not take into account the silting up of some of the harbours that had occurred. Only twice does it give distances in miles instead of stades (§§344, 346).

[10] Altomare 2013, 37; Pérez Martín 2016; Arnaud 2017a, 15–17.   [11] Arnaud 2017b, 714–20.

[12] Compiled from different navigational works: e.g. Medas 2013. Similarities to Menippos: Diller 1952, 149–50; and see Campbell in Ch. 21 above. Proposal of C1m AD date: Uggeri 1996, 45. Arnaud 2009, 166–70 (also Arnaud 2010) notes a relationship with the travels of St Paul and the Acts of the Apostles; and denies that *SMM* has a close connexion with the C3 BC work of Timosthenes (Ch. 10 above).

[13] '[M]odèle dynamique d'évolution': Arnaud 2009, 170; cf. Arnaud 2004. Cf. the updating of outdated itineraries by the explorers whom Nero sent up the Nile: Merrills 2017, 206–12.

Constantine Lascaris was born at Constantinople in 1434 or 1435 to a noble Byzantine family that had produced three emperors. After the fall of Constantinople in 1453, he stayed seven years on Corfù. He later travelled to Rhodes, where he acquired some manuscripts, and it is tempting to postulate that *SMM* originally came from there, although there is no direct evidence.[14] He then travelled to Italy with his library including this manuscript. Since *SMM* deals with sea travel from Alexandria and the majority of the surviving parts are from the eastern Mediterranean, the original of the work that was copied in Constantinople most likely came from the Greek east, perhaps even from Alexandria where the text begins.

TERMINOLOGY

SMM is unusual among our texts in the amount of detail it provides about the topography of places where ships can put in, and in occasionally including detail of the course to be steered for safe entry.[15] It uses several different terms for ports, harbours, and anchorages. Are the terms used interchangeably or do they denote specific meanings? By examining and analysing these terms the author's intentions may be gleaned. The suggestions of Leonard have much to commend them, though for the purposes of these volumes we have preferred to standardize with other chapters.[16]

limēn (λιμήν). This denotes a large or important, natural or artificial port, specifically in a commercial sense. It may contain architectural remains, breakwaters, or quays. It was sheltered either naturally or with manmade structures and is translated here as 'harbour', as it is throughout the volumes. As such, a *limēn* should be seen as a regional centre where commerce and shipping interacted with the countryside and provided jumping-off points for inter-regional commerce.

hormos (ὅρμος). In Leonard's view this denotes a medium natural or artificial harbour, generally circular or ring-shaped; it could also mean an inner basin containing a breakwater. The standard dictionary LSJ allows for these meanings, but in Greek geographical texts there seems little evidence to suggest that the word *normally* means a circular harbour or an inner basin. It is often variously translated as 'haven', 'anchorage', or 'roadstead'; but see below for 'roadstead'. Here it is translated 'anchorage'. From the signs in *SMM*, a *hormos* could be used as a territorial or smaller regional centre for commerce allowing ships to arrive and depart from the main regional centre or *limēn*, but still serving a region larger than that of the *hyphormos*.

hyphormos (ὕφορμος). As its name suggests (*hyp-* meaning 'under' or 'sub-'), this means a minor, never really predictable, natural anchorage; perhaps a concealed anchorage or

---

[14] For discussions of Constantine and the MSS, see Fernández Pomar 1966, 211–88; Martínez Manzano 1994; and now Pérez Martín 2016.
[15] On these practical details, see Medas 2013.
[16] Leonard 1997, 192–4. See the Introduction, §IX; and for a more detailed consideration of this and other points, see Shipley 2021b.

a place below a headland or promontory, somewhat sheltered from the environment or winds as a *hormos* is, but smaller and rougher. It could be translated as 'sheltered anchorage' or 'just anchorage', but here is translated as 'minor anchorage' to distinguish it from a sheltered anchorage or *hormos*. The *hyphormos* allowed a place for ships to be provisioned and to load and unload cargo for local markets.

emporion (ἐμπόριον). This was both a functional term referring exclusively to harbours of a type more commonly called *epineion* (ἐπίνειον, a 'dependent harbour' of a city), and denoted the commercial port of an inland city. For consistency with the rest of the book, we translate *emporion* as 'trading-place', though it may be the case that in *SMM* the term has a more precise meaning.

salos (σάλος). This technically denotes a 'tossing' or 'rolling' of the seas, but can also mean an open, natural anchorage. Either 'open anchorage' or 'roadstead' would serve to distinguish it from *hyphormos*; as in the other chapters, we have adopted 'roadstead'. Since it was unpredictable and tied to the weather, a *salos* was probably the least desirable spot for merchants, unless there was a need for water or the cargo was destined for the immediate area or for illicit trade. At §55 a place is described as *episalos*, which we have translated as 'with a rough roadstead'.[17]

Other terms for stopping-points are used more sparingly in *SMM*. *Ankyrobolia* (ἀγκυροβολία, lit. 'anchor-casting'), used only once (§25), means a 'temporary natural anchorage' and is translated as such; *cheiropoiētos hormos* (χειροποίητος ὅρμος, lit. 'handmade' *hormos*; §30), means an 'artificial manmade basin'; and *katagōgē* (καταγωγή, §§103, 134) means 'landing'. Finally the adjective *alimenos* (ἀλίμενος, §§3, 4, 70, etc.) literally means 'without a harbour', and is translated as such.

Besides the above terms discussed earlier, we translate *thīs* (θίς) as 'sandbank',[18] *skopelos* (σκόπελος) as 'peak',[19] and *chōrion* (χωρίον) as 'locality' (rather than 'settlement' as elsewhere in the volumes).[20]

For water there are several descriptive terms but two, *kalos* (καλός) and *glykys* (γλυκύς, literally 'sweet'), occur several times and can be translated in the same way each time: thus *kalos* is translated as 'good' and *glykys* as 'fresh'.[21] In *SMM*, *kalos* also describes anchorages or harbours and we have kept the same term there, 'good'. What these terms really meant, and whether there was any real distinction, is hard to determine.

The author uses three terms for projections of the coast. We have translated *akra* (ἄκρα) as 'cape', *aktē* (ἀκτή) as 'headland', and *akrōtērion* (ἀκρωτήριον) as 'promontory', as is the practice in other chapters. Did this author, however, mean them with different sense or interchangeably? In *SMM* the answer seems to be the latter, but we keep the distinction so that the reader will note the difference relayed in the text.

---

[17] Cf. *PME* §8 (Ch. 25 below). [18] §§36, 66–7, 93.
[19] §§10, 17–18, 25–6, 28, 73–4, 164, 284.
[20] §§129, 133, 169, 183, 187, 199–201, 206, 208–9, 224–5.
[21] In British English 'fresh', applied to water, is equivalent to 'sweet' in US English.

An internal analysis of the text can help show the complexity and differences in terms used by the author, especially for harbours. In §30, *salos* and *hormos* are both used, and in §9 both *limēn* and *salos* occur together, while in §3 and §99 *salos* and *alimenos* are mentioned. This last instance is important, since *salos* is used specifically with *alimenos* meaning 'no harbour'; therefore *salos* means here a roadstead. In §128 both *salos* and *koitōn* (κοιτών, lit. 'chamber') occur, the latter probably equivalent to *kōthōn* (κώθων, originally 'cup') and so meaning slips or chambers as we translate it; but it could also mean an artificial, protected inner harbour such as that of ancient Carthage, which was known as the Kōthōn. In both instances *salos* was used to indicate potential landing-places or docks; the instance still allows *salos* to mean 'roadstead' with 'cothons' or 'chambers' to indicate landing slips, land-based repair facilities, or even a protected, artificial inner harbour. In §§112 and 328 *limēn* occurs twice, while in §303 the terms *limēn* and *hyphormos* are given, and in §319 *hormos* and *limēn* occur. §336 has *hormos* twice, *limēn* twice, and *emporion* once. It appears, therefore, that these terms were not interchangeable but had distinct and definite meanings for the author of *SMM*.

PURPOSE OF THE WORK

While sea-captains know the way from A to B once they have sailed it, what do they do when they have no first-hand practical knowledge? Clearly, the captain would benefit from some kind of work. For the ancients a possibility would be a *periplous*. But could the surviving or mentioned *periploi* really help ancient captains? Hanno's work (Chapter 4 above) was a Carthaginian commemorative inscription which hung in a temple at Carthage, not something one would carry around on ship. Pseudo-Skylax (Chapter 7), although providing a more in-depth descriptive narrative than the *SMM*, beginning in the west and moving east to Italy, Asia Minor, and then Egypt—the exact opposite of *SMM*'s trajectory—does not help with concrete sailing information and, as argued in Volume One, was a desk-based exercise in geographical exposition. The *PME* (*Circumnavigation of the Erythraian Sea*, Chapter 25), though much closer in time to *SMM*, is more of a voyage summary than a 'how to sail' manual, and may have been intended for rich merchants and traders managing business at a high level rather than for practising sailors. Arrian's *Circumnavigation of the Black Sea* (Chapter 27), again, is a summary of his expedition and not necessarily a navigational manual, although it does present some ports and sites and was probably meant to be like Nearchos' work preserved in the *Indike*, appended by Arrian to his *Anabasis of Alexander* as its eighth book. These works, then, were created for the armchair geographer, administrator, military commander, or investor who wanted to be provided with a background to the ethnographical and historical environment of a region, and not a practical sailing manual. Is the *SMM*, then, a set of directions for an ancient sea-captain, or is it a work meant to be read in leisure in hopes of understanding the Mediterranean? The answer helps determine whether the text was meant to be a pilot's manual or a pedantic work for armchair geographers.

As Bunbury notes, even great cities like Leptis and Carthage have directions on how to approach. He further stresses that, unlike other existing *periploi*, *SMM* gives practical information even though it is irregular.[22] The purpose of *SMM*, as stated in the preface, is to describe what can be seen as one sails along the regions, not using legends but observations. Works by Herodotos, Pomponius Mela, and even Strabo presented material in the guise of histories and geographies in which local legends were meant to be factual. The *SMM* does not present material in a narrative: instead, the work provides descriptions. It does not present fanciful or outrageous ideas: rather, it provides material straightforwardly, even if many sections are monotonous repeats of one another. With the exception of the preface, there are no long narratives in the text, no great descriptions; instead there are just lists (e.g. §272).

While the material may or may not be accurate, it can be seen that there are no ludicrous additions, such as gold-digging ants or strange humans. For example, §112, dealing with the territory of the Lotus-eaters, does not provide any fanciful descriptions well known from mythology, but gives matter-of-fact geographical descriptions and distances of the islands and the surrounding region.

From the manuscript and an analysis of what kind of material is presented, therefore, some conclusions can be made. First, there are four main surviving sections: (1) Africa, (2) Asia Minor, (3) Cyprus, and (4) Crete. Second, Africa, Cyprus, and Crete have extensive descriptions concerning what a captain might see or how to navigate, while the second has the fewest. Third, Asia Minor (§§128–297) is the largest part of the document but has the smallest amount of descriptions. Finally, the individual descriptions in Africa, occupying the first 127 sections, provide the most detail in the entire work.

CONCLUSIONS

The *SMM* contains some detailed areas: (1) Africa, (3) Cyprus, and (4) Crete, while passage (2) on Asia Minor merely gives listings. The original *SMM* probably was a series of compilations, four or more, similar in style to what we have for Asia Minor, which probably just gave listings of ports and distances.[23] These may have then been reworked with supplementary details, as seen in parts 1, 3, and 4, occasionally under the influence of Latin sources.[24] Not all the information may be reliable; and some places may be doublets of others, potentially frustrating any attempt to locate them all cartographically.[25] Are there similar works in existence? While there are none in Greek exactly like the *SMM*, in Latin there is the *Maritime Itinerary*, dating from the late 3rd century, which gives a listing of cities, ports, and distances without details. Still

---

[22] Bunbury (n. 7 above).
[23] Arnaud's studies identify a plurality of sources to explain the variation in how entries are expressed. See Arnaud 2009; Arnaud 2010; and now Arnaud 2017a.
[24] Arnaud 2009, 186.
[25] See the cautions of Arnaud 2017a, focusing upon the Syrian section, esp. 28–9.

later, Diocletian's Price Edict (AD 301) gives ports and regions with prices instead of distances, although most likely based upon distances.

What, then, was the purpose of the *SMM*? There are three likely possibilities. (*a*) First, the *SMM* may have been a sea captain's piloting manual. As shown, the material only concerns the sea coasts and approaches to and from them. Also the descriptions do not contain frivolous points; they are all matter-of-fact. Additionally, in §2 there is a reference to merchant ships. Finally, in several sections there are references to winds and their directions. (*b*) A second possibility is that the *SMM* may have been similar to the *periploi* of Pseudo-Skylax and Arrian: a work primarily to be read at leisure as a geographical work, something produced by or for an armchair geographer; but if that were the case, it would have been a monotonous piece to read. (*c*) Finally, the *SMM* may have been used for official purposes by a tax or naval official, and it may have collected data to create some kind of official listing similar to Diocletian's Price Edict.

The first possibility is the most likely in view of the *SMM*'s scope and nature. It should be seen as an ancient pilot's or captain's manual, used either in the planning of voyages or even possibly onboard ships.

NOTE ON THE TEXT

The corrections by Cuntz, contained in Bauer's collection of Hippolytos' works,[26] represent an advance on the previously standard edition by Müller. They are incorporated into the most recent authoritative text, that by Helm,[27] which the present translation uses. In addition, we have checked the readings from photographs of the manuscript.

Modern place-names appear in parentheses where a simple equivalence is proposed. Names in the *Barrington Atlas* are in footnotes, with '*Barr.*' appended. Some names are inconsistent, especially when grammatical inflexions imply different nominative forms; if not clarified by a note, these are corrected silently by adopting the first form or a likely alternative (e.g. 20–1 Zephyrion).

The different wordings of summative distances[28] reflect the variations in the Greek.

The manuscript is inconsistent as regards the placing of the definite article before a name; we have generally omitted it.

Section numbers from 1 (the title) to 355 are Müller's; those in parentheses (beginning at 240, the preface) are those of Bauer, Cuntz, and Helm, which continue the numeration of Hippolytos' *Chronikon*. We have divided §§272, 279, and 282–4 into multiple paragraphs, as in the manuscript; it will be noted that in three of those sections all the entries refer to distances from the same departure point (Rhodes in §272, Kos in §279, and Delos in §284).

Part divisions are those of the manuscript.

---

[26] Cuntz 1905.   [27] Helm 1955.
[28] These are hardly ever the same: see §§19, 30 (33), 52, 57, 84, 93, 103, 124, 132, 153, 183, 213, 232, 254, 296, and 315. The only ones whose phrasings match are §93 = §103 and §153 = §232.

Special symbols in this chapter

⟨ ⟩   insertion by Helm
« »   insertion by Müller, rejected by Helm (may or may not be accepted by the present editors)
(90) numeral proposed by Müller

SELECTED FURTHER READING

Arnaud, P. (2009), 'Notes sur le Stadiasme de la Grande Mer (1): la Lycie et la Carie', *La cartografia degli antichi e dei moderni = Geographia antiqua*, 18: 165–93.

—— (2010), 'Notes sur le Stadiasme de la Grande Mer (2): rose des vents, systèmes d'orientation et Quellenforschung', *Geographia antiqua*, 19: 157–62.

—— (2017a), 'Playing dominoes with the Stadiasmus Maris Magni: the description of Syria. Sources, compilation, historical topography', in A. Külzer and M. S. Popović (eds), *Space, Landscapes and Settlements in Byzantium: Studies in Historical Geography of the Eastern Mediterranean presented to Johannes Koder* (Vienna–Novi Sad), 15–49 (map, 442).

—— (2017b) 'Un illustre inconnu: la Stadiasme de la (Grande) Mer', *Comptes-rendus des séances de l'Académie des Inscriptions et Belles-Lettres*, 2017. 2: 701–27.

*—— (forthcoming), 'Stadiasmos (2049)', in *FGrH* v.

*Helm, R. (1955), 'Der Stadiasmos des mittelländischen Meeres', in A. Bauer and R. Helm, *Die Chronik*, 2nd edn (Hippolytus' Werke, 4; Berlin), 43–69.

Medas, S. (2008), *Lo Stadiasmo o Periplo del Mare Grande e la navigazione antica: commento nautico al più antico testo portolanico attualmente noto*. Madrid. [Uses Müller's text, citing Helm's only in notes.]

—— (2009–10), 'Il più antico portolano attualmente noto: lo Stadiasmo o Periplo del Mare Grande', *Mayurqa*, 33: 333–64.

Pérez Martín, I. (2016), 'Chronography and geography in tenth-century Constantinople: the manuscript of the Stadiasmos (Madrid, BN, Mss/4701)', *Geographia antiqua*, 25: 79–97.

TEXT

Inconsistencies in the spelling of names are retained.

⟨PREFACE⟩

(240) These things having been demonstrated,[29] and as I admire those features of your love—your devotion to learning and your excellence—most honoured brother, it pleases me to show you this stade table (*stadiasmos*) or circumnavigation (*periplous*)

---

[29] In the preceding sections of his Christian chronology, Hippolytos enumerates prominent mountains and rivers in the world.

of the Great Sea[30] as accurately as possible so that, after reading these things, you may gain in experience. I have begun from Alexandria in the district of the Pharos (*Lighthouse*),[31] up to Dioskourias situated in the *Pontos*; and then in Europe from Hieron situated by Chalkedon, up to the Pillars of Herakles and Gadeira, as I want to help all men. I shall exhibit the division of Asia from Europe. I shall write about the distances of the islands from one another, how many they are, which ones are visible during the voyage, how large they are, and what winds they employ, what the voyage is like—(*all this*) I shall show you truthfully.

(241) STADE TABLE OF THE SEA[32]

Westwards from Alexandria[33]

1. (242) From Alexandria to Chersonesos: it is a harbour; 2 stades.

2. (243) From Chersonesos to Dysmai (?):[34] it is a harbour for merchant trade not exceeding a thousand (*measures*); 7 (*70*) ‹stades›.

3. (244) From Dysmai (?) to Plinthine: it is a roadstead (*salos*); the locality is without a harbour; 90 stades.

4. (245) From Plinthine to Taposiris:[35] it is a city without a harbour; a sanctuary of Osiris; 7 (*90*) stades.

5. (246) From Taposiris to Chio: it is a village; rocky shallows are apparent; 7 (*90*) stades.

6. (247) From Chio to Glaukos, 80 stades.

7. (248) From Glaukos to Antiphrai: the locality is a roadstead; 80 stades.

8. (249) From Antiphrai to Derrhon: it is a minor anchorage (*hyphormos*) in summer, and has water; 7 (*90*) stades.

9. (250) From Derrhon to Zephyrion: it is a harbour and has a roadstead; 400 (*170*) stades.

10. (251) From Zephyrion to Pezone,[36] 110 stades. At [—] stades from this, there is a peak called Myrmex, also a promontory called Tracheia (*Rough*).

11. (252) From Pezone to Pnigeus, 7 (*90*) stades. There is a low promontory; enter on the right into a flat rocky area.

---

[30] τῆς μεγάλης θαλάσσης σταδιασμὸν ἢ περίπλουν (*tēs megalēs thalassēs stadiasmon ē periploun*). 'Great' is omitted in the heading lower down, but it seems appropriate to retain it in the chapter title since this is how the author (be he Hippolytos or a predecessor) describes the work.

[31] Muller's expansion here, 'I will detail the places in Libyē up to the Pillars of Herakles, then those in Asia, again beginning from Alexandria in the district of the Pharos', is rejected by Helm.

[32] This title, Σταδιασμὸς τῆς θαλάσσης–*Stadiasmos tēs thalassēs*, is obelized by Cuntz as a later addition, but retained by Helm.

[33] Heading added by translators.

[34] *dysmai*, 'sunset', is presented as a place-name in the MS but is surely a directional indication, 'westwards'; a place-name has dropped out (Arnaud 2017b, 708).

[35] Taposiris Megale, *Barr*. But cf. also 'Taphosiris' in Eudoxos of Knidos?

[36] Pedonia, *Barr*.

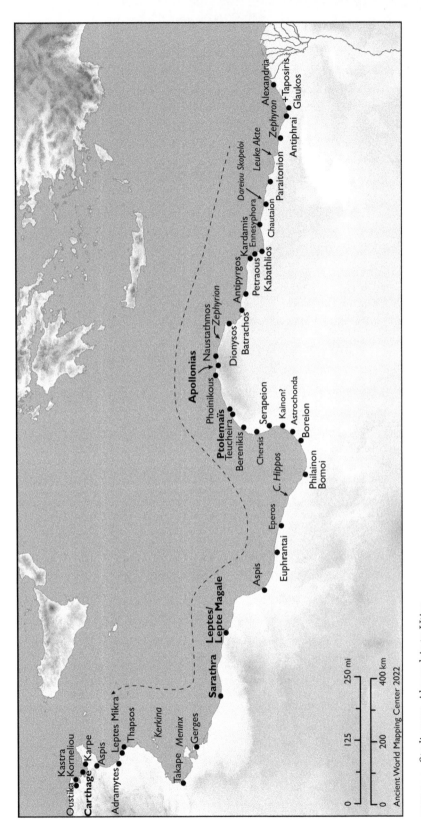

MAP 31.1. *Stadiasmos*: Alexandria to Utica.

12. (253) From Pnigeus to Phoinikous, 140 stades. There are the Didyma (*Twin*) islets; a minor anchorage is in front of them; it is deep enough for merchant ships; it has cistern (*lakkaion*) water in the ravine.

13. (254) From Phoinikous to Hermaia, 7 (90) stades; anchor while holding the cape on your right; it has water at the tower.

14. (255) From the Hermaia to Leuke Akte (*White Headland*),[37] 20 stades. A low islet lies off it, 2 stades distant from the land. It is a sheltered minor anchorage for merchant ships in the westerly winds. On the land under the promontory there is a long anchorage for ships of all kinds; (there is) a sanctuary of Apollo, with a well-known oracle, and it has water by the sanctuary.

15. (256) From Leuke Akte to Zygris, 7 (90) stades. It is an islet; hold it on the left as you drop anchor (*prosormizou*); it has water in the sand.

16. (257) From Zygris to Ladamantia, 20 stades. Beside it lies a large island; holding this to the right, bring your ship in (*katagou*). It is a sheltered harbour in any wind; it has water.

17. (258) From Ladamantia to the (*places of*) Kalamaios, 40 stades. It is a promontory with a peak; to the right of it there is a minor anchorage.

18. (259) From the (*places of*) Kalamaios to Graias Gony (*Old Woman's Knee*),[38] 9 (70) stades. It is a rough cape which has a peak on the heights; on the shore there is a tree. It is an anchorage (*hormos*) and it has water under the tree; watch out for the south wind.

19. (260) From Graias Gony to Artos, 120 stades. It is a rough promontory without a minor anchorage, and on the promontory there are two bulls[39] protruding like islands into the open sea. After rounding this you will see the city of Paraitonion.

(261) Together all the stades from Alexandria to Paraitonion become 1,550.

20. (262) From Paraitonion to Delphines (*Dolphins*), 7 stades.

(263) From Delphines to Zephyrion, 7 (90) stades. There are two islands and a promontory. It is a harbour in all winds, and it has water.

21. (264) From Zephyrion and Delphines to Apis, 30 stades; it is a village; if you sail 20 stades from this place there is an anchorage. It has water in the village.

22. (265) From Apis to Nesoi (*The Islands*), 7 (90) stades.

23. (266) From Nesoi to Linydai,[40] 70 stades. It is a cape which has a minor anchorage; it has shallows on the right; upon seeing the shallows, bring your ship in.

24. (267) From Linydai to Azy, 8 (50) stades.[41]

25. (268) From Azy to Dareios' ‹Peaks?›,[42] 120 stades. There are peaks; under these there is a temporary natural anchorage (*ankyrobolia*)[43] for cargo ships.

---

[37] Leuke Akte, *Barr.*   [38] Graias Gonu, *Barr.*
[39] i.e. features resembling bull's horns.   [40] Selenis, *Barr.*
[41] Helm misprints the number 50, emended by Müller instead of 8 in the MS.
[42] Tyndareioi Inss. *Barr.*; cf. Tyndareioi Skopeloi, Ps.-Skyl. §108. 1 *bis*.
[43] See chapter introduction.

26. (269) From ‹Dareios'› Peaks to Chautaion, 140 stades. It is a minor anchorage for small ships. It has drawn-up (*anaktos*) water gushing out into the fields.

27. (270) From Chautaion to Zygrai, 140 stades.

28. (271) From Zygrai to Ennesyphora, 200 (*210*) stades. It is a minor anchorage in summer. It has water in the sand, and a peak upon the sea.

29. (272) From Ennesyphora to Kabathlios,[44] 120 (*250*) stades. It is a high area; it is a harbour in all winds; it has water in the first valley towards the south part, in the fort, which is from rain (*ombrios*).

30. (273) From Kabathlios to Petraous,[45] 150 stades. Sailing along about 30 stades, you will see appearing next to you a high and large cape; and on the other side you will see a roadstead and a big lake. On the left side there is an artificial anchorage; it has water under the fig-tree, and because of this the place is called Sykē (*Fig-tree*).

31. (274) From Sykē to Panormos, 30 stades. It is a deep valley; under the fig-trees it has very good water.

32. (275) From Panormos to Eureia, 150 (*50*) stades. It is a ravine, but within is a beach, and there are fig-trees on it. It is a good anchorage; it has fresh water.

33. (276) From Eureia to Petreuōn,[46] ‹40 stades›; it has much water in both regions. [Together the stades from Alexandria as far as Petreuōn become 1,006 (*2,890*).][47]

[MARMARIKE FOLLOWS]

34. (277) From Petreuōn to Kardamis, 150 stades; it is an anchorage. It is a cape that tapers and has lookouts; anchor upon it with offshore winds. It has water on the mainland.

35. (278) From Kardamis to Menelaos, 100 stades; it is a harbour; it has brackish water in the sand.

36. (279) From Menelaos to Kataneai, 70 stades. Upon coming near you will see a white sandbank (*thīs*). It has brackish water in the sand.

37. (280) From Kataneai to Pyrthmanion,[48] 150 stades; sail 8 stades from the beach, for it has high shoals; it also has water.

38. (281) From Pyrthmanion to Antipyrgos, 220 stades; it is a summer anchorage. It is an island, and at it there is a tower; a sanctuary of Ammon; it has water on the opposite beach.

39. (282) ‹From Antipyrgos to Mikros (*Little*) Petreuōn[49] [—] (*380*) stades.›

40. (283) From Mikros Petreuōn to Batrachos (*Frog*), 30 stades. It is a minor anchorage in summer, there is a cape which has lookouts. It has much water in the valley.

---

[44] Catabathmus Maior, *Barr*.   [45] Petras Megas, *Barr*.   [46] Same as Petraous, §30.

[47] Helm places this, together with 'Marmarica follows', after §30 where they occur in the MS; Müller places it after §33 where it occurs geographically. Both probably derive from a later interpolation, as do the other bracketed headings below.

[48] Kyrthanion, *Barr*. The distance of 8 st. is one of several in *Stad*. which may have been converted from miles (Arnaud 2017b, 716).

[49] Petras Mikros, *Barr*. The distance has been added by both Müller and Helm; Müller gives the number.

41. (284) From Batrachos to Platea, 250 (*150*) stades. 30 stades out in the open sea lies an island called Sidonia—it has a minor anchorage in summer for cargo ships—at a distance of 30 stades; it has water towards the land in the tower.

42. (285) From Platea to Paliouros ‹— (*30*) stades›; it has brackish water.

43. (286) From Paliouros to Phaia, 90 stades; 15 stades from there it has collected (*synaktos*) water.

44. (287) From Phaia to Dionysos, 90 stades; afterwards bring your ship in on the left.

45. (288) From Dionysos to Cherronesos,[50] 90 stades.

46. (289) From Cherronesos to Azaris, 100 stades; sail from here at high tide: there are raised rocks; it has water and a great river.

47. (290) From Azaris, sailing close to shore, to the region of Zarine[51] is 150 stades.

48. (291) From Zarine to Zephyrion, 150 (*50*) stades; there is a forested cape; it is a minor anchorage in summer.

49. (292) From Zephyrion to Chersis, 70 stades; midway between Zephyrion and Chersis, 10 stades distant (*from the shore*), there is an anchorage called Aphrodisias; at it there is a sanctuary of Aphrodite.

50. (293) From Chersios to Erythron (*Red*), 90 stades; it is a village.

51. (294) From Erythron to Naustathmos (*Naval Station*), 70 stades; there is a broad roadstead; it has water in the sand.

52. (295) From Naustathmos to Apollonias, 120 stades.

(296) Altogether the stades from Paraitonios to Apollonias are 3,550.

[KYRENE FOLLOWS]

53. (297) From Apollonias to Phoinikous,[52] 100 (*160*) stades; it has a village. They anchor under here in the westerly winds. It is a summer anchorage. It has water.

54. (298) From Phoinikous to Nausis,[53] 190 stades; it is a village; it has water on the beach.

55. (299) From Nausis to Ptolemaïs, 250 stades; it is a very great city; it is a place with a rough roadstead (*episalos*),[54] and it has an island; it is called Ilos; make fast the ship.[55]

56. (300) From Ptolemaïs to Teucheira,[56] 250 (*200*) stades. It is an old city of the Pentapolis. This is called Arsinoë.

57. (301) From Teucheira to Ber(e)nikis,[57] 350 stades. The sailing voyage makes a bend. After sailing 90 (*6*) stades you see a promontory stretching out towards the west. Raised shallows lie beside it: keep watch as you sail alongside. You will see a low-lying black island. The promontory is called the Shallows (*Brachea*); on the left it has an anchorage for small boats.

---

[50] Chersonesos Akra, *Barr.* [51] Darnis, *Barr.* [52] Phykous, *Barr.* [53] Ausigda? *Barr.*
[54] See p. 856. [55] The same warning (*asphalizou*) occurs at §§126 and 302.
[56] Arsinoe/Taucheira, *Barr.* [57] Berenike, *Barr.*

(302) All the stades together out of Apollonias to Berenike are 1,150.

[SYRTIS OF THE KYRENAIANS FOLLOWS]

58. (303) From Berenike to Rhinon, 60 stades.

59. (304) From Rhinon to Pithos, 10 stades.

60. (305) From Pithos to Theotimaion, 1 stade; it is a summer anchorage; the beach is deep.

61. (306) From Theotimaion to Halai (*Salt-pans*), 710 (*10*) stades; it is a beach.

62. (307) From Halai to Boreion (*Northern*), 50 stades; it is a promontory which has a minor anchorage.

63. (308) From Boreion to Chersis, 140 stades; it has an anchorage from the Etesians (*annual winds*). It has water at the fort.

[SYRTIS OF KYRENE][58]

64. (309) From Chersion to Amastoros,[59] 110 stades.

65. (310) From Amastor to Herakleion,[60] 80 stades.

66. (311) From Herakleion to Drepanon (*Sickle*),[61] 7 stades; it is a high promontory of Herakles, with a white sandbank; it has water.

67. (312) From Drepanon to Serapeion,[62] 100 stades; running alongside, you will see a great white beach; out of which if you dig you will have fresh water.

68. (313) From Serapeion to Diarhoas, 50 stades.

69. (314) From Diarhoas to Apis, 1 stade; it is a minor anchorage.

70. (315) From Serapeion to Kainon (*New, sc. Place?*), 150 stades; it is a deserted fort; it has water; but it is without a harbour.

71. (316) From Kainon to Euschoinos, 70 stades; it is a deep beach; there is a round hill in the territory; it has water.

72. (317) From Euschoinos to Hyphaloi, 70 stades; it is an islet under the swell (*hyposalos*); it also has a wide beach.

73. (318) From Hyphaloi to Skopelites, 80 (*40*) stades; it is a peak, stretching out 15 stades from shore, high and similar to an elephant.

74. (319) From the peak towards the Lips (*SW wind*), at 2 (*20*) stades, is a high island; it is called Pontia.

75. (320) From Pontia to the south, at 7 (*90*) stades, is an island called Maia and under it a minor anchorage. It has drawn-up (*anaktos*) water.

76. (321) From Maia to Astrochonda, 50 stades.

77. (322) From Astrochonda to Korkodeilos (*sic*), 80 stades. It is a summer anchorage and has flowing water.[63]

---

[58] The MS and Helm have this heading after §63 while Müller has it after §62.
[59] Amastor, *Barr*.   [60] Probably a place with a sanctuary of Herakles.
[61] Probably a cape.   [62] A place with a sanctuary of Serapis.
[63] Lit. 'water containing streams' (*rheumata*).

78. (323) From Korkodeilos to Boreion (*Northern*),⁶⁴ 84 stades; it is a village; a deserted tower; it is a good anchorage against the Lips (*SW wind*); it has water.

79. (324) From Boreion to Antidrepanon, 20 stades; it is a promontory which has water.

80. (325) From Antidrepanon to Mendrion, 50 stades; it has no water.

81. (326) From Mendrion to Kozynthion, 120 (*20*) stades; it is a rough cape. It is a good anchorage, but has no water.

82. (327) From Kozynthion to Ammoniou Pegai (*Springs of Ammonios*), 110 stades; it is a beach.

83. (328) From Ammoniou Pegai to Automalakes, 180 stades.

84. (329) From Automalakes to Philainon Bomoi (*Altars of the Philainoi*),⁶⁵ 185 stades. It is a good summer anchorage, and it has water. Up to this promontory the mountains and country belong to the Kyrenaians.

(330) All the stades together from Berenike as far as Philainon Bomoi are 2,000.

[SYRTIS MEGALE (GREAT) FOLLOWS]

85. (331) From Philainon Bomoi as far as Cape Hippos (*Horse*),⁶⁶ 400 stades. It is a rugged promontory. It has a minor anchorage and water.

86. (332) From Cape Hippos to Eperos, 350 stades; it is a harbour for small ships. There is water. This is a fort belonging to barbarians.

87. (333) From Eperos to Korax (*Crow*),⁶⁷ 150 stades.

88. (334) From Korax to Euphrantai, 200 (*290*) stades; it is a harbour and has water.

89. (335) From Euphrantai to Dysopos, 150 stades.

90. (336) From Dysopos to Aspis, 350 stades.

91. (337) From Aspis to Tarichaiai (*Saltings*), 350 stades.

92. (338) From Tarichaiai to Kephalai (*Heads*), 400 stades.

93. (339) «From Kephalai to Neapolis⁶⁸ 550 stades.» Sailing into port from the open-sea, you will see a low area with islets; when you get near it, you will see the seaside city and a white sandbank and a beach, and the city is completely white, but it has no harbour; anchor securely at Hermaios. It is called Leptis.⁶⁹

(340) All the stades together from the Altars of the Philainoi to Lepte Megale are 4,200 (*3,090*).

94. (341) From Leptis to Hermaios, 5 (*15*) stades; it is an anchorage for small ships.

95. (342) From Hermaios to Gaphara, 300 (*200*) stades. It is a cape which has an anchorage on each side; it has water. It is called ‹Ai›neospora, for it is like an island.

96. (343) From Gaphara to Amaraias, 40 stades. It is a tower with a minor anchorage. It has river water. There are tilled lands near the river. The river is called Oinoladon.

97. (344) From Amaraias to Megerthis, 40 (*140*) stades. It is a city and it has a harbour and water.

---

⁶⁴ Boreum, *Barr.*   ⁶⁵ Arae Philaenorum, *Barr.*   ⁶⁶ Hippou Akra, *Barr.*
⁶⁷ Charax, *Barr.*   ⁶⁸ Neapolis/Lepcis Magna, *Barr.*   ⁶⁹ Same as Neapolis above.

98. (345) From Megerthis to Makaraia, 400 (250) stades.

99. (346) From Makaraia to Sarathra,[70] 400 stades; it is a city without a harbour. It has a roadstead.

[SYRTIS MIKRA (SMALL) FOLLOWS]

100. (347) From Alathre (*i.e. Sarathra*) to Lokroi, 300 stades. It is a village, and above it is a high tower.

101. (348) From Lokroi to Zeucharis,[71] 300 stades, a fort which has a tower; the tower [—]; it is a famous harbour.

102. (349) From Zeucharis to Gergis,[72] 350 stades. It is a tower and has a fort, a harbour, and water.

103. (350) From Gergis to Meninx, 150 stades; it is a city on an island. The island lies 8 stades from shore. It has considerable cities, and is a metropolis. This, then, is the island of the Lotophagoi (*Lotus-eaters*).[73] On it there is an altar to Hercules; he is called Greatest. There is a harbour and it has water.

(351) All the stades together from Leptis to Meninx are 2,300.

104. (352) From Meninx to Epeiros,[74] 200 stades. It is a city, and has a good harbour and water.

105. (353)[75] From Gergeis to Kidiphtha,[76] 180 stades; it is a city and has a harbour.

106. (354) ⟨From Kidiphtha to Takape, [—] (*200*) stades.⟩

107. (355) From Takape to Neapolis,[77] 100 (*400*) stades; it is a city and has a harbour.

108. (356) ⟨From Neapolis to Thythna, [—] (*220*) stades.

109. (357) From Thythna to Anchola, [—] (*500*) stades.⟩

110. (358) From Anchola to Halipota, 120 stades.

111. (359) ⟨From Halipota to Thapsos, [—] (*120*) stades.⟩

112. (360) These cities have harbours; and because shallows lie off these cities, moderate-sized boats sail to them. The island of Kerkina lies alongside Anchola and Halipota and Kidiphtha, 120 stades from shore. From the land of the Lotophagoi, which is Menix, to the island of Kerkina through the channel is 750 stades. From Thythna to the ⟨island and⟩ city of Kerkina, [—] stades. There are shoals running up to the city. From Kerkina to Thapsos is 700 stades. There is a beautiful island in the open-sea lying near Thapsos towards the north, about 80 stades distant. It has a harbour and water. These islands enclose the Ikarian open-sea.

[PHOINIKE (PUNICA) FOLLOWS]

113. (361) From Thapsos to Leptes Mikra,[78] 170 stades; it is a small city; it has conspicuous shallows, and the landing at the city is difficult.

---

[70] Abrotonum/Sabratha, *Barr.*   [71] Taricheiai/Zouchis/Praesidium, *Barr.*
[72] Gergis, *Barr.*   [73] Meninx/Lotophagitis/Girba, *Barr.*   [74] Gigthis, *Barr.*
[75] Helm omits '353' but clearly intended it to stand here.   [76] Gidaphta, *Barr.*
[77] Macomades Minores, *Barr.*   [78] Lepti Minus, *Barr.*

114. (362) From Lepteis to Thermai, 60 stades; it is a village, and here in the same way the shallows make landing difficult.

115. (363) Sailing 40 stades from Thermai, you will see the promontory which has two islets protected by palisades; it is a minor anchorage.

116. (364) From the promontory you will see the city of Adramytes[79] from 40 stades away; *(it is)* without a harbour.

117. (365) From Adramytes to Aspis (*Shield*),[80] 500 stades. It is a high and conspicuous promontory, like a shield. Keep the north on the left as you sail towards it, for there are in that open-sea many shallows and rocks. Then the Aspis will appear to you, and upon it Neapolis. From the gulf of Neapolis to Aspis, 200 stades.[81] It has a harbour towards the west, 10 stades beyond the city.

118. (366) From Aspis[82] ‹to Cape Hermaia, [—] (200) stades.›

119. (367) ‹From Cape Hermaia to Misoua harbour, [—] (120) stades.›

120. (368) ‹From Misoua harbour› to Therma, 60 stades; it is a village and the hot springs are above it.

121. (369) From Therma to Karpe, 160 stades; it is a city and has a harbour.

122. (370) From Karpe to Maxyla, 20 stades; it is a city and has a harbour.

123. (371) From Maxyla to Galabras, 50 stades; it is an anchorage as far as ‹the› onset of ‹the› sandy places.

124. (372) From Galabras to Karchedon (*Carthage*),[83] 120 stades; it is a very great city and has a harbour; in the city there is a tower; anchor on the right under the mole.

(373) All the stades together from Meninx, the island of the Lotophagoi, as far as to Carthage are 550 (*3,550*).

125. (374) From Carthage to Kastra Korneliou,[84] 303 stades; the harbour is fit for wintering; in it many ships can pass the winter.

126. (375) From Kastra Korneliou to Oustika,[85] 24 stades; it is a city; it does not have a harbour, but it has a roadstead. Make fast the ship.

127. (376) From Oustika [—].[86]

---

[79] Hadrumetum, *Barr.*   [80] Pupput, *Barr.*

[81] Here Helm deletes the words 'It is a high place and the city is there' from the MS; this passage is confusing.

[82] The error or 'lacuna' in transmission is probably due to the copyist losing his place when beginning the new folio.

[83] The MS reads *Chalkēdon*, which matches none of the usual forms of the name of Carthage (Arnaud 2017b, 708).

[84] Castra Corneli(ana), *Barr.*   [85] Utica, *Barr.*

[86] This is where the text for Africa breaks off. In the actual MS, however, this beginning and the following lines are connected as if one line. It is probable that the compiler or a previous copyist lost their place in the process and skipped over a folio (or a folio was missing) and acted as if the line here was really a continuation of the earlier African line.

Eastwards from Alexandria[87]

128. (377) [—] ⟨From Arados⟩ to Karnai, 24 stades; it is a roadstead; there are *kothōnes* (*slipways*) for small ships; go in carefully.

129. (378) From Karnai to the promontory of Balaneis, as it is called, 200 stades.

(379) ⟨From Balaneis⟩ to the localities of ⟨the Balaneotai, [—] stades.⟩[88]

130. (380) From the Balaneis promontory to Paltos promontory, 90 stades.

131. (381) From the Paltos promontory, curving round to the promontory of Branchion†,[89] 10 stades.

132. (382) From Cape Balaneis straight to Paltos,[90] 200 (*70*) stades.

(383) All the stades out of Ptolemaïs as you sail by the shore to Paltos are 2,000.

[AND KOILE (HOLLOW) SYRIA FOLLOWS]

133. (384) From Paltos to the locality of Pelleta,[91] 30 stades.

134. (385) From Pelleta to a harbour situated on the seashore, which has a ravine alongside it, 20 stades.

135. (386) From Pelleta to Gabala, 30 stades.

136. (387) From Gabala to the navigable river which is called [—], 40 (*80*) stades.

137. (388) From ⟨the⟩ navigable river to the cape upon which lies the city of Laodikeia, 200 (*70*) stades. From that river to Balaneis, 70 (*170*) stades. From Balaneis to Laodikeia (*Latakia*), running a straight course with the Leukonotos (*SSW wind*), (*travelling*) to the east of north, 200 stades.

138. (389) From ⟨Cape⟩ Laodikeia to Herakleia,[92] 20 (*120*) stades.

139. (390) As one rounds the promontory, there is a harbour called Leukos (*White*),[93] 30 stades.

140. (391) From Leukos Limen to the village called Pasieria (*Minet al-Farsi*),[94] 30 stades.

141. (392) From the village to the cape called Polia, 120 stades.

142. (393) From Herakleia to Poseidion[95] by the short way, 100 stades.

143. (394) From the cape at Poseidion to the city of Sidon, 300 (*80*) stades.[96] Above that is a high mountain called Thronos.[97]

---

[87] Heading added by translators.

[88] Helm reconstructs these lines as 'From Karna to the promontory called Balanea 200 stades ⟨from Balanea to the territory of Balanea [—] stades (40)⟩. Arnaud 2017a, 30, identifies Balaneis *vel sim.* as mod. *Banyas*, noting that its city status is attested by Augustan coins.

[89] Arnaud 2017a, 37, replaces Branchion with a reference to *brachea*, 'shallows', as originally suggested by Müller.

[90] Arnaud 2017a, 31, locates this at *'Arab al-Mulk* and *Belda al-Mulk*.

[91] Arnaud 2017a, 38–9, argues that Paltos and Pelleta are the same place.

[92] 'Herakleia?', *Barr.* 68 A2. Arnaud 2017a, 32, notes the important excavations at *Ras Ibn Hani*.

[93] Leukos Limen, *Barr.* 68 A2.   [94] Arnaud 2017a, 33.

[95] The prominent cape between Laodikeia and Seleukeia Pieria, *Barr.* 68. A2.

[96] Arnaud 2017a, 39–40, follows earlier scholars in taking *polin Sidōna* ('the city of Sidon') as a corruption of *Posideion*.

[97] Arnaud 2017a, 40, speculates that Mt Thronos is the same as Mt Kasios in the next entry.

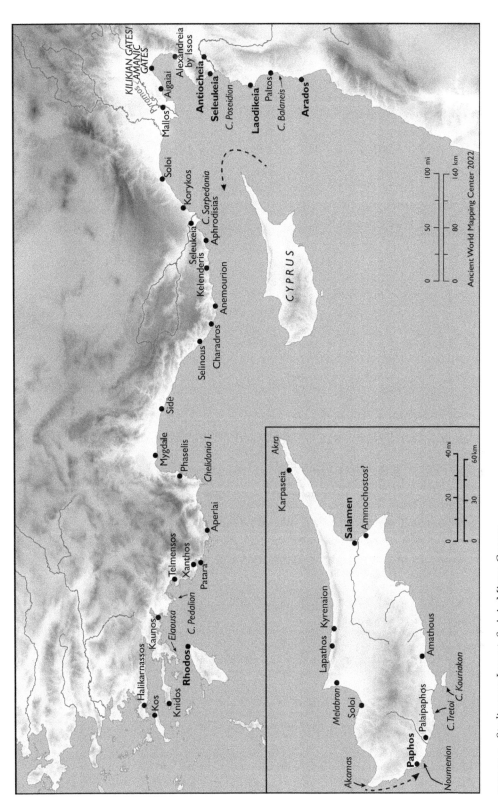

MAP 31.2. *Stadiasmos*: Levant, S. Asia Minor, Cyprus.

144. (395) From the city of Sidon to the place bordering Kasios[98] called Chaladropolis, 60 stades.

145. (396) From Chaladron to the island called Makra (*Long*), 10 stades.

146. (397) From Makra island to Nymphaion,[99] 50 stades. All of this circumnavigation is rugged from Kasios. Sail to this place (*keeping*) 20 stades from land.

147. (398) From Nymphaion to the city of Antiocheia (*Antioch*), which also has a trading-place and beside it a river called Orontes, 400 stades. The river is 15 stades away.

148. (399) From the river to Seleukeia,[100] 40 stades. From Poseidion, sailing the short way to Seleukeia with the west wind, 110 (*170*) stades.

149. (400) From Seleukeia to Georgia,[101] 142 (*40*) stades.

150. (401) From Georgia to the Peak of the Rhossaioi,[102] 300 (*80*) stades. From the Poseidion promontory to the gulf, with the fairest wind, 200 (*270*) stades.

151. (402) From Rhossos Terdnia to the city of Myriandros,[103] 90 stades.

152. (403) From Myriandros to Alexandreia by Issos, 120 (*80*) stades.

153. (404) From Alexandreia to the Kilikian Gates,[104] 200 (*45*) stades.

(405) Together all the stades from Paltos as far as the Kilikian Gates are 2,500 (*1,100*).

[KILIKIA FOLLOWS][105]

154. (406) From the Kilikian Gates to Hieron (*The Sanctuary*), 120 stades; that is, going from the place to (*the*) city.[106]

155. (407) From Hieron to the city of Aminsos,[107] 700 (*30*) stades.

156. (408) From Aminsos to the Amanic Gates[108] in the innermost part of the gulf, 90 stades.

157. (409) From the Gates to the village of Alai,[109] 50 stades; from Myriandros, running with a fair wind, 100 stades.

158. (410) From Alai to the city of Aigaiai, 100 stades; from Myriandros, running a straight course towards the (*North*) Pole with a south wind, 100 stades.

159. (411) From Aigaiai, the coastal sailing is beside cliffs to the village of Seretile,[110] 150 stades. From Rhosos, running a straight course towards the (*North*) Pole, to

---

[98] Cassius Mons, *Barr.*   [99] Nymphaion/Balaneion Tiberinon, *Barr.* 67 A4.

[100] Seleukeia Pieria, *Barr.* 67 A4.

[101] Arnaud 2017a, 40–1, suggests a corruption of Pterygion, another name for Pliny's Rossiorum montes (see next n.).

[102] Arnaud 2017a, 35–6, corrects *kolpon* ('gulf') to *skopelon*. Pliny 5. 18. 80 names the town of Rhosos near the 'mountains of the Rhossii' (*Rhossiorum montes*); cf. Ptolemy 5. 15. 2 Rhosos and Skopelos ho Rhosikos.

[103] Arnaud 2017a, 41–2, points out that the name Myriandos was assimilated to Greek *myriandros* ('of ten thousand men'), and that its existence as a city rather than a geographical location (cf. Ps.-Skyl. §102. 1; Artemidoros 4, from Strabo; Agathemeros iv. 16) is disputable.

[104] Kilikiai Pylai, *Barr.*

[105] Helm omits this heading in his text although it is clearly present in the MS.

[106] Or perhaps 'From there one may go beyond to the place near the city'.

[107] i.e. Amisos.   [108] Amanikai Pylai, *Barr.*   [109] (H)Alai, *Barr.*   [110] Serretillis, *Barr.*

Seretile, with a south wind, 250 stades. Opposite the village of Seretile, above it, is a village called Pyramos, and above that is the mountain called Parion, 60 stades away.

160. (412) From Seretilleus to the village at the end of Cape Ianouaria†,[111] 1 stade.

161. (413) From Cape Ianouaria† to the Didymoi (*Twin*) islands,[112] 30 stades.

162. (414) From the Didymoi islands to the city named Mallos, 100 stades.

163. (415) From Mallos to Antioch on the Pyramos river, 150 stades.

164. (416) From Antiocheia (*Antioch*) to Ionia, which they now call Kephale, 70 stades. Next to this promontory there is a navigable river; it is called Pyramos. †From the [—] peak, not running around the bay but sailing straight to Antiocheia, then to the east of the mainland with the south wind, raising (*the land?*) far to the left,† 350 stades.[113]

165. (417) From the Pyramos river, running a straight course to Soloi, being led to the west of north with a light south wind, 500 stades.

166. (418) From Kephale (*Head*) (*on*) the Pyramos to the river Saros, 120 stades.

167. (419) From the Saros river to the mouth of the lake, which is called Rhegmoi (*Breaches*),[114] 70 stades.

168. (420) From Rhegmoi to Tarsos (*Mersin*), 70 stades. The Kydnos river flows through the middle of the city.[115]

169. (421) From Tarsos to the locality of Zephyrion, 120 stades.

170. (422) ‹From Zephyrion to Soloi, [—] (50) stades.›

171. (423) And from Soloi to the village of Kalanthia, 50 (150) stades.

172. (424) From the village of Kalanthia to Elaious (*Olive City*),[116] 100 stades.

173. (425) From Elaiousa to the town called Korykos, 20 stades. And from Soloi to Korykos, 280 stades; above which at a distance is the cave called Korykion, 100 (20?) stades.

174. (426) From Korykos to the harbour called Kalon (*Fine*) Korakesion,[117] 125 (25) stades.

175. (427) From Korakesion to Poikile Petra (*Multi-coloured Rock*),[118] which has a stairway by which (*one reaches*) the road to Seleukeia on the Kalykadnos, 70 stades.

176. (428) From the stairway to the river Kalykadnos, 40 stades.

177. (429) From the river to a narrow, sandy cape called Sarpedonia, 80 stades. From it the shallows extend from Sarpedonia[119] for 20 stades.

---

[111] Possibly Magarsia (Müller) or Ionia as in §164 (Helm).   [112] Didymoi, *Barr.*

[113] This passage is corrupt; Helm's text differs substantially from Müller's. Müller reconstructs, somewhat speculatively, 'From the ‹Rhosic› headland, not running around the bay, but by sailing straight to Antiocheia toward the west ‹part of the promontory› by the south wind, retreating from the broad mainland on the left, 350 stades'. What may originally have been described, however, is a direct transit *from* Antioch (mod. *Antakya*) across the bay of İskenderun (bay of *Alexandretta*) to the mouth of the Pyramos (*Ceyhan*).

[114] The mouth, that is, not the lake.

[115] On the r. side the MS has the phrase περὶ Ταρσοῦ as given by Cuntz and seen in the photo.

[116] Elaioussa/Sebeste, *Barr.*   [117] Kalon Korakesion, *Barr.*   [118] Poikile Petra, *Barr.*

[119] These two words repeat information in the previous phrase and may not be original.

178. (430) From the cape—the closest (*point*) to Cyprus—to the city of Karpasia[120] by the most favourable winds, 400 stades.

179. (431) From Cape Sarpedonia to Seleukeia, 120 stades.

180. (432) And likewise to Holmoi, 120 stades.

181. (433) From Holmoi to the cape and village called Mylai, 40 stades.

182. (434) From the cape to the harbour of Nesoulion and the cape on the island, 60 stades.

183. (435) From the cape to the locality (*called*) Philaia, 20 stades.

(436) All the stades from Mylaia direct to Philaia are 500 (*50*).

184. (437) From Philaia to Pityousa (*Pine*) Island, 130 (*30*) stades. Pityousa is distant from the peninsula near Myle by 20 (*80*) stades. From the capes of Pityousa to Aphrodisias, 45 stades.

185. (438) From Aphrodisias, keeping Pityousa on the left, to the tower lying near the cape which is given the name Zephyrion, 40 stades. From Zephyrion to the cape and city of Aphrodisias, 40 stades. From Cape Sarpedonia to Aphrodisias, the sailing towards the setting of the Crab (*Karkinos*)[121] is 120 (*180*) stades.

186. (439) Aphrodisias lies nearest to Cyprus towards the headland of Aulion; as you hold the northerly regions to the stern, 500 stades.

187. (440) From Aphrodisias to the locality called Kiphisos ‹and the Melas (*Black*) river›, 35 stades.

188. (441) From the Melas river to Cape Kraunoi, 40 stades.

189. (442) From Kraunoi to Pisourgia, holding Krambousa on the left, 45 stades. And from Aphrodisias to the Pisourgia, 120 stades.

190. (443) From Pisourgia to the bay of Bernike,[122] 50 stades.

191. (444) ‹From Bernike to Kelenderis, 50 stades.›

192. (445) From Kelenderis to Mandane, 100 stades.

193. (446) From Mandane to the promontory called Poseidion, 60 stades.

194. (447) From Mandane to the (*Places of*) Dionysophanes, 30 stades.

195. (448) From the (*Places of*) Dionysophanes to Rhygmanoi, 50 stades.

196. (449) From Rhygmanoi to Anemourion, 50 stades.

197. (450) From Anemourion to the nearest part of Cyprus on Cape Krommyon, 300 stades.

198. (451) And from Anemourion to Platanous, 350 (*80*) stades.

199. (452) From Platanous to the locality (*called*) Charadros, 350 (*80*) stades. Above Charadros lies a great mountain called Androkos, 30 stades away.

200. (453) From Charadros to the locality called Kragos, 100 (*70*) stades.

---

[120] This site is mentioned in Cyprus in §314 below.

[121] i.e. Cancer. An unusual direction indicator: instead of the summer sunset or a NW wind, the reference is to the place where a particular constellation sets, valid for all the year. In antiquity, Cancer was the most northerly zodiacal constellation, so this is a reference to the NW horizon. Cf. §233.

[122] Bernikes (*sic*) Kolpos, Barr.

201. (454) From Kragos to the locality (*called*) Nephelion-by-the-Sea,[123] 25 stades.
202. (455) From Nephelion to Cape Nesiazousa (*Peninsular*), 80 stades.
203. (456) From Cape Nesiazousa to Selinous, 100 stades.
204. (457) From Selinous to Akamas in Cyprus, 1,200 stades.
205. (458) From Selinous to Nauloi, 120 stades.
206. (459) From Nauloi to the locality called Laërtes-on-the-Sea,[124] 320 (*20*) stades.
207. (460) From Laërtes to Korakesion, 100 stades.
208. (461) From Korakesion to Aunesis, to the locality (*called*) Hamaxia, 80 stades.
209. (462) From Anaxia to the locality called Augai, 70 stades.
210. (463) From Augai to the promontory of Leukotheios,[125] 50 stades.
211. (464) From Leukotheios to Kyberna,[126] 50 stades.
212. (465) From Kyberna to the temple of Artemis,[127] 50 stades.
213. (466) From the temple of Artemis to the navigable river Melanos, 9 stades.
(467) So all the stades together from the Kilikian Gates as far as the Melas river become **4,050**.

[PAMPHYLIA FOLLOWS]

214. (468) From the Melas river to Sidē, 50 stades.
215. (469) From Sidē to Attaleia,[128] 350 stades; from Attaleia to ‹Korykion›, a trading-place, 300 stades; from ‹the trading-place› of Korykion to Sidē, 50 (*450*) stades. From Sidē to Akamas, 1,200 stades.
216. (470) From Sidē to Seleukeia, 80 stades.
217. (471) From Seleukeia to the navigable river called Eurymedon ‹and Kynosarion›, 100 stades.
[218.][129]
219. (472) From Kynosarion to the river called Kestros, 60 stades; As you sail up the river there is the city of Perge.
220. (473) ‹From› the Kestros to Rhouskopous, ‹— (35?) stades›.
221. (474) From Rhouskopous to Masoura and the Cataracts, 50 stades.
222. (475) From Masoura to Mygdale,[130] 70 (*15*) stades.
223. (476) From Mygdale to Attaleia, 10 stades.
224. (477) From Attaleia to the locality (*called*) Tenedos, 20 stades.
225. (478) From Tenedos to the Lyrnas locality, 60 stades.
226. (479) ‹From Lyrnas to Phaselis, [—] (*170*) stades.› Above the city lies a great mountain.
227. (480) Out of Phaselis to Korykos, [—] (*80*) stades.

---

[123] Nephelis, *Barr.*   [124] Cebelires, *Barr.*   [125] Leucolla Pr., *Barr.*
[126] Kibyra Mikra, *Barr.*   [127] Artemision, *Barr.*   [128] Attalea, *Barr.*
[129] §218 in Müller is a supplement, 'From Eurymedon to Kynosarion, [—] stades.' This is rejected by Helm.
[130] Magydos, *Barr.*

228. (481) From Korykos to Phoinikous, 30 stades. Here lies a great and lofty mountain called Olympos.

229. (482) ‹From Phoinikous to Krambousa, 50 stades.› And out of Phaselis straight to Krambousa, 100 stades.

230. (483) From Krambousa to the territory of Posidarisous, 30 stades.

231. (484) From Posidarisous to the so-called Moron Hydor (*Foolish Water*), 30 stades.

232. (485) From Moron Hydor to Hiera Akra (*Sacred Cape; Taşlik Burnu*)[131] and the island of Chelidonia, 50 stades.

(486) Together all the stades from the river Melas as far as Chelidoniai, as you sail next to the land, are 500 (*900*). The short route through the straits to the Chelidoniai is 600 stades.

233. (487) There is from Chelidoniai ‹to› Marios and the promontory of Akamas in Cyprus, towards the rising of the Ram (*Krios*)[132] with the most favourable westerly wind, (*a voyage of*) 1,800 stades; and from Anemourion to the Chelidoniai islands, 1,200 (*1,900*) stades.

[‹LYKIA FOLLOWS[133]›]

234. (488) From Hiera Akra to Melanippe,[134] 30 stades.

235. (489) From Melanippe to Gagai (*Mavikent*),[135] 60 stades.

236. (490) From ‹Gagai› to the river Lamyros,[136] 60 stades. Above, 60 stades away, lies the city called Lamyra.[137]

237. (491) From Melanippe to the tower called Isios,[138] 60 stades.

238. (492) From the tower of Isios to Adriake (*Andraki*),[139] 60 stades.

239. (493) From Adriake to Somena (*Kale köy*),[140] 4 (*80*) stades.

240. (494) From Somena to Aperlai,[141] 60 stades.

241. (495) ‹From Aperlai to the [—] promontory (*Ulu Burun*),[142] (*50*) stades.›

242. (496) From the promontory to Antiphellos (*Kaş*),[143] 50 stades.

243. (497) From Antiphellos to the island of Megiste (*'Greatest'; Kastellórizo*),[144] 50 stades.

---

[131] Arnaud 2009, 178.

[132] i.e. Aries. As at §185, a direction is here indicated with reference to a constellation. Aries rose in the ENE in antiquity.

[133] The MS has 'Lycia follows' at the top of the folio, even though Helm places it after §233 where it occurs geographically.

[134] Melanippion, *Barr*. Melanippe is a copyist's error for Limyros. Leake 1824, 187.

[135] Arnaud 2009, 178.

[136] Limyra, *Barr*. (*Yuvalilar*, Arnaud 2009, 178–9.) Lamyros in the MS is a corruption of Limyros. See Leake 1824, 186.

[137] Also called Limyra (like the river), *Barr*.

[138] Arnaud 2009, 179: *Beymelek*, or *Pyrgo* further W.   [139] Arnaud 2009, 179.

[140] Arnaud 2009, 179, with detailed discussion; Simena, *Barr*.   [141] Aperlae, *Barr*.

[142] So Arnaud 2009, 179; Akroterion, *Barr*.   [143] So *Barr*.; Arnaud 2009, 179–80.

[144] Discussion at Arnaud 2009, 180.

244. (498) From Megiste to the island of Rhoge (*Agios Georgios*),[145] 50 stades.

245. (499) From Rhoge to the islands of Xenagoras, 300 (*80*) stades.

246. (500) From the islands of Xenagoras to Patara,[146] 60 stades.

247. (501) From Patara to the navigable river ‹Xanthos›—the city Xanthos lies beyond—60 stades.

248. (502) From the river Xanthos direct to Pydnai,[147] 60 stades.

249. (503) From Pydnai as far as Hiera Akra (*Sacred Cape; Kötü Burnu*),[148] 80 stades.

250. (504) From Hiera Akra to Kalabantia (*Sancaklı Liman*),[149] 30 stades.

251. (505) From Kalabantiai to Perdikiai,[150] 50 stades.

252. (506) From Perdikiai to Kissidai,[151] 50 stades.

253. (507) From Kissidai to the island of Lagousa (*Hare Island*),[152] 80 stades.

254. (508) From Lagousai to Telemensos (*Telmessos*), 5 (*15*) stades.

(509) Together all the stades ‹from the Sacred Cape› as far as Telemensos become 1,500 (*1,100*).[153]

[KARIA FOLLOWS]

255. (510) From Telemensos to Pedalion across from Rhopisa (*island*), 200 stades.

256. (511) Out of Telmensos to Daidala (*inlice*),[154] 50 stades.

257. (512) Out of Daidala to Kallimache, 50 stades.

258. (513) Out of Kallimache to Kroua (*Taşyaka*),[155] 60 stades.

259. (514) Out of Kroua to Kochlia (?),[156] 50 stades.

260. (515) Out of Klydai[157] to the promontory of Pedalion,[158] 30 stades.

261. (516) From Pedalion to the bend of the ‹bay of› Glaukos,[159] 80 stades.

262. (517) From the bend to Panormos of the people of Kaunos,[160] 120 stades.

---

[145] Arnaud 2009 180.

[146] Rhode: discussion at Arnaud 2009 180. Patara: Arsinoe, *Barr.*; Arnaud 2009, 180, notes that if this material derived from Timosthenes, we would expect to see the short-lived Ptolemaic name Arsinoë rather than the more usual Patara.

[147] Arnaud 2009, 180, discusses the coastal formation here, changed since antiquity.

[148] Arnaud 2009, 180–1; Hiera Akra/Kragos? *Barr.*

[149] Probably no more than a seasonal anchorage: Arnaud 2009, 181.

[150] Again, probably not a town: Arnaud 2009, 181, discussing epigraphic evidence.

[151] Unlocated: Arnaud 2009, 181.

[152] One of two islets E of Telemessos, *Kızıl Adası* or *Fethiye Adası*: Arnaud 2009, 181–2.

[153] Arnaud 2009, 182, notes the surprising absence from this Lykian passage of Mt Kragos, the city of Myra, and Mt Chimaira.

[154] Arnaud 2009, 182.

[155] Arnaud 2009, 182–3; same as Krya in Artem. 142 (from Steph. Byz.). Arnaud suggests a link with C. Kryassos, Ps.-Skyl. §99. 3, but the MS there has 'Kragos'; see Shipley 2019 ad loc.

[156] Lydai, *Barr.*; likewise Arnaud 2009, 183.

[157] Presumably the name should be the same as the second in §259.

[158] Uncertain; discussed by Arnaud 2009, 183.

[159] Uncertain; discussed by Arnaud 2009, 184.

[160] Panormos is tentatively identified as Pisilis, *Barr.*; Arnaud 2009, 183, locates this anchorage between *Baba Adası* (an island) and the mainland.

263. (518) From Panormos to the (*territory*) called Kymaria (*Kargıcık İskelesi?*),[161] 50 stades.

264. (519) From Kymaria to Pasadan,[162] 60 stades.

265. (520) From Pasadan to Kaunos, 30 stades.

266. (521) From Kaunos to Rhopousa,[163] 15 (*115?*) stades.[164]

267. (522) From Rhopousa to the opposite shore, to Leukopagos, 40 stades; and from Rhopousa to Samos (*Amos*),[165] 100 stades.

268. (523) From Samos (*Amos*) to ‹the› Poseidion,[166] 60 stades.

269. (524) From the Poseidion to ‹the› Phalaros†,[167] 50 stades.

270. (525) From the Phalaros† to the island called Elaousa,[168] 50 stades.

271. (526) From Elaousa to Rhodes, 150 stades.[169]

(*Rhodes*) makes (*the distance*) to Mallos **600** (*4,600*) stades, and to Hieron at Byzantion **600** (*4,600*) stades.[170]

272. (527) Out of Rhodes to Alexandria, 4,500 stades.

Out of Rhodes to Askalon, 3,600 stades.

Out of Rhodes to Kaisareia (*Caesarea*), 3,600 stades.

Out of Rhodes to Berytos (*Beirut*), 3,600 stades.

Out of Rhodes to Sidon, 3,600 stades.

Out of Rhodes to Byblos, 3,600 stades.

Out of Rhodes to Tripolis, 3,600 stades.

Out of Rhodes to Seleukeia, 3,600 stades.

Out of Rhodes to Kilikia, 1,500 stades.

Out of Rhodes to Korykos, 1,000 stades.

Out of Rhodes to western Cyprus towards the rising of Aries[171] with the fairest west wind, 2,800 stades.

Out of Rhodes to Patara, 700 stades.

---

[161] So, tentatively, *Barr.*; Arnaud 2009, 184, suggests a lacuna before this, and speculates that Kymaria may be a corruption of the city name Kalynda.

[162] Pasanda, *Barr.*; discussion, Arnaud 2009, 184–5.

[163] Probably the *Rhodasa* or *Rhodousa* of Pliny. 5. 35. 131.

[164] Arnaud 2009, 184–5: the entries immediately after Kaunos are confused, omitting well-known places and recording others unknown.

[165] Amos: Flensted-Jensen 2004, no. 872.

[166] Arnaud 2009, 185: the erroneous appearance of Samos led to the inclusion, here and in §269, of transects to and from Poseidion (a place in E Samos) and Phanaia (the S point of Chios, concealed within 'Phalaros'); Ptolemy 5. 2. 30 has the same places in the reverse order.

[167] See n. on §268.

[168] Elaioussa (*Barr.* 56. D4), an islet near the city of Elaia in mainland Ionia. See n. on §268.

[169] The distance is absurdly short if Ionian Elaioussa is meant. It appears that genuine place-names on the Karian coast have been suppressed (Arnaud 2009, 185).

[170] Arnaud 2009, 186: this out-of-place entry is a late interpolation, echoing §1 and reflecting an attempt to make good the loss of a passage between the Karian narrative and the catalogue of distances from Rhodes.

[171] See n. on §233.

Out of Rhodes to Kaunos, 450 stades.
Out of Rhodes to the island of Rhopousa, 350 stades.
Out of Rhodes to Physkos, 450 stades.
Out of Rhodes to Hagne (*Holy*), 350 stades.
Out of Rhodes to Knidos, 750 stades.
Out of Rhodes to Nisyros, 820 stades.
Out of Rhodes to Tilos (*i.e. Telos*), 550 stades.
Out of Lepataleis[172] to Poseidion on Karpasos (*i.e. Karpathos*), 420 stades.
Out of Rhodes to Kos, 850 stades.
Out of Rhodes to Chios, 3,000 stades.
Out of Rhodes to Myndos, 1,000 stades.
Out of Rhodes to Samos, 1,800 stades.
Out of Rhodes to Tenedos, 3,700 stades.

273. (528) ⟨There are from Rhodes to Cape Skylaion in the Argolid, sailing with a favourable wind, [—] stades.⟩ You will sail holding on the left the islands of Nesyros[173] and Astypalaia, on the right Kos, Leros, Amourgos, Ios, Sikinos, Daphne, Dera, Seriphos, and Kydnos (*Kythnos*). Further on, hold Donousa on the left, from where Skylaion is seen.[174]

274. (529) From Knidos to Kos, 180 stades.

275. (530) From Kos to Halikarnassos, 180 stades.

276. (531) From Halikarnassos to Myndos, 220 stades.

277. (532) From Myndos to Leros, 350 stades.

278. (533) From Myndos to Kos, 140 stades.

279. (534) And from Kos to Leros, 350 stades.
From Kos to Delos, 1,300 stades.
From Kos to Samos [through the strait],[175] 1,000 stades.

280. (535) From Kos to Delos ⟨through the strait⟩, one can sail ⟨towards the setting of⟩ Aries[176] with the most favourable east wind, 1,300 stades. You will sail to Kalydna;[177] then sailing back, holding on the right Hypsirisma, Kalydnai, [Keleris,] Leros, and Patmos ⟨and on the left⟩ Kinara and Amourgos, and you will sail to Donoussa, 8 stades to your left; taking the Melanthioi on the right and Mykonos, you would put in at Delos.

---

[172] Lapethos/Lepethis Phoinikon, *Barr.*   [173] Nisyrion Iss., *Barr.*, W of Nisyros.
[174] Müller emended the text to read as follows: '⟨There is from Rhodes to Scylla Argolis sailing to the west by a favourable east wind [—] stades.⟩ You sail holding on the left the islands Nisyrion and Astypalaia, on the right Kos and Leros ⟨and Kinara and Amorgos, and sailing to Donusa *5 stades⟩. The remainder ⟨from⟩ Donousa holding on the left Ios and Sikinos and Siphnos ⟨and Thera⟩ and Seriphos and Cydnus, where Skylla is seen.'
[175] Helm believes that this phrase should be deleted here and added to the next line.
[176] Cf. n. on §233. In this case, the direction indicated is WNW.   [177] Kalymna, *Barr.*

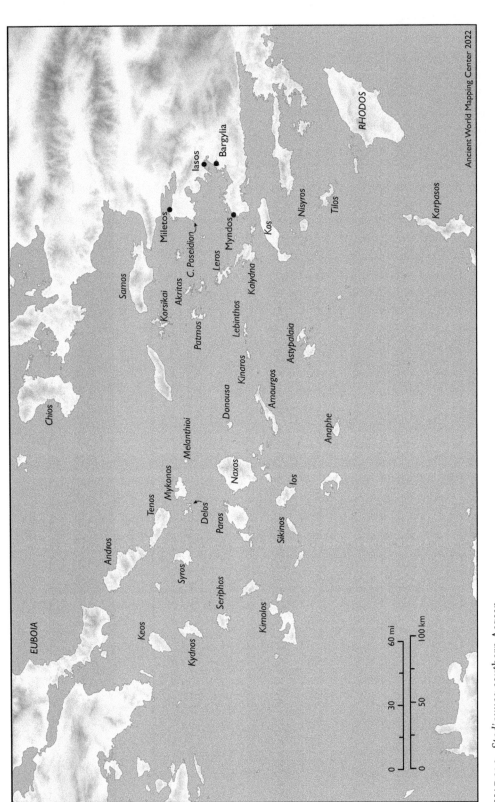

MAP 31.3. *Stadiasmos*: southern Aegean.

281. (536) From Myndos ‹to [—]›, which is in Attica, 1,500 stades. You will sail via the Korsiai (*Phoúrnoi*),[178] Leros, and Kalydnos and keeping ‹on the right› Horbidai (?) sail to Amourgiai (*Amorgos*); hold on the right Donoussa, Naxos, and Kydnos.

282. (537) If you wish to sail through the islands, you sail thus: from Kos to Lernos (*Leros*), 250 (*350*) stades.

Out of Lernos to Lebinthos, 250 stades.

Out of Lebinthos to Kinaros, 500 (*50*) stades.

Out of Kinaros to the nearest (*parts*) of Amourgiai[179] at the Kerata (*Horns*),[180] 85 stades. And the coastal sailing to[181] ‹Minoa›, 85 stades.

From [Korsiai to] Minoa ‹to the Kereia› (*territory of Keros*), 85 stades.[182] Out of the Kereia, holding the Kereia on the left, to Panormos of the Naxians, 65 stades.

From Panormos to Delos, 420 stades.

283. (538) From Kos to Leros, 320 stades.

From Leros to Parthenion,[183] 60 stades.

From ‹ Parthenion on› Leros to Amazonion on Patmos, 200 stades.

From Amazonion to Korsia, 400 (*100*) stades.

From the arc (?)[184] of Amazonion to Delos, 750 stades.

From Delos to Syros, 150 stades.

‹From Syros to Andros, [—] (*150*) stades.›

From Andros to the harbour of Gaurion, 80 stades.

From Gaurion to [—] (*Paionios?*)[185] promontory, 50 stades.

From the promontory ‹to Geraistos›, nearest to the cape ‹of Euboia?›, 450 (*150*) stades.

From Kregea†[186] to Karystos, 120 stades.

Out of Rhegea to Petaleai, 100 stades.

284. (539) I return once more to the distances out of Delos to the following islands.

Out of Delos to Thera, 350 (*550*) stades.

Out of Delos to Amourgia, to Minoa, 650 stades.

Out of Delos to Anaphe, 100 (*700*) stades.

Out of Delos to Ios, 650 (*450*) stades.

Out of Delos to the Korsiai, 650 (*750*) stades.

Out of Delos to Kimolos, 800 (*500?*) stades.

---

[178] The MS reads Korsikai.   [179] Amorgos, *Barr*.

[180] The MS has πέρατα–*perata*, perhaps meaning 'limit' or 'boundary' presented here, which Helm replaces with Κέρατα.

[181] The 'coastal sailing' is along Amorgos. The MS has Korsiaoi which Helm replaced with Minoa, a city on Amorgos.

[182] The MS has from 'Korsiai to Minoa' which Helm replaces with 'from Minoa to Kereia' (the territory of Keros, an island with a *polis* of the same name).

[183] Artemis Parthenos, *Barr*.

[184] The MS has ἄψης–*hapsēs*, possibly equivalent to ἄψις–*hapsis*, meaning any kind of circular object or structure; possibly referring to the arch or door of a temple.

[185] Andros, *Barr*.   [186] i.e. Geraistos?

Out of Delos to Siphnos, 640 (*340*) stades.
Out of Delos to Kydnos,¹⁸⁷ 350 (*450?*) stades.
Out of Delos to Tenos, 350 (*150*) stades.
Out of Delos to Naxos, 350 (*150*) stades.
Out of Delos to Donousa, 320 stades.
Out of Delos to Patmos, 850 stades.
Out of Delos to the Melanteoi Skopeloi (*Dark Peaks*), 180 stades.
Out of Delos to Keos, 300 (*450*) stades.
Out of Delos to Andros, 800 (*400*) stades.
Out of Delos to Paros, 400 (*200*) stades.

285. (540) I return once more to Myndos, from which I left. Out of Myndos to Panormos, 80 stades.

286. (541) Out of Myndos to Bargylia, 250 stades.

287. (542) From Panormos to Poseidion and Ankistron, 250 stades.

288. (543) From Bargylia to Iasos, 220 (*40*) stades.

289. (544) From Iasos to the Poseidion promontory, 120 stades.

290. (545) From Iasos to Akritas, 240 stades.

291. (546) Lying opposite ‹to Iasos› is the Passala spring, where one may depart to Mylassa, 20 (*80*) stades.

292. (547) From Poseidion to Panormos, 40 stades.

293. (548) From Panormos to Miletos, 80 stades.

294. (549) I return again to Myndos through the strait. From Panormos to Miletos, 300 stades.

295. (550) From Pharmakousa to Miletos, 120 stades.

296. (551) From Miletos to Samos, 300 (*200?*) stades.

(552) All the stades from Telemensos as far as Miletos are 2,500.

[‹AROUND CYPRUS›]¹⁸⁸

297. (553) From Akamas, holding Cyprus on the left, to Paphos,¹⁸⁹ 300 stades. It is a city lying towards the south. It has a triple harbour for all winds and a sanctuary of Aphrodite.

298. (554) From Paphos to Noumenion, which is an island that has a spring; the voyage is short. When you near the islet, press towards the land on the right, [1]25 (*55*) stades.

299. (555) From Noumenion to Palaipaphos, 25 stades.

300. (556) From Palaipaphos to Tretoi, which is a promontory, 50 stades.

301. (557) ‹From Tretoi to Kouriakon, [—] stades.›

---

¹⁸⁷ Kythnos, *Barr.*
¹⁸⁸ Not in the MS; Müller adds a heading 'Circumnavigation of Cyprus' here. *Stad.* performs an anti-clockwise coastal circuit of Cyprus.
¹⁸⁹ (Nea) Paphos, *Barr.*

302. (558) From Kouriakon[190] to Amathous, 150 stades; it is a city without a harbour; make fast the ship at the locality.

303. (559) From Kouriakon to Karaia, 40 stades; it is a promontory which has a harbour, a minor anchorage, and water.[191] [—]

304. (560) From Pedalion to the islands, 80 stades. It is a deserted city, called Ammochostos (*Famagusta*); it has a harbour for all winds; it has a hog's-back (*rock*) in the landing; beware.

305. (561) From the islands to Salamen,[192] 50 stades; it is a city; it has a harbour.

305a. (562) From Salamen to Palaia, 120 stades; it is a village and, has a harbour and water.

306. (563) From Palaia to Phileous, 300 stades.

307. (564) From Phileous to the Akra (*Capes*), 60 stades; there are two anchorages—one is bluish grey, the other white—each of which has water. Lying above is a sanctuary of Aphrodite. Also lying near are two islands, both of which have sailing channels.

308. (565) From Anemourion in Kilikia to Akamas in Cyprus, 700 stades.

309. (566) From Akamas, holding Cyprus on the right, to Arsinoë in Cyprus, 270 stades (*70*); it is a city; it has a deserted harbour, rough in the north wind.

310. (567) From Kromyakon to Melabron, 50 stades. It is a summer anchorage.

311. (568) From Melabron to Soloi, 300 stades. It is a city without a harbour.

312. (569) From Soloi to Kyrenaion (*Keryneia*), 350 stades. It is a city with a minor anchorage.

313. (570) From Kyrenaion to Lapathos, 450 (*50*) stades. It is a city which has an anchorage.

314. (571) From Lapathos to Karpaseia, 350 (*50 or 550*) stades. It is a city. It has a harbour for small boats; it is rough in the north wind.

315. (572) From Karpaseia to the Akra, 100 stades. From there we crossed over to Anemourion.[193]

(573) The entire circumnavigation of Cyprus is **1,250 stades** (*3,250*).

316. (574) From the Kouriakon to Pelousion,[194] 1,300 (*2,300*) stades.

317. (575) From Kition in Cyprus to Askalon, 3,300 stades.

[CIRCUMNAVIGATION OF CRETE]

318. (576) From Kasios[195] to Samonion in Crete, 500 (*300*) stades; it is a promontory of Crete rising up high towards the north; there is a sanctuary of Athena. It has a minor anchorage and water; other things have disappeared.

319. (577) From Samonion to Hiera Pydna,[196] 80 (*480*) stades; it is a city; it has an anchorage; it also has an island called Chrysea; it has a harbour and water.

---

[190] Marked in *Barr.* as the SW point of the island SE of the city of Kourion.
[191] The MS breaks off and then returns to Cyprus.   [192] Salamis, *Barr.*
[193] In Kilikia.   [194] In Egypt.
[195] In Egypt. *Stad.* begins the coastal tour of Crete at its NE tip and proceeds clockwise (westwards along the S coast, returning eastwards along the N coast).
[196] Hierapytna, *Barr.*

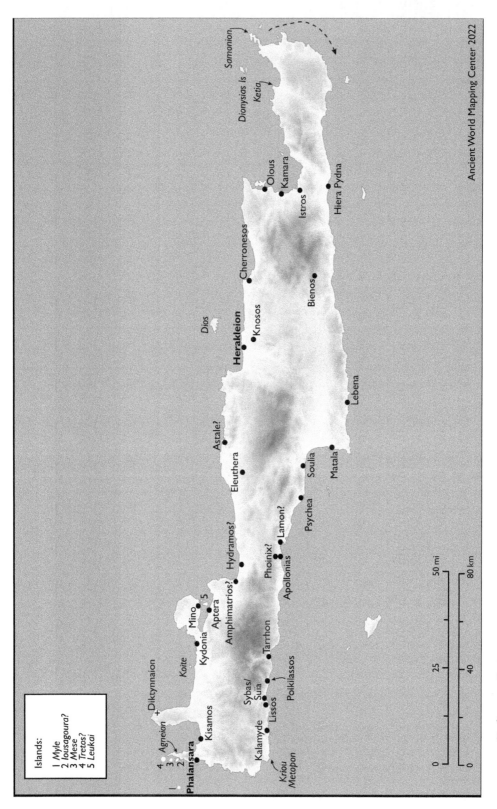

MAP 31.4. *Stadiasmos*: Crete.

320. (578) From Hiera Pydna to Bienos,[197] 70 (170) stades. It is a little city at a distance from the sea.

321. (579) From Bienos to Lebena, 70 (270) stades. There is an islet lying next to it, which is called Oxeia; it has water.

322. (580) From Lebena to Halai (*Saltings*), 20 (50) stades.

323. (581) From Halai to Matala,[198] 300 (80) stades. It is a city and has a harbour.

324. (582) From Matala to Soulia, 65 stades. It is a promontory rising up towards the south. There is a harbour; it has good water.

325. (583) From Soulena to Psychea, 12 stades.[199]

326. (584) From Psychea to Lamon, 150 stades. It is a harbour and has a city and water; from Pydna (*Hierapytna*) to Psychea, 350 (550) stades; (*there is*) a summer harbour, and it has water.

327. (585) From Psychea to Apollonias, 30 stades.

328. (586) From Apollonia to Phoinix, 100 stades. It is a city. It has a harbour and an island. From Klaudia[200] to Phoinike, 300 stades; it has a city and a harbour.

329. (587) From Phoinike to Tarrhon, 60 (160) stades. It is a small city and has an anchorage.

330. (588) From Tarrhon to Poikilassos,[201] 60 stades. It is a city and has an anchorage and water.

331. (589) From Poikilassos to Sybas,[202] 50 stades. It is a city and has a good harbour.

332. (590) ⟨From Suïa to Lissos, 30 stades⟩.

333. (591) From Lissos to Kalamyde, 250 (50) stades.

334. (592) From Kalamyde to Kriou Metopon (*Ram's Brow; C. Krios*), 30 stades. It is a high promontory; it has water and a minor anchorage.

335. (593) From Kriou Metopon there is a circumnavigation[203] to Biennos, 12 stades. It has a harbour and water.

336. (594) From Biennos to Phalansara (*Phalasarna*), 260 (160) stades.[204] It is an anchorage, trading-place, and an ancient city. The island of Iousagoura is 60 stades away, looking towards the east; it has a harbour, and has a sanctuary of Apollo in the harbour. There is another island 3 stades away called Mesē, and it has an anchorage. The third is called Mylē; the waterway is deep; there is a market-place.

337. (595) From Mylē to Tretos, 50 stades. It is a pierced (*tetrēmenon*) promontory, steep-sided and rugged, in Crete.

338. (596) From Tretos to Agneion, 50 stades. It is a harbour which has a sanctuary of Apollo; there is an interior bay, which is called Myrtilos; and it has water.

---

[197] Biannos, *Barr.*   [198] Matalon, *Barr.*   [199] Müller has §326 'from Pydna...' here.
[200] A line has clearly dropped out. Klaudia will be a copyist's for 'Gaudos' (Arnaud 2017b, 719 n. 44).
[201] Poikilasion, *Barr.*   [202] Syia, *Barr.*
[203] Müller gives the correct reading while Helm omits περίπλους seen in the MS.
[204] Müller replaces σξ' (260) with ρξ' (160); Helm has οξ' (meaningless), doubtless a misprint for one or other value.

339. (597) From Agneion to Kisamos, 80 stades. It is a city lying in the bay. It is a harbour and has water.

340. (598) From Kisamos to Tyros, 25 stades. It is a high promontory, thickly wooded; it faces towards the north.

341. (599) From Tyros to the Diktynnaion, 80 stades. It is an anchorage ⟨and⟩ beach.

342. (600) From the Diktynnaion to Koite, 170 stades. It is an island. It has an anchorage and water. It looks towards Crete towards the north.

343. (601) From Akoition[205] to Kydonia, 60 stades. It is a city; it has a harbour, and in the entrance it has shallows.

344. (602) From Kydonia to Aptera the circumnavigation is made in 150 stades,[206] but on foot it is 120 miles. The place is called Mino; by it there are three islands which are called the Leukai (*White Is.*).

345. (603) From Minos to Amphimatrios,[207] 150 stades. It is a river with a harbour around it suitable for winter, and has a tower.

346. (604) From Amphimatrios to Hydramos,[208] 100 (*30*) stades. It is a city. It has a beach. The city is called Eleuthera (*Eleutherna*). To go up by foot from Amphimatrios is 50 miles.[209]

347. (605) From Amphimatrios to Astale, 30 stades. There is a harbour on the left. It has water. [From there Eleuthera is 50 stades away.]

348. (606) From Astale to Herakleion, 100 (*300*) stades. It is a city. It has a harbour and water. 20 stades away lies the city of Knosos. An island lies 40 stades away towards the west; it is called Dios.[210]

349. (607) From Herakleion to the city of Cherronesos,[211] 30 (*130*) stades. It has water and an island that has a tower and a harbour.

350. (608) From Cherronesos to Olous, 60 (*260*) stades. It is a cape. It has a minor anchorage and good water. «An island» lies 20 stades from the land.

351. (609) From Olous to Kamara, 15 stades.

352. (610) From Kamara to Istros, 25 (*45?*) stades.

353. (611) From Istros to Cape Ketia, 15 (*150*) stades. It is a minor anchorage, but lacks water.

354. (612) From Cape Ketia[212] to Dionysias, 300 (*80*) stades. There are two islands, each of which has a harbour and water.

355. (613) From Dionysias to Sammonion, where we started to go round Crete, 120 stades. Promontory . . .[213]

---

[205] Koite/Akytos, *Barr.*   [206] About 19 mi (27 km).   [207] Amphimala, *Barr.*

[208] Müller restores the text to read 'From Amphimatrios to Hydramos ⟨30 stadia, then to Rithymna, 100 stadia; then to Pantomatrios⟩, 100 stadia; it is a city; it has a beach. ⟨Eleutherna lies there.⟩ Walking from Amphimatrios is 50 stadia.'

[209] The MS has *milia* or miles, but either the number is too large or *milia* should be replaced with *stadia* as Müller suggests.

[210] Dia, *Barr.*   [211] Chersonasos, *Barr.*   [212] Setaca, *Barr.*

[213] The MS breaks off; the word is a catchword for the next folio as seen on folios 66ᵛ and 74ᵛ, indicating that the work continued.

PART FIVE
LATE ANTIQUE PERIOD
~
(C. AD 300–600)

Too daring he who first did breach
untrustworthy straits with fragile craft,
and looking back upon his homeland
handed his soul to the fleeting winds,
and cleaving the waters with route unsure
felt able to trust the lightweight wood,
with such a slender frontier drawn
between the roads of life and death.

No one yet knew the constellations,
no use was made of stars with which
    the air is painted;
no craft was able yet to escape
    the showery Hyades,
nor yet the lights of Amalthea's goat,
nor yet the Arctic waggon which
the slow old man, Boötes, guides.
Nor yet did Boreas have a name,
    nor Zephyrus. . . .

But now the main (*pontus*) has given way
    and suffers laws.
No famous *Argo*, shaped by Pallas'
hand, carrying royal oarsmen home,
    is needed now;
    any skiff you like explores the deep.

Every frontier displaced, cities
have planted walls in new-found land.
Nothing remains upon the site
   where once it stood.
The Indian imbibes the icy Araxes,
Persians consume the Albis and Rhine.
An age shall come in later years
for Ocean to release the chains
of everything, Earth to lie open,
Tethys uncover new-found worlds,
   and Thule be no longer Furthest.

Seneca the Younger, *Medea*, 311–17, 364–79 (my translation)

32

AVIENUS (AVIENIUS), *ORA MARITIMA* (*THE SEA COAST*)

(MID-4TH C. AD)

Ralph Morley*

INTRODUCTION

The incomplete *Ora maritima* (*Sea Coast*) by Avienus is a description in Latin iambic trimeter verse of the coastline of Europe from Brittany (with a mention of Britain and Ireland) southwards as far as Marseille. It sits within the context of renewed interest in classical learning, sometimes expressed inexactly, in the 4th century AD. What justifies its place in the present book is the fact that it is reliant, directly or indirectly, on much earlier, lost Greek sources—the oldest of which, sometimes identified as the 'Massaliote *periplous*', likely dated from the 6th century BC—and so preserves for us some of the very earliest Greek knowledge about western Europe.

The poem survives only in the *editio princeps* (first printed edition) of Avienus, published by Victor Pisanus in 1488 and deriving from a now lost Carolingian manuscript. A facsimile of the *editio princeps* may be found in Murphy's edition.[1]

We can reconstruct something of the poet.[2] 'Avienus' is the traditional rendering of the *signum* (or additional name) of Postumius Rufius Festus. A 4th-century hexameter verse inscription that he authored tells us that his family were from Volsinii in Etruria; that he lived in Rome; that he was the author of many poems; and that he twice held proconsular appointments.[3] Two inscriptions offer clues to his proconsular career: one, from Bulla Regia (in modern-day Tunisia), records a Postumius Rufius Festus *signo* Abienius (*sic*) as proconsul;[4] another, from the Athenian Acropolis, records the thanks of the Areopagus for the services of a Rufius Festus as proconsul of Achaea.[5] Although the identification of our poet with the Rufius Festus of these inscriptions has been contested, it seems most likely; it also seems most likely that the spelling Avienius, rather than Avienus, is his *signum*. (The present edition continues to refer to Avienus, as the established English-language name.)

---

* I am grateful to Brady Kiesling for introducing me to the puzzles of Avienus and to Graham Shipley for his encouragement and patience. I am also indebted to the late Neil Hopkinson, Katherine Backler, Claire Hall, Philip Hardie, Robert Machado, Katherine Olley, and Hanneke Salisbury.

[1] J. P. Murphy, SJ 1977, 101–19.
[2] The fullest analysis of the sources for A.'s life is in Dorfbauer 2012.
[3] *CIL* VI 537 = *ILS* 2944 = *CLE* 1530.   [4] *AE* 2002, 1676.   [5] *IG* ii/iii 13274 = 422.

The inscriptions place Avienus' political career in the 330s AD. His poetry—at least the *Ora*—was the work of his later years, written when 'far gone in my life' (*prolixa die*, *Ora* l. 7).

Four of Avienus' poems survive apart from the inscription referred to above: (1) a short verse epistle to a Flavianus Myrmecius, which appears to have been a preface to an edition of the other three;[6] (2) the *Descriptio orbis terrae* (*Description of the Circle of the Earth*), a rendering into Latin hexameter verse of Dionysios Periegetes' *Periegesis* (Chapter 28 above); (3) the *Ora maritima*, translated below; and (4) the *Aratea*, a Latin hexameter version of Aratos' *Phainomena* (known to St Jerome, writing c. AD 386/7).[7] Servius records a fifth, a rendering in iambics of the myths in Virgil.[8]

Together, the *Descriptio*, the *Ora*, and the *Aratea* form a programmatic attempt to set in Latin verse prior (Greek) knowledge of the world, the sea, and the heavens respectively. The *Descriptio* must predate the *Ora*, because Avienus refers to it in the prologue to the latter poem (see ll. 71–3), and it is likely the earliest of the three poems. The dating of the *Aratea* relative to the *Ora* is uncertain, but the explicit reference to Avienus' old age in the *Ora* (above), that poem's unfinished nature, and its greater freedom with its material may point to it being last of all.

Avienus tells us that he wrote the *Ora* in response to a query from one Probus (possibly Sextus Petronius Probus, see note to line 1 below) about the Sea of Azov, and that he intended the *Ora* to be an account of the coast from the straits of Gibraltar through to the Black Sea. The surviving work instead starts beyond the straits, describing the Atlantic and then Mediterranean coast of Europe as far as Marseilles, at which point the text breaks off. It is unclear how much of the *Ora* no longer survives.

The extant text largely deals with the places and peoples of the coast in order, working round from Oestrymnis (*Finisterre* in Brittany) in an anti-clockwise direction:

A. *Prologue* (1–79): Avienus dedicates the work to Probus, introduces his sources, and sets out the structure of the poem

B. *The Atlantic coast of Europe and the Pillars of Hercules* (80–416): the Pillars of Hercules are introduced; the Atlantic coast from Oestrymnis (Brittany) and outlying islands (Britain and Ireland) down to Ophiussa (general area of NW Spain) (80–145); (in more detail) Atlantic coast of Spain, including Tartessus/Gades, as far as the Pillars of Hercules (146–318); extended discussion of the Pillars of Hercules (318–416)

C. *The Mediterranean coast from the Pillars of Hercules to Massalia*[9] (417–713): (in detail) the Mediterranean coast up to the Pyrenees (417–557); (in less detail) the coast from the Pyrenees to Massalia (558–713), including a digression on the source and course of the Rhône (631–99)

---

[6] The name transmitted to us is Flavianus Myrmeicus, but Woudhuysen 2019 corrects the error.
[7] Jerome, *Tit.* 1. 12. The *Aratea* is not mentioned by Firmicus Maternus, in a list of translations of the *Phainomena* in his *Mathesis*, written c. AD 335: *Math.* 2, pr. 2.
[8] Servius ad *Aen.* 10. 272.
[9] I employ the standard Greek name Massalia in the introduction and notes, but follow Avienus' Latin form *Massilia* in the translation.

As Avienus' willingness to engage in extended discussions that interrupt (and sometimes reverse) the logical progression around the coast demonstrates, the *Ora* is a poetic composition rather than a practical handbook. Its most striking feature is that Avienus sets out the places and peoples of the coast as they had once been, while showing no interest in the geography of his own day, even by way of explanation or to assist his reader; a by-product of this archaizing perspective is that the majority of the toponyms and ethnonyms he uses are not attested elsewhere.[10] He does not advert to this approach in the prologue.

In giving an account of the coast as it had been, the *Ora* is a poem reliant, sometimes unevenly, often uncritically (see, for example ll. 370–4 and note), on other sources. Avienus' approach to his sources, where he names them, appears to have been to mine later works for references to earlier writers. Save one reference to Dionysios Periegetes at line 331, he does not mention by name sources later than the 1st century BC. He lists several 6th- and 5th-century BC Greek writers in the prologue, not all of whom subsequently appear in the surviving text, but all of whom seem to be culled from a later source or sources such as Ephoros. Where he does cite an early source, he does not seem to have had access to that source itself: for example, although he makes repeated references to a *periplous* written by Himilco the Carthaginian, and stops to comment that he has drawn this 'deep from the ancient annals of the Carthaginians' (ll. 414–15), his use of Himilco indicates he only had access to a fragment, again most likely via an intermediary (see l. 117 and note).

Much of the focus of scholarship has been on trying to disentangle and date these sources. Above all, two interrelated questions about Avienus' use of sources arise: (1) whether Avienus has simply translated an immediate Greek predecessor into Latin, or has synthesized a treatment from a number of sources and (2) whether there is a single underlying archaic source for the surviving material which (via one or more intermediate stages, such as being turned into verse) forms the basis of any such Greek predecessor and thus of the surviving portion of the *Ora*.

As to the first question, Avienus is not a mere translator, who has faithfully turned a Greek model word-for-word into a Latin poem. Unlike the *Aratea* and the *Descriptio*, Avienus does not claim in the *Ora* to be translating a Greek model; to the contrary, insofar as he claims to be working off a text, it is Sallust's prose treatment of the Black Sea (see ll. 38–42), which he does not come to in the surviving text. Even if he were claiming to translate a Greek text, we should expect him to have made some additions and embellishments to the substantive content of the poem. By comparison, in the *Descriptio*, he lengthened the *Periegesis* by some 200 lines beyond the Greek original.

There are certain passages of the *Ora* that suggest Avienus' own work. In particular, the two extended discussions that disrupt the logical progression around the coast

---

[10] Guillaumin and Bernard 2021, xxxvi, identify 156 toponyms and ethnonyms, of which 79 are wholly unattested elsewhere and 39 are unattested elsewhere in the form Avienus uses but may be variants of names attested elsewhere, leaving 38 attested elsewhere.

(that concerning the Pillars of Hercules at ll. 318–416 and that concerning the Rhône at ll. 631–99) are markedly different from the surrounding sections, and appear to be Avienus' original poetic composition (though possibly drawing considerably on a single principal source for each). Both are demarcated (at ll. 416 and 631) by a reference to Avienus' 'pen' (*stilus*), drawing attention to the poet's own selection and arrangement of the material; they contain nearly all the express references to sources found in the main body of the poem; Avienus shows a greater willingness to comment on his material; and in the latter digression, he addresses Probus by name, evoking the prologue.[11]

These extended discussions aside, where Avienus' own observations can be tentatively identified, they are mostly book learning, marked by an interest in archaisms and linguistic points. Only once does he tantalizingly claim that he has visited a place he describes, namely Gades (see l. 274 and n.).

But nor does the fact that Avienus does not claim to be using a single source establish that the extant text is an original synthesis of individual points. Once the extended discussions and Avienus' own forays are stripped out, there is a consistent tenor to the underlying content of the *Ora*, progressing largely in order, with distances indicated by reference to duration,[12] and proceeding by reference to features of maritime interest (such as prevailing winds or unusual phenomena apparent to sailors),[13] all with no reference, direct or indirect, to any of the kinds of historical or poetic sources that we might expect Avienus, as a well-read Roman aristocrat, to advert to if he were producing his own synthesis. That indicates that, just as, for the later sections of the poem, Avienus intended to use Sallust as a base and elaborate on it, for the extant text, where Sallust did not supply a base, Avienus similarly used an earlier single source as his base, supplemented by his own additions.

It is not possible, without more information, to say what that source might be: Antonelli posits an iambic poem of Apollodoros dated to around the end of the 2nd century BC,[14] but Avienus need not have had a pre-existing poetic source and could equally have used a prose text (given that he intended to use Sallust for the Black Sea portion of the *Ora*). It is also likely that Avienus used different base sources in sequence for different stretches of coastline until Sallust took up the story: there is more non-maritime material in the later, Mediterranean sections of the poem, which may well be taken from a land-based itinerary from between the 4th and the 2nd century BC, possibly interpolated with further excerpts from the text Avienus has used for the remainder.[15]

As for the question of an underlying archaic source, in the late 19th century and early 20th century Müllenhoff and then Schulten posited a Massaliote *periplous* (which

---

[11] See l. 41 and n.

[12] Notably, all references to numerical geographical distances—stades and miles—in the poem are in Avienus' discussion of the Pillars of Hercules. By contrast, distance is expressed in the main progression of the poem solely in duration (how many days' journey it is from one place to another).

[13] For prevailing winds, ll. 174–7, 238–40; for unusual phenomena, ll. 166–70, 185–91.

[14] Antonelli 2013.   [15] See n. to l. 565.

Schulten dated to the late 6th century BC) as a foundational archaic source.[16] This is attractive, and has often been followed, although it is not without its problems: the details of Avienus' treatment of Massalia itself may be questionable, which would undermine this hypothesis, albeit that the ready answer would be that those details are embellishments at a later stage, and that any such original *periplous* would have been a more confined and less literary work. As an alternative, Antonelli suggests a Phokaian source: Herodotos (1. 163) credits the Phokaians as the first Greeks to make long sea voyages and the first to reach Tartessos.

A sceptical current in the scholarship, led by Berthelot, writing a decade or so after Schulten, prefers to give Avienus more credit, suggesting that there is no intermediate Greek base source and thus no underlying archaic source.[17] But this, though strongly argued in recent works, is not wholly persuasive. Aside from the features of the poem that suggest Avienus used an intermediate base source (indicated above), the repeated appearance (without explanation) of names of places and peoples not otherwise attested, the sometimes sketchy treatment of places beyond the Pillars of Hercules, and the focus on Tartessus—a pre-classical locality otherwise the stuff of myth—rather than on the later Carthaginian Gades (although see the note to l. 85)—as the centre for mining and trading precious metals all point to Avienus' base source ultimately deriving content from an archaic source, which likely dates to the latter part of the 6th century BC.

The *Ora* presents unique challenges among Avienus' surviving longer poems. It lacks an extant Greek comparandum to aid our analysis; his marshalling of his sources is sometimes confused; and his predilection for archaic names for peoples and places without providing context can be tiresome, if not infuriating. Yet the glimpses it affords of Greek knowledge of Britain, Ireland, and the Atlantic coast, of early stages of Iberia's development otherwise lost to the written sources, and of a late antique desire, at a time of religious and social change, to preserve in verse prior pagan learning all have continuing value.

This translation is a substantially updated and corrected edition of one first produced for the ToposText digital humanities project in 2018. For this edition, I have generally used Antonelli's edition of the text, but have dissented in a small number of places, which are identified in the notes.

To try to achieve consistency with other contributions, I have striven to use the same English translation for each Latin word by which Avienus designates a geographical feature (such as 'sea' or 'mountain'); sometimes, where Avienus himself is using different words interchangeably for the sake of poetic metre or effect, the effect may be infelicitous, but it is intended to illuminate, rather than obscure the Latin.

---

[16] Müllenhoff further suggested this was a Massaliote translation of a Carthaginian text: see Guillaumin and Bernard 2021, cxxii–cxxiii.

[17] A. Berthelot 1934, González Ponce 1995, and Guillaumin and Bernard 2021 are the best examples.

SELECTED FURTHER READING

Editions of Avienus

*Antonelli, L. (2013), 'Avienus, Ora maritima (2009)', in *FGrH* v. [Text, translation and detailed commentary (in Italian).]

*Berthelot, A. (1934), *Avienus, Ora maritima*. Paris. [French, with very conservative text; the commentary is the principal counterweight to Schulten.]

González Ponce, F. J. (1995), *Avieno y el periplo*. Ecija. [Text and Spanish trans., as appendix to monograph.]

*Guillaumin, J.-B., and Bernard, G. (2021), *Aviénus, Les Rivages maritimes*. Paris. ['Budé' edition; appeared too late to take into account fully.]

*Murphy, J. P., SJ (1977), *Rufus Festus Avienus, Ora Maritima: A Description of the Seacoast from Brittany to Marseilles [Massilia]*. Chicago. [Text, trans., commentary.]

Roller, D. W. (2022), *Three Ancient Geographical Treatises in Translation: Hanno, the King Nikomedes Periodos, and Avienus*. Abingdon–New York. [Appeared too late to be taken into account.]

*Schulten, A. (1922), *Avieni Ora maritima (periplus Massiliensis saec. VI. a. C.) adiunctis ceteris testimoniis anno 500 a. C. antiquioribus*. Berlin. (Repr. as *Ora marítima: junto con los demás testimonios anteriores al año 500 a. de J.C.*, Barcelona, 1955.) [The major C20 study of Avienus.]

TEXT

Headings are added.

PREFACE

Probus,[18] considering that you have often pondered
with heart and mind how the gulfs of the Tauric sea[19]
might be understood with reasonable confidence by those
whom the furthest expanses of the Earth separate,
I gladly entered upon this task so that what you
have longed for should become clear for you in song.
I did not think it right, now I am far gone in my life,
that that region's outline should not lie within

---

[18] Possibly Sextus Claudius Petronius Probus (c. AD 330–90), proconsul in Africa 357, consul 371. Schulten identifies Probus with Anicius Petronius Probus, consul in 406 (and the son of the former), but that sits less easily with the evidence for dating A.'s life to earlier in C4 AD (see introduction to chapter).

[19] The Black Sea. The name (not otherwise attested) is derived from the Tauri, who lived in the Crimean peninsula (Taurica Chersonesus). A. has possibly chosen this name, rather than more usual names such as Pontus Euxinus, because it identifies the sea by reference to the point furthest away, and so sets the scene for his intention to cover the extremes of east and west.

the compass of your understanding—a region
10 I have learned about from very old texts and
   my own private study, through every day of my life.
   I think it is the mark of a coarse and uneducated man
   to begrudge another what you possess without any expense.
   To those observations I add this too, that you stand in place of a child
   to me in my affections and in the bond of blood.
   Nor would that be enough, if I did not know
   that you had always avidly swallowed up
   literature's secrets, that you are of an open mind,
   that you are capable in your understanding,
20 that your thirst for such things is yoked to your heart,
   and that you beyond others remember what has been made known to you.
   Why would I pour out mysteries in vain to someone who could not
      remember them?
   Who would prattle[20] about deep mysteries to someone who could not
      comprehend?
   Yes, many things—many!—have driven me, Probus,
   to finish for you what you have demanded of me.
   Indeed, I also believed that this would be a parent's task,
   if my Muse were to make known to you what you long for
   more amply and more abundantly.
      To give what has been asked for is the mark of a man who is not mean;
30 but to increase further the sum of the gift with new things
   is the mark of a kindly and sufficiently generous mind.
   You asked, if you remember, what the region
   of the Maeotic sea[21] is. I knew that Sallust
   had reported this,[22] and I could not deny that his words
   are accepted by everyone to be of settled
   authority. So, to his famous description,
   where that writer, adept with his pen and truthful,
   set out in elegant words the layout and appearance
   of those places almost as though they were
40 before our sight, I have added many things
   taken from the commentaries of very many authors.[23]

---

[20] The word, *ogganiat* (strictly, 'yelps'), is an old comic word. The effect is jarring against the backdrop of A.'s treatment of his research as an initiation into secrets and mysteries, but its provenance may have appealed to his antiquarian cast of mind: he makes a knowing reference to the comic poet Plautus at l. 347 (see n.).

[21] The Sea of Azov.   [22] In book 3 of his *Histories* (frs 61–81 in Maurenbrecher 1891).

[23] All the authors A. lists date from C6 or C5. Of them, the surviving text cites only Phileas (at ll. 691–6); Scylax, i.e. Skylax (at ll. 372–4); Damastes (at ll. 370–2) and Euctemon (at ll. 350–69). Pausimachus and Bacoris are otherwise unknown.

Obviously, Hecataeus the Milesian will be found there,
Hellanicus of Lesbos, and Phileas
the Athenian, Scylax of Caryanda,
so too Pausimachus, whom ancient Samos bore,
and of course, Damastes, born in noble Sige,
Bacoris, sprung from Rhodes, Euctemon, too,
the citizen of Athens, Cleon the Sicilian,
Herodotus of Thurii himself, and then he who is
50   the great glory of oratory, the Athenian Thucydides.
     Here, Probus, half of my heart, you shall have in turn
whatever islands rise up in the waters—
I mean in those waters which, from the openings
of the world gaping wide from the Tartessian strait
and the waves of the Atlantic, push our sea[24]
right up to the land that lies far distant.
I shall tell of the curved gulfs and the headlands—
how the sloping shore stretches itself out,
how the mountain ridges entwine far off with the waves,
60   and how the noble cities are washed by the sea.
I shall tell you which sources pour forth the greatest rivers,
how the streams flow headlong into the flood of the sea,
how they then often surround islands
and how the harbours stretch out their sheltering reaches,
how the lagoons unfold, how the lakes lie,
how the high mountains lift up their rugged crest
and how the white wave of the flood laps the pastures.
But this will be the end of our work:
I shall explain in full the Scythian sea,[25] the waters of the Euxine sea,
70   and any islands which crop up there on the main.
We have written further about the remainder
more fully in that volume which we wrote
about the shores and regions of the world.[26]
So that you should have an open declaration
of my sweat and my labour,
let us begin the narrative of this work a little further away.[27]

---

[24] The prevailing current at the straits of Gibraltar is westerly, from the Atlantic, making it difficult to exit the straits by sail.

[25] The Sea of Azov again. The word Avienus uses for 'sea', *profundum* ('deep' or 'deep sea'), is not well chosen: the Sea of Azov is notoriously shallow.

[26] The *Descriptio orbis terrae*, for which see the introduction to this chapter.

[27] The Pillars of Hercules are one of the cardinal points of the world in A.'s *Descriptio* (for which see Selter 2010). His comment that he is beginning the work 'a little further away' and the swift

> You must store up in your innermost heart
> what I have set forth, for I have sought
> support far and wide, drawn from the authors.

THE ATLANTIC COAST BEYOND IBERIA

> 80 The circle of the broad Earth is widely spread,
> and waves surround the Earth.
> But where the deep main wends its way
> from the very Ocean, such that here the flood of our sea
> extends far, there is the Atlantic gulf.
> Here is the city of Gadir, previously called Tartessus;[28]
> here are the pillars of unyielding Hercules,
> Abila and Calpe:[29] The latter is on the left bank of the land I have mentioned;
> the former is next to Libya.[30] They ring
> with the harsh Septentrio,[31] but hold fast to their place.
> 90 And here rises the far point of a projecting ridge.[32]
> A more ancient age called it Oestrymnis,[33]
> and the lofty bulk of the rocky outcrops
> all turns towards the warm Notus.[34]
>   Beyond the point of this headland,

move to discuss places far beyond the Pillars mark his intention in the *Ora* to go beyond the account in the *Descriptio*.

---

[28] A. here follows a long-established tradition in the sources of treating 'Tartessus' as an older name for the Phoenician colony of Gadir (see e.g. Sallust *Hist.* 2 fr. 5 in Maurenbrecher 1891; Pliny 4. xxii. 120). The tradition is likely erroneous: the earliest Greek source (Stesichoros fr. 184 in Page and Davies 1991, at Strabo 3. 2. 11, C149) identifies Tartessus as the name of a river (the *Guadalquivir*); Herodotos (1. 163; 4. 152), also relying on older traditions, similarly uses the name to mean an indigenous settlement or territory around the *Guadiana* and *Guadalquivir*. The success of the Phoenician colonies and diminished Greek contact with the west from C5 onwards accelerated the identification of Tartessus with Gadir and later with Roman Gades. A. himself uses 'Tartessus' or 'Tartessian' elsewhere in the text indiscriminately to designate a sea (l. 54), a river (ll. 225–6, 283–5), people (ll. 114–15, referring both to Carthaginian colonists and, seemingly, the indigenous peoples; ll. 254–5), an estuary (ll. 265–7), and a mountain (ll. 308–9), not always intending it as a synonym for 'Gaditan'.

[29] Calpe is the Rock of Gibraltar. There is no comparable obvious promontory on the African side; Abila has been variously identified with *Jebel Musa* in Morocco and *Monte Hacho* in Ceuta. Strabo 3. 5. 5, C169–71, provides further debate on the origin of the Pillars.

[30] In this context, A. means Africa.

[31] The north wind. The prevailing winds at the straits of Gibraltar are in fact westerly (the Poniente) and easterly (Levante). A. Berthelot 1934, 57, suggests that the reason the north wind is named is because the Romans falsely believed the S coast of Spain ran directly W to E, placing Abila due W of Gibraltar (with the result that they believed the Poniente was the north wind).

[32] A. makes an abrupt transition from the Pillars of Hercules to Oestrymnis, in Brittany, while describing the latter as 'here' (*hic*), i.e. in the same region as the Pillars. Something has gone wrong here, either in A.'s sources or in his handling of them.

[33] In *Finisterre* in Brittany. Probably either *Pointe Saint-Mathieu* or *Pointe du Raz*.

[34] The south wind.

>   the Oestrymnian gulf spreads open for its inhabitants,
>   in which the Oestrymnian islands[35] spring up,
>   lying over a wide area and rich in deposits
>   of tin and lead. Great is the energy of the people here,
>   proud their character, pragmatic their skill.
> 100   All things are connected to affairs of business.
>   They cleave the tempestuous sea, and the flood
>   of the Ocean abounding in monsters, with woven boats.
>   In fact, these people do not know how to fashion keels with pine
>   and maple. They do not, as is usual, shape their boats from fir,
>   but—a miraculous thing—they always fit out
>   vessels by stitching hides together,
>   and often travel through the boundless swell in a skin.
>   Then from here it is two days' journey by boat
>   to the Holy Island—so the ancients called it.[36]
> 110   Amid the waves this island extends far in its fields,
>   and the people of the Hierni dwell all over it.
>   The island of the Albiones also lies nearby.[37]
>   It was the habit of the Tartessians to do business
>   among the furthest parts of the Oestrymnides.
>   The colonists from Carthage and the ordinary people, bearing on through
>   the pillars of Hercules, used to go to these waters.
>   Punic Himilco[38] declared that they
>   could scarcely be crossed in four months—
>   as he reported that he himself proved by sailing all the way.
> 120   This is so because no breezes drive the ship,
>   and the sluggish liquid of the inert waters stands still.
>   He adds this comment too: among the floods,

---

[35] Identified either with Britain (or islands off its coast) or with islands off the coast of Brittany. The references to rich deposits of tin and lead (not found in the islands of Brittany), to a distinct people, and to woven boats point to the identification of the islands with southern Britain. (Woven boats are a peculiarly British skill in ancient authors: see Caes. *BC* 1. 54; Pliny 4. xvi. 104.) Against that, the context requires that 'Oestrymnian islands' cannot mean 'the British Isles': A. subsequently refers to Britain as 'the island of the Albiones' (112), indicating that he (or his sources) understand that Britain is a single island; 'Oestrymnian islands' therefore does not reflect a belief in his sources that mainland Britain comprised several islands. Hdt. 3. 115 doubts the existence of the 'tin islands', which makes A.'s record of a Greek source especially important.

[36] Ireland. This is A.'s rendering of a Greek false etymology connecting the Greek name for it, *Iernē*, with *hierē nēsos*, 'holy island'. This etymology is otherwise unattested.

[37] See n. to l. 97 above.

[38] This is the first of three references to the voyage of the Carthaginian Himilco, who was tasked by Carthage with exploring the Ocean W of the Pillars of Hercules (Pliny 2. lxvii. 169); the others are at 380–4 and 412–15. A. has probably obtained a single fragment via an intermediate source: see the Introduction.

there is a lot of seaweed, and often it checks a ship
in the manner of a bush. He says that nonetheless here
the surface of the sea does not extend to a great depth,
and the seabed is scarcely covered with a little water.
Here and there sea creatures meet, and sea monsters
swim amid the slow ships sluggishly crawling along.
    If anyone dared to launch a light galley
130   into the waves from the Oestrymnian islands,
where the air grows stiff at Lycaon's pole,[39]
he would come upon the land of the Ligurians,[40]
devoid of inhabitants. Its fields have been empty
for a long time because of frequent battles with the Celts:
the Ligurians were driven out, as fortune often drives out others,
and came to those haunts, which they possess amid plenty
of bristling bushes. Round about these places are abundant
rough stone, rugged cliffs and mountains threatening the sky.
This tribe, avoiding contact, for some time led its life
140   amid the narrow confines of the rocks far from the waves.
For they were afraid of the main, on account of the danger
they had experienced in ancient times. Later, since freedom from care
fortified their boldness, peace and an untroubled life
coaxed them to be led down from their high dwelling-places
and to come down to their present places by the sea.

THE ATLANTIC COAST OF IBERIA, INCLUDING TARTESSUS

Then, after those places which we have set out above,
the great gulf of the open waters[41] extends up
to Ophiussa.[42] Then, from the shore of this place
to the inner waters, where the sea penetrates amid the land
150   (as I have said before), and which they call the sea of the Sardi,[43]

---

[39] The northern sky. From the myth of Callisto, daughter of Lycaon, catasterized into the Great Bear; her son by Zeus, Arcas, became the Little Bear. A. treats the Great Bear and the Little Bear in his rendition of Aratos at *Aratea* 105–37.

[40] Likely somewhere on the North sea coast, possibly *Jutland*. The stock of the Ligurians who dwelt in the Alps and N. Italy was unknown and a source of speculation (thus e.g. Dion. Hal. *Ant. Rom.* 1. 10). Possible corroboration for northern Ligurians is found in Plutarch (*Marius* 19), who records that at the battle of Aquae Sextiae in 102 BC the (Italian) Ligurians recognized the tribal name of the opposing Ambrones (which the Ambrones employed as their battle cry) and shouted it back, 'Ambrones' being their own ancestral name.

[41] The Bay of Biscay.

[42] NW Spain, a name seemingly of Greek (possibly Phokaian) origin and connected (as the story A. tells at ll. 156–7 relates) to *ophis*, 'snake'.

[43] The W portion of the Mediterranean, named for Sardinia's importance to trading routes. Pliny 3. x. 75 says this is the name the C3 geographer Eratosthenes of Cyrene used.

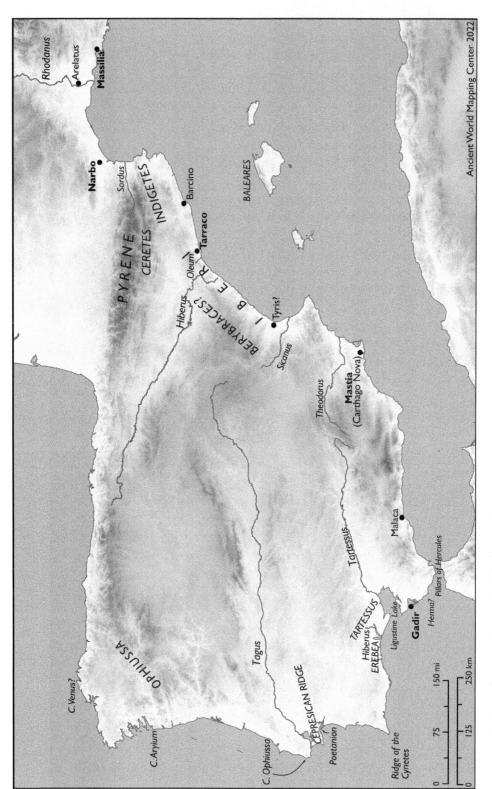

MAP 32.1. Avienus, *Ora maritima*: principal places in Iberia.

the journey coming back is seven days.
Ophiussa extends its side to a distance
as far as you hear the isle of Pelops[44] lies
in the land of the Greeks.[45] Ophiussa was first called Oestrymnis,[46]
since the Oestrymni inhabited its regions and fields.
Some time later a serpent forced the inhabitants to flee[47]
and imposed on the empty land its name.
    From there the ridge of Venus[48] extends into the floods,
and the main barks round two islands, which are inhospitable
160   because of the meanness of the land. Then the headland
of Aryium rises up in the harsh north.[49]
The journey from here for ships
as far as the pillars of powerful Hercules
is five days. After that there is a sea isle
abounding in grass and sacred to Saturn.[50]
But there is such great natural force in the island
that if anyone approaches it by sailing,
soon the sea in the region of the island is stirred up,
the island itself is shaken and all the Earth
170   leaps up, beginning to quake deeply.
Meanwhile, the rest of the open sea is still like a lagoon.
    Then the headland of Ophiussa[51] rises up to the air.
From the ridge of Aryium to this place is a journey of two days.
But the gulf which then unfolds its broad waters,[52] drawing back
from the sea, is not easy to sail with one wind:

---

[44] That is, the Peloponnese.

[45] The likely boundaries of Ophiussa are greater than those of the Peloponnese. The distance across the Peloponnese is just over 125 mi (200 km); by way of illustration, from C. *Ortegal* to C. *Silleiro*, creating a shallow triangle of which C. *Finisterre* is the apex, is c.155 mi (c.250 km).

[46] A. here appears to be confused. He has previously identified Oestrymnis with Brittany, but here treats it as a former name of NW Spain.

[47] There are many parallels for this tale, collected by Marx 1895, 339, including Hdt. 4. 105, Pliny 3. v. 59; Serv. ad *Aen.* 10. 564.

[48] There are several headlands on the N coast of Spain which could be the headland of Venus. Schulten and Murphy identify the headland of Venus as C. *Higuer*, at Irun on the Franco-Spanish border, but that is likely too far E; Berthelot places it further W at C. *Ortegal*, which is more probable.

[49] Likely either C. *Ortegal* (if the headland of Venus is identified as C. *Higuer*) or C. *Silleiro* (if the headland of Venus is itself identified with *Ortegal*).

[50] The *Berlenga* archipelago, which stands a few miles offshore. Antonelli cross-refers to a lush island in Strabo 3. 3. 1, C152, but that island is described as situated in the upper estuary of the Tagus, not a sea-isle, so Strabo and A. have different islands in mind (though the same tradition may have attached to both).

[51] C. *Roca*.

[52] The Tagus estuary, the geography of which fits with the mariner's need to have a westerly and a southerly wind in succession to navigate up it.

you will never reach the middle with the Zephyrus[53]
carrying you; the remainder requires the Notus.
Then from there, if someone made for the shore
of the Tartessians on foot, he would come
180   to the end of the journey on just about the fourth day.
If anyone should direct his path to our sea and Malaca's harbour,
it is a journey of five days.
        Then the Cepresican ridge[54]
looms large. Beneath it in turn lies the island
named by its inhabitants Achale.[55] Scarcely
can one trust the tale, because it is miraculous,
but plenty of sources provide support enough:
they say that in the bounds of this island
there is nothing equal in appearance to the rest of the flood.
Everywhere there is brightness in the waves
190   like the sheen of glass, and through the deep
main there is a bluish appearance.
But the ancients relate that there the waters
are thick with foul mud, and stick fast
with the dirt, like streams full of sediment.
    The Cempsi and the Sefes[56] inhabit the steep hills
in the country of Ophiussa. Nearby to these
the nimble Lusitanian and the offspring of the Draganes
had located their home beneath the snowy Septentrio.
Then, Poetanion is an island on the border of the Sefes,
200   and an accessible harbour.[57] After that, the peoples
of the Cynetes[58] lie next to the Cempsi. Then the ridge
of the Cynetes, looming on high where the starlight sets,
the furthest ridge of fertile Europe,
faces towards the main of the Ocean filled with monsters.

---

[53] The west wind.

[54] C. *Espichel*, just S of *Lisbon*.

[55] Now unknown; likely to have been located in the *Sado* estuary and silted up to form part of the mainland.

[56] The Cempsi are otherwise known only from Dionysios Periegetes 338 (and A.'s own *Descriptio* at 475). Dionysios, however, places them in the foothills of the Pyrenees. The Sefes are otherwise unknown. 'Nimble Lusitanian': the text reads *Lucis*, likely a variant or corruption of a name for Lusitanians. Antonelli adopts Schrader's *Ligus*, 'Ligurian'; but there is no record of Ligurians in this region. They are 'nimble' at Strabo 3. 3. 6, C154. The 'offspring of the Draganes' may be connected (cf. Greek *drakōn*, 'snake') to the tale of snakes driving the Oestrymni from Ophiussa at 154–7.

[57] The island is probably the present-day peninsula of *Tróia* opposite *Setúbal* at the mouth of the *Sado*, SE of *Lisbon*; the river's mouth is itself the port.

[58] Inhabitants of the Algarve, described by Hdt. 2. 33 and 4. 49 as the most westerly people in Europe. Unlike Hdt., A. does not mention the Celts in the same breath, which, Antonelli suggests, indicates that his source material pre-dates Hdt. The 'ridge of the Cynetes' is C. *St Vincent*, the most south-westerly point of Portugal.

There the river Anas[59] runs through the Cynetes
and cleaves the soil. The gulf opens up
and the land stretches out in a curve to the south.
From the river I have told you about, twin streams
suddenly separate themselves and push on
210   their slow courses through the dense water of
the aforementioned gulf. This is because all the deep here
is thick with mud. Here the crests of two islands
rise up high.[60] The smaller lacks a name.
Enduring tradition calls the other Agonis.
There a crag bristles with cliffs: it is sacred
to Saturn. The sea is struck against it and foams up.
The rocky shore stretches out over a wide area.
Here, the inhabitants' shaggy she-goats and many male goats
wander constantly among the brambles of the meadow.
220   They grow long, thick hair suited to military
use and to sailors' clothing.[61]
From here to the river I spoke about is a journey of one day.
Here too the tribe of the Cynetes have their border.

    The Tartessian region borders this,
and the river Tartessus flows through the country.[62]
Then there extends a mount sacred to the Zephyrus.[63]
In fact, the summit is called Zephyris.
The top of the peak rises high from the ridge.
Its great height reaches to the air, and something like
230   a mist sitting on top of it always covers its overcast tip.
From that point, all the country greatly abounds in grassy soil.
These inhabitants live on slopes that are always cloudy.
The upper air is denser, and the day more humid;
dew abounds, as though it were night. No breezes
blow through here, as is usual; no breath of wind
shakes the air upwards. A motionless mist sits on the land
and the earth is damp over a wide area.

---

[59] The *Guadiana*.

[60] Unknown. If the 'crag ... sacred to Saturn' is identified with *Sagres* Point, the islands could be its adjacent rocky islets: Strabo 3. 1. 4, C138, describing the 'sacred promontory' (usually taken to be C. St Vincent, but the features are not consistent), relates that Artemidoros reported three small islands nearby.

[61] A. borrows directly from Virgil, *Georgics* 3. 313. Like Virgil, he uses *velamina*, a poetical word for 'clothing', but other ancient sources suggest goat hair was used for ship's tackle rather than for sailors' clothing: Varro, *Rust.* 2. 11. See Mynors 1994 on this difficulty in A.'s Virgilian model.

[62] The *Guadalquivir*: see also n. to ll. 85–7 above.

[63] The west wind. The mountain is likely to be *Cerro de São Miguel* (alias *Monte Figo*).

If anyone were to set out from the crest of Zephyris by ship
and be carried towards the flood of our sea,
240   he would immediately be borne along by the breezes of Favonius.[64]
    Next, there is a mount sacred to the goddess of the lower world,
a wealthy sanctuary in a concealed hollow
and a lightless inner chamber. There is a great marsh nearby,
called Erebea.[65] In fact, the city of Herbi
is said to have stood in these parts in an ancient era;
this city, annihilated by the storms of battle,
left its reputation and its name to the salty ground.
From that place there flows the Hiberus river;[66] its waters
make the region fertile. Many people say
250   that the Hiberi are named for this, and not from that river
which glides past the restless Vascones.
For whatever part of this people lies towards the
sunset from this river, they call Hiberian.
The eastern side in turn contains the Tartessians
and Cilbiceni. After that is the island of Cartare.[67]
The Cempsi held it for a long time: there is sufficient reason
to believe this. Afterwards, since they were driven out
because of war with their neighbours, they set out in search
of different places. From there, Mount Cassius rises:[68]
260   the Greek tongue formerly called tin *cassiterum*
because of it. Then there is a headland shrine,
and the high citadel of Geron, which retains its Greek name
from of old. We have come across the tradition

---

[64] Another name for the west wind.

[65] At the junction of the *Odiel* and *Tinto* rivers. Both 'Erebea' and 'the city of Herbus' (named at the end of the line), unidentified and otherwise unknown, are likely to be Greek attempts to render local place-names, which may well have become fused in the tradition with the similar-sounding Greek Erebos, 'underworld'. Together with the adjacent mountain sacred to Proserpina (the goddess of the lower world), they point to a tradition identifying the places roundabout with a point of access to the underworld.

[66] The *Odiel* or the *Tinto*. The other Hiberus, which 'glides past the restless Vascones' (251) is the *Ebro*. Antonelli suggests that use of the same name corresponds to a time prior to C5 in which increasing Greek contact with the Iberian peninsula resulted in developing, but still imperfect, knowledge of the geography. 'Hiberus', like 'Erebea' and 'Herbus', may also be a Greek rendering of a local place name.

[67] A name found only in A. It is likely an island between the *Odiel* and the *Tinto*. For the Cempsi, see n. to l. 195.

[68] The fossil dunes of *Asperillo*. The etymology of the name (again a name found only in A.) is false, as tin was not mined in Tartessus but imported.

that Geryon was once named because of it.⁶⁹
Here are the wide-extending shores of the gulf of Tartessus.
From the river I have mentioned⁷⁰ to this place is
a journey of a day. Here is the town of Gadir,
for the Carthaginian tongue used to call a place
that had been enclosed 'Gadir'.⁷¹ It was previously named
270   Tartessus. It was a great and wealthy city
in ancient times. Now it is poor; now it is small;
now it is forsaken. Now it is a heap of ruins.
We saw nothing wonderful here, except
the festival of Hercules.⁷² But there was such power
in those rites, or such glory, in a former age
(if we believe the thing) that a proud king,
powerful beyond all those whom the Mauretanian
people chanced to have in that era,
most welcome to the emperor Octavian and always
280   applying himself to the study of literature—Juba⁷³—
although separated by the waters which flow between,
believed he was more illustrious because he held
the duumvirate of that city. The river Tartessus
flows through the outlets from the Ligustine lake⁷⁴
and winds round an island on all sides with its gliding course.

---

⁶⁹ Possibly (after Berthelot) located at the site of the fort of *Santa Catalina* on the NW tip of *Cádiz*; the shrine would be the temple of Saturn, mentioned by Strabo (3. 5. 3, C169). Geryon: a legendary three-headed giant killed by Hercules. Antonelli suggests that the name Geron may instead derive from a local custom of honouring old age, possibly associated with traditions about the longevity of Arganthonius, the legendary king of Tartessus (for whom see Hdt. 1. 163). However, Hesiod relates that Hercules killed Geryon in 'Erythia, surrounded by sea' (Hes. *Th.* 983), so the connection is of considerable antiquity.

⁷⁰ It is unclear whether A. means the Anas (ll. 205, 22) or the Hiberus (l. 248). Either is plausible.

⁷¹ This etymology is repeated in other sources (e.g. Pliny 4. xxii. 120) and appears to be true. For the conflation of Gades and Tartessus, see n. to ll. 85–7 above.

⁷² A.'s (otherwise unexplained) visit to Gades is the only point in the poem where he claims to have seen any of the places he describes. If he is to be identified with the proconsul commemorated at Bulla Regia (see the introduction), he may well have visited Gades while travelling to or from Africa Proconsularis. The festival of Hercules descends from worship of Melqart; Strabo 3. 5. 5, C169–70, relates the tradition that Gades was founded in obedience to an oracle commanding the Tyrians to set up a colony at the Pillars of Hercules, and that the temple to Hercules was founded with the city. In both the *Ora* and the *Descriptio* (see introduction to this chapter), A.'s only claims to first-hand sight of the places he describes relate to pagan religious rites: at *Descriptio* 603–4, A. refers to visiting the sanctuary of Apollo at Delphi.

⁷³ Juba II (*c*.48 BC–AD 23), installed by Augustus as king of Mauretania and famed for his learning (Pliny 5. i. 16). See Ch. 22 above. There is no other evidence for his appointment as *duumvir* of Gades, but epigraphic evidence establishes that he was appointed *duumvir* of Carthago Nova (*CIL* II.3417). However, he claimed descent from Hercules (Plut. *Sert.* 9), and may well have promoted a connection with Gades to give colour to those dynastic claims and abet his intellectual and political projects (for which, see Domínguez Monedero 2017).

⁷⁴ Possibly the lagoon S of *Coria* on the *Guadalquivir*. There is no other evidence for Ligurian settlement in this part of Spain (see n. to l. 195 above): either the text is corrupt or 'Ligustine' is a Greek attempt to render a local place-name by assimilating it to the name of a people already known to them.

Nor does that river flow on by a single course,
or in one body cut through the ground that lies nearby.
In fact, it carries three mouths into the land
in the east of the country, and it washes
290   the southern parts of the city with a twice twin mouth.
    Mount Argentarius[75] overhangs the marsh,
so named by the ancients from its appearance.
It shines upon its flanks with abundant tin,
and reflects more light into the air at a distance
when the sun beats down on the ridges with its glow from on high.
And the same river, its waves heavy with tin,
rolls fragments along and carries the rich metal
Down to the city walls. From here onwards, a great
expanse of territory[76] recedes from the waters' salty flood
300   through the middle of the land. The tribe of the Etmanes dwells here.
Then, after that, the Ileates spread themselves
up to the field of the Cempsi over the fruitful country,
but the Cilbiceni possess the coastal regions.
    The main in between separates the citadel of Geron
and the temple headland, as I have said above.[77]
The gulf curves inwards between the high points of the rocks.
By the next ridge a great river unfolds:
from here the mountain of the Tartessians rises on high,
shaded with woods. Then there is the island of Erythia[78]
310   spreading out its turf, once under the sway of Carthage,
since colonists of ancient Carthage first held it.
On the mainland side, Erythia is cut off
from the citadel by a channel five stades long.
Towards the sunset, the island is
consecrated to Venus of the Sea:[79]
    there is a temple of Venus on it, a deep hollow and an oracle.

---

[75] 'Silvery'. Strabo (3. 2. 10, C148) reports that the *Guadalquivir* rises in a 'Silver Mountain' near Cazlona. As with Mt Cassius (259), the account of which may well have its origins in the same single story about the Tartessus region, the description of Mt Argentarius with 'abundant tin' derives from some long-standing confusion about the sources of the metals shipped from Tartessus.

[76] The inland plain of the *Guadalquivir*. For the Cempsi and Cilbiceni see ll. 195–201, 255–7; the Ileates may be identifiable with the Igleti of Asklepiades of Myrlea (according to Strabo 3. 4. 19, C166); the Etmanes are not otherwise known.

[77] A. returns to the features of Gades which he mentioned in 261–4. Antonelli sees in this and the following lines another insertion which reflects A.'s first-hand sight of Gades.

[78] The smallest of the three islands (the others being Cotinoussa and Antipolis) which made up the Gaditan archipelago. Erythia and Cotinoussa are today one island.

[79] Pliny 4. xxii. 120 reports that Timaeus and Silenus called Erythia 'Aphrodisias'. Archaeological evidence supports the possibility that a temple to Astarte (later identified with Venus) was located in the W of Erythia.

THE PILLARS OF HERCULES

        Past that mountain—which I had told you bristles with woods
        when you reach it—there lies a shelving shore soft with sands,
320   into which the Besilus and Cilbus rivers drive on
        their streams.[80] After that, towards the sunset,
        the Sacred Ridge raises up its domineering rocks.[81]
        This place the Greeks once called the Herma,
        for Herma is a bulwark of earth,[82] and on both sides
        the place fortifies the strait that flows in between.
        Others, however, call it the Way of Hercules:
        Hercules, of course, is said to have smoothed over the seas,
        so that an easy route would lie open for the herd he had captured.[83]
        Many writers also relate that that Herma
330   was for a long time under Libya's sway.
        Nor should we reject Dionysius as a source:
        he explains that Tartessus is the border of Libya.[84]
        The headland, which I have mentioned is called
        Sacred by the inhabitants, rises up in European soil.
        A narrow strait flows between both places,
        which is called Herma and the Way of Hercules.
        Euctemon, an inhabitant of the city of Amphipolis,[85] says that
        it extends for no greater length than a distance of 108 miles,
340   and that the two of them are three miles apart.
        Here stand the Pillars of Hercules which, we have read,
        are reckoned to be the boundary of each continent.
        These are equally projecting rocks,[86]

---

[80] The *Barbate* and the *Salado de Conil*.

[81] This is either the 'crag sacred to Saturn' (ll. 215–16), which is C. *St Vincent* or *Sagres* Point (for which see n. to l. 212), or else C. *Trafalgar*. Neither is perfect. C. *Trafalgar* is preferable, as it is W of the *Barbate*, but it is E of the *Salado de Conil*. If the 'crag sacred to Saturn' were meant, the sudden shift far to the W after the extended description of Gades would be jarring. Ps.-Skyl. §112. 2 describes reefs extending from C. Hermaia in Libya to the 'Hieron (*Sacred*) Promontory'.

[82] In his effort to provide an etymology, A. has seemingly confused the Greek '*herma*' (a reef, so Hdt. 7. 183 and Thuc. 7. 25) with '*eruma*' (a fence or defence). The Herma will be shoals S of the Sacred Ridge of 322; a shallow reef called *Aceytera* in fact lies off C. *Trafalgar*.

[83] The herd of Geryon, which Hercules drove off (see also n. at l. 264 above). The tradition of Hercules crossing the Ocean appears in Hesiod (*Th.* 292), but not in the account of Hercules' labours in Apollodoros (2. 5. 10).

[84] A. again runs together Tartessus and Gades. Dion. Peri. in fact says (at 176) that Libya 'begins at Gadeira' (which A. accurately renders at *Descriptio* 22).

[85] Otherwise unknown. It is unclear whether this is (as Murphy suggests) simply Euctemon the Athenian (who appears at l. 350 and is mentioned in the prologue, see n. to l. 42) by another name, reflecting a move to Amphipolis, or a different Euctemon. The source for these comments, and the later comments of Euctemon the Athenian, is probably Ephoros.

[86] Here I read *paria* 'equal', i.e. 'equally projecting', and so differ from Antonelli, who reads *parva*, 'small'.

Abila and Calpe.[87] Calpe is in Hispania;
Abila is in the land of the Mauretanians. For the Carthaginian race
calls 'Abila' what is a 'high mountain' in the barbarian tongue—
I mean of course the Latin tongue; the term is from Plautus.[88]
'Calpe', on the other hand, in Greek is the name of a type of water-pitcher,
hollow and smoothed in appearance.[89]

350 Euctemon the Athenian says, though,
that there are no rocks or peaks rising
on either side: he relates that two islands
lie between Africa's soil and Europe's shore.
He says that these are named the Pillars
of Hercules, and reports that thirty stades
separate these two; they bristle all over with woods,
and are always inhospitable for sailors. In fact,
he says that there are temples and altars to Hercules
on these islands, and that foreigners carried there by ship
360 make offerings to the god and depart with hastening sail;[90]
it is thought sinful to linger on the islands.
He relates that the shallow sea lying round about
these islands stands still over a wide expanse.
Laden ships are not able to approach the place
because of the shallow flood and the thick mud of the shore.
But if anyone's will happens to impel him to approach
the temple, he hastens to direct his ship to the island
of the Moon,[91] to remove the loads from his vessel,
and thus to be carried across the sea in a light craft.
370   But as to the heaving waves that flow between
the Pillars, Damastes says they are scarcely
seven stades across. Scylax of Caryanda maintains
that the flood flowing between the Pillars
is as wide as the swell of the Bosphorus.[92]

[87] See n. to l. 88.
[88] Plautus in several places refers to Latin as the 'barbarian' tongue: *Asin.* 11, *Trin.* 19, *Mil.* 2. 2. 58.
[89] A.'s Greek is, as we would expect, correct.
[90] 'Sail' translates *pes*, lit. 'foot' but also 'sheet' in the sense of the rope controlling a sail.
[91] See n. to l. 429.
[92] For Damastes and Skylax, see n. to l. 41. The comparison between the strait of Gibraltar and the Bosporus is puzzling, for two reasons. First, if the strait still known as the Bosporos in Istanbul is meant, the comparison is grossly inaccurate: the straits of Gibraltar are c.8 mi (13 km) wide, whereas the Bosporos is on average 1 mile (1.5 km) wide (tolerably close to 7 stades). Second, although Ps-Skyl. §67. 8 does give the width of the Bosporos as 7 stades, that text does not draw the comparison A. records, but says only that the Pillars are a day's sail apart (§§1; 111. 7). Panchenko 2005 suggests that the original, and correct, comparison may have been with the Kimmerian Bosporos (strait of *Kerch*), which is c.9 mi (15 km) wide at its widest point. This is again an indicator of A.'s habit of referring directly to earlier authors whom he knows only through later intermediaries.

Beyond these Pillars, on the European side,
inhabitants from Carthage once possessed the villages
and cities: it was their custom to build ships
with flatter keels by means of which a boat
wider in the beam could glide along the shallower bed
380 of the sea.[93] Beyond, to the west, Himilco relates
that from the Pillars the flood is without end:[94]
the open sea extends wide, and the main is spread out.
No man has entered upon these seas; no man
has ever set ships on those waters, because
the deep lacks the winds to drive a ship along,
and no breath from heaven favours a ship.
From here on, because a mist clothes the air
with a kind of cloak, fog always conceals the deep
and lasts through the day, which is altogether thick with clouds.
390   That is the Ocean, which roars far off around
the vast Earth. That is the great open sea.[95]
This flood encircles the shores. This is the source
of the inner saltwater; this is the parent of our sea.
From the outside it stirs up almost every gulf,
and the power of the deep penetrates our world.
But let us tell you about the four greatest gulfs.
Now, the first narrow entry point of this Ocean
in between the dry land is the western swell and the Atlantic main;
then there are the Hyrcanian waves, the Caspian sea;
400 the Indian main, the spread of the Persian waves;
and the Arabian gulf[96] beneath the south wind, already warm.
An old usage once called this the Ocean;
another custom called it the Atlantic sea.
The flood of this sea spreads out in a great circle,
and extends its wandering flank far and wide.
For the most part, in fact, that main is shallow:
it scarcely covers the sands which lie beneath it.
Thick seaweed dominates the flood,
and the swell here is checked by the marshy seabed.
410 Abundant sea creatures swim all through the open sea,
and great terror abides in the deep because of these creatures.
Punic Himilco reported that he had once seen these

---

[93] For this custom, see also Silius Italicus, 3. 473.
[94] The second mention of Himilco: see n. on l. 117.
[95] At ll. 390–406, A. strays from his subject matter to describe the Ocean and the four greatest gulfs. He has already done this at *Descriptio* 71–90 (a reworking of Dion. Peri. 43–55).
[96] Mod. *Red Sea*.

creatures in the Ocean and proved their existence.[97]
We have made these things known to you, drawn deep
from the ancient annals of the Carthaginians.

THE MEDITERRANEAN COAST OF IBERIA

Now let my pen return to my prior subject.[98]
Opposite the African Pillar, as I have said,
there rises up another in European soil.
Here the river Chrysus[99] enters the deep flood;
420 on this side and that four tribes dwell.
In this place are the fierce Libyphoenicians,[100]
the Massieni, and the kingdoms of the Cilbiceni
in fertile country, and the rich Tartessians,
who extend into the Calactic gulf.[101]
 Hard by these lie the Barbetian ridge[102]
and the river of Malaca, with the city of the same name,
which in an earlier age was called Menacē.[103]
There an island under the sway of the Tartessians
lies opposite the city, consecrated by the inhabitants
430 to Noctiluca a long time ago.[104] On the island is a pool
and a safe harbour: the town of Menacē lies above it.
Where the region I speak of draws away from the waves,
Mount Silurus swells up with its lofty peak.[105]
There a great rock rises up and extends
into the deep sea. The pines which once
covered this gave it its name in the Greek tongue.[106]
The shore is downward sloping as far as the shrine of Venus

---

[97] The third and final citation of Himilco: see n. on l. 117.
[98] A. returns to the description of the coast which he left at l. 323.   [99] The *Guadiaro*.
[100] According to Livy (21. 22. 3) a people of mixed Carthaginian and Libyan descent. The Massieni inhabited the territory up to Mastia (see n. to l. 449). 'Cilbiceni' is an amendment of the text by Schulten, which accords with the prior description of the Cilbiceni as inhabiting the coastal regions at 303.
[101] Unknown, though the name is likely to derive from the Greek *kalē aktē* (beautiful shore). A. Berthelot 1934 suggests it may be a reference back to the bay of *Huelva* (which would make sense as the locality of Tartessus), on the basis of a cognate place name Calathe in Hekataios.
[102] C. *Calaburras*, at the W end of the gulf of *Malaga*.
[103] A. (or his source) is wrong to conflate Malaca (mod. *Malaga*) with Menace/Mainakē. The latter was the Phokaians' most westerly colony. Strabo 3. 4. 2, C156, reports that it lay to the E of the Phoenician foundation of *Malaga* and that its ruins were distinctly visible.
[104] The cult is otherwise undocumented. The island is possibly the same as the 'Island of the Moon' in 367, but the precise geography is difficult to reconstruct. The reference confirms that A. or his source does not here have in mind Malaca, which did not have an island opposite the town.
[105] The *Sierra Nevada*.
[106] The 'great rock' is C. *Sabinal*, at the W of the gulf of *Almeria*. Its name in Greek was Pityoussa, from *pitys*, 'pine'. Murphy notes that the modern name *Sabinal* is similarly derived from the pine-trees.

and the ridge of Venus.¹⁰⁷ There on that stretch
of coast stood numerous cities in times past,
440 and many Phoenicians dwelt in these places a long time ago.
Now the empty land offers inhospitable sand.
Bereft of farmers, the ground lies neglected.
From the aforementioned ridge of Venus
the African Herma is seen at a distance,¹⁰⁸
as I have said before. Here again the shore lies bare,
now devoid of inhabitants, and the soil is degraded.
Here, too, stood very many cities in days of old,
and many peoples thronged these parts.
  Next the harbour of Namnatius curves in from the deep waters
450 in the vicinity of the city of the Massieni;¹⁰⁹
in the innermost part of the gulf rises the Massienan
city with its high walls. After this, the ridge of Traete
rises up,¹¹⁰ and the small island of Strongyle¹¹¹
stands nearby. On the edge of this island,
a marshy level extends its great flanks.¹¹²
There the Theodorus river oozes out;¹¹³
do not be puzzled that in this fierce place,
barbarian enough, you should hear the name of this river
in the Greek tongue. The Phoenicians formerly inhabited
460 those places. From here again the sands
of the shore spread themselves out, and three islands
surround this shore on all sides: here once stood
the boundary of the Tartessians. Here once was the city of Herna.¹¹⁴
The tribe of the Gymnetes had settled those places.
Now forsaken, and for a long time lacking inhabitants,
the river Alebus flows, burbling to itself.¹¹⁵
Next, the island of Gymnesia lies amidst the waves,¹¹⁶

---

¹⁰⁷ C. *Gata* at the E end of the gulf of *Almeria*.
¹⁰⁸ A. here means C. *Tres Forcas* in Morocco (adjacent to *Melilla*). His apparent identification of this with the Herma of l. 322, W of the Pillars, is an error.
¹⁰⁹ The city of the Massieni is Mastia (described as 'Tartessian' in Polyb. 3. 24. 1); Carthago Nova (mod. *Cartagena*) was founded on the site by Hasdrubal in 228 BC.
¹¹⁰ C. *Palos*, E of *Cartagena*.
¹¹¹ There are a number of small islands which could be Strongyle (Greek: 'round'). The most obvious are *Isla Grosa* and the *Isla del Barón*.
¹¹² The 'marshy level' is the *Mar Menor*, a saltwater lagoon bounded by C. *Palos*.
¹¹³ The *Segura*. Theodoros is a Greek rendering of Tader, the indigenous name (used at Pliny 3. iii. 19).
¹¹⁴ Unknown; possibly *La Fonteta* near *Guardamar*.   ¹¹⁵ The *Vinalopo*.
¹¹⁶ The Gymnesiae were *Majorca* and *Menorca*. A. does not appear to appreciate either that there was more than one island or that 'the broad backs of the Baleares' (l. 471) encompass the same islands. The Pityusae are *Ibiza* and *Formentera*.

which gave its old name to the population,
who dwell right up to the channel of the flowing Sicanus.¹¹⁷

470 There too the islands of Pityusae appear
and the broad backs of the Baleares islands.

    On the far side, the Iberi extend their sway right up
to the ridge of Pyrene, settled over a wide area
near the inner sea. Ilerda rises, the first of their cities:¹¹⁸
from here stretch out the barren sands of the shore:
Here, too, a long time ago the city of Hemeroscopium
was inhabited.¹¹⁹ Nowadays the ground, devoid
of inhabitants, is a stagnant swamp.

    Next, the city of Sicana rears its head,¹²⁰
480 so named by the Iberians from the neighbouring river.
Not far from the fork in this river
the Tyrius river touches the town of Tyris.¹²¹
But where the land draws far back from the main,
there extends a wide region full of thickets.
There the Berybraces, a fierce and savage tribe,¹²²
used to wander amid their herds of many cattle.
These people, feeding themselves hardily
with milk and fatty cheese, used to live
like wild beasts. Beyond that the ridge of Cabrasia
490 stretches on high,¹²³ and the shores lie bare
right up to the boundary of the empty Cherronesus.¹²⁴

    The marsh of the Naccarares spreads out along those shores.
Custom, in fact, gave this name to that marsh.
In the middle of the lagoon there also rises a small island
abounding in olives: for this reason, it is sacred to Minerva.

---

[117] The *Júcar*. Thucydides 6. 2 suggests that the Sicani who inhabited Sicily originally lived along the Iberian Sicanus and were expelled by the Ligyans.

[118] Possibly *Jávea*.

[119] i.e. 'place for keeping day watch', a Phokaian or Massaliote fort, mentioned by Strabo 3. 4. 6, C159, who places it at Dianium, mod. *Denia*, but no definite Greek settlements have been found.

[120] Possibly located on C. *Cullera* at the mouth of the *Júcar*.

[121] The Tyrius is the modern river *Turia*, which would place Tyris at *València* (Roman Valentia).

[122] A Celtic tribe, likely to be identified with the tribe elsewhere named as the 'Bebrykes' (e.g. *Nik.* 201) and sometimes in the same breath as a tribe of the same name living in Asia Minor.

[123] Possibly *Oropesa*.

[124] Identified variously as *Peniscola* or as the land around the *Ebro* delta. Both identifications are problematic: if the former is accepted, it is not clear where the 'marsh of the Naccarares' is located (the solution Schulten puts forward, that it is the *Albufera de València*, S of Saguntum, seems strained given that the marsh must be 'on these shores'); as for the latter, while the location is more logical and the marsh would then evidently be in the region of the *Ebro*, Strabo 3. 4. 6, C159 identifies Cherronesus as a city near Saguntum and before the crossing of the *Ebro* delta (where a different city, Dertosa, is situated). If the 'marsh of the Naccarares' is in *Albufera*, the island is to be identified with *Palmar*.

There were many cities nearby. It was here, in fact,
that Hylactes, Hystra, Sarna, and noble Tyrichae
stood.[125] The town had an old name, and the inhabitants'
treasure was greatly renowned through all the lands
500 of the Earth since, quite apart from the richness
of the soil, by which the ground sustained cattle,
vines, and the gifts of flaxen Ceres,
foreign goods were carried up the Hiberus river.[126]
  Very near, the Sacred Mountain raises its proud peak[127]
and the Oleum river flows between the twin crests
of the ridges, dividing up the neighbouring country.[128]
Soon Sellus—this is the old name for the mountain—[129]
reaches as far as the heights of the clouds.
The city of Lebedontia[130] stood near the mountain
510 in an earlier age; now the country, devoid of dwellings,
is home to the haunts and dens of wild beasts.
After these places lies a vast expanse of sand:[131]
amid these sands the town of Salauris once stood;
in them once lay ancient Callipolis.
That is the Callipolis which with the great height
of its walls and its lofty gables once drew near
to the winds; it used to touch on both sides, with the edge
of its great expanse of dwellings, a pool which was always
rich in fish.
  Then there is the town of Tarraco
520 and the charming seat of the wealthy Barcilones.[132]

---

[125] Nothing is known of Hylactes, Hystra, and Sarna. Tyrichae could be an old name for Dertosa, mod. *Tortosa*.

[126] The *Ebro*.

[127] If the Oleum is taken to be the *Llastres* (see next n.), this may be, as Berthelot suggests, the *Coll de Balaguer*; if the Oleum is the *Ebro*, it is possibly in the *Serra del Montsià* range located just S of the *Ebro*.

[128] Sometimes taken to be the *Ebro* by another name, but that creates problems for reconciling the subsequent settlements and mountains with the geography of the coastline immediately NE of the *Ebro*, which (from the sea) is largely flat. An alternative candidate is the *Llastres* (anc. *Subi*), which flows into the sea at *L'Hospitalet de L'Infant*. 'Llastres' derives from Oleastrum, which is also the name of a settlement mentioned in Strabo 3. 4. 6, C159 (albeit, with Cherronesus, before the *Ebro*).

[129] C. *Salou* or (if the Oleum is the *Ebro*) a hill inland from *L'Ampolla* (see next n.) such as *Coll de l'Alba*.

[130] Unknown. Schulten places it in the vicinity of mod. *L' Ampolla*, N of the *Ebro*, but the difficulty with this location is that there is no obvious nearby height which could be Mt *Sellus*; the hills inland that could be candidates are some way distant.

[131] This is the sandy bight from C. *Salou* along to *Tarragona*. Salauris and Callipolis would be located within the bight.

[132] *Tarragona* and *Barcelona*. These places are later foundations: Pliny describes Tarraco as founded by the Scipios (3. 3. 21), while Colonia Barcino was an Augustan foundation. Their mention appears to be an insertion by A.

There a harbour spreads out its sheltering reaches,
and the land is always wet with pleasant water.
After that, the harsh Indigetes show themselves:
that tribe is hardy, a fierce tribe in hunting
and one which sticks to its haunts. Then the Celebandic
ridge[133] extends its spine right up to salty Thetis.[134]
It is now only hearsay that here stood the city
of Cypsela: for the rugged land preserves
no traces of the earlier city.

530   There a harbour opens wide in a great gulf,
and the main laps the broad curve of the land.
After that, the shore of the Indigetes[135] slopes down to the sea
As far as the peak of projecting Pyrene.
After that shore, which as I said slopes down
to the sea, Mount Malodes rears itself
amid the waves where two crags stand proud,
and the twin peak seeks the lofty clouds.[136]
Between these lies a large harbour[137]
and the waters are exposed to no breezes.

540   That is so because, since rocky outcrops lie in front of it,
the summits of the crags surround it on all sides
and the motionless gulf lies hidden between the rocks.
The waters lie still: shut in, the ocean is struck dumb.
    Then the lagoon of Tonon lies at the foot of the mountains,
and the ridge of the Tononian cliff rises:
through that region the roaring Anystus river whirls along
its foaming water and cuts through the main with its flow.
These places are near the waves and the salty deep.
All the countryside inland from the flood

550   the Ceretes and the hardy Ausoceretes
previously held.[138] Now, under one name, the tribe

---

[133] *Tossa de Mar* or C. *Begur*. The location of Cypsela is unknown: it could be *San Feliu de Guixol*, the mouth of the *Ter* or *Ullastret*.

[134] The mother of Achilles; hence the sea.   [135] Also mentioned at Pliny 3. iii. 21.

[136] Possibly Mt *Montgó*, at the S end of the gulf of Roses. This could be the 'Mount of Jupiter' identified by Pomponius Mela, 2. 634.

[137] This is the gulf of Roses itself, which provides some protection against winds in all directions. The lagoon of Tonon is to be identified with the marshes between the Fluvia and Muga rivers at the NW point of the gulf (today *Aiguamolls de l'Empordà*); the Anystus is generally taken to be the *Muga*, although (as Berthelot observes) A.'s comments about the river's current are inapposite for the river's mouth.

[138] Inland peoples to be identified with the Carretanians of Strabo 3. 4. 11, C162. Strabo praises these people for their cured ham.

are the Hiberi. Then beyond that point the Sordan
people once lived among out-of-the-way places.
Spreading out right up to the inner sea,
where the pine-bearing crests of the Pyrenees stand
and bear down on the fields on all sides and the flood of the sea,
they lived their lives amid the haunts of beasts.

THE MEDITERRANEAN COAST FROM THE PYRENEES TO MASSALIA, INCLUDING THE RHÔNE

On the border of the Sordicene land
on the flanks of Pyrene, a wealthy city
560   is said once to have stood.[139] Here the inhabitants of Massilia
often used to engage in affairs of business.
    But to Pyrene from the Pillars of Hercules,
from the Atlantic flood and from the edge
of the western shore, is a journey of seven days
for a swift ship.[140] After the Pyrenean range
there lie the sands of the Cynetic shore:[141]
the river Roschinus furrows them over a long distance.[142]
Here is the territory of the Sordiceni, as I have said.
Here, in fact, a lagoon and a swamp extend wide:[143]
570   the inhabitants give it the name of Sordice.
Beyond the rattling waters of its great flood—
for on account of the broad circumference of
its open border, it swells up with stormy winds—
from this very lagoon the river Sordus flows out.
575   From the mouths of this watercourse
    ... (*text corrupt*) ...
578   it is penetrated by the sea, and through its own destruction
the earth is eroded; the waves creep more slowly,
580   and the great bulk of the flood is spread out.

---

[139] Schulten identifies this as Emporion ('trading station', mod. *Empúries*).

[140] This is the first sailing time given for the Mediterranean coast, and one of only two for the Mediterranean, together with that at l. 699. This lends support to the theory that large parts of the Mediterranean portions of the poem come from a different source from the Atlantic portions. Ugolini and Olive suggest that this is to be dated to a C4–C2 land-based journey (Ugolini and Olive 1987).

[141] Unknown. Something appears to have gone wrong: the Cynetes are named as the inhabitants of the Algarve in l. 201 (see n.), but here we have crossed the Pyrenees. Either the text is corrupt or (as Antonelli suggests) it is a clumsy misreading of the description of the Pyrenees, the Celts, and the Cynetes in Hdt. 2. 33.

[142] The *Têt*, which flows through *Perpignan*.

[143] The *Étang de Leucate*; the river Sordus (l. 574) is the *Agly*.

Moreover, three islands of great size stand in it,
And the open sea flows amid the harsh rocks. Not far
from that place where the land is split apart,
another gulf opens up,[144] which surrounds four islands—
an old tradition called these all the Piplae—
with the deep. Once, the tribe of the Elesyces
inhabited these parts,[145] and the city of Narbo[146]
was the great capital of a warlike kingdom.
Here the river Attagus[147] rushes into the salt waters
590   and adjacent here is the marsh of Helice.
An old tradition records that Besara stood next,[148]
but now in fact the Heledus and Orobus rivers[149]
wander through the empty fields and the mounds of ruins,
witnesses to its ancient loveliness.
595   Not far from those the Thyrius is borne into the deep sea
. . . Cinorus (*text corrupt*) . . .[150]
599   ⟨such that⟩ the eddies of the waters are never roused up,
600   and the halcyon calm always levels the flood.[151]
But the peak of this crag extends from this region
to that promontory which I have said is called
Candidum.[152] Nearby is the island of Blasco,
and the land is eroded by the main to a smooth
shape. On the mainland, in between the tops
of the ridges that rise up, a plain of sandy soil
unfolds: these shores stretch out devoid of inhabitants.
   Then high, pine-bearing Mount Setius puffs up
its crest.[153] The ridgeline of Setius stretches up
610   to Taurus, since its foot spreads over a wide area:
to explain, the local people call the marsh

---

[144] The *Étang de Bages-Sigean*; Berthelot suggests that the Piplae are now silted up and part of the mainland.

[145] Hdt. 7. 165 lists this tribe among the Carthaginian allies at the battle of Himera in 480 BC.

[146] *Narbonne.*

[147] The *Aude*. Helice in the next line would then be the *Étang de Vendres*.

[148] *Béziers.* This settlement was only founded in C6e. The description of it as having flourished and then collapsed is another pointer to the later date of the source material for this section.

[149] The Orobus is the *Orb*; the Heledus is possibly the *Lirou*, which joins the *Orb* at *Béziers*.

[150] Thyrius and Cinorus are possibly the *Libron* and the *Hérault* respectively.

[151] The myth of the halcyon days. As told in Ovid, *Metamorphoses* 11. 410–748, Alcyone's husband, Ceyx, was drowned at sea. The gods transformed the couple into kingfishers and quietened the sea for seven days in December while Alcyone brooded on her nest.

[152] 'White'. Identified by Schulten with the *Cap d' Agde*. A. must have referred to it in the corrupt portion of the text. Blasco is *Brescou*, lying off the headland.

[153] *Mont St-Clair*, behind *Sète*. The marsh called Taurus is the *Étang de Thau*.

next to the river Oraris 'Taurus'.[154] The Iberian land
and the rugged Ligyes are separated by the channel
of this river. Here is the city of Polygium,
a rather small town of slender means.
Then there are the village of Mansa and the town of Naustalo[155]

617 and the city ... (*text corrupt*) ...
621 ... and the river Classius flows into its waters.[156]

But the country of Cimenice[157] extends far
from the salty current. The ground covers a wide area,
shaded with woods. The source of the name
is the mountain range with its lofty summits: the Rhodanus
touches the lowest foothills of this, and its waters
wend their way through the rugged mass of the overshadowing range.

The Ligures stretch over a great distance[158]
up to the waves of the inner sea from the crest
630 of Setius and the crags of the rocky ridge.

But the subject almost demands
that I should more fully explain to you
the flow of the Rhodanus.[159] Probus, bear with this discussion
from my lingering pen. I shall speak of the source of the river,
the cascade of the immense flood, the tribes which it laps
with its waves, how great is the gain for the inhabitants
it waters, and the forks of its mouths.

The Alps raise their snowy ridge to the sky
from the sunrise. The fields of the country of Gaul
are divided up by rocky outcrops,
640 and storm winds blow there all the time.[160]

---

[154] I read, following Guillaumin and Bernard ad loc., *Orari* rather than *Orani*. Murphy suggests that this is the *Lez*, but A. says that the marsh is next to the river, and the *Lez* flows into the sea at *Montpellier*, which is too far E. Other candidates for the Oraris might be the *Pallas* and the *Vène*, streams which empty into the *Étang de Thau*.

[155] Berthelot offers for the locations of Polygium, Mansa, and Naustalo *Bouzigues*, *Mèze*, and *Maguelone* respectively.

[156] Possibly either the *Coulazou*, a tributary of the *Mosson*, which feeds into the *Lez*, or one of the rivers which flow into the *Étang de l'Or*, E of *Montpellier*.

[157] The mountain region of *Cévennes*, which lies inland and to the W of the *Rhône*. The mountain which is the 'source of the name' is called Cemmenus by Strabo 4. 1. 1, C177.

[158] While later 'Liguria' came to be applied to the portion of N. Italy between Gaul and Etruria, earlier authors conceived of the Ligurians as extending as far as the *Rhône*; so, for example, Aeschylus imagined Hercules fighting Ligurians there, quoted at Strabo 4. 1. 6, C183.

[159] At ll. 631–99, A. digresses to discuss the source, and course, of the *Rhône*. This is largely a more original synthesis, marked by an antiquarian's interest in using obscure names for tribes and places. As in the prologue, A. addresses Probus directly and makes explicit reference to his 'pen', drawing attention to the digression as A.'s particular composition.

[160] The Mistral.

>   The river pours out bursting forth from the opening
>   of a cave,[161] furrowing the Earth with savage force.
>   It is navigable at the source of its waters and at its very beginning.
>   The tribes name that flank of the rock
>   rising on high, which brings forth the river,
>   the Column of the Sun.[162] That is because from so great
>   an outcrop its great summit reaches right up to the lofty
>   clouds, such that the midday sun cannot be seen
>   from the opposite ridge when it is about to bring back
> 650   the day and approaches the borders of the north.
>   You know that the Epicureans' opinion
>   was of this sort:[163] that the Sun is not brought down
>   at sunset—it enters no flood, is never hidden, but traverses
>   the world, runs through the corners of the sky,
>   gives life to the lands, and nurtures all the vaults
>   of heaven with the fodder of its light,
>   and in turn the white torch of Phoebus
> 657   is denied to the regions in a sure pattern.
>   ... (text corrupt) ...
> 662   When it has cut itself a southern track
>   and turned its light towards the Atlantic clime
>   to bring its fire to the Hyperboreans
>   and carry itself from its Achaemenian[164] rising,
>   it is bent towards other parts of the sky by its curving
>   circuit, and crosses the turning-post. And when the Sun denies
>   its splendour to our sight, horrid night rushes down on the sky,
>   and blind darkness immediately covers our lands.
> 670   But then the bright day shines its light on those
>   who stand stiff beneath the Septentrio.
>   Then, when the shadow of night holds the northern regions,

---

[161] The source of the *Rhône* is in fact the Rhône Glacier, which is not navigable. Sebastian Münster, who visited in 1546, did not notice the *Rhône* bursting through a cave. (An ice grotto has been artificially created since the mid-C19 as a tourist attraction.)

[162] This would be the *Dammastock*, the W side of which is covered by the Rhône Glacier (although, as per the previous note, it is not clear to what extent A.'s account of the source is based on accurate testimony). Antonelli notes that several peaks of the Western Alps (in which the *Rhône* rises) have the name *Sonnenhorn*: such a peak may well have been identified, inaccurately, with the source of the *Rhône*.

[163] A digression from the digression to discuss the motion of the sun. As Murphy observes, A.'s description has more in common with the pre-Socratic Ionian philosophers than with the Epicureans. Contrary to what A. says, Lucretius (*DRN* 5. 650–65) in his exposition of Epicurean doctrine is, in fact, prepared to consider the possibility that the sun sank underground at sunset and returned to the E beneath the land (*DRN* 5. 654 and 658) as one of his alternative explanations for the motions of the sun.

[164] The Hyperboreans were mythical inhabitants of the far N; Achaemenian, i.e. Persian, refers to the E.

the whole of our race enjoys the shining day.
   Then the river passes from its source through the Tylagii,
the Daliterni, the fields of the Clahilcori,
and the Lemenican fields. The names are harsh enough,
and all are wounding when first heard,[165] but you must not
fail to say them, on account of your enthusiasm
and my effort. From there it extends through ten
680   bends in the meandering of its floods, and then
it flows into a sluggish lagoon—many authors report this—
a huge marsh which an old Greek custom used to call
Accion.[166] It drives its waters headlong through
the calm of the lagoon. Then, flowing out
and bending itself into the shape of a river, from there
it is borne into the floods of the Atlantic,
facing our sea and the west, and cuts
through the wide-spreading sands with its five mouths.[167]
There arises the city of Arelatus,[168]
690   called Theline in an earlier age, when the Greeks
inhabited it.
           Many things have compelled me
to treat the Rhodanus at length above.
But my mind is never taken with that
proposition that Europe and Africa are divided
by that river. Phileas may say, and it may be an old proposition,
that the inhabitants thought so:[169] let such barbarian
ignorance be an object of scorn and derision.
   ... (*text corrupt*) ...
       It is a journey of two days and two nights for a ship.[170]
700   From here lie the tribe of the Nearchi, the city of Bergine,[171]
the fierce Salyes, the ancient town of Mastrabala,

---

[165] A. uses obscure or archaic names for Gallic or Germanic tribes. The Tylagii are possibly the *Tulingi* mentioned by Caesar at *BG* 1. 5. 4; Daliterni has been proposed as a name for a tribe around the *Dala*, a tributary of the *Rhône*; of the Clahilcori, nothing is known; and Lemenican (a correction of *Temenicum* in the *editio princeps*: I differ from Antonelli on this point) would refer to the inhabitants of the area around L. *Geneva* (which Caesar, *BG* 1. 8, calls Lake Lemannus).

[166] The *Plaine de Fourques* betweens *Arles* and *Tarascon*, now dry land.

[167] In this view, A. follows Timaeus, as detailed at Strabo 4. 1. 8, C183.

[168] *Arles*. The Greek name of Theline is not otherwise attested in surviving texts.

[169] On Phileas, see n. to 42. Antonelli suggests that Phileas posited the *Rhône* as the border of the 'Ligyes' and that this was misread as 'Libyes', from which the notion that Phileas thought the *Rhône* the border of Europe and Africa may arise.

[170] Berthelot suggests this journey is from the 'wealthy city' of l. 559 as far as the *Rhône* or Massalia. The reference to distance is the first since ll. 564–5; see n. there.

[171] Probably *Berre*, W of Massalia. Mastrabala is likely a settlement on the Étang de Berre.

the marshes, the peak with its projecting back
which the inhabitants call Cecylistrium.[172]
　　And there is Massilia[173] itself. The city's layout is as follows:
the shore lies in front of it; a slender passage
lies amid the waves. The waters bathe the sides;
the lagoon laps the city, and waves extending on all sides
lap the settlement and its dwellings. The city is almost an island,
since to such an extent have men's hands mingled water and land

710　but the careful labour a long time ago of the founders
overcame the shape of the place and the natural terrain
by skill. If at all it pleases you to translate
these old names into new ones [—]
(*text breaks off*)[174]

---

[172] Berthelot suggests this is *L'Estaque*.　　[173] *Marseille*.
[174] The surviving text breaks off midway through A.'s description of Massalia. It is not clear how accurate his description is, or what the source for it is: Antonelli sets out the archaeological evidence. The 'slender passage' (l. 705) may refer to the narrow channel into the old port between *Pointe du Pharo* and *Fort St-Jean*.

33

EXPOSITIO TOTIUS MUNDI ET GENTIUM (ACCOUNT OF THE WHOLE WORLD AND ITS PEOPLES) AND IUNIOR PHILOSOPHUS

(MID-4TH C. AD)

*Richard J. A. Talbert**

INTRODUCTION

There are many obvious questions to ask about this curious Latin work, but few definite answers to them.[1] With the title *Expositio totius mundi et gentium* (*Account of the Whole World and its Peoples*), it survived—incomplete—in only one manuscript, which has been lost since the 17th century. The scholar who found it at an unrecorded location early in that century passed it to a fellow scholar, who passed it in turn to Jacques Godefroy (Jacobus Gothofredus) in Geneva, a formidable Swiss public figure and scholar. His publication of it there in 1628 is painstaking to a fault.[2] The text's deplorable Latin distressed him greatly. In his book he printed it to the right of the vertical line dividing each right-hand page in two. Then to the left of that line he printed his own version in polished Latin. Meantime the entire left-hand page was occupied (in larger type) by his own further translation of the Latin into Greek, because he believed that the work had originally been written in Greek. Loss of the manuscript has long since made it impossible to check how accurately he reproduced its text. Moreover, while there are reasons to suspect that the work as preserved is indeed a translation from another language, which language that may have been remains uncertain; and there is equally the possibility that it may not be a translation at all (see further below). The division of the work into sections that continues standard today was made by Godefroy.

In 1830 the Vatican librarian Angelo Mai prolonged his visit to the library of the Benedictine monastery at Cava, near Salerno (Italy), for an extra day because of heavy rain, and then found there a 12th-century manuscript entitled *Orbis descriptio* (*Description of the Globe*), the work of Iunior Philosophus. Mai published this the following year.[3] As he recognized, it amounts to little more than a précis of the *Expositio* (although in better Latin), but it does include four opening sections and a short

---

* *I acknowledge the advice of Raymond Davis.*

[1] Note the recent discussions by Grüll 2014; Lebreton 2017.   [2] Gothofredus 1628.
[3] In his *Classicorum auctorum e Vaticanis codicibus editorum*, vol. iii (Rome, 1831), 385–409.

concluding one, all of which the manuscript of the *Expositio* had lacked. It has become editors' regular practice, therefore, to graft on these sections from the *Descriptio* when presenting the *Expositio*,[4] and this translation does the same. Nothing else is known of the philosopher Iunior, but he was presumably not the author of the *Expositio*.

In his *Geographi Graeci minores*, Carl Müller presented both texts together for the first time, the *Descriptio* at the top of the page, with the corresponding passage of the *Expositio* below.[5] He reprinted Godefroy's 'Prolegomena', and was able to make use of a second, better manuscript of the *Descriptio*, datable to the early 14th century; he had found this himself in the Bibliothèque Nationale, Paris.

The Latin text of the *Expositio* translated here is that of Jean Rougé's thoughtful, painstaking edition (1966), which presents the corresponding passage of the *Descriptio* below on each page. Rougé offers a lengthy introduction and notes, as well as a translation into French. He is also the first editor to take into account a third manuscript of the *Descriptio*, one reckoned to be of 12th-century date, that had been found in the Spanish national library in Madrid. For the *Expositio*, however, there is still nothing more than Godefroy's edition. The two existing English translations—Vassiliev (1936) and Woodman (1964)—both predate Rougé's edition, and are overdue for replacement. A German translation by Peter Franz Mittag based on Rougé's text with some amendments appeared in 2011.[6]

Suspicion that the *Expositio* is a translation from another language stems from the occurrence of many Greek words in one form or other, as well as of Greek and Semitic grammatical constructions: consequently, Greek, Hebrew or Syriac could have been the original language of the work. Yet the notion of a translation can equally well be dismissed. In that event, while the author's native language was no doubt Greek or Semitic, he also had a working grasp of Latin and for whatever reason chose to write in that language, even if still in a distinctly Greek or Semitic style.[7] Either way, the Latin has a gauche character, often ungrammatical, which (I confess) seems impossible to replicate adequately. Readers should be cautioned, therefore, that the style and syntax of the English being presented to them are of superior quality to the Latin prose from which the translation derives. In particular, I offer a comprehensible formulation in the many instances where the meaning of the Latin is unclear as a consequence of either the author's bad grammar or copyists' slips, or both. However, such best guesses at his meaning may not be invariably correct. By contrast, the sense of his repetitiveness, as well as his limited vocabulary, can still be conveyed.

The *Expositio* can at least be dated approximately (or, if we have a translation made at some later date, the original work can be). It must postdate Constantine's refoundation

---

[4] As did Alexander Riese in his *Geographi Latini minores* (Heilbronn, 1878), 104–26, who otherwise omits the *Descriptio* from his collection.

[5] *GGM* ii. 513–28, with 'Prolegomena' at pp. xliv–li.

[6] *FGH* V, no. 2023 Iunior Philosophus.

[7] Note that, at a much more elevated level, the easterner Ammianus Marcellinus opted to write his lengthy history in Latin.

of Byzantium as Constantinople, and his major construction activity there (around 330), praised in §50. Then mention of Nisibis as a Roman city, celebrated for its successful repulse of all Persian efforts to take it (§22), can fairly be reckoned to predate its handover to Persia in 363 following Julian's disastrous Mesopotamian campaign—a loss bitterly lamented by the contemporary historian Ammianus Marcellinus (25. 7. 11). To date the *Expositio* to around the mid-4th century seems reasonable, therefore.

The author of the *Expositio* offers next to no clues to his identity, so his background and profession, where he wrote, and with what audience in mind can only be inferred from the work itself. At the start, he casts himself as a father attempting to advance an unnamed son's education and prospects, but this self-identification could simply be a pose. By the same token, the confused mention of a half-dozen philosophers and historians in §3 is presumably just name-dropping, because the tone of the work overall is far from learned, although it does often reflect some historical awareness. The opening sentence promises 'astonishing inquiries—some arising from autopsy, others from accounts by experts that I have heard, and certain ones learned from reading'. Yet to distinguish in what follows between these three types of source is hardly possible. In particular, the ring of personal experience or engagement is persistently lacking. Rather, platitudes abound, and the insights offered are shallow. Non-Romans and their behaviour are mostly disparaged for one reason or other, whereas the opinions expressed of places and peoples within Roman territory are almost all laudatory. Altogether, the author identifies strongly with Rome, Roman power, and Roman values, but without elaboration; so, for example, no comment is made on why emperors should live where they do, in Antiochia, Pannonia, and Triveris (§§32, 57–8). The author shows no special concern for religion, but at least his remarks about deities, myths, and festivals make it most unlikely that he was Christian or Jewish.[8]

In its coverage, and in the relative amount of attention given to the places and peoples described, the work is preoccupied with the East far more than the West. Whether it follows therefore that the author was an easterner, rather than a westerner who wanted to draw special attention to the East, is impossible to establish, although he has commonly been identified as an easterner. The work begins with a succession of largely fabulous peoples in the Far East, next advances rapidly through India and Persia, then becomes fuller once 'our' (Roman) territory is reached in Mesopotamia, Osrhoene, and Syria (§22). Because Syria and Palestine are the region of the empire in which the most cities are mentioned (twenty in all), the natural inference has been drawn that it was the author's home region, but this too can only be plausible conjecture. In view of the exceptionally favourable reference made with pride to the character and talents of men from Pontus, Paphlagonia, Cappadocia, and Galatia and their leading role at both

---

[8] The translation omits a few passages that blatantly reflect a Christian outlook; these must be additions made to the original at some stage. In a few further instances where editors have found cause to suspect that a passage is a later addition to the original, the translation omits it if it adds little or nothing of substance.

Western and Eastern imperial courts (§44), one could equally infer that the author came from this part of Asia Minor.

The course which the work takes beyond Syria and Palestine—mostly by Roman province or geographical region—reflects an interesting, yet puzzling, world-view on the author's part.[9] He proceeds next to Egypt, which he states to be 'on the left-hand side of Syria' (§34), and then to Arabia ('to the right of Syria and above', §38), thus indicating a perspective oriented north. This is by no means the norm in antiquity, although it happens to be shared by Ptolemy in his *Geography* and by the Peutinger Map. Alexandria warrants special attention. Next come the regions of Asia Minor from Cilicia to Bithynia. Then come Thrace and the regions of Greece from Macedonia round to Epeiros. Dalmatia gains token mention next, followed at once with similar brevity by Calabria, Bruttium, Lucania, and Campania (§§53–4). 'After it (*Campania*) is Italy', states the author curiously. Here the only region named is Tuscia; Rome warrants special attention. Then he offers the briefest coverage of Moesia, Dacia, Pannonia (bordered by the Danube river), and Noricum (categorized as a city), followed by marginally more attention to Gaul and Spain, although in neither is any region named, let alone any river. From here, the author continues through Africa eastwards from Mauretania back to Alexandria. Appended almost as an afterthought are brief, eclectic references to 'islands situated in the open sea', again from east to west: Cyprus, the Cyclades and others in their vicinity, Crete, Cythera, Zacynthus, Cephalonia, Sicily, one whose name is irrecoverable, Sardinia, and Britannia—this last described as briefly and favourably as Sardinia (§§66–7).

It is natural to ask whether the author used a map or some comparable image, but the means to determine with confidence whether or not he did so is lacking. On balance, the likelihood must surely be that he did not use one, especially given the typical lack of interest in maps even among Romans far better educated than he seems to be.[10] His was a mental map.[11]

The geographical grasp he assumes on his own part and that of his son or audience is a related matter. Notably, he distinguishes between the regions east of the Roman empire and those within it by stating the extent of each people's territory in the former, expressed as the number of days' journey required to traverse it—information somehow at his disposal but, it seems, in his view unlikely to be familiar to others. For regions within the empire, by contrast, he offers no such information. It is true that Alexandria and Nicopolis are mentioned for their sea-fish, the Danube river as separating Pannonia from the Sarmatians, and Spain as bordering the Ocean (§§35, 53, 57, 59). However, there is not even the most cursory reference to such major defining physical features of the Roman world as the Mediterranean, Adriatic, Aegean, or Black Seas, the Alps, Pyrenees, or Taurus mountains, or the Euphrates, Po, Rhine, or Rhône

---

[9] For comparison with other geographic works, see Salway 2012, 214–17.
[10] See, for example, Talbert 2017, 340–2, and references there.
[11] Further discussion by Lebreton 2017, 282–5.

rivers. Yet presumably the author did not imagine that, for example, it was just a land journey from Dyrrachium to Calabria and Bruttium (§53), or from Arelatus to Triveris (§58). Even so, it remains an open question whether his grasp of the West was genuinely as sketchy as we may be tempted to infer, or whether his perfunctory coverage of it towards the end is just the consequence of his deliberate effort to fix attention primarily on the East while not ignoring the West altogether.

From our perspective, an unquestionably distinctive aspect of the work is the author's interest in the crops, products, commerce, and manpower of provinces, regions, and cities as well as in the cults, architecture, and entertainments of the latter. To be sure, most of what he has to say on these topics is general, unremarkable, and uncritical. However, his repeated references to the production and trading of textiles, dyes, and clothing in both East and West are striking. At the least they must reflect a special interest of his, or of a source (written or oral) on which he opted to rely throughout. Does it follow that he was himself involved professionally in these activities?[12] Maybe, although in that case he might be expected to mention even a few figures or details, which he never does. Last but not least, the work offers no clear indication of what audience its author had in mind for the work beyond himself and his son. Quite possibly he never intended that it should circulate further.

SELECTED FURTHER READING

Grüll, T. (2014), 'Expositio totius mundi et gentium: a peculiar work on the commerce of Roman empire from the mid-fourth century—compiled by a Syrian textile dealer?', in Z. Csabai (ed.), *Studies in Economic and Social History of the Ancient Near East in Memory of Péter Vargyas* (Budapest), 629–42.

Lebreton, S. (2017), 'Cartes et discours géographiques: à propos de l'Expositio totius mundi et gentium', in N. Bouloux *et al.* (eds), *Orbis disciplinae: hommages en l'honneur de Patrick Gautier Dalché*, 281–309. Turnhout.

*Mittag, P. F. (2011), 'Iunior Philosophus (2023)', in *FGrH* v. [The main commentary, however, will be by Ruffing (below).]

*Rougé, J. (1966), *Expositio totius mundi et gentium: introduction, texte critique, traduction, notes et commentaire*. Paris.

*Ruffing, K. (forthcoming), 'Expositio totius mundi et gentium (2020)', in *FGrH* v.

Salway, B. (2012), 'Putting the world in order: mapping in Roman texts', in R. J. A. Talbert (ed.), *Ancient Perspectives: Maps and their Place in Mesopotamia, Egypt, Greece, and Rome* (Chicago), 193–234.

Vassiliev, A. A. (1936), 'Expositio totius mundi: an anonymous geographic treatise of the fourth century AD', *Seminarium Kondakovianum*, 8: 1–39.

Woodman, J. E. (1964), 'The Expositio totius mundi et gentium: its geography and its language.' MA thesis, Ohio State University.

---

[12] On the 'hellenistic' character of the author's economic categories, see Ruffing 2004.

TEXT

Headings are added.

PREFACE

1. Dearest son, after all the sound recommendations I have given you for improving your way of life, I now wish to begin telling you about a great number of astonishing inquiries—some arising from autopsy, others from accounts by experts that I have heard, and certain ones learned from reading. So, with a mental grasp of this material not only will you learn much of value, but you will also succeed in enhancing your knowledge thanks to the variety of such matters.

2. Intent as we are upon writing, we should state first the disposition of peoples from the East all the way to the West; then how many types of barbarian there are, then the entirety of Roman territory—the number of provinces worldwide, their resources and strength; what cities are in each province, and what is of special note in each individual province or city. This is a work that I consider to be well motivated and scholarly.

PEOPLES OF THE EAST

3. So where else should we begin except with the Magi first? Those predecessors of ours who tried to write about these matters were able to make some contribution; later, information about provinces and periods was supplied by the Chaldaean philosopher Berosus and his literary successor the Egyptian prophet Manethon, also Apollonius, likewise an Egyptian philosopher. Otherwise, the Ephesian Menander and Herodotus and Thucydides wrote comparable works, but not really about the distant past. So much for their contributions. Now I for my part will try to summarize for you what those I have just mentioned wrote.

4. The Camarini people are said to be located in eastern regions, where also, according to reports, a really great river reaches its mouth. These are notably devout, fine people, free of all vices, physical or mental. Should you want more definite information, accounts say that they don't make use of normal bread like ours, let alone comparable food or fuel like the fire we use. Instead, we are told, bread rains down on them day-by-day, and they drink wild honey and pepper. Their fire is provided by the sun and with such intensity[13] that, as soon as it spreads over the earth from the sky, they are all liable to be burnt up unless they quickly plunge into the river, where they stay until this fire goes back again to where it belongs.   5. Evidently they are not subjects, but autonomous. Their food is not like that of everyone else. This is because they do not have our bodily defects. Among them, fleas, lice, bugs, and nits are not to be

---

[13] Reading *flagrantiae* rather than *fragrantiae*.

found, nor any sickness of the body. Their clothes, too, are not like those of everyone else. In fact so perfect is their clothing that it cannot be dirtied. Should that happen, they clean it close to a fire, since it is improved by being heated.   6. They neither sow nor reap. They have first-rate resources, a wide range of high-value ones such as precious stones, namely in the mountains emeralds, pearls, jacinths, and carbuncles and sapphires. These all emerge in the following way: the river in its course flows along in the mountains day and night, and cuts away mountain-tops by flooding their slopes with quantities of water. The people closest are ingenious enough to have found a means of discovering what is produced as a result; by placing nets where the river narrows, they collect whatever comes into these.   7. In such favourable circumstances they neither work nor fall ill; uniquely, when they die, they know on what day that will happen. They all die aged 118 and 120; an older person does not see a younger one die, nor parents their sons. With advance knowledge of the day they will die, each individual makes a coffin from a range of scented woods—they have plenty of these, of all kinds—lies in it and awaits what removes their life. When the moment is impending, they greet everyone, bid them all farewell, and calmly expire. I have given only a partial account of this people's good fortune; there is much that I could have said, but have omitted. The territory they occupy is the length of a seventy-day journey.[14]

8. After this people, what else is there? Moving West, there is where the Braxmani live. These people are not subjects; they manage their affairs well and maintain their neighbours' goodwill. The territory they occupy is the length of a five-day journey.   9. Next after them comes another region, that of the Euiltae. They too are not subjects and live the life almost of gods. The territory they occupy is the length of a thirty-two-day journey.   10. After them comes another people, whose name is Emer. They do not live as subjects, and behave in a law-abiding way. The territory they occupy is the length of a forty-seven-day journey.   11. After them is a region called Nebus, the first one where there are despots; its rulers are elders. It is the length of a sixty-day journey.

12. From here onwards sowing and reaping occur. With the exception of the Camarini, the people mentioned thus far live on fruit, pepper, and honey. Camarini receive bread daily from heaven. Among them without exception, rage is unknown, nobody brings a lawsuit, and there are no brawls; nor is there avarice or treachery or any wicked behaviour.

13. The region next to the Nebus people is Disaph, whose inhabitants are governed well, as are their neighbours. The territory they occupy is the length of a 240-day journey.   14. Next is a people called Choneum, a community whose way of life matches that of their neighbours; hence they think it a good life because it is not different. The territory they occupy is the length of a 120-day journey.   15. Then comes the Diua people, ruled likewise by elders; the territory they occupy is the length of a 210-day journey.   16. Then comes Greater India, the source, we are told, of silk and every vital item.

---

[14] Literally, from here through §18 a territory's extent is reckoned in terms of how many overnight stays at a *mansio* (stopping-place with lodging) would be required to traverse the distance.

The people here live like their neighbours and manage their affairs well. The territory they occupy is a large, fine one, the length of a 210-day journey.   17. The region situated next is Exomia: its men are said to be brave, very energetic warriors, and altogether versatile. Lesser India, whenever under attack from Persians, seeks help from here. They (*Exomians*) have everything in profusion. The territory they occupy is the length of a 150-day journey.   18. After them is Lesser India, where the people are ruled by elders; they have elephants beyond number, and for this reason Persians acquire their elephants from them. The territory they occupy is the length of a fifteen-day journey.

19. After these are the Persians, the Romans' neighbours. By all accounts they are noted for every kind of wickedness and for being brave warriors. They are also said to be perpetrators of major sacrilege. Without regard for what is naturally fitting, like dumb creatures they sleep with their mothers and sisters, and behave profanely towards the god who made them. Otherwise, however, they are said to have plenty of everything; evidently this complete abundance stems from their ability to do business with the peoples bordering their region.

20. Near them live the Sarraceni people, whose hope is to support themselves by bowmanship and rape. Like Persians, they are sacrilegious perjurers, uncommitted to any agreement they make on campaign or in any other dealing. It is further said that their rulers are women.

ROMAN PROVINCES

21. So that is an inquirer's report on the peoples mentioned thus far. With the need now to cover our territory too—Roman, that is—I shall attempt to offer an account that can be helpful to its readers. Let us begin therefore.

Mesopotamia and Osdroena

22. After these peoples it is our territory. Mesopotamia and Osdroena come first. Mesopotamia has many different cities, of which I want to mention the outstanding ones. These are Nisibis and Edessa, whose men are the best in all respects, both very sharp in matters of business and fine huntsmen. In particular, they are wealthy and have a complete range of goods at their disposal. They import from the Persians and sell throughout Rome's entire territory; whatever they buy, they then trade again, except for bronze and iron, because providing the enemy with bronze or iron is illegal. Thanks to the wisdom of the gods and the emperor, their cities are always in good order, their walls are celebrated, and in war the Persians just waste their worth on them. They are energetic businessmen, and their relationship with the entire province is a good one. Then Edessa itself in Osdroena is a splendid city.

Syria

23. Next the entire region of Syria is now divided into three Syrias: Punica and Palestina and Coela. These have various superb great cities, and it will please my audience

if I mention some of them. First is Antiochia, a royal city, excellent in every respect, the residence too of a world-ruler. This is a fine-looking city, renowned for its public buildings; it draws masses of people from every direction, and can support them all. Its resources are altogether plentiful.

24. Tyrus, like the other cities, throbs with trading activity of all kinds, and is exceptionally flourishing; probably no other city in the East is as densely populated; it has wealthy businessmen of outstanding ability in all respects.

25. Next is Berytus, a really delightful city with its law-schools which ensure the universal maintenance of Roman courts. Experts from here advise judges worldwide, and with their legal knowledge protect the provinces; the texts of laws are sent to them.

26. Likewise delightful is the city of Caesarea, with everything plentiful there, and a location for the city outstanding in many respects. Everyone has heard of its tetrapylon, a unique and unusual sight.

27. Of all the other cities, the names of at least some should be mentioned because they have notable individual points. So there is the fine city of Laodicia, a commercial hub which exports to Antiochia and has rendered outstanding assistance to the military.

28. Seleucia is likewise a first-rate city which offers all its imports to Antiochia, already mentioned, as well as taxes and private contributions. The emperor Constantine, world-ruler, realizing its value to himself and his army, split a huge mountain, let in the sea, and made a great, fine harbour (*portus*) where incoming ships might shelter and the government's cargoes escape loss.

29. Now for all the other cities. Ascalon and Gaza, superior cities and thriving centres of commerce with plenty of everything, export to everywhere in Syria as well as sending the finest wine to Egypt.

30. Neapolis is a glorious, thoroughly noble city. Tripolis and Scythopolis and Byblus are bustling cities. Heliopolis next to Mount Libanus produces beautiful women—everyone calls them Libanitides (*daughters of Lebanon*)—and maintains a superb cult of Venus; they claim that she resides there and bestows the gift of beauty on women. Further likewise outstanding cities are Sidon, Sarepta, Ptolemais and Eleutheropolis; so, too, is Damascus.

31. So, now that we have offered a partial description of the cities mentioned and have stated ... ⟨*text missing*⟩[15] Noted for their cloth are: Scythopolis, Laodicia, Byblus, Tyrus, Berytus; they export cloth worldwide and stand out for their full range of resources. A comparable reputation for genuine purple-dyed cloth is enjoyed by Sarepta, Caesarea, and Neapolis, as well as by Lydda. All the cities mentioned are famous for their bumper crops of grain, wine, and oil. In the Palestina region—at the location actually called Jericho—they have the Nicolaus date, likewise the Damascus date and another smaller one, as well as pistachios and every sort of fruit.

---

[15] In the corresponding passage of the *Descriptio* the author moves on to say that he will now go into detail about individual cities.

32. Since their distinctive features ought to be described, I must state what it is that makes individual cities delightful. Take Antiochia with its wealth of every kind of delight, circuses above all. Why every kind? Because this is an emperor's residence, and for him there must be everything. To be sure, Laodicia, too, and Tyrus, Berytus, and Caesarea have circuses. But Laodicia sends the best charioteers to other cities, Tyrus and Berytus mimes, Caesarea pantomimes, and Heliopolis pipers—mainly because the Muses on Mount Libanus inspire them with divine powers of expression. Sometimes too, Gaza has fine spokesmen and, so it is said, pancratists; also Ascalon has athletic wrestlers, and Castabala trapeze-artists.

33. These cities all depend on their commerce, they have men gifted in every way, including their speech, energy and valour. Their climate, too, is mild. This is as much as I have to say about Syria. There is plenty we have omitted so as not to give the impression of going on unseasonably, and to allow the chance to write about other regions and cities too.

Egypt

34. So, on the left-hand side of Syria you have the regions of Egypt, Alexandria, and the entire Thebais: these must now be described. You have the entire region of Egypt garlanded by the river called the Nile, which advances to water the entire expanse of land so that every kind of crop grows except olives—plenty of wheat, barley, vegetables, and vines. Similarly, the men here are outstanding, in their worship of the gods especially. Nowhere else are the divine mysteries conducted like here right from antiquity to the present; it is from here virtually that the whole world has learned how to worship the gods. The Chaldaeans' way is said to be better, but our admiration is for those we have seen,[16] and we claim that they are the best in all respects. We know, too, that gods once lived there and even still do. According to some, letters were their (*Egyptian*) invention, although others say it was a Chaldaean one, others still a Punic one, and there are those who urge that Mercury was the one to invent letters. Amid these many claims, no-one knows the truth or can be believed. This said, Egypt does have more sages than anywhere else in the world. In its capital Alexandria you will find every sort of philosopher and every type of learning. Thus at some point when there was a competition organized between Egyptians and Greeks over which should have the Museum, the Egyptians emerged as the sharper and more mature, so they won and the Museum was awarded to them. On any topic you like it is impossible to find anyone as expert as an Egyptian. This is why all the superior philosophers and experts on literary culture have always stayed there. With them there is no pretentiousness. Rather, each of them is the master of what he professes. Far from any claiming to be omniscient, each minds his own business, striving to gain a polished grasp of his specialty.

35. Alexandria is definitely the largest city, with a superior layout and everything in plenty, food especially. In fact, unlike in any other province, three types of fish are

[16] i.e. the Egyptians.

eaten here—from river, lake, and sea. There is every kind of product here, including spices and certain commodities acquired through trade with barbarians. Beyond the border of Thebais the city has contact with the Indian people, and everything it imports it then exports in all directions. Worship of the gods is very prominent, and the temple of Serapis is here, in all the world a singular, unique, unusual sight. Nowhere else on Earth is such a structure or temple layout or sacred space to be found. It seems to be universally known that the Museum belongs here.

36. Amid all Alexandria's resources, one is found only there and in its region, something indispensable for managing courts and private business, indeed evidently depended upon by almost the entire human race. And what is this that we are praising so? It's the sheets[17] that the city itself manufactures and exports worldwide, demonstrating its value to all. Despite being unique among all cities and provinces in having this product, it includes it among its exports ungrudgingly. Again unlike any other province, it has the Nile's generosity—the Nile being a river that, as it flows down in summertime, soaks the entire land and makes it ready for sowing. The people there derive great benefit from this sowing: one measure yields 100 to 120 measures. And because the land is this productive every year, it is of service to other provinces too. Thus Constantinople in Thrace is fed by it almost entirely, so also the regions of the East, principally because of the emperor's army and the war with the Persians, and because the only province with sufficient capacity is divine Egypt. I term it so because I think it receives particular favour from the gods, and, as already mentioned, its worshippers render special service by so ably offering images of them. It has sacred sites and its temples are fully decorated; there are numerous temple-guardians, priests, attendants, diviners, and worshippers, as well as the best devotees. Everything, too, proceeds in orderly fashion: so there you will find altars always glowing with fire, sacrifices, and incense in plenty, also headbands, and divine fragrance wafting from censers filled with spices.

37. You will also find it to be a city noted for disciplining governors; the readiness with which the people of Alexandria show them disrespect is unique. This is a city that governors enter with fear and trembling, because they fear the justice of a populace which does not hesitate to let loose firebrands and stones on crooked governors. The city and its region are altogether impossible to comprehend. Among the whole world's cities, there is almost no match for the amount of philosophical truth here, where so many schools of philosophers are to be found. Hence Aesculapius willingly bestowed on it the expertise in medicine which it has. He deigned to provide it with the best doctors anywhere on Earth, so much so that this city is very widely acknowledged to be the source of health for mankind. Its climate, too, is very mild. This is as much as I have to say about the region and city above; to write a complete account is impossible.

---

[17] i.e. of papyrus, the pith of a Nile marsh-plant, which was cut into strips to make the ancient equivalent of paper today.

Arabia

38. Next to the right again of Syria and above you will find Arabia. Its greatest city is Bostra, which is said to be a major commercial centre, as well as being near the Persians and Saraceni, and having a tetrapylon which is much admired among its public buildings.

Asia Minor

39. Next again is the region of Cilicia, which brings joy to other provinces with its large-scale production of wine, and has a fine great city called Tarsus.

40. After this in an upper part is Cappadocia, with its outstanding men and Caesarea its greatest city. The cold here is said to be really intense, such that for those without local knowledge life here is impossible unless they show some ingenuity. However, opportunities for trade here are excellent and exports apparently go everywhere, including hare-fur clothing and beautiful specimens of 'Babylonian' hides and those divine creatures.[18]

41. Next to be encountered is the fine, self-sufficient province of Galatia. It trades clothing on a major scale, and periodically provides rulers with fine soldiers. Its greatest city is called Ancyra, where apparently they consume quite remarkable divine bread.

42. Then there is Phrygia, also a fine region whose men are brave according to the writers of old, Homer, Vergil, and others, who describe the war between these Phrygians and the Greeks. The greatest city is said to be Laodicia, which exports a single-piece costume specifically called by the name Laodicene.

43. Next above here there is Lesser Armenia, which, we are told, provides cavalrymen and archers fit for campaigns.

44. Then are Paphlagonia and Pontus, the home of wealthy men really distinguished for their learning and all their resources like Cappadocians and Galatians. Their women are lovely too. By all accounts they are so lovely and so very pale that the sight of them creates the impression they are goddesses. As for men, the provinces and cities just mentioned—Pontus, Paphlagonia, Galatia, Cappadocia—produce clever men too. Should you want confirmation of their cleverness, look to the two courts of East and West, and there you will find more men from Pontus, Paphlagonia, Cappadocia, and Galatia than from any other city or province. Hence the impression is created that matters are handled by them on the emperors' instructions. They are very trustworthy, and they reckon Nature's riches to be intrinsically good; hence they are impelled to assist their superiors and their betters. At this point, however, I have spoken enough about them, and shall begin on what is to be said next.

45. The regions concerned are inland. But there is the need to point out areas with a seaboard, namely Cilicia and then Isauria, whose men evidently are brave; they also

---

[18] Horses may be meant.

attempted brigandage periodically, even aiming to be hostile to the Romans, but they were unable to beat their invincible name. After this is Pamphylia, a fine, self-sufficient region whose extensive production of olive-oil serves other regions also. It has two superb cities, Perge and Side.

46. After it is the self-sufficient region of Lycia. It has a truly massive mountain called Caucasus; according to reports, this mass is unsurpassed anywhere else on Earth.

47. After Lycia is Caria. So here we are in Asia, which stands out as the greatest of all the provinces and has countless cities. These include very large ones and many on the sea, two of which must be specified: Ephesus, which is said to have an exceptional harbour, as well as the superb city of Smyrna. The entire region is vast, and productive in every way, with different wines, oil, rice, fine purple and spelt. It really is marvellous, and thus difficult to praise enough.

48. After this is the Hellespont, a productive region with an abundance of grain, wine and oil. It has those ancient cities Troy and Ilium, and—larger than them—Cyzicus, which exceeds all praise for its location, size, grandeur and loveliness. For it was here that Venus, equipped with Cupid's dart, opted to bestow beauty on women.

49. After the Hellespont one finds marvellous Bithynia, the greatest and finest (*of regions*), which produces every kind of crop. It has the marvellous great cities Nicaea and Nicomedia. Nicaea's city-plan is one hard to find elsewhere; its uniformity and loveliness make one think that it has been applied to the entire city with a ruler, and it is altogether magnificent and permanent. Nicomedia, too, is superb, marvellous and thoroughly prosperous. Its fine civic building is an ancient basilica, which is said to have been ignited by divine fire coming down from the sky, and was subsequently restored by Constantine. It has a circus, a specially fine structure for watching the circus shows, which are a serious attraction.

Thrace to the Adriatic

50. Next after Bithynia is the province of Thrace, it too made wealthy by its crops, and with outstanding men, brave warriors; for this reason, soldiers are often recruited here. It has the superb cities Constantinople and Heraclea.[19] At one time this Constantinople used to be Byzantium, (*but then*) Constantine bestowed his name on the city he founded. Heraclea's excellent buildings are a theatre and a royal palace. Thanks to Constantine, Constantinople has lots of outstanding things. What's more, spectators here watch the circus shows most passionately.

51. Moving on from Thrace you will encounter Macedonia which, with its full resources, has an export trade in iron and feathers,[20] also sometimes bacon and Dardanian cheese; Dardania is a neighbouring region. It has, too, the superb city of Thessalonica, which ranks among the distinguished ones.

---

[19] Named Perinthus prior to C3l AD.   [20] For pillows.

52. After Macedonia there is Thessaly, which produces ample grain and for other commodities is said to be self-sufficient. It has Mount Olympus, which according to Homer is the home of the gods.

After Thessaly is the land of Achaia, Graecia, and Laconica, which has schools, though otherwise is not self-sufficient, since it is confined and mountainous and has only limited productive capacity. But it does yield oil from meagre resources as well as Attic honey, yet it has more cause to take pride in learning and oratory, and nowhere near as much in anything else. The cities it has are Corinth and Athens. Corinth is a very thriving commercial city, and its amphitheatre a remarkable structure. Athens, in addition to its schools and ancient literature, has something else that merits mention, namely an arch which is a marvellous sight with many standing statues representing a war of old. Laconica's resources are reckoned to be limited to Crocinus stone, which is called Lacedaemonian.

53. To be found next after Achaia are the regions of Epirus and the city which is thus called Epirus; some call the province Epirus, others Aetolia. After this city, the city of Nicopolis has so much fish caught from the sea that even the sight of a quantity of them proves repellent. Next, a little further up, is Dalmatia, reckoned to be outstanding for business. Three useful products that it has plenty of for export are Dalmatian cheese, roofing-timber, and also iron. It has the superb city of Salona. A god destroyed Dyrrachium because of its people's vice, or more probably, according to the accounts, it sank (*into the sea*) and disappeared.

Italy

Next, in order, are provinces: Calabria which, since it produces wheat, has everything in plenty; then Bruttium, outstanding for its export trade in woollen clothing[21] and a large amount of outstanding wine; after Bruttium, Lucania, an outstanding region; it too has everything in plenty, and exports bacon far and wide because in its mountains there are all kinds of food for animals.

54. After this is the province of Campania; although not a specially large one, it has wealthy men and is self-sufficient, as well as being a storeroom for Rome the ruler.

55. After it is Italy, which displays its glory when mentioned by just this word or name. It has many different cities, all of them with ample resources, and Foresight is its ruler. In Italy you will find many types of wine: Picene, Sabine, Tiburtine, Tuscan; in fact Tuscia—whose loveliness we shall describe shortly—borders the province just mentioned. So Italy with its incomparable prosperity also possesses this, the greatest of resources: the greatest, most outstanding and royal city, which is called Rome, a name that displays its strength.[22] Romulus is said to have founded it as a boy. It is enormous

---

[21] The rare Latin word here, *byrrus*, is used elsewhere of a woollen overcoat worn in Britain and Gaul: see Grüll 2014, 635 n. 8.

[22] Greeks were impressed by the coincidence that the name 'Rome' was their word for strength or force.

and filled with quite divine buildings. All previous emperors, and the present ones too, have wanted to leave their mark there in one way or other, and so each commissions a construction-project named for himself. Should Antoninus be of interest to you, you will find any number of his projects; consider too the forum named after Trajan, which has a superb, famous basilica. There is also a well-sited circus much enhanced by bronze (*ornaments*). In Rome are the seven virgins of free birth from senatorial families who conduct ceremonies in honour of the gods for the city's preservation, in accordance with the practice of the ancients; they are called Vestal Virgins. Likewise it has the well-known river Tiber, which is valuable to the city just mentioned; after passing through there, it reaches the sea, and serves as the means by which everything imported from abroad is conveyed as far as eighteen miles upstream. Hence the city has all resources in plenty. It also has the greatest senate of wealthy men. Should you care to investigate them individually, you will find that all were, or will be, governors, or have the potential but are unwilling to exercise it because of a wish to live risk-free enjoying what they have. The gods they worship are, for example, Jupiter, Sol, and others. They are said also to perform rites for the Mother of the Gods; it is certain that they have diviners.

56. After this you come to the neighbouring region of Tuscia. Tuscia is quite the greatest of names bestowed by the gods. It is said that the origin of divination is to be found here, and this was said to be a benefit from the gods. It does have every resource in plenty as well as, above all, marked capacity to divine the gods' will: certainty in this matter is said to be theirs. So much for Rome and Tuscia. Italy has other superb cities, those called Aquileia and Mediolanum.

Danube lands

57. So after Italy we should mention provinces and cities omitted earlier. Moesia and Dacia are self-sufficient provinces, but really cold ones; their major city is called Naissus. Then there is the region of Pannonia, a land rich in all respects—crops, livestock and commerce, some of it in slaves. It is also where emperors regularly live. It has two major cities, Sirmium as well as Noricum, from which Norican clothing is said to be exported. So much for the region of Pannonia. Bordering it across the river Danube is a barbarian people, the Sarmatians.

Gaul

58. After Pannonia is the province of Gaul which, because of its immense size, is in constant need of an emperor and has one of its own. It is amply supplied with everything because he is here, but prices are very high. It is said to have a major city called Triveris (*Trier*), an inland one, where they say a ruler resides. Equally, it has another city which supports it (*Triveris*) in every way, on the coast, whose name is Arelatus, which imports commodities from across the world and then exports them to the city just mentioned. The entire region has brave, outstanding men; so in war an army of Gauls is said to be very large and brave. In all respects it is an admirable province. Bordering it is a barbarian people, the Goths.

Spain

59. From Gaul, next is Spain, a vast, very great, wealthy territory, provided with educated men and altogether thriving commercially, as we can illustrate from such exports—in sufficient quantities for the whole world—as oil, fish-sauce, clothing of different types, bacon and livestock. Along with such complete resources, and all of outstanding quality, it also has rope of quality unrivalled anywhere: this is a product widely regarded as essential, because it secures every type of ship and thus affects all commerce. Yet many do not agree, and regard (*Spain*) as a weak region.

After this is said to be the Ocean, a part of it which no human can describe. After all, what can be there? It is, as they say, a waste, and it's here that the world ends.

African provinces and beyond

60. Next, turning to southern land, you will find the land of Mauretania. Its inhabitants have the lifestyle and morals of barbarians, despite being Roman subjects. This province trades in clothing and slaves, has plenty of grain, and the city of Caesarea. After Mauretania, next is Numidia, a province of bumper crops and self-sufficient, also commercially active in clothing of various types and top-quality animals.

61. After this province one finds Africa, a wealthy region in all respects; it is provided with every resource, including crops and livestock, and almost on its own it supplies oil for every people's use. While it has many different cities, one called Kartago is quite outstanding and marvellous; it was founded by a Tyrian woman named Dido, who on coming to Libya purchased an area called Byrsa, as large as a cow-hide could enclose, says Virgil.[23] Its layout is quite magnificent, and it has a harbour which makes an incomparably unusual sight and evidently provides—in complete security—a calm briny[24] that ships need not fear. You will also find a superb civic structure there, a silversmiths' quarter. For entertainment there is just one type of show that the inhabitants insistently press for: gladiatorial games. Outstanding, fine and wealthy the region of Africa may be, but its men are not worthy of their homeland: they do not live up to the region's many good things. The word is that not a single one of them can be trusted—they say one thing, but do another. It is hard to find a good man among them, although there may be a few good ones among so many.

62. Next, bordering the entire region of Africa, is a vast desert land to the South; according to reports, in a very small part of this desert live wretched barbarian people called Mazices and Aethiopes. After them one finds the region of Pentapolis, which is small, but has crops and livestock in plenty; it also has two ancient cities, Ptolemais and Cyrene, which are said to have been royal once. After this there is another province called Libyē, near Alexandria and west of it; no water falls from the sky here,

---

[23] i.e. when the hide was cut into strips.
[24] This poetic English word is an inadequate attempt to convey the tone of *Neptunus* (the god's name used of the sea itself) in the Latin here.

because it doesn't rain year in year out. It has few men, although they are fine, devout, clever. In my view their innate merit can only be a lesson from god. Then we are back again in Alexandria, after this partial description which we have been able to make of Roman and barbarian territory. Quite emphatically it has not been feasible to cover everything. Even so, if some region has by chance escaped our notice, I do not think it can amount to very much.

Islands

63. However, so as not to create the impression of overlooking one entire part of these inquiries, I should end the account by also mentioning islands situated in the open sea. So, from the East you have the following islands: first and largest is Cyprus, which regularly builds ships. They say that for this ship-building there is nothing it needs from another province. The island itself has everything required, namely: wood, bronze, iron, pitch, as well as cloth for sails and what is needed for cables. According to reports, there is no lack of other fine resources too. Next, the island of Euboea is said to be outstanding. Then what are called the Cyclades, a very numerous group, fifty-three islands, each with its own magistrate. Some must be mentioned by name. Thus there is Rhodes, an island and major city which according to the Sibyl's prophecy is going to be destroyed by divine wrath. In the city itself there is the statue that everyone calls a Colossus, a massively unusual sight; yet, according to the prophecy of the Sibyl just mentioned, there was wickedness in it. Another island, Delos, located at the centre of the Cyclades, is where Latona gave birth to Diana and Apollo. Then there is Tenedos, Apollo's island. Nearby you will find Imbrus; Imbrus is an island from which hare-skin clothing is the major export because it has so much of this and plenty of those animals, but really only a moderate amount of anything else. Then there is Lemnus, which is self-sufficient; it produces plenty of wine, which it exports to the region of Macedonia and Thrace.

64. After this is the island of Crete, distinguished for having 100 cities; in all respects it is wealthy and admirable, and produces excellent wine. Its greatest city is called Gortyna, one where there are said to be circus games; it has some rich and learned men. Next Cythera, another island, then Zacynthus and Cephalonia, islands that have all resources in plenty.

65. After all these islands Sicily is the best and largest, reckoned superior to all other islands because of its dense soil. Sicily produces much of quality, and exports quantities of useful commodities: wool and grain, similarly livestock. Also, it has men who are wealthy and well-informed about all branches of philosophy, both Greek and Latin. It has the superb cities of Syracuse and Catana, where fine circus games thrive. Each city has fine, sturdy animals (*horses*), and in their rivalry they delight in the animals' strength. In this island there is also a mountain called Etna. The presence of a divinity on this mountain seems quite credible, because day and night the mountain-peak is ablaze, with smoke to be seen ascending. All around this mountain are numerous vineyards which produce superb wine.

66. Then [—].²⁵ After it is another island, one named Sardinia, very rich in crops and livestock, and really quite splendid.

67. Then is another island, one named Britannia and—so those who have been there tell—really superb. It has every resource in plenty, as well as brave fighting-men.

CONCLUSION

Here ends the *Account of the Whole World and its Peoples*.

68. This—so far as humanly possible—is my description. If there are provinces or cities or islands which have escaped our notice, my sense is they are not numerous. Any such escape reflects the fact that no mortal can possibly be omniscient; only the god who created everything can be omniscient.

---

²⁵ Name irrecoverable; perhaps Corsica, since 'another island . . . Sardinia' follows?

34
MARKIANOS OF HERAKLEIA
(c. AD 390–410)

D. Graham J. Shipley

εὐτυχῶς Μαρκιανῷ[1]

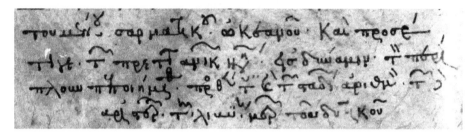

FIG. 34.1. End of the preserved portion of Markianos' *Periplous*, p. 48 (detail).

INTRODUCTION

Markianos (often anglicized as 'Marcian'), from Herakleia in the Black Sea, is a key figure in the transmission of ancient Greek geographical writing: were it not for his efforts, we would possess significantly fewer texts of the 'minor' authors. Working in a Neoplatonic rather than a Christian tradition, probably at Constantinople, he compiled—perhaps partly on the basis of work by Menippos (Chapter 21 above)—the original corpus of geographers of which substantial parts survive in the mid-13th-century manuscript D (see Introduction, §VIII. 2. b). His own works, in Greek, formed the first part of that corpus.

If Markianos is correctly identified with the man of that name who was active at Constantinople immediately before and after 400,[2] he was a scholar with an established reputation well before then. The city was an intellectual powerhouse already under Theodosios I (r. 379–95, in Constantinople from 380) and Arkadios (r. 395–408), and remained so under Theodosios II (sole r. 408–50).[3] In a letter dated 401–5, Synesios (c.370–c.415), future bishop of Ptolemaïs in Libya, lauds a certain Markianos as an expert, advanced in years, whose lectures he used to hear in Constantinople (B. 6 below on p. 977). If this is our Markianos,[4] we have here a rare, perhaps unique,

---

[1] See Chapter 11 n. 2.
[2] This possible link is not mentioned by *PLRE* ii. 714, s.v. Marcianus 3.
[3] See e.g. Traina 2013 for geography under Theodosios II.
[4] Marcotte 2000b, xxxvii, approves this suggestion by the early modern editors of Markianos.

personal testimony to a geographer from another writer who knew him. In a letter from 406, Synesios refers to a Markianos, presumably the same man, as a philosopher and former governor of Paphlagonia (B. **8**, on p. 977).

We know of several works, designated here by letters to indicate the relevant section of this chapter:

A. *Epitome of Artemidoros*. The work of Markianos' most frequently cited in the sources is his *Epitome* of the 11-book *Geographoumena* of Artemidoros (often abbreviated to *Epit. Art.*), which originally occupied most of the first 32 pages of manuscript D but is now lost. It is referred to many times by Stephanos of Byzantion; 19 such citations will be found in Chapter 18 above (also listed below as 'Epitome of the *Geographoumena* of Artemidoros').

B. *Circumnavigation (Periplous) of the Outer Sea*. The first surviving part of manuscript D contains most of Markianos' abridgement of his own *periplous* in two books. It lacks its opening as well as about one-quarter of the text at the end; but at around 13,000 words it remains substantial, even in this truncated form.

C. *Epitome of Menippos* (*Epit. Men.*). Next in D (after 16 missing pages) we have (*a*) the last few lines of a table of contents for Markianos' abridgement of Menippos' *Periplous*, translated in Chapter 21 above; (*b*) Markianos' introduction to that abridgement, which amounts to a general history of geographical writing; then (*c*) the abridgement itself, printed in Chapter 21 above. (*b*) makes reference to works A and B above, showing that they are earlier.

D. *Preface to (Pseudo)-Skylax*. In the next part of manuscript D, we have the preface, almost certainly by Markianos, to the *Periplous* he attributes to Skylax of Karyanda; this preface (represented by a 'blind' heading at IV below) is printed as no. 6 in Chapter 7 above. The acuity of his scholarly judgement has been noted in the introduction to that chapter. We may note a verbal echo of *Epit. Men.* 3: in both prefaces, Markianos notes the expansion of geographical knowledge brought about by Roman military power. The *Periplous* (1. 11, 14, and 17; 2. 2 and 46), the *Epitome of Menippos* (§§4 and 6), and the preface to Ps.-Skylax (§3) are linked together stylistically by the use of the unusual adverb προσέτιγε (*prosetige*),[5] for which the rendering 'what is more' is reserved in these volumes.[6]

E. *Distances from Rome*. We have one apparent reference to a work of this name; see 'F Other sources' below.

---

[5] Perhaps to be regarded as two words, προσέτι γε, but, if so, still distinctive.

[6] Mark. is also fond of the verb τυγχάνω–*tynchanō*, using it 34 times in the surviving abridgement of the *Periplous* (23 times in book 1, 11 times in book 2) and 3 times in *Epit. Men.* In Classical Greek its meanings include the strong senses of 'happen' or 'chance', but also a weaker sense close to 'be' or 'exist' (LSJ s.v.) or, in the case of geographical features, 'be set' or 'lie' (CGL s.v.). However, (*a*) in Mark. it is often combined with the participle 'lying' (*keimenos*), so 'lie' is not an option for the translator; and (*b*) it may be intended to convey the idea that he is 'observing' phenomena by looking at a map. So I have translated it as 'happen', which is adequately colloquial.

Like his epitome of Menippos, Markianos' *Periplous of the Outer Sea* has undergone abridgement between his compilation of the corpus and the making of the 13th-century copy.[7] Eight times in book 1 we read that a detailed description has been omitted; this reflects subsequent editing. Citations by Stephanos of Byzantion (B. 2–40, including what appear to be direct quotations of Markianos' words at **8, 10, 14, 16, 18,** and **40**) indicate that regions were covered in the original whose descriptions are now lost. Nevertheless it seems that Markianos was more interested in systematic enumeration of numerical data than in ways of life, to judge from the more detailed sections we have (e.g. B. 1. 26–30 on Karmania).

The chief sources for the *Periplous* were Artemidoros,[8] Strabo, and Ptolemy; he also four times (B. **1**, book 1 §1; book 2 §§2, 5, 38) names Protagoras, thought to be a successor of Ptolemy.[9] Markianos' aims, however, are more descriptive than mathematical,[10] and in general he bases his account chiefly on Greek writers of the hellenistic period.[11] The structure of the work is of his own devising. A very reflective writer, he often pauses to discuss his working methods,[12] including his and his predecessors' handling of distance measurements (book 1 §2; book 2 §§5, 9). He says he aims to cover the coasts of the world in double *periplous* format: book 1 will be a *periplous* of 'the eastern and southern Ocean', that is, the eastern and western parts of the Indian Ocean; book 2 a *periplous* of 'the western and northern Ocean', that is, the Atlantic coasts but also the Mediterranean. The main discussion is preceded by a prologue whose first part (book 1 §§1–4) covers the form of 'our sea', that is, the Mediterranean. In each main *periplous*, he also gives details of the most important island or group of islands in each part of the Ocean: Taprobane (Sri Lanka) in the first, the British Isles in the second.

In both books, Markianos is led by historical information rather than by the administrative realities of his own day, whether that be the 3rd, 4th, or 5th century AD—most likely the end of the 4th, by which time there had been many rearrangements in provinces and jurisdictions.[13] Thus in the east he largely follows the historic kingdoms of the Persian and post-Alexander empires, while in the west he operates with the Roman provinces that had existed in the early Imperial or even the late Republican period. In

---

[7] C16 copies of D remained in circulation while D itself was lost to public view; while they are not an independent authority for the text, they can contribute to a reconstruction of M.' s plan for the geographical corpus (Altomare n.d.).

[8] Pontani 2010 confirms M.' s close reliance upon Artemidoros in 2. 2–7, for example.

[9] Protagoras wrote a *Geometry of the Inhabited World* in C2/C3 AD, known only from references in Photios and Tzetzes and the four citations by Mark. in his *Periplous*. See Dueck 2011 (misattributing M.' s citations to his epitome of Menippos).

[10] In the case of Iberia at least, authors after Ptolemy reverted to a periplographic rather than scientific, geometric approach to cartography (Bianchetti 2008, esp. 50–2).

[11] Altomare n.d. (project outline; I have not seen the related thesis, Altomare 2010).

[12] The brief overview of the *Periplous* offered here is indebted to Altomare 2013 and especially Altomare 2014–15.

[13] See e.g. Eutropius, *Breviarium* 9. 15, for the relocation of the population and name of Dacia from N of the Danube to S of it.

this he is no doubt guided by Artemidoros (Chapter 18 above), as the citation of the earlier author at 2. 19 suggests. The eastward limits of knowledge are, however, those of Ptolemy, based on the trade contacts with South-east Asia and China already mentioned in *PME* (Chapter 25 above).[14]

Whereas Ptolemy in the 2nd century AD had structured his work by region, giving within each region a list of places with their longitude and latitude, Markianos thus envisages two independent *periploi*. Although our main source for his work is the mid-13th-century manuscript D (see Introduction, §VIII. 2. b), it is likely that the red initial letters and marginal signs, as well as the headings (retained in the translation below), broadly reflect his own subdivisions of the work (such signposting was conventional by the late antique period).[15] The decisive role played by the *periplous* format in his conception is confirmed by the fact that Stephanos of Byzantion does not cite the *Periplous* by book number but by region, referring to each regional account as a *periplous* or *periodos*; when he uses a form such as 'in his first *Circumnavigation*', as he does four times, all with reference to Aithiopia (there are no references of the form 'in his second *Circumnavigation*'), this is probably not a book number but a reference to the regional description that stood first.[16]

Each regional subsection of the *Periplous* as we have it (at least, each subsection that appears complete) is introduced and closed by similar formulaic expressions and has a standard structure, except where Markianos announces that he will give less than full information (as at B. 1, book 1 §10; book 2 §§38, 46). Several times he implicitly refers the reader to his epitome of Artemidoros (book 1 §§1, 3; book 2 §2).

The *Periplous* was probably accompanied by a map, such as Markianos may have used as an aid to his lectures; since at least Ptolemy's time, maps were a familiar adjunct to geographical texts.[17] But the texture of his geography was different from that of Ptolemy: more descriptive than mathematical.[18] The example of his organization of his material, and his use of a map, were followed by Greek and Roman geographers of the succeeding generations.[19] His descriptive approach was doubtless more engaging than Ptolemy's more technical exposition of scientific data.

The *Periplous* should be seen as one component of a larger project embodied in Markianos' 'corpus' (Introduction, §VIII. 2. b), and as designed to complement his own and the other works therein.[20] His coverage of the east coast of Africa is less

---

[14] On China, see Dueck 2012, 62–3. Roman knowledge and understanding of SE Asia was not necessarily any greater than at the end of the Republic: see Dionysios Periegetes 752–7 for a dismissive mention of the 'barbarian' Seres. For a far more admiring portrayal from C4, see Ammianus Marcellinus 23. 6. 64–8, which includes an allusion to the Great Wall of China (64), mentions ten peoples (*gentes*) and four major cities (66) including Sera (see n. on 1. 44 'mother-city', below), and paints an idyllic (idealized?) picture of a peaceful civilization (67–8).

[15] Altomare 2014–15, 40.   [16] Altomare 2014–15, 50–1.   [17] Altomare 2013, 19–20.

[18] Bianchetti 2008, esp. 50–2, argues that only Ptolemy picked up on the methods developed by Eudoxos of Knidos, Pytheas, and Eratosthenes, and that later authors such as Mark. reverted to a periplographic rather than geometric approach.

[19] Altomare 2013, 20–1.   [20] Altomare 2014–15, 37.

detailed by design (1. 10; 2. 46); he may have covered it more fully in the *Epitome of Artemidoros*,[21] though Stephanos finds enough material on Aithiopia to cite this missing part of the *Periplous* six times (B. 7, 9–10, 13, 37, 39).

Although there is as yet no full study of Markianos, scholars are now actively starting to elucidate his aims and to recognize his talents more fully than before. The version of the *Periplous* below necessarily follows the Greek of Müller and González Ponce.[22] I have rearranged Müller's text, however, by removing his reconstructed table of contents to book 1, and taking the quotations from Stephanos into their own section (with those entries which Müller did not include).

SELECTED FURTHER READING

Altomare, B. M. (2014–15), 'Périples dans le Périple: notes sur la structure du Périple de la Mer extérieure de Marcien d'Héraclée et sur sa tradition indirecte', *Revue des études tardo-antiques*, 4: 35–53.
*—— (forthcoming), 'Marciano di Eracleia (2027)', in *FGrH* v.
Diller, A. (1952), *The Tradition of the Minor Greek Geographers*. Lancaster, Pa.–Oxford. [Menippos epitome at pp. 147–64.]
*González Ponce, F. J. (2008b), *Periplo de Hanón y autores de los siglos VI y V a.C.* Zaragoza. [Edition and translation of *Epit. Men.* 1–5 at pp. 50–69 (the Greek matches Müller's).]
*Müller, *GGM* i, pp. cxxix–cxxxvii (addendum, cxlv), 515–76.
Schoff, W. H. (1927), *Periplus of the Outer Sea: East and West, and of the Great Islands Therein, by Marcian of Heraclea*. Philadelphia. [A work of modest ambition, but included as one of the few studies in English.]

A. EPITOME OF THE *GEOGRAPHOUMENA* OF ARTEMIDOROS

Lost from the beginning of manuscript D (see introduction to this chapter, and the Introduction, §VIII. 2. b). For citations of the *Epitome*, see Chapter 18 nos 10 (by Markianos himself), 14, 16–17, 26, 48, 129, 131, 139, 141–4, 147–9, 151, 155–6, and 164.

B. *PERIPLOUS* OF THE OUTER OCEAN

1 Codex Parisinus supplément grec 443, pp. 1. 1–49. 3
Headings are original unless enclosed in angle brackets 〈 〉.

---

[21] Altomare 2014–15, 48.
[22] *GGM* i. 515–62; checked against passages quoted by Altomare 2014–15, who is preparing a new critical edition.

BOOK 1

⟨Preface⟩

1. [—] ⟨Within the Pillars of Herakles⟩ lies a sea whose western end is marked by the Ocean surrounding the Earth, which makes its inflow at the so-called Herakleian strait—the circumnavigation of this was composed by the geographer Artemidoros of Ephesos, to the best of his ability, in the eleven books of the *Geography*.[24] We, however, leaving aside the superfluous digressions by the previously noted man in these books, and also the Aithiopian cities of the barbarians, made the circumnavigation for ourselves, in summary form,[25] very clearly and with the precise addition of supplementary discoveries, in order that nothing might be lacking that could contribute to perfect clarity for those studying this aspect of geography.

For both Oceans, however, both eastern and western—knowledge of which, insofar as it is attainable by human beings, has been rendered clear by the zeal and learning of many—we preferred to compose the circumnavigation of these in two books, on the basis of the geography of the most divine and most wise Ptolemy;[26] of the measurement of stades by Protagoras,[27] which he has appended to his own books of geography; and, moreover, of numerous other ancient men. (*We cover*) the eastern and southern Ocean in the first of the two books, the western and northern in the second; as well as the largest islands lying in them, and the so-called Taprobane, formerly called Palaisimoundou,[28] and both the Prettanic (*British*) islands. The first of these is agreed to lie in the very middle of the Indian open-sea (*pelagos*), the other two in the northern Ocean.

⟨MEASUREMENT IN STADES⟩

2. Knowing that others among the old authors zealously dealt with this subject—some making certain partial expositions, others touching on several regions—I devoted much consideration in order not to be seen as second to any of them, hoping that the precision of what we are about to say might be a clear sign of our zeal in this matter. Because of this, I deemed it necessary also to present to those who encounter my book the cause of the disagreement concerning the measurement of stades.

---

[23] At this point we are at the start of the first surviving quaternion (originally the third quaternion) of MS D, where any list of contents—probably by Markianos himself—has been lost along with the beginning of the Prologue (I have inverted the syntax of the first sentence to reflect the word order of the original). Müller's list of contents (*GGM* i. 515–16), not translated here, is only his reconstruction of what may have stood here, on the analogy of the beginning of book 2.

[24] Cf. similar statements at 1. 3; 2. 2.

[25] Mark. here refers to his epitome of Artemidoros' eleven books of *Geographoumena*; see Ch. 18, including many citations of the epitome by Steph. Byz.

[26] For Ptolemy's major work, see Introduction, §VI. 1. e.

[27] See n. 9 above.

[28] For the variation Simoundou–Palaisimoundou, see Artem. 48; *PME* §61; 1. 8 and 1. 35 below; and *Hypotyposis* §25.

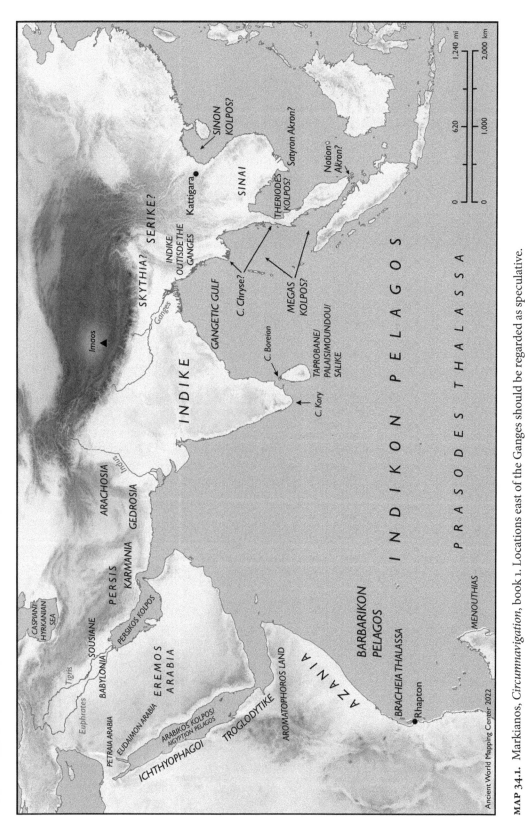

MAP 34.1. Markianos, *Circumnavigation*, book 1. Locations east of the Ganges should be regarded as speculative.

For, since a subject of this kind has its precision not only in the locations of localities, cities, islands, and harbours but also, and above all, in the stades and the computation of places, I deem it consistent to give an account of it that will appear true even to those who wish to contemplate, according to the nature of the matter, measurement during the circumnavigation of the sea; although none of those who have devoted themselves to these matters has observed this, but (*all of them*) have reported the numbers of the stades as if the sea had been measured with a cord. I declare, indeed, that is not easy to discover, in all parts of the sea, the number of the stades with high accuracy; but if a particular coast happens to be straight, with no indentations or protrusions, the measurement of the voyage beside it is generally easy. It is not, however, possible to represent accurately the circumnavigation of the gulfs, and of the promontories or peninsulas. For one does not, in the way that people make a journey by land using the main roads, perform one's voyage on the sea by way of recognized places.

Let us imagine, for the sake of example, a gulf drawn in outline as occupying 100 stades along the actual seashore. If one were to (*sic*) sail round this and keep close in to the actual beach, one will (*sic*) find that the stades are fewer than will a man walking along the same shore, but will not stray far from the truth. If, however, someone were to sail round the same gulf further into the middle, he will find the stades to be fewer than will the man who has sailed along beside the shore, and would find that the effect was multiplied the more he shortened the circle of his circumnavigation. Similarly with circumferences: if, after the outer line, one were to outline a second (*segment of*) circumference inside it with the same extremities, and then another, and after that another, the second circumference would be found to be less than the previous one, and again the third than the second, and similarly the fourth than the third, and by analogy they would be shown to be so if one did this successively. Thus with gulfs, as in a drawing of circumferences, it is possible for those sailing round to make their voyage in either more, or fewer, stades.

One could clearly establish this also in the case of direct voyages. For if one wished not to sail round the gulf but to sail directly across, the crossing would be seen as very short, so that in all likelihood the number of stades involved in the gulfs and promontories would depend on the opinion of those making the circumnavigation. For this reason it happens that some reckon one way and some another. The miscalculation concerning what number of stades is observed is therefore forgivable—unless the error be a very great one—because one would mostly not find, among all the old authors who have written circumnavigations (*periploi*), that in all the seas the number of the stades is in harmony. The causes of such disagreement would take a long time to tell. This being so, the maritime nations and cities and their dependent harbours [—]

⟨THE OIKOUMENĒ⟩

3 [— *The Ocean* ...] the west [—] runs into [—], taking its inflow from the so-called Atlantic open-sea (*pelagos*), and advances far into the land in an easterly direction up to the Issic gulf, which is among the Kilikian nation. This entrance to our sea is narrowest

at the so-called Pillars of Herakles or Herakleian strait, which occupies 80 stades; and this is the mouth of this gulf, that is, of the sea: for one could not sail out from the inner sea into the Ocean from any other point but via the said Herakleian strait. This sea of ours also extends up to Egypt, which lies under the south so as to lie opposite the Arabian gulf (*Red Sea*)—called by us the Egyptian open-sea (*pelagos*)—and so that a great isthmus is formed by the land between the Arabian gulf and our sea at this point. We have established clearly the circumnavigation of this sea with our epitome of the eleven books of Artemidoros the geographer, as stated earlier; but as for the outer seas or eastern and western Ocean, we have chosen to compose its circumnavigation by submitting to the laborious task ourselves.

4. Eratosthenes of Kyrene says the greatest circumference of all the ⟨known⟩ Earth is 259,200 stades.[29] Dionysios son of Diogenes has measured it similarly. But the most divine Ptolemy, senior in experience and true learning but younger in date than Eratosthenes, has proved that the (*inhabited portion of the*) Earth measures 180,000 stades (*sc. south to north*), and has established that there are 80 meridional degrees (*south to north*) in the breadth of the (*inhabited portion of the*) Earth and 180 in its length (*west to east*).

In this measurement is contained the inhabited world, divided into three continents—into Asia, Libyē, and Europe—as is known to all. Europe is divided from Libyē by the mouth of the Ocean located at Gadeira, which they called the Herakleian strait and through which, as we have said before, the inflow of the Ocean into our sea takes place. Again, the river Tanaïs (*Don*) similarly separates Europe from Asia in the northern part, flowing out into Lake Maiotis, which discharges into the Pontos called Euxeinos. Libyē, with Asia, is separated from Europe by the aforementioned Herakleian strait, but from Asia by the so-called Kanobic mouth of the Nile. Asia is separated in relation to Europe by the aforementioned river Tanaïs, and in relation to Libyē by the above-mentioned Kanobic mouth of the Nile, as we have said before.

Now our sea, conjoining with the western Ocean via the Herakleian strait, outlines the three continents in the following way.

5. Europe's coastal territory, if its gulfs in our sea are sailed round, has its beginning at the river Tanaïs and ceases at the Herakleian strait and the island of Gadeira; and the whole circumnavigation is 69,000 stades.[30]

The circumnavigation of Libyē from the city of Tingis up to the Kanobic mouth of the Nile is 30,280 stades.

The circumnavigation of Asia with Egypt, from the Kanobic mouth of the Nile up to river Tanaïs, is 40,120 stades.

---

[29] Given as 252,000 by Strabo (Eratosthenes 29 above; cf. Hipparchos 40a) and Pliny (Erat. 34); also *Hyp.* §1. Though differing from the usual figure of 252,000, this may not be a MS error in Markianos as it is divisible by 12. Dionysios is unknown (Roller 2010, 144).

[30] This and the next two numbers (but not the total) have been edited by Müller.

Thus the complete coastal territory of our sea is, including Europe, Libyē, and Asia, **139,400 stades.**

6. First among the continents in terms of size is Asia, second Libyē, and third Europe. Of the three seas, the first in size happens to be the one beside the Indian open-sea (*pelagos*); second our sea between Libyē and Europe, beginning from Gadeira or the Herakleian strait and running through up to Asia; and third the Hyrkanian (*sea*).

The size of the inhabited world, from east to west, has been measured at 78,545 stades; this is from the outlets of the river Ganges, the easternmost river among the Indians, to the westernmost promontory of the whole inhabited world, which is called Hieron (*Sacred*) Point and belongs to the Lousitanian nation in Iberia. This (*promontory*) happens to be further west than Gadeira or the Pillars of Herakles by 3,000 stades.[31] The straight line of the breadth (*of the inhabited world*), at the point where it happens to be widest, has been measured at 43,060 stades; this is from south to north, as far as it is from the Aithiopian sea up to the island of Thoule.

7. Of the largest gulfs[32] the first is the Gangetic,[33] the second the Persian, the third the one called by the name of Megas (*Great*),[34] the fourth the Arabian, the fifth the Aithiopic,[35] the sixth that of the Pontos (*Black Sea*), the seventh that of the Aegean open-sea (*pelagos*), the eighth that of Lake Maiotis (*Sea of Azov*), the ninth the Adriatic or Ionian gulf, the tenth that of the Propontis.

8. Among the largest islands or peninsulas, those of the first class, the first is the island of Taprobane, formerly called Palaisimoundou and now Salike; the second is Albion, one of the Prettanic islands; the third the Chryse (*Golden*) Peninsula,[36] the fourth Iouernia (*Hibernia, Ireland*), one of the Prettanic islands, the fifth the Peloponnese, the sixth Sicily, the seventh Sardo (*Sardinia*), the eighth Kyrnos (*Corsica*), the ninth Crete, the tenth Cyprus. So much for these matters; we shall move on to the tasks before us.

---

[31] 9,000 in the MS; corrected by Müller.

[32] *Kolpos*, the regular word for 'gulf' or 'bay', is here used for (*a*) major indentations within the divisions of the outer Ocean—thus the Gangetic and Megas gulfs are parts of the 'Indian open-sea' (cf. 1. 10); (*b*) enclosed bodies of water such as the Black Sea and Maiotis; (*c*) the Aegean as a 'gulf' within the Mediterranean.

[33] The N part of the *Bay of Bengal*.

[34] At 1. 16 the Megas gulf follows C. Chryse, plausibly part of the *Malay* peninsula. See, further, n. on 1. 16 Chryse. (Thus I set aside the *gulf of Thailand*, proposed by Wheeler 1954, 172, using the older name *gulf of Siam*.) Mark. here lists the Megas in 3rd place, smaller than the Persian gulf, so it cannot be (in his conception) the major sea off China but should be a 'gulf' within it. In any case, he regards that major sea as the eastern part of the Indikon Pelagos (or Indike Thalassa), comprising the Prasodes Thalassa (or part therefore; 1. 12 and 44 are ambiguous) and extending S to the 'southern unknown land'. Stückelberger and Graßhoff 2006, ii. 733, on Ptol. 7. 3. 3, make the Megas the *South China sea*; at 91 with n. 83 (on Ptol. 1. 13. 1; cf. their trans. of 7. 3. 1), they make the gulf of the Sinai (1. 44) the *gulf of Tonkin* (in the NW part of the *S. China sea*), which indeed it should be if Kattigara (1. 46) is correctly located near *Hanoi*. They offer no location, however, for the Theriodes gulf (1. 45) between those two; I propose the *gulf of Thailand*. (The name 'Megas' need not imply that the gulf of that name was the largest gulf.) In fact, therefore, the Megas gulf, Theriodes gulf, and gulf of the Sinai are probably all gulfs within the eastern Indikon Pelagos.

[35] The eastern Atlantic—the great bight of west-central Africa.   [36] See 1. 16 below.

⟨SCOPE OF BOOK 1⟩

9. We shall begin the circumnavigation, as we have said before, from the Arabian gulf and its head, the so-called Ailanites (*gulf of Aqaba*). Hereabouts, as has been said above, is the narrowest part of the continent, which prevents it joining up with our sea at the head of the Arabian. This head happens to adjoin Egypt and what is called Petraia (*Rocky*) Arabia, which joins onto what is called Ioudaia (*Judaea*), in which Palaistine is the nation lying beside our sea. For from the city of Gaza in Palaistine to the head of the Arabian gulf ⟨and⟩ the aforementioned Aïla (*Aqaba*), if the journey is on foot towards the south, it is 1,260 stades.

10. For the left-hand parts of Asia,[37] that is, of Arabia Eudaimon (*Arabia Felix*) and the Erythraian sea, and after it the Persian gulf and all the Indian open-sea (*pelagos*)[38] as far as ⟨the⟩ nation of the Sinai[39] and the extremity of the known Earth,[40] we shall construct the most accurate possible circumnavigation and reckoning of stades.

For the right-hand parts of Libyē,[41] up to the so-called Prasos (*Green*) promontory and the island of Menouthias (*Madagascar*), we shall show the appellations of the cities and the dependent harbours; moreover, we shall point out the namings of the seas, gulfs, promontories, and islands; but only on the large scale shall we append to distances the number of stades.

For some of these right-hand parts we have clarified their measurement in a cursory fashion, purely for the sake of the position that the land and the sea occupy in relation to the territory of Asia opposite them—that is, the land of the Arabs, Indians, and other nations. For the left-hand parts, however, in accordance with our aforesaid declaration, we have made the circumnavigation carefully.

Circumnavigation of the right-hand parts of the 'Arabian gulf', 'Erythraian sea', and 'Indian sea'

11. So the position and outline of the right-hand parts of Libyē have this character; before the part-by-part (*account*) we must, of course, show its designation in general and

---

[37] i.e. the parts of Asia one passes on one's left hand when sailing S from the head of the Arabian gulf (mod. *Red Sea*).

[38] For its eastward extent, see 1. 12.

[39] Mark. returns to the Sinai at 1. 43–4 and 46. Ptol. 7. 5. 2 makes the Sinai and Serike the last *ethnē* before the eastern unknown lands. In the view of Stückelberger and Graßhoff 2006, i. 91 n. 83 (on Ptol. 1. 31. 1), Ptolemy distinguishes the Sinai (approached from the sea) from the Seres (approached overland from the W) without realizing they are the same culture. Casson 1989, 238, accepts that the name Sinai and that of their capital, Thina (1. 16 below), are (like 'China') derived via Sanskrit from name of the Qin (Ch'in) dynasty (221–206 BC); for the same view in detail, see Bodde 1978, 20 and n. 2.

[40] If we had only his abridged *periplous* but not Ptol., it would be tempting to set the E limit of M.' s geography at around Burma (Myanmar); but P. names so many intervening places, giving definite longitudes and latitudes (even if his 'route' mistakenly goes SE rather than NE from the *Malay* peninsula), that a field of view extending well into China is likeliest. Roman artefacts of Imperial and late antique date have been found on the *Malay* peninsula, in Vietnam (cf. n. on 1. 46 Kattigara), and now as far E as *Bali* (Calo, Bellwood et al. 2020).

[41] i.e. the parts of Africa to the right when one sails S from the head of the Arabian gulf (mod. *Red Sea*).

the positions of the places. As one sails the Arabian gulf towards the south, deviating slightly towards the east and keeping the mainland on the right, the first place is Egypt, which in part adjoins the gulf; along this part live the Arab–Egyptian Ichthyophagoi (*Fish-eaters*). After this Troglodytike extends very far; for it runs beside the Arabian gulf itself, and beside the Erythraian sea; after the mouth of the Arabian gulf the Erythraian sea (*western Indian Ocean*) is next. As one sails round the latter, likewise keeping the land on one's right, there is the Aualites gulf,[42] which happens to be in the right-hand parts of the Erythraian sea; the nations living beside it are the aforementioned Troglodytai, the Aualitai, and, what is more, the Mossyloi.

12. After one has sailed out of the gulf and the Erythraian sea, which gradually narrows at the promontory after the gulf, there is the Indian open-sea (*pelagos*), spreading out wide (*eastern Indian Ocean*); in its length it goes towards the east and the risings of the sun up to the nation of the Sinai, who happen to lie at the end of the inhabited world beside the unknown land towards the east. In its breadth it spreads out very far towards the south, continuing up to the other unknown land that exists at the south. Beside this there extends the so-called Prasodes Thalassa (*Green Sea*), lying all beside the southern unknown land up to the east, and occupying (*part of*) the Indian open-sea (*pelagos*); it has taken its designation from its colour.

13. Now after the Erythraian sea, as one bends towards the south and likewise keeps the land on the right, there happen to lie Mt Elephas (*Ivory*) and the Aromatophoros (*Spice-bearing*) Land. After this there follows the nation named Barbarikon and the so-called Barbarikon Pelagos (*open-sea*), in which there are several gulfs and the sea-roads of the so-called Azania. The first of the notable places is the gulf in it called Apokopa (*Cut-off; El-Hazin?*); next in order are the Mikros Aigialos (*Small Shore*) and the Megas (*Great*); after these is another great gulf up to the promontory of Rhapton (*Stitched; C. Puna?*). After these places is the so-called Bracheia (*Short*) sea (*thalassa*)[43] and the extremely large gulf around it, which the barbarian Anthropophagoi (*Man-eaters*) occupy. At the end of the gulf lies the very large promontory which is called Prason Akron (*Green Point*),[44] and the island of Menouthias (*Madagascar*), which happens to be not far from the promontory.[45]

14. And the whole situation and outline of the right-hand parts of the Arabian gulf and the Erythraian sea, and, what is more, the Indic open-sea (*pelagos*) which deviates towards the south, has this character. The part-by-part character is as follows. (The part-by-part (*description*) is omitted.)[46]

---

[42] Cf. *PME* §7: the narrows of the *Red Sea*.
[43] lit. 'Short Sea', i.e. shallow; identified with *Menai Bay*.
[44] Schoff 1927, 47, suggests *Kilwa* or C. *Delgado*.
[45] On Mediterranean contact with Madagascar, see Altomare 2014.
[46] This and seven more such sentences are notes by the excerptor who altered M.'s text between its composition in the late antique period and the making of our C13 copy. Müller suggests we can reconstruct the contents of the missing passage from Ptolemy book 4.

Circumnavigation of the left-hand parts of both the Arabian gulf and the Erythraian sea and all of the Indic open-sea (pelagos)

15. For the left-hand parts of Asia, the position of the continent and the seas is organized more or less in the following way. For here, too, before the part-by-part namings we must show the general designations, and note the position of the places. So as one sails out of[47] the Arabian gulf and keeps the mainland on the left, the first place is so-called Eudaimon Arabia (*Arabia Felix*), which runs through along all of the Arabian gulf up to the above-mentioned Arabian Strait. After the narrows of the Arabian gulf there follows the Erythraian sea; as one sails round this keeping the mainland on the left, there follows the above-mentioned nation of the Arabs, living all along this mainland. In this part of the sea, there also happens to exist the nation of the Homeritai,[48] occupying (*part of*) the land of the Arabs and running through up to the beginning of the Indian open-sea (*pelagos*).

Next after the Erythraian sea is the Indikon Pelagos. So, as one sails round the left-hand parts of this as well, which are spread out towards the land of the Arabs up to the mouth of the Persian gulf, there follows Mt Syagros (*Ras Fartak?*) and the Sachalites gulf,[49] which is very large and runs through as far as the mouth of the Persian gulf.

After one has sailed into the Persian gulf and is circumnavigating this, keeping the mainland on the left up to the outlets of the river Tigris, [—] In the Persian gulf itself, the nation of Sousiane is next; but also Persis happens to lie after Sousiane, after which is the largest part of Karmania as far as the narrows of the Persian gulf itself. The Persian gulf lies opposite the Caspian sea (*thalassa*), also called the Hyrkanian; making the land between them narrow, it forms the great isthmus of Asia.

16. After one has sailed out of the gulf and makes a voyage towards the east, likewise keeping the mainland on the left, the next in sequence is the Indian open-sea (*pelagos*), by which the remainder of the nation of Karmania lives. And after this there happens to lie the nation of Gedrosia; next after them is the Indike (*India*) lying within the river Ganges, opposite which, by the very centre of the continent, lies a very great island called Taprobane (*Sri Lanka*).

After this[50] is the other Indike, that outside (*i.e. east of*) the river Ganges, which happens to be the boundary of both the Indian terrains.[51] In Indike outside the Ganges

---

[47] Reading ⟨ἐκ⟩πλέοντι with Lucarini 2020, 224.

[48] This and many other places named in the text are also the subject of entries in Steph. Byz. citing Mark. Homeritai, for example, is at B. **33** below.

[49] Schoff 1927, 47, notes that the ancients mistakenly believed there was a large bay in the Oceanic coast of Arabia. He equates Sachalites with a stretch of coast, *Es-Shehr*.

[50] After India 'within the Ganges', i.e. bounded by the R. Ganges (rather than after Taprobane).

[51] i.e. between India within and outside the Ganges. 'Terrain' is chosen to represent the unusual word γαιῶν–*gaiōn* (from *gaia*, a form of *gē*, 'Earth').

is the peninsula called Chryse (*Golden*),⁵² after which is the so-called Megas gulf.⁵³ By the very centre of this⁵⁴ are the boundaries of Indike outside the Ganges and of the Sinai. Next in order is the nation of the Sinai⁵⁵ and their mother-city, which is designated Thinai;⁵⁶ it happens to be the frontier of the known and ⟨the⟩⁵⁷ unknown land (*gē*).

17. And the overall position and outline of the places in the left-hand parts of Asia—the Arabian gulf, the Erythraian sea, and, what is more, the Persian gulf and all the Indian open-sea (*pelagos*)—have this character; but the part-by-part (*account*) is somewhat as follows.⁵⁸

CIRCUMNAVIGATION OF THE LEFT-HAND PARTS OF THE ARABIAN GULF
BESIDE EUDAIMON ARABIA

Eudaimon Arabia is bounded on the north by the sides of Petraia (*Rocky*) Arabia and Eremos (*Desert*) Arabia, and by the southern part of the Persian gulf up to the outlets of the Tigris river; ⟨on the west by the Arabian gulf; on the east by a part of the Persian gulf⟩⁵⁹ and a part of the Indian sea; on the south by the Erythraian sea; ⟨and on the west by the Arabian gulf⟩.

Its position is somewhat as follows: it projects very far towards the south into the Erythraian sea and the Indian open-sea (*pelagos*), and like a very large peninsula attached by a very wide isthmus it is surrounded by the sea. On both parts of this isthmus two gulfs are juxtaposed. Of these the one from the westward parts is called the Arabian gulf, as already mentioned; but that inclined towards the east is named the Persian gulf. The (*parts*) in between, from the head of the Arabian (*gulf*) up to the aforementioned Persian gulf, the part at which the Tigris river makes its outlets, can be sailed round; it happens to be peninsular in form, as has been mentioned earlier. It contains very many large nations, of which those adjoining the sea during the circumnavigation will be shown. The (*places*) around the neck of Eudaimon Arabia, after Petraia and Desert Arabia, are occupied by the so-called Sarakenoi (*Saracens*), who have many designations but possess much desert land. These people are neighbours of Arabia Petraia, Desert Arabia, Palaistine, and Persis, and then in sequence the aforementioned Eudaimon Arabia. (The part-by-part (*description*) is omitted.)

---

⁵² At *PME* §63 Chryse is an island; by Ptolemy's time, improved knowledge made it a peninsula, probably one projecting from the *Malay* peninsula, e.g. the outflow of the R. *Irrawaddy* (*Ayeyarwady*) or the *Phuket* peninsula; the fact that at 1. 8 Mark. makes Chryse larger than Ireland favours the former. Thus Megas Kolpos may be the *Andaman sea* or the *Malacca strait*. Ptol. distinguishes a region called Chryse and a peninsula of the same name; at 7. 2. 5 he lists places in Chryse (including *Maleou kōlon*) with latitudes straddling the Equator. See further Casson 1989, 235–6.
⁵³ See n. on 1. 7 Megas Kolpos.   ⁵⁴ This detail reappears at 1. 50.   ⁵⁵ See n. on 1. 10 Sinai.
⁵⁶ Cf. Thina at *PME* §64. Mark. returns to this region at 1. 46–8 below. It is called the Metropolis of the Sinai by Ptol. 1. 14. 10; 1. 17. 5; Stückelberger and Graßhoff 2006 do not propose a specific location.
⁵⁷ 'the' is plausibly added by Lucarini 2020, 224–5.
⁵⁸ In this instance, the 'part-by-part' description has not been removed.
⁵⁹ Müller's reconstruction, modified by Lucarini 2020, 225.

19.[60] The length of Eudaimon Arabia is 11,700 stades; its breadth is 8,850 stades. It contains 54 nations or satrapies, 164 notable cities and villages, 15 notable mountains, 4 notable rivers, 6 notable harbours, 5 notable gulfs, 2 large seashores, and 35 notable islands previously mentioned in the circumnavigation. The total, from the promontory of Asabōn up to the Maisanites gulf, which happens to be beside Eudaimon Arabia, is 5,140 stades.[61]

The grand total of the whole circumnavigation of the coast of the land of the Eudaimones Arabes (*Fortunate Arabs*), from the Ailanites head of the Arabian gulf up to the Maisanites gulf and the extremity of the Persian gulf by Desert (*Arabia*), and also (*up to*) the outlets of the river Tigris, is **38,150 stades.**

⟨CIRCUMNAVIGATION⟩ OF SOUSIANE

20. Sousiane lies in the Persian gulf. It is bounded on the north by Assyria; on the west by the aforementioned Babylonia, beside this part of the river Tigris as far as the sea; on the east by Persis; and on the south by the Persian gulf from the outlets of the river Tigris up to the outlets of the river Oroatis (*Zoreh*) into the Persian gulf. And the overall outline of the territory is of this kind; but the part-by-part coastal sailing is somewhat as follows.

21. From the eastern mouth of the river Tigris to Charax Spasinou[62] is 80 stades. Beside this part lies the island called Apphana; some assign this to the circumnavigation of Eudaimon Arabia, numbering it among the 35 islands.

From Charax of Pasinos (*sic*) to the outlets of the river Mogaios is 700 stades.

From the river Mogaios to the gulf called Pelodes (*Muddy*) is 400 stades. Beside this gulf and the places around it live the Elymaioi, belonging to the territory of Sousiane. By this gulf lies an island called Taxiana.

From the gulf to the outlets of the river Eulaios is 690 (?) stades. By this river, in the interior, lies a city, the mother-city of Sousiane, Sousa.

From the river Eulaios to ⟨Ammodes (*Sandy*)⟩ Lagoon ⟨is 110 stades.

From⟩ Ammodes ⟨Lagoon⟩ to the outlets of the river Oroatis is ⟨1⟩,450 stades.

22. The length of Sousiane is 3,500 stades; its breadth is 2,350 stades. It contains 6 nations or satrapies 6, 17 notable cities and villages, 4 notable rivers, the Pelodes gulf, Sandy Lagoon, and the Pillars of Herakles.

The total of the coastal sailing of the territory of Sousiane, from the mouth of the river Tigris up to the outlets of the river Oroatis, is **3,430.**

COASTAL SAILING BESIDE PERSIS

23. Persis itself also lies on the Persian gulf, and is bounded on the north by Media; on the west by the aforementioned Sousiane; on the east by Karmania; and on the south by the Persian gulf. It begins ⟨from⟩ the river Oroatis (*and goes*) up to the outlets of

---

[60] §18 was a group of 'fragments' placed here by Müller.   [61] Müller suggests 8,140.
[62] 'Charax of Spasinos' ('Pasinos' in the MS). For Charax, cf. Juba 20.

Bagradas,[63] the river. And the overall outline of the territory is of this kind; but the part-by-part circumnavigation has this character:

24. From the outlets of the river Oroatis to the cape called Taoke (*Tawwaj?*) is 500 stades.

From Cape Taoke to the outlets of the river Rhogomanis is 700 stades. On the coastal sailing lies an island called Sophtha.

From the river Rhogomanis to Chersonesos is 500 stades. Beside this lies the so-called Alexander's Island.

From Chersonesos to the outlets of the river Brisoanas is 650 stades.

From the river Brisoanas to Ausinza (*Sausinda*) is 600 stades.

From Ausinza ⟨to⟩ the outlets of the river Bagradas is 450 stades. Here we have mentioned previously that the boundaries of Persis come to their end.

25. The length of Persis is 4,000 stades; its breadth is 1,400. It contains 10 nations or satrapies, 32 notable cities and villages, 3 notable rivers, 1 notable promontory, 1 notable peninsula, and 2 notable islands. The total of the coastal sailing of the territory of the Persians, from the Oroatis up to the outlets of the river Bagradas, is **3,400 stades**.

CIRCUMNAVIGATION OF KARMANIA

26. Karmania lies in part by the Persian gulf, in part beside the Indian open-sea (*pelagos*) ⟨that is⟩ after the Persian gulf. It is bounded on the north by Eremos (*Desert*) Karmania; on the west by the above-mentioned Persis and the aforementioned river Bagradas, and also by the remaining part of the Persian gulf, called the Karmanic; on the east by the nation of Gedrosia beside the Parsic mountains; and on the south, after the narrows of the Persian gulf, by the Indian open-sea (*pelagos*). And the overall outline of the territory is of this kind; but the part-by-part circumnavigation is as follows.

27. From the outlets of the previously mentioned river Bagradas to the river Dara is 300 stades. Beside this the Kameloboskoi (*Camel-herders*), belonging to the territory of Karmania.

From the river Dara to the outlets of the river Kathraps is 500 stades. ⟨From the river Kathraps⟩ to the outlets of the river Korios is 700 stades. By these places lies an island called Agedana, in which much red ochre occurs.

From the river Korios to the outlets of the river Achidana is 400 stades.

From the river Achidana to the outlets of the river Andanis[64] is 500 stades. Beside these places lies the island of Oörachtha.

From the river Andanis to the outlets of the river Saganos, 400 stades.

From the outlets of the river Saganos to the city of Armouza,[65] 200 stades.

From Armouza to the promontory called Armozōn (*C. Hormuz*),[66] 800 stades.

---

[63] Unidentified, like several of the following places.
[64] Near the narrows of the Persian gulf.
[65] Called Harmouza at Ptolemy, *Geography* 6. 8. 5; 8. 22. 21.
[66] Harmozon Akron, Ptolemy, *Geography* 6. 8. 5.

From the Armozōn promontory to the promontory of Karpella, 750 stades. Beside here lies the above-mentioned Strongylon Oros (*Round Mountain*) of Semiramis, opposite which, as we said, lie the mountain and promontory of Asabōn by Eudaimon Arabia; these two mountains and promontories (*i.e. Strongylon and Asabōn*) form the narrows of the Persian gulf.

The total of the circumnavigation of Karmania, which turns out to be along the Persian gulf, from the river Bagradas up to the Round Mountain and Cape (*sic*) Karpella, happens to be **4,250 stades**.

The grand total of the whole circumnavigation of the Persian gulf, from Mt Asabōn and the promontory of Asabōn up to the Round Mountain of Semiramis and the promontory of Karpella, is ⟨**16,790 stades**.[67]

28. After Cape Karpella⟩ there follows the Indian open-sea (*pelagos*), extending towards the east; beside it the remaining part of Karmania runs up to the land of the Mousarnaioi. In fact there follows, after Cape Karpella, a very large gulf, the so-called Paragōn, running through up to the promontory called Alambater and the island called Zibe. The place-by-place (*account*) is as follows.

From Cape Karpella to the city of Kanthatis, 1,000 stades. Beside here live the people called Pasargadai, being of the race of Karmanians.

From the city of Kanthatis to the city of Agrisa, 250 stades.

From the city of Agrisa to the trading-place of Ommana, one of the notable ones, 600 stades.

From Ommana to Rhogana, 150 stades.

From Rhogana to the outlets of the river Salaros, 150 stades.

From the river Salaros to Pasis, 200 stades.

From Pasis to the city of Samydake, 200 stades. Beside here live the Chelonophagoi (*Tortoise-eaters*), who also happen to be in Karmania.

From the city of Samydake to the outlets of the river Samydakos, 500 stades.

From the river Samydakes to the city of Tesa, 400 stades.

From the city of Tesa to the outlets of the river Hydriakes, 200 stades.

From the outlets of the river Hydriakes to Cape Bagia (*anc. Bagisara?*), 400 stades.

From Cape Bagia to the harbour of Kyiza, 250 stades.

From the harbour of Kyiza to the promontory of Alambater, 400 stades. In these parts lies a deep-sea (*pelagia*) island called Pola. Beside the promontory of Alambater lies an island called Zibe. Here we have mentioned previously that the gulf called Paragōn ends.

The total circumnavigation thereof (*of the gulf*), from Cape Karpella to the promontory of Alambater, is **4,700 stades**.[68]

---

[67] Müller prints ͵α Ϛψζ′ (16,707) within an insertion, but his translation gives 16,790, which Schoff also prints; Mark. explains in a note, cross-referring to his n. on §51.

[68] 1,700 in the MS; corrected by Müller.

29. From the promontory of Alambater to Derenobilla, 250 stades. Beside here lies an island called Karmina (*Asthala?*).

From Derenobilla to the harbour of Kophas, 250 stades.

From the harbour of Kophas to the outlets of the river Zorambos, 200 stades.

From the river Zorambos to Badara,[69] 250 stades.

From Badara to the city of Mousarna, 300 stades.

30. The length of Karmania is 7,000 stades; its breadth is 1,500. It contains 10 nations or satrapies, 23 notable cities and villages, 3 notable mountains, 10 notable rivers, 3 notable promontories, and 5 notable harbours.

The total of the circumnavigation of the (*part of*) Karmania beside the Indian open-sea (*pelagos*), from the promontory of Karpella up to the city of Mousarna, is **5,950 stades**.[70]

The grand total of the circumnavigation of all the coast of the Karmanians, from the river Bagrada up to the city of Mousarna, is **10,200 stades**.

CIRCUMNAVIGATION OF GEDROSIA

31. Gedrosia is bounded on the north by Drangiane and Arachosia; on the west by the aforementioned Karmania up to the sea; on the east by the part of Indike beside the river Indos, up to the frontier of the previously noted Arachosia; and on the south by the Indian open-sea (*pelagos*). And the overall outline is of this kind; but the part-by-part (*account*) is as follows.

32. From the city of Mousarna to the outlets of the river Artabis, 1,300 stades. After one has sailed up the river, a city lies on the right during the voyage upstream, called Arbis; and still further up, and likewise on the right of the river, is the city of Parsis, the mother-city of Gedrosia.

From the river Artabis to the city of Rhapraua, 550 stades.

From the city of Rhapraua to Gynaikōn Limen (*Women's Harbour; Morontobara*), 500 stades. Here lie the villages of the Arabitai.

From Gynaikōn Limen to Koiamba, 400 stades. ⟨From Koiamba to Rhizana, 1,100 stades.⟩ Here begins the territory of Patalene (*Sind*), most of which the river Indos has surrounded with its mouths; and it has come about that the mother-city itself, called Patala, (*now*) lies after the third mouth of the river Indos as an island, as do numerous other cities.

33. The length of Gedrosia is 6,600 stades; its breadth is 5,250 stades. It contains 8 nations or satrapies, 12 notable cities and villages, 1 very large mountain, 1 great river, 1 notable harbour, and 2 notable islands.

The total, from the city of Mousarna to Rhizana on the coast of the Gedrosians, is **3,850 stades**.

---

[69] Possibly the place also called Barna?   [70] 5,350 in MS; corrected by Müller.

Circumnavigation of Indike within the river Ganges and the gulfs and islands therein

34. Indike within the river Ganges[71] is bounded on the north by Mt Imaos (*Himalaya*), beside the Sogdianians and Sakai who lie beyond it; on the west, towards the sea, by the aforementioned Gedrosia, but in the interior by Arachosia and further up by the Paropanisadai; on the east by the river Ganges; and on the south by the Indian open-sea (*pelagos*). And the overall outline is of this kind: ⟨but the part-by-part (*account*) is as follows. The part-by-part (*description*) is omitted.⟩

The total circumnavigation of the aforementioned part, Indike within the Ganges, from the harbour of Naustathmos (*Naval Station*)[72] up to the promontory of Kory (*C. Comorin/Kanyakumari*),[73] is ⟨2⟩1,725 stades.

CIRCUMNAVIGATION OF THE ISLAND OF TAPROBANE

35. Opposite the promontory of Indike called Kory lies the promontory of the island of Taprobane called Boreion (*Northern*). The island of Taprobane was formerly called Palaisimoundou, but now Salike. This promontory of the island, the one lying opposite Kory, which as we said is called Boreion Akron (*Point*), is distant from the eastern horizon (*i.e. limit of the oikoumenē*) 26,460 stades; from the western horizon 61,626 stades; from the south and the equator, roughly to the north, 6,350 stades. (The part-by-part (*description*) is omitted.)

36. After the promontory of Boreion, the overall outline and circumnavigation of the island of Taprobane has this character: along its diameter, 9,500 stades in length and 7,500 stades in breadth. It contains 13 nations or satrapies, 22 notable cities and trading-places, 2 notable mountains, 5 notable rivers, 8 notable promontories, 4 notable harbours, 2 great gulfs, and 1 great seashore.

The total of the circumnavigation of the island of Taprobane is **26,385 stades.**[74]

And concerning the island of Taprobane let so much be said; but we shall come back to the coastal sailing of Indike within the Ganges. (The part-by-part (*description*) is omitted.)

CIRCUMNAVIGATION OF THE GANGETIC GULF

37. From this Apheterion (*Departure Place*) there follows the gulf called Gangetic, which is extremely large. By its head the river Ganges discharges, making its outlet in five mouths; as we have said, it is the frontier between Indike within the Ganges and outside. (The part-by-part (*description*) is omitted.)

---

[71] i.e. northern Indike, including mod. Bangladesh and Nepal.

[72] Not mentioned up to now; presumably part of the details omitted at an earlier point, e.g. the end of 1. 18.

[73] The S tip of India; not the point closest to Sri Lanka, despite the next sentence.

[74] In reality *c*.833 mi (1,340 km, www.cia.gov/the-world-factbook/countries/sri-lanka/#geography), which at 8 st. to the mile would make *c*.6,660 st.—almost exactly one-quarter of the figure in the MS.

38. The length of Indike within the Ganges, where it happens to be longest—from the fifth mouth of the river Ganges, called Antibole, as far as the harbour of Naustathmos, the one in the gulf of Kanthi[75]—is 18,290 stades. Its breadth, from the promontory called Apheterion as far as the sources of the river Ganges, is 13,000 stades. It contains 54 nations or satrapies, 216 notable cities, villages, and trading-places, 6 notable mountains, 23 notable rivers, 2 notable promontories, 1 notable harbour, 5 notable gulfs, 12 notable river mouths, 1 notable departure place, 10 notable river confluences, and 9 notable islands.

39. The total of the circumnavigation of the region[76] of the Gangetic gulf, from Apheterion up to the fifth mouth of the river Ganges, the one called Antibole, is **5,660 stades**.

The grand total of the circumnavigation of all of Indike within the Ganges, from the harbour of Naustathmos as far as the fifth mouth of the river Ganges, which is called Antibole, is **35,695 stades**.

Circumnavigation of Indike outside the river Ganges and the gulfs therein

40. Indike outside the river Ganges is bounded on the north by the parts of Skythia and Serike (*Silk Land*);[77] on the west by the river Ganges itself; on the east by the Sinai[78] up to the so-called Megas (*Great*) gulf and by the gulf itself;[79] and on the south by the Indian open-sea (*pelagos*) and a part of the Prasodes Thalassa (*Green Sea*) which, beginning from the island of Menouthias (*Madagascar*), extends on a parallel line up to the parts of the Great gulf lying opposite, as we have mentioned before.[80] (The part-by-part (*description*) is omitted.)

41. The length of Indike outside the Ganges, where it happens to be longest, is 11,650 stades; its breadth, where it is widest, is 19,000 stades.[81] It contains 50 nations or satrapies, 67 notable cities, villages, and trading-places, 18 notable mountains, 5 notable promontories, 3 notable harbours, 1 very large gulf, and 30 notable islands.

42. The total of the circumnavigation of the part of the Great gulf that happens to be beside Indike outside the Ganges, from the ⟨Great⟩ promontory up to the frontier with the Sinai, is **12,550**.

The grand total of the whole circumnavigation of the coast of Indike outside the Ganges, from the fifth mouth of the river Ganges, which is called Antibole, up to the boundaries with the nation of the Sinai, is **45,350 stades**.[82]

---

[75] Apparently near *Bhuj* in *Gujarat*.   [76] Or possibly 'of this part'.

[77] The derivation of 'Serike' and 'Seres' (1. 17) from a word for silk is implicitly accepted by Stückelberger and Graßhoff 2006, ii. 743 n. 170 (to Ptol. 7. 5. 2).

[78] See n. on 1. 10. Ptol. 1. 17. 5 locates the Seres N of the Sinai.   [79] See n. on 1. 16.

[80] For the relationship between the Prasodes Thalassa and the Indikon Pelagos, see n. on 1. 12.

[81] It does not seem possible to reconcile the different figures in 1. 41–2.

[82] At 8 st. to the mile, this would be *c.*5,668¾ miles. Even allowing for coastal indentations, this is several times the circuit of Indo-China including the elongated *Malay* peninsula; taken at face value, the figure would imply knowledge of China at least as far as Taiwan or, in another direction, *Bali* (see n. on 1. 7 Megas Kolpos).

Circumnavigation of the Sinai and the gulfs among them

43. The nation of the Sinai is bounded on the north by a part of Serike; on the west by Indike outside the Ganges, at the aforementioned frontier in the Megas (*Great*) gulf; on the east by unknown land; and on the south by the southern sea and the southern unknown land. And the overall outline has this character; ⟨but the part-by-part (*account*) is as follows⟩. (The part-by-part (*description*) is omitted.)

44. Here there begin to live beside (*the sea*), up to the southern unknown land, the Ichthyophagoi (*Fish-eating*) Sinai.[83] For one must understand that there are two unknown lands: that running through along the east, beside which we have stated that the Sinai live, and that beside the south,[84] which runs through beside all the Indike Thalassa (*Indian sea*), also called the Prasodes, which is part of the Indike Thalassa;[85] so that in joining together each of the unknown lands it (*the southern one*) forms a sort of angle at the Sinōn kolpos (*gulf of the Sinai*).[86] Beyond the Sinai lies the territory of the Seres and their mother-city.[87] The places further east than these are unknown land containing marshy lakes, in which great reeds grow so thickly that people effect their passage by holding onto them.

CIRCUMNAVIGATION OF THE THERIODES GULF

45. So as one sails beyond the Megas (*Great*) gulf and Notion Akron (*South Point*)[88] in a southerly direction, keeping the land of the Sinai and the east on the left, there follows a gulf called Theriodes (*Of Wild Animals*),[89] which runs through up to the promontory called Satyrōn Akron (*Satyrs' Point*).[90] The total of the circumnavigation of the Theriodes gulf, from Notion Point up to the promontory of the Satyrs, is **10,503†** stades.[91]

CIRCUMNAVIGATION OF THE GULF OF THE SINAI

46. From Satyrs' Point there follows a very large gulf called Sinōn kolpos (*gulf of the Sinai*).[92] This runs along up to the southern unknown land where it joins the unknown land in the east beside which, as we have mentioned, the Sinai live. So from the

---

[83] Ptol. 7. 3. 3 locates 'Fish-eating Aithiopes' around the gulf of the Sinai.
[84] A dim awareness of Borneo and islands beyond?
[85] These phrases are not consistent; that one or other is an intrusive gloss seems a possibility.
[86] Not mentioned by Mark. until now. The explanation probably reflects the ancient belief in a land bridge from SE Asia to Africa; cf. Stückelberger and Graßhoff 2006, ii. 733 n. 139; cf. Introduction, §III. 3. g; but it remains confusing unless Mark. is thinking of the southern unknown land as joining SE Asia about here.
[87] Ptol. 1. 11. 4 calls it Sera. Stückelberger and Graßhoff 2006, ii. 669 n. 229 (on Ptol. 6. 16. 8), note that while the official Chinese view today is that Sera is *Xi'an*, the capital in Ptolemy's day was *Luoyang*.
[88] Not mentioned up to now; presumably details were omitted at the end of 1. 43. If Megas is the *Andaman sea* or the *Malacca strait* (see n. on 1. 7 Megas), then Notion Akron may be Singapore (*c*.1° N).
[89] *Gulf of Thailand*? See n. on 1. 7 Megas.
[90] If Theriodes is the *gulf of Thailand*, Satyron Akron should be *Mui Ca Mao*, the S extremity of Vietnam, though it at *c*.8° N whereas Ptol. 7. 3. 3 locates Satyron Akron on the Equator.
[91] Müller suggests 4,550; but all reconstructed distances depend on what locations we assign to named places and features.
[92] Probably the *gulf of Tonkin*; see n. on 1. 7 Megas.

promontory of the Satyrs to the outlets of the river Kottiaris, which discharges in the gulf of the Sinai, is 1,250 stades.

From the river Kottiaris there follows Kattigara,[93] representing an anchorage (*hormos*) of the Sinai but also the frontier of the known and inhabited land in the parts towards the south. The number of stades in this circumnavigation it is not easy to compute. It will not be easy for anyone other than some divine intelligence to show clearly the subsequent circumnavigation, the one after the anchorage of the Sinai, nor to render clear[94] for people the parts towards the south that run along beside the unknown land, nor the unknown land beside the eastern (*land*) after the Sinai.

47. The greatest length of the (*territory of the*) Sinai is 3,000 stades; its greatest breadth is 17,250 stades. It contains 5 nations or satrapies, 7 notable cities and villages, 1 notable mountain, 4 notable rivers, 2 notable gulfs, and 2 notable promontories. ⟨Altogether the cities and villages of the eastern Earth are 560.⟩

48. The total of the whole circumnavigation of the coast of the Sinai, from the frontier in the Great gulf of the Sinai, lying towards Indike outside the Ganges, to the outlets of the river Kottiaris, is **12,650 stades**.[95]

Recapitulation of all the aforementioned distances

49 (50 M.).[96] It is established that the whole circumnavigation and outline of the maritime territory of (*this*) part of Asia—the Arabian gulf, the Erythraian sea, and also the Persian gulf and the Indian open-sea (*pelagos*)—has this character.

The grand total of the distance, if all the gulfs are sailed round, from the Ailanites head as far as the outlets of the river of Kottiaris that happens to be in the gulf of the Sinai, is **153,295 stades**.[97] The part-by-part (*account*) of the coast of the left-hand parts has this character:

50 (51 M.). From the Ailanites head, from which we made a start on the circumnavigation of the left-hand parts of Asia, up to the narrows of the Arabian gulf, 11,670 stades.[98]

From the narrows of the Arabian gulf, the stades of the circumnavigation of the Erythraian sea and a part of the Indian open-sea (*pelagos*) are 21,530.[99]

From the mouth of the Persian gulf back up to the same mouth again, the ⟨stades⟩ of the circumnavigation of the whole Persian gulf are ⟨16,790.

---

[93] Probably near *Hanoi* (Stückelberger and Graßhoff 2006, e.g. 733 (on Ptol. 7. 3. 3); cf. their map at i. 18. An earlier view identified Kottiara with *Óc Eo* (*O Keo*) in the *Mekong* delta (10° 15′ N, 105° 9′ E)). For C2 AD Roman finds there, see Wheeler 1954, 172; Brentjes 2006b; cf. Calo, Bellwood *et al.* 2020, 111, 114, etc.; for trade in SE Asia during the Sasanid era (AD 224–651), Ritter 2011; and for R finds further E, see n. on 1. 10 'the known Earth'.

[94] Reading καταστῆσαι for καταστῆναι, with Lucarini 2020, 225.

[95] This information is soon repeated in the overview at 1. 50.

[96] There is no section 1. 49 in Müller.   [97] 123,395 in MS; corrected by Müller.

[98] 11,609 in MS; corrected by Müller.   [99] 10,530 in MS; Müller suggests 21,340.

From the Persian gulf⟩ up to the boundaries of the coast of the Karmanians, 5,950 stades.¹⁰⁰

From the aforementioned boundaries of Karmania up to the city of Rhizana on the coast of the Gedrosians, 3,850 stades.

From the above-mentioned boundaries of Gedrosia and also the first and westernmost mouth of the river Indos, called Sagapa, up to the fifth mouth of the river Ganges, which is called Antibole, the stades of the coast of Indike within the Ganges are 35,695.

From the fifth mouth of the river Ganges, which is called Antibole, up to the boundaries with the Sinai, who happen to be in the very middle¹⁰¹ of the so-called Great gulf, the stades of Indike outside the river Ganges are 45,350.¹⁰²

From the frontier of the Sinai in the Great gulf to the outlets of the river Kottiaris on the coast of the Sinai, 12,650 stades.

The total stades of the aforementioned total circumnavigation of the left-hand parts of Asia, from the Ailanites head up to the nation of the Sinai and the outlets of the river Kottiaris, are gathered together into **153,295**.

51 (52 M.). Here, then, we shall make an end of our first book, after composing the circumnavigation of all of the Arabian gulf, all of the Erythraian sea, not to mention the Indian open-sea (*pelagos*) in both its right-hand and, moreover, its left-hand parts—such as have become attainable by human diligence and scholarship—up to the unknown land by both continents, the eastern and the southern. Now we shall begin the circumnavigation of the western Ocean; for that was what we promised to do at the beginning of the book.

Markianos of Herakleia in the Pontos, his *Circumnavigation* of the outer sea, eastern and western, and of the largest islands in it. Of the two books, the first (*ends here*).

BOOK 2¹⁰³

⟨Contents of Book 2⟩

⟨The following things are in Markianos' 2nd *Periplous* of the eastern and western Ocean.

Preface (*prooimion*).⟩

Circumnavigation of the parts of Iberia and Hispania beside the western and northern Ocean. The part-by-part (*account*) is as follows: Circumnavigation of Baitike from the parts around Kalpe up to the boundaries of Lousitania. Circumnavigation of Lousitania. Circumnavigation of Tarrakonesia.

Circumnavigation of the so-called Keltogalatia. The part-by-part (*account*) is as follows: Circumnavigation of Akytania (*Aquitania*). Circumnavigation of Lougdounesia (*Lugdunensis*). Circumnavigation of Belgike with upper and lower Germania.

Circumnavigation of Great Germania.

---

¹⁰⁰ 5,750 in MS; corrected by Müller.
¹⁰² 15,330 in MS; corrected by Müller.
¹⁰¹ The same location is indicated at 1. 16.
¹⁰³ Book 2 begins on p. 28 of codex D.

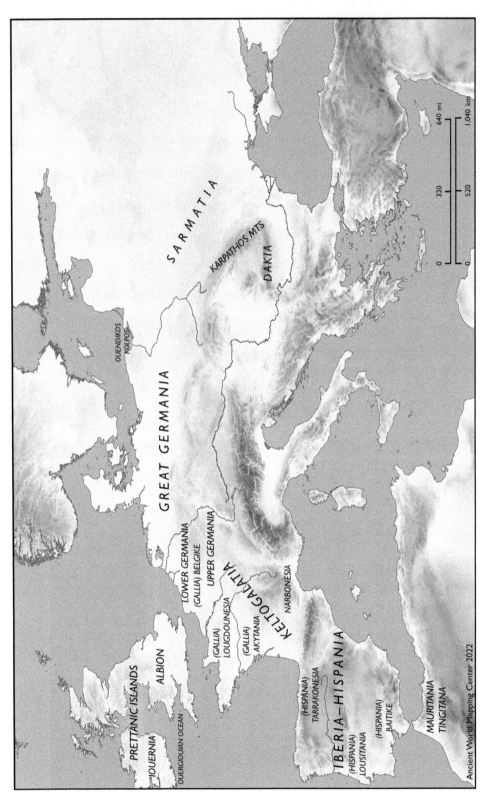

MAP 34.2. Markianos: *Circumnavigation*, book 2.

Circumnavigation of the Sarmatia in Europe.

On the Prettanic (*British*) islands. Circumnavigation of the Prettanic island of Iouernia (*Hibernia*). ⟨Circumnavigation of the Prettanic island of Albion.⟩

Circumnavigation of the parts of Libyē beside the western and northern Ocean up to Aithiopia. The part-by-part (*account*) is as follows: Circumnavigation of Mauritania Tingitana. Circumnavigation of inner Libyē.[104]

On the distances from Rome to the notable cities of the inhabited world.[105]

⟨Preface⟩

1. The second book will contain the whole circumnavigation from the Herakleian strait along the western and northern Ocean up to the northernmost parts; and, moreover, of the southern parts as far as the unidentified land in both continents. This (*circumnavigation*) will be, first, of the right-hand parts along Iberia—which is also called Hispania—(*namely*) the places in it that lie beside the Ocean; and moreover along Akytania, Lougdounesia (*Lugdunensis*), and Belgike; and Great Germania up to the (*part of*) Sarmatia that is in Europe, after which there follows the unknown land towards the north. In addition to these, however, (*it will also be a circumnavigation*) of the two islands lying in the northern Ocean that they commonly call (*the*) Prettanikai, though one of them is called Iouernia and the other Albion; and of the left-hand parts along Libyē and the western and southern Ocean, and the places adjoining these up to the so-called Aithiopian Hypodromos (*Run-in*),[106] where it is established that the Ocean, spreading towards the south, has its end and the unknown land then follows.

2. The accurate circumnavigation of all the sea within the Pillars of Herakles, as we have mentioned before, has been made accurately by us, we deem, in the summaries of the eleven books by Artemidoros of Ephesos, the geographer, whom we believe has made the most diligent circumnavigation of our sea in the (*books*) of his *Geography*.[107] As for the outer sea, which is called Ocean by most (*writers*), even if the aforementioned Artemidoros has to some extent noted certain parts, nevertheless we, extracting the most accurate circumnavigation of this (*sea*) from the *Geography* of the divine Ptolemy and, what is more, from Protagoras and other ancient men—that is, of the Arabian gulf and the Erythraian sea in both continents and, moreover, of the whole Indian open-sea (*pelagos*) up to the eastern and unknown land—have gone through it in our former book, as far as possible in sequence.

Now, however, we shall arrive at the parts around the western Ocean.

3. So we shall make a beginning of the circumnavigation of the outer sea from the Herakleian strait. This strait divides the two continents: both Iberia, ⟨which⟩ they also designate Hispania, and which represents a part of Europe, and Libyē, lying directly

---

[104] The areas in this paragraph are lost from the end of the surviving text.

[105] This may have been a separate work (F. 42 below).

[106] Cf. Ptolemy, *Geography*, 4. 6. 7: 'the *hypodromos* of Aithiopia', following Mauretania and preceding a list of mountains in Libyē.

[107] Much of this paragraph repeats the statement at 1. 1.

opposite it. For as one sails out of the Herakleian strait and presses on towards the Ocean, on one's right is the nation of Baitike in Hispania, but on the left, in Libyē, are the Mauritaniai, as they are called. The ⟨open sea⟩ (*pelagos*) between these ⟨in the inner sea is called⟩ the Iberic. After one has sailed out through the Herakleian strait and (*past*) the temple of Hera[108]—this lies on the right during the voyage out of the strait— there follows the Ocean, opening out towards both continents, Iberia and Libyē, and also extending westwards to a limitless and unknown magnitude.

4. The first place on the right happens to be the island of Gadeira, where it is established that the Pillars of Herakles are. For those at Mt Kalpe, which lies inward from the Herakleian narrows, say that this is the Pillars; but those at Gadeira (*say that*) the island is, as does Artemidoros the geographer. But there is no obstacle to making the circumnavigation of Iberia from Mt Kalpe, which most people would like to be the Pillar of Herakles.

Kalpe is in the province called Baitike.[109] The end and frontier of this nation is occupied by the river Anas (*Guadiana*), making its outlets at the western Ocean. After this, the subsequent nations of Hispania happen to lie by the outer sea and the Ocean.[110] So the circumnavigation will have its beginning from Kalpe in Iberia and from ⟨this⟩ part of the province of Baitike.

5. Since many of those who have circumnavigated these parts made mistakes about the number of stades—indeed, we have gone through the causes of such errors in our previous book—nevertheless, for the sake of greater accuracy, we have generally chosen to append the number of stades in double form, adding 'not more than' and 'not less than' next to a line placed beneath. Thus the interval between both numbers will be available,[111] as a kind of definition of the truth, for those pursuing accuracy. Protagoras, too, by doing this in a clear manner in his *Geography*, seems to have avoided the error with reference to the stades.

Circumnavigation of the parts of Iberia or Hispania beside the Ocean

6. Iberia, which is also called Hispania, begins from the Pyrenaian mountains and runs very far, surrounded by both seas: the northern and western Ocean, and our sea. Mt Pyrene, beginning from our sea, stretches up to the northern Ocean. One extremity of the mountain projects into our sea; but its other extremity is thrust forth towards the north and the northern Ocean. It disconnects and divides Iberia with respect to the region that follows, namely Keltogalatia, so that Iberia appears to be a very large

---

[108] Cf. 2. 3 above.

[109] Hispania Baetica, created by Augustus when he reorganized the Spanish provinces (cf. 2. 7 below).

[110] Not that they have only an Atlantic coast: Mark. refers below to the Mediterranean coasts of Baetica and Tarraconensis.

[111] 'The interval' translates τὸ μεταξύ–*to metaxý*, literally 'the between'. It does not seem that Mark. is referring to the mean (average) of the two data; cf. Geus 2014 for the absence of averaging in ancient geography.

peninsula attached by the neck to Pyrene. The mountain curves somewhat towards Hispania.

7. Formely Iberia has been divided by the Romans into two provinces, but now into three: Hispania Baitike (*Baetica*), Hispania Lousitania (*Lusitania*), and Hispania Tarrakonesia (*Tarraconensis*). The majority of Baitike lies in front of our sea (*and*) within the Pillars of Herakles, but part (*lies*) beside the western Ocean. Of the two remaining nations, the whole of Lousitania happens to lie by the western Ocean; but Tarrakonesia over its greatest part is adjacent to the northern Ocean, though in a certain part to our sea: it runs through from the south to both seas, up to the Pyrenaean mountains. So we shall write the circumnavigation of the parts of Iberia beside the Ocean; for this is what we undertook to do.[112]

CIRCUMNAVIGATION OF BAITIKE FROM THE PARTS AROUND KALPE UP TO THE BOUNDARIES OF LOUSITANIA

8. Hispania Baitike is bounded on the north and west by Lousitania and part of the province of Tarrakonesia; but on the east by the so-called Balearic open-sea (*pelagos*), which is attached to the Iberian sea (*thalassa*); on the south, at the outer sea and the Herakleian strait, by the western Ocean; but at the inner sea by the Iberian open-sea (*pelagos*). And the overall outline is of this kind; but the part-by-part circumnavigation has this character:

9. From the mountain and pillar of Kalpe—which is at the beginning of the inner sea—as one sails out to the strait and the Ocean, keeping the mainland of Iberia on the right, it is 50 stades to Karteia. Beside this lives the nation of ⟨the⟩ Bastouloi called Poinoi (*Punic*).

From Karteia to Barbesola, 100 stades.

From Barbesola to Transducta (*or Iulia Traducta*), not more than 200 stades; not less than 145 according to the line placed beneath.

From Transducta to Menralia (*or Mellaria*), not more than 115 stades;[113] not less than 123 stades.

From Menralia to the city of Belon, not more than 140 stades; not less than 100 stades. Here begins the nation of the Tourdouloi.

From the city of Belon to the outlets of the river Belon, not more than 75 stades;[114] not less than 50 stades.

From the outlets of the river Belon to the promontory at which lie the strait and the temple of Hera, 200 stades/150 stades.

From here on, only the stades will adjoin (*the text*), and the first of the two numbers will show the greatest, and the following (*number*) the lesser, so that we shall not write 'more than' and 'less than' before each instance.[115]

---

[112] Quoted inaccurately by Steph. Byz. 1 19 'Iberiai: two': see at end of chapter.
[113] Müller suggests 155 st.
[114] Müller translates as 75 and has evidently misprinted σε (205) for οε.
[115] I use an oblique stroke (/) to join these double measurements.

From the promontory at which are the strait and the temple of Hera, as one sails the Ocean northwards and similarly keeps the mainland on the right and the western Ocean on the left, there follows Menestheos Limen (*Menestheus's Harbour*).[116] Up to it there are 225 stades/160 stades.

By these places lies an island in the outer sea, Gadeira (*Cádiz*), on which is also a city of the same name, Gadeira. From the promontory where the strait is to Gadeira, the island, 270 stades/240 stades.

From Menestheos Limen to the estuary at Astan, 210 stades. From here the Tourdetanoi begin to live beside (*the coast*).

From the estuary at Astan to the more easterly mouth of the river Baitis (*Guadalquivir*), 385 stades/285 stades. From the outlets of the river Baitis to the sources of the same river, 3,350 stades/2,400 stades.

From the more easterly mouth of the river Baitis to Onoba Aistouria,[117] 420 stades/300 stades.

From Onoba Aistouria to the outlets of the river Anas, 210 stades/150 stades. From the outlets of the river Anas to the sources of the same river, 2,145 stades/1,550 stades.

This is the extremity of the part of Baitike Hispania that runs along beside both the seas that happen to be in the area of the Herakleian strait: the one on our side and the outer one, that is, the Ocean.

10. The length of the whole of Baitike begins from the outlets of the river Anas and passes through as far as the sources of the same river Anas, so that the stades in its length, via the greater line, are 3,709.

The breadth of Baitike begins from the sources of the same river, but terminates towards the south in the direction of the aforementioned temple of Hera, or the city of Belon or Portos Magnos (*Portus Magnus*), so that the stades in the distance of the breadth, via the greater line, are 1,158.

The boundary circuit of inland Baitike is 6,709 stades/5,140 stades. It contains 5 nations, 85 notable cities, 3 notable mountains, 5 notable rivers, 2 notable promontories, and 1 notable harbour.

11. The total stades of the circumnavigation of the whole of Baitike are gathered together into not more than 4,345 stades/⟨not less than [—] stades⟩. Of this part of Baitike whose circumnavigation we have made, from the mountain and pillar of Kalpe up to the outlets of the river Anas on the same coast beside the Ocean, the stades are not more than 2,380, not less than 1,245.[118]

CIRCUMNAVIGATION OF LOUSITANIA

12. Of the Hispanias, Lousitania is bounded on the north by Tarrakonesia Hispania, along the western part of the river Dorion (*Douro*); on the east by the same Tarrakonesia; on the west by the western Ocean; on the south by the aforementioned Baitike,

---

[116] Apparently at *Cádiz*.   [117] Near *Huelva*. Probably the same as Ossonoba in 2. 11.
[118] Müller suggests 1,745.

⟨which, as we stated, lies beside the western Ocean,⟩ and by our sea. And the overall outline has this character; but the part-by-part (*account*) is as follows.

13. From the outlets of the aforementioned river Anas to Balsa, 380 stades/⟨... 240 (?) stades⟩. And beside these parts live the Tourdetanoi.

From Balsa to Ossonoba,[119] 340 stades/300 stades.

From Ossonoba to the Hieron (*Sacred*) Promontory (*C. St Vincent?*), 360 stades/260 stades. This projects far out into the Ocean, and is among the most famous (*promontories*).

From Hieron Promontory to the outlets of the river Kalipous, 1,350 stades/950 stades.

From the outlets of the river Kalipous to Salakra, 230 stades/210 stades.

From Salakra to Kaitobrix (*Alentejo*), 105 stades/90 stades.

From Kaitobrix to Barbarion Point,[120] 190 stades/160 stades.

From Barbarion Point to Oliosipon (*Lisbon*), 380 stades/250 stades.

From Oliosipon to the outlets of the river Tagos (*Tagus*), 155 stades/⟨... 130 (?) stades⟩. To the sources of the same river, ⟨... stades⟩.

From the outlets of the river Tagos to the Mountain and Point of Selene (*the Moon*), there are 150 stades/120 stades. Beside here lies ⟨an island⟩ called Lanobris; and from the promontory of Selene to this is 940 stades/670 stades. From Hieron Promontory to this is 1,510 stades/1,130 stades.

From Mount Selene to the outlets of the river Monda, 150 stades/120 stades.

From the river Monda to the outlets of the Ouakos,[121] 380 stades/275 stades.

After the river Ouakos there follow the outlets of the river Dorion, at which it is established that Lousitania Hispania has its end.

From the outlets of the river Dorion to the sources of the same river, 1,370 stades.

⟨From the outlets of the Ouakos to the outlets of the river Dorion, ... stades/... stades.⟩

14. The length of Lousitania begins from the western side and the promontory of Hieron and passes through towards the sources of the river Dorion, so that the stades of its length, via the greatest line, are 3,335. The breadth of Lousitania begins from the sea by the northern side at the outlets of the river Ouakos, and ceases in the direction of the south at the city of Balsa, so that in addition the stades of the breadth, via the greater line, are 1,793. The boundary circuit of Lousitania in the interior has a grand total of 4,400 stades/4,000 stades. It contains 4 nations, 56 notable cities, 5 notable mountains, 6 notable rivers, and 2 notable promontories.

---

[119] Probably the same as Onoba in 2. 9.   [120] Near *Lisbon*.
[121] A number of names in book 2 begin with Ou-, similar to consonantal *u* in Latin. As such, they may be pronounced as if spelled with *w* (in English), e.g. 'Wakos' in this case.

15. The total of the circumnavigation of the coast of Lousitania facing the Ocean, from the outlets of the river Anas up to the outlets of the river Dorion, is not more than **4,140 stades**; not less than **3,265 stades**.

CIRCUMNAVIGATION OF TARRAKONESIA

16. Of the Hispaniai, Tarrakonesia is bounded on the north by the Kantabrian ocean, and this belongs to the northern parts; but in the direction of the summer sunrises (*north-east*) by the whole of (*Mt*) Pyrene, from Oiasso (*Irun*), a promontory of Pyrene, up to its other promontory lying beside our sea, upon which has been founded the sanctuary of Aphrodite; ⟨in the direction of the winter sunrises (*south-east*) by the Baliaric (*sic*) open-sea (*pelagos*)⟩; on the south by the aforementioned Lousitania and ⟨the (*part of*) Baitike lying upon⟩ our sea; and on the west by the western Ocean. And the overall outline has this character: ⟨but the part-by-part (*account*) is as follows.⟩

17. The length of Tarrakonesia begins on the western side from the promontory of Nerion (*or Artabrum*), but passes by the promontory of Pyrene in our sea, where the sanctuary of Aphrodite is, so that the length of the province, via the section through the middle, is 7,230 stades. The breadth of Tarrakonesia ⟨begins by the northern side from the Kantabrian ocean and the Pyrenaian mountain, and ceases in a southerly direction at the northern parts of Lousitania⟩ and Baitike, ⟨and at the city of Ourke in Baitike⟩, so that the distance of the breadth, via the greater line, is 4,250 stades.

Its boundary circuit by land is 4,500 stades/3,300 stades. It contains 55 nations, 273 notable cities, 5 notable mountains, 23 notable rivers, 8 notable promontories, and 2 notable harbours.

18. And the circumnavigation of Tarrakonesia, the parts lying towards the Ocean on the western and northern side, has been told; but the remaining part of it, beside the Baliaric (*sic*) open-sea (*pelagos*), beginning from the Pyrenaean mountain and its promontory, on which, as we have mentioned before, lies the ⟨sanctuary of⟩ Aphrodite, and ceasing at Ourke, after which there follows the province of Baitike, whose parts towards the Herakleian strait and western Ocean we went through at the start; ⟨in the summary of Artemidoros' *Geography* or *Circumnavigation* we went through it clearly⟩.

The total of the circumnavigation of the coast of Tarrakonesia beside the Ocean, from the outlets of the river Dorion to the promontory of Pyrene named Oiasso, is not more than **10,327 stades**/not less than **8,012 stades**.

The grand total of the whole circumnavigation of Iberia lying beside the Ocean, from Mt Kalpe lying by the Herakleian strait up to the promontory of Pyrene (*named*) Oiasso, is not more than **16,845 stades/13,282 stades**.[122]

Therefore the circumnavigation of Iberia that happens to be beside the western and northern Ocean, from Mt Kalpe and the Herakleian strait up to Mt Pyrene and its

---

[122] The MS has 16,045 and 13,286; corrected by Müller.

northern extremity, ⟨the promontory⟩[123] called Oiasso, has this character; but we shall proceed to the subsequent matters.

Circumnavigation of Keltogalatia

19. The so-called Keltogalatia goes through very far by land and ⟨by⟩ sea. It has been divided into four provinces: Gallia Akytania, Gallia Lougdounesia (*Lugdunensis*), Gallia Belgike (*Belgica*), and ⟨Gallia⟩ Narbonesia (*Narbonensis*). But the aforementioned three provinces live towards the Ocean, turned towards the north, while Narbonesia lies in our sea, the inner one, and looks towards the south.

So we shall tell the circumnavigation in sequence, beginning from the nations of Akytania living beside the northern Ocean in Keltogalatia; for we undertook to compose this circumnavigation. We have clearly expounded the circumnavigation of Narbonesia in the epitome of Artemidoros' *Geography* or *Circumnavigation*, even if the aforementioned Artemidoros did not make the division between the provinces in ⟨Keltogalatia and those in⟩ Iberia.

CIRCUMNAVIGATION OF AKYTANIA

20. Akytania is bounded on the north by part of the succeeding province, Lougdounesia, and by the northern Ocean after it; on the east, likewise, by the part of Lougdounesia at the river Liger (*Loire*) up to its sources, and by part of Narbonesia up to its extremity towards Pyrene; on the west by the Akytanian ocean; on the south by the part of Pyrene inclining towards the Ocean at the promontory of Oiasso, and by part of the province of Narbonesia from the head of the Liger up to the aforementioned extremity at Pyrene. And the overall outline is of this kind; but the part-by-part (*account*) of the coast at the Akytanian ocean is as follows.[124]

21. After Oiasso, the promontory of Pyrene, there follow the outlets of the river Atouris; to this it is not more than 1,250 stades/not less than 785 stades.

From the outlets of the Atouris to the outlets of the river Signatis, 500 stades/450 ⟨stades⟩.

From the outlets of the river Signatis to the promontory of Kouriannon is 500 stades/370 stades.

From Kouriannon to the outlets of the river Garounna (*Garonne*), which is 50 stades in size (*i.e. width*), 600 stades/430 ⟨stades⟩. From the outlets of the Garounna to its sources, 900 stades/600 stades.

After one has sailed up the river Garounna, there lies a city in Akytania, Bourdigala (*Bordeaux*). Beside here live the Santones, to whom belongs the city of Mediolanion (*Mediolanum Santonum; Saintes*),[125] lying upon the sea beside the river Garounna.

From the outlets of the river Garounna to the Santones' Point, 475 stades/325 stades.

---

[123] Added by Lucarini 2020, 225.   [124] Cf. B. 4 below.
[125] Müller comments on the inaccuracy of this, not denying the name of Mediolanion and giving its modern name as *Saintes*, but saying it lies on the R. *Charente*.

From the Santones' Point to the outlets of the river Kanentellos (*Charente*), 560 stades/550 (?) stades.

From the outlets of the river Kanentellos to Piktonion Point,[126] 210 stades/150 stades.

From Piktonion Point to the harbour of Sikor (*Nantes?*), 300 stades/290 stades.

From the harbour of Sikor to the river Liger (*Loire*), which happens to be very large and has a size of ⟨... stades (*in width*)⟩, 185 stades/155 stades. Beside the river live the nation of the Samnitai.

22. The length of Akytania begins from the outlets of the river Atouris, passing on to the city of Auarikon (*Avaricum*),[127] so that via the longest line there are 1,408 stades. The breadth of Akytania begins from its extremity towards Pyrene, and ceases at the southward bend of the river Liger, so that the stades are 2,250. Its boundary circuit in the interior is not more than 4,770 stades/not less than 3,370. It contains 16 nations, 16 notable cities, 5 notable rivers, 4 notable promontories, and 1 notable harbour.

23. The total circumnavigation of the coast of Akytania, from Oiasso, the promontory of Pyrene, up to the outlets of the river Liger, is not more than **4,800** stades/not less than **3,525** stades.

CIRCUMNAVIGATION OF LOUGDOUNESIA

24. Lougdounesia Gallia is bounded on the north by the Prettanic ocean; on the east by the province of Belgike at the river Sekoanos (*Seine*); but on the west by the Akytanian ocean; and on the south by part of the province of Narbonesia. And the overall outline of the nation has this character; ⟨but the part-by-part (*account*) is as follows [—]...⟩

25. The length of Lougdounesia begins from the promontory of Gabaion and leaves off by its eastern side where it is attached to Belgike at the river Sekoanos, so that the stades of its length are 3,376. The breadth of Lougdounesia begins on the south from the city of Kabyllinon, but ceases at the outlets of the river Sekoanos, so that the stades of its breadth are 3,080. The circuit of the province by land is 7,290 stades/5,420 stades. It contains 25 nations, 26 notable cities, 1 notable mountain, 4 notable rivers, 1 notable promontory, and 3 notable harbours.

26. The total circumnavigation of the coast of Lougdounesia, from the outlets of the river Liger up to the outlets of the river Sekoanos, is **3,370 stades/3,065 stades.**

CIRCUMNAVIGATION OF BELGIKE WITH UPPER AND LOWER GERMANIA

27. Belgike with the two Germaniai is bounded on the north by the northern Ocean that comes through beside Prettania (*Britain*); but on the east by the river Rhenos (*Rhine*) beside Great Germania as far as the head of the river, and also by the mountain, from its source to the Alps, that is called Adoulas; on the west by the province of Lougdounesia and the aforementioned river Sekoanos; on the south by the remaining part of Narbonesia. And the overall outline of the nation is roughly of this kind; ⟨but the part-by-part (*account*) is as follows.⟩

---

[126] Near *Nantes*.   [127] Near *Bourges*.

28. For (*the territory*) from the sea up to the river Obrinka is called Lower Germania, but that from the river Obrinka (*onwards*) is called Upper Germania.

29. The length of Belgike, with the two Germaniai, begins from the outlets of the river Phroudis and passes eastwards by the river Rhenos beside Great Germania as far as the head of the river, so that the stades of the length are 2,685.

Its breadth begins from Mt Adoulas and the common extremity of the Alps, and ceases at the western mouth of the Rhenos, so that the stades of the breadth become 4,375. The total boundary circuit by land of the province of Belgike ⟨with the two Germaniai⟩ is 15,160 stades/12,300 stades. Belgike with the two Germaniai contains 24 nations, 38 notable cities, 2 notable mountains, 7 notable rivers, and 1 notable promontory.

30. The total of the whole circumnavigation of the coast of Belgike with Upper and Lower Germania, from the river Sekoanos up to the river Rhenos—⟨that is,⟩ its so-called western mouth—is not more than **3,850 stades**/not less than **3,180 stades**.

Circumnavigation of Great Germania[128]

31. Great Germania is bounded on the north by the so-called Germanic ocean; but on the east by the Sarmatic mountains and ⟨the part of Sarmatia⟩ after the mountains ⟨up to⟩ the head of the river Ouistoula (*Vistula*)[129] and also by the river itself; on the south by the western part of the river Danoubios (*Danube*),[130] and on the west by the river Rhenos. And the overall outline of the territory is as follows; but we shall (*now*) tell it part by part.

32. From the outlets of the river Rhenos—that is, from its so-called western mouth—to the outlets of the river Ouidros[131] is 380 stades/⟨... stades⟩.

From the river Ouidros to the harbour of Mararmanos, 350 stades/250 stades.

From the harbour of Mararmanos to the outlets of the river Amasios (*or Amisia; Ems*), 655 stades/470 stades.

From the outlets of the river Amasios to the sources of the same river, 2,350 stades/1,300 stades.

From the outlets of the river Amasios to the outlets of the river Ouisourgios (*Weser*), 560 stades/⟨... stades⟩.

From the outlets of the river Ouisourgios to the sources of the same river, 1,780 stades/1,600 stades.

---

[128] This 'Great Germania' is across the *Rhine* from the Roman provinces of Upper and Lower Germany just described.

[129] Reaching the sea E of *Gdańsk*.

[130] At this point, Müller plausibly brackets the following words as a marginal gloss: 'the Danoubios where it begins has a size (*i.e. width*) of 1 stade, then 2 stades, next 3 stades, and also changes its name, being called Istros as well'.

[131] Presumably one of the distributaries of the *Rhine*; perhaps the *IJssel*, which is slightly less than halfway from the main *Rhine* outlet and the *Ems*.

From the river Ouisourgios to the outlets of the river Albis (*Elbe*), 625 stades/⟨... stades⟩.

From the outlets of the river Albis to the sources of the same river, 5,370 stades/3,300 stades. By this part lie the so-called Islands of the Saxones. To them from the outflow of the river Albis is 750 stades/⟨... stades⟩.

33. After the river Albis there follows the so-called Kimbric peninsula (*Jutland*), which happens to be very great.

From the outlets of the river Albis to the peninsula's first projection, the one lying after the river Albis, there are 570 stades/400 stades.

From the peninsula's first projection to the projection of the same peninsula that lies next, 1,600 stades/1,100 stades.

From the peninsula's second projection to the next and northernmost projection of the same peninsula, 1,450 stades/1,150 stades.

From the northernmost projection of the peninsula to the first projection after its bend, 650 stades/550 stades.

From the first projection after its bend to its easternmost part, 720 stades/520 stades.

From the easternmost part of the peninsula itself to its (*projection*) next beneath ⟨this one⟩, 2,000 stades/1,500 stades.

From the (*projection*) next beneath its (*projection*) to its (*the peninsula's*) eastward bend, 1,600 stades/750 stades.

Here the circumnavigation of the Kimbric peninsula is completed; it runs a long way into the Ocean and lies obliquely parallel to the eastward mainland, so that at the river Suebos (*Oder?*) it creates a very large gulf that extends to its inner part. The total circumnavigation of the peninsula is 8,050 stades/5,970 stades.

34. The neck of the peninsula is occupied by the nation called Axones,[132] though numerous nations occupy the peninsula itself. Beyond the peninsula lie three islands called the Alokiai; from the peninsula to these is 550 stades/500 stades.

To the east of the peninsula lie the so-called Skandiai islands: three small ones, from which to the middle of the peninsula there are 2,000 stades/1,700 stades; one very large, the easternmost, and this is specifically called Skandia.[133] It lies by the outlets of the river Ouistoula, from which to it there are 1,600 stades/1,200 stades. The total circumnavigation of Skandia is 2,500 stades/2,000 stades.

35. From the eastward bend of the peninsula to the ouflow of the river Suebos,[134] 1,260 stades/⟨... stades⟩.

From the river Suebos to the outlets of the river Ouiados (*Oder*), 850 stades/⟨... stades⟩.

---

[132] Not necessarily a corruption of *Saxones* (Müller ad loc.).

[133] Presumably these are eastern islands of Denmark, including *Fyn* and *Sjælland*; the easternmost, given the reference to the *Vistula*, might be Bornholm.

[134] Perhaps the *Peene* or the *Warnow* in NE Germany, E of *Rostock*.

From the outlets of the river Ouiados to the outlets of the river Ouistoula there are 700 stades/⟨... stades⟩.

From the outlets of the river Ouistoula to the head of the same river there are 2,000 stades/1,850 stades.

36. The length of Germania begins from the west and the city of Askibourgion (*Asberg*) and passing though to the outlets of the river Ouistoula, so that the total length of the province is ⟨... stades⟩/4,350 stades. Its breadth begins from the deviation of the river flowing south which is called Arrhabon (*Raab/Rába*), and ceases towards the north, via the longer line: that is, at the Kimbric peninsula and its northernmost projection, so that the stades of the breadth are 6,250.

The boundary circuit of Great Germania by land is 12,300 stades/11,250 stades. It contains within itself 68 nations, 94 notable cities, 7 notable mountains, 14 notable rivers, the Kimbric peninsula, ⟨1⟩[135] notable harbour, the Orkynios (*Hercynian*) forest, the wood of Gabretas.

37. The total circumnavigation of the coast of Great Germania, from the river Rhenos—that is, from its so-called western mouth up to the outlets of the river Ouistoula—is **13,400 stades/10,300 stades**.

Circumnavigation of the Sarmatia in Europe

38. The Sarmatia in Europe is bounded on the north by the Sarmatic ocean at the Ouendic gulf,[136] and by part of the unknown land; on the east by the isthmus ⟨beginning at the river Karkinites⟩[137] and Lake Byke,[138] and by part of Lake Maiotis (*Sea of Azov*) up to the river Tanaïs (*Don*), and subsequently by ⟨the⟩ river Tanaïs itself, and also by its ⟨southern part⟩ from the sources of the river Tanaïs up to the unknown land; on the west by the river Ouistoula and Great Germania after the Sarmatic mountains, and by the mountains themselves; on the south by the Metanastai (*Migrant*) Iazyges from the southern extremity of the Sarmatic mountains up to the beginning of Mt Karpathos (*Carpathian Mts*), and also by Dakia (*Dacia*) up to the outlets of the river Borysthenes, and by the coastal district of the Euxeinos Pontos from this (*river*) up to the head of the Karkinitic gulf.

And the overall outline is of this kind; but we have arranged the part-by-part (*account*) of Sarmatia in a more summary fashion, not appending the number of the stades, for the reason that the exact circumnavigation of this northern Ocean happens to be almost unknown: for it (*the Ocean*) approaches in the north the unknown land that lies beyond Lake Maiotis, and this land is not easily comprehended by the great majority of people, especially given that even Protagoras appears to have left to one

---

[135] Numeral added by Lucarini 2020, 226.

[136] If this is reference to the Veneti or Venedi, who turn up in different parts of N. Europe, their 'gulf' may be the eastern Baltic. Schoff 1927, 55, suggests the 'Gulf of Danzig', now *Bay of Gdańsk*; but the mention at 2. 39 suggests a larger body of water (including this bay), e.g. SE Baltic as a whole.

[137] In the northern Black Sea; see Arrian §19. 5.

[138] Cf. the R. *Byk*, a tributary of the *Dnieper* in E. Ukraine.

side the number of the stades. And the outline of the places will be expressed purely by the outlets of rivers, for the same reasons.

39. After the outlets of the river Ouistoula, there follows the outlets of the river Chronos (*Pregolya*). From the river Chronos the next thing is the outlets of the river Rhoudon (*Neman*). These rivers discharge into the Ouendic gulf, which begins from the river Ouistoula and runs along very far. From the river Rhoudon the next thing is the outlets of the river Tourountes;[139] and from the river Tourountes there follows the river Chesynos (*Daugava?*) and its outlets.

After the river Chesynos, the next thing is the unknown Hyperborean ocean,[140] connecting with the Hyperborean unknown land. Beside the river Chesynos lives the nation of the Agathoursoi, belonging to the Sarmatia in Europe. The river Chesynos and the Tourountes run down from the mountains lying beyond, which are called the Rhipaian mountains and lie in the interior between Lake Maiotis and the Sarmatic ocean.

The river Rhoudon runs from Mt Alanos. Over a long distance there live beside the mountain and this territory the nation of the Alanian Sarmatai,[141] beside whom the sources of the river Borysthenes, which comes out into the Pontos, happens to be. Beside the territory around the Borysthenes, after the Alanoi, live the so-called Chounoi, the ones in Europe.

40. The length of Sarmatia is **7,700 stades**; its breadth is 7,650 stades. It contains 56 nations, 53 notable cities, 9 notable mountains, 4 notable rivers, 3 notable promontories, 3 notable harbours, 4 notable gulfs, and the previously mentioned Ouendic gulf and 3 others.

We have now, as we undertook to do, made the circumnavigation of the right-hand parts of Europe with appropriate diligence. We shall now cross over to the Prettanic islands.

On the Prettanic Islands

41. The Prettanic islands are two: the so-called Albion, and Iouernia (*Ireland*). But Albion happens to be much larger;[142] it lies opposite Keltogalatia, extending beside Lougdounesia and Belgike up to Great Germania. For it is not compact like the other islands, but rather divided and scattered; it runs in large part into the northern Ocean, having two particularly long isthmuses almost like feet; the larger of these runs ⟨up to the Kimbric peninsula⟩, the shorter to Akytania. The other island, Iouernia, lies beyond it and happens to be further west; it is lesser in size and has the same position

---

[139] *Barr.* 2 H2 places this tentatively in Latvia.

[140] Possibly the *White sea* (around 65½° N, 38° E), where the *Barents sea* projects into NW Russia, E of *Murmansk*.

[141] Or Alanoi, a people W of the Caspian between 43° and 45° N (*Barr.* 85 B3; 88 C1). On the evidence for the Sarmatai, see now Grumeza 2021.

[142] Cf. B. 5 below.

as the aforementioned one. So we shall compose the circumnavigation of this one first; then we shall come to the greater.

CIRCUMNAVIGATION OF THE PRETTANIC ISLAND OF IOUERNIA

42. The Prettanic island of Iouernia is bounded on the north by the so-called Hyperborean ocean lying beyond it; but on the east by the so-called Iouernian ocean; on the west by the western Ocean; on the south by the so-called Ouergiouian ocean. And the overall position of the island has this character; ⟨but the part-by-part (*account*) is as follows⟩.

43. The greatest length of the Prettanic island of Iouernia in Prettanike begins from Notion (*Southern*) Promontory and ceasing at Rhobogdion Point,[143] so that the length of the island is 2,170 stades.[144] Its breadth begins from Hieron (*Sacred*) Point and passes through to Rhobogdion Point, so that the breadth of the island is 1,834 stades.

The distances between its extremities and the horizons (*of the Earth*) have the following character: its northern point is 14,250 stades from the northern horizon; but its western point ⟨is [—] stades from the western horizon; its southern point⟩ is 38,317 stades from the equator; its eastern 40,317 from the east. It contains 16 nations, 11 notable cities, 15 notable rivers, 5 notable promontories, and 6 notable islands. The total of the circumnavigation of Iouernia is not more than **9,085** stades/not less than **6,845** stades.

CIRCUMNAVIGATION OF THE PRETTANIC ISLAND OF ALBION

44. In sequence, we shall now expound the circumnavigation of the island of Albion. The Prettanic island of Albion is bounded on the north by the Ocean called Douekaledonian; on the east by the Germanic ocean; on the west by the Iouernian ocean, after which is the island of Iouernia, and also by the Ouergiouian ocean (*Celtic sea*);[145] on the south by the Prettanic ocean and the aforementioned mainlands (*sic*) and nations of Gallia. And the overall outline of the island has this character; ⟨but the part-by-part (*account*) is as follows⟩.

45. The length of the island of Albion in Prettanike begins from the western horizon at Damnonion Point, also called Okrion (*The Lizard*), and passing through as far as Tarouedounon, also known as Cape Orkas (*Dunnet Head*), so that the stades of its greatest length are 5,225. Its breadth begins at Damnonion Point, also called Okrion, and ceases at the peninsula of the Neouantai[146] and the promontory of the same name, so that the stades of its breadth, via the longest line, are 3,083.[147]

It contains within itself 33 nations, 59 notable cities, 40 notable rivers, 14 notable promontories, 1 notable peninsula, 5 notable gulfs, and 3 notable harbours. The total

---

[143] Marked E of *Ballycastle* by Pleiades.   [144] Müller suggests 3,170.
[145] That is, the sea S of Ireland.
[146] Presumably the Novantae of SW Scotland; though one expects an eastward extremity of Great Britain.
[147] Müller doubts both figures.

of the complete circumnavigation of Albion is not more than **28,604** stades/not less than **20,526** stades.

⟨*Summary of the above*⟩

46. And the circumnavigation of the western and northern Ocean, the parts beside Europe, and of the Prettanic islands in it, has its end here.

Just as in the previous book on the parts of the Arabian gulf and Erythraian sea next to Libyē, and on the Indian Ocean (*sic*) looking to the south, we made the circumnavigation in summary—rendering the number of the stades only at intervals for the sake of clarity—but composed accurately the circumnavigation of all the left-hand parts beside Asia, up to the nation of the Sinai and the unknown land, noting the stades of all the distances: so too, here, we have made to the best of our powers the circumnavigation of the right-hand parts of the Ocean that is beside Europe, from the Pillars of Herakles up to the unknown land, the Sarmatic ocean that terminates beside it, and, what is more, the Prettanic islands; also adding ⟨the⟩ number of stades.

Of the left-hand parts of Libyē on the western [—] (*text breaks off*)[148]

CITATIONS OF THE *PERIPLOUS* BY STEPHANOS OF BYZANTION

For Stephanos of Byzantion's citations of *Epit. Art.* and *Epit. Men.*, see Chapters 18 and 21 above. The 39 further extracts included here are arranged in the order of Stephanos' text, which usually follows Greek alphabetical order. Müller distributes them through his text of the *Periplous*, apart from twelve which we add here for the first time: 3–4, 11, 14–15, 21–2, 29, 31, 34, 36, and 39. All but the last two are clearly from book 2.

2   Stephanos of Byzantion α 56

Adaroupolis: a Persian city, as Markianos (*says*) in *Periplous of the Persian Gulf*.

3   Stephanos of Byzantion α 90

Aiboudai: five islands in Prettanike, as Markianos (*says*) in *Periplous*.

4   Stephanos of Byzantion α 180

Akytania: a province in Keltogalatia, one of the four. Markianos, in (*the*) *Periplous* of it.[149]

5   Stephanos of Byzantion α 197

Albiōn: a Prettanic island. Markianos, in (*the*) *Periplous* of it.[150]

---

[148] Müller reconstructs a hypothetical closing sentence here by analogy with that in book 1. The next quaternion (no. 7) is lost; it contained the substantial end of Markianos' *periplous* of the Outer Ocean, namely the Atlantic coast of Libyē, and the beginning of his table of contents for his précis of Menippos (see Ch. 21).

[149] Cf. *Peripl.* 2. 20.   [150] Cf. *Peripl.* 2. 41.

6   Stephanos of Byzantion α 360

Apokopa, neuter: a gulf at the head of the Barbaric gulf. Markianos, in *Periplous*.[151]

7   Stephanos of Byzantion α 468

Aroma: a city of Aithiopes, as Markianos (*says*).

8   Stephanos of Byzantion α 478

Askitai: a nation living beside the Indic gulf and sailing upon *askoi* (*skins*), as Markianos (*says*) in the *Periplous* of it: 'There lives beside ⟨the Sachalitic gulf⟩ a nation, itself called that of the Sachalitai; indeed, there is another nation, that of the Askitai.' So in parallel to *askos* we have Askites, as to *astos* (*townsman*) *astitēs* (*town-dweller*),[152] and to *mesos* (*middle*) *mesitēs* (*mediator*).[153]

9   Stephanos of Byzantion α 485

Aspis: ... There is also a promontory in the (*part of*) Aithiopia by Egypt, as Markianos (*says*), first (*book*) of *Periodoi* (*Circuits*).

10   Stephanos of Byzantion α 499

Astarte: an island in Aithiopia. Markianos, in *Periplous*, 1st (*book*): 'Here begins the (*part of*) Aithiopia beyond Egypt; after Bazion Point (*akron*) follows Mt Prionoton (*Sawn, 'jagged'*); by this is the island of Astarte.'

11   Stephanos of Byzantion β 1

Babai: a city in Libyē. Markianos, in (*the*) *Periplous* of it (*the region*).

12   Stephanos of Byzantion β 169

Brettia: ... Others (*write it*) as follows, using a pi: 'Pretanides islands', as Markianos and Ptolemy (*do*).

13   Stephanos of Byzantion γ 121

Gypseïs: an island in Aithiopia, as Markianos (*says*) in *Periplous*, 1st (*book*).

14   Stephanos of Byzantion ζ 5

Zadrame: kingdom of the Kinaidokolpitai.[154] ... They are a nation of Eudaimon Arabia. Markianos, in (*the*) *Periplous* of it (*the region*): 'Zadramitai of (*the*) Kinaidokolpitai'. The ethnic is Zadramaios.

15   Stephanos of Byzantion ι 4

Iazyges: a European nation, as Markianos (*says*) in *Periplous*.[155]

---

[151] Cf. *Peripl.* 1. 13.   [152] The two terms are really synonymous; the second rare.
[153] 'Circumnavigation' here is a descriptive term for a passage in a work, not the title of a separate work.
[154] No explanation is available for this apparently derogatory name (*kinaidos* 'sodomite', *kolpos* 'gulf'), also used by Ptol. *Geog.* 6. 7. 5; the entry referred to is lost.
[155] Cf. *Peripl.* 2. 38.

16 Stephanos of Byzantion ι 19a (Constantine Porphyrogennetos, *De administrando imperio*, 23)[156]

Iberiai (*Iberias*), two: . . . Iberia used to be divided into two ⟨provinces⟩, but now into three, as Markianos (*says*) in (*the*) *Periplous* of it: 'Formely Iberia was divided into two ⟨provinces⟩ by the Romans, but now into three: Baitike, Lousitania, and Tarrakonesia.'[157]

17 Stephanos of Byzantion ι 113

Istriana: a city beside the Persian sea (*thalassa*; Persian gulf), as Markianos (*says*) in (*the*) *Periplous* of it (*the gulf*).

18 Stephanos of Byzantion κ 112

Kassanitai: a nation on the coast of the Erythraian sea. Markianos, in (*the*) *Periplous* of it: 'Here follows the nation of the Kassanitai.'

19 Stephanos of Byzantion κ 168

Koromane: a city beside the Persian gulf. Markianos, in (*the*) *Periplous* of it (*the gulf*).

20 Stephanos of Byzantion κ 240

Ktesiphon: a city in Assyria. Markianos, in *Periplous*.

21 Stephanos of Byzantion λ 13

Ladisakites Kolpos: a gulf in the Persian sea (*thalassa*). Markianos, in (*the*) *Periplous* of it.

22 Stephanos of Byzantion λ 72

Lindonion:[158] a city in Brettania. Markianos, in (*the*) *Periplous* of it (*the island*).

23 Stephanos of Byzantion λ 89

Lousitania: bordering upon Baitike. Markianos, in (*the*) *Periplous* of it.[159]

24 Stephanos of Byzantion μ 39

Mallada: a Persian city. Markianos, in *Periplous of the Persian Gulf*.

25 Stephanos of Byzantion μ 64

Margana: a city in Indike. Markianos, in *Periplous*. It is also Marganai, plural.

26 Stephanos of Byzantion μ 100

Mauritaniai: there are two. One is Tingitane, the other Kaisaresia (*sic*), as Markianos (*says*) in the *Periplous*.[160]

27 Stephanos of Byzantion μ 152

Mesanites Kolpos; Markianos, in *Periplous of the Persian Sea* (*thalassa*).[161]

---

[156] Cf. Artem. 23 and 31.   [157] Almost a verbatim quotation from *Peripl.* 2. 8.
[158] Evidently 'Londinion' (Lat. *Londinium*) is meant.   [159] Cf. *Peripl.* 2. 8 and 12.
[160] Cf. *Peripl.* 2. 3.   [161] Schoff 1927, 47, suggests the area of *Maisan* near *Basra*.

28 Stephanos of Byzantion μ 191

Minaioi: a nation on the coast of the Erythraian sea. Markianos, in (*the*) *Periplous* of it.

29 Stephanos of Byzantion μ 213

Mosylon: a promontory and trading-place in Aithiopia. Markianos, in (*the*) 1st (*book*) of *Periodos* (*Circuit*).[162]

30 Stephanos of Byzantion μ 247

Myrike: an island in the Erythraian sea. Markianos, in (*the*) *Periplous* of it.

31 Stephanos of Byzantion ν 13

Narbōn: a trading-place and Keltic city. . . . But Markianos refers to it as Narbonesia.[163]

32 Stephanos of Byzantion ν 59

Nikopolis: a city in Epeiros, as Markianos (*says*).

33 Stephanos of Byzantion ο 66

Homeritai: a nation [—] Aithiopes.[164] Markianos, in (*the*) 1st *Periplous*.[165]

34 Stephanos of Byzantion ο 73

Onne: a trading-post in Eudaimon Arabia. Markianos, in *Periplous*.

35 Stephanos of Byzantion σ 126

Siagathourgoi: a nation of which Markianos speaks in *Periplous of Sarmatia*.

36 Stephanos of Byzantion σ 151

Sithenoi: a nation lying beside the Erythraian sea, as Markianos (*says in*) *Periplous*.

37 Stephanos of Byzantion σ 165

Sinai: the capital city of the Sinai, of whom Markianos speaks in *Periploi* (*sic*).[166]

38 Stephanos of Byzantion τ 121

Tingis: a city in Maurousia. . . . But Markianos calls it (*the region*) Mauritania.[167]

39 Stephanos of Byzantion χ 3

Chadramotitai: a nation around the Indian gulf, living beside the river Prion, as Markianos (*says*) ⟨in (*the*) *Periplous* of it⟩ (*the gulf*).[168]

---

[162] Cf. Mossyloi, the people, at *Peripl.* 1. 11. 'First *Circumnavigation*' means book 1 of his *Circumnavigation*.

[163] Not so: Mark. uses Narbonesia for the province, not the city, at *Peripl.* 2. 19.

[164] A word such as 'near' has dropped out (Billerbeck).

[165] Cf. *Peripl.* 1. 15. The Greek is ἐν περίπλῳ αʹ; one expects ἐν περίπλου αʹ, 'in (*the*) 1st (*book*) of *Periplous*'.

[166] *Periploi* is the plural of *periplous*. Mark. in fact calls the city Thinai: *Peripl.* 1. 16.

[167] Cf. *Peripl.* 2. 3.

[168] The words in angle brackets are supplied from the complementary version in manuscript N (Billerbeck 2006–17, v. 65 n. 1).

40 Stephanos of Byzantion χ 57

Chryse: . . . There is also another (*Chryse*), a peninsula in Indike. Markianos, in *Periplous*: 'In the (*part of*) Indike outside the Ganges (*is*) a peninsula called Chryse.'[169]

C. PREFACE TO THE *EPITOME* OF MENIPPOS

For the surviving part of Markianos' epitome of Menippos, see Chapter 21. Here we print Markianos' preface to that epitome (translated by J. Brian Campbell).[170]

41 Codex Parisinus supplément grec 443, pp. 49. 4–56.15

1. Markianos to his friend Amphithalios, greetings.

Those who read the works of the ancients uncritically, or who do not understand how to work out the value of the argument or follow the train of thought, provide considerable license, so it seems, for those who want to write loosely and superficially.[171] I leave the rest (*of these*) to be examined by others, who through careful training know how to do this more effectively than (*I could*) by my judgement. But those who have written *periploi* carelessly and, wishing to convince their readers, run through the names of locations and the number of stades, and all this in respect of barbarian places or peoples, the names of which no one could even pronounce, seem to me to have surpassed even Antiphanes of Berge himself in mendacity.[172] Now, in the case of those who produce particular descriptions of *periploi*, where they know the locations clearly and understand something of the measurement of distance by sea, and have thoroughly examined the cities, harbours, and distances between them, these men seem to have written everything, or nearly everything, as truthfully as possible. But in the case of those who, either putting their trust in what others have reported without having seen it, or following those who wrote about something without having accurately found out the facts, have selected some of the *periploi* of the inhabited world, it is clear that they have not only deceived themselves but also those who trust what they have written.

2. I write this having encountered many *periploi* and having spent a lot of time acquiring knowledge of these topics. It is essential in the case of those who have acquired deep learning to examine this kind of knowledge, so as not to trust carelessly their words, or place our own uncertain opinion in opposition to their considered views. Therefore we will examine these (*writers*) more carefully. Those who in my view have investigated these matters intelligently are Timosthenes of Rhodes, who was chief helmsman of the second Ptolemy; and after him Eratosthenes, whom the officials of the Mouseion

---

[169] Cf. *Peripl.* 1. 8 and 16.

[170] A revised Greek text of M.' s prologue, with Spanish translation, is at González Ponce 2008b, 50–69.

[171] The present passage can be seen as a polemical response to the unknown author of the *Stadiasmos* (Arnaud 2017b, 707).

[172] Antiphanes collected fantastical stories about distant places and was criticized by Strabo (2. 3. 5, C102) for indulging in deliberate fabrications.

(*at Alexandria*) called Beta (*Number Two*); in addition to these Pytheas of Massalia, Isidoros of Charax, Sosandros the helmsman, who wrote about Indian matters, and Simmeas, who composed a circumnavigation of the entire world (*oikoumenē*). Then there are Apellas of Kyrene, Euthymenes of Massalia, Phileas of Athens, Androsthenes of Thasos, Kleon of Sicily, Eudoxos of Rhodes,[173] and Hanno of Carthage. Some wrote about the circumnavigation of individual parts, some of the entire inner sea, others of the external sea. Then again there are Skylax of Karyanda and Botthaios:[174] for both of these men used the daily sailings, not the stades, to show the sea distances. And there are many more whom I consider it superfluous to enumerate.[175]

3. Next to most of these writers, Artemidoros of Ephesos the geographer, and Strabo, who combined geography and circumnavigation, and Menippos of Pergamon, who wrote about sea crossings (*diaploi*), are in my view more accurate than all those mentioned above. I have to discuss these authors so that those who have an interest in this aspect of geography are not left in ignorance of anything.

For Timosthenes, when most parts of the sea were still unknown, since the Romans had not yet conquered them in war, wrote treatises *On Harbours*, in which he did not deal accurately with all the nations living round our sea. Of course, in the European area his *periplous* of the Tyrrhenic (*Etruscan*) open-sea (*pelagos*) was incomplete, and he was unable to obtain knowledge of the area around the strait of Herakles (*straits of Gibraltar*), in respect of either our sea or the outer sea. In respect of Libyē he encountered the same problem, in that he was ignorant of all the places beyond Carthage and round the outer sea.[176] From these ten books, an epitome in one book has been made. Furthermore, he also wrote a summary of the so-called stade distances (*stadiasmoi*) in another, single book. In all these works, however, he has failed to convey anything completely or clearly. But Eratosthenes of Kyrene—I don't know what possessed him—transcribed Timosthenes' book, adding a few items but in such a way that he did not even keep his hands off the prologue of the author mentioned, but placed that at the start of his book in those very words. Others have done the same thing, offering obscure and unfocused accounts.

Artemidoros of Ephesos the geographer, who lived around the 169th Olympiad (*104–100 BC*), sailed out round the largest part of the inner sea and our sea, and saw the island of Gadeira and some parts of the external sea, which they call Ocean. It

---

[173] Probably E. of Knidos.

[174] Müller speculates that the name of a geographer has fallen out of the text and that *Bottiaios* referred to his origin in a district in Macedonia; but Nenci 1953 emends to 'Hekataios' and is followed by Orth 2011a.

[175] Of writers who are known, Timosthenes, Eratosthenes, Pytheas, Isidoros, Hanno, and Skylax (i.e. Ps.-Skylax) are treated in these volumes (Chs 10, 12, 8, 23, 4, and 7 respectively). Euthymenes of Massalia, probably C6, sailed along the coast of NW Africa and wrote an account of his travels; Phileas of Athens, C5, is attested as a geographer; Androsthenes of Thasos sailed in the fleet of Alexander the Great, explored the Persian gulf, and wrote an account of his voyage; Kleon of Sicily, according to Steph. Byz., wrote a work on harbours; Eudoxos of Rhodes (i.e. Knidos) is described as an historian by Diogenes Laërtios (8. 90).

[176] Excising 'around the strait of Herakles and the outer sea', with Lucarini 2020, 226.

falls short of an accurate geographical description; but in eleven books he covered with proper diligence the circumnavigation of the sea within the strait of Herakles and the measurement of this, and so seems to have written very clearly and accurately the circumnavigation of our sea. Menippos of Pergamon,[177] ⟨who⟩ himself treated the circumnavigation of the inner sea in three books, produced an account combining history and geography.

4. Now, I placed Artemidoros of Ephesos ahead of all those mentioned, and I made an epitome of his eleven books, adding from other old writers material that was lacking, while keeping the arrangement of the eleven books, so as to produce a reasonable geographical account but a complete *periplous*. When I saw that the majority of old writers either did not mention the outer sea at all or only to a limited degree, and since even this description was obscure and not in harmony with the truth, I gave my own scrutiny to the entire eastern and southern ocean of both continents, Africa and Asia, from the Arabian gulf as far as the nation of the Sinai. I also included in two books the *periplous* of the western and northern ocean and the parts of both Europe and Africa. Since I learned that Menippos too offered a reasonable account to his readers from his own volumes, but had not carefully explained everything, I appended a great deal of material that had been left out, and furthermore added clarity in respect of places and descriptions of peoples, which usually provide a complete understanding for readers, and made an account in three volumes. However, I did not take away the author's paternity from this work, nor did I claim for myself someone else's work, just as I did not suppress the name of Artemidoros when he set out everything carefully, but I wrote the names of these authors in the books so that I should seem to have done nothing wrong in respect of the gods of writing, giving the epitomes of these works and corrections which resulted from my own efforts a clear designation, so that those who read them cannot fail to recognize what was written by those authors and the material added by me or thought worthy of careful correction.

5. The discrepancy in the measurement of the number of stades was already discussed in my previous book, in which I have dealt with the circumnavigation of the entire eastern ocean, but there is nothing to prevent me from now setting out the main points. More or less all those who have written circumnavigations in respect of cities, places (*chōria*), harbours, and islands either differ not at all or in a few details easily capable of correction. But in respect of the number of stades between these same cities, ⟨settlements (*chōria*)⟩,[178] islands, and harbours, they differ widely. In the case of bays and promontories the discrepancy can easily be explained. For some circumnavigated the bay and promontories closer to the mainland, others further away, and therefore the circumnavigation covered more or fewer stades. In the case of a direct voyage one

---

[177] For Menippos' date see Introduction to Ch. 21. [178] Added by Lucarini 2020, 226–7.

could not easily explain the reason for a different calculation, unless one wished to attribute the mistake to the speed or slowness of the vessel. It is agreed that a ship with a following wind can cover 700 stades in one day, but one might find that a ship could even cover 900 stades by picking up speed from the skill of its construction, while another could scarcely manage 500 because of opposing features in its construction. Nevertheless, we should accept that errors of this kind should be pardoned. For they were not establishing the measurement for some places on the mainland, but on water and the open seas (*pelagē*), making the calculation of stades more from customary practice than from any other skill.

6. Menippos has divided up the circumnavigation of the three continents, Asia, Europe, and Libyē (*Africa*), in the following way. He withheld and dealt with in a separate circumnavigation the Hellespont and Propontis, with the Thracian Bosporos and furthermore the Euxeinos Pontos on both continents, Asia and Europe: first the Pontos, after that the Thracian Bosporos and the Propontis along with the Hellespont. He made the start of the circumnavigation of both continents from the sanctuary called Zeus Ourios,[179] which is situated right at the mouth of the Pontos. After this, starting from the remaining parts of Europe he circumnavigates all of it up to the strait of Herakles and the island of Gadeira (*Cádiz*). Then, crossing to the mainland opposite at the strait of Herakles, that is, to Libyē, he sails round this area too and adds to it the circumnavigation of Asia up to the Hellespont, which I mentioned above. The entire arrangement of the circumnavigation has the following plan: it will go through each part in turn and receive correction to make it clearer, as mentioned above.

(For §§7–10 of the Epitome of Menippos, see Chapter 21 section A above.)

D. PREFACE TO PSEUDO-SKYLAX

See Chapter 7, no. B. 6.

E. *DISTANCES FROM ROME TO THE NOTABLE CITIES OF THE INHABITED WORLD* (?)

42 Stephanos of Byzantion α 271

Amisa: a city in Germania. Markianos, in the ⟨*Distances*⟩ *from Rome to the Important Cities*.[180]

---

[179] The settlement was called Hieron: see §7 of this Preface at Ch. 21 above, no. A. 1.
[180] See also the end of the table of contents to *Periplous*, book 2, above.

F. OTHER SOURCES

43 Synesios, *Letter* 101, *To Pylaimenes* (AD 401–2 or 405)[181]

Address yourself very warmly from me to the most venerable Markianos. If I had adopted the style of (*Aelius*) Aristeides and said 'that the image of Hermes, that master of language, had appeared among humankind', I should hardly have hit the mark of his value, in that he is more than the image. Though desirous of appending a letter direct to him, I grew numb and so cannot make myself answerable to the encyclopaedic men who would try to polish my words; for there is no little danger of the letter being read at the Panhellenion. For thus I refer to that place in which I was often anxious with weighty anxieties[182] as the eloquent men from all over the world gather to hear the old man's sacred voice as it hunts down narratives (*diēgēmata*) old and new.

44 Synesios, *Letter* 119, *To Tryphon* (AD 406)

Address yourself from me to the philosopher Markianos, who has governed the Paphlagonians; and if he has any power—as I reckon he does—let him prevent my relative, a very close cousin, from becoming material for sycophantic complainants, the common scourges of the land.

45 Priscian of Lydia, *Solutions to Chosroës*, p. 42 lines 8–14 Bywater

We have also used what is useful in Strabo's *Geography* . . . and Ptolemy's *Geography* on latitudinal zones, . . . and Marcianus' *Periegesis*, and the *Heavenly Phenomena* of Arrian.

---

[181] Synesios of Cyrene (*c*.370–*c*.413), Neoplatonist philosopher and active member of his city's aristocracy, represented Cyrene's interests at Constantinople for three years around 400 (399–402, Garzya 1989, 10–11; either 397–400 or 399–402, Rist 2006). This letter is written soon after he returned to Cyrene. It is not certain that the Markianos to whom he refers is the geographical writer, but *c*.400 is a plausible date for Mark.

[182] The echo is in the Greek.

35

HYPOTYPŌSIS TĒS GEŌGRAPHIAS EN EPITOMĒI (OUTLINE OF GEOGRAPHY IN SUMMARY)

(AFTER AD 565)

D. Graham J. Shipley

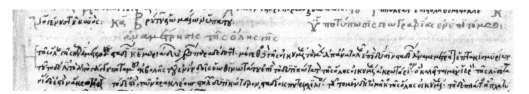

FIG. 35.1. Opening of the anonymous *Hypotyposis*, fo. 1ʳ (detail).

INTRODUCTION

This late antique *Outline of Geography in Summary* (*Hypotypōsis tēs geōgraphias en epitomei*),[1] a Greek text of mixed quality, survives near the beginning of the Vatopedi codex (B).[2] From the table of contents in the manuscript,[3] it stood first in what we call corpus A of the geographers, before the similarly titled work of Agathemeros (Chapter 29 above). The work was, like Agathemeros and the still later *Diagnosis* (see Introduction, §VIII. 2. a), an addition to the front of the corpus: in this case, to make good the absence of information from Ptolemy in Agathemeros' treatise.[4] The unknown author may be the same as the compiler of the Pseudo-Arrianic *Periplous of the Euxine* (*Eux.*, Chapter 36).[5]

The treatise opens by defining the size of the Earth and its inhabited part (§§1–2), a topic to which the author returns later (§39). Next come the names and boundaries of

---

[1] The same name, *hypotypōsis*, is given to the text of Agathemeros (Chapter 29 above).
[2] More precisely, on the first of the detached pages now in London. It is missing from the Heidelberg MS of the same corpus, whose front sections are lost.
[3] The so-called *Pinax* (*Table*) to the *Hypotyposis*, not actually part of *Hyp.* but standing immediately before it, is a list of the entire contents of corpus A of the geographers as they were when complete. See Diller 1952, 6–7, 12. Mittenhuber 2011c (*FGrH* 2021a) is a critical edition of the *Pinax*.
[4] Mittenhuber 2011b, 'Quellenautoren'.
[5] Marcotte 2000b, cxxxv, would attribute *Hyp.* and *Eux.* to the same author; at cxxx he dates *Hyp.* later than the reign of Justinian (i.e. post-565). For the interpretation of *Hyp.*, I have drawn in various ways upon Mittenhuber 2011b, though my interpretation does not always coincide with his.

the continents (§§3–4), another subject that recurs (§46). There follows a brief statement of aims (§5): to outline the nations (*ethnē*) of each continent and the seas within those continents—an incomplete description of what actually follows: in particular, it ignores §§27–39 on islands, mountains, rivers, the 'Great Sea', winds, and the dimensions of the *oikoumenē*. Furthermore, although the author here says that no picture (*eikōn*) is needed to understand his account, much of what follows suggests he is working with a visual counterpart such as a map,[6] which would explain his use of relational terms such as 'above' and 'below'. Furthermore, the 'nations' in the three continents are geographical areas, not human populations.

Europe is treated first (§§6–14), from the Hispaniai in the west to Greece in the east, with the British Isles and the major Mediterranean islands appended.[7] Libyē comes next (§§15–18), from the Mauritaniai[8] in the west to eastern Africa in the east, the many 'nations' of the latter being covered from north to south. Asia is then described (§§19–25), from Sarmatia in the north via Asia Minor to Mesopotamia, Arabia, and the rest of western Asia eastwards as far as the Sinai—the western Chinese[9]—and ending with India and Sri Lanka (here called Salike). Regional names, where applicable, are those of Roman provinces rather than ethnographic units. The continents are then compared in size (§26, first part) and prosperity; on the latter criterion Europe is ranked first, ahead of those parts of Asia under 'Roman' rule and the maritime parts of Libyē. The 'largest' nations in each continent are listed (§26, second part), followed by the largest islands (§27), mountains (§28), and rivers (§§29–31).

Next, the gulfs of the outer Ocean are briefly characterized from east to west (§§32–6), ending with the Erythraian sea. A more theoretical perspective is briefly readopted with an account of the wind rose (§§37–8), here in Timosthenes' twelvefold version but with each wind occupying an equal portion of the compass circle (that is, 30 degrees in our terms).[10] This is illustrated by a sketch in the manuscript that may derive from an original drawing. The author then returns to the geometrical form of the *oikoumenē* and its dimensions in degrees and stades (§39).

---

[6] Mittenhuber 2011b observes that the enumeration of regions and peoples (§§5–25) is broadly cartographic rather than following a traditional *periplous* or *periodos* format: sometimes the author appears to conceive of a two-dimensional representation: e.g. §19 'the meridian dividing the Caspian sea into two lengthways'; §39, where if not using a map directly he must be imagining a cartographic view similar to that implied in Ptolemy's prescription for mapmaking.

[7] The heading before §5, referring to Europe, would better stand before §6.

[8] The spelling of this name appears to have changed from Mauretania to Mauritania around C4.

[9] Cf. *PME* §§64, 66. For Sinai or Thinai in Greek and Roman sources (probably derived from the name of the Qin dynasty, 221–206 BC), Brentjes 2006a, or perhaps more likely from the much earlier and long-lasting Qin state in western China, whose people were also known to the Greeks and Romans as Seres (*Silk People*) who traded with the Mediterranean world via India, Brentjes 2006b. Zhang 2004 argues (contra Kordosis 1999) that Kosmas Indikopleustes, slightly earlier than *Hyp.*, has a relatively clear notion of China's extent (he calls it Tzinitza or Tzinista).

[10] In Timosthenes (Ch. 10 above) the cardinal and ordinal winds were supplemented with the four that separate each polar direction from its ordinal neighbours (i.e. omitting ENE, ESE, WSW, and WNW), implying a division into 16 parts of which 4 have no name.

The treatise closes with a focus on bodies of water, as promised in §5, beginning with the dimensions of the Mediterranean (§40), the Black Sea (§41), the Caspian (§42), and some gulfs of the Ocean (§§43–4). Then the author tells us, schematically, of the three latitudinal divisions of the Ocean (northern, southern, and southernmost) and their respective subdivisions (defined longitudinally, so to speak, as eastern and western in each case; §45).

The text now returns to the question of continental boundaries, giving the usual two versions of the Europe–Asia division, either at the Tanaïs or at the Phasis (§46); then turns to dimensions. The length of the Mediterranean is given in stades, followed by the shorter distances that make it up, from east to west (§47); then its breadth (§48, first part) and all its divisions from west to east, ending with the Propontis (§§49–51). The treatise ends with the form and coastal dimensions of the Black Sea (§§51–3). After the memorable comparison of the latter to a drawn bow (§53),[11] the text concludes abruptly with the circumference of Lake Maiotis (*Sea of Azov*) and the name of its entrance.

Multiple sources have been used in the compilation of the text, as shown by inconsistencies in the spelling of names and the rendering of distances, which are sometimes converted from stades into miles at the rate of 8 : 1 (§2) but sometimes at 7½ : 1 (§40 onwards).[12] Much of the material is derived from Strabo and Ptolemy, such as the figure for the circumference of the world (§1; cf. e.g. Eratosthenes 27); but the author often modifies his sources or adds to them. For example, his citation of the river Ganges as one end of the central parallel of the *oikoumenē*, in the same passage, is not in the equivalent passage of Strabo (1. 4. 5, C64); while his '1,000 less than 30,000 stades' (§1) for the breadth of the *oikoumenē* is more precise than Strabo's 'a little less than 30,000' (2. 4. 3). For some material, an oral source seems likely (e.g. at §33). In the central part of the work (§§5–25), the sequence of regions is mostly the same as in books 3–7 of Ptolemy's *Geography*, but the British Isles and Mediterranean islands are held back to the end, perhaps in order to bring together a special category of landmass. There are echoes of Dionysios Periegetes, such as the Frozen Sea (§45; cf. Dionysios lines 32, 316), but for the most part the account of the constituent seas of the Mediterranean and the Black Sea (§§47–53) reflects Strabo in a very condensed form (2. 4. 3; 2. 5. 19–26). Markianos, too, appears: the beginning of §36, for example, echoes almost verbatim the first sentence of book 1 §9 of his *Periplous*, probably written over a century before the *Hypotyposis*.

A strictly topological focus is maintained for the most part, though occasionally the author varies his material: for example, with the briefest discussions of the Nile flood (§31), the unusual characteristics of the southernmost parts of the Ocean (§§32–3), and—the longest 'digression', this—the cause of the red colour of the 'Arabian gulf'

---

[11] Also seen at Hekataios 59; Eratosthenes 107; Dionysios Periegetes ll. 157–62.
[12] Arnaud 1993, 241.

(mod. *Red Sea*; §36), a favourite topic of ancient geography.[13] The overall tone, however, is severely scientific rather than literary, making it suitable as a preface to the corpus and a complement to the pre-Ptolemaic treatise by Agathemeros. As such, we would not expect it to have had an influence upon later works; its legacy is limited to six extracts preserved in certain manuscripts of the *De thematibus* by Constantine VII Porphyrogennetos in the 9th century.[14]

The Greek text translated is that of Mittenhuber.

SELECTED FURTHER READING

Diller, A. (1952), *The Tradition of the Minor Greek Geographers*. Lancaster, Pa.–Oxford. [Pp. 6–7, 12.]

Marcotte, D. (2000), *Introduction générale; Ps.-Scymnos, Circuit de la terre*. Paris. ['Budé' edition.] [Pp. xl–xlii.]

*Mittenhuber, F. (2011), 'Hypotyposis (2021)', in *FGrH* v.

TEXT

The headings are in the manuscript, and probably original.

MEASUREMENT OF THE WHOLE EARTH

1. The circumference of the whole Earth has been handed down as 252,000 stades.[15]

The length of the inhabited world from east to west has been measured at 70,000 stades; and this is from the outlet of the river Ganges, the easternmost among the Indians, to the westernmost promontory of the whole inhabited world, which is called Hieron (*Sacred*) and is a cape in Lysitania; this is further west than the Pillars of Herakles by some 3,000 stades.

This is the length of the whole inhabited world; but the breadth, where it happens to be broadest, is measured at 1,000 less than 30,000 stades, from the south to the north.

2. The 36 degrees from the Arctic pole to the Arctic Circle are all uninhabited on account of the cold; but they amount to 25,200 stades.[16] Also uninhabited are the parts up to 8⟨,800⟩ stades from the equator, where we have supposed the beginning of our inhabited world to be; and likewise, in the northern region, the parts directly after the Arctic Circle. Thus the total uninhabited stades of this surface are 34,000.

---

[13] Cf. Agatharchides 2a–5b; Artemidoros 100.   [14] Diller 1952, 42–3.

[15] Cf. Erat. 29 and 34; Hipparchos 40a; slightly different figures at Dikaiarchos 8 (Kleomedes); Markianos, *Peripl.* (Ch. 34 above), 1. 4. §§1–2, probably derive from Strabo apart from the brief characterization of the mouths of the Ganges, which differs from that at Strabo 15. 1. 11, C689 (Mittenhuber 2011b).

[16] i.e. $1/_{10}$ of 360° and $1/_{10}$ of Eratosthenes' figure of 252,000 st. for the circumference of the Earth. The author here works with a value of 700 st. to the degree, but in later chapters he uses 500.

There remains, therefore, a habitable distance falling under the temperate (*part*) of 29,000 stades, which is 3,625 miles,[17] or a little over 900 *schoinoi* of 30 stades each; which is also the breadth of our inhabited world.

ON THE DIVISION OF THE INHABITED WORLD

3. The whole inhabited world is divided into three continents: Asia, Libyē, and Europe. The division is by isthmuses or straits (*porthmoi*). The boundaries of the continents are these: of Europe with Libyē, the Pillars and the Herakleian Strait by which our sea flows in; but of Asia with Europe, the isthmus that goes through from the head of Lake Maiotis (*Sea of Azov*) to the sea towards the north; the Tanaïs (*Don*) flows through this isthmus. Asia, too, is separated from Libyē by a narrow isthmus again: this is formed by the line that goes up from the sea at Pelousion to the head of the Arabian gulf. The old writers, however, called Libyē and Europe, as if they were one (*continent*), both by the sole and single name of Europe.

WHAT RELATION THE THREE CONTINENTS HAVE TO THE HORIZON OF THE INHABITED CIRCLE

4. Again, of the three continents Europe is all towards the north and west, Libyē towards the south and west, while Asia, lying towards the east, extends alongside the other two continents: for it stretches from the northernmost to the southernmost parts of the known world.

ON THE NATIONS IN EUROPE

5. These things have been set out, we shall trace in full, in the most summary fashion, the nations in each continent and the seas contained within them, so that one may most easily survey the whole inhabited world in one's mind through their relation to one another, needing no picture (*eikōn*).[18]

6. Thus, to give the principal ones, the nations in Europe are the following. The three Hispaniai (*Spains*), which were formerly called Iberiai. These have the sea flowing round them in the manner of a peninsula, with a very narrow isthmus upon which are the Pyrenaia mountains separating the Galliai (*Gauls*) from them. Lysitania is by the western Ocean, but Baitike by the inner sea (*Mediterranean*), also including a little of the land outside the Strait (*of Gibraltar*); and Tarrakonesia (*Tarraconensis*) extends from the Ocean, or outer sea, to the inner sea.

7. Of the Galliai, which people used formerly to call Galatiai and which lie next, Akouitania (*Gallia Aquitania*), Lougdounesia (*Gallia Lugdunensis*), and Belgike (*Gallia Belgica*), in the last of which are the two Germaniai, are oriented towards the outer sea; but they include quite a large part of the interior, especially Lougdounesia. Towards the inner sea, extending alongside these, lies Narbonesia. 8. Again, after

---

[17] At 8 st. to the mile.
[18] The long enumeration of regions and their peoples (§§5–25) is based on Ptolemy, with variations in sequence (see introduction to chapter).

Belgike Germania[19] reaches a fair distance eastwards, and like the others is oriented towards the outer sea. After Narbonesia is Italia, surrounded by two seas. Germania is bounded by the river Rhenos (*Rhine*), which rises from the mountains beyond the Alps and discharges into the outer sea.

Towards Narbonesia, Italia is bounded by the coastal Alps; these rise up to the north, then turning towards the east they also separate the rest of Italia from the nations lying beyond.   9. Not much further on from the sources of the Rhenos, the Istros (*Danube*) has its beginnings. As far as the city of Nouiodounon (*Noviodunum*) they call it the Danoubis. It bounds Germania in the direction of the nations lying below: Rhaitia (*Rhaetia*), Ouindelikia (*Vindelicia*), and Norikon (*Noricum*), which lie beyond the Alps and Italy; and outside the Alps the two Pannonias, below which is ⟨Illyris, which⟩ in its eastern parts is called Dalmatia.

10. Next to Germania, after the river Ouistoula (*Vistula*) there follows Sarmatia; it includes much land and many nations, has a share in the next continent, and bounds Europe somewhere beside Lake Maiotis. Next, after the isthmus of the Taurike Chersonesos (*Crimea*)—which juts out and makes a strait towards Asia, the so-called Kimmerian Bosporos—it (*Sarmatia*) includes the parts of the Pontos up to the river Borysthenes (*Dnieper*).

11. Below the westernmost parts of Sarmatia, a region descends to the south after the Iazyges (*called*) Metanastai (*Migrants*). This is Dakia (*Dacia*); it, too, is bounded by the Istros. Below the remaining parts and to the east is placed Lower Mysia (*i.e. Moesia*); this, too, includes a fair amount of the land beyond the Istros, and occupies all the coast that lies between the Borysthenes and the city of Mesembria.   12. Below Dakia, too, and after the Istros lies Upper Mysia (*i.e. Moesia*), which on its east joins Lower Mysia and on its west Dalmatia. Below[20] Dalmatia and part of Upper Mysia is Macedonia; and below the remainder of that and the Lower (*Mysia*) is Thrace. Next to this is the Chersonese specially called by that name. To the south of Macedonia lie, on the west, Epeiros and, on the east, Thessaly. Below these lies Hellas, which beside the isthmus in the Krisaian gulf forms the Peloponnese.

13. The notable islands of this continent[21] are, in the outer sea, the two Brettanikai, Iouernia (*Hibernia, Ireland*) and Alouion[22] (*Albion, Great Britain*); but Iouernia is in the westernmost position, extending some way opposite Hispania. Alouion, in which the military camps have been founded, is the largest and most elongated; for beginning from the north it reaches ⟨west to the⟩ middle parts of Tarrakonesia, and east almost to the middle of Germania. Also notable would be Thoule[23] and the great

---

[19] i.e. 'greater Germania', E of the two provinces (Mittenhuber ad loc.).

[20] One of the indications that the author is consulting a map, presumably with N at the top.

[21] The author returns to islands at §27.

[22] As in book 2 of Mark. *Periplous*, it may be helpful to think of the diphthong *ou* as a *w*, as if 'Iwernia' and 'Alwion' stood here.

[23] Probably the *Shetland Is.*, as in Ptolemy (Breeze and Wilkins 2018). Cf. Erat. 29; Pytheas 6–7, 13, 23, 26, 28.

Skandeia (*Sweden*) which lies below²⁴ the Kimbric peninsula (*Jutland*); for it projects from Germania, mostly towards the north and the ocean of the former.²⁵ 14. In the inner sea, below the more westerly parts of Italia, is Kyrnos, also called Korsike, which has Sardonia (*sic*) below it. Below the more easterly parts (*of Italia*) and towards the strait (*of Herakles*) is Sicily; and beside Attica and the Peloponnese is Crete, extending to the east; and beside Achaia²⁶ is Euboia.

ON THE NATIONS IN LIBYĒ

15. In Libyē, as it begins from the Pillars of Herakles, are the two Mauritaniai: the western being Tingitana, but following this (*to the east*) Kaisarensia (*Caesariensis*). After the latter is Afrike, next Kyrenaïke (*Cyrenaica*) Pentapolis, ⟨next⟩ Marmarike (*Marmarica*), next Egypt. Below the Mauritaniai is Gaitoulia (*Gaetulia*); below Afrike and the Pentapolis is the rainless and completely sandy land. This desert is located so as to extend up to the beginning of Egypt.

16. ⟨The nations of Inner Libyē⟩, in the west, are the following: the Daradai, Perorsoi, Odrangidai, Mimakes, Noubai (*Nubians*), Garamantes, Derbikai, Melanogaitouloi (*Black Gaitouloi*), Girrhoi, Nigritai, Afrikerones, and Leukaithiopes (*White Ethiopians*).²⁷

17. In the Aithiopia below Egypt, the whole region beside the sea that runs from Beronike (*sic*)²⁸ up to the narrows of the Arabian gulf (*Red Sea*) is called Troglodytike. Inward from this lies Azania, in which are all kinds of elephants, and the Spice-bearing (*Aromatophoros*) Land. 18. And after the Great Cataract, to the west of the Nile, are the Euonymitai,²⁹ Sebridai, and Katoipoi; and beside Meroë Island the Memnones, after whom are the Elephant-eating Aithiopes. Next the Pesendarai and the Cinnamon-bearing Land; and further west than these is Phazania. To the east (*of the Nile*) are the Koloboi (*Mutilated*), Atteroi, other Noubai, Blemmyes, Strouthophagoi (*Ostrich-eaters*), and the Myrrh-bearing Land.

The remaining, most southerly region, after which is the unknown region, is occupied, beside the so-called Aithiopes, by the Horse-eating (*Hippophagoi*) Aithiopes. Further south than the latter are the people commonly called the Western (*Hesperioi*; sc. *Aithiopes*).³⁰ Further east than these are the Athakai, and in the area round the gulf of the Bracheia (*Short*) sea³¹ the Anthropophagoi (*Man-eating*) Aithiopes. To the east and south of these, and approaching the unknown land, is the wide land called Agisymba.

---

²⁴ Here, perhaps, in the nautical sense of 'beyond'.   ²⁵ i.e. of Germania; the *North Sea*.
²⁶ The Roman province of that name, embracing all of mainland Greece.
²⁷ The sequence differs from Ptolemy's text, suggesting that the author is consulting a map (Mittenhuber 2011b on §16).
²⁸ i.e. Berenike, *Benghazi*.   ²⁹ *Left-handers? Auspicious People?*
³⁰ An example of the persistent belief that a swathe of Africa, from the W coast to the E, was occupied by Aithiopes.
³¹ i.e. Shallow Sea; probably the same as Ptolemy's 'Green Sea', part of the Indian Ocean; cf. Mark. *Peripl.* 1. 10, 12, and 40. See §33 & n. below.

ON THE NATIONS IN ASIA

19. The nations in Asia are as follows. For after the isthmus and the Tanaïs, Sarmatia, extending in the aforementioned way, is limited by the meridian dividing the Caspian sea into two lengthways; but then, coming round Lake Maiotis and the parts of the Pontos up to its inner end, it arrives at the Caspian via the interior. It (*Sarmatia*) is followed on the east by Skythia. Around its beginning it does not have a great breadth, but around its eastern part it is very wide; for it is not far short of joining up with Indike. After the whole of Skythia is Serike, which in its easternmost part terminates the known world.

20. Below Sarmatia on the Pontic side lies Kolchike, but on the Caspian side Albania; between them lies Iberia. The next place in the continent after the Propontis and the straits is the projection called Pontobithynia, also called Inner Pontos, alongside which is Paphlagonia. Below Pontobithynia, advancing up to Mt Dindymos, is Asia,[32] after which are Lykia and ⟨Pamphylia⟩. Between Pamphylia and Pontos lies Galatia. Enfolding this section and going up to the north beside Kolchis is Kappadokia, below which is Kilikia, lying beside the Tauros. The mainland (*ēpeiros*) containing the aforementioned nations itself resembles a peninsula with a broad neck, which would extend from the gulf of Issos to the city of Trapezous lying in Pontos.

21. Again, below Iberia and a part of Albania is Armenia, separated from Kappadokia by the Euphrates. Below this lies Mesopotamia, which has Syria further west. Below Syria is Ioudaia (*Judaea*). This lying southwards, there extends opposite and beside it the Arabia around Petra, up to the head of the Arabian gulf. The (*land*) between the aforementioned nations and the western side of the Persian gulf is called the Desert (*Eremos, i.e. Arabia Deserta*); it, too, contains Arabian nations. The mainland (*ēpeiros*) drawn around the southernmost part of the Desert, Arabia Petraia, the Arabian gulf and Erythraian sea, and part of the Persian gulf, is called Arabia Eudaimon (*Arabia Felix, Fortunate Arabia*) and is very great in size.

22. Below the Caspian sea and after the frontiers of Armenia is Media. Below this, to the east of the Tigris, is Assyria, in which is Ktesiphon. After the confluence of the Euphrates and Tigris, Babylonia descends to the sea with the Desert on its west. Below Assyria lies Sousiane up to the sea; likewise below Media Persis. To the east of Media lies Hyrkania, beside the sea of the same name; and below this Parthia. Below this is placed Empty (*i.e. Desert*) Karmania, after which lies True Karmania up to the sea.

23. Again, below the Skythia that runs up to Mt Imaos (*Himalaya?*) there lie, beginning from the west, Margiane, next Sogdiane, next Sakia. Below Margiane and east of Parthia lies Aria; below Sogdiane is placed Baktria; next, below Aria, which is oblong, lies Drangiane, and below Baktria the Paropanisadai (*or Paropamisadai*). Below them is Arachosia, which has the western (*or eastern?*) parts of Gedrosia lying below it, which in turn has (*below it*) Karmania, below which lies Drangiane.

---

[32] i.e. the Roman province, only part of Asia Minor.

24. All the remainder of the continent up to the Thinai, being very great and occupied by many nations, is ruled by the Indians and [—] being bounded on the east by the Sinai (*Chinese*), but on the west by Gedrosia, and on the north by the Paropanisadai and Arachosia, by the Sogdians and Sakai, and by Skythia and Serike.

25. Also belonging to this continent, in the Indian open-sea (*pelagos*) (*Indian Ocean*), is a very large island, the one called Simounda of old but now Salike (*Sri Lanka*).[33] In it, they say, all things grow that are useful for life, and it has mines of all kinds, and the men occupying it have their heads bound in feminine tresses. And in our sea is Cyprus.

COMPARISON OF THE THREE CONTINENTS

26. When the three continents are compared with one another, the greatest would appear to be Asia, then Libyē, but last Europe. Again, in terms of well-being and prosperity, and in terms of the constitution of the winds, the universal availability of water, and the varied abundance of plants, one would conclude from the records that the one that is pre-eminent over the others is, by a long way, Europe; next, out of all of Asia, almost exclusively the parts under the Romans; and of Libyē, the parts by the sea.

Of the nations in them, in Europe the largest[34] are Hispania and Italia, also Germania and Sarmatia; of those in Libyē Afrike and Egypt; and of the Asians above all Indike especially, though also very large are Skythia, Serike, and Eudaimon (*Arabia Felix*).

ON THE LARGEST ISLANDS

27. Among the particularly large islands, in comparison with all those in the inhabited world, the one in the first rank is Salike (*Sri Lanka*); but in second place is Alouion (*Albion*); and the third prize would be taken by Iouernia (*Hibernia*). Again, of the others that are large but lesser compared with those mentioned, the one placed first will be Sicily, the second Sardonia, the third Cyprus, the fourth Crete, and the fifth Euboia. Of the remainder, occupying as it were the third class in size, the first would be Korsike, also called Kyrnos, the second Lesbos, and the third Rhodos.[35]

ON THE LARGEST MOUNTAINS

28. The greatest mountains are (*as follows*): in Asia Imaos, the Emoda (*plural*), and the Kaukasia (*plural*); they say that these, and the Rhipaia, are the highest in comparison with all others. A very great mountain, too, is Paropanisos (*Hindu Kush*), as is Tauros and the majority of those in India. Of the Libyan ones, the highest are the great Atlas and Theon Ochema (*Chariot of the Gods*),[36] but the Aithiopian ones are great, and

---

[33] Cf. Palaisimoundou, *PME* 61; Markian, *Periplous*, 1. 1; 1. 8; 1. 35. The longer name may have been misunderstood as two words: *palai* means 'of old' in Greek.

[34] sc. in terms of population.

[35] For §§27–9, the author appears to have made his own list and rankings, rather than draw directly on Ptolemy (Mittenhuber 2011b ad loc.).

[36] Possibly Mt *Cameroon*; cf. Hanno §16.

are the longest: for beginning from the border with Egypt they descend to the south, extending equally as far as the course of the Nile.

In Europe they say the largest are the Sarmatika and the Alps, if one were to take them in combination. Also high, they say, are the Pyrenaia and Idoubaida (*Sistema Ibérico*)[37] in Hispania, the Macedonian Olympos, Athos, and the Akrokeraunia in Epeiros; the last, they say, can even be seen from Kanysion (*Canusium*).

ON THE LARGEST RIVERS

29. Of the rivers in the inhabited world the largest are, to begin with Asia where there are many, the Ganges and Indos above all; for these, arising from the northernmost parts of the inhabited world and taking in (*the water of*) nearly all the notable ones that flow through the whole of Indike—these, too, are numerous—they discharge into the southern sea. Of the remaining rivers in Asia, [—] and flowing into different seas, the Iaxartes (*Syr Darya*), Oxos, Rhymmos (*Ural?*), Rhas (*Volga?*), Kyros (*Kura*), and Araxes (*Aras*) make for the Caspian sea, but the Phāsis (*Rioni?*), Thermodon (*Terme Çay*), and Sangaris (*Sakarya*) for the Pontos. These have their outlets almost in the same places as their sources.

30. Of those in Europe the one that might be in first place is probably the Istros, which, running from the places to the west and passing through so many nations and places, discharges into the Pontos. Next, very large, are the Borysthenes (*Dnieper*), Ouistoulas (*Vistula*), Tanaïs (*Don*), and Rhenos (*Rhine*). There are other rivers that are large in respect of their outlets, especially the Eridanos (*Po*), Iber (*Ebro*), Baitis (*Guadalquivir*), Sekoanos (*Saône*), Dorias (*Douro*), and those around the Rhenos.

31. In Libyē the largest is the Nile; for after rising from the parts beyond the equator in the depth of the southern regions, it issues into our sea, drawing a curve, as seems likely, which is a characteristic of rivers [—] as is probable that it is by the rains that occur there during our summer, rather than by the formation of snow, that its flooding at the same time each year is caused. The Bagradas,[38] too, flowing in the area of Carthage, and the Kinyps[39] appear to come from the southernmost parts. Of those flowing through Inner Aithiopia and having both their sources and their ends within the continent, the largest is the Gir, together with the Nigir.[40]

ON THE GREAT SEA

32. Within the Greatest Sea,[41] the one towards the east, its southernmost parts towards the unknown land are called the Prasodes (*Leek-green*) sea;[42] for it is said to be something like that in colour, and to contain an enormous quantity of very large seaweed similar to the leek (*prason*), from which its leek-green appearance probably derives.

---

[37] The range running SE across NE Spain to the area of *València*.
[38] Unidentified; see n. on Mark. *Peripl.* 1. 23.   [39] Cf. Ps.-Skylax §109. 4 & n.
[40] For these two, cf. Juba 4.
[41] The Indian Ocean as a whole, not the outer Ocean (called 'Great Sea' at §45).
[42] Part of the Indian Ocean; cf. Mark. *Peripl.* 1. 12 and 44.

33. After this, roughly to the north, lies the Bracheia sea, which has gained this name not because of shortness of size[43]—for it is very large—but because of the *brachē* (*shallows*) within it. For the ebb-tides are (*said to be*) very large there: they do not change within the same day, but the water withdraws over a very long period, and after its withdrawal the rocky shores dry out, so that sailors, if they ever fall into this misfortune, may underprop the boat and climb off as if onto the mainland.[44]

34. Beyond this sea lies the remaining one, which is beside the continent (*of Asia*). The largest part of this is the Indian open-sea (*pelagos*), in which there are very large peninsulas and gulfs: the Theriodes (*Of Wild Animals*), the Megas (*Great*), and the Gangetic.[45]

35. But the Indian open-sea (*pelagos*) is followed by the Karmanian, projecting roughly westwards; and this is followed by the Erythraian sea. At the confluence of these lies the mouth of the Persian gulf. This gulf is enclosed on the east and south by Karmania; on the north, for those travelling west, by Persis, Sousiane, and Babylonia; and on the west by Empty (*Erēmos*) Arabia (*Arabia Deserta*),[46] and then again on the south by Eudaimon Arabia (*Arabia Felix*).

36. From the Erythraian sea as far as Egypt is the Arabian gulf. At about this point lies the narrowest part of the continent (*of Asia*), the part that prevents (*the gulf*) from joining onto our sea. They say it[47] does not take its red colour, as people sketchily assert, from the adjacent mountains, which are red ⟨and from which⟩ an influence influences (*sic*) the water when it is calm and creates the image of redness: rather—since this open sea (*pelagos*) is usually calm because the winds that occur there, so the story goes, are neither great nor continuous—when the sun is close to the zenith accumulations of watery clouds accumulate (*sic*), and the rays of the sun which fall upon these colour them; just as in our region the parts along the horizon are usually affected when the sun is rising or has already set, so that the sea receives the colours when it has a smooth surface.[48] After the Arabian gulf and the remainder of the Erythraian sea is the Aithiopic sea by Barbaria.[49]

ON THE WINDS OF THE INHABITED WORLD

37. The positions of the winds and airs around the inhabited world, and the parts from which each arises and through which each passes, are as follows.   38. Let a very large circle be conceived,[50] containing the known world and divided into twelve equal parts by six diameters, so that two of those that are at right angles to each other

---

[43] The adjective *brachys*, of which *bracheia* is the feminine form, means 'short'.
[44] This account is unique in ancient literature and may derive from sailors' tales (Mittenhuber 2011b, on §33). Cf. §§18 and 43.
[45] Cf. e.g. Mark. *Peripl*. 1. 45, 40, and 7 respectively.   [46] Cf. §21.   [47] The Erythraian sea.
[48] For discussion of the redness or otherwise of the Erythraian sea, cf. Agatharch. 2–5; Artem. 100 §2.
[49] Cf. *PME* §2.
[50] Not a 'great circle' round the whole Earth, but a line circumscribing the *oikoumenē* on part of its surface.

form the equator and the meridian.[51] Along the equator towards the east these define the Apeliotes, but towards the west the Zephyros; and again along the meridian to the north the Aparktias, but to the south the Notos. Next, on each side of the Apeliotes, to the south is the Euros, to the north the Kaikias; but again to the east of the Aparktias the Boreas, and to the west the Thraskias or Mesē (*Middle Wind*); and to the south of the Zephyros the Lips, but to the north the Iapyx or Argestes; and to the east of the Notos the Euronotos, but to the west the Libonotos. And there are those diametrically opposed, blowing against each other: Apeliotes against Zephyros, but Kaikias against Lips, and Boreas against Libonotos; then again Aparktias against Notos, but Thraskias against Euronotos, and Iapyx against Euros.

ON THE LENGTH AND BREADTH OF THE WHOLE INHABITED WORLD

39. It is also necessary to state the length and breadth of the whole inhabited world. So we shall grasp the length of it, not as the ⟨length⟩ that follows the form of a parallelogram, but as ⟨that which follows⟩ a certain segment of a circle and is greater than all the others that run through its whole length. For it has been shown that the ⟨area lying⟩ on the equator and falling away from it ⟨on each side, and extending⟩ from west to east, is similar ⟨in shape⟩ to the known world, and is much more prominent than the parts further south or north than this ⟨the equator⟩.[52] Let the ⟨size⟩ of that which is distant from the equator to its north be 23 degrees and a half plus one-third (23° 50′). This differs from ⟨the⟩ greatest ⟨circle by one hour and a half (*in the length of the longest day*), and has a length of⟩ 82,336 ⟨stades⟩. Thus the length via the great circle enclosing the known world is almost 90,000 stades. The breadth upon the meridian drawn through the Hippic mountains of Sarmatia is 32,500 stades or 4,333 miles.

ON THE LENGTH AND BREADTH OF THE SEAS IN THE INHABITED WORLD

40. The lengths and breadths of the seas of the inhabited world have the following character.[53] The parts of our sea from Kotes, the extremity of Mauritania Tingitana, up to Issos measure 25,400 stades or 3,386 miles. Its breadth from Massilia (*sic*)—since it is here that the Gallic sea[54] is most greatly indented towards the north—to the colony of Igilgilis in Mauritania, is 5,500 stades or 733 miles.

41. The Pontos has a length, from Tomis at the outlets of the Phasis, of 6,200 stades or 826 miles. Its breadth from the Phanagoria in the Bosporos to the outlets of the Halys, where the Pontos is also widest, is 2,400 stades or 320 miles.

---

[51] This is similar to Timosthenes' scheme but not identical: see introduction to chapter.

[52] This section returns to the discussion in §1. The thought is not expressed with perfect clarity; but Mittenhuber notes that the second half of §39 depends on Ptolemy's conic projection.

[53] Mittenhuber, commentary on §39, notes that the sizes of seas in §§40–4 appear to have been read off a map, since they depend on knowing that lines of longitude converge away from the equator.

[54] Called 'Galatic' at 48–9 below.

42. The Caspian sea has a length, from the outlets of the Kyros, which comes down from Armenia, to the outlets of the Iaxartes, of 8,200 stades or 1,094 miles, and a greatest breadth of 2,500 stades, 334 miles.

43. (*The length*) of the Bracheia (*Short, i.e. Shallow*) sea[55] in the Indian open-sea (*pelagos*)—since this in comparison to the others extends furthest to east and west—from the trading-post of Esinau in Barbaria,[56] or (*from*) the capital of the Rhaptoi,[57] to the river Kottiaris[58] among the Sinai, is 52,500 stades or 7,000 miles. Its breadth from the head of the Great gulf to the unknown land is 10,500 stades or 1,400 miles.

44. (*The length of*) the Arabian gulf, which inclines eastwards in the parts up to the narrows, is not less than 10,000 stades, which is 1,333⅓ miles.[59]

45. This Great Sea flowing round the whole inhabited world is called by the name Okeanos, but has different appellations corresponding to latitudinal zones. The (*Ocean*) under the north (*arktoi*) is said to be the Arktikos or Boreios (*both meaning Northern*), but its more easterly part the Skythian ocean, and the more westerly is called the Germanic or Bretannic. The same one in its entirety is also named the Kronian open-sea (*pelagos*), the Pepegos (*Solid, i.e. Frozen*), or the Nekron (*Corpse or 'Dead'*).[60] But the whole (*Ocean*) below the south is called the Mesembrinos or Notios (*both meaning Southern*) Ocean; again, its more easterly part is designated the Erythraian sea, but the more westerly as the Aithiopic ocean. The eastward part of the remaining two latitudinal zones is the Heōos (*Eastern*) open-sea (*pelagos*) or Indian Ocean; but the westward, from which our own sea is filled, is designated the Hesperios (*Western*) Ocean or most properly the Atlantic open-sea (*pelagos*).

46. The Earth round which these flow is distributed three ways by those who divide the inhabited world in the best way: into Europe, Asia, and Libyē.[61] The boundaries of Europe with Libyē are the strait at the Pillars of Herakles and the Middle (*Mediterranean*) open-sea (*pelagos*) that is filled up eastwards through it, up to the Kanopic mouth of the Nile. Those of Asia with Libyē are the very same mouth of the Nile and the straight course of that river towards the south, but that with Europe is the river Tanaïs discharging into Lake Maiotis; this runs out into the Euxeinos Pontos, this (*in turn*) into the Propontis, and this into the Hellespont, after which the Aegean open-sea (*pelagos*) likewise unfolds to the south. But some divide the preceding continents by isthmuses: Europe from Asia by that between the Caspian sea and the Pontos, Libyē (*from Asia*) by that between the Arabian gulf and the sea at Pelousion.

47. Such are the complete sections of the inhabited world. The (*length*) of the open seas (*pelagē*) contained within it, extending eastwards from the Iberian capes in the west as far as the Issic gulf by Kilikia, is 29,000 stades or ⟨3,867⟩ miles. For from the Issic gulf up to Rhodian (*territory*) 5,000 (*stades*) are counted, or 667 miles; from here to the eastern promontory of Crete, which is called Samonion, is 1,000 stades or

---

[55] Cf. §18 and n. to §33 above. [56] Cf. §36. [57] Cf. *PME* §16; Mark. *Peripl.* 1. 13.
[58] Cf. Mark. *Peripl.* 1. 46. [59] At 7½: 1.
[60] These names are a clear echo of Dion. Peri. 29–33.
[61] This is not a digression; it leads to the enumeration of component bodies of water.

133 miles; from Samonion to Kriou Metopon (*Ram's Brow; C. Krios*), the other, western promontory of Crete, is 1,500 (*stades*), which is also the length of the island. The passage from here to Pachynos Point, the extremity of Sicily, is 4,500, which is also the length of the Sicilian open-sea (*pelagos*). From Pachynos to the strait is more than 1,000; the passage from here to the Pillars is 13,000. From the Pillars to the Hieron (*Sacred*) Promontory, 3,000. This, then, is the length.[62]

48. But the breadth of the (*Mediterranean*) open-sea (*pelagos*) is, at its largest, 5,000 stades, from the Galatic (*Gallic*) gulf between Narbo and Massalia to the part of Libyē directly opposite. The whole of it has names corresponding to different places. For the mouth of the open sea (*pelagos*) is itself called the Strait beside the Pillars of Herakles; this is 120 stades in length, or 16 miles; and where it is narrowest, 70 stades. But to those who have sailed into this strait, our sea is at once revealed. The part of it beside Libyē, up to Egypt, is called the Libykon Pelagos (*Libyan Open-sea*), in which two gulfs exist, the ones designated the Syrteis. Of these the lesser, lying further west than the other, has a circumference of 1,600 stades or ⟨213⟩ miles, while the greater is 5,000. The depth of the latter is 1,500, which is also the size of its mouth.

49. The open sea (*pelagos*) beside Europe has several appellations. The first from the west is called the Iberic; after that is the Galatic gulf beside Massalia and Narbo. Next, by the beginning of what is now Italia, there follows the Ligystic (*Ligurian*) open-sea (*pelagos*); after this the Sardoan; succeeding this is the Tyrrhenic (*Etruscan*); next the Sicilian. The last arrives at Pachynos towards the south, at the extremities of Crete towards the east, and at Iapygia in a northerly direction. After this the Adriatic spreads a long way towards the north, then deviates to the west; it has a length of 6,000 stades or ⟨800⟩ miles, and a breadth where it is widest of 1,200. The parts ⟨on the right⟩ of this are Illyris, those on the left Italia as far as the head of the sea by Akouileia (*Aquileia*) and Polai.

50. After the Sicilian open-sea (*pelagos*) there follows the Cretan, with which the Egyptian connects, after which is the Phoenician. Next it inclines towards the north, grazing upper Syria and Kilikia. After this it turns away towards the west and is designated the Pamphylian open-sea (*pelagos*) up to the Chelidoniai islands and Cape Lykiake. From the Chelidoniai there unfolds the Aegean to the north, having a length towards the north of 4,000 stades or 533 miles, and a breadth where it is widest of 2,000. Afterwards the Hellespont is drawn together into a narrow place, having a width of 7 stades by Sestos and Abydos.

51. Next after this the Propontis broadens out, having a length from the Troad to Byzantion of 1,500 stades or ⟨200⟩ miles, and being roughly equal in breadth. After the Propontis, the mouth of the Pontos narrows again to a four-stades distance, which is called the Thracian Bosporos.

---

[62] §§48–53 are closely based on various passages of Strabo, but in §50 the author varies from Strabo's sequence (Mittenhuber 2011b).

From here the Pontos itself now opens up, being in a certain sense a double sea: for in the middle of it two capes project, about 2,500 stades distant from one another. The one extending north from Asia is called Karambis; the one (*extending*) south from Europe is designated Kriou Metopon (*Ram's Brow*).   52. Also the left-hand parts of the Pontos, which are towards the west, have a length from Byzantion up to the outlets of the Borysthenes of 3,800 stades, ⟨507⟩ miles, and a breadth of 2,000. The eastern part, which is also on the right hand for those sailing in, has a length of 5,000, or a little more, from the mouth to the head of the sea at Dioskourias, and a breadth of 3,000. 53. The circumference of the whole Pontos is 25,000 stades, similar to a Skythian bow: for the right-hand parts resemble the string, for it is everywhere straight except for the projecting Karambis; the remainder all (*resembles*) the horn of the bow, having its curve in double form so that two gulfs exist, of which the western is generally more rounded than the more easterly. To the north of this and beyond lies Lake Maiotis, with a circumference of 9,000 stades;[63] its mouth is called the Kimmerian Bosporos.

Such, then, is the nature of our sea.

---

[63] As at *Eux.* §121.

36

PSEUDO-ARRIAN,
CIRCUMNAVIGATION OF THE EUXINE

('*EUX.*')

(AFTER AD 565)

D. Graham J. Shipley

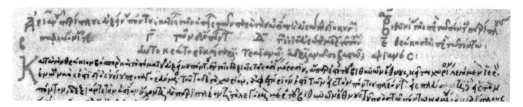

FIG. 36.1. Opening of Pseudo-Arrian, *Circumnavigation of the Black Sea*, fo. 4ʳ (detail).

INTRODUCTION

If we accept the title in the main manuscript at face value,[1] this treatise in Greek (often known as *Eux.* for short) masquerades as Arrian's *Periplous of the Euxeinos Pontos* (Chapter 27 above), reproducing part of his introductory salutation to the emperor Hadrian and even extensive passages of his text. Its real author is unknown, though possibly he is the same as the author of the *Hypotyposis* (Chapter 35), which would place it in the late 6th century AD.[2] The structure of its narrative of the Black Sea, however, is quite different from that of Arrian's: it proceeds anti-clockwise like his, but in one complete circuit beginning at the Thracian Bosporos and returning there,[3] as opposed to Arrian's three stages of which one is a 'flashback'. The anonymous *periplous* stands immediately before that by Arrian in the main manuscript; but internal evidence shows that it postdates it by several centuries: sometimes echoing the language of Procopius (who worked in Byzantion in the mid-6th century), sometimes referring

---

[1] The work is preserved complete only in pp. 8ʳ–11ᵛ of the Vatopedi codex, B (pp. 4ʳ–7ᵛ of those now in London), with parts in two other MSS (see Introduction, §VIII. 2. a).

[2] See n. 5 to Chapter 35 above.

[3] What Diller 1952, 102–17, repeatedly calls a tour 'to the right', referring to the direction in which one turns upon entering the Black Sea.

to place-names not otherwise attested before that time, notably Danapris for the river Borysthenes (mod. *Dnieper*; §87).⁴

At first sight, the work may appear to be no more than a patchwork of cut-outs: extracts not only from Arrian (*c*.31 per cent of the text, comprising roughly half of Arrian's original words) but also from three authors much earlier than Arrian: in descending order, the *Nikomedean Periodos* at *c*.26 per cent, Menippos at *c*.18 per cent, and Pseudo-Skylax at less than 1 per cent; in addition, there are 17 short passages, adding up to a few hundred words, where *Eux.* has concocted statements about the 'nations' (*ethnē*) along the shores of the sea by blending information from Ps.-Skylax and the others.⁵ With their aid the author has attempted to augment Arrian's, in places jejune, account—the new *periplous* is roughly two-thirds longer than Arrian's original. Less than one-quarter of the text is new; closer examination, however, reveals much of interest and value. He surely had access to a major library or book collection, and exercised considerable scholarly acumen in interweaving four sources—two of them, Ps.-Skylax and the *Nikomedean Periodos*, 'travelling' in the opposite direction to the others—as well as deploying new information.

At some points, however, the compiler's adaptation of Arrian and Ps.-Skylax has perpetuated or created inaccuracy; this is less the case with reference to Menippos' detailed prose.⁶ For example, the author fails (§71) to correct the misunderstanding by Arrian (19. 1) which makes the Tanaïs emerge from Lake Maiotis into the main Black Sea (rather than into Maiotis itself, which then debouches into the sea). He is sometimes confused about the identification of features with alternative names, at one point (§86) falsely equating the Danapris (or Borysthenes; *Dnieper*) with the Istros (*Danube*). When using an extract from one of the two clockwise sources, he sometimes forgets to invert the local order of places: Pantikapaion, for example, is called the last place in Europe rather than the first, as it should be (§78; the author here follows *Nik.*). In several cases he defines the homeland of a people in relation to adjacent places in such a way as to betray the clockwise progression of his source (e.g. §§37, 42–3, 49, 58, 60, 62, 64, 66, 74, 83).⁷

Despite these failings, however, the work's marginalization in scholarship is unjustified. On the positive side, its arrangement as a single circuit is an improvement on Arrian's (see above). They both proceed anti-clockwise,⁸ but Arrian begins at Trapezous in the south-east, proceeds north as far as Dioskourias (chs 1–11), then jumps back to insert the first part of the circuit (the north coast of Asia Minor as far as Trapezous, chs 12–16) before resuming, in less detail, from Dioskourias (chs 18–25).

---

⁴ Diller 1952, 110–12. At p. 113 Diller dates the work no earlier than AD 550–600.
⁵ All between §31 and §79; see Diller 1952, 107–9. These 'ethnographic' passages are marked ᵉ by Diller and in our translation.
⁶ Diller 1952, 112.   ⁷ Podossinov 2011, n. on §10; *GGM* i, p. cxvii.
⁸ Or 'to the left' in Diller's terminology.

The *periplous* is important, moreover, for the material from *Nik.* and Menippos which it preserves, including evidently most of the Black Sea passage of *Nik.*⁹ The author also supplies abundant factual details, chiefly new place-names, to update the text for geopolitics of his day. He adds value, too, to the information he has gathered: as well as place-names, he supplies conversions of stades into miles, and gives new summative distances (e.g. §§69, 79, 85, 92, and in a sustained sequence at §§120–1, though a close examination suggests some use of Menippos in these passages).¹⁰ A particular cluster of new pieces of information, of unknown origin, occurs in the sections describing the coast below the Caucasus (§§62–4): this passage and Procopius (the two being independent of one another) are the only sources for a migration of Gothic peoples east of the Kimmerian Bosporos in the mid-6th century AD (Procopius, *On the Wars*, 8. 4. 12; 8. 18. 22).¹¹

Indeed, a prime difference between Arrian's *periplous* and *Eux.* is the much greater level of detail—albeit with some new errors—in the later work, especially about the western Black Sea, where Arrian's verbal journey (17. 2–25. 4) is a relative sprint. Here *Eux.* supplements the information mainly with data from Menippos' obviously much fuller account. At §87 he avoids Arrian's confusion (20. 1, 21. 1) about the peninsula known as Achilles' Racetrack, only to repeat at §93 the error of Arrian 21. 1, who transfers the name to Leuke, Achilles' Island.¹²

In light of these features, we may consider *Eux.* an improvement on Arrian in some respects. None of the additional details is such as to prove that the author knew the coasts of the Black Sea at first hand, but the work is a serious attempt to update and enrich Arrian's letter to Hadrian; the opening reproduced from Arrian may not be intended to deceive but, on the contrary, to attribute the new, greatly enlarged edition of the work to its original author; perhaps thereby to give it credibility. Revision must have been a laborious task for its compiler—who surely had access to a library of imperial quality—as it entailed checking at least four source texts, updating numerous details, and converting stades to miles at a ratio of 7½ : 1 (except in one case, which may be accidental).¹³ By coincidence, he has preserved substantial material from lost geographers.

The translation follows Diller's transcription (taking into account his *apparatus criticus* and commentary),¹⁴ with occasional changes. The text published by Müller in *GGM* i (1855) had 92 sections, comprising §§1–42 from manuscript V (which preserves

---

⁹ Given the character of *Nik.* as we have it, it is apparent that there was little that *Eux.* would have had to omit: Diller 1952, 106. Müller, *GGM* i. 226–9, reconstructs 234 additional lines of *Nik.*, many forming continuous extracts; Diller 1952, 165–76, no fewer than 279 lines.

¹⁰ Diller 1952, 105.   ¹¹ Diller 1952, 111.   ¹² On this confusion, see Braund 2000, 351.

¹³ See §74, where it is 8 to the mile if the MS is correct. At §15 the distance from Herakleia to Amastris is given as 90 mi; there is no stade figure in manuscript B, but the relevant shorter distances in §§12–15 add up to 630, suggesting that the author 'must have converted carelessly at the rate of 7' (Diller 1952, 105).

¹⁴ Diller 1952 prints the MS text without emendations, but it is vastly superior to those of Müller (*GGM* i. 402–23; *FHG* v. 174–87). Podossinov 2011 also follows Diller's text.

only this part of the *Periplous*)¹⁵ and §§43–92 from the Heidelberg manuscript, A (which preserves only this final part).¹⁶ Fifteen years later, Müller published the central portion of the work from the London pages of manuscript B (which had come to light in 1853 and contains the whole *Periplous*), dividing it into 29 subsections numbered '§42. 1–29' since this passage stands between the original §§42 and 43;¹⁷ Diller later renumbered these subsections as 1B–29B. Podossinov's recent edition, more conveniently, continues the numeration after §42, designating this passage §§43–71 and the final part of the work §§72–121 (rather than §§43–92). We adopt his numeration, but give Diller's earlier numbers in parentheses where they differ.

NOTE ON THE TRANSLATION

Locators of the forms $_{A12.1}$, $_{M7}$, and $_{PS90}$ indicate corresponding passages in Arrian, Menippos, and Ps.-Skylax respectively.

Additionally, words drawn from Arrian or Menippos, or (from §29 onwards) attributed to Menippos by Diller in his bold reconstruction of that author's lost passages, are marked ^{a} or ^{m} unless immediately preceded by one of the above subscript locators. Words taken from Arrian will normally match the translation in Chapter 27. Lines of the surviving portion of *Nik.* (the *Nikomedean Periodos*, Chapter 17) are marked in the form $_{N747}$, fragments in the form $_{Nf38}$. As in Chapter 17, metrical phrases or lines attributed to *Nik.* are in double quotation marks " " with line breaks marked |. In 17 places between §31 and §79, ^{e} marks words that Diller identifies as blending material from Ps.-Skylax and the other sources (see introduction, above).¹⁸

Italics within parentheses ( ), as elsewhere in the volumes, are editorial explanations such as modern place-names. *Italics not in parentheses* are text apparently originated by the compiler of *Eux.*, not taken from one of his four sources. Where such words interrupt text marked ^{a} or ^{m}, the subsequent resumption of the text taken from Arrian or Menippos is not normally marked.

Headings, unless placed in angle brackets ⟨ ⟩, are in the manuscripts and may be original.

SELECTED FURTHER READING

*Diller, A. (1952), *The Tradition of the Minor Greek Geographers*. Lancaster, Pa.–Oxford. [Ch. 4 (pp. 102–46) with Greek transcription; map opp. p. 176.]
*Podossinov, A. V. (2011), 'Anonymi Periplus Ponti Euxini (2037)', in *FGrH* v.
[The first edition (2022) of Brodersen 2023a appeared too late to be taken into account.]

---

[15] V = codex Vaticanus graecus 143 in Rome (dated C15). Diktyon no. 66774.
[16] For manuscript A, see Introduction, §VIII. 2. a.
[17] *FHG* v. 1. 174–87 (with corrections to the previously published passages at pp. xix–xxiii).
[18] See Diller 1952, 107–9.

TEXT

^aArrian's Circumnavigation of the Euxeinos Pontos, _{M7}of both continents, of the places both along Asia and along Europe, thus: (*a*) circumnavigation of the (*part of*) Bithynia beside the *Pontos*, (*b*) circumnavigation of Paphlagonia, (*c*) circumnavigation of the two Pontoses, (*d*) circumnavigation of the parts of the Pontos in Europe, (*e*) circumnavigation of ^mthe (*part of*) Thrace beside the Pontos.[19]

1. _{A.preface}To the Emperor Caesar Trajan Hadrian Sebastos (*Augustus*), Arrian (*sends greetings*).[20] _{M7}Near the Thracian Bosporos and the mouth of the Euxeinos Pontos in the right-hand parts of Asia, which belongs to the nation of the Bithynians, lies a settlement called Hieron (*Sanctuary*), in which is a temple designated that of Zeus Ourios. This place is the point of departure for those sailing into the Pontos. As one sails into the Pontos, holding Asia on the right side and circumnavigating the remaining part of the nation of the Bithynians that lies towards the Pontos, the circumnavigation is somewhat as follows.

2. _{A12.1}The sanctuary (*Hieron*) of Zeus Ourios is 120 stades from Byzantion, and it is here that the so-called mouth of the Pontos is narrowest, where it enters the Propontis.

^MFIRST (PART): CIRCUMNAVIGATION OF THE PART OF BITHYNIA TOWARDS THE PONTOS

3. _{M8}^aAs one sails ^mfrom the sanctuary (*Hieron*) of Zeus Ourios ^aon the right side, ^mit is 90 stades, *12 miles* towards the river Rhibas (*Riva Kalesi*). From the river Rhibas to Cape Melaina (*Black; Kara Burunu*), now called Kalē (*Good*), 150 stades, *20 miles*. From Cape Kalē to the river Artanas (*or Artana; Kuzgun*) and the settlement there, 150 stades, *20 miles*. ^aThere is an anchorage (*hormos*) for small vessels near the sanctuary of Aphrodite; ^mand an islet lies nearby which shelters the harbour.

4. ^mFrom the river Artanos (*or Artanon*) ^ato the river ^mand settlement of ^aPsilis (*Gök Su*), 150 stades, *20 miles*. And small boats might be anchored near the rock that emerges not far from the outlet of the river.

5. From the river Psilis to the harbour ^mand river ^aof Kalpes (*Kerpe Limani*) is 210 stades, *28 miles*. ^mThis is a trading-place of the Herakleians. ^aOf Kalpes Limen, of the nature of the place and of its anchorage; of the spring there of cold, pure water; and of the forest, infested with wild beasts, of shipbuilding wood near the sea, Xenophon the Elder spoke.[21]

6. _{A13.1}From Kalpes Limen to the Rhoë (*Stream; Kumkagız Dere*), in which there is an anchorage for small ships, 20 stades, *2⅔ miles*. From Rhoë to the small island of

---

[19] In the main MS, this paragraph is in red and the five phrases are numbered using the letters αβγδε. At each of (*c*)–(*e*) MS B omits 'circumnavigation'.

[20] Here the MS changes to black ink for normal text (apart from the large initial letter, which is in red).

[21] Xen. *Anab.* 6. 4. 3–5.

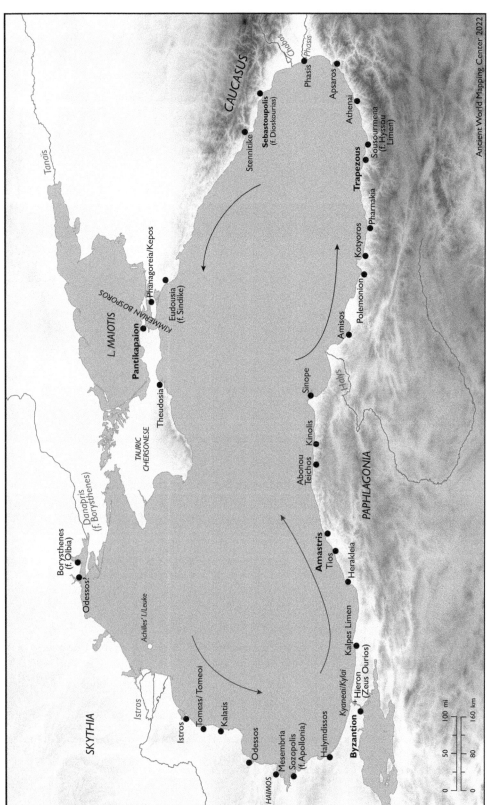

MAP 36.1. Pseudo-Arrian, *Euxine*: principal places. Includes names altered since the time of Arrian.

Apollonia (*Kefken Adası*), *now called Daphnousia, a short distance from the mainland, in which is a harbour at the bottom of the islet,* 20 stades, *2⅔ miles. This Apollonia* _{Nf38}*has within it a city called Thynias, a colony of the Herakleiots. From the island of Apollonia or Daphnousia* ^a*to Chelai,* 20 stades, *2⅔ miles. This is the one still also called Chele of the Medianoi.*

7. From Chelai ^mto the Sangarios (*Sakarya*), a navigable (*plōtos*) river, ^a180 stades, 24 miles. _{Nf37}(*The river Sangarios*), *running from the land about the Thynoi and from Phrygia, debouches through the Thynian territory.*

8. ^mFrom the river Sangarios to the river Hypios (*Büyuk Melen Çayı*), 180 stades, 24 miles. _{Nf36}This river has upon it an inland city called Prousias.

9. ^mFrom the river Hypios to the city of Dia, in which there is also an anchorage for small ships, 60 stades, *8 miles.*

From the city of Dia ^ato the trading-place of Lilaion (*Akçakoca*), 40 stades, *5⅓ miles.*

From Lilaion ^mto the trading-place of Elaion (*Aftun Deresı?*) and the river, ^a60 stades, *8 miles.*

^mFrom Elaion to the river Kalēs (*Alaph*) and its trading-place, 120 stades, *16 miles.*

^mFrom the river Kalēs ^ato the river Lykos (*Gülüç Çay?*), 80 stades, *10⅔ miles.*

From the river Lykos to the city of Herakleia (*Ereğli*), a Hellenic, Dorian one and a colony of the Megarians, 20 stades, *2⅔ miles.*

10. _{Nf35}Herakleia is "a foundation of the Boiotians | and Megarians; they are founding this within | the Kyaneai, starting out from Hellas | at the times when Cyrus took control of Media".

11. ^mAltogether, from Hieron as far as Herakleia, 1,550 stades, *206⅔ miles*; but to someone sailing directly, 1,200 stades, *160 miles.*

From Herakleia to the city of Apollonia in Europe, lying opposite in the Thracian nation, *and now called Sozopolis,* 1,000 stades, *123⅓ miles.*[22]

12. _{A13.3}From *the city of* Herakleia to the so-called Metroön, *now called Aulia,* 80 stades, *10⅔ miles.*

From *the* Metroön to the Posideon *now called Potistia,* 40 stades, *5⅓ miles.*

From the *Posideon* to Todaridai (*i.e. Tyndaridai*), *now called Kyrsaïta,* 45 stades,[23] *6 miles.*

From *Todaridai* to the Nymphaion, 15 stades, *2 miles.*[24]

From the Nymphaion to the river Oxinas (*Ilık Su*), 30 stades, *4 miles.*

13. From the *river* Oxinas to Sindarache (*Zonguldak*), *in which is* an anchorage for ships, ^m40 stades, *5⅓ miles.*

From Sindarache to Krenides (*Kilimli*), in which is an anchorage for small ships, 20 stades, *2⅔ miles.*

---

[22] This distance is a temporary interruption of the eastward progress: it looks back west, past the Bosporos, to a city on the W shore.

[23] The first distance in stades that is not a multiple of 10.

[24] The four places just named were probably local sanctuaries.

From Krenides to the settlement of Psylla (*Çatal Ağzi*), *ᵃ*30 stades, *4 miles*.

From *Psylla* to Tios (*Filyos/Hisarönü*), a Hellenic, Ionian city built on the sea, another colony of the Milesians, 90 stades, *12 miles*.

From Tios to the river Billaios (*Filyos Çayı/Yenice Ç.*), 20 stades, *2⅔ miles*. ᵐThis river Billaios, some say, forms the boundary of Bithynia. Beyond this belongs to Paphlagonia. Some, however, wish the river Parthenios (*Bartin Çayı*) to be the boundary between Bithynia and Paphlagonia.

SECOND (PART): ⟨CIRCUMNAVIGATION OF PAPHLAGONIA⟩

ᵃFrom the *river* Billaios ᵐto the river *Psilis, now called Papanios*, 60 stades, *8 miles*.

From the river Psilis, *also Papanios*, to the river Parthenios, 70 stades, *8⅓ miles*. 14. ₙ𝑓₃₄This river Parthenios is navigable, descending with a very quiet current. In it, so the story goes, "there is a very famous bath of Artemis".

15. ₘ₉ ₐ₁₄.₁ᵐFrom the river Parthenios to Amastris (*Amasra*), *ᵃa Hellenic city that also has* ᵐa river, ₚₛ₉₀formerly called Sesamos, ᵐ90 stades, *12 miles. From Herakleia to Amastris, 90 miles.*²⁵ 16. ₙ𝑓₃₃(*The city of Amastris:*) "they say Phineas ruled over these places, | son of Phoinix the Tyrian". In later times an expedition of Milesians came from Ionia and founded these cities, "which Amastris later brought together | into Amastris, a city of this name she founded | upon this site. She is reported as | the Persian Oxathres' daughter, the story goes, | and Herakleian" tyrant Dionysios' wife.

17. ᵃFrom Amastris to *Chele* Erythinoi (*by Çakraz Burunu*), 90 stades, *12 miles*.

From *Chele* Erythinoi *to* ᵐthe settlement of ᵃKromna (*Korç Şile/Tekeönü*), *90 stades, 12 miles*.

ᵐFrom Kromna to *the trading-post of* Kytoros (*Kidros*), an anchorage *for ships*, 90 stades, *12 miles*.

ₐ₁₄.₂From Kytoroi²⁶ *to the settlement of* Aigialos (*Karaagaç Limanı*), 60 stades, *8 miles*.
ᵐFrom Aigialos to the *village* of Klimax, *30 stades, 4 miles*.

From Klimax to the settlement of Timolaion, *40 stades, 5⅓ miles*.

From Timolaion ᵃto Thymina (*Timne*), 20 stades, *2⅔ miles*.

ₐ₁₄.₃From Thymina ᵐto the promontory of Karambis (*C. Kerempe*), which is lofty and huge, ᵃ120 stades, *16 miles*.

18. ᵐOpposite Karambis, in Europe, lies ₙ𝑓₃₂a high mountain falling steeply into the sea, the so-called Kriou Metopon (*Ram's Brow*), distant from Karambis the voyage of a night and a day.

19. ᵐFrom Karambis to the village of Kallistratis, *also (called) Marsylla*, 20 stades, *2⅔ miles*.²⁷

From Kallistratis ᵃto Zephyrion (*near Doganyurt*), *40 stades, 5⅓ miles*.

From Zephyrion ᵐto the settlement of Garion, *30 stades, 4 miles*.

---

²⁵ *Sic*; no distance in stades is given in the MS. ²⁶ Or Kytora; here plural.
²⁷ For its location, see Dana 2018, attributing hitherto unidentified amphora stamps to it.

From the settlement of Garion to the city of Abonou Teichos (*Inebolu*), called Ionoupolis, 120 stades, *16 miles*. *ᵃThe anchorage is not secure for ships; though they could ride at anchor (*saleuoien*) without harm, unless a large storm occurred.

20. ᵐFrom *Ionoupolis* ᵐto the small town and river of Aiginetes (*Hacıveli Burunu*), *120 stades, 16 miles.*

From Aiginetes to the village of Kimolis (*Ginoğlu*), ᵃcalled Kinolis,[28] 60 stades, *8 miles*. At Kinolis ships could ride at anchor in season; ᵐand it has a minor anchorage in the so-called Antikinolis.

_{A14.4}From Kinolis ᵐto the village and harbour of Stephane (*Usta Burunu*), ᵃ180 stades, *24 miles*. From Stephane ᵐto the settlement of Potamoi,[29] 150 stades, *20 miles*. ᵐFrom Potamoi to Syrias, a narrow cape,[30] 120 stades, *16 miles*. After Syrias, the *narrow cape*, there follows a gulf; someone sailing into it comes to the village of Armene (*Ak Limanı*) and a large harbour; ᵃ60 stades, *8 miles*. ᵐBeside the harbour is a river called Ochthomanes.

21. _{A14.5}ᵐFrom Armene to the city of Sinope (*Sinop*), ᵃa colony of the Milesians, 40 stades, *5⅓ miles*. ᵐThere is situated at the outskirts an islet called Skopelos (*Crag*); it has a way through for smaller ships, but bigger ships must sail round it and in this way reach the city. For those who sail round the island, there is an additional distance of 40 stades, *5⅓ miles*.   22. _{Nf31}Sinope is named after one of the Amazons living nearby who occupied it of old; they were kindred of the Syroi. "After that, it is said, those Hellenes who came over | against the Amazons, Autolykos and Phlogios, | who followed Deïleon and were Thessalians". Next Abron (*i.e. Habron?*), by race a Milesian; he appears to have been killed by Kimmerians. "After the Kimmerians in turn, Kretines of Kos", and those who had become exiles from the Milesians. This people are founding it when the army of the Kimmerians overran Asia.

23. ᵐFrom Sinope to the river Euarchos, *also called Euēchos*, 80 stades, *10⅔ miles*; this river *Euarchos* forms the boundary of Paphlagonia and neighbouring Kappadokia. For the ancient (*writers*) wish Kappadokia to stretch right to the Euxeinos Pontos; but some called them Leukosyroi (*White Syrians*). Now, after Paphlagonia, the land up to the frontier of the barbarian regions is properly called Pontos. It is divided into two provinces.

THIRD (PART): CIRCUMNAVIGATION OF THE TWO PONTOSES

24. _{M10}From the river Euarchos to the trading-post of Karousa (*Gerze*), with a harbour in winds from the west, *formerly named Polichnion (Little Town), 70 stades, 8⅓ miles*.

From Karousai (*sic*) to Gourzoubathe, *60 stades, 8 miles*.

---

[28] The first name is perhaps from a false association with the Aegean island of Kimolos.

[29] 'Rivers'; by *Cebelit Burunu*.

[30] Or, as in Arr. §14. 4, Lepte Akra, 'Narrow Cape' (*İnce Burunu*), perhaps another name for Syrias; or perhaps a word such as *ētoi* ('also') has dropped out. One MS reads *akron* ('point') instead of *akran* ('cape').

From Gourzoubathe to the settlement of Zagora (Çayağzi), *also called Kallipous*, *ᵃ*150 stades, *20 miles*.

*ᵃ*From Zagoron (*sic*) *ᵐ*to the river Zalikos and the village, which has no harbour, *90 stades, 12 miles*.

From the river Zalikos to the navigable river *Halys* (*Kızıl Irmak*), *210 stades, 28 miles*. 25. ₐ₁₅.₁This river was of old the boundary between the kingdoms of Kroisos (*Croesus*) and of the Persians, and now flows under Roman rule—not from the south, as Herodotos says, but from the rising sun. And there, where it flows into the Pontos, it separates the territories of the Sinopeans and the Amisenians. ₙf₃₀ Being 300 stades distant from Amisos, running between the Syroi³¹ and Paphlagonians it debouches into the Pontos.

26. ₐ₁₅.₂From the river Halys to Naustathmos (*Ship Station*), in which is also a harbour (*or 'lake'*), *40 stades, 5⅓ miles*.

From the harbour of Naustathmos to Konopion (*Mosquito Place*),³² a lake (*or 'harbour'*), *50 stades, 6⅔ miles*.

From Lake Konopion to Eusene, *also called Dagalis*, *120 stades, 16 miles*.

From Eusene to the city of Amisos (*Samsun*), *160 stades, 20⅔ miles*. 27. ₐ₁₅.₃Amisos, a Hellenic city and a colony of the Athenians, is built on the sea, ₙf₂₉lying in the land of the Leukosyroi, a colony of the Phokaians: for being settled four years earlier than Herakleia it received an Ionian founding; and by this city is the neck of Asia that is almost the narrowest, "passing through | to the Issic gulf (*gulf of Issos*) and Alexandroupolis, | founded by the Macedonian; it has a road | of seven days in total to Kilikia". For it is said that the most isthmus-like part of Asia "draws together into the corner around it (*the city*); | but Herodotos seems not to know it, saying | that a straight road of five days exists | from Kilikia, as he reports in his writing", to Sinope, a city further on.³³ "The peninsula, comprising almost the best locations | in Asia, has fifteen races, three Hellenic: | the Aiolic, next the Ionic, and the Doric"; but otherwise the rest of the mixed peoples are barbarian. "There live here Kilikians, Lykians, and in addition | Karians and maritime Mariandynoi | and Paphlagonians and Pamphylians; | Chalybes in the interior, Kappadokians near them, | and those that hold Pisidia, and Lydians, | and in addition Mysians and Phrygians."

28. *ᵐ*From Amisos to the river Lykastos, *20 stades, 2⅔ miles*.

From the river Lykastos to the village and river of Chadisios, *40 stades, 5⅓ miles*.³⁴

From the river Chadisios *ᵃ*to Ankon's harbour, into which the river Iris (*Yeşil Irmak*) pours, *ᵐ*100 stades, *13⅓ miles*.

---

³¹ *Sic*, not 'Syrians'.
³² This, like Eusene, is not definitely identified, though the mosquitoes fit the marshy area E of the Halys.
³³ Hdt. 2. 34. See n. on Ps.-Skylax §102. 2.
³⁴ The surviving fragment of Menippos breaks off here.

29. From the river Iris to the sanctuary and promontory of Herakleia (*at Caltı Burunu*), ^a360 stades, *48 miles*; ^mhere is a large harbour, the one called Lamyron; ^athere is anchorage for ships, and water for an expedition.

From Herakleia to the river Thermodon (*Terme Suyu*), *accessible for ships* (*nausiporos*), 40 stades, *5⅓ miles*. This Thermodon is in the (*area*) in which, they say, the Amazons lived. ^mIt also has by its outlet a city called Themiskyra;[35] and the river Thermodon flows through it.

_{A16.1}From the river Thermodon to the river Beris (*Miliç Suyu*), 60 stades, *8 miles*.

From the river Beris to the river Thoaris (*Zindan Dere*), 90 stades, *12 miles*.

30. From the river Thoaris ^mto the river Oinios (*Ünye Dere*) in the Pontos, in which there is also a minor anchorage for ships, ^a30 stades, *4 miles*.

From the river Oinios ^ato the river Phigamous (*Yevis Dere?*), 40 stades, *5⅓ miles*.

From the river Phigamous ^mto the location (*called*) Amylitos, 20 stades, *2⅔ miles*.

From the location (*called*) Amylitos ^ato Phidasane (*Fatsa*) ^mor Phadissa, *130 stades, 17⅓ miles*; ^mhere is a harbour and a city nearby called Polemonion.[36]

_{A16.2}^mFrom Phadissa ^ato the city of Polemonion, 10 stades, *1⅓ miles*.

31. ^e*From Polemonion nearly*[37] *as far as the banks of the river Thermodon was formerly settled by the nation of the Chalybes.*

32. From Polemonion to the promontory called Iasonion (*Yasun Burunu*), 130 stades, *17⅓ miles*.

From Iasonion to the island of Kilikos (*Hoynat Kale*), 15 stades, *2 miles*.

_{A16.3}From the island of Kilikos ^mto the river Genepos, 55 stades, *7⅓ miles*.

From the river Genepos to the promontory and land of Boön (*Persembe/Vona*), ⟨20 stades, *2⅔ miles*⟩; here is a harbour in all winds ^aand an anchorage for ships.

From Boön to Kotyoros (*Ordu*), 90 stades, *12 miles*. Of this Kotyoros Xenophon,[38] the Pylades,[39] made mention, and says that it was a colony of the Sinopeans; now it is a village, and not a large one.

33. ^e*From Kotyoros nearly as far as Polemonion*[40] *there lived formerly the nation of the Tibarenoi,* _{Nf28}*sharing space* [—] *"to play, loving to laugh in every fashion"*, *having judged that this is the greatest blessing.*

34. ^mFrom Kotyoros a gulf follows; when one sails into it, (*the voyage*) to the river Melanthios (*Melet Irmak*) is 60 stades, *8 miles*.

From Kotyoros, if one does not sail round the gulf but sails straight across the mouth of the gulf, to the settlement of Hermonassa (*Akçaabat*) of the Trapezountians (*is*) 300 stades, *40 miles*.

---

[35] Not located.   [36] See n. on Arr. §16. 2.
[37] Diller 1952, 142, explains the Greek here.   [38] Cf. Xen. *Anab.* 5. 5. 3.
[39] Pylades was the best friend of the hero Orestes (son of Agamemnon); Diller 1952, 142, reports Müller's suggestion that Arrian referred to Xenophon of Athens, his literary hero, as his Pylades. (The author of *Eux.* may have introduced the idea.)
[40] One of a number of places where the author has, perhaps inadvertently, not inverted the local order of a source text.

*a*From the river Melanthios to the river Pharmantos (*Bazar Suyu*), *called Pharmantinos*, 140 stades, *20 miles*.

From the river Pharmantinos to Pharnakia (*Giresun*), *called Pharnakion*, 120 stades, *16 miles*. $_{A16.4}$This Pharnakeia used to be called Kerasous, and was another colony of the Sinopeans, $_{Nf27}$founded †by which an empty place is lying, opposite which† extends an island called Ares' Isle.

35. *eFrom Pharnakia, which used to be Kerasous, nearly as far as Kotyoros*[41] *there lived formerly* $_{Nf26}$the nation called the Mosynoikoi (*Hut-dwellers*), with harsh customs, most barbaric in their deeds; "for, it is said, they all reside in lofty | towers of wood, but everything they do | is always done in public; while their king, | bound and shut away within a tower, | watches with care—his tower is the one | with the highest roof of all— but those who guard him | ensure that all of his commands are lawful; | if he transgresses, he receives a punishment"—the greatest, they say, as they give him no food.

36. *aFrom Pharnakia to the island of Aristias,*[42] *which has a minor anchorage against the winds from the west*, 30 stades, *4 miles*; this island of Aristias is called Ardous, also Areonesos.[43]

*m*From the island of Aristias to the settlement of Zephyrion (*Çam Burunu*), *a*120 stades, *16 miles*; there is an anchorage (*Zefre Liman*) for ships.

From the settlement of Zephyrion to Tripolis (*Tirebolu*), 90 stades, *12 miles*.

From Tripolis to Argyria[44] 20 stades, *2⅔ miles*.

$_{A16.5}$From Argyria to Philokaleia, 90 stades, *12 miles*.

From Philokaleia to Koralla, 100 stades, *13⅓ miles*.

From Koralla *m*to the city and river of Kerasous, 60 stades, *8 miles*.

From Kerasous to Hieron Oros (*Sacred Mountain; Yoros Burunu*), in which is a city and a minor anchorage, 90 stades, *12 miles*.

From Hieron Oros to the settlement of Kordylion (*near Akçakale*), *a*in which is also an anchorage, 40 stades, *5⅓ miles*.

$_{A16.6}$From Kordyle *m*to the settlement of *a*Hermonassa (*Akçaabat*), in which is also an anchorage, 45 stades, *6 miles*.

From Hermonassa to the city of Trapezous (*Trabzon*), *m*in which is an anchorage called Daphnous, *a*60 stades, *8 miles*. $_{A1.1}$Trapezous is a Hellenic city, a colony of the Sinopeans, founded on the sea.

37. *eSo from Trapezous as far as the island of Aristias or ⟨Pharnakia⟩, which used to be Kerasous, there lived formerly* $_{Nf25}$the nation called the Makrones (*Long Men*) or Makrokephaloi (*Long-heads*).

38. $_{A7.1}$From Trapezous to the Hyssou Limen, *now called Sousourmena* (*Araklıçarşısı/Sürmene*), 180 stades, *24 miles*.

---

[41] Another reverse direction. [42] 'Aretias', Arr. §16. 4.
[43] Ares Isle was already mentioned at §34.
[44] i.e. 'the *argyria*', silver-mines (at *Halkavala*), as at Arr. §16. 4, end.

From Sousourmena ᵐto the river Ophious (*Of*), in which there is a moderately sized roadstead (*salos*) for ships, 90 stades, *12 miles*. This river Ophious ᵃseparates the territory of the Kolchoi from Thianitike. ᵉ*So* (*the land*) *from the Ophious river as far as the Trapezountes* (sic) *was formerly occupied by the nation called Becheires, but now Kolchoi occupy it.* ᵐSo up to the river Ophious are the nations of the two Pontoi, but the ones after it are of different barbarian nations.

39. ₐ₇.₂From the river Ophious ᵃto the river called Psychros (*Cold; Baltacı Dere*), 30 stades, *4 miles*.

From the river Psychros to the river Kalos,⁴⁵ now called *Kalē Parembolē* (*Good Camp*), *is* 30 stades, *4 miles*.

From *Kalē Parembolē to the river* Thrizeos ᵐor Rhizeos (*Rize*), *and a harbour*, ᵃ120 stades, *16 miles*.

₍ₐ₇.₃₎From the Rhizeos to the river Askourna (*Taşlı Dere*), 30 stades, *4 miles*.

From the river Askournos (*sic*) to the river ᵐAdinaios (*Kanlü Dere/Kıbledağı Dere*), ᵃalso called Adienos, 60 stades, *8 miles*; ᵐand it has a moderately sized roadstead for ships.

From the river Adinaios to the settlement of Kordyle, 100 stades, *13⅓ miles*.

From Kordyle to the settlement of Athenai, 80 stades, *10⅔ miles*; here is an anchorage for ships. ₐ₄.₁For there is in the Euxeinos Pontos a land called *Athenai* (*Athens*),⁴⁶ *in which is also a Hellenic sanctuary of Athena, from which I imagine the place got that name, and also an abandoned fort.* ₐ₄.₂The anchorage at the right time of year can accommodate only a few ships and shelters them from the south wind, and even the east; it may also save ships that are anchoring from the Boreas (*NNE wind*), but not from the Aparktias (*north wind*), nor from the wind called the Thraskios (*NNW wind*) in the Pontos, and the Skiros (*i.e. Skiron*) in Hellas.

40. ₐ₇.₃From Athenai to the river Zangales (*Pazar Dere/Susa D.*), 7½ stades,⁴⁷ *1 mile*.

From *the river Zangales, or* Athenai, *to the river Pyrtanes*,⁴⁸ 40 stades, *5⅓ miles, where Anchialos' palace is.*

From the river Pyrtanes ᵐto the location (*called*) Armene, 24 stades, *3⅓ miles*.⁴⁹

₍ₐ₇.₄₎From the settlement of Armene ᵃto the river Pyxites (*Piskala Dere?*), 66 stades, *8⅔ miles*.⁵⁰

From the *river* Pyxites to the *river* Archabis (*Arhavi*), 90 stades, *12 miles*.

From the *river* Archabis to the *river* Apsaros (*Gonio*), 60 stades, *8 miles*. 41. ₐ₆.₃And it is said that *the settlement of* Apsaros was long ago called Apsyrtos; for it was there that Apsyrtos was killed by Medea, and the tomb of Apsyrtos is pointed out. The name was subsequently corrupted by the barbarians who live around there, just as many

---

⁴⁵ *Good; İyi Dere/Kalopotamos.* ⁴⁶ See n. on Arr. §4. 1.

⁴⁷ The first distance in stades that is not a multiple of 5.

⁴⁸ i.e. Prytanes? Prytanis would mean 'Chief'. *Büyük Dere/Furtuna Dere.*

⁴⁹ The first distance in stades that is not a multiple of 2½, which is one-third of a mile at the ratio of 7½ to 1 which *Eux.* employs. 3⅓ miles would actually be 25 st.

⁵⁰ Incorrect, like the preceding calculation: should be 65 st.

others were corrupted too; _{A6.4}since they say that Tyana in Kappadokia was named Thoana after Thoas, king of the Tauroi, who, *they claim*, while pursuing Orestes and Pylades, came as far as this region and died here of a disease.

42. *ᵉSo from the river Archabis as far as the river Ophious*[51] *was formerly occupied by the nation named Ekecheirieis, but is now occupied by the Machelones and Heniochoi.* 43. (1B). *And from the river Apsaros as far as the river Archabis was formerly occupied by the nation called Bouseres, but is now occupied by the Zydritai.*

44. (2B). _{A7.4}From the river Apsaros to the Anakampsis (*Çoruh*), a river accessible to ships, 15 stades, *2 miles*.

_{A7.5}From *the river Anakampsis to the river Bathys* (*Deep; Qorolistsqali*), 75 stades, *10 miles*.

From *the river Bathys* to the river Kinasos (*Kintrish?*),[52] 90 stades, *12 miles*.

From *the river Kinasos* to the Isis (*Natanebi*), a river accessible to ships, 90 stades, *12 miles*. Being accessible to ships, both the Akampsis and the Isis send out strong winds in the morning.

From the river Isis to the Mogros (*Supsa*), ⟨a river⟩ accessible to ships, ᵐalso called Nygros, ᵃnavigable, 90 stades, *12 miles*.

_{A8.1}⟨From the river Mogros to the river *Phasis* (*Rioni?*), 90 stades, *12 miles*.⟩ 45. (3B). This river Phasis _{Nf24}has a current "that runs down out of Armenia, near which | Iberians live who once were relocated | from Iberia to Armenia. As one goes into" a river "to the left of the Phasis", there lies beside it a Hellenic city of the Milesians, called Phasis, into which it is said sixty nations come down, all using different tongues, "among whom they say that some from India" and Baktria have come together, both barbarian. Between these the Koraxic land is barbarian; the places following it are the so-called Kolike, the nation of Melanchlainoi, and that of the Kolchoi. 46. (4B). _{PS81}The river admits upstream sailing (*for*) 180 stades, *24 miles*; in it is a great city called Aia, from where Medea came. 47. (5B). _{A8.2}The Phasis, having ᵃvery light water, floats on the sea, not mixing with it, _{A8.3}and just below the surface it is very fresh to draw up, but if one sinks the cup deeper, it is salty. Moreover, the whole Pontos has much fresher water than the sea outside it; the reason for this is its rivers, being so many and so great in volume. _{A8.4}The proof of this freshness—if proof of perceptible phenomena be necessary—is that those who live next to the sea lead all their cattle down and water them from this; they drink happily, and the opinion is it is more beneficial to them than fresh water is. _{A8.5}The colour of the Phasis is *strange*, like that of water that has been tainted with lead or tin; but, being left to stand, it becomes extremely clear. Furthermore, those who sail *into it* are traditionally forbidden from importing water into the Phasis, and as soon as they enter its stream they are ordered to pour out all water that is on the ships; and if they do not, it is said, they will not sail on favourably. And

---

[51] In the reverse direction.   [52] Akinases at Arr. §7. 5.

the water of the Phasis does not stagnate, but remains unchanged for upwards of ten years—if anything, it becomes fresher.

48. (6B). $_{A10.1}$From the river Phasis to the Charieis (*Khobi*), a river accessible to ships, 90 stades, *12 miles*.

From the *river* Charieis to *the Chobos* (*Inguri*), *a river accessible to ships*, 90 stades, *12 miles*.

$_{A10.2}$From the river Chobos to the river Segame (*Galizga*), *ᵐ*also called Zeganis, 210 stades, *28 miles*.

*ᵃ*From the river Zeganis to the river Tarsouras (*Tanoush*), *ᵐ*called Moche, 120 stades, *16 miles*.

*ᵃ*From the river Tarsouras to the river Hippos (*Horse*), *now called Lagoumpsa*, 150 stades, *20 miles*.

$_{A10.3}$From the river Hippos *ᵐ*to the river Atelaphos,[53] *now called Euripos—there is a way in to the ferry-point*[54]—30 stades, *4 miles*. $_{A10.4}$From the river Atelaphos to the city of Dioskourias, which has a lake[55] *ᵃ*and is now called Sebastoupolis (*Sukhumi*), a colony of the Milesians, *ᵐ*135 stades, *18 miles*.

49. (7B). *ᵉSo from Dioskourias Sebastoupolis as far as the river Apsaros was formerly occupied by the nation called Kolchoi, the ones who were renamed Lazoi*. 50. (8B). $_{A11.1}$We passed the following nations. The Kolchoi border on the Trapezuntines, just as Xenophon says.[56] And the people he records[57] as being most warlike $_{A11.2}$and hostile towards the Trapezountines, he calls Drillai, but I think they are actually the Sannoi. For they too are very warlike, even to this day, and are extremely hostile to the Trapezountines, live in fortified places, and *as* a nation without a king they were formerly liable for tribute to the Romans, although, being pirates, they are not anxious to pay their tribute. After *the Kolchoi* come the Machelones and Heniochoi; their king is Anchialos. 51. (9B). $_{Nf23}$The nation of the Heniochoi (*Charioteers*) hates foreigners. Some say these people were called Heniochoi after Amphitos and Telchis, the charioteers of Polydeukes (*Pollux*) and Kastor. "These men appear" to have arrived in the expedition with Jason, but "to have settled around these places | after being left behind, so the myth says". Beyond the Heniochoi and inland lies the Kaspia, "as the sea is called, which has living around it | horse-eating (*hippophaga*) races of barbarians; | the frontiers of the Medes are close to it". 52. (10B). *ᵃ*Coming after the Machelones and Heniochoi are the Zydritai; these are subject to the Pharesmanoi. *Coming after the Zydritai are the Lazoi; the king of the Lazoi is Malassas, who has his kingdom from you*. $_{A11.3}$Following the Lazoi are the Apselai; the king of the Apselai is Ioulianos

---

[53] Both branches of the *Kodor*?

[54] This phrase, *eisplous porthmiōi*, is slightly elliptical; it is a parenthetical remark of the kind seen in *Stadiasmos* (Chapter 31 above).

[55] Müller in a note suggests *limena* 'harbour' in place of *limnēn* 'lake'; both are features *Eux*. mentions elsewhere, and he sometimes says a settlement 'has a harbour' or does not; but certainty is impossible, as at §26 (twice).

[56] Xen. *Anab*. 4. 8. 22.   [57] Xen. *Anab*. 5. 2.

(*Julian*); he holds his kingdom from your father. Bordering on the Apselai are the Abasgoi; the king of the Abasgoi is Rhimagas, and he holds his kingdom from you. Following the Abasgoi come the Sannitai, *in which area* Sebastoupolis was founded: the king of the Sanigai is Spadagas, who holds his kingdom from you.[58]

53. (11B). _{A11.4}As far as Apsaros we were sailing *towards the east and the eastern*, right-hand part of the Pontos; and Apsaros seemed to me to be the limit of the length of the Pontos; for from there our voyage was northwards *to* the Chobos ⟨river, and beyond the Chobos⟩ to the Sigames. From the Sigames we veered towards the left-hand flank of the Pontos *to* the river Hippos. From the *river* Hippos in the direction of Atelaphos and Dioskouris (*sic*) we clearly sailed directly towards the left of the Pontos, and our voyage was into the setting sun; then, turning *under* the Astelephos towards Dioskouris, we saw the Caucasus mountain, which is just as high as the Keltic Alps. And one summit of the Caucasus—the summit called Strobilos—was pointed out, where, legend has it, Prometheus was hung up by Hephaistos, as instructed by Zeus.[59]

54. (12B). _{A17.2}Thus, then, is the voyage sailing to the right from Byzantion to Dioskourias (*sic*), the camp which is the limit of Roman control when one *now* sails to the right of the Pontos. _{A17.3}But when I heard that Kotys, king of the so-called Kimmerian Bosporos, had died, I decided that it was my duty to explain the voyage as far as the *Kimmerian* Bosporos to you, so that, if you *are* planning something with regard to the Bosporos, you would be able to *make the* plan without being ignorant of the voyage.

55. (13B). . . . *e*†*the places up to Sebastoupolis and Abasgia, fulfilling thus the remaining places as follows*†.[60] _{A18.1}For those who have ⟨started out⟩[61] from Dioskourias Sebastoupolis, the first anchorage would be at Pityous (*Pitzunda*). So from Sebastopolis (*sic*) *m*⟨to Pityous⟩, where is an anchorage for ships, 350 stades, *46⅔ miles*.   56. (14B). Up to this place is the Pontic kingdom of the barbarians and the places around Tibaranion, Sannike, and Kolchis; but the places following them belong to the autonomous barbarians.

57. (15B). From Pityous *a*to *the land of* Stennitike (*Gagra?*),[62] *once also called Triglites*, 150 stades, *20 miles*; *in it* a Skythian tribe used to live of old, of whom the writer Herodotos makes mention;[63] _{A18.2}he says that they are the eaters of fir-cones (*or 'lice'*); and still people hold that opinion concerning them.

From Stennitike to the river Abaskos, 90 stades, *12 miles*.

From the river Abaskos to the river Mozygos,[64] *now called Brouchon*,[65] 120 stades, *16 miles*.

---

[58] See n. on §11. 3.   [59] See n. on Arr. §11. 5.
[60] Diller 143 regards this passage as 'corrupt and unintelligible'.
[61] *hormistheisin . . . ek*, 'having anchored . . . from', a patent error for Arrian's *hormētheisin . . . ek*, 'having started out from'.
[62] 'Nitike', Arr. §18. 1.   [63] Diller cites 4. 109.
[64] 'Borgys', Arr. §18. 2; unlocated.
[65] Probably related to the Brouchoi people of the Caucasus: Procopius 8. 4. 1 (Podossinov 2011, on §57).

From *the Brouchon* to the river Nesis, in which is Cape Herakleion (*C. Adler?*), *the one called Pyxites, 60 stades, 8 miles.*

~A18.3~From the *river* Nesis to the *river* Masetikes (*Matsesta*), 90 stades, 12 miles.

From *the river Masetikes* to the river Achaious (*Sochi*), *into which there is a voyage for ferry-boats,* 60 stades, 8 miles; this river *Achaious is called Basis, and* separates the Zichoi and Sanichai. The king of the Zichoi is Stachemphlas, and he holds his kingdom from you.

58. (16B). ᵉ*So from the river Achaious as far as the river Abaskos, dwell the Saniches.*⁶⁶

59. (17B). From the river Achaious to the promontory of Herakleion (*Mys Kodosh?*), *now called Ta Erēma* (*The Deserted Places*), 150 stades, 20 miles.

From the promontory of Herakleion *to a cape* (*Mys Gryaznova?*) *on which is now said to be the castle of Bagas,* 10 stades, 1⅓ miles.

From ⟨the cape⟩ to a cape at which there is shelter from the Thraskios (*NNW wind*) *and the north wind,* (*and*) *at which Laiai is now said* (*to lie*), 80 stades, 10⅔ miles.

~A18.4~From *Laiai to Palaia* (*Old*) *Lazike, as it is named, in which has been founded the so-called Nikopsis, near which is the so-called river Psachapsis,* 120 stades, 16 miles.

From Old Lazike to Palaia (*Old*) Achaia,⁶⁷ *in which is the river now called Topsidas,* ᵃ150 stades, *20 miles.*

60. (18B). ᵉ*So from Palaia Achaia as far as Palaia Lazike, and beyond as far as the river Achaious, was formerly occupied by the nations called Heniochoi, Koraxoi and Korikoi, Melanchlainoi, Machelones, Kolchoi, and Lazoi, but is now occupied by the Zichoi.*

61. (19B). From Palaia Achaia to Pagras Limen (*Harbour of Pagra*; *Gelendzhik?*), *now called Heptalos's Harbour,* 350 stades, 46⅔ miles.

62. (20B). ᵉ*From Pagras's harbour as far as Palaia Achaia was formerly occupied by the nations called the Achaioi* (*Achaians*), *but is now occupied by the Zichoi.*

63. (21B). From Heptalos's Harbour ᵃto Hiera Limen (*Sacred Harbour*; *Novorossisk*), *now called Hierios's* (*Harbour*) *or Nikaxis,* ᵃ180 stades, *24 miles.*

From the Sacred Harbour *or Nikaxis* to Sindike⁶⁸ ᵐ*or Sindikos Harbour, but now called Eudousia,*⁶⁹ ᵃ300 stades, *40 miles.*

64. (22B). ᵉ*From Sindikos Harbour as far as Pagras Limen was formerly occupied by the nations called Kerketai or Toxitai, but is now occupied by the so-called Eudousianoi, using the Gothic and Tauric language.*⁷⁰

65. (23B). ᵐ*After the harbour of Sindikon there follows the village called Korokondame, lying on an isthmus or 'narrow' of* (*i.e. between*) *the lake and the sea, after which is Lake Korokondamitis, now called Opissas, making a quite large gulf;* 630 stades, *84 miles. As one sails into this lake and sails round it,* (*the distance*) *to the city of Hermonassa* (*is*) 440 stades (*sic*), *58⅔ miles.*

---

⁶⁶ 'Sanigai', Arr. §18. 3.   ⁶⁷ For Palaia Lazike and Palaia Achaia, see n. on Arr. §18. 4.
⁶⁸ Sindike is probably a region.   ⁶⁹ 'Eulysia' in Procopius 8. 4 7 (Diller 1952, 111, citing Müller).
⁷⁰ On the significance of this for Gothic history, see the chapter introduction.

66. (24B). *^eSo from Hermonassa as far as Sindikos Harbour,* _{Nf22}certain Maiotai live alongside, called the nation of the Sindoi, after whom Sindike is named. These Sindoi are barbarians, but civilized in their customs. After the Sindoi are the Kerketai called Toritai, a just and reasonable nation, very dedicated to nautical matters. After the Kerketai, the land bordering on these is held by Achaians, "whom they say, being Hellenes by race", are called the Barbarized Achaians. For they say that once the Orchomenian host "of Ialmenos, and the Minyans, sailing | in full strength from Ilion, by the breaths" of the wind of the Tanaïs "came perforce into the Pontic area, | barbarian land; thus forced into exile, | they are outside the law and, in their customs, | strongly malevolent towards the Hellenes". Many of the Achaians are enemies of the Kerketai.

67. (25B). *^mSailing from Hermonassa into the gulf upon the mouth of Lake Maiotis and the village of Achilleion, 515 stades, 68⅔ miles.* 68. (26B). _{A19.1}*^mSailing straight ^afrom Sindike ⟨to the Bosporos⟩ called Kimmerion and the city of Pantikapaion (Kerch) on the Bosporos, 540 stades, 72 miles.*

69. (27B). *Altogether, sailing round from Hieron as far as the mouth of Lake Maiotis or the village of Achilleion, 12,487 stades, 1,653⅓ miles.*[71]

70. (28B). *^mFrom the village of Achilleion, which is lying at the end of Asia and of the channel at the mouth of Lake Maiotis or the Tanaïs, to the village lying opposite at the end of Europe, called Porthmios (Ferry), which similarly lies upon the channel at the mouth of Lake Maiotis, the voyage across the mouth is 20 stades, 2⅔ miles.* 71. (29B). *^aThis river Tanaïs is said to divide Europe from Asia. And it starts from the Maiotis lake, and flows into the sea of the Euxeinos Pontos.* _{A19.2}Aeschylus, however, in *Prometheus Unbound*, makes the Phasis the boundary of Europe and Asia. In his play the Titans, at any rate, tell Prometheus, 'We have come, Prometheus, to witness | Your struggle, and your torment in chains'.[72] 72. (43). Then they recount the lands they have come through: 'Where the soils of Europe and Asia | have a twin limit in the great *river* Phasis'. _{A19.3}It is said that the circumnavigation round the Maiotis lake is about 9,000 stades, *1,200 miles.* 73. (44). _{PS68.5}Lake Maiotis is said to be half (*the size*) of the Pontos. 74. (45). _{Nf19}The river Tanaïs, which is the frontier of Asia, cutting each continent apart, is possessed, first, by Sarmatai, continuing for 2,000 stades, *which becomes 250 miles;*[73] next after the Sarmatai is the race of Maiotai called Iazamatai, as Demetrios has said, after whom lake Maiotis is called; but as Ephoros calls it, the nation of the Sauromatai. The Amazons mingled with these "Sauromatai, they say, when once they came" from the battle that took place around the Thermodon; after them the Sauromatai were surnamed Gynaikokratoumenoi (*Woman-ruled*).

---

[71] Should be 1,664.93 (1,664 ¹⁴/₁₅) miles. See §92 for the same figure correctly converted (albeit with rounding).
[72] MS A begins at 'Your'.
[73] This figure is converted at the rate of 8 stades to the mile, unlike others.

75. (46). ₚₛ₇₂Next is Phanagoras's city, (or) the city of Kepos (Garden).[74]   76. (47). ₙ𝒻₂₁"Next is Hermonassa, and Phanagoreia, | which they say the Teians founded at some date; | and Sindikos Harbour, having for its founders | Hellenes who came out from nearby places. | These cities have their sites enclosed within" an island (*i.e.* peninsula) "beside Maiotis as far as the Bosporos; | it occupies a large amount of plain-land, | in part impassable by reason of marshes | and rivulets, by lagoons in the further part, | which form within the sea and in the lake".

77. ⟨48⟩[75] ₙ𝒻₂₀"As you sail out of the mouth, the city of Kimmeris (or *Kimmerikon*),[76] | called after the barbarian Kimmerioi"; it is a foundation by the tyrants of the Bosporos; "and Kepos (or *Kepoi*),[77] colonized by Milesians". *And these are in the Asiatic part.*

FOURTH (PART). ⟨CIRCUMNAVIGATION OF THE EUROPEAN PARTS OF THE PONTOS⟩[78]

78. (49). ₙ𝒻₁₇The last place in Europe, on the very mouth of Lake Maiotis, is Pantikapaion (*Kerch*), named a royal residence by the people of the Bosporos. Above these people, Skythike is barbarian; "it is bordering upon the unlived-in land, | and is a land unknown to all the Hellenes. | The first people by the Istros are the Karpides, | says Ephoros; the Aroteres" (*Ploughmen*) are "further off, | and the Neuroutai, as far as the empty, frozen land. | Towards the east, when one leaves the Borysthenes" (*Dnieper*) river, they say that in so-called Hylaia "the inhabitants are Skythai; then the Georgoi (*Farmers*) follow above these, | then again emptiness over a wide place, | and beyond this the nation of the Anthropophagoi (*Man-eating*) Skythai", and beyond these again a desert follows. "Across the Pantikapes, the nation of the Limnaioi (*Lake-men*) | and several others not having their own names | but with the surname Nomadic, very pious; | none of them would be unjust to a living person; | house-carriers, it has been said, they feed | upon the milk" from the Skythian milk-mares, "their way of life involves declaring property | and social relations to be common to all. | They say wise Anacharsis was born of those | Nomads that are by far the most pious of all".

ₙ𝒻₁₈(*Ephoros has said that*) "some also came to Asia | and settled in it, whom in fact they call | Sakai";[79] and he says the most conspicuous (*race*) is that of the Sauromatai, (*then*) the Gelones, "and third | the race of the Agathyrsoi, as they are named". Taking its name from the Maiotai, "lying next is the Maiotis lake" into which the Tanaïs (*Don*), "taking the current from the river Araxes, | is mingled, as Hekataios of Teos[80] said, | or, as Ephoros reports, from a certain lake | whose limit is unstated. It (*the Tanaïs*)

---

[74] Not named by Arrian where one would expect it, at 19. 1 or 19. 3.
[75] Müller and Diller do not mark a section 48; Podossinov places the break here.
[76] On the *Taman* peninsula.   [77] On the gulf of *Taman*.   [78] i.e. as far as the Istros.
[79] The MSS have 'Sabakai', which would not fit the metre of *Nik.*, from which the words are quoted, as only two syllables are wanted. Marcotte 2000b, 140 (his fr. 15b = our fr. 18) and 250 (commentary) accepts Holsten's emendation to 'Sakai', a known Skythian people.
[80] A mistake (by the poet of *Nik.*?) for either Miletos (see Hekataios 61) or Abdera.

debouches, | with double-mouthed stream, into the so-called Maiotis | and (*then*) into the Kimmerian Bosporos". 79. (50). *The mouth of the lake is called Bosporos.*

^mFrom the settlement of Porthmios (*Ferry*), *or the mouth of Lake Maiotis, to the small city called Myrmekion, 60 stades, 8 miles.*

From Myrmekion to the distinguished city of Pantikapaion in the Bosporos, 25 stades, 3⅓ miles; it has a large harbour and shipsheds.

As one sails straight from the Bosporos into the mouth of Lake Maiotis, or of the Tanaïs, ^a*60 stades, 8 miles.*

From the city of Pantikapaion to the city of Tyristake, 60 stades, *8 miles*.

From the city of Tyristake to the city of Nymphaion, 25 stades, *3⅓ miles*.

From Nymphaion to the small village of Akrai (*The Capes*), 65 stades, *8⅔ miles*.

From Akrai to the city of Kytai, _PS68.3_formerly called Kydeakai†, ^m*30 stades, 4 miles*. ^eSo from Athenaiōn up to Kytai the Skythians occupy it. After these is the Kimmerian Bosporos.

From Kytai to the city of the Kimmerikoi, 60 stades, 8 *miles*; here is an anchorage for ships from the winds from the west. _Nfi6_Opposite in the sea are rocky islands, not very large, two in number, a little distant from the mainland.

Altogether, from the mouth of Lake Maiotis as far as the Kimmerikos (sc. Bosporos?), **300 stades,** *40 miles. From the city of Pantikapaion ⟨as far as⟩ the Kimmerikos,* **240 stades,** *32 miles.*

80. (51). _A19.3_*From the Kimmerikos* ^a*to the village of Kazeka* (*Katschik*), *built on the sea,* ^m*180 stades, 24 miles.*

^a*From Kazeka to the city of Theudosia* (*Feodosiya*), *a deserted city* ^m*that has a harbour,* ^a*280 stades, 37⅓ miles.* _A19.4_It used to be a Hellenic city, a colony of the Milesians, and there is a mention of it in many works. *Now Theudosia is called, in the Alanic or Tauric dialect, Ardabda: that is, Seven Gods. In this Theudosia,* _Nfi5_it is said, exiles from the people of the Bosporos, too, once settled.

81. (52). ^m*From Theudosia to the harbour of Athēnaiōn* (*Sudak*), *also known as* ^a*Harbour of the Skythotauroi, a deserted one, 200 stades, 26⅔ miles;* ^m*here is an anchorage without waves for ships.* ^e*So from Athenaiōn ⟨up to Kalos Limen the Tauroi occupy it.*

From⟩ the harbour of ⟨Athēnaiōn⟩, ^a*also known as Skythotauroi, to Lampas* (*Biyuk Lambat*), *600 stades, 80 miles;* ^m*here is an anchorage for ships.*

_A19.5_^m*From Lampades* (*sic*) *to Kriou Metopon* (*Ram's Brow*), _PS68.2_*the promontory of Taurike* ^m*and a high mountain, 220 stades, 29⅓ miles.* 82. (53). _Nfi4_In this land in Taurike "some say that after her abduction" Iphigeneia came here from Aulis; the Tauroi are dense with crowds of people, "and are devoted to a life on the land, a pastoral one, | but in cruelty they are barbarians, murderers, | placating the divinities with their impieties. | 83. (54). The so-called Taurike Chersonesos | is attached to these, and has a Hellenic city | which Herakleiots and Delians colonized | after an oracle came to the Herakleiots | who lived in Asia within the Kyaneai" that they should settle the Chersonese together with the Delians.

84. (55). ₐ₁₉.₅ ᵐFrom Kriou Metopon to Euboulos's Harbour, ᵃanother Tauric one, also known as Symboulon,⁸¹ ᵐ300 stades, *40 miles*; here is a harbour without waves.

ᵃFrom the harbour of Symboulon ᵐto the city of Cherronesos, ᵃalso known as Taurike Chersonesos, ᵐa colony of the Herakleians in the *Pontos,* ᵃ180 stades, *24 miles*; ᵐhere is an anchorage and good harbours.

85. (56). A coastal sailing is involved by the boundaries of Taurike, from the harbour of Athēnaiōn up to Kalos Limen (*Good Harbour; Chernomorskoye*), of 2,600 stades, *346⅔ miles.*

From the village of Porthmitis (Ferry) at the end of Europe, lying in the mouth of Lake Maiotis or the Tanaïs, as far as Cherson, 2,260 stades, 301⅓ miles.

Altogether, from the city of Bosporos, also known as Pantikapaion, as far as Cherson, **2,200 stades,** *293⅓ miles.*

86. (57). *From Cherson* ᵐto Koronitis, ᵃalso called Kerkinitis (*near Evpatoria*), 600 stades, *80 miles.*

ᵐFrom Koronitis, ᵃalso known as Kerkinitis, to the Skythian Kalos Limen *of Chersonitis,* 700 stades, *93⅓ miles.* ᵉ*So from Kalos Limen up to the river Istros, also called Danapris, again the Skythians occupy it.*

ₐ₂₀.₁ ᵐFrom Kalos Limen a gulf follows, called Karkinites, passing through the Tamyriakoi; the gulf is 2,250 stades, *300 miles.* If one does not sail round but sails straight for the isthmus, the stades are 300, *40 miles.* ᵃWithin the (*land of*) Tamyriake is a lake, which is not large.

87. (58). ᵐFrom the promontory, ₙf₁₃the Achilleios Dromos (*Achillean Racetrack*), which is a beach, that is, a shore, is truly long and narrow, ᵐpasses by the Tamyriakoi, passing through the channel for 1,200 stades, *160 miles*, with a width of 4 *plethra* (*c.400 feet*); its extremities form islands, and it is separated from the mainland by 60 stades, *8 miles.* In the middle of it a neck in the form of an isthmus, *that is, of narrow form,* joins the mainland, *in other words the land,* for 40 stades, *5⅓ miles* in length.

From Tamyriake, indeed, if one sails the aforesaid course (*dromos*) towards the other promontory of Dromos Achilleos (*Racetrack of Achilles*),⁸² which is called the Hieron Alsos (*Sacred Grove*) of Hekate, the aforesaid stades are 1,200, *160 miles.*

From the Sacred Grove of Hekate to the *Borysthenes,* a river accessible to ships, now called *Danapris,* 200 stades, *26⅔ miles.* 88. (59). ₙf₁₂This river Borysthenes "is the most serviceable of all, | bearing many great monsters and the crops | that grow here and pastures for herd animals. | They say the flow of its stream is navigable | for forty days; though in its upper parts | it is unnavigable" and not passable, "for it is blocked by snow and frosts". 89. (60). At the confluence on (*sic*) the Hypanis and Borysthenes †with their two rivers† a city was founded, formerly called Olbia but after that again called Borysthenes by Hellenes. The Milesians are founding this during the Median

---

⁸¹ In the bay of *Balaklava.*
⁸² Oller Guzmán 2021 equates the Dromos with the *Tendra* peninsula.

empire. It has an upstream voyage of 240 stades from the sea, by the river Borysthenes, *the one now called Danapris; the distance is 32 miles.*

90. (61). $_{A20.2}$From the Borysthenes to a *very* small island, deserted and nameless, is 60 stades, *8 miles.*

From *the very small island, deserted and nameless (Berezan),* to Odessos,[83] 80 stades, *10½ (sic) miles.*

From Odessos ᵐto the settlement of Skopeloi (*Reefs*), 160 stades, *21⅓ miles.*

From Skopeloi ᵃto the harbour of the Istrianoi (*Luzanovka?*), 90 stades, *12 miles.*

$_{A20.3}$From *the Harbour of the Istrianoi* ᵃto the harbour of Iako (*Odessa?*),[84] *90 stades, 12 miles.*

From *the harbour of Iako* ᵐto the settlement of Nikonion, 300 stades, *40 miles.*

From the settlement of Nikonion to the Tyras (*Dniester*), a river accessible to ships, 30 stades, *4 miles.*   91. (62). $_{Nf11}$This river Tyras, being deep and nourishing in pastures for flocks, "has resources for traders" in fish | "and for cargo ships it offers a safe voyage upstream. | A city sharing its name with the river lies here, | Tyras", said to be a colony of the Milesians.

92. (63). *Altogether, from the river Borysthenes as far as the river Tyras, 810 stades, 108 miles; and from Cherson to the river Tyras, 4,110 stades, 548 miles.*

ᵐArtemidoros the geographer writes that from the city of Cherson up to the river Tyras, with the circumnavigation of the gulf of Karkinitis, is 4,420 stades, *589⅓ miles.*

From the river Tyras to the area of Neoptolemos, 120 stades, *16 miles.*

From Neoptolemos to Kremniskoi, 120 stades, *16 miles.* Artemidoros the geographer says that from the river Tyras to Kremniskoi is 480 stades, *64 miles.*

From Kremniskoi as far as the (*Places*) of Antiphilos, 330 stades, *44 miles.*

From Antiphilos ᵃto the mouth of the river *Istros* called Psilon, 300 stades, *40 miles.* $_{Nf10}$These people are Thracians and immigrant Bastarnai.

93. (64). $_{A21.1}$Just about opposite this mouth *of the Istros, Psilon*—straight across the open sea (*pelagos*), especially when you sail with the Aparktias wind—lies an island *in front*, which some call Achilles' Island (*Zmiinyi*),[85] others Dromos Achilleos,[86] and others still Leuke (*White*) because of its colour.   94. (65). $_{Nf9}$It "has also a tame multitude of birds", a sacred sight to people who arrive. From this it is not possible to see land, even though it is distant from land 400 stades, *53⅓ miles,* as indeed Demetrios (*of Kallatis*) writes.   95. (66). ᵃThetis is said to have set up *this island* for her son, and that Achilles lived there. And there is a temple of Achilles there, and a wooden image (*xoanon*), *that is, a statue,* of ancient workmanship. $_{A21.2}$The island is deserted of humans, but a few goats live there—they say that those who *from time to time* put in there dedicate one to Achilles—and there are many other votive offerings set up in the temple—bowls and rings and rather costly stones. These *are all* thank-offerings to

---

[83] Unlocated; see n. on Arr. §20. 3.   [84] 'Harbour of the Isiakoi', Arr. §20. 3.
[85] See n. on Ps.-Skyl. §68. 4.   [86] See §87 for the actual location of Achilles' Racetrack.

Achilles. Also *laid up are inscribed items*, some in the Roman fashion (*i.e. in Latin*), some in the Greek, in one metre or another, praising Achilles.

96. (67). _{A24.1}From the mouth of the Istros (*Danube*) called Psilon to the second mouth is 60 stades, *8 miles*.

From *the second mouth* to the mouth called Kalon (*Good*), 40 stades, *5⅓ miles*.

And from Kalon to Arakos, *as they call* the fourth mouth of the Istros, 60 stades, *8 miles*.

_{A24.2}From *Arakos* ᵐto the Hieron (*Sacred*) mouth, ᵃthe fifth *mouth of the Istros*, 120 stades, *16 miles*.

ᵐFrom here the parts of Thrace facing the Pontos are succeeded by the borders of the Thracians, and the former nations are barbarian.

FIFTH (PART): ⟨CIRCUMNAVIGATION OF THE PART OF THRACE TOWARDS THE PONTOS⟩

97. (68). *This river Istros, also called Danoubis,* _{Nf8}comes down from the western places "making its outflow in five mouths"; but splitting into two it also flows into the Adriatic. It is also "recognized", actually, as far as "Keltike, | and persists all the time, even in summer; | for in the winter it is increased and filled | by the rains that occur" †and by the snow, as they say, taking the inflows of the generated frosts, but in summer† "it emits a stream that is exactly equal; | and it also has islands lying within itself, | numerous and of great size, so the story goes, | of which the one that lies between the sea | and the mouths" is no lesser in size than Rhodes. It is called Peuke because of the multitude of pines there; then immediately after it, lying in the open sea, is the aforementioned Achilles' Island.

98. (69). ᵐFrom the Hieron (*Sacred*) mouth of the river Istros to the city of Istros (*near Istria*), ᵃ500 stades, *66⅔ miles*. 99. (70). _{Nf7}(*The city of Istros*) took its name from the river; and this city "the Milesians are founding when the army | of the barbarian Skythai crossed into Asia, | pursuing the Kimmerians from the Bosporos".

100. (71). ᵐFrom the city of Istros to the city of Tomeas (*Tomis; Costanţa*), which has a minor anchorage, ᵃ300 stades, *40 miles*. 101. (72). _{Nf6}Tomeoi, "being a colony of the Milesians, | was settled by Skythai" †in a circle round about†.

102. (73). _{A24.3}From Tomeoi (*sic*) to the city of Kalatis (*Mangalia*), which has an anchorage for ships, 300 stades, *40 miles*. 103. (74). _{Nf5}Kallatis, a colony of the Herakleotai that came into being according to an oracle: "and they founded this when | Amyntas took over the rule of the Macedonians".

104. (75). ᵃFrom *Kalatis* to Karōn Limen,[87] 180 stades, *24 miles*. And the land in a circle around the harbour is *washed over*. †Karai is now called Kareai†.

---

[87] 'Karians' Harbour', *Nos Shabla*.

From Karōn Limen to Tetrisias (*Nos Kaliakra*), *ᵐ*also called Tirizanakros†, which also has a minor anchorage against the winds from the west *and is now called Akra*, *ᵃ*120 stades, *16 miles*.

From *Tetrisias or Akra* *ᵐ*to the small city of Bizone,[88] in which there is a roadstead, *ᵃ*60 stades, *8 miles*.   105. (76). This small city, ₙf₄some say, is barbarian, "others that it came into being as a colony of Mesembria".

106. (77).   ₐ₂₄.₄From Bizone to Dionysospolis (*Balchik*), 80 stades, *10⅔ miles*.   107. (78).   ₙfᵦThis Dionysopolis "was first named | Krounoi through the outflow of the nearby waters"; next it was renamed Matiopolis; and next the statue of Dionysos having fallen from the sea onto the place "they say it was in turn called Dionysopolis". | Lying "on the frontier of the land of the Krobyzoi and Skythai, | it has mixed Hellenic settlers".

108. (79).   *ᵃ*From *Dionysopolis* to the city of Odessos (*Varna*), *in which is* an anchorage for ships, 200 stades, *26⅔ miles*.   109. (80). ₙf₁The Milesians are founding Odessos when Astyages ruled Media; and in a circle around it, it has the Thracian Krobyzoi.

110. (81).   *ᵃ*From Odessos to the foothills of Haimos,[89] which fall right down to the Pontos, *and in which is* an anchorage for ships, 260 stades, *34⅔ miles*.   111. (82).   ₙ₇₄₃₋₇"A mighty mountain rises above it, Haimos, | comparable to Cilician Tauros in size | and in extension of the places lengthwise; | for from the Krobyzoi and the Pontic boundaries | it projects as far as the Adriatic places."

112. (83).   ₐ₂₄.₅From Haimos to the city of Mesembria (*Nesebur*), 90 stades, *12 miles*.   113. (84).   ₙ₇₃₈₋₄₂This city of Mesembria, "at the feet of the mountain known as Haimos . . ., | bordering on the Thrakian and Getic land; | Kalchedonians and Megarians settled this | when Darius sent his force against the Skythai."

114. (85).   *ᵃ*From Mesembria to the city of Anchialos, *ᵐ*which also has a harbour against the winds from the west, 70 stades, *9⅓ miles*.

From Anchialos to the city of Apollonia, *now called Sozopolis* (*Sozopol*), which also has two large harbours, *ᵃ*180 stades, *24 miles*.   115. (86).   ₙ₇₃₁₋₇This city of Apollonia's "founders . . ., some fifty years | before the reign of Cyrus, were Milesians | after their arrival at this place. | For they sent many colonies from Ionia | to the Pontos, which was previously called Axenos (*Friendless*) | because of the attacks by the barbarians, | but they caused it to take a new name, Euxeinos (*Friendly*)."

116. (87).   ₐ₂₄.₆This is all of the Hellenic cities founded in Skythia, on the left-hand side as one sails into the *Pontos*.

From Apollonia, *also* (*known as*) *Sozopolis*, to Cherronesos,[90] *in which is* an anchorage for ships, 60 stades, *8 miles*.

From Cherronesos to Aulaiou Teichos (*Aulaios's Fort; Akhtopol*), *ᵐ*called the Settlement of Therai (*Hunts?*), in which is also a minor anchorage, *ᵃ*250 stades, *33⅓ miles*.

---

[88] See n. on Arr. §24. 4.   [89] See n. on Arr. §24. 4.   [90] See n. on Arr. §24. 6.

*ᵐFrom here the parts belonging to the Byzantines follow, (but) the previous parts are in the (part of) Thrace that extends to the Pontos.*⁹¹

From the Settlement of Therai, *ᵃcalled Aulaiou Teichos, to Thynias (C. Tuna; Kora Burunu), ᵐa promontory and ᵃheadland ᵐin which is also an anchorage for ships, ᵃ120 stades, 16 miles.* ₙ₇₂₈₋₉Thynias is *ᵃa cape with a good harbour . . . the furthest place in Astic Thrace*.

117. (88). ₐ₂₅.₁*ᵐFrom Thynias to Halmydissos (or Salymdessos; Midye), ᵃ200 stades, 36⅔ miles.* Xenophon the Elder⁹² makes mention of this place: it was to here, he says, that the Greek army of the Hellenes came which he led when he campaigned for the last time with Seuthes the Thracian. And he wrote much concerning the place's lack of harbours, the fleet's shipwreck when forced by a storm, and the neighbouring Thracians' fighting among themselves over the wreckage.⁹³   118. (89). ₙ₇₂₄₋₇ "Then a certain shore called Salmydessos | extends for 700 stades; very marshy, | difficult to anchor on, and wholly | harbourless, a place most hostile to ships".

119. (90). ₐ₂₅.₃*ᵐFrom Halmydissos ᵃto the (Cape) Phrygia ᵐalso called Philia (Friendship; Kara Burunu), a place and ᵃpromontory ᵐof the Byzantines, ᵃ310 stades, 41⅓ miles.*

From Phrygia *ᵐor Philea (sic) ᵃto Kyaneai, also known as Kylai, 320 stades, 42⅔ miles.* These Kyaneai are those (rocks) that the poets say once used to wander, and through which the first ship to pass was the Argo when it carried Jason to Kolchis.

ₐ₂₅.₄From the Kyaneai to the Sanctuary (Hieron) of Zeus Ourios, *at which lies the mouth of the Pontos, is 40 stades, 5⅓ miles.*

From *Hieron to the harbour of Daphne Mainomene (The Mad), now called Sosthenes,*⁹⁴ *40 stades, 5⅓ miles.*

From *Sosthenes to Byzantion, 80 stades, 10⅔ miles.*

These, then, are the things from the so-called Kimmerian Bosporos to Thrace and Byzantion.

120. (91). *Altogether, from the Hieron (Sacred) mouth of the river Istros as far as the sanctuary of Zeus Ourios, or the mouth of the Pontos,* **3,640 stades,** *485⅓ miles.*

From the river Borysthenes, also called Danapris, as far as the sanctuary (Hieron) of Zeus Ourios, **5,600 stades,** *746⅔ miles.*

From Cherson as far as the sanctuary of Zeus Ourios, **8,900 stades,** *1,186⅔ miles.*

From the village of Porthmia (Ferry) at the end of Europe in the Pontos region, lying in the mouth of Lake Maiotis or Kimmerian Bosporos, as far as the sanctuary of Zeus Ourios, **11,100 stades,** *1,480 miles.*

*It is said that the circumnavigation of Europe is the same as the circumnavigation of the Pontic part of the Asian region.*⁹⁵

---

⁹¹ Diller makes a paragraph here; the preceding paragraph ends with words he excises as unintelligible and duplicated, which appear to be a form of heading introducing a new section of the *periplous*.
⁹² See Xen. *Anab*. 7. 5. 12–14.   ⁹³ See Xen. *Hell*. 7. 5. 13.
⁹⁴ See n. on Dionysios of Byzantion §95 'Insana Laurus'.
⁹⁵ i.e. the European and Asian coasts of the Black Sea are of the same length. Cf. Diller 1952, 107, who rejects Müller's ascription of these words to Ps.-Skylax.

121. (92). *From the sanctuary of Zeus Ourios as far as Amisos*, **4,660 stades**, 621⅓ *miles*.

From Amisos as far as the river Phasis, **3,802 stades,** *507 miles.*[96]

From the river Phasis as far as the mouth of Lake Maiotis, or the village of Achilleion, **4,025 stades,** *536⅔ miles.*

So from the sanctuary of Zeus Ourios as far as the mouth of Lake Maiotis is **12,487 stades,** *1,665 miles.*[97]

Altogether, the whole circumnavigation of the Euxine Pontos, both the right-hand parts of the Pontos, beside Asia, and the left-hand parts of the Pontos, beside Europe, from the sanctuary of Zeus Ourios as far as the same sanctuary of Zeus Ourios again, is **23,587 stades,** *3,145 miles.*[98]

And the circumnavigation of Lake Maiotis is 9,000 stades, 1,200 miles.

APPENDIX: *ANAMETRESIS* OF THE *OIKOUMENĒ* AND *PERIMETROS* OF THE *PONTOS*

A work partly related to *Eux.* is this short and unreliable text known by the cumbersome title *Anametresis* (*Mensuration*) *of the Inhabited World and Perimetros* (*Circumference*) *of the Black Sea*, preserved in a 14th- or 15th-century MS in Copenhagen but probably late antique in origin. It begins with a note on Eratosthenes (also printed as Eratosthenes 41 in Chapter 12 above), and continues with some 250 words inaccurately drawn from *Eux.* and adding nothing to our knowledge of that work. It closes with inaccurate notes on measures of distance.

Section numbers are modern.[99]

One must realize that the whole Earth's circumference in stades is 2,035† myriads; the length of our inhabited (*part*) from the mouth of the Ganges as far as Gadeira is 8,308†; the width from the Ethiopian sea as far as the river Tanaïs (*Don*) is 3,500† stades; and the part between the Euphrates and the Tigris river, called Mesopotamon, has a dimension of 3,000 stades. This calculation (*anametrēsis*) was made by Eratosthenes, the most mathematical of the ancients.[100]

(2) From Byzantion to Sosthenion: 80 stades, 10½ miles.

From Sosthenion to Hieron (*The Sanctuary*): 40 stades, 5½ miles. Total: 16 miles.

From the Hieron of Zeus Ourios, that is, the mouth of the Pontos, as far as the sacred mouth of the river Istros (*Danube*): 3,640 stades, 485½ miles.

---

[96] Actually 506.93 (506 ¹⁴⁄₁₅).

[97] Actually 1,664.93 (1,664 ¹⁴⁄₁₅). The same figure of 12,487 is at §27B, where it is wrongly converted to 1,653⅓ mi.

[98] Actually 3,144.93 (3,144 ¹⁴⁄₁₅).

[99] Diller 1952, 39–40, prints the MS text unaltered, which is preferable to the heavily corrected text at *GGM* i. 424–6.

[100] 2,035 myriads = 20,350,000, which at 7½ st. to the mile is 271,333⅓ miles (*c.*437,000 km), about ten times too large. Müller, *GGM* i. 424–6 emends this and the preceding two numbers to match other sources (8,308 to 83,800; 3,500 to 35,000).

(3) From the sanctuary of Zeus Ourios as far as the river Bosphoros† (*i.e. Borysthenes*), also called Anapris† (*i.e. Danapris, mod. Dniepr*): 5,670† stades,¹⁰¹ 746½ miles.

From the sanctuary of Zeus Ourios as far as the city of Porthmia at the European end of the Pontic area ⟨at the mouth of⟩ Lake Maiotis, also called the Kimmerian Bosporos: 1,100 stades, 480 miles.¹⁰²

The circumnavigation of Pontic Europe is said to be equal to the circumnavigation of the Asian parts (*sc. of the Pontos*).

(4) From the sanctuary of Zeus Ourios as far as Amisos: 4,660 stades, 621½ miles.

From Amisos as far as the river Baphis† (*i.e. Phasis*): 3,820¹⁰³ stades, 507 miles.

From the river Basis† (*i.e. Phasis*) to the mouth of Lake Maiotis, ⟨that is, as far as the village of Achilleion: 4,025 stades, 536½ miles.

So the figure from the sanctuary of Zeus Ourios as far as the mouth of Lake Maiotis is⟩ 1,487 stades, 665½ miles.¹⁰⁴

(5) Together the circumnavigation of the Euxine Pontos, both the right-hand parts along Asia and the left-hand parts along Europe, from the sanctuary ⟨of Zeus Ourios, is 23,587 stades⟩, 3,145 miles.

The circumnavigation of Lake Maiotis is ⟨9,000 stades,⟩ 3,003¹⁰⁵ miles.

(6) *On the stade.* The stade (*stadion*) contains 400 cubits, 800 feet, (*or*) 133½ fathoms.¹⁰⁶

(7) *On the mile.* The mile (*milion*) contains 7½ stades, 3,000 cubits, (*or*) 6,000 feet.

(8) *On the year.* A whole one contains 8,706¹⁰⁷ hours (*or*) 365¼ days.

---

¹⁰¹ 5,600, Müller.
¹⁰² Müller emends the figures to 11,000 and 1,480 respectively.
¹⁰³ 3,802, Müller.
¹⁰⁴ Müller emends the figures to 12,487 and 1,665½ respectively.
¹⁰⁵ 1,200, Müller.
¹⁰⁶ The figure should be 133⅓.   ¹⁰⁷ 8,766, Müller.

ἑπτάλοφον ποτὶ ἄστυ Γαδειρόθεν, ἕκτον ὁδοῖο
    Βαίτιος εὐμύκους ἄχρις ἐς ἠιόνας·
κεῖθεν δ' αὖ πέμπτον Πυλάδου μετὰ Φώκιον οὖδας·
    Ταύρη χθών, βοέης οὔνομ' ἀπ' εὐετίης·
Πυρήνην δέ τοι ἔνθεν ἐπ' ὀρθόκραιρον ἰόντι
    ὄγδοον ἠδὲ μιῆς δωδέκατον δεκάτης.
Πυρήνης δὲ μεσηγὺ καὶ Ἄλπιος ὑψικαρήνου
    τέτρατον· Αὐσονίης αἶψα δυωδέκατον
ἀρχομένης ἤλεκτρα φαείνεται Ἠριδανοῖο.
    ὦ μάκαρ, ὃς δισσὰς ἤνυσα χιλιάδας,
πρὸς δ' ἔτι πέντ' ἐπὶ ταῖς ἑκατοντάδας ἔνθεν ἐλαύνων·
    ἣ γὰρ Ταρπείη μέμβλετ' ἀνακτορίη.

To seven-hilled city from Gadeira, one-sixth of the road
    is all the way to the shores of the lowing Baitis.[1]
Next, from there one-fifth towards Pylades' Phokian ground
    is Taurē the land, named for a bountiful bovine season.[2]
5   Thence—mark well!—as you go to straight-horned Pyrene,
    one-eighth, plus one-twelfth of a single tenth.
Betwixt Pyrene and the high-headed Alp,
    one-fourth. In a twelfth, Ausonia suddenly
beginning, Eridanos' amber pieces shine out.[3]
10 O blessed am I, who completed a double thousand,
    as well as five hundreds above them, voyaging hence:[4]
    for imperial Tarpeia had been my concern.[5]

Metrodoros (C3s AD or later),
in *Anthologia Graeca*, 14. 121 (my translation)

---

[1] The banks of the R. *Guadalquivir*, with cattle.
[2] See *Eux.* §36 & n.; Massalia was founded from Phokaia, a name often interchanged with Phokis in legend (Kubitschek 1933, 175). Taurē, from *tauros* 'bull', may be a play upon Tarraco (*Tarragona*) or upon the Vaccaei (cf. Lat. *vacca* 'cow'), a Hispanic people.
[3] Ausonia is Italy, Eridanos the river *Po*.
[4] 'hence': from the Eridanos to Rome. Stades, rather than miles, are to be understood. The fractions as far as l. 9 total ⅚ of the journey; since the remaining ⅙ is defined as 2,500 st., the total distance is 15,000 st. or 1,875 miles. The riddle is elucidated by M. Schmidt 2011; see also Kubitschek 1933, 174. I translate the text of Beckby 1965, iv, p. 232 (with nn. at 538).
[5] The Tarpeian rock was a prominent cliff in Rome.

Sources of Extracts (Selected)

Where an extract (such as a testimonium or a fragment) comes from a text or author that is the subject of a chapter in the present work readers will find context and further information about scholarly publications in that chapter. Below is a selective list of editions that will enable readers to explore further the original texts of source-authors (and some others), together with a selection of translations into modern languages where they exist (including at least one in English when there is one that is known to me and can be recommended). Many of the older works listed are available for download at Internet Archive and elsewhere.

Within each section, modern works are listed by date. Series titles are included only selectively, and serial numbers generally omitted as are some subtitles. Places of publication, and Latin forms of modern names, are anglicized.

SYMBOLS AND SERIES ABBREVIATIONS

¶ original text plus English translation
† English translation without original text
‡ original text plus non-English translation
Budé = Collection des universités de France (Paris: Les Belles Lettres/Association Guillaume Budé), text, French translation.
Loeb = Loeb Classical Library (Cambridge, Mass.), text, English translation.
OCT = Oxford Classical Texts (Oxford)
OWC = Oxford World's Classics (Oxford), English translation
Teubner = Bibliotheca scriptorum Graecorum et Romanorum Teubneriana (Stuttgart, Leipzig, or Berlin)
Tusculum = Sammlung Tusculum (Munich, Zürich, etc.), text, German translation

Achilles Tatius, *Introduction to Aratos' Phainomena*

Aelian, *On the Nature of Animals*

E. Maaß, *Commentariorum in Aratum reliquiae* (Berlin, 1898), 27–75

R. Hercher, *Claudii Aeliani De natura animalium libri XVII; Varia historia; Epistolae; Fragmenta*, i (Leipzig, 1864)

¶ A. F. Scholfield, *Aelian, On Animals*, 3 vols (Loeb) (1958–9)

M. García Valdés et al., *Claudius Aelianus, De natura animalium* (Teubner) (2009)[1]

---

[1] Extracts are numbered according to this edition; where the traditional numeration differs, it is in parentheses.

Aelius Aristeides	B. Keil, *Aelii Aristidis Smyrnaei quae supersunt omnia*, ii (Berlin, 1898) [*Orations* 17–52; vol. i not published]
Aëtios, *De placitis* (*On Acceptable Opinions*)	'De placitis reliquiae', in H. Diels, *Doxographi Graeci* (Berlin, 1879), 275–443
Ammianus Marcellinus	¶ J. C. Rolfe, *Ammianus Marcellinus, History*, 3 vols (Loeb) (1939–50)
	W. Seyfarth *et al.*, *Ammianus Marcellinus*, 2 vols (Teubner) (1999)
Ammonios	K. Nickau, *Ammonii qui dicitur liber De adfinium vocabulorum differentia* (Teubner) (1966)
Anametresis tes oikoumenes	A. Diller, *The Tradition of the Minor Greek Geographers* (Lancaster, Pa., 1952), 39–40
Anthologia Graeca	‡ H. Beckby, *Anthologia Graeca*, 4 vols (Tusculum) (Munich, ²1965)
	¶ W. R. Paton, *The Greek Anthology*, 5 vols (Loeb) (1916–18; vol. i ²2014)
Antigonos of Karystos	*see* Pseudo-Antigonos of Karystos
Apollonios Paradoxographos, *Stories about Wonders*	A. Giannini, *Paradoxographorum Graecorum reliquiae* (Classici greci e latini: testi e commenti, 3; Milan, 1965), 120–42
Aristotle	(*see also* Pseudo-Aristotle)
Meteorologica	¶ H. D. P. Lee, *Aristotle, Meteorologica* (Loeb) (1952)
Politics	W. D. Ross, *Aristotelis Politica* (OCT) (1957)
	† E. Barker–R. F. Stalley, *Aristotle, Politics* (OWC) (1995)
Arnobius	C. Marchesi, *Arnobii adversus nationes libri VII* (Turin, 1953)
	‡ J. Champeaux, *Arnobe, Contre les gentils (Contre les païens)*, iii: *Livre III* (Budé) (2007)
Arrian, *Anabasis* and *Indike*	(*see also* Pseudo-Arrian, *bis*)
	A. G. Roos–G. Wirth, *Flavii Arriani quae exstant omnia*, 2 vols (Teubner) (1976)
	¶ P. A. Brunt, *Arrian, Anabasis of Alexander* (Loeb) (1976–83)
Athenaios	¶ S. D. Olson, *Athenaeus, The Learned Banqueters*, 8 vols (Loeb) (2007–12)
Caesar, *Gallic War*	W. Hering, *C. Iulii Caesaris Commentarii rerum gestarum*, i: *Bellum Gallicum* (Teubner) (1987)
	† C. Hammond, *Julius Caesar, Seven Commentaries on the Gallic War: With an Eighth Commentary by Aulus Hirtius* (OWC) (2008)

Catalogus codicum astrologorum Graecorum	F. Cumont–F. Boll, *Catalogus codicum astrologorum Graecorum*, 12 vols (Brussels, 1898–1953)
Cicero, *Letters to Atticus*	¶ D. R. Shackleton Bailey, *Cicero's Letters to Atticus*, 7 vols (Cambridge, 1965–70)
	¶ —— *Cicero, Letters to Atticus*, 4 vols (Loeb) (1999)
Clement of Alexandria	¶ G. W. Butterworth, *Clement of Alexandria* (Loeb) (1919)
	M. Marcovich, *Clementis Alexandrini Protrepticus* (Leiden, 1995)
Cleomedes	see Kleomedes
Constantine VII Porphyrogennetos	
De administrando imperio	¶ G. Moravcsik–R. J. H. Jenkins, *Constantine Porphyrogenitus, De administrando imperio* (Washington, DC, ²1967)
De thematibus	A. Pertusi, *Constantine Porphyrogenitus, De thematibus* (Vatican City, 1952)
Didymos, *On Demosthenes*	¶ P. E. Harding, *Didymos on Demosthenes: Introduction, Text, Translation, and Commentary* (Oxford, 2006)
Diodoros, book 3	¶ C. H. Oldfather, *Diodorus of Sicily*, ii: *Books II 35–IV 58* (Loeb) (1935)
	‡ B. Bommelaer, *Diodore de Sicile, Bibliothèque historique*, iii: *Livre III* (Budé) (1989)
Diogenes Laërtios	¶ R. D. Hicks, *Lives of Eminent Philosophers*, i–ii (Loeb) (1925)
	T. Dorandi, *Diogenes Laertius, Lives of Eminent Philosophers* (Cambridge, 2013)
	† P. Mensch–J. Miller, *Lives of the Eminent Philosophers, Diogenes Laertius* (Oxford–New York, 2018)
	† S. A. White, *Diogenes Laertius, Lives of Eminent Philosophers: An Edited Translation* (Cambridge–New York, 2021) [not taken into account in the present work]
Diogenianos	E. L. von Leutsch–F. G. Schneidewin, *Corpus paroemiographorum Graecorum*, i (Göttingen, 1839), 177–320
Dionysios of Halikarnassos, *On Thucydides*	¶ S. G. Usher, *Dionysius of Halicarnassus, Critical Essays*, i (Loeb) (1974), 456–633
Dioskorides	see Pedanios Dioskorides

Epimerismoi Homerikoi	A. R. Dyck, *Epimerismi Homerici*, ii: *Epimerismos continens qui ordine alphabetico traditi sunt* . . . (Berlin, 1995)
Eustathios	
On Dionysios Periegetes	'Εὐσταθίου Παρεκβολαί—Eustathii Commentarii', Müller, *GGM* ii. 201–407
On Homer, Iliad	M. van der Valk, *Eustathii archiepiscopi Thessalonicensis commentarii ad Homeri Iliadem pertinentes*, 4 vols (Leiden, 1971–87)
On Homer, Odyssey	J. G. Stallbaum, *Eustathii archiepiscopi Thessalonicensis commentarii ad Homeri Odysseam*, 2 vols (Leipzig, 1825–6)
Fulgentius, *Mythologiae*; *Expositio sermonum antiquorum*	R. Helm with J. Préaux, *Fabii Planciadis Fulgentii V. C. opera: accedunt Fabii Claudiani Gordiani Fulgentii V. C. De aetatibus mundi et hominis, et S. Fulgentii episcopi Super Thebaiden* (Teubner) (1898, repr. with addenda 1970), 3–80, 111–26
Galen, *On Compound Drugs according to Places* (*De compositione medicamentorum secundum locos*)	C. G. Kühn, *Claudii Galeni tomus XIII* (Medicorum Graecorum opera quae exstant, 13; Leipzig, 1827), 1–361
	‡ G. Santana Henríquez, *Galen, Sobre la composición de los medicamentos según los lugares libros II* (Las Palmas de Gran Canaria, 2005) [not a critical edition; uses Kühn's text][2]
Geminos	‡ G. Aujac, *Géminos, Introduction aux Phénomènes* (Budé) (1975)
	† J. Evans–J. L. Berggren, *Geminos's Introduction to the Phenomena* (Princeton, 2006)
Harpokration	W. Dindorf, *Harpocrationis Lexicon in decem oratores Atticos*, i (Oxford, 1853)
	J. J. Keaney, *Harpocration, Lexeis of the Ten Orators* (Amsterdam, 1991)
Herodian, *General Prosody*; *On the Unique Word*	A. Lentz, *Herodiani Technici reliquiae* (Grammatici Graeci, 3. 2; Leipzig, 1867–70), i. 1–547; ii. 908–52
	H. Hunger, 'Palimpsest-Fragmente aus Herodians Καθολικὴ προσῳδία, Buch 5–7: Cod. Vindob. Hist. Gr. 10', *Jahrbuch der Österreichischen Byzantinischen Gesellschaft*, 16 (1967), 1–33

---

[2] See Petit 2007.

Herodotos	N. G. Wilson, *Herodoti Historiae* (OCT) (2015)
	† R. Waterfield, *Herodotus, The Histories* (OWC) (1998)
Hesychios	K. Latte *et al.*, *Hesychii Alexandrini Lexicon* (Copenhagen/Berlin, 1953–)
Hipparchos, *On Aratos and Eudoxos*	C. Manitius, Ἱππάρχου τῶν Ἀράτου καὶ Εὐδόξου Φαινομένων ἐξηγήσεως βιβλία τρία—*Hipparchi in Arati et Eudoxi Phaenomena commentariorum libri tres* (Leipzig, 1894)
Iohannes Lydos, *On the Months*	R. Wünsch, *Ioannis Lydi liber de mensibus* (Teubner) (1898)
Josephus	B. Niese, *Flavii Iosephi Opera*, 7 vols (Berlin, 1885–95)
	S. A. Naber, *Flavii Iosephi Opera omnia*, 6 vols (Teubner) (1888–96)
	¶ H. St. J. Thackeray, *Josephus, The Life; Against Apion* (Loeb) (1926)
	¶ —— *et al.*, *Josephus, Jewish Antiquities* (Loeb) (1930–65)
Julian of Ascalon	J. Geiger, 'Julian of Ascalon', *Journal of Hellenic Studies* 112 (1992), 31–43
Kleomedes	R. B. Todd, *Cleomedes, Caelestia (Μετέωρα)* (Teubner) (1990)[3]
	† A. C. Bowen–R. B. Todd, *Cleomedes' Lectures on Astronomy* (Berkeley, 2004)
Kosmas Indikopleustes	‡ W. Wolska-Conus, *Cosmas Indicopleustès, Topographie chrétienne*, 3 vols (Paris, 1968–73)
Longinus	see Pseudo-Longinus
Lucian	M. D. Macleod, *Luciani opera* (OCT) (1972–87)
	¶ A. M. Harmon *et al.*, *Lucian*, 8 vols (Loeb) (1913–67)
Martianus Capella	J. Willis, *Martianus Capella* (Teubner) (Leipzig, 1983)
	‡ B. Ferré, *Martianus Capella, Les Noces de Philologie et de Mercure*, vi: *Livre VI. La Géometrie* (Budé) (2007)
	‡ L. Cristante *et al.*, *Martiani Capellae De nuptiis philologiae et Mercurii, Libri I–II* (Hildesheim, 2011)
Maximus of Tyre	M. B. Trapp, *Maximus Tyrius, Dissertationes* (Teubner) (1994)

---

[3] Numbers in extracts are those of lines in Todd's text.

Natalis Comes (Natale Conti)	Natalis Comes, *Mythologiae, sive explicationis fabularum, libri decem* (Geneva, 1651; repr. 1653; originally Venice, 1568)
	† J. Mulryan–S. Brown, *Natale Conti's Mythologiae*, 2 vols (Tempe, Ariz., 2006)
P. Oxy.	B. P. Grenfell, *et al.*, *Oxyrhynchus Papyri* (London, 1896–)
Palaiphatos	N. Festa, *Palaephati Περὶ ἀπίστων: Heracliti qui fertur libellus Peri apiston; excerpta Vaticana (vulgo Anonymus De incredibilibus)* (Leipzig, 1902)
	¶ J. Stern, *Palaephatus, On Unbelievable Tales* (Wauconda, Ill., 1996)
	‡ A. Santoni, *Palefato, Storie incredibili* (Pisa, 2000)
	‡ K. Brodersen, *Die Wahrheit über die griechischen Mythen: Palaiphatos' 'Unglaubliche Geschichten'* (Stuttgart, 2002)
Pedanios Dioskorides	M. Wellmann, *Pedanii Dioscuridis Anazarbei De materia medica libri quinque*, 3 vols (Berlin, 1906–14)
	† L. Y. Beck, *Pedanius Dioscorides of Anazarbus, De materia medica* (Hildesheim, 2005)
Perimetros tou Pontou	A. Diller, *The Tradition of the Minor Greek Geographers* (Lancaster, Pa., 1952), 39–40
Philostratos	¶ C. P. Jones, *Philostratus, The Life of Apollonius of Tyana*, 2 vols (Loeb) (²2005)
	G. Boter, *Philostratus, Vita Apollonii Tyanei* (Teubner) (Berlin, 2022) [not taken into account in the present work]
Photios	
Lexikon	C. Theodoridis, *Photii Patriarchae Lexicon* (Berlin, 1982–2013)
Library	‡ R. Henry, *Photius, Bibliothèque*, iii: *Codices 186–222* (Budé) (1962)
	‡ —— *Photius, Bibliothèque*, vii: *Codices 246–256* (Budé) (1974)
	† N. G. Wilson, *Photius, The Bibliotheca* (London, 1994) [selection]
	‡ L. Canfora *et al.*, *Fozio, Biblioteca* (Pisa, ²2019)
Pliny the Elder	¶ H. Rackham *et al.*, *Pliny, Natural History* (Loeb) (1938–80)
	‡ A. Ernout *et al.*, *Pline l'Ancien, Histoire naturelle* (Budé) (1947–)

	‡ R. König *et al.*, *C. Plinius Secundus d. Ä., Naturkunde, lateinisch–deutsch* (Sammlung Tusculum) (Munich–Zurich, 1979–2007)
	† B. Turner–R. J. A. Talbert, *Pliny the Elder's World: Natural History, Books 2–6* (Cambridge, 2022) [not taken into account in the present work]
Plutarch	(*see also* Pseudo-Plutarch)
Isis and Osiris; The Oracles at Delphi	¶ F. C. Babbitt, *Plutarch, Moralia*, v (Loeb) (1936), 3–191; 256–345
Quaestiones convivales	¶ P. A. Clement–H. B. Hoffleit, *Plutarch, Moralia*, viii: *Table-talk, Books 1–6* (Loeb) (1969)
That it is Not Possible to Live Contentedly while Following Epicurus	¶ B. Einarson–P. H. De Lacy, *Plutarch, Moralia*, xiv (Loeb) (1967), 2–149
Polybios	T. Büttner-Wobst, *Polybius, Historiae*, 5 vols (Teubner) (1882–1904)
	¶ W. R. Paton, rev. F. W. Walbank–C. Habicht, *Polybius, Histories*, 6 vols (Loeb) (2010–12)
Pomponius Mela	‡ A. Silberman, *Pomponius Mela, Chorographie* (Budé) (1988)
	‡ K. Brodersen, *Pomponius Mela, Kreuzfahrt durch die alte Welt* (Darmstadt, 1994)
	† F. E. Romer, *Pomponius Mela's Description of the World* (Ann Arbor, 1998)
Porphyrius *De antro Nympharum*	R. M. van Goens, Πορφυρίου περὶ τοῦ ἐν τῇ Ὀδυσσείᾳ τῶν Νυμφῶν ἄντρου—*Porphyrius De antro Nympharum* (Utrecht, 1765)
	¶ Seminar Classics 609 (J. M. Duffy *et al.*), *Porphyry, The Cave of the Nymphs in the Odyssey* (Buffalo, NY, 1969)
	† R. Lamberton, *Porphyry on the Cave of the Nymphs* (Barrytown, NY, 1983)
	T. Dorandi (ed.), *Porphyre, L'Antre des Nymphes dans l'Odyssée* (Paris, 2019) [not taken into account in the present work]
Vita Pythagorae	‡ É. Des Places, *Porphyre, Vie de Pythagore; Lettre à Marcella* (Budé) (1982)
Priscianus Lydus, *Solutions for Chosroës*	I. Bywater, *Prisciani Lydi quae extant, Metaphrasis in Theophrastum et Solutionum ad Chosroem Liber* (Berlin, 1886)

Proclus	
On the Timaios	E. Diehl, *Procli Diadochi in Platonis Timaeum commentaria*, i–iii (Teubner) (1903–6)
On Hesiod, Works & Days	T. Gaisford, *Poetae minores Graeci* (Leipzig, 1823), ii. 3–447
	A. Pertusi, *Scholia vetera in Hesiodi Opera et dies* (Milan, 1955), 1–259
	P. Marzillo, *Der Kommentar des Proklos zu Hesiods 'Werken und Tagen'* (Classica Monacensia, 33; Tübingen, 2010)
Proverb in Bodleian manuscript	T. Gaisford, 'Παροιμίαι δημώδεις κατὰ στοιχεῖον', in his *Paroemiographi Graeci* (Oxford, 1836), 1–120
Pseudo-Antigonos	O. Musso, *[Antigonus Carystius], Rerum mirabilium collectio* (Naples, 1986)
	‡ D. Eleftheriou, *Pseudo-Antigonos de Carystos, Collection d'histoires curieuses*, 2 vols (diss. Paris Nanterre, 2018)
Pseudo-Aristotle, *On Miraculous Things Heard* (*De mirabilibus auscultationibus*)	¶ W. S. Hett, *Aristotle, Minor Works* (Loeb) (1936)
Pseudo-Longinus	¶ W. H. Fyfe–D. A. Russell, 'Longinus, On the Sublime', in S. Halliwell *et al.*, *Aristotle, Poetics; Longinus, On the Sublime; Demetrius, On Style* (Loeb) (²1995), 145–305
Pseudo-Lucian	*see* Lucian
Ptolemy of Alexandria	P. Kunitzsch, *Der Almagest: die Syntaxis mathematica des Claudius Ptolemäus in arabisch-lateinischer Überlieferung* (Wiesbaden, 1974)
	† J. L. Berggren–A. Jones, *Ptolemy's Geography: An Annotated Translation of the Theoretical Chapters* (Princeton, 2000)
	‡ A. Stückelberger–G. Graßhoff, *Ptolemaios, Handbuch der Geographie (Griechisch-Deutsch)*, 2 vols (Basel, 2006)
scholia to Aeschylus, *Persians*	O. Dähnhardt, *Scholia in Aeschyli Persas* (Leipzig, 1894)
scholia to Apollonios of Rhodes	C. Wendel, *Scholia in Apollonium Rhodium vetera* (Berlin, 1935)
scholia to Dionysios Periegetes	Müller, *GGM* ii. 427–57
scholia to Dionysios Thrax	A. Hilgard, *Scholia in Dionysii Thracis Artem grammaticam* (Grammatici Graeci, i. 3; Leipzig, 1901)

scholia to Euripides	E. Schwarz, *Scholia in Euripidem*, 2 vols (Berlin, 1887–91)
scholia to Homer	H. Erbse, *Scholia in Iliadem (scholia vetera)*, 7 vols (Berlin, 1969–88)
	W. Dindorf, *Scholia graeca in Homeri Odysseam*, 2 vols (Oxford, 1855)
scholia to Lucan	H. Usener, *M. Annaei Lucani Commenta Bernensia* (Scholia in Lucani Bellum civile, 1; Leipzig, 1869)
scholia to Lucian	H. Rabe, *Scholia in Lucianum* (Leipzig, 1906)
scholia to Pindar	A. G. Drachmann, *Scholia vetera in Pindari carmina*, 3 vols, i: *Scholia in Olympionicas* (1902); ii: *Scholia in Pythionicas* (Teubner) (1910)
scholia to Ptolemy, *Geography*	V. I. Tsiotras, Ἡ ἐξηγητικὴ παράδοση τῆς Γεωγραφικῆς ὑφηγήσεως τοῦ Κλαυδίου Πτολεμαίου: οἱ ἐπώνυμοι σχολιαστές (Athens, 2006)
	—— 'The oldest anonymous scholia on Ptolemy's Geography', in R. Ceceña (ed.), *Claudio Ptolomeo, Geografía: capítulos teóricos* (Mexico City, 2018), 251–79 (texts, 272–4)
scholia to Theokritos	C. Wendel, *Scholia in Theocritum vetera* (Teubner) (Leipzig, 1914)
Seneca the Younger, *Natural Questions*	¶ T. H. Corcoran, *Seneca, Natural Questions*, 2 vols (Loeb) (1971–2)
	† H. M. Hine, *Lucius Annaeus Seneca, Natural Questions* (Chicago, 1995)
	—— *Lucius Annaeus Seneca, Naturalium quaestionum libri* (Teubner) (1996)
Servius, *On Vergil, Georgics*	G. Thilo, *Servii grammatici qui feruntur in Vergilii Bucolica et Georgica commentarii* (Leipzig, 1887)
Sextus Empiricus	
Against the Professors	¶ R. G. Bury, *Sextus Empiricus*, iv (Loeb) (1949)
Outlines of Pyrrhonism	¶ —— *Sextus Empiricus*, i (Loeb) (1933)
Solinus	T. Mommsen, *C. Iulii Solini Collectanea rerum memorabilium* (Berlin, 1895)
	‡ K. Brodersen, *Solinus, Wunder der Welt* (Darmstadt, 2014)
Stephanos of Byzantion	W. Dindorf, *Stephanus Byzantinus*, 4 vols (Leipzig, 1825)
	‡ M. Billerbeck, *Stephani Byzantii Ethnica*, 6 vols (Berlin, 2006–17)
Stobaeus	C. Wachsmuth, *Ioannis Stobaei Anthologii libri duo priores*, i: *Anthologii librum primum continens* (Berlin, 1884)

Strabo	¶ H. L. Jones, *The Geography of Strabo*, 8 vols (Loeb) (1917–32)
	‡ S. L. Radt, *Strabons Geographika* (Göttingen, 2001–11)
	† D. W. Roller, *The Geography of Strabo* (Cambridge, 2014)
Suda	A. Adler, *Suidae Lexicon* (Stuttgart, 1928–38)
	† D. M. Whitehead *et al.*, *Suda On Line* (www.stoa.org/sol/) (2000–)
Symeon Seth, *On the Usefulness of the Heavenly Bodies* (*De utilitate corporum caelestium*)	'Περὶ χρείας τῶν οὐρανίων σωμάτων', in A. Delatte, *Anecdota Atheniensia*, ii: *Textes relatifs à l'histoire des sciences* (Liége–Paris, 1939), 90–126
Synesios	N. Terzaghi, *Opuscula* (Synesii Cyrenensis hymni et opuscula, 2. 1; Rome, 1944)
	‡ A. Garzya, *Opere di Sinesio di Cirene: epistole, operette, inni* (Turin, 1989)
	‡ A. Garzya–D. Roques, *Synésios de Cyrène, Lettres I–CLVI* (Budé) (2000)
Theon of Alexandria	A. Rome, *Commentaires de Pappus et de Théon d'Alexandrie sur l'Almageste* (Vatican City, 1936–43), vols 2–3
Theon of Smyrna	E. Hiller, *Theonis Smyrnaei philosophi Platonici Expositio rerum mathematicarum ad legendum Platonem utilium* (Teubner) (1878)
	‡ K. Brodersen, *Theon von Smyrna, Mathematik für die Platonlektüre* (Darmstadt, 2021)
Tzetzes	
(Ioannes) *Chiliades*	P. L. M. Leone, *Tzetzes, Chiliades* (Naples, 1968)
(Isaak or Ioannes) *On Lykophron, Alexandra*	E. Scheer, *Lycophronis Alexandra*, ii: *Scholia* (Berlin, 1908)
Vita Arati	'Γένος Ἀράτου καὶ βίος' ('Ancestry and life of Aratos'), in E. Maaß, *Commentariorum in Aratum reliquiae* (Berlin, 1898), 76–9
Zenobios	E. L. von Leutsch–F. G. Schneidewin, *Corpus paroemiographorum Graecorum*, i (Göttingen, 1839), 1–175
	W. Bühler, *Zenobii Athoi Proverbia vulgari cetera memoria aucta*, 3 vols (i, iv–v only) (Göttingen, 1982–99)

Works Cited

Series titles are included only selectively. The terms 'ed.' and 'eds' are reserved for multi-authored works.

Abulafia, D. (ed. 2004), *The Mediterranean in History*. London.
—— (2011), *The Great Sea: A Human History of the Mediterranean*. Oxford.
Adams, C. E. P. (2007a), *Land Transport in Roman Egypt 30 BC–AD 300: A Study in Administration and Economic History*. Oxford.
—— (2007b), 'Transport', in W. Scheidel, I. Morris, and R. P. Saller (eds), *The Cambridge Economic History of the Greco-Roman World* (Cambridge), 218–40.
—— and Laurence, R. (eds 2001), *Travel and Geography in the Roman Empire*. London–New York.
—— and Roy, J. (eds 2007), *Travel, Geography and Culture in Ancient Greece, Egypt and the Near East*. Oxford.
Adams, P. C. (2017), 'Tuanian geography', in B. P. Janz (ed.), *Place, Space and Hermeneutics* (Berlin), 275–88.
Adler, A. (ed. 1928–38), *Suidae Lexicon*. 5 vols. Stuttgart.
Adornato, G. (ed. 2016), *I disegni* (Intorno al Papiro di Artemidoro, 3). Milan.
Albaladejo Vivero, M. (2011), 'Eudoxos von Kyzikos (2206)', in *FGrH* v.
Alcock, S. E., Cherry, J. F., and Elsner, J. (eds 2001), *Pausanias: Travel and Memory in Roman Greece*. New York.
Alonso-Nuñez, J.-M. (1997), 'Approaches to world history in the hellenistic period: Dicearchus [*sic*] and Agatharchides', *Athenaeum*, n.s. 75. 1: 53–67.
Altomare, B. M. (2010), 'Per una nuova edizione di Marciano di Eraclea', Ph.D. thesis. Université de Reims Champagne-Ardennes.
—— (2013), 'Géographie et cosmographie dans l'Antiquité tardive: la tradition grecque et les modèles latins', *Dialogues d'histoire ancienne*, 39. 1: 9–34.
—— (2014), 'Madagascar avant Madagascar: l'île Ménouthias des anciens et les premières représentations de l'île de Saint Laurent', *Anabases*, 19: 227–41.
—— (2014–15), 'Périples dans le Périple: notes sur la structure du Périple de la Mer extérieure de Marcien d'Héraclée et sur sa tradition indirecte', *Revue des études tardo-antiques*, 4: 35–53.
—— (n.d.), 'For a new critical edition of Marcianus of Heraclea', *Academia.edu*.
—— (forthcoming), 'Marciano di Eracleia (2027)', in *FGrH* v.
Álvarez Delgado, J., Mederos Martín, A., and Escribano Cobo, G. (eds 2015), *Descubrimiento, colonización y primer poblamiento de las Islas Canarias: oro, púrpura y pesca en el litoral atlántico norteafricano y las Islas Canarias en época fenicia, cartaginesa y romana republicana*. Santa Cruz de Tenerife/Las Palmas de Gran Canaria.

Álvarez Martí-Aguilar, M. (2017a), 'Talismans against tsunamis: Apollonius of Tyana and the stelai of the Herakleion in Gades (VA 5.5)', *Greek, Roman and Byzantine Studies*, 57. 4: 968–93.
—— (2017b), 'La tradición historiográfica sobre catástrofes naturales en la Península Ibérica durante la Antigüedad y el supuesto tsunami del Golfo de Cádiz de 218–209 a.C.', *Dialogues d'histoire ancienne*, 43. 2: 117–45.
Aly, W. (1956), with F. Sbordone, *De Strabonis codice rescripto cuius reliquiae in codicibus vaticanis Vat. Gr. 2306 et 2061 A servatae sunt*. Vatican City.
—— (1957), *Strabon von Amaseia: Untersuchungen über Text, Aufbau und Quellen der Geographika*. Bonn.
Amato, E. (2004), 'Note esegetiche e testuali alla Descriptio orbis di Dionisio d'Alessandria (III)', *Göttinger Forum für Altertumswissenschaft*, 7: 1–9.
—— (2005), *Dionisio di Alessandria, Descrizione della terra abitata*. Milan.
Ameling, W. (2008), 'Ethnography and universal history in Agatharchides', in T. C. Brennan and H. I. Flower (eds), *East and West: Papers in Ancient History presented to Glen W. Bowersock* (Cambridge, Mass.), 13–59.
Ampolo, C., and Michelini, C. (eds 2009), *Immagine e immagini della Sicilia e di altre isole del Mediterraneo antico: atti delle seste giornate internazionali di studi sull'area elima e la Sicilia occidentale nel contesto mediterraneo*, i. Pisa.
Anderson, J. C. (ed. 2013), *The Christian Topography of Kosmas Indikopleustes: Firenze, Biblioteca Medicea Laurenziana, Plut. 9.28. The Map of the Universe Redrawn in the Sixth Century*. Rome.
Anderson, J. K. (1995), 'The Geometric catalogue of ships', in J. B. Carter and S. P. Morris (eds), *The Ages of Homer: A Tribute to Emily Townsend Vermeule* (Austin), 181–91.
André, J., and Filliozat, J. (1980), *Pline l'Ancien, Histoire naturelle, livre VI, 2e partie [§§46–106]: l'Asie centrale et orientale; l'Inde* (Collection des universités de France, série latine, 244). Paris. ['Budé' edition.]
anon. (2019), 'Papiro di Artemidoro, report rivela in esclusiva le analisi sull'opera: "improbabile che gli inchiostri siano antichi"', *Finestre sull'arte* (18 June).
Antonelli, L. (2013), 'Avienus, Ora maritima (2009)', in *FGrH* v.
Arafat, K. W. (1996), *Pausanias' Greece: Ancient Artists and Roman Rulers*. Cambridge.
Aranegui, C., and Mar, R. (2009), 'Lixus (Morocco): from a Mauretanian sanctuary to an Augustan palace', *Papers of the British School at Rome*, 77: 29–64.
Arenz, A. (2006), *Herakleides Kritikos, Über die Städte in Hellas: eine Periegese Griechenlands am Vorabend des chremonideischen Krieges*. Munich.
—— (2013), 'Herakleides Kritikos (2022)', in *FGrH* v.
Arnaud, P. (1989), 'Pouvoir des mots et limites de la cartographie dans la géographie grecque et romaine', *Dialogues d'histoire ancienne*, 15. 1: 9–29.
—— (1993), 'De la durée à la distance: l'évaluation des distances maritimes dans le monde gréco-romain', *Histoire et mesure*, 8. 3–4: 225–47.

—— (2004), 'Entre Antiquité et Moyen-Âge: l'Itinéraire Maritime d'Antonin', in L. De Maria and R. Turchetti (eds), *Rotte e porti del Mediterraneo dopo la caduta dell'impero romano d'occidente: continuità e innovazioni tecnologiche e funzionali* (Rubettino), 3–20.

—— (2005), *Les Routes de la navigation antique: itinéraires en Méditerranée*. Paris.

—— (2007–8), 'Texte et carte de Marcus Agrippa: historiographie et données textuelles', *Geographia antiqua*, 16–17.

—— (2009), 'Notes sur le Stadiasme de la Grande Mer (1): la Lycie et la Carie', *Geographia antiqua*, 18: 165–93.

—— (2010), 'Notes sur le Stadiasme de la Grande Mer (2): rose des vents, systèmes d'orientation et Quellenforschung', *Geographia antiqua*, 19: 157–62.

—— (2014), 'Marseille grecque et les routes du commerce maritime', in S. Bouffier and D. Garcia (eds), *Les Territoires de Marseille antique: Actes Sud, septembre 2014* (Arles–Paris).

—— (2016), 'Marcus Vipsanius Agrippa and his geographical work', in S. Bianchetti, M. R. Cataudella, and H.-J. Gehrke (eds), *Brill's Companion to Ancient Geography: The Inhabited World in Greek and Roman Tradition* (Leiden–Boston), 205–22.

—— (2017a), 'Playing dominoes with the Stadiasmus Maris Magni: the description of Syria. Sources, compilation, historical topography', in A. Külzer and M. S. Popović (eds), *Space, Landscapes and Settlements in Byzantium: Studies in Historical Geography of the Eastern Mediterranean presented to Johannes Koder* (Vienna–Novi Sad), 15–49 (map, 442).

—— (2017b), 'Un illustre inconnu: la Stadiasme de la (Grande) Mer', *Comptes-rendus des séances de l'Académie des Inscriptions et Belles-Lettres*, 2017. 2: 701–27.

—— (2020), 'Aides à la navigation, pratique de la navigation et construction des paysages maritimes en Atlantique du Nord-Est: quelques éléments de réflexion', *Gallia: archéologie de la France antique*, 77. 1: 29–43.

—— (forthcoming), 'Stadiasmos (2049)', in *FGrH* v.

Arnim, *see* von Arnim.

Arnold, J. H. (2000), *History: A Very Short Introduction*. Oxford–New York.

Arnott, W. G. (1996), *Alexis, The Fragments: A Commentary* (Cambridge Classical Texts and Commentaries, 31). Cambridge.

—— (2007), *Birds in the Ancient World from A to Z*. London.

Asirvatham, S. R. (2012), 'Pausanias of Antioch (854)', in *BNJ*.

Ast, R., and Bagnall, R. S. (2015), 'The receivers of Berenike: new inscriptions from the 2015 season', *Chiron*, 45: 171–85.

Aujac, G. (2000), 'Strabon et son temps', in W. Hübner (ed.), *Geographie und verwandte Wissenschaften* (Stuttgart), 103–39.

—— (2016), 'The "revolution" of Ptolemy', in S. Bianchetti, M. R. Cataudella, and H.-J. Gehrke (eds), *Brill's Companion to Ancient Geography: The Inhabited World in Greek and Roman Tradition* (Leiden–Boston), 313–34.

—— (2020a), 'En Grèce ancienne, le ciel enseignait la terre', in G. Maddoli, M. Nafissi, and F. Prontera (eds), Σπουδῆς οὐδὲν ἐλλιποῦσα: *Anna Maria Biraschi. Scritti in memoria* (Perugia), 1–12.

—— (2020b), *Hipparque de Nicée et l'astronomie en Grèce ancienne*. Florence.

Austin, M. M. (2006), *The Hellenistic World from Alexander to the Roman Conquest: A Selection of Ancient Sources in Translation*, 2nd edn. Cambridge.

Avram, A. (2009), 'Héraclée du Pont et ses colonies pontiques: antécédents milésiens (?) et empreinte mégarienne', in M. Lombardo and F. Frisone (eds), *Colonie di colonie: le fondazioni sub-coloniali greche tra colonizzazione e colonialismo* (Galatina), 209–27.

Ayodeji, K. (2009), 'Maritime identities', in G. R. Boys-Stones, B. Graziosi, and P. Vasunia (eds), *The Oxford Handbook of Hellenic Studies* (Oxford), 340–51.

Bagnall, R. S. (ed. 2012), *The Encyclopedia of Ancient History*. 13 vols. Malden, Mass.–Chichester.

Baksa, I. (2020), 'Meteorology (Chapter 4)', in P. Gregorić and G. Karamanolis (eds), *Pseudo-Aristotle, De Mundo (On the Cosmos): A Commentary* (Cambridge), 121–48.

Baladié, R. (1980), *Le Péloponnèse de Strabon: étude de géographie historique*. Paris.

Banchich, T. (2010), 'Artemidoros of Ephesos (438)', in *BNJ*.

—— (2019), 'Artemidoros of Ephesos (438)', in *BNJ*^{2}.

Bartelink, G. J. (ed. 1971), *Callinicus, Vie d'Hypatios*. Paris.

Basham, A. A. (1968), *The Wonder that was India*, 3rd edn. New York.

Bats, M. (2009), 'Le colonie di Massalia', in M. Lombardo and F. Frisone (eds), *Colonie di colonie: le fondazioni sub-coloniali greche tra colonizzazione e colonialismo* (Galatina), 203–8.

Bayer, K. (1993), 'Der Fahrtenbericht des Hanno', in G. Winkler (ed.), *C. Plinius Secundus d. Ä., Naturkunde, lateinisch–deutsch, Buch V: Geographie. Afrika und Asien* (Sammlung Tusculum; Munich), 337–53.

Beagon, M. (1992), *Roman Nature: The Thought of Pliny the Elder*. Oxford.

—— (2005), *The Elder Pliny on the Human Animal: Natural History Book 7*. Oxford.

Bean, G. E. (1979), *Turkey's Southern Shore*, 2nd edn. London.

Bearzot, C. (2020), 'Aminta e gli Stathmoi (FGrH/BNJ 122): bematista o pseudo-bematista?', in G. Maddoli, M. Nafissi, and F. Prontera (eds), Σπουδῆς οὐδὲν ἐλλιποῦσα: *Anna Maria Biraschi. Scritti in memoria* (Perugia), 13–22.

Beaujeu, J. (1951), *Pline l'Ancien, Histoire naturelle, livre II: cosmologie, astronomie et géologie* (Collection des universités de France, série latine, 133). Paris. ['Budé' edition.]

Beaulieu, M.-C. (2016), *The Sea in the Greek Imagination*. Philadelphia.

Beccaria, A. (1477), *Dionysius Periegetes, De situ orbis*. Venice.

Beck, L. Y. (ed. 2005), with J. Scarborough, *Pedanius Dioscorides of Anazarbus, De materia medica*. Hildesheim–Zürich–New York.

Beckby, H. (ed. 1965), *Anthologia Graeca*, 2nd edn. (Sammlung Tusculum). 4 vols. Munich.

Bekker-Nielsen, T. (1988), 'Terra incognita: the subjective geography of the Roman empire', in A. Damsgaard-Madsen, E. Christiansen, and E. Hallager (eds), *Studies in Ancient History and Numismatics presented to Rudi Thomsen* (Aarhus), 148–61.

—— and Gertwagen, R. (eds 2016), *The Inland Seas: Towards an Ecohistory of the Mediterranean and the Black Sea*. Stuttgart.

—— and Jensen, M. (2015), 'Two Pontic rivers', *Cedrus: The Journal of MCRI*, 3: 231–42.

Belfiore, S. (2009), *Il Periplo del Ponto Eusino di Arriano e altri testi sul Mar Nero e il Bosforo: spazio geografico, mito e dominio ai confini dell'impero romano*. Venice.

—— (2013), 'Periplus maris Erythraei (2036)', in *FGrH* v.

Belke, K. (2020), *Bithynien und Hellespont*, i. (Tabula imperii Byzantini, 13). Vienna.

—— (2021), 'Gates to Asia Minor: the harbours of Chalcedon, Chrysopolis, Hiereia and Eutropiu Limen opposite Constantinople', in F. Daim and E. Kislinger (eds), *The Byzantine Harbours of Constantinople* (Heidelberg), 223–33.

Bentley, R. (1699), *Dissertations upon the Epistles of Phalaris: With an Answer to the Objections of the Honourable Charles Boyle, Esquire*. London.

Bereti, V., Consagra, G. et al. (2013), 'Orikos—Oricum: final report on the Albano-Swiss excavations, 2007–2010', *Mediterranean Archaeology*, 26: 95–185.

Berger, A. (2013), *Accounts of Medieval Constantinople: The Patria*. Cambridge, Mass.

Berger, F. X. (1804), 'Artemidori geographi fragmentum de Nilo: e codice ms. bibliothecae electoralis Monacensis nunc primum editum a Fr. Xav. Berger', *Beyträge zur Geschichte und Literatur*, 1. 2: 49–53.

Berger, H. (1880), *Die geographischen Fragmente des Eratosthenes*. Leipzig.

—— (1903), *Geschichte der wissenschaftlichen Erdkunde der Griechen*, 3rd edn. Leipzig.

—— (1964), *Die geographischen Fragmente des Eratosthenes*. Amsterdam.

Berggren, J. L., and Jones, A. (2000), *Ptolemy's Geography: An Annotated Translation of the Theoretical Chapters*. Princeton.

Bernabé, A. (2016), 'Transfer of afterlife knowledge in Pythagorean eschatology', in A.-B. Renger (ed.), *Pythagorean Knowledge from the Ancient to the Modern World: Askesis, Religion, Science*.

Bernardakis, G. N. (1896), *Plutarchos, Moralia*, vii. *Plutarchi fragmenta vera et spuria multis accessionibus locupletata*. Leipzig.

Bertelli, L. (2001), 'Hecataeus: from genealogy to historiography', in N. Luraghi (ed.), *The Historian's Craft in the Age of Herodotus* (Oxford), 67–94.

Berthelot, A. (1934), *Avienus, Ora maritima*. Paris.

Berthelot, H., *et al.* (eds 2016), *Vivre et penser les frontières dans le monde méditerranéen antique: actes du colloque tenu à l'Université Paris-Sorbonne, les 29 et 30 juin 2013*. Bordeaux.

Betegh, G., and Gregorić, P. (2020), 'God's relation to the cosmos (Chapter 6)', in P. Gregorić and G. Karamanolis (eds), *Pseudo-Aristotle, De Mundo (On the Cosmos): A Commentary* (Cambridge), 176–212.

Bianchetti, S. (1998), *Pitea di Massalia, L'Oceano*. Pisa–Rome.

—— (2005), 'La geografia di Pitea e la diorthosis di Polibio', in G. Schepens and J. Bollansée (eds), *The Shadow of Polybius: Intertextuality as a Research Tool in Greek Historiography* (Leuven), 255–70.

—— (2008), 'Geografía e cartografía dell'estremo occidente da Eratostene a Tolemeo', *Mainake*, 30: 17–58.

—— (2013), 'Peripli e periegesi: strumenti indispensabili a "disegnare" il mondo?', in F. Raviola *et al.* (eds), *L'indagine e la rima: scritti per Lorenzo [Braccesi]* (Rome), 221–39.

—— (2014), 'Aspetti di geografia eforea nei Giambi a Nicomede', *La parola del passato*, 69. 394-400: 751–80.

—— (2015), 'Il "Grande Nord" tra scienza e letteratura fantastica da Pitea a Antonio Diogene', *Orbis Terrarum*, 13: 11–31.

—— (2019), 'Le rotta delle Estrimnidi: dallo spazio mitico allo spazio cartografico', in E. Ferrer Albelda (ed.), *La ruta de las Estrímnides: navegación y conocimiento del litoral atlántico de Iberia en la Antigüedad* (Alcalá de Henares), 85–102.

——, Cataudella, M. R., and Gehrke, H.-J. (eds 2016), *Brill's Companion to Ancient Geography: The Inhabited World in Greek and Roman Tradition*. Leiden–Boston.

Bichler, R. (2018), 'On the traces of Onesicritus: some historiographical aspects of Alexander's Indian campaign', in K. Nawotka *et al.* (eds), *The Historiography of Alexander the Great* (Wiesbaden), 51–69.

—— (2021), review of M. Waters, *Ctesias' Persica and its Near Eastern Context*, in *Bryn Mawr Classical Review*, 2021.01.05.

Bilić, T. (2012), 'Crates of Mallos and Pytheas of Massalia: examples of Homeric exegesis in terms of mathematical geography', *Transactions of the American Philological Association*, 142. 2: 295–328.

—— (2020), 'Pytheas and Hecataeus: visions of the north in the late fourth century BC', *Greek, Roman and Byzantine Studies*, 60. 4: 574–93.

Billerbeck, M. (ed. 2006–17), with J. F. Gaertner *et al.*, *Stephani Byzantii Ethnica*. 5 vols. Berlin–New York.

—— (2009), 'Artemidorus' Geographoumena in the Ethnika of Stephanus of Byzantium: source and transmission', in Brodersen and Elsner (below), 65–87.

Bing, P. (2005), 'The politics and poetics of geography in the Milan Posidippus, section one: in stones', in K. J. Gutzwiller (ed.), *The New Posidippus: A Hellenistic Poetry Book* (Oxford), 119–40.

Bintliff, J. L. (ed. 1991), *The Annales School and Archaeology*. Leicester–London.
Blakesey, J. W. (1854), *Herodotus: With a Commentary*. London.
Blomqvist, J. (1979), *The Date and Origin of the Greek Version of Hanno's Periplus*. Lund.
—— (1992), 'Alexandrian science: the case of Eratosthenes', in P. Bilde *et al.* (eds), *Ethnicity in Hellenistic Egypt* (Aarhus), 53–75.
Bodde, D. (1978), 'The state and empire of Ch'in', in D. Twitchett and J. K. Fairbank (eds), *The Ch'in and Han Empire, 221 BC–AD 220* (The Cambridge History of China, 1; Cambridge), 20–102.
Boechat, E. M. B. (2018), 'Geographical systems in the first century BC: Posidonius' F 49 E-K and Vitruvius' On Architecture VI 1. 3–13', *Prometeus: filosofia em revista*, 11: 37–61.
Bollansée, J., Haegemans, K., and Schepens, G. (2008), 'Mnaseas of Patara (215–175 BCE)', *Encyclopedia of Ancient Natural Scientists* 559.
——, ——, and —— (2008), 'Plutarch, pseudo, De Fluuiis (300 CE?)', *Encyclopedia of Ancient Natural Scientists* 676–7.
—— and Schepens, G. (eds 1998–), *Felix Jacoby, Die Fragmente der griechischen Historiker Continued*, iv. *Biography and Antiquarian Literature*. Leiden–Boston–Cologne.
Bolton, J. D. P. (1962), *Aristeas of Proconnesus*. Oxford.
Bommelaer, B. (1989), *Diodore de Sicile, Bibliothèque historique*, iii. *Livre III* (Collection des universités de France, série grecque, 327). Paris. ['Budé' edition.]
Bonneau, D. (1993), *Le Régime administratif de l'eau du Nil dans l'Égypte grecque, romaine et byzantine*. Leiden–New York–Cologne.
Bos, A. P. (2020), review of P. Gregorić and G. Karamanolis, *Pseudo-Aristotle, De Mundo*, in *Bryn Mawr Classical Review*, 2021.06.24.
Bosak-Schroeder, C. (2019), 'Making specimens in the Periplus of Hanno and its imperial tradition', *American Journal of Philology*, 140. 1: 67–100.
Boshnakov, K. (2004), *Pseudo-Skymnos (Semos von Delos?), Τὰ ἀριστερὰ τοῦ Πόντου: Zeugnisse griechischer Schriftsteller über den westlichen Pontosraum*. Stuttgart.
Bourtembourg, R. (2013), 'Was Uranus observed by Hipparchus?', *Journal for the History of Astronomy*, 44. 4: 377–87.
Bowen, A. C., and Todd, R. B. (2004), *Cleomedes' Lectures on Astronomy: A Translation of The Heavens*. Berkeley.
Bowersock, G. W. (1983), *Roman Arabia*. Cambridge, Mass.–London.
Bowie, E. L. (1970), 'Greeks and their past in the Second Sophistic', *Past and Present*, 46: 3–41.
—— (1990), 'Greek poetry in the Antonine age', in D. A. Russell (ed.), *Antonine Literature* (Oxford), pp. 53–90.
—— (2000), 'The reception of Apollonius in imperial Greek literature', in M. A. Harder (ed.), *Apollonius Rhodius* (Leuven).

—— (2001), 'Inspiration and aspiration: date, genre, and readership', in S. E. Alcock, J. F. Cherry, and J. Elsner (eds), *Pausanias: Travel and Memory in Roman Greece* (New York), 21–32.

—— (2004), 'Denys d'Alexandrie: un poète grec dans l'empire romain', *Revue des études anciennes*, 106: 177–86.

Bowra, C. M. (1956), 'A fragment of the Arimaspea', *Classical Quarterly*, n.s. 6: 1–10.

Bradshaw, P. F. (ed. 2020), with A. McGowan, *Egeria, Journey to the Holy Land*. Turnhout.

Braudel, F. (1972), *The Mediterranean and the Mediterranean World in the Age of Philip II*. 2 vols. London.

Braun, T. F. R. G. (2004), 'Hecataeus' knowledge of the western Mediterranean', in K. Lomas (ed.), *Greek Identity in the Western Mediterranean: Papers in honour of Professor B. B. Shefton* (Leiden), 287–347.

Braund, D. C. (1994), *Georgia in Antiquity: A History of Colchis and Transcaucasian Iberia 550 BC–AD 562*. Oxford.

—— (2000), 'Map 23 Tomis–Olbia–Chersonesos', in R. J. A. Talbert (ed.), *Map-by-map Directory: To accompany Barrington Atlas of the Greek and Roman World*, i (Princeton–Oxford), 350–68.

—— (2004), 'Herodotus' Spartans and Scythians', in C. J. Tuplin (ed.), *Pontus and the Outside World: Studies in Black Sea History, Historiography, and Archaeology* (Leiden), 25–41.

—— (2019a), 'Dancing around the Black Sea: Xenophon, Pseudo-Scymnus and Lucian's bacchants [Epilogue]', in D. C. Braund, E. M. Hall, and R. Wyles (eds), *Ancient Theatre and Performance Culture around the Black Sea* (Cambridge), 470–89.

—— (2019b), 'Theatre and performance in the Bosporan kingdom', in D. C. Braund, E. M. Hall, and R. Wyles (eds), *Ancient Theatre and Performance Culture around the Black Sea* (Cambridge), 82–105.

—— (2020), 'Между Вифинией и Борисфеном: от ристалища Ахилла на Кальпе к прибытию Афродиты в Гилею' ['Between Bithynia and Borysthenes: from Achilles' racecourses on the Kalpe to the arrival of Aphrodite in Hylaea'], *Археологические вести—Archaeological News*, 29: 175–90.

—— (2021), 'Gyenos: reflections on etymology in Colchis and tales of Argonauts and giants', in D. C. Braund and V. F. Stolba (eds), *Environment and Habitation around the Ancient Black Sea* (Berlin–Boston), 321–34.

—— and Kakhidze, E. (2022), 'Reflections on the southeastern coast of the Black Sea in the Roman period', in D. C. Braund, A. Chaniotis, and E. K. Petropoulos (eds), *The Black Sea Region in the Context of the Roman Empire: International Symposium dedicated in memory of Victor I. Sarianidi, Athens 5–8 May 2016* (Athens), 59–73.

—— and Kryzhitskiy, S. D. (eds 2007), *Classical Olbia and the Scythian World: From the Sixth Century BC to the Second Century AD*. Oxford/London.

Bravo, B. (2009), *La Chronique d'Apollodore et le Pseudo-Skymnos: érudition antiquaire et littérature géographique dans la seconde moitié du IIe siècle av. J.-C.* Leuven.

Breeze, D. J., and Wilkins, A. (2018), 'Pytheas, Tacitus and Thule', *Britannia*, 49: 303–8.
Bremmer, J. N. (1983), *The Early Greek Concept of the Soul*. Princeton.
—— (2002), *The Rise and Fall of the Afterlife*. New York.
Brentjes, B. (2006a), 'China', in H. Cancik, H. Schneider, and C. F. Salazar (eds), *Brill's New Pauly* (Leiden).
—— (2006b), 'Seres', in H. Cancik, H. Schneider, and C. F. Salazar (eds), *Brill's New Pauly* (Leiden).
Brillante, S. (2017), 'Pseudo-Scylax: édition, traduction et commentaire', Ph.D. thesis. Bari/Reims: Università di Studi di Bari/Université de Reims Champagne-Ardennes.
—— (2020), *Il Periplo di Pseudo-Scilace: l'oggettività del potere*. Hildesheim–Zürich–New York.
Broadhead, H. D. (1960), *The Persae of Aeschylus*. Cambridge.
Brodersen, K. (1994a), *Dionysios von Alexandria, Das Lied von der Welt*. Hildesheim–Zürich–New York.
—— (1994b), *Pomponius Mela, Kreuzfahrt durch die alte Welt*. Darmstadt.
—— (1996), *C. Plinius Secundus d. Ä., Naturkunde, lateinisch-deutsch, Buch VI: Geographie: Asien* (Sammlung Tusculum). Zürich–Düsseldorf.
—— (2001), 'Savage's savages: how the gorilla became a savage beast because of Hanno's Periplus', in K. Geus and K. Zimmermann (eds), *Punica—Libyca—Ptolemaica: Festschrift für Werner Huß* (Leuven), 87–98. Repr. in K. Brodersen, *Classics outside Classics* (Heidelberg, 2015), ch. 5.
—— (2002), *Die Wahrheit über die griechischen Mythen: Palaiphatos' 'Unglaubliche Geschichten'*. Stuttgart.
—— (2006), 'Hierokles [8]', *Brill's New Pauly*.
—— (2012), 'Cartography', in D. Dueck (ed.), *Geography in Classical Antiquity* (Cambridge), 99–110.
—— (2015), 'Savage's savages: how the gorillas became savage beasts because of Hanno's Periplus', in id., *Classics outside Classics* (Heidelberg), 61–8.
—— (2016a), *Aetheria/Egeria, Reise ins Heiliges Land* (Sammlung Tusculum). Berlin–Boston.
—— (2016b), 'The geographies of Pliny and his "ape" Solinus', in S. Bianchetti, M. R. Cataudella, and H.-J. Gehrke (eds), *Brill's Companion to Ancient Geography: The Inhabited World in Greek and Roman Tradition* (Leiden–Boston), 298–310.
—— (2019), *Apuleius, Aristoteles, Über die Welt* (Sammlung Tusculum). Berlin.
—— (2021), *Periplus Maris Erythraei: zweisprachige Ausgabe*. Speyer.
—— (2023a), *Arrianos/Anonymos, Periplus Ponti Euxini: zweisprächige Ausgabe*. 2nd edn. Speyer.
—— (2023b), *Theophrastos, Wind und Wetter* (Sammlung Tusculum). Berlin.
—— and Elsner, J. (eds 2009), *Images and Texts on the 'Artemidorus Papyrus': Working Papers on P.Artemid*. Stuttgart.

Broggiato, M. (2013), 'Krates of Mallos (2113)', in *FGrH* v.
—— (ed. 2001), *Cratete di Mallo: i frammenti*. La Spezia.
Bruce, J. (1790), *Travels to Discover the Source of the Nile in the Years 1768, 1769, 1770, 1771, 1772, and 1773*. 3 vols. London.
Brunt, P. A. (1980), 'On historical fragments and epitomes', *Classical Quarterly*, 74 (n.s. 30): 477–94; repr. in J. M. Alonso-Nuñez, *Geschichtsbild und Geschichtsdenken im Altertum* (Darmstadt, 1991), 334–62.
—— (ed. 1976–83), *Arrian, Anabasis of Alexander*, revised edn (Loeb Classical Library, 236; 239). 2 vols. Cambridge, Mass.–London.
Bucciantini, V. (2012), 'The limits of knowledge: explorations of and information from the Horn of Africa to the East African coast in the Graeco-Roman tradition', in M.-F. Boussac, J.-F. Salles, and J.-B. Yon (eds), *Autour du Périple de la mer Érythrée* (Lyons), 159–76.
—— (2013), 'Misurazioni e distanze marittime nel Periplo di Nearco', in K. Geus and M. Rathmann (eds), *Vermessung der Oikoumene* (Berlin–Boston), 65–76.
—— (2016), 'Geographical description and historical narrative in the tradition on Alexander's expedition', in S. Bianchetti, M. R. Cataudella, and H.-J. Gehrke (eds), *Brill's Companion to Ancient Geography: The Inhabited World in Greek and Roman Tradition* (Leiden–Boston), 98–109.
Bucher, G. S. (2016), 'Anonymous, On Rome and Italy (840)', in *BNJ*.
Buisseret, D. (ed. 2007), *The Oxford Companion to World Exploration*. 2 vols. Oxford.
Bulloch, A. W. (1985), 'Hellenistic poetry', in P. E. Easterling and B. M. W. Knox (eds), *The Cambridge History of Classical Literature*, i (Cambridge), 541–621. Greek Literature.
Bunbury, E. H. (1879), *A History of Ancient Geography: Among the Greeks and Romans from the Earliest Ages till the Fall of the Roman Empire*, 1st edn. 2 vols. London.
—— (1883), *A History of Ancient Geography*, 2nd edn. 2 vols. London.
Burri, R. (2014), 'The geography of De mundo', in J. C. Thom (ed.), *Cosmic Order and Divine Power: Pseudo-Aristotle, On the Cosmos* (Tübingen), 89–106.
Burstein, S. M. (1986), 'The Ethiopian war of Ptolemy V: an historical myth', *Beiträge zur Sudanforschung*, 1: 17–23; repr. as 'The Aithiopian war of Ptolemy V: an historical myth?', in id., *Graeco-Africana: Studies in the History of Greek Relations with Egypt and Nubia* (Rochelle, NY), 97–104 (ch. 8).
—— (1989), *Agatharchides of Cnidus, On the Erythraean Sea*. London.
—— (1995), 'The Aithiopian war of Ptolemy V: an historical myth?', in id., *Graeco-Africana: Studies in the History of Greek Relations with Egypt and Nubia* (Rochelle, NY), 97–104.
—— (2008), 'Elephants for Ptolemy II: Ptolemaic policy in Nubia in the third century BC', in P. McKechnie and P. Guillaume (eds), *Ptolemy II Philadelphus and his World* (Leiden–Boston), 135–47.

—— (2009), 'Agatharchides of Knidos (86)', in *BNJ*.
—— (2009), 'Hecataeus of Miletus and the Greek encounter with Egypt', *Ancient West and East*, 8: 133–46.
—— (2012a), 'Agatharchides of Cnidus, On the Erythrean Sea F 20: a note on the history of cavalry in Kush', *Beiträge zur Sudanforschung*, 11: 15–19.
—— (2012b), 'Aithiopia, appendix (673)', in *BNJ*.
—— (2021a), 'Greek and Roman views of ancient Nubia', in G. Emberling and B. Beyer Williams (eds), *The Oxford Handbook of Ancient Nubia* (Oxford), 697–711.
—— (2021b), 'The African encounter with Greece', *Acta Classica*, 64: 48–71.
Butterworth, G. W. (ed. 1919), *Clement of Alexandria* (Loeb Classical Library, 92). Cambridge, Mass.

Čače, S. (1999), 'Manijski zaljev, Jadastini i Salona', *Vjesnik za arheologiju i historiju dalmatinsku*, 90–1: 57–87.
—— (2015), 'Jadranski otoci u Pseudo Skimnovoj Periegezi—The Adriatic islands in the Periegesis of Pseudo-Scymnus: dvije napomene—two remarks', *Miscellanea Hadriatica et Mediterranea*, 2: 9–23.
Calame, C. (1992), 'Espaces limineaux et voix discursives dans l'Idylle 1 de Théocrite', in C. Calame (ed.), *Figures grecques de l'intermédiaire* (Lausanne), 58–85.
—— (2011), 'Myth and performance on the Athenian stage: Praxithea, Erechtheus, their daughters, and the aetiology of autochthony', *Classical Philology*, 106: 1–19.
Calo, A., et al. (2020), 'Trans-Asiatic exchange of glass, gold and bronze: analysis of finds from the late prehistoric Pangkung Paruk site, Bali', *Antiquity*, 94. 373: 110–26.
Campbell, D. A. (ed. 1988), *Greek Lyric*, ii. *Anacreon, Anacreontea, Choral Lyric from Olympus to Alcman* (Loeb Classical Library, 143). Cambridge, Mass./London.
Campbell, J. B. (1996), 'Shaping the rural environment: surveyors in ancient Rome', *Journal of Roman Studies*, 86: 74–99.
—— (2000), *The Writings of the Roman Land Surveyors*. London.
—— (2012), *Rivers and the Power of Ancient Rome*. Chapel Hill.
Canfora, L. (2013), 'The so-called Artemidorus papyrus: a reconsideration', *Museum Helveticum*, 70. 2: 157–79.
—— Micunco, S. et al. (2016), with M. R. Acquafredda, B. M. Altomare et al., *Fozio, Biblioteca*. Pisa.
Canter, D. (1977), *The Psychology of Place*. London.
Cappelletto, P. (2003), *I frammenti di Mnasea*. Milan.
Carey, S. (2004), *Pliny's Catalogue of Culture: Art and Empire in the Natural History*. Oxford.
Casson, L. B. (1980), 'Periplus Maris Erythraei: three notes on the text', *Classical Quarterly*, 74 (n.s. 30): 495–7.
—— (1986), *Ships and Seamanship in the Ancient World*, 2nd edn. Princeton, NJ; repr. with revisions, Baltimore–London, 1995.

—— (1989), *The Periplus Maris Erythraei*. Princeton.
Castelli, E. (2020), *La nascita del titolo nella letteratura greca: dall'epica arcaica alla prosa di età classica*. Berlin–Boston.
Castiglioni, Alfredo, Castiglioni, Angelo, and Vercoutter, J. (1995), *L'Eldorado dei Faraoni: alla scoperta di Berenice Pancrisia*. Novara.
Castiglioni, M. P. (2008), 'The cult of Diomedes in the Adriatic: complementary contributions from literary sources and archaeology', in J. Carvalho (ed.), *Bridging the Gaps: Sources, Methodology and Approaches to Religion in History* (Pisa), 9–28.
Cataudella, M. R. (2016), 'Some scientific approaches: Eudoxus of Cnidus and Dicaearchus of Messene', in S. Bianchetti, M. R. Cataudella, and H.-J. Gehrke (eds), *Brill's Companion to Ancient Geography: The Inhabited World in Greek and Roman Tradition* (Leiden–Boston), 115–31.
—— (forthcoming), 'Dicearco (2015)', in *FGrH* v.
Chaniotis, A., and Mylonopoulos, J. (2003), 'Epigraphic bulletin for Greek religion 2000', *Kernos*, 16: 247–306.
Charles, M. B. (2020), 'The African elephants of antiquity revisited: habitat and representational evidence', *Historia*, 69. 4: 392–407.
Chiai, G. F. (2021), 'Perception of diversity and exploration of the environment: Greeks and Scythians in the archaic period', in D. C. Braund and V. F. Stolba (eds), *Environment and Habitation around the Ancient Black Sea* (Berlin–Boston), 195–212.
Christ, W. (1890), *Geschichte der griechischen Literatur: bis auf die Zeit Justinians*, 2nd edn. Munich.
—— Schmid, W., and Stahlin, O. (1924), *Geschichte der griechischen Literatur*, ii. 2. Munich.
Christesen, P. (2019), *A New Reading of the Damonon Stele*. Newcastle upon Tyne.
Clarke, K. (1999), *Between Geography and History: Hellenistic Constructions of the Roman World*. Oxford.
—— (2007), 'Les fragments de Posidonios chez Athénée', in D. Lenfant (ed.), *Athénée et les fragments d'historiens: actes du colloque de Strasbourg (16–18 juin 2005)* (Paris), 291–302.
—— (2018), *Shaping the Geography of Empire: Man and Nature in Herodotus' Histories*. Oxford.
—— (2020), 'Minding the gap: mimetic imperfection and the historical enterprise', in A. Turner (ed.), *Reconciling Ancient and Modern Philosophies of History* (Berlin), 183–206.
Cohen, G. M. (2006), *The Hellenistic Settlements in Syria, the Red Sea Basin, and North Africa*. Berkeley–Los Angeles.
Cohen, S. M., and Burke, P. (1990), 'New evidence for the dating of Aristotle Meteorologica 1–3', *Classical Philology*, 85. 2: 126–9.
Cole, T. (1967), *Democritus and the Sources of Greek Anthropology*. Cleveland.

Compatangelo-Soussignan, R. (2016), 'Poseidonios and the original cause of the migration of the Cimbri: tsunami, storm surge or tides?', *Revue des études anciennes*, 118. 2: 451–68.

Condello, F. (2011), 'Artemidoro 2006–2011: l'ultima vita, in breve', *Quaderni di storia*, 37. 74: 161–256.

—— (2018), 'P. Artemid. e i suoi avvocati [review of Gallazzi et al. 2012; Adornato 2016]', *Eikasmos*, 29: 510–46.

Constable, G., and Kazhdan, A. P. (1982), *People and Power in Byzantium: An Introduction to Modern Byzantine Studies*. Washington.

Conte, G. B., and Most, G. W. (1996), 'Genre', *Oxford Classical Dictionary*³ 630–1.

Coo, L., and Finglass, P. J. (2020), 'Introduction', in P. J. Finglass and L. Coo (eds), *Female Characters in Fragmentary Greek Tragedy* (Cambridge), 1–16.

Cook, A. B. (1914–40), *Zeus: A Study in Ancient Religion*. 3 vols. Cambridge.

Cook, J. (2008), 'Ptolemy Philadelphus and Jewish writings: Aristobulus and Pseudo-Aristeas as examples of Alexandrian Jewish approaches', in P. McKechnie and P. Guillaume (eds), *Ptolemy II Philadelphus and his World* (Leiden–Boston), 193–206.

Corda, P. (2019), *Pitea, il figlio degli oceani*. Place not stated.

Cordovana, O. D., and Chiai, G. F. (eds 2017), *Pollution and the Environment in Ancient Life and Thought*. Stuttgart.

Cory, W., with Benson, A. C. (1905), *Ionica*, 3rd edn. (London), 12–14.

Counillon, P. (1981), 'Un autre acrostiche dans la Périégèse de Denys', *Revue des études grecques*, 94: 514–22.

—— (1983), 'Édition critique de la Périégèse de Denys', thèse de 3ᵉ cycle. Université de Langue et des Lettres de Grénoble III.

—— (1991), 'À propos de l'histoire du texte de Denys le Périégète', *Revue des études anciennes*, 93: 365–71.

—— (1998a), 'Datos en Thrace et le périple du Pseudo-Skylax', *Revue des études anciennes*, 100. 1: 115–24.

—— (1998b), 'Λιμὴν ἔρημος', in P. Arnaud and P. Counillon (eds), *Geographica historica* (Bordeaux–Nice), 55–67.

—— (2001a), 'Dionysos dans la Description de la terre habitée de Denys d'Alexandrie', in I. Zinguer (ed.), *Dionysos: origines et resurgences* (Paris), 105–14.

—— (2001b), 'Les Cyclades chez les géographes grecs', *Revue des études anciennes*, 103. 1–2: 11–23.

—— (2004a), 'La Périégèse de la terre habitée et l'Hymne à Délos de Callimaque', *Revue des études anciennes*, 106: 187–202.

—— (2004b), *Pseudo-Skylax, Le Périple du Pont-Euxin: texte, traduction, commentaire philologique et historique*. Bordeaux.

—— (2007), 'Le Périple du Pseudo-Skylax et l'Adriatique (§17–24)', in S. Čače, A. Kurilič, and F. Tassaux (eds), *Les Routes de l'Adriatique antique/Putovi antičkog Jadrana: géographie et économie—geografija i gospodarstvo* (Bordeaux), 19–29.

Cramer, J. A. (1835), *Anecdota Graeca e codd. manuscriptis bibliothecarum Oxoniensium*, i. Oxford.
Crow, J. (2007), 'The infrastructure of a great city: earth, walls and water in late antique Constantinople', in L. Lavan, E. Zanini, and A. Sarantis (eds), *Technology in Transition AD 300–650* (Leiden–Boston), 251–85.
—— Bardill, J., and Bayliss, R. A. (2008), *The Water Supply of Byzantine Constantinople*. London.
Cruz Andreotti, G. (2016), 'Rome and Iberia: the making of a cultural geography', in S. Bianchetti, M. R. Cataudella, and H.-J. Gehrke (eds), *Brill's Companion to Ancient Geography: The Inhabited World in Greek and Roman Tradition* (Leiden–Boston), 274–97.
—— Le Roux, P., and Moret, P. (eds 2006), *La invención de una geografía de la península ibérica*, i. *La época republicana*. Málaga/Madrid.
—— (eds 2007), *La invención de una geografía de la península ibérica*, ii. *La época imperial*. Málaga/Madrid.
Cunliffe, B. (1983), 'Ictis: is it here?', *Oxford Journal of Archaeology*, 2. 1: 123–6.
—— (2001), *The Extraordinary Voyage of Pytheas the Greek*. London.
—— (2002), *The Extraordinary Voyage of Pytheas the Greek: The Man who Discovered Britain*, 2nd edn. London.
Cuntz, O. (1905), 'Der Stadiasmus Maris Magni', in A. Bauer (ed.), *Die Chronik des Hippolytus im Matritensis Graecus 121* (Leipzig), 243–76.
—— (ed. 1929), *Itineraria Antonini Augusti et Burdigalense*. Leipzig.
—— and J. Schnetz (1940), *Ravennatis Anonymi Cosmographia et Guidonis Geographica*. Leipzig.
Cusset, C. (2004), 'Denys lecteur d'Apollonios de Rhodes? L'exemple de la description des fleuves', *Revue des études anciennes*, 106: 203–16.

Dähnhardt, O. (1894), *Scholia in Aeschyli Persas*. Leipzig.
D'Alessio, G. B. (2009), 'On the "Artemidorus" papyrus', *Zeitschrift für Papyrologie und Epigraphik*, 171: 27–43.
Dagron, E. (1984), *Constantinople imaginaire: études sur le recueil des Patria*. Paris.
Dan, A.-C. (2008), 'Aristeas of Proconnesus', in Εγκυκλοπαιδεία Μείζονος Ελληνισμού: Εύξεινος Πόντος.
—— (2014), 'Xenophon's Anabasis and the common Greek mental modelling of spaces', in K. Geus and M. Thiering (eds), *Features of Common Sense Geography: Implicit Knowledge Structures in Ancient Geographical Texts* (Berlin), 157–98.
—— (2016), 'The rivers called "Phasis"', *Ancient West and East*, 15: 245–77.
——, et al. (2016), 'Common sense geography and ancient geographical texts', *eTOPOI*, 6: 571–97.
Dana, D. (2018), 'Un groupe de timbres amphoriques méconnus: les timbres de Myrsileia. 2, Le toponyme Myrsileia et l'onomastique de ses fabricants', *Revue archéologique*, n.s. 2: 331–48.

Davis, D. L. (2009), 'Commercial navigation in the Greek and Roman world', Ph.D. thesis. University of Texas at Austin.

De Andres, G. (1987), *Catalogo de los codices griegos de la Biblioteca Nacional Madrid*. Madrid.

De Boer, J. G. (2006), 'The Cimmerian invasions in Anatolia and the earliest Greek colonies in the Black sea area', *Eirene*, 42: 43–55.

de Bruijn, C. (1700), *Voyage au Levant*. Delft.

De Callataÿ, G. (2006), 'The colossus of Rhodes: ancient texts and modern representations', in C. R. Ligota and J.-L. Quantin (eds), *History of Scholarship: A Selection of Papers from the Seminar on the History of Scholarship held Annually at the Warburg Institute* (Oxford–London), 39–73.

De Romanis, F. (1997), 'Hypalos: distanze e venti tra Arabia e India nella scienza ellenistica', *Topoi: Orient-Occident*, 7: 671–92.

—— (2016), 'An exceptional survivor and its submerged background: the Periplus Maris Erythraei and the Indian Ocean travelogue tradition', in G. Colesanti and L. Lulli (eds), *Submerged Literature in Ancient Greek Culture: Case Studies* (Berlin–Boston), 97–110.

—— (2020), *The Indo-Roman Pepper Trade and the Muziris Papyrus*. Oxford.

de Stoop, E. (1911), *Vie d'Alexandre l'Acémète*. Paris.

Delehaye, H. (1923), *Les Saints stylites*. Brussels.

Derow, P. S. (2012), 'Polybius (1)', *Oxford Classical Dictionary*[4] 1174–5.

Desanges, J. (1978), *Recherches sur l'activité des Méditerranéens aux confins de l'Afrique'*. Rome.

—— (1980), *Pline l'Ancien, Histoire naturelle, livre V, 1re partie [§§1–46]: géographie. L'Afrique du Nord* (Collection des universités de France, série latine, 245). Paris. ['Budé' edition.]

—— (1983), 'Des interprètes chez les "Gorilles": réflexion sur un artifice dans le Périple d'Hannon', in *Atti del I congresso internazionale di studi Fenici e Punici, 1981*, i, 267–75.

—— (2008), *Pline l'Ancien, Histoire naturelle, livre VI, 4e partie [§§163–220]: l'Asie africaine sauf l'Egypte; les dimensions et les climats du monde habité* (Collection des universités de France, série latine, 390). Paris. ['Budé' edition.]

Desclos, M.-L., and Fortenbaugh, W. W. (eds 2011), *Strato of Lampsacus: Text, Translation, and Discussion*. New Brunswick.

Dettori, E. (2006), 'Aristea "corvo" e "sciamano" (?): Herodot. 4. 15', *Seminari romani di cultura greca*, 9: 87–103.

Dewing, H. B. (1924), 'Argonautic associations of the Bosporus', *Classical Journal*, 19. 8: 469–83.

Dey, H. W., and Goodman-Tchernov, B. (2010), 'Tsunamis and the port of Caesarea Maritima over the longue durée: a geoarchaeological perspective', *Journal of Roman Archaeology*, 23. 1: 265–84.

Dickey, E. (2011), 'Epimerismi Homerici', *The Homer Encyclopedia*, i: 255–6.
Dickinson, O. T. P. K. (2011), 'Catalogue of Ships', in M. Finkelberg (ed.), *The Homer Encyclopedia*, i (Chichester), 150–5.
Dicks, D. R. (1960), *The Geographical Fragments of Hipparchus*. London.
Diels, H. (1952), with W. Kranz, *Die Fragmente der Vorsokratiker*, 6th edn. 3 vols. Berlin.
—— and Kranz, W. (1959–60), *Die Fragmente der Vorsokratiker*, 9th edn, i–iii. Berlin.
Dierksmeier, L., et al. (eds 2021), *European Islands between Isolated and Connected Worlds: Interdisciplinary Long-term Perspectives*. Tübingen.
Dilke, O. A. W. (1985), *Greek and Roman Maps*. London/Ithaca.
—— (1987a), 'Cartography in the ancient world: a conclusion', in J. B. Harley and D. Woodward (eds), *The History of Cartography*, i (Chicago–London), 276–9.
—— (1987b), 'Cartography in the ancient world: an introduction', in J. B. Harley and D. Woodward (eds), *The History of Cartography*, i (Chicago–London), 105–6.
—— (1987c), 'Cartography in the Byzantine empire', in J. B. Harley and D. Woodward (eds), *The History of Cartography*, i (Chicago–London), 258–75.
—— (1987d), 'Itineraries and geographical maps in the early and late Roman empires', in J. B. Harley and D. Woodward (eds), *The History of Cartography*, i (Chicago–London), 234–57.
—— (1987e), 'Maps in the service of the state: Roman cartography to the end of the Augustan era', in J. B. Harley and D. Woodward (eds), *The History of Cartography*, i (Chicago–London), 201–11.
—— (1987f), *Mathematics and Measurement*. London.
—— (1987g), 'Roman large-scale mapping in the early empire', in J. B. Harley and D. Woodward (eds), *The History of Cartography*, i (Chicago–London), 212–33.
—— (1987h), 'The culmination of Greek cartography in Ptolemy', in J. B. Harley and D. Woodward (eds), *The History of Cartography*, i (Chicago–London), 177–200.
Diller, A. (1936), 'Two Greek forgeries of the sixteenth century', *American Journal of Philology*, 57. 2: 124–9.
—— (1937), 'The Vatopedi manuscript of Ptolemy and Strabo', *American Journal of Philology*, 58. 2: 174–84.
—— (1943), 'The anonymous Diagnosis of Ptolemaic geography', in anon. (ed.), *Classical Studies in honor of William Abbott Oldfather* (Urbana, Ill.), 39–49.
—— (1949), 'The ancient measurements of the Earth', *Isis*, 40: 7–8.
—— (1950), 'Julian of Ascalon on Strabo and the stade', *Classical Philology*, 45. 22–5.
—— (1952), *The Tradition of the Minor Greek Geographers*. Lancaster, Pa.–Oxford.
—— (1955), 'The authors named Pausanias', *Transactions and Proceedings of the American Philological Association*, 86: 268–79.
—— (1958), review of W. Aly, *De Strabonis codice rescripto; Strabon von Amaseia*, in *Gnomon*, 30. 7: 527–32.
—— (1969), 'Some false fragments', in anon. (ed.), *Classical Studies presented to Ben Edwin Perry: By his Students and Colleagues at the University of Illinois, 1924–60*

(Urbana), 27–30. Repr. in A. Diller, *Studies in Greek Manuscript Tradition* (Amsterdam, 1983), 63–6.

—— (1975a), 'Agathemerus, Sketch of Geography', *Greek, Roman and Byzantine Studies*, 16. 1: 59–76; repr. in id., *Studies in Greek Manuscript Tradition* (Amsterdam, 1983), 69–86.

—— (1975b), *The Textual Tradition of Strabo's Geography*. Amsterdam.

Dindorfius, G. (1825), *Stephanus Byzantinus cum annotationibus L. Holstenii, A. Berkelii et Th. Pinedo*. 4 vols. Leipzig.

Dion, R. (1977), *Aspects politiques de la géographie antique*. Paris.

Dobesch, G. (1995), *Das europäische 'Barbaricum' und die Zone der Mediterrankultur: ihre historische Wechselwirkung und das Geschichtsbild des Poseidonios*. Vienna.

Domínguez Monedero, A. J. (2010), 'El viaje de Hanón de Cartago y los mecanismos de exploración fenicios', in F. Marco Simón et al. (eds), *Viajeros, peregrinos y aventureros en el mundo antiguo* (Barcelona), 77–93.

—— (2017), 'Rex Iuba, monarca e intellectual helenistico, y la Hispania de Augusto', *Gerión*, 35: 61–85.

Doody, A. (2010), *Pliny's Encyclopaedia: The Reception of the Natural History*. Cambridge.

Dorfbauer, L. J. (2012), 'Der Dichter und zweimalige Proconsul Postumius Rufius Festus signo Avienius', *Mnemosyne*, 65. 2: 251–77.

Dover, K. J. (1983), 'Thucydides "as history" and "as literature"', *History and Theory*, 22. 1: 54–63.

Dowden, K. (2013), 'Poseidonios (87)', in *BNJ*².

—— (2016), 'Aristeas (35)', in *BNJ*².

Draelants, I. M. C. (2000), 'Le dossier des livres sur les animaux et les plantes de Iorach: tradition occidentale et orientale', in B. van den Abeele, A. Tihon, and I. M. C. Draelants (eds), *Occident et Proche-Orient: contacts scientifiques au temps des Croisades* (Turnhout), 191–276.

Draycott, J. L. (2010), 'The sacred crocodile of Juba II of Mauretania', *Acta Classica: Verhandelinge van die Klassieke Vereniging van Suid-Afrika—Proceedings of the Classical Association of South Africa*, 53: 211–17.

—— (2012), 'The symbol of Cleopatra Selene: reading crocodiles on coins in the late republic and early principate', *Acta Classica: Verhandelinge van die Klassieke Vereniging van Suid-Afrika—Proceedings of the Classical Association of South Africa*, 55: 43–56.

Drews, R. (1963), 'Ephorus and history written κατὰ γένος', *American Journal of Philology*, 84: 244–55.

Droß-Krüpe, K. (2013), 'Textiles and their merchants in Roman eastern trade', in M. Gleba and J. Pásztókai-Szeöke (eds), *Making Textiles in Pre-Roman and Roman Times* (Oxford), 149–60.

Dübner, F. (1856), *Plutarchi scripta moralia: ex codicibus quos possidet regia bibliotheca omnibus ab Konto cum Reiskiana edition collatis*. Paris.

Dueck, D. (2000), *Strabo of Amasia: A Greek Man of Letters in Augustan Rome*. London–New York.

—— (2005), 'The parallelogram and the pinecone: definition of geographical shapes in Greek and Roman geography on the evidence of Strabo', *Ancient Society*, 35: 19–57.

—— (2008a), 'Marinos of Tyre (100 CE)', *Encyclopedia of Ancient Natural Scientists* 533.

—— (2008b), 'Pausanias of Damaskos (125–95 BCE)', *Encyclopedia of Ancient Natural Scientists* 630–1.

—— (2009), 'Poetic citations in Latin prose works of philosophy', *Hermes*, 137. 3: 123–35.

—— (2011), 'Protagoras (2044)', in *FGrH* v.

—— (2012), with K. Brodersen, *Geography in Classical Antiquity*. Cambridge.

—— (2016), 'Travelling literature alphabetically: literary hodology in Giovanni Boccaccio', in F. J. González Ponce, F. J. Gómez Espelosín, and A. L. Chávez Reino (eds), *La letra y la carta: descripción verbal y representación gráfica en los diseños terrestres grecolatinos. Estudios en honor de Pietro Janni* (Seville), 321–35.

—— (2020), 'A lunar nation: the meaning of an Arcadian epithet, or, who is the most ancient of them all?', *Philologus*, 164. 1: 133–47.

—— (ed. 2017), *The Routledge Companion to Strabo*. London–New York.

—— Lindsay, H., and Pothecary, S. (eds 2005), *Strabo's Cultural Geography: The Making of a Kolossourgia*. Cambridge.

Duff, J. W., and Duff, A. M. (1934), *Minor Latin Poets* (Loeb Classical Library, 284.) London/Cambridge, Mass.

—— and —— (1982), *Minor Latin Poets* (Loeb Classical Library, 284; 434). 2 vols. Cambridge, Mass.

Dumitru, A. (2006), 'Byzance et les Philippes de Macédoine', *Revue des études grecques*, 119: 139–56.

Dyck, A. R. (1995), *Epimerismi Homerici*, ii. *Epimerismos continens qui ordine alphabetico traditi sunt. Lexicon αἱμωδεῖν quod vocatur seu verius ἐτυμολογίαι διάφοροι*. Berlin–New York.

Edelstein, L., and Kidd, I. G. (1989), *Posidonius*, 2nd edn, i: *The Fragments*. Cambridge.

Eichel, M. H., and Todd, J. M. (1976), 'A note on Polybios' voyage to Africa in 146 BC', *Classical Philology*, 71. 3: 237–43.

Eichholz, D. E. (1962), *Pliny, Natural History*, x. *Libri XXXVI–XXXVII* (Loeb Classical Library, 419). Cambridge, Mass.–London.

Eleftheriou, D. (2015), 'L'hétérogénéité du Palatinus Heidelbergensis gr. 398: nouvelles approches sur le manuscrit et la "collection philosophique"', in L. M. Ciolfi and

J. Devoge (eds), *VIIIe rencontres annuelles internationales des doctorants en études byzantines (2015)*, 37–45.

—— (2018), 'Pseudo-Antigonos de Carystos, Collection d'histoires curieuses', Ph.D. thesis. Université Paris Nanterre.

Ellmers, D. (2010), 'Der Krater von Vix und der Reisebericht des Pytheas von Massalia: Reisen griechischer Kaufleute über die Rhône nach Britannien im 6.–4. Jahrhundert v. Chr.', *Archäologisches Korrespondenzblatt: Urgeschichte, Römerzeit, Frühmittelalter*, 40. 3: 363–81.

Elsner, J. (2000), 'The Itinerarium Burdigalense: politics and salvation in the geography of Constantine's empire', *Journal of Roman Studies*, 90: 181–95.

Engels, J. (2004), 'Agatharchides von Knidos' Schrift Über das Rote Meer', in H. Heftner and K. Tomaschitz (eds), *Ad fontes! Festschrift für Gerhard Dobesch zum 65. Geburtstag am 15. September 2004* (Vienna), 179–92.

—— (2012), 'Artemidoros of Ephesos and Strabo of Amasia: common traditions of Greek cultural geography and Strabo's decisive importance in the history of reception of Artemidoros' Geographoumena', in C. Gallazzi et al. (eds), *Geografia e cartografia* (Intorno al papiro di Artemidoro, 2) (Milan), 139–55.

Ercolani, A., and Nicolai, R. (2011), 'Polybios von Megalopolis (2117)', in *FGrH* v.

Etiope, G., et al. (2006), 'The geological links of the ancient Delphic oracle (Greece): a reappraisal of natural gas occurrence and origin', *Geology*, 34. 10: 821–4.

Eustratiades, S., and Arcadios (1924), *Catalogue of the Greek Manuscripts in the Library of the Monastery of Vatopedi on Mt. Athos*. Cambridge, Mass.–Paris–London.

Evans, J., and Berggren, J. L. (2006), *Geminos's Introduction to the Phenomena: A Translation and Study of a Hellenistic Survey of Astronomy*. Princeton.

Evelyn-White, H. G. (1919), *Decimus Ausonius, Poems and Letters*, i: *Books 1–16* (Loeb Classical Library, 96). Cambridge, Mass./London.

Evers, K. G. (2017), *Worlds Apart Trading Together: The Organisation of Long Distance Trade Between Rome and India in Antiquity*. Oxford.

Fabricius, B. (1848), *Scylacis Periplus: ex recensione B. Fabrici . . .* Dresdae.

Fabricius, E. (1890), 'Über die Abfassungszeit der griechischen Städtebilder des Herakleides', in *Bonner Studien: Aufsätze aus der Alterthumswissenschaft Reinhard Kekulé zur Erinnerung an seine Lehrthätigkeit in Bonn gewidmet von seinen Schülern* (Berlin), 58–66.

Farrer, J. A. (1907), *Literary Forgeries*. London.

Faucher, T. (2018), 'Ptolemaic gold: the exploitation of gold in the eastern desert', in J.-P. Brun, et al. (eds), *The Eastern Desert of Egypt during the Greco-Roman Period: Archaeological Reports*, https://books.openedition.org/cdf/5241.

Febvre, L. (1925), with L. Bataillon, *A Geographical Introduction to History*. London.

Federspiel, M., and Levet, J.-P. (2018) with A. Cohen-Skalli and M. Cronier, *Pseudo-Aristote, Du monde; Positions et dénominations des vents; Des plantes*. Paris.

Fedi, M., et al. (2010), 'The Artemidorus papyrus: solving an ancient puzzle with radiocarbon and ion beam analysis measurements', *Radiocarbon*, 52. 2–3: 356–63.

Fernández Pomar, J. M. (1966), 'La colección de Uceda y los manuscritos griegos de Constantino Láscaris' *Emerita*, 34: 211–88.

Ferrari, G. (2008), *Alcman and the Cosmos of Sparta*. Chicago.

Ferrer Albelda, E. (ed. 2019), *La ruta de las Estrímnides: navegación y conocimiento del litoral atlántico de Iberia en la Antigüedad*. Alcalá de Henares.

Fıratlı, N., and Robert, L. (1964), *Les Stèles funeraires de Byzance gréco-romaine: avec l'édition et l'index commenté des épitaphes par Louis Robert*. Paris.

Fischer-Hansen, T., Nielsen, T. H., and Ampolo, C. (2004), 'Sikelia', in M. H. Hansen and T. H. Nielsen, *An Inventory of Archaic and Classical Poleis* (Oxford), 172–248.

Fleischer, K. (2020), *The Original Verses of Apollodorus' Chronica: Edition, Translation and Commentary on the First Iambic Didactic Poem in the Light of New Evidence*. Berlin–Boston.

Flensted-Jensen, P. (2004), 'Karia', in M. H. Hansen and T. H. Nielsen, *An Inventory of Archaic and Classical Poleis* (Oxford), 1108–37.

—— and Hansen, M. H. (1996), 'Pseudo-Skylax' use of the term polis', in M. H. Hansen and K. Raaflaub (eds), *More Studies in the Ancient Greek Polis* (Stuttgart), 137–67.

—— and —— (2007), 'Pseudo-Skylax', in M. H. Hansen (ed.), *The Return of the Polis: The Use and Meanings of the Word Polis in Archaic and Classical Sources* (Stuttgart), 204–42.

Folkerts, M. (2006), 'Eudoxus [1] of Cnidus', in H. Cancik, H. Schneider, and C. F. Salazar (eds), *Brill's New Pauly* (Leiden).

Fontenrose, J. (1988), *Didyma: Apollo's Oracle, Cult, and Companions*. Berkeley–Los Angeles–London.

Forster, E. S., and Furley, D. J. (1955), *Aristotle, On Sophistical Refutations; On Coming-to-be and Passing Away; On the Cosmos* (Loeb Classical Library, 400). London.

Fortenbaugh, W. W., and Schütrumpf, E. (eds 2000), *Dicaearchus of Messana: Text, Translation, and Discussion*. New Brunswick–London.

—— White, S. A. (eds 2004), *Lyco of Troas and Hieronymus of Rhodes: Text, Translation, and Discussion*. New Brunswick, NJ–London.

Foss, C. (2000), 'Map 52 Byzantium', in R. J. A. Talbert (ed.), *Map-by-map Directory: To accompany Barrington Atlas of the Greek and Roman World*, ii (Princeton–Oxford), 785–95.

Fossey, J. M. (1988), *Topography and Population of Ancient Boiotia*, i. Chicago.

Fowler, R. L. (2000), *Early Greek Mythography*, i. *Texts*. Oxford.

—— (2001), 'Early historiē and literacy', in N. Luraghi (ed.), *The Historian's Craft in the Age of Herodotus* (Oxford), 95–115.

—— (2013), *Early Greek Mythography*, ii. *Commentary*. Oxford.

Fraser, P. M. (1972), *Ptolemaic Alexandria*. 3 vols. Oxford.

—— and Matthews, E. (eds 1987), with A. Griffin, *et al.*, *The Aegean Islands, Cyprus, Cyrenaica* (A Lexicon of Greek Personal Names, 1). Oxford.

Frick, O. (1865), 'Conjecteanorum in Dionysii Byzantii Anaplum Bosporum particulam I', *Programm des Gymnasiums zu Burg*.

Frisk, H. (1927), *Le Périple de la mer Érythrée*. Gothenburg.

Furley, D. J. (1955), 'Aristotle, On the Cosmos', in E. S. Forster and D. J. Furley (eds), *Aristotle, On Sophistical Refutations; On Coming-to-be and Passing Away; On the Cosmos* (Loeb Classical Library, 400; London), 333–409.

Gärtner, H. A. (2006), 'Pytheas [4]', in *Brill's New Pauly*.

—— (2006), 'Scymnus [1]', in *Brill's New Pauly*.

Gagné, R. (2020), 'Mirages of ethnicity and the distant north in book IV of the Histories: Hyperboreans, Arimaspians, and Issedones', in T. J. Figueira and C. Soares (eds), *Ethnicity and Identity in Herodotus* (Abingdon), 237–57.

Gail, J. F. (1826–31), *Geographi Graeci minores*. 3 vols. Paris.

Gaisford, T. (1836), *Paroemiographi Graeci: quorum pars nunc primum ex codicibus manuscriptis vulgatur*. Oxford.

Gallazzi, C., Kramer, B., and Settis, S. (eds 2008), with G. Adornato, A. C. Cassio, and A. Soldati, *Il papiro di Artemidoro (P. Artemid.)*. 2 vols. Milan.

——, ——, and —— (eds 2010), *Contesto culturale, lingua, stile e tradizione* (Intorno al papiro di Artemidoro, 1). Milan.

——, ——, and —— (eds 2012), *Geografia e cartografia* (Intorno al papiro di Artemidoro, 2). Milan.

Garzón Díaz, J. (2008), *Geógrafos griegos: Escílax de Carianda; Hannón de Cartago; Heraclides crético; Dionisio, hijo de Califonte*. Oviedo.

Garzya, A. (1963), *Dionysii Ixeuticon seu de Aucupio libri tres*. Leipzig.

—— (1989), *Opere di Sinesio di Cirene: epistole operette inni*. Turin.

Gawlikowski, M. (1996), 'Thapsacus and Zeugma: the crossing of the Euphrates in antiquity', *Iraq*, 58: 123–33.

Gehrke, H.-J. (2016), 'The "revolution" of Alexander the Great: old and new in the world's view', in S. Bianchetti, M. R. Cataudella, and H.-J. Gehrke (eds), *Brill's Companion to Ancient Geography: The Inhabited World in Greek and Roman Tradition* (Leiden–Boston), 78–97.

—— (n.d.), 'About Die Fragmente der Griechischen Historiker continued Part V', in *FGrH* v.

—— and Meier, F. (eds 2011–), *Fragmente der griechischen Historiker*, v (Leiden).

Geiger, J. (1992), 'Julian of Ascalon', *Journal of Hellenic Studies*, 112: 31–43.

Gelenius, S. (1533), Ἀρριανοῦ Περίπλους Εὐξείνου Πόντου, τοῦ αὐτοῦ Περίπλου Ἐρυθρᾶς θαλάσσης, Ἄννωνος Περίπλους Λιβύης, Πλουτάρχου Περὶ ποταμῶν καὶ ὀρῶν, Ἐπιτομὴ τῶν τοῦ Στράβωνος Γεωγραφικῶν/*Arriani et Hannonis Periplus, Plutarchus De fluminibus et montibus, Strabonis Epitome*. Basel.

Geus, K. (2002), *Eratosthenes von Kyrene: Studien zur hellenistischen Kultur- und Wissenschaftsgeschichte*. Munich.

—— (2007), 'Die Geographika des Eratosthenes von Kyrene: Altes und Neues in Terminologie und Methode', in M. Rathmann (ed.), *Wahrnehmung und Erfassung geographischer Räume in der Antike* (Mainz am Rhein), 111–22.

—— (2011), review of D. W. Roller, *Eratosthenes' Geography*, in *Isis*, 102. 3: 554.

—— (2014), 'A "day's journey" in Herodotus' Histories', in K. Geus and M. Thiering (eds), *Features of Common Sense Geography: Implicit Knowledge Structures in Ancient Geographical Texts* (Berlin), 147–56.

—— (2014–15), 'Alexander und Eratosthenes: der Feldherr und der Geograph', *Geographia antiqua*, 23–4: 53–61.

—— (2016), 'Progress in the sciences: astronomy and Hipparchus', in S. Bianchetti, M. R. Cataudella, and H.-J. Gehrke (eds), *Brill's Companion to Ancient Geography: The Inhabited World in Greek and Roman Tradition* (Leiden–Boston), 150–60.

—— (2017), 'Wer ist Marinos von Tyros? Zur Hauptquelle des Ptolemaios in seiner Geographie', *Geographia antiqua*, 26: 13–22.

—— (forthcoming), 'Hipparchos von Nikaia (2112)', in *FGrH* v.

—— and Dan, A.-C. (2018), 'Ein "vielteiliges" Meer? Der Pontos Euxeinos in Pseudo-Aristoteles, De mundo, 393a31. Ein Beitrag zur "platonischen" Geographie und armenischen Nebenüberlieferung', *Mediterraneo antico*, 21. 1–2: 399–416.

—— and Rathmann, M. (eds 2013), *Vermessung der Oikoumene*. Berlin–Boston.

—— and Thiering, M. (2014), 'Common sense geography and mental modelling: setting the stage', in K. Geus and M. Thiering (eds), *Features of Common Sense Geography: Implicit Knowledge Structures in Ancient Geographical Texts* (Berlin), 5–15.

—— and —— (eds 2014), *Features of Common Sense Geography: Implicit Knowledge Structures in Ancient Geographical Texts*. Berlin.

Geyer, P., et al. (1965), *Itineraria et alia geographica*. Turnhout.

Gibson, R. K., and Morello, R. (eds 2011), *Pliny the Elder: Themes and Contexts*. Leiden–Boston.

Gill, D. W. J. (1988), 'Silver anchors and cargoes of oil: some observations on Phoenician trade in the western Mediterranean', *Papers of the British School at Rome*, 56: 1–12.

Giovannini, A. (1993), 'Greek cities and Greek commonwealth', in A. W. Bulloch, *et al.* (eds), *Images and Ideologies: Self-definition in the Hellenistic World* (Berkeley–Los Angeles–London), 265–86.

Gisinger, F. (1927), 'Skymnos 1', *Pauly–Wissowa, Realencyclopädie der classischen Altertumswissenschaft* ²iii. 1. 661–87.

—— (1937), 'Timosthenes (3) von Rhodos', *Pauly–Wissowa, Realencyclopädie der classischen Altertumswissenschaft* ²vi. 2. 1310–22.

Giustetti, O. (2018), 'Il Papiro di Artemidoro è un falso: venne pagato quasi tre milioni di euro', *La Repubblica* (18 Dec.).

—— (2019), 'Torino, il Mibac chiude il caso: "ecco perché è falso il Papiro di Artemidoro"', *La Repubblica* (5 Jan.).

Gleede, B. (2021), *Antiochenische Kosmographie? Zur Begründung und Verbreitung nichtsphärischer Weltkonzeptionen in der antiken Christenheit*. Berlin.

Gómez Espelosín, F. J. (2021), 'Alexander and the Ocean', *Karanos*, 4: 91–7.

González Ponce, F. J. (1995), *Avieno y el periplo*. Ecija.

—— (2008a), 'Los huidizos gorilas de Hanón y la tradición helenística sobre la zoología fabulosa de la India', in J. M. Candau Morón *et al*. (eds), *Libyae lustrare extrema: realidad y literatura en la visión grecorromana de* África. *Hommaje al Prof. Jehan Desanges* (Seville), 291–304.

—— (2008b), *Periplo de Hanón y autores de los siglos VI y V a.C.* (Periplógrafos griegos, 1: Épocas arcaica y clásica, 1). Zaragoza.

—— (2011), 'Hanno von Karthago (2208)', in *FGrH* v.

—— (2013a), 'Euthymenes of Massalia (2207)', in *FGrH* v.

—— (2013b), 'Phileas von Athen (2038)', in *FGrH* v.

—— (2019a), 'Agatémero y las reminiscencias de una literatura náutica', *Geographia antiqua*, 28: 87–104.

—— (2019b), 'Los restos del periplo de Himilcón en el contexto de la literatura grecolatina', in E. Ferrer Albelda (ed.), *La ruta de las Estrímnides: navegación y conocimiento del litoral atlántico de Iberia en la Antigüedad* (Alcalá de Henares), 185–204.

—— and Chávez Reino, A. L. (eds 2021), *El espacio en el tiempo: geografía e historiografía en la antigua Grecia* (= *Estudios clásicos*, 160). Madrid.

Gothofredus, J. (1628), *Vetus orbis descriptio*. Geneva.

Gould, P. R. (1972), 'On mental maps', in P. W. English and R. C. Mayfield (eds), *Man, Space, and Environment: Concepts in Contemporary Human Geography* (New York–London–Toronto), 260–82.

Gow, A. S. F., and Page, D. L. (1965), *The Greek Anthology: Hellenistic Epigrams*. 2 vols. Cambridge.

Gozzoli, S. (1978), 'Etnografia e politica in Agatarchide', *Athenaeum*, 56: 54–79.

Graham, D. W. (2010), *The Texts of Early Greek Philosophy: The Complete Fragments and Selected Testimonies of the Major Presocratics*. 2 vols. Cambridge.

Greaves, D. D. (1994), 'Dionysius Periegetes and the hellenistic poetic and geographic traditions', Ph.D. thesis. Stanford University.

Gregorić, P. (2020), 'The eternity of the cosmos (Chapter 5)', in P. Gregorić and G. Karamanolis (eds), *Pseudo-Aristotle, De Mundo (On the Cosmos): A Commentary* (Cambridge), 149–75.

—— and Karamanolis, G. (2020a), 'Introduction', in iid. (eds), *Pseudo-Aristotle, De Mundo (On the Cosmos): A Commentary* (Cambridge), 1–13.

—— and —— (eds 2020b), *Pseudo-Aristotle, De Mundo (On the Cosmos): A Commentary*. Cambridge.

Grélois, P. (2007), *Pierre Gilles, Itinéraires byzantins; Lettre à un ami; Du Bosphore de Thrace; De la topographie de Constantinople et de ses antiquités: introduction, traduction du latin et notes*. Paris.

Griffith, M. (1983), 'Personality in Hesiod', *Classical Antiquity*, 2: 37–65.

Gronovius, J. (1697), *Geographica antiqua: hoc est Scylacis Periplus Maris Mediterranei, Anonymi Periplus Maeotidis paludis et Ponti Euxini, Agathemeri Hypotyposis geographiae, omnia Graeco-Latina. Anonymi Expositio totius mundi, Latina*. Leiden.

Groom, N. (1981), *Frankincense and Myrrh: A Study of the Arabian Incense Trade*. London–New York/Beirut.

Grüll, T. (2014), 'Expositio totius mundi et gentium: a peculiar work on the commerce of Roman empire from the mid-fourth century—compiled by a Syrian textile dealer?', in Z. Csabai (ed.), *Studies in Economic and Social History of the Ancient Near East in Memory of Péter Vargyas* (Budapest), 629–42.

Grumeza, L. (2021), 'Sarmatae and Sarmatia: from the north Pontic area to the Great Hungarian Plain', in D. C. Braund and V. F. Stolba (eds), *Environment and Habitation around the Ancient Black Sea* (Berlin–Boston), 157–76.

Gualandri, I. (1982), 'Avieno e Dionisio il Periegeta: per un riesame del problema', in *Studi in onore di Aristide Colonna* (Perugia), 151–65.

Güngerich, R. (1927), *Dionysii Byzantii Anaplus Bospori*. Berlin; repr. with revisions 1958.

Guillaumin, J.-B., and Bernard, G. (2021), *Aviénus, Les Rivages maritimes* (Collection des universités de France, série latine, 433). Paris. ['Budé' edition.]

Guzmán Guerra, A. (1977), 'Agatémero y su ὑποτύπωσις: a propósito de la edición de A. Diller y los recentiores españoles, Scorialensis Ω I. 11 (512 Revilla-de Andrés) y Matritensis N 138 (4759) B. N.', *Habis*, 8: 19–22.

Gyllius, P. (1561), *De Bosporo Thracio Libri III*. Lyons.

Gysembergh, V. (2015), 'Eudoxe de Cnide: une édition traduite et commentée des fragments et testimonia', Ph.D. thesis. Université de Reims Champagne-Ardennes.

—— (2016), 'Frontières et confins dans la cartographie d'Eudoxe de Cnide', in H. Berthelot, *et al.* (eds), *Vivre et penser les frontières dans le monde méditerranéen antique: actes du colloque tenu à l'Université Paris-Sorbonne, les 29 et 30 juin 2013* (Bordeaux), 31–41.

—— (2019), 'A synoptic study of the number of stars in the constellations of Hipparchus' star catalogue', in A. Hadravová, P. Hadrova, and K. Lippincott (eds), *The Stars in the Classical and Medieval Traditions* (Prague), 13–23.

—— (2020), 'La réputation sulfureuse de Natale Conti, helléniste faussaire', in C. Bohnert and R. Darmon (eds), *La Mythologie de Natale Conti éditée par Jean Baudoin, livre I (1627)* (Reims), 183–202.

Habicht, C. (1998), *Pausanias' Guide to Ancient Greece*. Berkeley–Los Angeles–London.

—— (2013), 'Eudoxus of Cyzicus and the Ptolemaic exploration of the sea route to India', in K. Buraselis, M. Stefanou, and D. J. Thompson (eds), *The Ptolemies, the Sea and the Nile: Studies in Waterborne Power* (Cambridge), 197–206.

Hadas, M. (1935), 'Utopian sources in Herodotos', *Classical Philology*, 30: 113–21.

Hammerstaedt, J. (2009), 'Warum Simonides den Artemidorpapyrus nicht hätte fälschen können: eine seltene Schreibung für Tausender in Inschriften und Papyri', *Chiron*, 39: 323–37.

—— (2012), 'Artemidorus fr. 21 Stiehle and its relationship to the Artemidorus papyrus', *Historia*, 61. 3: 309–24 (bibl., 357–61).

—— (2013), 'Geographische Raumerfassung und Weltdarstellung im Artemidorpapyrus', in D. Boschung, T. Greub, and J. Hammerstaedt (eds), *Geographische Kenntnisse und ihre konkreten Ausformungen* (Paderborn), 137–68.

Hammond, M. (2013), with J. Atkinson, *Arrian, Alexander the Great: The Anabasis and the Indica* (Oxford World's Classics). Oxford.

Hammond, N. G. L. (1967), *Epirus: The Geography, the Ancient Remains, the History and the Topography of Epirus and Adjacent Areas*. Oxford.

Hanigan, D. R. (2022), 'Geography in couplets? A note on the fragment(s) of Zenothemis' Periplous', *Mnemosyne*, 75: 521–30.

—— and Kynaston, G. R. (2023), 'Autopsy and didactic authority: rethinking the prologue of the Periodos to Nicomedes', *Classical Quarterly*, 72. 2: 558–72.

Hannah, R. (2008), *Time in Antiquity*. Abingdon.

Hansen, M. H. (1995), 'Kome: a study in how the Greeks designated and classified settlements which were not poleis', in M. H. Hansen and K. A. Raaflaub (eds), *Studies in the Ancient Greek Polis* (Stuttgart), 45–81.

—— (1997), 'Hekataios' use of the word polis in his Periegesis', in T. H. Nielsen (ed.), *Yet More Studies in the Ancient Greek Polis* (Stuttgart), 17–27.

—— and Nielsen, T. H. (2004), *An Inventory of Archaic and Classical Poleis*. Oxford.

Harley, J. B., and Woodward, D. (eds 1987), *The History of Cartography*, i. *Cartography in Prehistoric, Ancient, and Medieval Europe and the Mediterranean*. Chicago–London.

Harris, W. V. (ed. 2005), *Rethinking the Mediterranean*. Oxford.

Harrison, S. J. (2000), *Apuleius: A Latin Sophist*. Oxford–New York.

—— (2007), 'The primal voyage and the ocean of epos: two aspects of metapoetic imagery in Catullus, Virgil and Horace', *Dictynna*, 4 (unpaginated).

Hartmann, U. (2017), 'Die Parthischen Stationen des Isidor von Charax: eine Handelsroute, eine Militärkarte oder ein Werk geographischer Gelehrsamkeit?', in J. Wiesehöfer and S. Müller (eds), *Parthika: Greek and Roman Authors' Views of the Arsacid Empire* (Wiesbaden), 87–125.

Hartog, F. (1988), *The Mirror of Herodotus: The Representation of the Other in the Writing of History*. Berkeley–London.

Hasluck, F. W. (1909), 'The Marmara islands', *Journal of Hellenic Studies*, 29: 6–18.

Hatzilambrou, R. (2022), 'A new papyrus of Strabo's Geographica (12.3.1)', *Pylon*, 2.

Hauben, H. (1996), 'Timosthène et les autres amiraux de nationalité rhodienne au service des Ptolémées', in G. Gkizelis (ed.), Πρακτικά του διεθνούς επιστημονικού συμποσίου 'Ρόδος: 24 αιώνες'—*Proceedings of the International Scientific Symposium 'Rhodes: 24 Centuries': 1–5 Οκτωβρίου 1992—Oct. 1–5, 1992* (Athens), 220–42.

Hauser, S. R. (2017), 'Isidor von Charax Σταθμοί Παρθικοί: Annäherungen an den Autor, den Routenverlauf und die Bedeutung des Werkes', in J. Wiesehöfer and S. Müller (eds), *Parthika: Greek and Roman Authors' Views of the Arsacid Empire* (Wiesbaden), 127–87.

Head, B. V. (1911), with G. F. Hill, G. Macdonald, and W. Wroth, *Historia Numorum: A Manual of Greek Numismatics*, New and enlarged edn. Oxford.

Healy, J. F. (1999), *Pliny the Elder on Science and Technology*. Oxford.

Helm, R. (1955), 'Der Stadiasmos des mittelländischen Meeres', in A. Bauer and R. Helm, *Die Chronik*, 2nd edn (Hippolytus' Werke, 4; Berlin), 43–69.

Henry, R. (1959), *Photius, Bibliothèque*, i. *Codices 1–83* (Collection des universités de France, série grecque, 137). Paris. ['Budé' edition.]

—— (1974), *Photius, Bibliothèque*, vii. *Codices 246–256* (Collection des universités de France, série grecque, 229). Paris. ['Budé' edition.]

Hercher, R. (1851), *Plutarchi Libellus de fluviis*. Leipzig.

—— (1855–6), 'Über die Glaubwürdigkeit der Neuen Geschichte des Ptolemaeus Chennus', in A. Fleckeisen (ed.), *Jahrbücher für classische Philologie*, 1. Supplementband (Leipzig), 269–93.

Hexter, J. H. (1972), 'Fernand Braudel and the monde braudellien', *Journal of Modern History*, 44. 4: 480–539; repr. in J. H. Hexter, *On Historians* (Cambridge, Mass., 1979), 61–145 (ch. 3).

Hillgruber, M. (2019), review of S. L. Radt, *Strabons Geographika*, in *Gnomon*, 91. 2: 108–25.

Hladký, V. (2020), 'God's many names (Chapter 7)', in P. Gregorić and G. Karamanolis (eds), *Pseudo-Aristotle, De Mundo (On the Cosmos): A Commentary* (Cambridge), 213–30.

Hoffmann, S. F. W. (1838), 'Fragmente der Geographie des Artemidorus', in his *Die Iberer im Westen und Osten: eine Ethnographische Untersuchung [. . .]* (Leipzig), 221–88.

Hofmann, I. (1970), 'Zur Kombination von Elephant und Riesenschlange in Altertum', Ἄνθρωπος, 65: 625–6.

Honigmann, E. (1939), *Le Synekdèmos d'Hiéroklès: et l'opuscule géographique de Georges de Chypre*. Brussels.

Hope Simpson, R., and Lazenby, J. F. (1970), *The Catalogue of Ships in Homer's Iliad*. Oxford.

Horden, J. N. P. B., and Purcell, N. (2000), *The Corrupting Sea*. Oxford–Malden, Mass.

—— and —— (2006), 'The Mediterranean and "the new thalassology"', *American Historical Review*, 111. 3: 722–40.

—— and —— (2020), *The Boundless Sea: Writing Mediterranean History*. London–New York.

Hornblower, S., and Spawforth, A. J. S., with E. Eidinow (eds 2012), *The Oxford Classical Dictionary*, 4th edn. Oxford–New York.

Hosgormez, H., Etiope, G., and Yalçin, N. (2008), 'New evidence for a mixed inorganic and organic origin of the Olympic Chimaera fire (Turkey): a large onshore seepage of abiogenic gas', *Geofluids*, 4. 8: 263–73.

Householder, F. W., Jr, and Prakken, D. W. (1945), 'A Ptolemaic graffito in New York', *Transactions of the American Philological Association*, 76: 108–16.

Howard, A. A. (1893), 'The αὐλός or tibia', *Harvard Studies in Classical Philology*, 4: 1–60.

Hubbell, H. M. (1935), 'Ptolemy's zoo', *Classical Journal*, 31: 68–76.

Hudson, J. (1698–1712), with H. Dodwell, *Geographiae veteris scriptores Graeci minores: cum interpretatione Latina, dissertationibus, ac annotationibus*. 4 vols. Oxford.

Hübner, W. (2006), 'Hipparchos [6]', in *Brill's New Pauly*.

Huitink, L. (2019), '"There was a river on their left-hand side": Xenophon's Anabasis, arrival scenes, reflector narrative and the evolving language of Greek historiography', in A. Willi (ed.), *Formes et fonctions des langues littéraires en Grèce ancienne: neuf exposés suivis de discussions* (Vandœuvres, Geneva), 185–226.

Hunger, H. (1967), 'Palimpsest-Fragmente aus Herodians Καθολικὴ προσῳδία, Buch 5-7: Cod. Vindob. Hist. Gr. 10', *Jahrbuch der Österreichischen Byzantinischen Gesellschaft*, 16: 1–33.

Hunt, D. (2004), 'Holy Land itineraries: mapping the Bible in late Roman Palestine', in R. J. A. Talbert and K. Brodersen (eds), *Space in the Roman World: Its Perception and Presentation* (Münster), 97–110.

Hunter, R. L. (1989), *Apollonius of Rhodes, Argonautica, Book III* (Cambridge Greek and Latin Classics). Cambridge.

—— (2004), 'The Periegesis of Dionysius and the traditions of hellenistic poetry', *Revue des études anciennes*, 106: 217–32.

—— (2006), 'The prologue of the periodos to Nicomedes ("Pseudo-Scymnus")', in M. A. Harder et al. (eds), *Beyond the Canon* (Leuven), 123–40.

Huntingford, G. W. B. (1980), *The Periplus of the Erythraean Sea: By an Unknown Author*. London.

Huß, W. (1993), 'Das afrikanische Unternehmen des Hanno', in G. Winkler (ed.), *C. Plinius Secundus d. Ä., Naturkunde, lateinisch–deutsch, Buch V: Geographie. Afrika und Asien* (Sammlung Tusculum; Munich), 354–63.

—— and Huß, B. (2006), 'Genre, genre theory', in H. Cancik, H. Schneider, and C. F. Salazar (eds), *Brill's New Pauly* (Leiden).
Hutchinson, G. O. (1988), *Hellenistic Poetry*. Oxford.
Hutton, W. (2005), *Describing Greece: Landscape and Literature in the Periegesis of Pausanias*. Cambridge.

Ilyushechkina, E. (2010), 'Studien zu Dionysios von Alexandria'. Ph.D. thesis. Universiteit van Groningen.
—— (2011) 'Die sakrale Geographie: zu einigen Passagen des Apollonios Rhodios in der Bearbeitung des Dionysios Periegetes', in M. A. Harder *et al.* (eds), *Gods and Religion in Hellenistic Poetry* (Leuven), 165–79.
——, Görz, G., and Thiering, M. (2014), 'Towards a cognitive-linguistic reconstruction of the spatial orientation in ancient texts: the example of Dionysius Periegetes', in K. Geus and M. Thiering (eds), *Features of Common Sense Geography: Implicit Knowledge Structures in Ancient Geographical Texts* (Berlin), 245–63.
Ippolito, A. (2006), 'Hestiaea', in *Lexikon of Greek Grammarians of Antiquity* (Leiden).
Irby, G. L. (2012), 'Mapping the world: Greek initiatives from Homer to Eratosthenes', in R. J. A. Talbert (ed.), *Ancient Perspectives: Maps and their Place in Mesopotamia, Egypt, Greece, and Rome* (Chicago), 81–107.
—— (2020), 'Tracing the orbis terrarum from Tingentera', in D. W. Roller (ed.), *New Directions in the Study of Ancient Geography*, 103–34.
—— (2021), *Using and Conquering the Watery World in Greco-Roman Antiquity*. London.
Irwin, E. (2015), 'Imperialism, ethics and the popularization of medical theory in later fifth-century Athens: Airs, Waters, Places', Ἀριάδνη, 22: 57–92.
Isaac, B. (2004), *The Invention of Racism in Classical Antiquity*. Princeton.
Ivantchik, A. I. (1993), 'La datation du poème l'Arimaspée d'Aristéas de Proconnèse', *L'Antiquité classique*, 62: 35–67.

Jacob, C. (1981), 'L'œil et la mémoire: sur la Périégèse de la Terre habitée de Denys', in C. Jacob and F. Lestringant (eds), *Arts et légendes d'espaces: figures du voyage et rhétoriques du monde* (Paris), 21–97.
—— (1990), *La Description de la terre habitée de Denys d'Alexandrie: ou la leçon de géographie*. Paris.
Jacoby, F. (1923–58), *Die Fragmente der griechischen Historiker*. 3 in 16 vols. Berlin–Leiden.
Jameson, S. (1968), 'Chronology of the campaigns of Aelius Gallus and C. Petronius', *Journal of Roman Studies*, 58: 71–84.
Janin, R. (1964), *Constantinople byzantine: développement urbain et répertoire topographique*, 2nd edn. Paris.

—— (1969), *Les Églises et les monastères*, 2nd edn (La Géographie écclésiastique de l'empire byzantine, 1: Le Siège de Constantinople et le patriarcat œcuménique, 3). Paris.

—— (1975), *Les Églises et les monastères des grands centres byzantins: Bithynie, Hellespont, Latros, Galèsios, Trébizonde, Athènes, Thessalonique* (La Géographie écclésiastique de l'empire byzantine, 2). Paris.

Janko, R. (2009), review of L. Canfora, C. Gallazzi *et al.*, [1] *The True History of the So-called Artemidorus Papyrus;* [2] *Il papiro di Artemidoro;* [3] *Il papiro di Artemidoro*, in *Classical Review*, 59. 2: 403-10.

—— (2022), 'Response: Janko on Bondí on Thomas, Art, Science, and the Natural World in the Ancient Mediterranean, 300 BC to AD 100', *Bryn Mawr Classical Review*, 2022.12.27.

Janni, P. (1982), review of A. Peretti, *Il periplo di Scilace*, in *Ath.*, 66: 602-7.

—— (1984), *La mappa e il periplo: cartografia antica e spazio odologico*. Rome.

—— (2016), 'The sea of the Greeks and Romans', in S. Bianchetti, M. R. Cataudella, and H.-J. Gehrke (eds), *Brill's Companion to Ancient Geography: The Inhabited World in Greek and Roman Tradition* (Leiden-Boston), 21-42.

Jeffreys, E., Jeffreys, M., and Scott, R. (1986), with B. Croke, *et al.*, *The Chronicle of John Malalas: A Translation*. Melbourne.

Jirsa, J. (2020), 'The sublunary domain (Chapters 2-3, 392a31-393a8)', in P. Gregorić and G. Karamanolis (eds), *Pseudo-Aristotle, De Mundo (On the Cosmos): A Commentary* (Cambridge), 62-79.

Jones, G. D. B., and Little, J. H. (1971), 'Coastal settlement in Cyrenaica', *Journal of Roman Studies*, 61: 64-79.

Jones, H. L. (ed. 1917-32), with J. R. S. Sterrett, *The Geography of Strabo* (Loeb Classical Library, 49-50; 182; 196; 211; 223; 241; 267). 8 vols. Cambridge, Mass./London.

Jones, N. F. (2010), 'Timosthenes of Rhodos (354)', in *BNJ²*.

Jouanna, J. (1996), *Hippocrate, Airs, eaux, lieux* (Collection des universités de France, série grecque, 374). Paris. ['Budé' edition.]

Kaiser, S. I. (2010), *Die Fragmente des Aristoxenos aus Tarent*. Zürich.

Kaldellis, A. (2005), 'The Works and Days of Hesychios the Illustrious of Miletos', *Greek, Roman and Byzantine Studies*, 45: 381-403.

Kaplan, P. G. (2008), 'The function of the early periploi', *Classical Bulletin*, 84. 2: 27-44.

—— (2009), 'Skylax of Karyanda (709)', in *BNJ*.

—— (2018), 'Early Greek geography', in P. T. Keyser and J. Scarborough (eds), *Oxford Handbook of Science and Medicine in the Classical World* (Oxford), 195-213.

—— (2019), 'Skylax of Karyanda (709)', in *BNJ²*.

Karamanolis, G. (2020), 'On philosophy and its proper subject (Chapter 1)', in P. Gregorić and G. Karamanolis (eds), *Pseudo-Aristotle, De Mundo (On the Cosmos): A Commentary* (Cambridge), 14-32.

Karttunen, K. (1997), *India and the Hellenistic World*. Helsinki.

Katsonopoulou, D. (2016), 'Natural catastrophes in the gulf of Corinth, northwestern Peloponnese, from prehistory to late antiquity: the example of Helike', in J. Borsch and L. Carrara (eds), *Erdbeben in der Antike: Deutungen—Folgen—Repräsentationen* (Tübingen), 137-52.

Kelder, J. (2017), 'Catalogue of Ships', in R. S. Bagnall, *et al.* (eds), *Encyclopedia of Ancient History* (Malden, Mass.).

Kelly, G. (2004), 'Ammianus and the great tsunami', *Journal of Roman Studies*, 94: 141-67.

Kessler, D. (2001), 'Monkeys and baboons', in D. B. Redford (ed.), *The Oxford Encyclopedia of Ancient Egypt*, ii (New York), 428-32.

Kessler, K., and Burian, J. (2006), 'Itinerare', in *Brill's New Pauly*.

Keyser, P. T. (2000), 'The geographical work of Dikaiarchos', in W. W. Fortenbaugh and E. Schütrumpf (eds), *Dicaearchus of Messana: Text, Translation, and Discussion* (New Brunswick-London), 353-72.

—— (2008a), 'Massiliot periplous (520-350 BCE?)', *Encyclopedia of Ancient Natural Scientists* 535.

—— (2008b), 'On the Kosmos (80-20 BCE)', *Encyclopedia of Ancient Natural Scientists* 487-8.

—— and Irby-Massie, G. L. (2008), *The Encyclopedia of Ancient Natural Scientists: The Greek Tradition and its Many Heirs*. London-New York.

Khan, Y. Z. N. (2002), 'A commentary on Dionysius of Alexandria's Guide to the Inhabited World, 174-382', Ph.D. thesis. University College London.

—— (2004), 'Denys lecteur des Phénomènes d'Aratos', *Revue des études anciennes*, 106. 1: 233-46.

Kidd, I. G. (1988), *Posidonius*, ii. *The Commentary* (Cambridge Classical Texts and Commentaries, 14 a-b). 2 vols. Cambridge.

—— (1999), *Posidonius*, iii. *The Translation of the Fragments* (Cambridge Classical Texts and Commentaries, 36). Cambridge.

Kindstrand, J. F. (1981), *Anacharsis: The Legend and the Apophthegmata*. Uppsala.

Kinneging, A. A. M. (2009), *The Geography of Good and Evil: Philosophical Investigations*. Wilmington, Del.

Kirk, A. (2021), *Ancient Greek Lists: Catalogue and Inventory Across Genres*. Cambridge.

Kislinger, E. (2021), 'Neorion and Prosphorion: the old harbours on the Golden Horn', in F. Daim and E. Kislinger (eds), *The Byzantine Harbours of Constantinople* (Heidelberg), 133-9.

Klostermann, E. (1904), *Das Onomasticon der biblischen Ortsnamen* (Eusebius' Werke, 3. 1). Leipzig.

Klotz, A. (1930-1), 'Die geographischen Commentarii des Agrippa und ihre Überreste', *Klio*, 24 (n.s. 6): 38-58 and 386-466.

Knapp, A. B. (ed. 1992), *Archaeology, Annales and Ethnohistory*. Cambridge.
Kock, T. (1880–8), *Comicorum Atticorum fragmenta*. 3 vols. Leipzig.
Koelsch, W. A. (2013), *Geography and the Classical World: Unearthing Historical Geography's Forgotten Past*. London.
König, R. (1981), with G. Winkler, *C. Plinius Secundus d. Ä., Naturkunde, lateinisch–deutsch, Bücher XIV/XV: Botanik. Fruchtbäume* (Sammlung Tusculum). Berlin.
—— (1994), with J. Hopp and W. Glöckner, *C. Plinius Secundus d. Ä., Naturkunde, lateinisch–deutsch, Buch XXXI: Medizin und Pharmakologie. Heilmittel aus dem Wasser* (Sammlung Tusculum). Berlin.
—— (2007), with J. Hopp and W. Glöckner, *C. Plinius Secundus d. Ä., Naturkunde, lateinisch–deutsch, Buch XXXVII: Steine. Edelsteine, Gemmen, Bernstein*, 2nd edn (Sammlung Tusculum). Berlin.
Kolb, A. (2016), 'The Romans and the world's measure', in S. Bianchetti, M. R. Cataudella, and H.-J. Gehrke (eds), *Brill's Companion to Ancient Geography: The Inhabited World in Greek and Roman Tradition* (Leiden–Boston), 223–38.
Kordosis, M. S. (1999), 'The limits of the known land (Ecumene) in the east according to Cosmas Indicopleustes: Tzinista (China) and the Ocean', *Byzantion*, 69. 1: 99–106.
Korenjak, M. (2003), *Die Welt-Rundreise eines anonymen griechischen Autors ('Pseudo-Skymnos')*. Hildesheim.
—— (2003), 'Textkritische und interpretatorische Bemerkungen zu Pseudo-Skymnos', *Philologus*, 147. 2: 226–37.
—— (2011), 'Pseudo-Skymnos (2048)', in *FGrH* v.
Koukouvelas, I. K., Piper, D. J. W. *et al.* (2020), 'Earthquake-triggered landslides and mudflows: was this the wave that engulfed ancient Helike?', *The Holocene*, 30. 12: 1653–68.
Kowalski, J.-M. (2012), *Navigation et géographie dans l'antiquité gréco-romaine: la terre vue de la mer*. Paris.
Kramer, N. (2003), 'Das Itinerar Stathmoi Parthikoi des Isidor von Charax: Beschreibung eines Handelsweges?', *Klio*, 85. 1: 120–30.
Kraye, J. (1990), 'Aristotle's god and the authenticity of "De mundo": an early modern controversy', *Journal of the History of Philosophy*, 28. 3: 339–58.
Kruse, T. (2018), 'The transport of goods through the eastern desert of Egypt: the archive of the "camel driver" Nikanor', in B. Voytek (ed.), *Infrastructure and Distribution in Ancient Economies* (Vienna), 369–80.
Kubitschek, W. (1933), 'Ein arithmetisches Gedicht und das Itinerarium Antonini', *L'Antiquité classique*, 2. 1: 167–74.
Külzer, A. (2008), *Ostthrakien* (Tabula Imperii Byzantini, 12). Vienna.

Laffranque, M. (1964), *Poseidonios d'Apamée: essai de mise au point*. Paris.
Lafond, Y. (1998), 'Die Katastrophe von 373 v.Chr. und das Verschwinden der Stadt Helike in Achaia', in E. Olshausen and H. Sonnabend (eds), *Naturkatastrophen in*

der antiken Welt: Stuttgarter Kolloquium zur historischen Geographie des Altertums 6, 1996 (Stuttgart), 118–23.

Laqueur, R. (1932), 'Mnaseas 6', *Pauly–Wissowa, Realencyclopädie der classischen Altertumswissenschaft*, xv. 2, 2250–2.

Lasserre, F. (1966), *Die Fragmente des Eudoxos von Knidos: herausgegeben, übersetzt und kommentiert*. Berlin.

Lateiner, D. (1986), 'Early Greek medical writers and Herodotus', *Antichthon*, 20: 1–20.

Leake, W. M. (1824), *Journal of a Tour in Asia Minor: With Comparative Remarks on the Ancient and Modern Geography of that Country*. London.

Lebreton, S. (2017), 'Cartes et discours géographiques: à propos de l'Expositio totius mundi et gentium', in N. Bouloux, A.-C. Dan, and G. Tolias (eds), *Orbis Disciplinae: hommages en l'honneur de Patrick Gautier Dalché* (Turnhout), 281–309.

Lee, H. D. P. (1952), *Aristotle, Meteorologica* (Loeb Classical Library, 397). London–Cambridge, Mass.

Lenfant, D. (1999), 'Peut-on se fier aux "fragments" d'historiens? L'exemple des citations d'Hérodote', *Ktèma*, 24: 103–21.

—— (2004), *Ctésias de Cnide, La Perse, L'Inde, autres fragments* (Collection des universités de France, série grecque, 435). Paris. ['Budé' edition.]

—— (2017), 'Les "Asiatiques" du traité hippocratique Airs, Eaux, Lieux ont-ils été les premiers "Orientaux"?', *Archimède*, 4: 19–25.

Leon, M. L. S. (1981), 'En torno a la transmision de la obra de Agatarqides', *Hispania antiqua*, 11–12: 183–95.

Leonard, J. R. (1997), 'Harbor terminology in Roman periploi', in S. Swiny, R. L. Hohlfelder, and H. W. Swiny (eds), *Res Maritimae: Cyprus and the Eastern Mediterranean from Prehistory to Late Antiquity* (Nicosia/Atlanta, Ga.), 163–200.

Leroy, P.-O. (2011), review of B. Bravo, *La Chronique d'Apollodore et le Pseudo-Skymnos*, in *Bryn Mawr Classical Review*, 2011.01.27.

—— (2018), 'Agathemeros (2102)', in *FGrH* v.

Leue, G. (1884), 'Zeit und Heimath des Periegeten Dionysios', *Philologus*, 42: 175–8.

—— (1925), 'Noch einmal die Akrosticha in der Periegese des Dionysios', *Hermes*, 60: 367–8.

Leutsch, *see* von Leutsch.

Levi, P. (1971), *Pausanias: Guide to Greece*. 2 vols. Harmondsworth.

Lewin, K. (1934), 'Der Richtungsbegriff in der Psychologie: der spezielle und allgemeine hodologische Raum', *Psychologische Forschung*, 19: 249–99.

Lewis, M. (2012), 'Greek and Roman surveying and surveying instruments', in R. J. A. Talbert (ed.), *Ancient Perspectives: Maps and their Place in Mesopotamia, Egypt, Greece, and Rome* (Chicago), 129–62.

Lewis, N. (1960), 'On timber and Nile shipping', *Transactions of the American Philological Association*, 91: 137–41.

Liddle, A. (2003), *Arrian, Periplus Ponti Euxini*. London.

Lightfoot, Jane L. (1999), *Parthenius of Nicaea*. Oxford.
—— (2014), *Dionysius Periegetes, Description of the Known World: With Introduction, Text, Translation, and Commentary*. Oxford.
—— (2017), 'Man of many voices and of much knowledge: or, in search of Strabo's Homer', in D. Dueck (ed.), *The Routledge Companion to Strabo*, 251–62.
Lightfoot, Jessica (2020a), '"Not enduring the wanderings of Odysseus": poetry, prose, and patronage in Pseudo-Scymnus's Periodos to Nicomedes', *Transactions of the American Philological Association*, 150. 2: 379–413.
—— (2020b), 'Tacitus' Germania and the limits of fantastic geography', *Histos*, 14: 116–51.
—— (2021), *Wonder and the Marvellous from Homer to the Hellenistic World*. Cambridge.
Lipiński, É. (2003), *Itineraria Phoenicia*. Leuven.
Livrea, E. (1973), *Dionysii Bassarikon et Gigantiadis fragmenta*. Rome.
Llewellyn-Jones, L., and Robson, J. (2009), *Ctesias' History of Persia: Tales of the Orient* (Routledge Classical Translations).
Lloyd, G. E. R. (1978) with J. Chadwick *et al.*, *Hippocratic Writings*. Harmondsworth.
López Pardo, F., and Mederos Martín, A. (2008), *La factoría fenicia de la isla de Mogador y los pueblos del Atlas*. Seville–Tenerife.
Louis, P. (1982), *Aristote, Météorologiques*, i: *Livres I et II* (Collection des universités de France, série grecque, 290). Paris. ['Budé' edition.]
Loukopoulou, L. D. (1989), *Contribution à l'étude de la Thrace propontique*. Athens.
Lozowsky, N. (2008), 'Kosmās of Alexandria, Indikopleustēs (530–570 CE)', *Encyclopedia of Ancient Natural Scientists* 487.
Lucarini, C. M. (2015), 'I due stili asiani (Cic. Br. 325; P. Artemid.) e l'origine dell'Atticismo letterario', *Zeitschrift für Papyrologie und Epigraphik*, 193: 11–24.
—— (2017), 'I viaggi iberici di Artemidoro: le guerre cantabriche in Strabone e alcune opinioni sulla Spagna di Pitea ed Eratostene', in W. Kofler and A. Novokhatko (eds), *Verleugnete Rezeption: Fälschungen antiker Texte* (Freiburg im Breisgau–Wien), 373–87.
—— (2020), 'Textkritisches zu Agatharchides von Knidos und zu Markianos von Heraklea', *Hyperboreus*, 26. 2: 221–7.
—— (2021), 'Zu Ps.-Skylax, Periplus 94', *Hermes*, 149. 2: 232.
—— and Scermino, M. (2018), 'Il ruolo di Posidonio e della dossografi a per la datazione del Περὶ κόσμου e i rapporti di quest'ultimo con l'Elogium geographiae, I', *Hyperboreus*, 24. 2: 198–228.
—— and —— (2019), 'Il ruolo di Posidonio e della dossografi a per la datazione del Περὶ κόσμου e i rapporti di quest'ultimo con l'Elogium geographiae, II', *Hyperboreus*, 25. 1: 27–55.

Luppe, W. (2008), review of C. Gallazzi, B. Kramer, and S. Settis, *Il papiro di Artemidoro (P. Artemid.)*, in *Gnomon*, 81. 8: 686–91.
Lytle, E. (2006), 'Marine fisheries and the ancient Greek economy', Ph.D. thesis. Duke University.

McDermott, W. C. (1938), *The Ape in Antiquity*. Baltimore.
McGowan, A., and Bradshaw, P. F. (2018), *The Pilgrimage of Egeria: A New Translation of the Itinerarium Egeriae with Introduction and Commentary*. Collegeville.
McInerney, J. J. (2007), 'Herakleides Kritikos (369A)', in *BNJ*².
—— (2012), 'Heraclides Criticus and the problem of taste', in I. Sluiter and R. M. Rosen (eds), *Aesthetic Value in Classical Antiquity* (Leiden–Boston), 243–64.
—— (2019), 'Herakleides Kritikos (369A)', in *BNJ*².
McKechnie, P. (2000), 'The career of Joshua Ben Sira', *Journal of Theological Studies*, 51. 1: 3–26.
McLeod, W. (1970), review of R. Hope Simpson and J. F. Lazenby, *The Catalogue of Ships in Homer's Iliad*. In *Phoenix*, 24: 256–60.
Macochius, I. (1512), *Dionysius Periegetes, De situ orbis*. Ferrara.
McPhail, C. (2014), 'Pytheas of Massalia's route of travel', *Phoenix*, 68. 3: 247–57.
—— (2016), 'The roles of geographical concepts in the construction of ancient Greek ethno-cultural identities, from Homer to Herodotus: an analysis of the continents and the Mediterranean sea', Ph.D. thesis. University of Otago.
—— and Hannah, R. (2008–11), 'Eratosthenes' perception of the Caspian sea: a gulf or an inland sea?', *Orbis Terrarum*, 10: 155–72.
Maehler, H. (1989), *Pindari Carmina*, ii. Leipzig.
Magie, D. (1950), *Roman Rule in Asia Minor: To the End of the Third Century after Christ*. 2 vols. Princeton.
Mandelbrot, B. (1967), 'How long is the coast of Britain? Statistical self-similarity and fractional dimension', *Science*, 156. 3775: 636–8.
Mango, C. A. (1965), 'Constantinopolitana', *Jahrbuch des Deutschen Archäologischen Instituts*, 80: 305–36; repr. in id., *Studies on Constantinople* (Aldershot/Brookfield, Vt., 1993), 305–36 (ch. 2).
—— (1985), *Le Développement urbain de Constantinople (IVe–VIIe siècles)*. Paris.
—— (2001), 'The shoreline of Constantinople in the fourth century', in N. Necipoğlu (ed.), *Byzantine Constantinople: Monuments, Topography and Everyday Life* (Leiden–Boston–Cologne), 17–28.
Mansfeld, J. (1992), 'Περὶ κόσμου: a note on the history of a title', *Vigiliae Christianae*, 46. 4: 391–411.
Marcone, A. (2020), 'L'idea di confine in Strabone', in G. Maddoli, M. Nafissi, and F. Prontera (eds), Σπουδῆς οὐδὲν ἐλλιποῦσα: *Anna Maria Biraschi. Scritti in memoria* (Perugia), 393–7.

Marcotte, D. (1986), 'Le périple dit de Scylax: esquisse d'un commentaire épigraphique et archéologique', *Bollettino dei classici*, 7: 166–82.
—— (1990), *Le Poème géographique de Dionysios, fils de Calliphon: édition, traduction et commentaire*. Louvain.
—— (1998), 'La climatologie d'Ératosthène à Poséidonios: genèse d'une science humaine', in G. Argoud and J.-Y. Guillaumin (eds), *Sciences exactes et sciences appliquées à Alexandrie* (Saint-Étienne), 263–77.
—— (2000a), 'Avienus, témoin de Julien: pour une interprétation et une datation nouvelles de la Descriptio orbis terrae', *Revue des études latines*, 78: 195–211.
—— (2000b), *Introduction générale; Ps.-Scymnos, Circuit de la terre* (Collection des universités de France, série grecque, 403). Paris. ['Budé' edition.]
—— (2001), 'Structure et caractère de l'œuvre historique d'Agatharchide', *Historia*, 50. 4: 385–435.
—— (2010), 'Le papyrus d'Artémidore', *Revue d'histoire des textes*, n.s. 5: 333–71.
—— (2012), 'Le Périple de la mer Érythrée dans son genre et sa tradition textuelle', in M.-F. Boussac, J.-F. Salles, and J.-B. Yon (eds), *Autour du Périple de la mer Érythrée* (Lyons), 7–25.
—— (2016), 'The Indian Ocean from Agatharchides of Cnidus to the Periplus Maris Erythraei', in S. Bianchetti, M. R. Cataudella, and H.-J. Gehrke (eds), *Brill's Companion to Ancient Geography: The Inhabited World in Greek and Roman Tradition* (Leiden–Boston), 163–83.
—— (2020), 'Chercheurs de topaze: sur un passage de Strabon', in G. Maddoli, M. Nafissi, and F. Prontera (eds), Σπουδῆς οὐδὲν ἐλλιποῦσα: *Anna Maria Biraschi. Scritti in memoria* (Perugia), 399–417.
—— (2021), 'Plutarque et le dragonneau', *Revue des études grecques*, 134. 1: 97–120.
Marcovich, M. (1995), *Clementis Alexandrini Protrepticus*. Leiden.
Marek, C. (1993), 'Die Expedition des Aelius Gallus nach Arabien im Jahre 25 v.Chr.', *Chiron*, 23: 121–56.
Marenghi, G. (1958), *Arriano, Periplo del Ponto Eusino*. Naples.
Mariotta, G. (2017), 'Una spedizione di Onesicrito nello Sri Lanka?', *Sileno*, 43: 113–20.
Marshall, E. (2000), 'Synesius, Homer, and the sea: the sea and the representation of Libyans in Synesius' letters', in G. J. Oliver, et al. (eds), *The Sea in Antiquity* (Oxford), 13–18.
Martínez Manzano, T. (1994), *Konstantinos Laskaris: Humanist, Philologe, Lehrer, Kopist*. Hamburg.
Marx, F. (1895), 'Aviens Ora Maritima', *Rheinisches Museum*, n.s. 50: 321–47.
Mathieu, J. (2017), 'The European Alps—an exceptional range of mountains? Braudel's argument put to the test', *European Review of History—Revue européenne d'histoire*, 24. 1: 96–107.
Matijašić, I. (2016), 'Scylax of Caryanda, Pseudo-Scylax, and the Paris Periplus: reconsidering the ancient tradition of a geographical text', *Mare Nostrum*, 7: 1–19.

Maurenbrecher, B. (1891), *C. Sallusti Crispi Historiarum reliquiae*, i. *Prolegomena*. Leipzig.
Mauro, C. M. (2021), 'Identificazione e analisi dei contenuti nautici nel Periplo dello Ps.Scilace', *Habis*, 52: 9–29.
—— (2022a), 'An analysis of the "closed harbours" in Strabo's geography: background, nature and meaning of the expression', *Annual of the British School at Athens*, 117: 285–309.
—— (2022b), 'The Periplus of Pseudo-Skylax and its relationship with earlier nautical knowledge', *The Mariner's Mirror*, 108. 1: 6–30.
—— and Durastante, F. (2022), 'Evaluating visibility at sea: instrumental data and historical nautical records. Mount Etna from the Calabrian Ionian coast (Italy)', *Journal of Island and Coastal Archaeology*, 17. 1: 21–42.
—— and Gambash, G. (2020), 'The earliest "limenes kleistoi": a comparison between archaeological–geological data and the Periplus of Pseudo-Skylax', *Revue des études anciennes*, 122: 55–84.
Mavrogordato, J. (1916), 'A chronological arrangement of the coins of Chios, part III', *Numismatic Chronicle*, 16: 281–355.
Mayhoff, K. F. T. (1875–97), *C. Plini Secundi Naturalis historiae libri XXXVII*. 5 vols.
Mazzarino, S. (1997), 'On the name of the Hipalus (Hippalus) wind in Pliny', in F. De Romanis and A. Tchernia (eds), *Crossings: Early Mediterranean Contacts with India* (New Delhi), 72–9.
Mc-: *indexed as* Mac-.
Medas, S. (2008), *Lo Stadiasmo o Periplo del Mare Grande e la navigazione antica: commento nautico al più antico testo portolanico attualmente noto*. Madrid.
—— (2009–10), 'Il più antico portolano attualmente noto: lo Stadiasmo o Periplo del Mare Grande', *Mayurqa*, 33: 333–64.
—— (2013), 'Contenuti nautici nel "Periplo del mare interno" di Menippo di Pergamo', in F. Raviola (ed.), *L'indagine e la rima: scritti per Lorenzo [Braccesi]* (Rome), 985–96.
Mederos Martín, A., and Escribano Cobo, G. (2015), *Oceanus Gaditanus: oro, púrpura y pesca en el litoral atlántico norteafricano y las Islas Canarias en época fenicia, cartaginesa y romana republicana*. Santa Cruz de Tenerife–Las Palmas de Gran Canaria.
Meineke, A. (1846), *Scymni Chii Periegesis et Dionysii descriptio Graeciae*. Berlin.
—— (1849), *Stephani Byzantii Ethnicorum quae supersunt*, i. Berlin.
Mele, A. (2009), 'Tra sub-colonia ed epoikia: il caso di Neapolis', in M. Lombardo and F. Frisone (eds), *Colonie di colonie: le fondazioni sub-coloniali greche tra colonizzazione e colonialismo* (Galatina), 183–201.
—— (2016), 'Eforo e le colonie greche d'Occidente, 2', *Incidenza dell'antico: dialoghi di storia greca*, 14. 2: 9–70.

Mendell, H. (2008), 'Eudoxos of Knidos (ca 365–340 BCE)', *Encyclopedia of Ancient Natural Scientists* 310–13.
Merkelbach, R., and West, M. L. (1967), *Fragmenta Hesiodea*. Oxford.
Merrills, A. H. (2005), *History and Geography in Late Antiquity*. Cambridge.
—— (2017), *Roman Geographies of the Nile: From the Late Republic to the Early Empire*. Cambridge–New York.
—— (forthcoming 2023), *War, Rebellion and Epic in Byzantine North Africa: A Study of Corippus' Iohannis*. Cambridge.
Mette, H. J. (1978), 'Die "kleinen" griechischen Historiker heute', *Lustrum*, 21: 5–43.
Meuli, K. (1935), 'Scythica', *Hermes*, 70: 121–76.
Meyer, D. (1998), 'Hellenistische Geographie zwischen Wissenschaft und Literatur: Timosthenes von Rhodos und der griechische Periplus', in W. Kullmann *et al.* (eds), *Gattungen wissenschaftlicher Literatur in der Antike* (Tübingen), 193–215.
—— (2008), 'Apollonius as a hellenistic geographer', in T. D. Papanghelis and A. Rengakos (eds), *A Companion to Apollonius Rhodius*, 2nd edn (Leiden), 267–85.
—— (2013), 'Timosthenes von Rhodos (2051)', in *FGrH* v.
—— (forthcoming), 'Kleon von Syrakus (2025)', in *FGrH* v.
Micunco, S. (2007), 'Artemidoro: osservazioni a partire da colonna V, 1–16', *Quaderni di storia*, 65: 399–403.
Mirhady, D. C. (2000), 'Dicaearchus of Messana: the sources, text and translation', in W. W. Fortenbaugh and E. Schütrumpf (eds), *Dicaearchus of Messana: Text, Translation, and Discussion* (New Brunswick–London), 1–142.
Miski, M. (2021), 'Next chapter in the legend of silphion: preliminary morphological, chemical, biological and pharmacological evaluations, initial conservation studies, and reassessment of the regional extinction event', *Plants*, 10. 1: no. 102.
Mitford, T. B. (2000), 'Thalatta, thalatta: Xenophon's view of the Black Sea', *Anatolian Studies*, 50: 127–31.
Mittag, P. F. (2011), 'Iunior Philosophus (2023)', in *FGrH* v.
Mittenhuber, F. (2011a), 'Diagnosis (2107)', in *FGrH* v.
—— (2011b), 'Hypotyposis (2021)', in *FGrH* v.
—— (2011c), 'Pinax zu Hypotyposis (2021a)', in *FGrH* v.
Mommsen, T. (1895), *C. Iulii Solini Collectanea rerum memorabilium*. Berlin.
Montanari, F. (2006a), 'Apollodoros [7] of Athens', in *Brill's New Pauly*.
—— (2006b), 'Hypomnema', in *Brill's New Pauly*.
—— (2015), with M. Goh and C. M. Schroeder, *The Brill Dictionary of Ancient Greek*. Leiden–Boston.
Mooren, L. (1972), 'The date of SB V 8036 and the development of Ptolemaic maritime trade with India', *Ancient Society*, 3: 127–33.
Morello, R., and Gibson, R. K. (eds 2003), *Re-imagining Pliny the Younger* (= *Arethusa*, 36. 2).

Morellus, F. (1606), Μαρκιανοῦ Ἡρακλεώτου περιήγησις/*Marciani Heracleotae Poema de situ orbis: Fed. Morellus profess, & interpres reg. Graeca recensuit, et Latine eodem genere versuum expressit. Cum notis & indice duplici*. Paris.

Moreno, A. (2008), 'Hieron: the ancient sanctuary at the mouth of the Black Sea', *Hesperìa: studi sulla grecità di occidente*, 77. 4: 655–709.

Moret, P. (2012), 'Posidonius et les passions de l'or chez les Gaulois', in S. Péré-Noguès (ed.), *L'Antiquité en partage: itinéraires d'histoire et d'archéologie. Mélanges offerts à Jean-Marie Pailler* (Toulouse), 143–58.

Most, G. W. (2007), *Hesiod, The Shield; Catalogue of Women; and Other Fragments*, 2nd edn (Loeb Classical Library, 503). Cambridge, Mass.

Müller, C. W. L. (1841–70), *Fragmenta historicorum Graecorum*. 5 vols. Paris.

—— (1846), 'Ἀρριανοῦ Ἐπιστολή πρός Τραιανὸν [Ἀδριανὸν]: ἐν ᾗ καὶ Περίπλους Εὐξείνου Πόντου (Arriani Epistula ad Trajanum [Adrianum] in qua etiam Periplus Ponti Euxini)', in F. Dübner and C. W. L. Müller (eds), *Anabasis et Indica [. . .]; reliqua Arriani, et scriptorum de rebus Alexandri M. fragmenta [. . .]; pseudo-Callisthenis Historiam fabulosam [. . .]; Itinerarium Alexandri [. . .]* (Paris), 254–65.

—— (1855–61), *Geographi Graeci minores*. 3 vols. Paris.

—— (1883), *Claudii Ptolemaei Geographia*, i. 1. *Libri I–III*. Paris.

Müller, S. (2011), 'Onesikritos und das Achaimenidenreich', *Anabasis*, 2: 45–66.

Mulryan, J., and Brown, S. (2006), *Natale Conti's Mythologiae*. 2 vols. Tempe, Ariz.

Mund-Dopchie, M. (2011), review of B. Bravo, *La Chronique d'Apollodore et le Pseudo-Skymnos*, in *L'Antiquité classique*, 80. 1: 270–2.

Murphy, J. P., SJ (1977), *Rufus Festus Avienus, Ora Maritima: A Description of the Seacoast from Brittany to Marseilles [Massilia]*. Chicago.

Murphy, T. (2004), *Pliny the Elder's Natural History: The Empire in the Encyclopedia*. Oxford.

Musso, O. (1986), *[Antigonus Carystius], Rerum mirabilium collectio*. Naples.

Mynors, R. A. B. (1994), with R. G. M. Nisbet, *Virgil, Georgics*. Oxford.

Myres, J. L. (1953), *Herodotus: Father of History*. Oxford; repr. (in Italian) of ch. 3 (pp. 32–46) in F. Prontera (ed.), *Geografia e geografi nel mondo antico: guida storica e critica* (Rome, 1983), 115–34.

Nagy, G. (1973), 'Phaethon, Sappho's Phaon, and the white rock of Leukas: "reading" the symbols of Greek lyric', *Harvard Studies in Classical Philology*, 77: 137–77. Reprinted with revisions in G. Nagy, *Greek Mythology and Poetics* (Ithaca, NY, 1990), 223–62 (ch. 9).

Nappo, D. (2010), 'On the location of Leuke Kome', *Journal of Roman Archaeology*, 23: 335–47.

—— (2015), 'Roman policy on the Red Sea in the second century CE', in F. De Romanis and M. Maiuro (eds), *Across the Ocean: Nine Essays on Indo-Mediterranean Trade* (Leiden–Boston), 55–72.

—— (2018a), *I porti romani nel Mar Rosso da Augusto al Tardoantico*. Naples.

—— (2018b), 'Money and flows of coinage in the Red Sea trade', in A. I. Wilson (ed.), *Trade, Commerce, and the State in the Roman World* (Oxford–New York), 557–78.

Nauck, A. (1889), 'Zu Dionysios Periegetes', *Hermes*, 24: 325.

Nenci, G. (1953), 'Due nuovi frammenti di Ecateo di Mileto', *La parola del passato*, 8: 225–9.

Nichols, A. (2011), *Ctesias, On India: And Fragments of his Minor Works*. London.

Nicolai, R. (1992), review of I. O. Tsavari, *Histoire du texte de la Description de la terre de Denys le Périégète*, in *Rivista di filologia e di istruzione classica*, 120: 478–83.

Nicolet, C. (1988), *L'Inventaire du monde: géographie et politique aux origines de l'empire romain*. Paris.

—— (1991), *Space, Geography, and Politics in the Early Roman Empire*. Ann Arbor.

Nisetich, F. (2005), 'The poems of Posidippus', in K. J. Gutzwiller (ed.), *The New Posidippus: A Hellenistic Poetry Book* (Oxford), 17–66.

Nixon, C. E. V., and Rodgers, B. S. (1994), with R. A. B. Mynors, *In Praise of Later Roman Emperors: The Panegyrici Latini*. Berkeley.

Nobbe, C. F. A. (1843–5), *Claudii Ptolemaei Geographia*. 3 vols. Leipzig; repr. in 1 vol., with introduction by A. Diller, Hildesheim, 1966.

Oberhummer, E. (1897), 'Bosporos 1', in *Pauly–Wissowa, Realencyclopädie der classischen Altertumswissenschaft*, iii. 1, 742–57.

—— (1921), 'Keras 1', in *Pauly–Wissowa, Realencyclopädie der classischen Altertumswissenschaft*, xi. 1, 257–62.

Ogden, D. (2001), *Greek and Roman Necromancy*. Princeton.

—— (2006), 'Lucian's tale of the sorcerer's apprentice in context', in K. Szpakowska (ed.), *Through a Glass Darkly: Magic, Dreams and Prophecy in Ancient Egypt* (Swansea), 121–43.

Oikonomides, A. N., and Miller, M. C. J. (1995), *Hanno the Carthaginian, Periplus or Circumnavigation [of Africa]*, 3rd edn. Chicago.

Oldfather, C. H. (1935), *Diodorus of Sicily*, ii. *Books II 35–IV 58* (Loeb Classical Library, 303). Cambridge, Mass./London.

Oleson, J.-P. (2008), 'Testing the waters: the role of sounding weights in ancient Mediterranean navigation', in R. L. Hohlfelder (ed.), *The Maritime World of Ancient Rome* (Ann Arbor), 119–76.

Oller Guzmán, M. (2021), 'Racing for love: Achilles and Iphigenia in the Black Sea', in D. C. Braund and V. F. Stolba (eds), *Environment and Habitation around the Ancient Black Sea* (Berlin–Boston), 225–34.

Olshausen, E. (2010), 'Exploration in the ancient world', in C. F. Salazar, et al. (eds), *Historical Atlas of the Ancient World* (Brill's New Pauly Supplements, 1. 3; Leiden).

—— (2012), 'Chalyben: Autonym oder Xenonym', in E. Olshausen and V. Sauer (eds), *Die Schätze der Erde: natürliche Ressourcen in der antiken Welt* (Stuttgart), 337–44.

—— (2016), 'News from the east? Roman-age geographers and the Pontus Euxinus', in S. Bianchetti, M. R. Cataudella, and H.-J. Gehrke (eds), *Brill's Companion to Ancient Geography: The Inhabited World in Greek and Roman Tradition* (Leiden–Boston), 259–73.

—— and Sauer, V. (eds 2014), *Mobilität in den Kulturen der antiken Mittelmeerwelt*. Stuttgart.

Omont, H. (1916), 'Minoïde Mynas et ses missions en Orient (1840–1855)', *Mémoires de l'Institut national de France*, 40: 337–421.

Orth, C. (2011a), 'Botthaios (2011)', in *FGrH* v.

—— (2011b), 'Skymnos (2047)', in *FGrH* v.

Oudot, E. (2004), 'Athènes dans la Périégèse de Denys d'Alexandrie ou la mutation d'une image', *Revue des études anciennes*, 106: 247–61.

Page, D. L. (1959), *History and the Homeric Iliad*. Berkeley–Los Angeles–London.

—— and Davies, M. (1991), *Alcman, Stesichorus, Ibycus* (Poetarum melicorum Graecorum fragmenta, 1). Oxford.

Pajón Leyra, I. (2021), 'Un frammento di prosa del IV secolo a.C. sugli Autariati: etnografia, storiografia e movimenti di popolazione in P.Oxy. IV 681', *Rationes rerum*, 17: 85–97.

—— and Bartoš, H. (2020), 'Geography (Chapter 3, 393a9–394a6)', in P. Gregorić and G. Karamanolis (eds), *Pseudo-Aristotle, De Mundo (On the Cosmos): A Commentary* (Cambridge), 80–120.

Pàmias i Massana, J., and Zucker, A. (2013), *Eratosthène de Cyrène, Catastérismes* (Collection des universités de France, série grecque, 497). Paris. ['Budé' edition.]

Panchenko, D. V. (1998), 'Scylax' circumnavigation of India and its interpretation in early Greek geography, ethnography and cosmography, I', *Hyperboreus*, 4. 2: 211–42.

—— (2002), 'Scylax in Philostratus' Life of Apollonius of Tyana', *Hyperboreus*, 8. 1: 5–12.

—— (2003), 'Scylax' circumnavigation of India and its interpretation in early Greek geography, ethnography and cosmography, II', *Hyperboreus*, 9. 2: 274–94.

—— (2005), 'Scylax of Caryanda on the Bosporus and the strait at the Pillars', *Hyperboreus*, 11. 2: 173–80.

—— (2013), 'Anaximandros of Miletos (2103)', in *FGrH* v.

Panichi, S. (2013), 'Dall'India all'Iberia: Artemidoro di Efeso misura l'ecumene (frr. 1 e 125 Stiehle)', in K. Geus and M. Rathmann (eds), *Vermessung der Oikoumene* (Berlin–Boston), 101–6.

—— (forthcoming), 'Artemidoros von Ephesos (2008)', in *FGrH* v.

Parker, G. R. (2008), *The Making of Roman India*. Cambridge–New York.

Paton, W. R., Walbank, F. W., and Habicht, C. (2010), *Polybius, Histories*, revised edn, ii. *Books 3–4* (Loeb Classical Library, 137). Cambridge, Mass./London.

—, —, and — (2010–12), *Polybius, Histories*, revised edn (Loeb Classical Library, 128; 137–8; 159–61). 6 vols. Cambridge, Mass.

—, —, and — (2011), *Polybius, Histories*, revised edn, iv. *Books 9–15* (Loeb Classical Library, 159). Cambridge, Mass./London.

Peremans, W. (1967), 'Diodore de Sicile et Agatharchide de Cnide', *Historia*, 16: 432–55.

Peretti, A. (1979), *Il periplo di Scilace: studio sul primo portolano del Mediterraneo*. Pisa.

Pérez Martín, I. (2016), 'Chronography and geography in tenth-century Constantinople: the manuscript of the Stadiasmos (Madrid, BN, Mss/4701)', *Geographia antiqua*, 25: 79–97.

Petersen, J. H. (2011), 'Constructing identities in multicultural milieux: the formation of Orphism in the Black sea region and southern Italy in the late 6th and early 5th centuries BC', in M. Gleba and H. W. Horsnæs (eds), *Communicating Identity in Italic Iron Age Communities* (Oxford), 167–76.

Petit, C. (2007), review of G. Santana Henríquez, *Galen, Sobre la composición de los medicamentos según los lugares libros II*, in *Classical Review*, 57. 2: 559–60.

Pfeiffer, R. (1949–53), *Callimachus*. 2 vols. Oxford.

— (1968), *History of Classical Scholarship: From the Beginnings to the End of the Hellenistic Age*. Oxford.

Pfister, F. (1951), *Die Reisebilder des Herakleides: Einleitung, Text, Übersetzung und Kommentar mit einer Übersicht über die Geschichte der griechischen Volkskunde*. Vienna.

Phillips, C. R., III (2006), 'Tellus [2]', in *Brill's New Pauly*.

Piérart, M. (2004), 'Argolis', in M. H. Hansen and T. H. Nielsen, *An Inventory of Archaic and Classical Poleis* (Oxford), 599–619.

Pisanus, V. (1488), ⟨*Avienus, Aratea; Descriptio Orbis terrae; Ora maritima; Germanicus, Aratea; Cicero, Aratea*⟩; *Quinti Sereni Medicinae liber, prohoemium*. Venice.

Pitts, M., and Versluys, M. J. (2015), *Globalisation and the Roman World*. Cambridge.

Pococke, R. (1745), *A Description of the East and some other Countries*. London.

Podossinov, A. V. (2011), 'Anonymi Periplus Ponti Euxini (2037)', in *FGrH* v.

— (ed. 2014), *The Periphery of the Classical World in Ancient Geography and Cartography*. Leuven.

— (2016), 'Karte und Text: zwei Wege der Repräsentation des geographischen Raums in der Antike und im frühen Mittelalter', in F. J. González Ponce, F. J. Gómez Espelosín, and A. L. Chávez Reino (eds), *La letra y la carta: descripción verbal y representación gráfica en los diseños terrestres grecolatinos. Estudios en honor de Pietro Janni* (Seville), 3–32.

— (2019), 'A concept "Riphaean mountains" in ancient geocartography: myth, cosmology, symbol and/or reality?', *Miscellanea Geographica: Regional Studies on Development*, 23. 3: 194–8.

Poiss, T. (2014), 'Looking for bird's-eye view in ancient Greek sources', in K. Geus and M. Thiering (eds), *Features of Common Sense Geography: Implicit Knowledge Structures in Ancient Geographical Texts* (Berlin), 69–87.

Pontani, F. (2010), 'Minima Marcianea', *Archiv für Papyrusforschung und verwandte Gebiete*, 56. 1: 45–50.

Pothecary, S. (1995), 'Strabo, Polybios, and the stade', *Phoenix*, 49. 1: 49–67.

Potter, P. (2022), *Hippocrates, Ancient Medicine; Airs, Waters, Places; Epidemics 1 and 3; The Oath; Precepts; Nutriment*, 2nd edn (Loeb Classical Library, 147). Cambridge, Mass.

Pownall, F. (2009), 'Eratosthenes of Cyrene (241)', in *BNJ*².

—— (2013), 'Hekataios of Miletos (1)', in *BNJ*².

Pretzler, M. (2007), *Pausanias: Travel Writing in Ancient Greece*. London.

Proeva, N. (1993), 'Enchéléens–Dassarètes–Illyriens: sources littérarires, épigraphiques et archéologiques', in P. Cabanes (ed.), *L'Illyrie méridionale et l'Épire dans l'Antiquité*, ii (Paris), 191–9.

—— (2021), 'Les Encheleis/Encheleai/Engelanes reconsidérés', in A. Guieu-Coppolani, M.-J. Werlings, and J. Zurbach (eds), *Le Pouvoir et la parole: mélanges en mémoire de Pierre Carlier* (Nancy/Paris), 577–94.

Prontera, F. (2011), *Geografia e storia nella Grecia antica*. Florence.

—— (2013), 'Timosthenes and Eratosthenes: sea routes and hellenistic geography', in K. Buraselis *et al.* (eds), *The Ptolemies, the Sea and the Nile: Studies in Waterborne Power* (Cambridge), 207–17.

—— (2016), 'Strabo's Geography', in S. Bianchetti, M. R. Cataudella, and H.-J. Gehrke (eds), *Brill's Companion to Ancient Geography: The Inhabited World in Greek and Roman Tradition* (Leiden–Boston), 239–58.

—— (2017), 'The Indian Caucasus from Alexander to Eratosthenes', in C. Antonetti and P. Biagi (eds), *With Alexander in India and Central Asia: Moving East and Back to West* (Oxford), 212–21.

Purcell, N. (1996), 'Rome and the management of water: environment, culture and power', in D. G. J. Shipley and J. B. Salmon (eds), *Human Landscapes in Classical Antiquity: Environment and Culture* (London–New York), 180–212.

—— (2010), review of R. J. A. Talbert, *Rome's World: The Peutinger Map Reconsidered*, in *Imago mundi*, 65. 1: 129–30.

Raaflaub, K. A. (2002), 'Philosophy, science, politics: Herodotus and the intellectual trends of his time', in E. J. Bakker *et al.* (eds), *Brill's Companion to Herodotus* (Leiden), 149–86.

—— and Talbert, R. J. A. (eds 2010), *Geography and Ethnography: Perceptions of the World in Pre-modern Societies*. Malden, Mass.–Oxford–Chichester.

Rackham, H. (1938), *Pliny, Natural History*, i. *Libri I–II* (Loeb Classical Library, 330). Cambridge, Mass.–London.

—— (1942), *Pliny, Natural History*, ii. *Libri III–VII* (Loeb Classical Library, 352). Cambridge, Mass.–London.
Radt, S. L. (1985), *Aeschylus* (Tragicorum Graecorum fragmenta, 3). Göttingen.
—— (1999), *Sophokles* (Tragicorum Graecorum fragmenta, 4). Göttingen.
—— (2001–11), *Strabons Geographika*. 10 vols. Göttingen.
Rae, A. (2016), 'How long is the coastline of Great Britain?'. *Stats, Maps n Pix*.www.statsmapsnpix.com/2016/08/how-long-is-coastline-of-great-britain.html [last accessed 14 March 2023].
Ramin, J. (1976), *Le Périple d'Hannon—The Periplus of Hanno*. Oxford.
Raschieri, A. (2007), 'Il numero delle isole Stecadi in un frammento papiraceo di Artemidoro (P.Oxy. 2694)', in *Quaderni del Dipartimento di Filologia Linguistica e Tradizione Classica 'Augusto Rostagni'*, n.s. 6 (Bologna), 87–93.
Raschke, M. G. (1978), 'New studies in Roman commerce with the east', in *Aufstieg und Niedergang der römischen Welt*, ii. 9. 2, 604-1361.
Rathbone, D. W. (1983), 'Italian wines in Roman Egypt', *Opus*, 2: 81–98.
—— (2000), 'Ptolemaic to Roman Egypt: the death of the dirigiste state?', in E. Lo Cascio and D. W. Rathbone (eds), *Production and Public Powers in Classical Antiquity* (Cambridge), 44–54.
—— (2012), review of K. Brodersen, J. Elsner, and L. Canfora, *[1] Images and Texts on the 'Artemidorus Papyrus'; [2] Artemidorus Ephesius; [3] Il papiro di Artemidoro: convegno internazionale di studio Rovereto*, in *Classical Review*, 62. 2: 442–8.
Rathmann, M. (2006), 'Milestones', in *Brill's New Pauly*.
—— (ed. 2007), *Wahrnehmung und Erfassung geographischer Räume in der Antike*. Mainz am Rhein.
—— (2011–12), 'Neue Perspektiven zur Tabula Peutingeriana', *Geographia antiqua*, 20–1: 83–102.
—— (2013a), 'The Tabula Peutingeriana in the mirror of ancient cartography', in K. Geus and M. Rathmann (eds), *Vermessung der Oikoumene* (Berlin–Boston), 203–22.
—— (2013b), 'Die "Tabula Peutingeriana" und die antike Kartographie', in J. Cobet (ed.), *Weltwissen vor Kolumbus* (Berlin), 92–120.
—— (2016a), *Tabula Peutingeriana: die einzige Weltkarte aus der Antike*, 1st edn. Darmstadt.
—— (2016b), 'The Tabula Peutingeriana and antique cartography', in S. Bianchetti, M. R. Cataudella, and H.-J. Gehrke (eds), *Brill's Companion to Ancient Geography: The Inhabited World in Greek and Roman Tradition* (Leiden–Boston), 337–62.
—— (2017), *Tabula Peutingeriana: die einzige Weltkarte aus der Antike*, 2nd edn. Darmstadt.
—— (2018), *Tabula Peutingeriana: die einzige Weltkarte aus der Antike*, 3rd edn. Darmstadt.

Reale, G., and Bos, A. P. (1995), *Il trattato Sul cosmo per Alessandro attribuito ad Aristotele*, 2nd edn. Milan.

Redon, B., Faucher, T., and Versnel, H. S. (2017), 'Forts et mines d'or du désert oriental d'Égypte: découvertes récentes dans le district de Samut', *Revue archéologique*, n.s. 1: 101–9.

Reeve, M. D. (1992), review of I. O. Tsavari, *Histoire du texte de la Description de la terre de Denys le Périégète*, in *Classical Review*, 41. 2: 306–9.

—— (1994), 'Some manuscripts of Dionysius the Periegete', *Illinois Classical Studies*, 19: 209–20.

Reger, G. (1997), 'Islands with one polis versus islands with several poleis', in M. H. Hansen (ed.), *The Polis as an Urban Centre and as a Political Community* (Copenhagen), 450–92.

Reinhardt, K. (1926), *Kosmos und Sympathie: neue Untersuchungen über Poseidonios*. Munich.

Reuters, F. H. (1957), *Anacharsidis epistulae*. Inaug.-Diss., Bonn.

—— (1963), *Die Briefe des Anacharsis*. Berlin.

Reynolds, L. D. (1983), *Texts and Transmissions: A Survey of the Latin Classics*. Oxford.

Richter, D. S., and Johnson, W. A. (eds 2017), *The Oxford Handbook of the Second Sophistic*. Oxford–New York.

Riese, A. (1878), *Geographi Latini minores*. Heilbronn.

Rihll, T. E. (1999), *Greek Science*. Oxford.

Rist, J. (2006), 'Synesios (1)', in *Brill's New Pauly*.

Ritter, N. C. (2011), 'Perser am Mekong: die maritimen Fernhandelskontakte der Sasaniden', *Antike Welt*, 42. 2: 71–8.

Robert, L. (1960), *Hellenica: recueil d'épigraphie, de numismatique et d'antiquités grecques*, xi–xii. Paris.

Roberto, U. (2005), *Ioannis Antiocheni fragmenta ex Historia Chronica*. Berlin.

Roberts, W. R. (1902), *Demetrius, On Style*. Cambridge.

Robin, C. (1997), 'The date of the Periplus of the Erythraean sea in the light of South Arabian evidence', in F. De Romanis and A. Tchernia (eds), *Crossings: Early Mediterranean Contacts with India* (New Delhi), 41–65.

Robinson, M. (2013), 'Ovid and the Catasterismi of Eratosthenes', *American Journal of Philology*, 134. 3 (535): 445–80.

Rocha-Pereira, M. H. (1989–90), *Pausaniae Graeciae descriptio*, 2nd edn. 3 vols. Leipzig.

Rogers, G. M. (2014), *The Sacred Identity of Ephesos: Foundation Myths of a Roman City*, 2nd edn. London–New York.

Roller, D. W. (2003), *The World of Juba II and Kleopatra Selene: Royal Scholarship on Rome's African Frontier*. London.

—— (2006), *Through the Pillars of Herakles: Greco-Roman Exploration of the Atlantic*. London–New York.

—— (2008a), 'Hanno and Pytheas: problems with obscure geographical texts [unpublished abstract]', American Philological Association, 139th Annual Meeting (Chicago), 6 January.
—— (2008b), 'Juba II of Mauretania (275)', in *BNJ*.
—— (2010), *Eratosthenes' Geography: Fragments Collected and Translated*. Princeton.
—— (2013), review of J.-M. Kowalski, *Navigation et géographie dans l'antiquité gréco-romaine*, in *Bryn Mawr Classical Review*, 2013.01.07.
—— (2014), *The Geography of Strabo: An English Translation, with Introduction and Notes*. Cambridge.
—— (2015), *Ancient Geography: The Discovery of the World in Classical Greece and Rome*. London–New York.
—— (2018), *A Historical and Topographical Guide to the Geography of Strabo*. Cambridge–New York.
—— (2018), 'Juba II of Mauretania (275)', in *BNJ²*.
—— (2019), 'Isidoros of Charax (781)', in *BNJ²*.
—— (ed. 2020a), *New Directions in the Study of Ancient Geography*. Sarasota.
—— (2020b), 'Timosthenes of Rhodes', in id. (ed.), *New Directions in the Study of Ancient Geography* (Sarasota), 56–79.
—— (2022a), *A Guide to the Geography of Pliny the Elder*. Cambridge.
—— (2022b), *Three Ancient Geographical Treatises in Translation: Hanno, the King Nikomedes Periodos, and Avienus*. Abingdon–New York.
Romer, F. E. (1998), *Pomponius Mela's Description of the World*. Ann Arbor.
Romm, J. S. (1989), 'Herodotus and mythic geography: the case of the Hyperboreans', *Transactions of the American Philological Association*, 119: 97–117.
—— (1992), *The Edges of the Earth in Ancient Thought: Geography, Exploration, and Fiction*. Princeton.
Ronchey, S. (2018), 'È un falso, una truffa: la fine del Papiro di Artemidoro', *La Repubblica* (18 Dec.).
Rood, T. (2011), 'Black sea variations: Arrian's Periplus', *Cambridge Classical Journal: Proceedings of the Cambridge Philological Society*, 57: 137–63.
Roos, A. G., and Wirth, G. (1968), *Flavii Arriani quae exstant omnia*, ii. *Scripta minora et fragmenta*. Leipzig.
Rose, V. (1886), *Aristotelis qui ferebantur librorum fragmenta*. Leipzig.
—— (1967), *Aristotelis qui ferebantur librorum fragmenta*. Stuttgart.
Roseman, C. H. (1994), *Pytheas of Massalia, On the Ocean*. Chicago.
Rossetti, L. (2020), 'Il "mappamondo" di Anassimandro', in G. Maddoli, M. Nafissi, and F. Prontera (eds), Σπουδῆς οὐδὲν ἐλλιποῦσα: *Anna Maria Biraschi. Scritti in memoria* (Perugia), 521–33.
Rougé, J. (1966), *Expositio totius mundi et gentium: introduction, texte critique, traduction, notes et commentaire*. Paris.
Rubincam, C. R. (2021), *Quantifying Mentalities: The Use of Numbers by Ancient Greek Historians*. Ann Arbor.

Ruffing, K. (1993), 'Das Nikanor-Archiv und der römische Süd- und Osthandel', *Münstersche Beiträge zur antiken Handelsgeschichte*, 12: 1–26.

—— (2004), 'Ökonomie als Kategorie in der antiken deskriptiven Geographie: Berichtsweise und Eigenart der Expositio totius mundi et gentium', *Münstersche Beiträge zur antiken Handelsgeschichte*, 23. 1: 88–130.

—— (2013), 'The trade with India and the problem of agency in the economy of the Roman empire: Studi ellenistici: supplementi, 1', in S. Bussi (ed.), *Egitto: dai Faraoni agli Arabi* (Pisa–Rome), 199–210.

—— (forthcoming), 'Expositio totius mundi et gentium (2020)', in *FGrH* v.

Russell, J. B. (1991), *Inventing the Flat Earth: Columbus and Modern Historians*. New York.

Russell, T. (2012), 'The land of Inachus: Byzantium's early coinage and two Bosporus toponyms', *Zeitschrift für Papyrologie und Epigraphik*, 180: 133–8.

—— (2017), *Byzantium and the Bosporus: A Historical Study, from the Seventh Century BC until the Foundation of Constantinople*. Oxford.

Russo, L. (2013), 'Ptolemy's longitudes and Eratosthenes' measurement of the earth's circumference', *Mathematics and Mechanics of Complex Systems*, 1. 1: 67–79.

Ryan, F. X. (2007), 'Der sogenannte Pseudo-Skymnos', *Quaderni urbinati di cultura classica*, n.s. 87: 137–43.

Sallmann, K. G. (2006), 'Varro [2] Terentius, M. (Reatinus)', in *Brill's New Pauly*.

Salway, R. W. B. (2004), 'Sea and river travel in the Roman itinerary literature', in R. J. A. Talbert and K. Brodersen (eds), *Space in the Roman World: Its Perception and Presentation* (Münster), 43–96.

—— (2012), 'Putting the world in order: mapping in Roman texts', in R. J. A. Talbert (ed.), *Ancient Perspectives: Maps and their Place in Mesopotamia, Egypt, Greece, and Rome* (Chicago), 193–234.

Sánchez-Román, A., et al. (2012), 'Spatial and temporal variability of tidal flow in the Strait of Gibraltar', *Journal of Marine Systems*, 98–9: 9–17.

Sandys, G. (1621), *A Relation of a Journey begun An: Dom: 1610*, 2nd edn. London.

Sannino, G., Pratt, L., and Carillo, A. (2009), 'Hydraulic criticality of the exchange flow through the Strait of Gibraltar', *Journal of Physical Oceanography*, 39. 11: 2779–99.

Šašel Kos, M. (2005), *Appian and Illyricum*. Ljubljana.

—— (2013), 'The "great lake" and the Autariatai in Pseudo-Skylax', *Mélanges de l'École Française de Rome: Antiquité*, 125. 1: 247–57.

Savino, E. (1991), 'La datazione del cap. 168 del De mirabilibus auscultationibus e la più antica citazione dei Germani nella letteratura classica', *Annali di archeologia e storia antica*, 13: 231–6.

Schamp, J. (1991), *Photius, Bibliothèque*, ix. *Index* (Collection des universités de France, série grecque, 339). Paris. ['Budé' edition.]

Schepens, G. (1998), '1000 (= 709) Skylax of Karyanda', in J. Bollansée, G. Schepens *et al.* (eds), *Felix Jacoby, Die Fragmente der griechischen Historiker Continued*, iv: *Biography and Antiquarian Literature. A: Biography. Fascicle 1: The Pre-hellenistic Period* (Leiden–Boston–Cologne), 2–24.

Schiano, C. (2010), *Artemidoro di Efeso e la scienza del suo tempo*. Bari.

Schliephake, C., Sojc, N., and Weber, G. (eds 2020), *Nachhaltigkeit in der Antike: Diskurse, Praktiken, Perspektiven*. Stuttgart.

Schmidt, K. (1980), *Kosmologische Aspekte im Geschichtswerk des Poseidonios*. Göttingen.

Schmidt, M. (2011), 'A Gadibus Romam', *Bulletin of the Institute of Classical Studies*, 54. 2: 71–86.

Schmitt, R. (2012), 'Isidorus of Charax', *Encyclopaedia Iranica* xiv. 2. 125–7.

—— (2017), 'Isidors "Stathmoi Parthikoi" aus Sicht der iranischen Toponomastik', in J. Wiesehöfer and S. Müller (eds), *Parthika: Greek and Roman Authors' Views of the Arsacid Empire* (Wiesbaden), 189–220.

Schneider, P. (2004), *L'Éthiopie et l'Inde: interférences et confusions aux extrémités du monde antique (VIIIe siècle avant J.-C.–VIe siècle après J.-C.)*. Rome.

—— (2006), 'L'élimination des vieillards et des malades: regard grec sur les sociétés des confins de l'oikoumenê', in M. Molin (ed.), *Les Régulations sociales dans l'Antiquité: actes du colloque d'Angers, 23 et 24 mai 2003* (Rennes), 43–53.

—— (2016), 'The so-called confusion between India and Ethiopia: the eastern and southern edges of the inhabited world from the Greco-Roman perspective', in S. Bianchetti, M. R. Cataudella, and H.-J. Gehrke (eds), *Brill's Companion to Ancient Geography: The Inhabited World in Greek and Roman Tradition* (Leiden–Boston), 184–202.

—— (2017), '"On the Red Sea the trees are of a remarkable nature" (Pliny the Elder): the Red Sea mangroves from the Greco-Roman perspective', in D. A. Agius, et al. (eds), *Human Interaction with the Environment in the Red Sea: Selected Papers of Red Sea Project VI* (Leiden–Boston), 9–29.

—— (forthcoming), 'Denys le Périégète (2019)', in *FGrH* v.

Schoff, W. H. (1927), *Periplus of the Outer Sea: East and West, and of the Great Islands Therein, by Marcian of Heraclea*. Philadelphia.

Schorn, S. (2011–), *Biography and Antiquarian Literature* (Felix Jacoby, Die Fragmente der griechischen Historiker Continued, iv). Leiden.

Schütrumpf, E. (ed. 2008), *Heraclides of Pontus: Texts and Translation*. New Brunswick, NJ–London.

Schulten, A. (1922), *Avieni Ora maritima (periplus Massiliensis saec. VI. a. C.) adiunctis ceteris testimoniis anno 500 a. C. antiquioribus*. Berlin. (Repr. as *Ora marítima: junto con los demás testimonios anteriores al año 500 a. de J.C.*, Barcelona, 1955.)

Schulzski, H.-J. (2006), 'Stadion (1)', in *Brill's New Pauly*.

Schuol, M. (2017), 'Isidor von Charax und die literarische Gattung der Stathmoi', in J. Wiesehöfer and S. Müller (eds), *Parthika: Greek and Roman Authors' Views of the Arsacid Empire* (Wiesbaden), 71–85.

Scott, L. (2021), *Pytheas*. Abingdon–New York.
Scott, R. D. (1990), 'Malalas' view of the classical past', in G. W. Clark (ed.), *Reading the Past in Late Antiquity* (Canberra), 147–64.
Scruton, R. (2001), *Kant*. Oxford.
Scullard, H. H. (1974), *The Elephant in the Greek and Roman World*. London–Ithaca, NY.
Seaford, R. (2009), 'The fluttering soul', in U. Dill and C. Walde (eds), *Antike Mythen: Medien, Transformationen und Konstruktionen* (Berlin–New York), 406–14.
Seamon, D. (2015), 'Humanistic geography: lived emplacement and the locality of being. A return to humanistic geography?', in S. Aitken and G. Valentine (eds), *Approaches to Human Geography*, 2nd edn (London), 35–48.
—— (2022), 'Sense of place', in D. Richardson *et al.* (eds.), *International Encyclopedia of Geography: People, the Earth, Environment, and Technology* (New York).
Sedley, D. N. (2010), 'Philosophy in the Artemidorus Papyrus', in C. Gallazzi, B. Kramer, and S. Settis (eds), *Contesto culturale, lingua, stile e tradizione* (Intorno al papiro di Artemidoro, 1; Milan), 29–53.
Seeck, O. (1876), *Notitia dignitatum: accedunt Notitia urbis Constantinopolitanae et Laterculi provinciarum*. Berlin.
Segal, C. (1974), 'Death by water: a narrative pattern in Theocritus', *Hermes*, 102: 20–38.
Selter, B. (2010), 'Through the looking glass of memory', *Quaderni urbinati di cultura classica*, 95. 2: 113–30.
Seminar Classics 609 (1969), *Porphyry, The Cave of the Nymphs in the Odyssey: A Revised Text with Translation*. Buffalo, NY.
Şengör, A. M. C. (2002), 'Is the Symplegades myth the record of a tsunami that entered the Bosphorus? Simple empirical roots of complex mythological concepts', in R. Aslan (ed.), *Mauerschau: Festschrift für Manfred Korfmann* (Grunbach), 1005–28.
Shackleton Bailey, D. R. (1968), *Cicero's Letters to Atticus, iii. 51–50 BC. 94–132 (Books V–VII. 9)* (Cambridge Classical Texts and Commentaries, 5). Cambridge.
Sharples, R. W. (2006), 'Dicaearchus', in *Brill's New Pauly*.
Shcheglov, D. A. (2005), 'Hipparchus on the latitude of southern India', *Greek, Roman and Byzantine Studies*, 45. 4: 359–80.
—— (2006), 'Posidonius on the dry west and the wet east: fragment 223 EK reconsidered', *Classical Quarterly*, 56. 2: 509–27.
Shipley, D. G. J. (1987), *A History of Samos 800–188 BC*. Oxford.
—— (2000), *The Greek World after Alexander: 323–30 BC*. London–New York; repr. with corrections 2001; 2004 (twice); 2006.
—— (2005), 'Little boxes on the hillside: Greek town planning, Hippodamos, and polis ideology', in M. H. Hansen (ed.), *The Imaginary Polis* (Copenhagen), 335–403.
—— (2006), 'Landscapes of the ancient Peloponnese: a human-geographical approach', *Leidschrift*, 21. 1: 27–43.

—— (2010), 'Pseudo-Skylax on Attica', in N. V. Sekunda (ed.), *Ergasteria: Works presented to John Ellis Jones on his 80th Birthday* (Gdańsk), 100–14.
—— (2011), *Pseudo-Skylax's Periplous: The Circumnavigation of the Inhabited World*, 1st edn. Exeter.
—— (2012), 'Pseudo-Skylax and the natural philosophers', *Journal of Hellenic Studies*, 132: 121–38.
—— (2017), 'Pseudo-Skylax (2046)', in *FGrH* v.
—— (2018), *The Early Hellenistic Peloponnese: Politics, Economies, and Networks, 338–197 BC*. Cambridge.
—— (2019), *Pseudo-Skylax's Periplous: The Circumnavigation of the Inhabited World*, 2nd edn. Liverpool.
—— (2021a), 'Periplus (περίπλους, ὁ)', in C. A. Baron (ed.), *The Herodotus Encyclopedia*, iii (Hoboken), 1085–6.
—— (2021b), 'Scylax (Σκύλαξ, ὁ) of Caryanda', in C. A. Baron (ed.), *The Herodotus Encyclopedia*, iii (Hoboken), 1300–1.
—— (2021c), 'Sun, sea, and sky: on translating directions (and other terms) in the Greek geographers', in E. Boutsikas, S. C. McCluskey, and J. M. Steele (eds), *Advancing Cultural Astronomy: Studies in honour of Clive Ruggles* (Cham, Switzerland), 105–36.
—— (2023), 'Rules of engagement with Greek geographical writing', *Histos*, 17: xxii–xl.
—— and Salmon, J. B. (eds 1996), *Human Landscapes in Classical Antiquity: Environment and Culture*. London–New York.
——, Vanderspoel, J., Mattingly, D. J., and Foxhall, L. (eds 2006), *The Cambridge Dictionary of Classical Civilization*. Cambridge.
Sickinger, J. P. (2020), 'Anonymous Periegete (P. Haw., 80–81) (Anonymus periegeta) (369)', in *BNJ*².
Sidebotham, S. E. (2011), *Berenike and the Ancient Maritime Spice Route*. Berkeley–Los Angeles.
Sider, D. (2015), review of J. C. Thom, *Cosmic Order and Divine Power: Pseudo-Aristotle, On the Cosmos*, in *Bryn Mawr Classical Review*, 2015.08.34.
Silberman, A. (1978), 'Quelques remarques sur la composition du Périple d'Arrien', *Revue des études grecques*, 91: 158–64.
—— (1988), *Pomponius Mela, Chorographie* (Collection des universités de France, série latine, 283). Paris. ['Budé' edition.]
—— (1993), 'Arrien, "Périple du Pont-Euxin": essai d'interprétation et d'évaluation des données historiques et géographiques', in *Aufstieg und Niedergang der römischen Welt*, ii. 34. 1, 276–311.
—— (1995), *Arrien, Périple du Pont-Euxin* (Collection des universités de France, série grecque, 371). Paris. ['Budé' edition.]

Sourvinou-Inwood, C. (2003), 'Herodotos (and others) on Pelasgians: some perceptions of ethnicity', in P. Derow and R. Parker (eds), *Herodotus and his World: Essays from a Conference in Memory of George Forrest* (Oxford), 103–44.

Speidel, M. P. (2016), 'Wars, trade and treaties: new, revised, and neglected sources for the political, diplomatic, and military aspects of imperial Rome's relations with the Red Sea basin and India, from Augustus to Diocletian', in K. S. Mathew (ed.), *Imperial Rome, Indian Ocean Regions and Muziris: New Perspectives On Maritime Trade* (New Delhi), 83–128.

Stavrou, D. (2021), 'Insularity and religious life: the case of hellenistic Ikaros/Failaka island', *Religions*, 12. 11: 1002.

Stenger, J. (2013), 'Eusebios' Erfassung des Heiligen Landes: die Evidenz des Raumes im Onomastikon der biblischen Ortsnamen', in K. Geus and M. Rathmann (eds), *Vermessung der Oikoumene* (Berlin–Boston), 223–41.

Stevenson, E. L. (1932), *Geography of Claudius Ptolemy*. New York; repr. as *Claudius Ptolemy: The Geography*, New York, 1991.

Stiehle, R. (1856), 'Der Geograph Artemidorus von Ephesos', *Philologus*, 11. 2: 193–244.

Stoneman, R. (2021), *Megasthenes' "Indica": A New Translation of the Fragments with Commentary*. Abingdon–New York.

Strasburger, H. (1966), *Die Wesensbestimmung der Geschichte durch die antike Geschichtsschreibung*. Wiesbaden.

Stronk, J. P. (2010), *Ctesias' Persian History*, i. *Introduction, Text and Translation*. Düsseldorf.

Stuckius, J. G. (1577), *Arrianus Flavius, Ponti Euxini et maris Erythraei periplus, ad Adrianum Caesarem: nunc primum e Graeco sermone in Latinum versus, plurimisque mendis repurgatus . . . addita est praeter loca, que solers Lusitanorum penetravit navigatio, omnium cum oppidorum, quae Danubius irrigat: . . . observatio, praeterea ipsius Ponti Chorographica tabula*. 2 in 1 vols. Geneva.

Stückelberger, A., and Graßhoff, G. (2006), with F. Mittenhuber, R. Burri *et al.*, *Ptolemaios, Handbuch der Geographie*. 2 vols. Basel.

Sundwall, G. A. (1996), 'Ammianus geographicus', *American Journal of Philology*, 117. 4: 619–43.

Szpakowska, K. (ed. 2006), *Through a Glass Darkly: Magic, Dreams and Prophecy in Ancient Egypt*. Swansea.

Talbert, R. J. A. (1989), review of J. B. Harley and D. Woodward, *The History of Cartography*, in *American Historical Review*, 94. 2: 407–8.

—— (1994), 'Carl Müller (1813–1894), S. Jacobs, and the making of classical maps in Paris for John Murray', *Imago mundi*, 46. 1: 128–50.

—— (ed. 2000), *Barrington Atlas of the Greek and Roman World*. Princeton–Oxford.

—— (ed. 2000), *Map-by-map Directory: To accompany Barrington Atlas of the Greek and Roman World*. 2 vols. Princeton–Oxford. [http://mail.nysoclib.org/Digital_Archives/ebooks/Barrington_Atlas/ (map-by-map chapters, also BATL-GAZ.PDF, the complete *Directory*).
—— (2007), 'Author, audience and the Roman empire in the Antonine Itinerary', in R. Haensch and J. Heinrichs (eds), *Herrschen und Verwalten: der Alltag der römischen Administration in der hohen Kaiserzeit* (Cologne–Weimar–Vienna), 256–70.
—— (2009), 'P.Artemid.: the map', in K. Brodersen and J. Elsner (eds), *Images and Texts on the 'Artemidorus Papyrus': Working Papers on P.Artemid.* (Stuttgart), 57–64, 158–63 figs 66–70.
—— (2010), *Rome's World: The Peutinger Map Reconsidered*. Cambridge.
—— (2012a) *Ancient Perspectives: Maps and their Place in Mesopotamia, Egypt, Greece, and Rome*. Chicago.
—— (2012b), review of D. Dueck and K. Brodersen, *Geography in Classical Antiquity*, in *Bryn Mawr Classical Review*, 2012.12.29.
—— (2012c), 'The unfinished state of the map: what is missing, and why?', in C. Gallazzi, B. Kramer, and S. Settis (eds), *Geografia e cartografia* (Intorno al papiro di Artemidoro, 2; Milan), 185–96.
—— (2013), 'Worldview reflected in Roman military diplomas', in K. Geus and M. Rathmann (eds), *Vermessung der Oikoumene* (Berlin–Boston), 163–70.
—— (2015), review of W. A. Koelsch, *Geography and the Classical World: Unearthing Historical Geography's Forgotten Past*, in *Geographical Review*, 105. 2: 255–8.
—— (2017), 'Communicating through maps', in F. S. Naiden and R. J. A. Talbert (eds), *Mercury's Wings: Exploring Modes of Communication in the Ancient World* (Oxford), 340–62.
—— (2019a), 'Carl Müller (1813–1894), S. Jacobs, and the making of classical maps in Paris for John Murray: in R. J. A. Talbert, *Challenges of Mapping the Classical World* (Abingdon–New York), 20–48.
—— (2019b), *Challenges of Mapping the Classical World*. Abingdon–New York.
—— (2019c), 'William Smith and George Grove, eds., Atlas of Ancient Geography Biblical and Classical (1872–1874): introduction to the 2013 reissue (London: I. B. Tauris, 2013, pp. v–xii)', in id., *Challenges of Mapping the Classical World* (Abingdon–New York), 8–19.
—— (2020), 'An English translation of Pliny's geographical books for the 21st century', *Shagi—Steps: The Journal of the School of Advanced Studies in the Humanities* [Moscow], 6. 1: 214–28.
Tarte, S. M. (2012), 'The digital existence of words and pictures: the case of the Artemidorus papyrus', *Historia*, 61. 3: 325–36 (bibl., 357–61).
Thein, K. (2020), 'The heavenly sphere (Chapter 2, 391b9–392a31)', in P. Gregorić and G. Karamanolis (eds), *Pseudo-Aristotle, De Mundo (On the Cosmos): A Commentary* (Cambridge), 33–61.

Thom, J. C. (2014a), *Cosmic Order and Divine Power: Pseudo-Aristotle, On the Cosmos*. Tübingen.

—— (2014b), 'Introduction', in id. (ed.), *Cosmic Order and Divine Power: Pseudo-Aristotle, On the Cosmos* (Tübingen), 4–17.

—— (2014c), 'Text, translation and notes', in id. (ed.), *Cosmic Order and Divine Power: Pseudo-Aristotle, On the Cosmos* (Tübingen), 20–66.

Thomas, R. (2000), *Herodotus in Context: Ethnography, Science and the Art of Persuasion*. Cambridge.

—— (2006), 'The intellectual milieu of Herodotus', in C. Dewald and J. M. Marincola (eds), *The Cambridge Companion to Herodotus* (Cambridge), 60–75.

Thompson, D'A. W. (1936), *A Glossary of Greek Birds*, new edn. Oxford.

—— (1947), *A Glossary of Greek Fishes*. London.

Thomson, J. O. (1948), *A History of Ancient Geography*. Cambridge.

Thonemann, P. J. (2011), *The Maeander Valley: A Historical Geography from Antiquity to Byzantium*. Cambridge.

Tierney, J. J., and Bieler, L. (1967), *Dicuili, Liber de mensura orbis terrae*. Dublin.

Traina, G. (2013), 'Mapping the world under Theodosius II', in C. Kelly (ed.), *Theodosius II: Rethinking the Roman Empire in Late Antiquity* (Cambridge), 155–71.

Trautmann, T. (2015), *Elephants and Kings: An Environmental History*. Chicago.

Trevor-Roper, H. R. (1972), 'Fernand Braudel, the Annales, and the Mediterranean', *Journal of Modern History*, 44. 4: 468–79.

Trowbridge, C. C. (1913), 'On fundamental methods of orientation and imaginary maps', *Science*, 38. 990: 888–97.

Tsavari, I. O. (1990), *Histoire du texte de la Description de la Terre de Denys le Périégète*. Ioannina.

Tsiotras, V. I. (2018), 'The oldest anonymous scholia on Ptolemy's Geography', in R. Ceceña (ed.), *Claudio Ptolomeo, Geografía: capítulos teóricos* (Mexico City), 251–79.

Tuan, Y.-F. (1974a), 'Space and place: humanistic perspective', *Progress in Geography*, 6: 211–52.

—— (1974b), *Topophilia: A Study of Environmental Perception, Attitudes, and Values*. Englewood Cliffs, NJ–London.

—— (1975), 'Images and mental maps', *Annals of the Association of American Geographers*, 65. 2: 205–13.

—— (1977), *Space and Place: The Perspective of Experience*. London/Minneapolis.

—— (1990), *Topophilia: A Study of Environmental Perception, Attitudes, and Values*, new edn. New York.

Tuck, S. L. (2018), 'Was the tempestas of AD 62 at Ostia actually a tsunami?', *Classical Journal*, 114. 4: 439–62.

Turner, B., and Talbert, R. J. A. (2022), *Pliny the Elder's World: Natural History, Books 2–6*. Cambridge–New York.

Tzvetkova-Glaser, A. (2014), 'The concepts of οὐσία and δύναμις in De mundo and their parallels in hellenistic–Jewish and Christian texts', in J. C. Thom (ed.), *Cosmic Order and Divine Power: Pseudo-Aristotle, On the Cosmos* (Tübingen), 133–52.

Uggeri, G. (1996), 'Stadiasmus maris magni: un contributo per la datazione', in M. Khanoussi, P. Ruggeri, and C. Vismara (eds), *L'Africa romana: atti dell'XI convegno di studio, Cartagine, 15–18 dicembre 1994* (Ozieri), 1, 277–85.

Ugolini, D., and Olive, C. (1987), 'Béziers et les côtes languedociennes dans l'Ora maritima d'Avienus', *Revue archéologique de Narbonnaise*, 20: 143–54.

van de Woestijne, P. (1961), *La Descriptio orbis terrae d'Avienus*. Bruges.

van Minnen, P. (1986), 'The volume of the Oxyrhynchite textile trade', *Münstersche Beiträge zur antiken Handelsgeschichte*, 5. 2: 88–95.

—— (2009), 'Less Artemidorus and more', *Bulletin of the American Society of Papyrologists*, 46: 165–74.

Vassiliev, A. A. (1936), 'Expositio totius mundi: an anonymous geographic treatise of the fourth century AD', *Seminarium Kondakovianum*, 8: 1–39.

Verlinsky, A. (2019), 'Posidonius' linguistic naturalism and its philosophical pedigree', in G. Pezzini and B. Taylor (eds), *Language and Nature in the Classical Roman World* (Cambridge), 15–45.

Vian, F. (1974), 'Légendes et stations argonautiques du Bosphore', in R. Chevallier (ed.), *Littérature gréco-romaine et géographie historique: mélanges offerts à Robert Dion* (Paris), 91–104.

Villani, D. (2009), 'La Méditerranée, l'Océan et l'oikouménè dans l'œuvre de Posidonius et à travers le personnage de Pompée', *Pallas*, 79: 283–93.

Visser, E. (2021), 'The catalogue in early Greek epic', in R. Laemmle, C. Scheidegger Laemmle, and K. Wesselmann (eds), *Lists and Catalogues in Ancient Literature and Beyond* (Berlin), 197–210.

Vivero, M. A. (2013), 'Textile trade in the Periplus of the Erythraean sea', in M. Gleba and J. Pásztókai-Szeöke (eds), *Making Textiles in Pre-Roman and Roman Times* (Oxford), 142–8.

Vött, A. (2011), 'Die Olympia-Tsunami-Hypothese: neue sedimentologische und geoarchäologische Befunde zur Verschüttung Olympias', *AntW*, 42. 5: [4 pp.].

—— (2013), *Neue geoarchäologische Untersuchungen zur Verschüttung Olympias: eine Einführung in die Olympia-Tsunami-Hypothese*, 23. Wiesbaden.

von Arnim, H. (1903–24), with M. Adler, *Stoicorum veterum fragmenta*. 4 vols. Leipzig.

von Leutsch, E. L., and Schneidewin, F. G. (1839), *Corpus paroemiographorum Graecorum*, i. *Zenobius, Diogenianus, Plutarchus, Gregorius Cyprius cum appendice proverbiorum*. Göttingen.

Vossius, G. I. (1624), *De historicis Graecis libri quatuor*. Leiden.

Vossius, I. (1639), *Periplus Scylacis Caryandensis: cum tralatione, & castigationibus Isaaci Vossii. Accedit anonymi Periplus Ponti Euxini è bibliotheca Claudii Salmasii, cum ejusdem Is. Vossii versione, ac notis*. Amsterdam.

Wachsmuth, C. (1884), *Ioannis Stobaei Anthologii libri duo priores: qui inscribi solent Eclogae physicae et ethicae*, i. *Anthologii librum primum continens*. Berlin.
—— (1889), 'Zu den Akrostichen des Dionysios Periegetes', *Rheinisches Museum*, 44: 151–3.
Wainwright, G. A. (1946), 'Zeberged: the shipwrecked sailor's island', *Journal of Egyptian Archaeology*, 32: 31–8.
Walbank, F. W. (1948), 'The geography of Polybius', *Classica et mediaevalia*, 9: 155–82; repr. in id., *Polybius, Rome and the Hellenistic World: Essays and Reflections* (Cambridge, 2002), 31–52.
—— (1957–79), *A Historical Commentary on Polybius*. 3 vols. Oxford.
—— (1972), *Polybius*. Berkeley–Los Angeles–London.
—— (1980), 'The idea of decline in Polybius', in S. Koselleck and P. Widmer (eds), *Niedergang: Studien zu einem geschichtlichen Thema* (Stuttgart), 41–58.
—— (2002), 'The idea of decline in Polybius: in F. W. Walbank, *Polybius, Rome and the Hellenistic World: Essays and Reflections* (Cambridge), 193–211.
Waldherr, G. H. (1997), *Erdbeben: das außergewöhnliche Normale. Zur Rezeption seismischer Aktivitäten in literarischen Quellen vom 4. Jahrhundert v. Chr. bis zum 4. Jahrhundert n. Chr.* Stuttgart.
Warmington, E. H. (1934), *Greek Geography*. London/Toronto/New York.
Warren, P. (1992), 'Lapis Lacedaemonius', in J. M. Sanders (ed.), *Φιλολάκων: Lakonian Studies in honour of Hector Catling* (London), 285–96.
Wasserman, T. (2018), 'Papyrus Artemidorus in the news again'. *Evangelical Textual Criticism*. http://evangelicaltextualcriticism.blogspot.com/2018/12/papyrus-artemidorus-in-news-again.html [last accessed 14 March 2023].
Waters, M. (2020), *Ctesias' Persica and its Near Eastern context*. Madison.
Wehrli, F. (1967), *Dikaiarchos*, 2nd edn. Basel–Stuttgart.
Weißenberger, M. (2006), 'Hegesias [2] of Magnesia', in *Brill's New Pauly*.
Wendel, C. (1935), *Scholia in Apollonium Rhodium vetera*. Berlin.
Wenkebach, E. (1936), *Galeni in Hippocratis Epidemiarum librum III commentaria III*. Leipzig–Berlin.
Wenskus, O., and Daston, L. (2006a), 'Paradoxographi', in *Brill's New Pauly*.
—— and —— (2006b), 'Paradoxographoi', in *Der Neue Pauly*.
Wescher, C. (1874), *Dionysii Byzantii de Bospori navigatione quae supersunt: una cum supplementis in geographos Graecos minores*. Paris.
West, M. L. (2003), *Greek Epic Fragments: From the Seventh to the Fifth Centuries BC* (Loeb Classical Library, 497). Cambridge, Mass.–London.

—— (2009), 'All Iberia is divided into two parts', in K. Brodersen and J. Elsner (eds), *Images and Texts on the 'Artemidorus Papyrus': Working Papers on P.Artemid.* (Stuttgart), 95–101.

West, S. R. (1991), 'Herodotus' portrait of Hecataeus', *Journal of Hellenic Studies*, 111: 144–60.

—— (2003), '"The most marvellous of all seas": the Greek encounter with the Euxine', *Greece and Rome*, 50. 2: 151–67.

—— (2004), 'Herodotus on Aristeas', in C. J. Tuplin (ed.), *Pontus and the Outside World: Studies in Black Sea History, Historiography, and Archaeology* (Leiden–Boston), 43–67.

—— (2012), 'Skylax's problematic voyage: a note on Hdt. IV 44', *Eikasmos*, 23: 159–67.

Wheeler, R. E. M. (1954), *Rome beyond the Imperial Frontiers*. London.

Whitby, L. M. (2011), 'Onesikritos (134)', in *BNJ*.

White, S. A. (2002), 'Happiness in the hellenistic Lyceum', in R. A. Shiner and L. J. Jost (eds), *Eudaimonia and Well-being* (Kelowna, BC), 69–93.

Whittaker, C. R. (2004), *Rome and its Frontiers: The Dynamics of Empire*. London–New York.

Wiesehöfer, J., and Müller, S. (eds 2017), *Parthika: Greek and Roman Authors' Views of the Arsacid Empire*. Wiesbaden.

Wijsman, H. J. W. (1998), 'Thule applied to Britain', *Latomus*, 57. 2: 318–23.

Wilcken, U. (1910), 'Die attische Perigese von Hawara', in *Genethliakon Carl Robert zum 8. März 1910* (Berlin), 189–226.

Wilkinson, J. (1999), *Egeria's Travels: Translated with Supporting Documents and Notes*, 3rd edn. Oxford.

Williams, M. F. (2018), 'Apollodoros of Athens (244)', in *BNJ*².

Wilson, A. I. (2015a), 'Red Sea trade and the state', in F. De Romanis and M. Maiuro (eds), *Across the Ocean: Nine Essays on Indo-Mediterranean Trade* (Leiden–Boston), 13–32.

Wilson, N. G. (2015b), *Herodoti Historiae* (Oxford Classical Texts). 2 vols. Oxford.

Winiarczyk, M. (2007), 'Das Werk Die Erziehung Alexanders des Onesikritos von Astypalaia (FGrHist 134 F 1–39): Forschungsstand (1832–2005) und Interpretationsversuch', *Eos*, 94: 197–250.

Winkler, G. (1993), with R. König, *C. Plinius Secundus d. Ä., Naturkunde, lateinisch-deutsch, Buch V: Geographie. Afrika und Asien* (Sammlung Tusculum). Munich.

—— (2002), with R. König, *C. Plinius Secundus d. Ä., Naturkunde, lateinisch-deutsch, Bücher III/IV: Geographie. Europa*, 2nd edn (Sammlung Tusculum). Düsseldorf–Zürich.

—— and König, R. (1997), *C. Plinius Secundus d. Ä., Naturkunde, lateinisch-deutsch, Buch II*, 2nd edn (Sammlung Tusculum). Düsseldorf–Zürich.

Wipszycka, E. (1965), *L'Industrie textile dans l'Égypte romaine*. Breslau.

Wittmann, A. (1979), 'The obliquity of the ecliptic', *Astronomy and Astrophysics*, 73. 1–2: 129–31.
Wiznura, A., and Williamson, C. G. (2018–20), 'Mountains of memory: triangulating landscape, cult and regional identity through Zeus', *Pharos*, 24: 77–112.
Wolff, É. (ed. 2020). *Rutilius Namatianus, aristocrate païen en voyage et poète*. Bordeaux.
Wolska-Conus, W. (1968–73), *Cosmas Indicopleustès, Topographie chrétienne*. 3 vols. Paris.
Woodman, J. E. (1964), 'The Expositio totius mundi et gentium: its geography and its language.' MA thesis, Ohio State University.
Worthington, I. (ed. 2007–), *Brill's New Jacoby*. Leiden.
Woudhuysen, G. (2019), 'Myrmeicus or Myrmecius?', *Mnemosyne*, 72. 5: 840–60.

Xian, R. (2020), 'The Cyrus anecdote in Herodotus 9.122', *Classical Quarterly*, 70. 1: 16–26.

Yarrow, L. M. (2005), *Historiography at the End of the Republic: Provincial Perspectives on Roman Rule*. Oxford.

Zadorojnyi, A. V. (2013), 'Shuffling surfaces: epigraphy, power, and integrity in the Graeco-Roman narratives', in P. Liddel and P. Low (eds), *Inscriptions and their Uses in Greek and Latin Literature* (Oxford), 365–86.
Zaikov, A. V. (2004), 'Alcman and the image of Scythian steed', in C. J. Tuplin (ed.), *Pontus and the Outside World: Studies in Black Sea History, Historiography, and Archaeology* (Leiden–Boston), 69–84.
Zehnacker, H. (2004), *Pline l'Ancien, Histoire naturelle, livre III: géographie des mondes connus: Italie, Espagne, Narbonnaise*, revised edn (Collection des universités de France, série latine, 347). Paris. ['Budé' edition.]
—— and Silberman, A. (2017), *Pline l'Ancien, Histoire naturelle, livre IV: géographie de l'Europe, suite* (Collection des universités de France, série latine, 409). Paris. ['Budé' edition.]
Zhang, X.-S. (2004), 'The name of China and its geography in Cosmas Indicopleustes', *Byzantion*, 74. 2: 452–62.
Zhmud, L. (2004), 'Dikaiarchos aus Messene', in H. Flashar (ed.), *Philosophie der Antike* (Basel), 568–75.
—— (2016), 'Pythagoras' northern connections: Zalmoxis, Abaris, Aristeas', *Classical Quarterly*, 66. 2: 446–62.
Zimmermann, K. (2002), 'Eratosthenes' chlamys-shaped world: a misunderstood metaphor', in D. Ogden (ed.), *The Hellenistic World: New Perspectives* (Swansea/London), 23–40.

Zucker, A. (2008), 'Iouba II of Mauretania, C. Iulius (ca 20 BCE–24 CE)', *Encyclopedia of Ancient Natural Scientists* 441–2.

Zweifel, U. (2012), 'Diomedes in der Adria: ein Vergleich archäologischer und schriftlicher Quellen', Seminararbeit. Universität Zürich. www.archaeologie.uzh.ch/static/onlineart/DiomedesAdria.htm [last accessed 14 March 2023].

Concordances

ABBREVIATIONS

In these Concordances, abbreviations follow the *Oxford Classical Dictionary*, with these additions:

Agatharch.	Agatharchides
Agathem.	Agathemeros
[Antig. Car.]	Ps.-Antigonos of Karystos
Artemid.	Artemidoros
Avien. *OM*	Avienus, *Ora maritima*
Const. Porph.	Constantine Porphyrogennetos
Adm. imp.	*De administrando imperio*
Them.	*De thematibus*
Dikaiarch.	Dikaiarchos
Dion. Kall.	Dionysios son of Kalliphon
Eratosth.	Eratosthenes
Eux.	Ps.-Arrian, *Periplous of the Euxine*
Hekat.	Hekataios
Herakl. Krit.	Herakleides Kritikos
Hipparch.	Hipparchos
Markian.	Markianos
Mart. Cap.	Martianus Capella
Menipp.	Menippos
Nik.	the *Nikomedean Periodos* ['Ps.-Skymnos']
Poseidon.	Poseidonios
Ps.-Skyl.	Pseudo-Skylax
Σ	scholion, scholia
Str.	Strabo
Timosth.	Timosthenes

I. CONCORDANCE OF EXTRACTS BY CHAPTER

Includes displayed quotations found in the Introduction. Where a reference locator stands with blank cells to its left, understand the locator in the first column to be the same as in the row above (see e.g. Artemidoros 44b).
‡ = not yet published (in *FGrH*)

before Introduction			
	Anth. Gr. 9. 144 (Anyte)		
Introduction			
§VI. 1. e	Ptol. *Geog.* 3. 17. 1–2		
§VI. 2. a	Hdt. 4. 85. 2–86. 3		
§VI. 2. c	Xen. *Anab.* 4. 4. 1–3		
§VI. 2. c	Xen. *Anab.* 4. 8. 1		
§VI. 2. e	Str. 1. 2. 8, C34 (Eudoxos)		
§VI. 2. g	Polyb. 3. 39. 6–11		
§VI. 2. g	Polyb. 3. 47. 9		
§VI. 2. g	Polyb. 3. 48. 10–12		
§VI. 4. c	Str. 13. 1. 36, C599 (Hestiaia)		
§III. 3. m	Phot. *Bibl.* cod. 72. 49b 39–50a 4 (Ktesias)		
§III. 3. n	Plin. *HN* 37. lxxvii. 201–2		
§V. 3	Arist. *Mete.* 2. 6, 363a 25–b 1		

before Prologue			
	Hom. *Od.* 11. 121–34		

1 Aristeas of Prokonnesos		*BNJ*² 35	Bolton
1	Hdt. 4. 13	F 2	F 1
1	Hdt. 4. 13–14		T 12
1	Hdt. 4. 13–15	T 2	
1	Hdt. 4. 16		F 2
2	[Longinus] 10. 4	F 7	F 7
3	Maximus of Tyre, *Dissertatio* 10. 2	T 1b	T 19
4	Maximus of Tyre, *Dissertatio* 38. 3	T 1a	T 20
5	Suda α 3900 Aristeas	T 1	T 11

6	Tzetz. *Chil.* 7. 678–84	F 4	T 3
6	Tzetz. *Chil.* 7. 678–9	F 4	F 3
6	Tzetz. *Chil.* 7. 680–2	F 4	F 4
6	Tzetz. *Chil.* 7. 683–4	F 4	F 5

2 Skylax of Karyanda		*BNJ*² 709	
1	Hdt. 4. 44	T 3; F 1	
2	Arist. *Pol.* 7. 13, 1332b 12–27	F 5	
3	Str. 12. 4. 8, C566	F 11	
4	Str. 13. 1. 4, C583	F 12	
5	Str. 14. 2. 20, C658	T 2a	
6	Harp. s.v. *hypo gēn oikountes*	F 6	
7	Ath. 2. 82, 70a–c	FF 3–4	
8	Philostr. *VA* 3. 47	F 7a	
9	Markian. pref. to Ps.-Skyl.	T 4; F 2	*FGrH* 2046 T 6
10	Markian. *Epit. Men.* 2	T 6	
11	Steph. Byz. κ 102 Karyanda	T 2b	
12	Const. Porph. *Them.* 1. 2	F 13	*FGrH* 2046 T 7
13	*Suda* σ 710 Skylax of Karyanda	T 1	*FGrH* 1000 T 1; 2046 T 8
14	Tzetz. *Chil.* 7. 621–36	F 7b	

3 Hekataios of Miletos		*BNJ* 1	Fowler
1	Hdt. 2. 143. 1	T 4	T 4
2	Agatharch. 64	T 14	
3	Dion. Hal. *Thuc.* 5	T 17a	T 17a
4	Str. 1. 1. 1, C1	T 11a	T 11a
5	Str. 1. 1. 11, C7	T 11b	T 11b
6	Str. 7. 3. 6, C298–9	T 13	T 13
7	Plin. *HN* 1. 4	T 25a	T 25a
7	Plin. *HN* 1. 5	T 25b	T 25b
7	Plin. *HN* 1. 18	T 25c	T 25c
8	Aët. *Placita* 2. 20. 6	F 302d	

9	Agathem. 1. 1	T 12a	T 12
10	Σ Dionys. Per. p. 428, col. i. 7–9	T 12b	
11	Ath. 2. 82, 70a–b	T 15a	
12	Ath. 9. 79, 410e	T 15b	T 15b
13	Avien. *OM* 32–42	T 23	T 23
14	*Suda* ε 360 Hekataios	T 1	T 1a
15	Σ Hom. *Od.* 10. 139	F 35c	F 35A
16	Σ Ap. Rhod. 1. 551 A	F 2	F 2
17	Σ Ap. Rhod. 4. 257–62 B	F 18a	F 18a
18	Σ Ap. Rhod. 4. 282–91 B	F 18b	F 18b
19	Steph. Byz. α 288 Amphanai	F 3	F 3
20	Steph. Byz. o 25 Oine	F 4	F 4
21	Steph. Byz. φ 12 Phalanna	F 5	F 5
22	Str. 8. 3. 9, C341	F 25	
23	Σ Ap. Rhod. 2. 998–1000	F 7b	F 7b
24	Steph. Byz. χ 2 Chadisia	F 7a	F 7a
25	Steph. Byz. ψ 21 Psophis	F 6	F 6
26	Natalis Comes 7. 2	F 35b	
27	Natalis Comes 9. 9	F 6b	
28	Ath. 4. 31, 148f	F 9	F 9
29	Σ Ap. Rhod. 2. 946–54 C	F 34	F 34
30	Steph. Byz. μ 126 Melia	F 11	F 11
31	Steph. Byz. μ 227 Mygissos	F 12	F 12
32	Steph. Byz. τ 178 Tremile	F 10	F 10
33	Harp. s.v. *rhodōniá*	F 37	
34	Steph. Byz. ε 55 Elibyrge	F 38	
35	Steph. Byz. υ 30 Hyops	F 48	
36	Steph. Byz. κ 138 Kaulonia	F 84	
37	Steph. Byz. α 65 Adria	F 90	
38	Str. 7. 5. 8, C316	F 102b	
39	Steph. Byz. χ 22 Chaonia	F 105	
40	Steph. Byz. δ 52 Dexaroi	F 103	
41	Steph. Byz. ω 15 Orikos	F 106	
42	Str. 6. 2. 4, C271	F 102c	
43	Steph. Byz. χ 7 Chalaion	F 113a	

44	Steph. Byz. χ 6 Chaironeia	F 116	
45	Steph. Byz. γ 68 Gephyra	F 118	
46	Steph. Byz. χ 17 Chalkis	F 129	
47	Ath. 10. 67, 447d	F 154	
48	Steph. Byz. χ 8 Chalastra	F 146	
49	Hdn. *General Prosody* 5 fr. 34 Hunger	F 145a	
50	Steph. Byz. μ 81 Maroneia	F 159	
51	Steph. Byz. χ 40 Cherronesos	F 163	
52	Steph. Byz. λ 46 Lemnos	F 138a	
53	Steph. Byz. τ 91 Tenedos	F 139	
54	Steph. Byz. μ 262 Mytilene	F 140	
55	Steph. Byz. χ 44 Chios	F 141	
56	Hdn. *On the Unique Word* 2. 31. 26 (937. 10–11 Lentz)	F 166	
57	Steph. Byz. μ 119 Melanchlainoi	F 185	
58	Plin. *HN* 4. xiii. 94	F 370	
59	*Epimerismi Homerici* s.v. *memetreatai*	F 196	
60	Amm. Marc. 22. 8. 10–13	F 197	T 12A
61	*Eux.* 49 (*Nik.* 865 ff.)	F 195	
62	Steph. Byz. ε 123 Hermonassa	F 208	
63	Steph. Byz. χ 47 Choi	F 207	
64	Steph. Byz. χ 48 Choirades	F 204	
65	Steph. Byz. χ 19 Chalybes	F 203	
66	Str. 12. 3. 25, C552–3 (Eust. *Il.* 2. 852)	F 199	T 25B
67	Str. 12. 3. 22, C550–1	F 217	T 25C
68	Steph. Byz. α 4 Abarnos	F 220	
69	Steph. Byz. μ 249 Myrikous	F 222	
70	Steph. Byz. α 245 Amazoneion	F 226	

71	Steph. Byz. κ 313 Korykos	F 231	
72	Steph. Byz. μ 125 Meleteios kolpos	F 227	
73	Hdn. *On the Unique Word* 1. 13. 19–20 (920. 7–8 Lentz)	F 234	
74	Str. 14. 1. 8, C635	F 239	
75	Steph. Byz. ξ 2 Xanthos	F 255	
76	Steph. Byz. ι 29 Idyros	F 260	
77	Steph. Byz. ν 3 Nagidos	F 266	
78	Steph. Byz. σ 143 Side	F 262	
79	Steph. Byz. χ 24 Charadros	F 265	
80	Steph. Byz. κ 313 Korykos	F 267	
81	Steph. Byz. δ 150 Doros	F 275	
82	Steph. Byz. κ 287 Kyre	F 281	
83	Steph. Byz. π 49 Parikane	F 282	
84	Harp. s.v. *kypassis*	F 284	
85	Steph. Byz. υ 57 Hyope	F 287	
86	Steph. Byz. μ 232 Mykoi	F 289	
87	Ath. 2. 82, 70a	F 291	T 15a
88	Ath. 2. 82, 70b	F 292a	
89	Ath. 2. 82, 70b	F 296	
90	Steph. Byz. γ 31 Gandarai	F 294a	
91	Steph. Byz. ω 13 Opiai	F 299	
92	Arr. *Anab.* 5. 6. 5	F 301	T 15c
93	Steph. Byz. φ 8 Phakousa	F 303	
94	Steph. Byz. α 79 Atharrhabis	F 304	
95	Steph. Byz. χ 39 Chemmis	F 305	
96	Hdn. *On the Unique Word* 2. 36. 29–31 (942. 11–13 Lentz)	F 307	
97	Aelius Aristeides, *Oration* 36. 108	F 308	
98	Steph. Byz. ε 43 Heleneios	F 309	
99	Steph. Byz. ε 179 Ephesos	F 310	

100	Ath. 10. 67, 447c	F 323a	
101	Ath. 10. 13, 418e	F 323b	
102	Steph. Byz. υ 49 Hysaeïs	F 326	
103	Steph. Byz. σ 204 Skiapodes	F 327	
104	Ath. 9. 79, 410e	F 358	T 15b
105	Steph. Byz. μ 86 Maskotos	F 333	
106	Steph. Byz. φ 86 Phoinikoussai	F 278	
107	Steph. Byz. μ 108 Megasa	F 335	
108	Steph. Byz. κ 246 Kybos	F 343	
109	Steph. Byz. θ 60 Thrinke	F 356	
110	Hdn. *On the Unique Word* 2. 31. 25-6 (937. 9-10 Lentz)	F 355	
111	Steph. Byz. μ 131 Melissa	F 357	

before chapter 4		
	Anth. Gr. 7. 256 (Plato)	

4 Hanno of Carthage		*BNJ* 673	*FGrH* 2208
A	cod. Heidelbergensis 398, 55ʳ–56ʳ		F 1
B 1	Palaiphatos 31		F 4
B 2	Ps.-Arist. *Mir. ausc.* 37		F 6
B 3	Pomponius Mela 3. 89–99	F 24	FF 5a, 7a
B 4	Plin. *HN* 2. lxvii. 169		T 2b
B 5	Plin. *HN* 5. i. 8		T 3
B 6	Plin. *HN* 6. xxxvi. 200		T 5b
B 7	Arr. *Ind.* 43. 11–12		F 2
B 8	Ath. 3. 25, 83c		T 7
B 9	Markian. *Epit. Men.* 2		T 4

6 Eudoxos of Knidos		Lasserre (fr.)	Pfeiffer, *Kallimachos* (fr.)	Eleftheriou (fr.)
1	Str. 1. 1. 1	273b		

2	Plut. *Non posse suaviter vivere secundum Epicurum*, 10 (*Mor.* 1093b–c)	272		
3	Agathem. 1. 1	273a		
4	Agathem. 1. 2	276a		
5	Tzetz. *Chil.* 7. 633–8	274		
6	[Antig. Car.] 123	337		A20.8
7	[Antig. Car.] 162	333	407 XXXIV	B05.5
8	Ps.-Arist. *Mir. ausc.* 173	338		
9	Str. 12. 3. 42, C562–3	329, 335		
10	Str. 13. 1. 4, C582	336		
11	Zen. *Proverbs* 5. 56	284b		
12	Sext. Emp. *Pyrrh. hypot.* 1. 152	278b		
13	Ath. 9. 47, 392d–e	284a		
14	Diogenes Laërtios 8. 8. 90	339		
15	Diogenes Laërtios 9. 11. 83	278a		
16	Steph. Byz. α 437 Armenia	279		
17	Steph. Byz. α 476 Askalon	285		
18	Steph. Byz. μ 212 Mossynoikoi	281		
19	Steph. Byz. σ 237 Syrmatai	277		
20	Steph. Byz. χ 1 Chabarenoi	283		
21	Steph. Byz. χ 19 Chalybes	282		
22	Str. 11. 7. 5, C510	344a		
23	Aët. *Placita* 4. 1. 7	288		
24	Plut. *De Is. et Os.* 6 (*Mor.* 353a–c)	300		
25	Plut. *De Is. et Os.* 21 (*Mor.* 359c)	291		
26	Plut. *De Is. et Os.* 64 (*Mor.* 377a)	298		
27	Ael. *NA* 10. 16	301		

28	Proclus, *In Ti.* 1. 31f (on 22b), i. 102 Diehl	302		
29	Steph. Byz. α 472 Asdynis	286		
30	Σ Hom. *Od.* 4. 477 ΕΡQHT	287		
31	Plin. *HN* 7. ii. 24	340 [*FGrH* 2206 Eudoxos of Kyzikos F3]		
32	[Antig. Car.] 129	347	407 I	B01.1
33	[Antig. Car.] 147	331	407 XIX	B03.11
34	Str. 7, fr. 21a	306		
35	Str. 12. 3. 21, C550	345		
36	Clem. Al. *Protrept.* 5. 64. 5 (5. 56 Butterworth)	303		
37	Steph. Byz. α 6 Abdera	307		
38	Steph. Byz. κ 26 Kale Akte	370		
39	Steph. Byz. σ 174 Sintia	308		
40	Steph. Byz. σ 229 Skymniadai	304		
41	Steph. Byz. φ 77 Phlegra	310		
42	Steph. Byz. χ 17 Chalkis	309		
43	Phot. *Lexikon* s.v. Haimon	346		
44	Σ Ap. Rhod. 1. 922	305		
45	Σ Hom. *Od.* 11. 239 HQT [rather than *Il.* 2. 158]	349		
46	[Antig. Car.] 138	355	407 X	B03.02
47	[Antig. Car.] 148	351	407 XX	12
48	Str. 9. 1. 1, C390–1	350		
49	Str. 9. 2. 35, C413	353		
50	Plut. *De Pyth. or.* 17 (*Mor.* 402d)	352		
51	Proclus, *In Hesiodi Opera* 640	354		
52	Steph. Byz. κ 119 Kastanaia	356		
53	Steph. Byz. π 176 Plataiai	311		
54	[Antig. Car.] 153	368	407 XXV	B04.4
55	Apollonius, *Mir.* 38	323		
56	Str. 8. 6. 21, C378–9	357		

57	Plin. *HN* 31. xiii. 16	314		
58	Ath. 7. 31, 288c	318		
59	Steph. Byz. α 21 Agathe	359		
60	Steph. Byz. α 71 Azania	313		
61	Steph. Byz. α 108 Aigion	317		
62	Steph. Byz. α 475 Asine	316		
63	Steph. Byz. ζ 30 Zygantis	322		
64	Steph. Byz. κ 211 Kremmyon	312		
65	Steph. Byz. o 79 Opikoi	321		
66	Steph. Byz. σ 227 Skylletion	320		
67	Steph. Byz. σ 263 Spina	358		
68	Steph. Byz. φ 46 Phelessaioi	319		
69	Σ Ap. Rhod. 4. 263–4 B	315		
70	Σ Eur. *Tro.* 221	360		
71	[Antig. Car.] 129	362	407 I	B01.1
72	[Antig. Car.] 161	363	407 XXXIII	B05.4
73	[Antig. Car.] 163	366	407 XXXV	B05.6
74	Str. 10. 4. 2, C474	365		
75	Plin. *HN* 6. xxxvi. 198	369 [*FGrH* 2206 Eudoxos of Kyzikos F 2]		
76	Plin. *HN* 31. ix. 13	364		
77	Harp. s.v. Lipara	326		
78	Porph. *Life of Pythagoras*, 7	325		
79	Hsch. s.v. *bous Kyprios*	361a		

7 Ps.-Skylax		*BNJ*² **709**	*FGrH* **2046**
1	Str. 13. 1. 4, C583	F 12	T 1
2	Σ Ap. Rhod. 1. 1177–8 A	F 10	T 2
3	Σ Ap. Rhod. 4. 1215	F 9	T 3
4	Avien. *OM* 32–44	T 5	T 4
5	Avien. *OM* 370–4	F 8	T 5
6	Markian. pref. to Ps.-Skylax	T 4; F 2	T 6

7	Const. Porph. *Them.* 1. 2	F 13	T 7

8 Pytheas of Massalia (*FGrH* 2215‡)		Roseman	Bianchetti
1	Hipparch. *Arat.* 1. 4. 1	F 1	F 1
2	Str. 1. 4. 2, C62–3	F 2	F 7a+8a+18a
2	Str. 1. 4. 3, C63	F 3; T 1a	F 7a+8a+18a
2	Str. 1. 4. 4, C63–4	T 2	F 7a+8a+18a
2	Str. 1. 4. 5, C64	T 3; F 4	F 6a
3	Str. 2. 1. 12, C71–2	T 4	F 8b
4	Str. 2. 1. 18, C75	T 5	F 11
5	Str. 2. 3. 5, C102	T 6	F 20
6	Str. 2. 4. 1–2, C104	TT 7–8; F 5	F 7b+8d+21
7	Str. 2. 5. 7–8, C114–15	T 9; F 6	F 8c
8	Str. 2. 5. 43, C136	T 10	F 14
9	Str. 3. 2. 11, C148	T 11	F 4
10	Str. 3. 4. 4, C157–8	T 12	F 22
11	Str. 4. 2. 1, C190	T 13	F 5
12	Str. 4. 4. 1, C195	T 14	F 6b
13	Str. 4. 5. 5, C201	T 15; F 7	F 8e
14	Str. 7. 3. 1, C295	T 16	F 8g
15	Geminos 6. 8–9	F 8	F 13a
16	Plin. *HN* 1. 2	T 17	F 3+10
17	Plin. *HN* 1. 4	T 20	F 7d
18	Plin. *HN* 1. 37	T 24	F 17
19	Plin. *HN* 2. lxxvii. 186–7	T 18a	F 9a
20	Plin. *HN* 2. xcix. 217	T 19	F 7e
21	Plin. *HN* 4. xiii. 95	T 21	F 16?
22	Plin. *HN* 4. xvi. 102	T 22	F 7c
23	Plin. *HN* 4. xvi. 104	T 23	F 8f
24	Plin. *HN* 37. xi. 35–6	T 25	F 15
25	Aët. *Placita* 3. 17. 3	T 26	F 2a–b
26	Kleomedes 1. 4. 208–10 Todd (1. 7. 37 Ziegler)	T 27	F 12a
27	Σ Ap. Rhod. 4. 761–5 A	T 30	F 19
28	Markian. *Epit. Men.* 2	T 28	F 23
29	Mart. Cap. 6. 595	T 18b	F 9b

30	Mart. Cap. 6. 608–9	T 29	F 12b	
31	Kosmas Indikopleustes 11. 80. 6–9	F 9	F 13b	
32	Steph. Byz. ω 21 Ostiones	T 1b	F 18b	

before chapter 9

Kallimachos, *Epigrams*, 18

9 Dikaiarchos of Messana (*FGrH* 1400 and 2015‡)		Mirhady	Wehrli	
1	Cic. *Att.* 6. 2. 3 (*Letter* 116 Shackleton Bailey)	F 79	F 20	
2	Geminos 17. 5	F 119	F 106	
3	Str. 1. 1. 1, C1–2	F 117	F 104	
4	Str. 2. 4. 1–3, C104–5	F 124	F 111	
5	Str. 3. 5. 5, C170	F 125	F 112	
6	Plin. *HN* 1. 2; 1. 4; 1. 5; 1. 6	F 116	F 116	
7	Plin. *HN* 2. lxv. 162	F 118	F 105	
8	Kleomedes 1. 5. 57–75 Todd (1. 8. 42–3 Ziegler)	Keyser pp. 361–2		
9	Theon of Smyrna 3. 3	F 120	F 107	
10	Agathem. 1. 2	F 122	F 109	
11	Agathem. 1. 5	F 123	F 110	
12	Mart. Cap. 6. 590–1	F 121	F 108	
13	Stob. *Flor.* 1. 38. 2	F 127 (misnumbered 128 by Keyser p. 368)	F 114	
14	Ioannes Lydus, *Mens.* 4. 107 Wünsch	F 126	F 113	
15	*Suda* δ 1062 Dikaiarchos	F 2	F 1	

10 Timosthenes of Rhodes		*FGrH* 2051	Roller	Wagner
1	*Nik.* 109–20	T 9	F 5	
2	Didymos, *Dem. Phil.* 11. 11. 28–37	F 12	F 18	
3	Str. 1. 2. 21, C29 (*BNJ* 87 F 74)	F 4	F 7	F 6

4	Str. 2. 1. 40, C92	T 7	F 3	F 2
5	Str. 2. 1. 41, C93	T 5	F 31	F 18
6	Str. 2. 1. 41, C94	T 8	F 4	F 4
7	Str. 3. 1. 7, C139–40	F 16	F 34	F 19
8	Str. 9. 3. 10, C421–2	T 3	F 37	p. 52
9	Str. 13. 2. 5, C618	F 24	F 22	F 35
10	Str. 17. 3. 6, C827	F 29	F 33	FF 20+11
11	Plin. *HN* 1. 4	T 10a	F 38	
11	Plin. *HN* 1. 5	T 10c		
11	Plin. *HN* 1. 6	T 10b		
12	Plin. *HN* 5. ix. 47	F 2	F 15	F 30
13	Plin. *HN* 5. xxxv. 129	F 23	F 16	F 36
14	Plin. *HN* 6. v. 15	F 11	F 27	F 25
15	Plin. *HN* 6. xxxiii. 163	F 21	F 13	F 9
16	Plin. *HN* 6. xxxv. 183	F 19	FF 12–13?	F 37
17	Plin. *HN* 6. xxxvi. 198	F 22	F 14	F 10
18	Agathem. 2. 6–7	F 3	F 6	F 6+13
19	Agathem. 5. 20	F 27	F 30	F 15+22+23
20	Ptol. *Geog.* 1. 15. 3	F 28	F 29	F 14
21	Ptol. *Geog.* 1. 15. 5	F 20	F 11	F 16
22	Harp. s.v. *eph' hieron*	F 9	F 24	F 27
23	Markian. *Epit. Men.* 2	T 1	F 1 init.	F 1
23	Markian. *Epit. Men.* 3. 10–21	T 4; F 15	F 2 init.	FF 5+12+21?
23	Markian. *Epit. Men.* 3. 21–4	T 2	F 2 med.	p. 5
23	Markian. *Epit. Men.* 3. 24–7	T 6	F 2 fin.	F 3
24	Steph. Byz. α 21 Agathe	F 17	F 32	F 38
25	Steph. Byz. α 200 Alexandreiai	F 6	F 21	F 34
26	Steph. Byz. α 357 Apia	F 7	F 20	F 33
27	Steph. Byz. α 457 Artake	F 8	F 23	F 31
28	Steph. Byz. χ 13 Chalkeia	F 30	F 35	
29	Σ Aesch. *Per.* 303	F 13	F 19	F 40
30	Σ Theoc. 13. 22–3 AB	F 25	F 26	F 26
31	Σ Ap. Rhod. 2. 296–7 B	F 14	F 28	F 39
32	Σ Ap. Rhod. 2. 498–527 Q	F 31	F 9	F 42

33	Σ Ap. Rhod. 2. 498–527 v	F 5	F 8	F 7
34	Σ Ap. Rhod. 2. 531–2	F 10	F 25	F 28
35	Σ Ap. Rhod. 3. 846–7 A	F 18	F 36	F 41?
36	Σ Ap. Rhod. 4. 1712	F 26	F 17	F 24
37	Σ Lucan 9. 411	F 1	F 10	F 8
38	Aristotle, *Mete.* 2. 6. 363a 21–365a 14			
intr.	Theophr. *On Winds*, 62: Ch. 10 n.3			

11 Herakleides Kritikos (*FGrH 2022*)		*BNJ*²	
1	cod. Par. suppl. gr. 443, pp. 114. 13–121. 23 (Herakl. Krit.)	369a F 1	
2	cod. Par. gr. 571, fos. 417–30	369a F 2	
3	cod. Par. suppl. gr. 443, pp. 121. 24–123. 19 (Herakl. Krit.)	369a F 3	
4	Apollonius. *Mir.* 19	369a T 1	
5	*P. Hawara* 80–1 (Anonymus Periegetes)	369 1–2	

12 Eratosthenes of Cyrene (*BNJ* 241; *FGrH* 2109‡)		Roller	Berger (frs)
epigraph	*Anth. Gr.* 7. 78 (Dionysios of Kyzikos)		
1	Str. 1. 1. 1, C1–2	F 1	IA 1
2	Str. 1. 1. 11, C7	F 12	IB 5
3	Str. 1. 2. 3, C15–17	F 2	IA 14+19+21
4	Str. 1. 2. 7, C18	F 3	IA 11
5	Str. 1. 2. 11–14, C21–3	F 6	IA 2+12, IB 3, IIIB 115
6	Str. 1. 2. 15, C24	F 5	IA 16
7	Str. 1. 2. 17, C25	F 4	IA 17
8	Str. 1. 2. 18–19, C26	F 7	IA 14
9	Str. 1. 2. 20–4, C28–30	FF 10–11	IA 7–8, IB 1
10	Str. 1. 2. 31, C38	F 17	IB 18
11	Str. 1. 2. 37, C44	F 9	IA 3

12	Str. 1. 3. 1–2, C47–8	F 13	IB 6+8, IIA 9, IIIB 93+114
13	Str. 1. 3. 3–4, C48–50	F 15	IB 7, IIIB 1+96
14	Str. 1. 3. 11–15, C54–7	F 16	IA 8 + IB 16+19+20
15	Str. 1. 3. 22, C61–2	F 20	IB 21
16	Str. 1. 3. 23–1. 4. 1, C62	F 19	IB 22
17	Str. 2. 1. 9, C70	F 22	IB 23
18	Str. 2. 4. 1–2, C104	F 14	IB 7+1+96
19	Str. 7. 3. 6–7, C298–300	F 8	IA 5–6, IB 4
20	Str. 11. 7. 4, C509–10	F 24	IC 23
21	Str. 15. 1. 7, C687	F 21	IB 23
22	Str. 16. 2. 44, C764	F 18	IB 17
23	Arr. *Anab.* 5. 3. 1–4	F 23	IB 24
24	Str. 1. 1. 8–9, C5–6	F 39	IIA 13
25	Str. 1. 4. 1–2, C62–3	F 25	IIA 1
25	Str. 1. 4. 1–2, C62–3	F 35	IIC 2
26	Str. 1. 4. 6–8, C64–6	F 33	IIA 6
26	Str. 1. 4. 6–8, C64–6	F 37	IIC 18
27	Str. 2. 1. 20, C77	F 40	IIB 36
28	Str. 2. 3. 2, C97	F 45	IIA 5
29	Str. 2. 5. 5–9, C112–16	F 30	IIB 27
29	Str. 2. 5. 5–9, C112–16	F 34	IIB 15+23, IIIA 39
30	Str. 2. 5. 13, C118	F 31	IIA 7
31	Str. 2. 5. 42, C135	F 36	IIC 5
32	Geminos 15	F 44	IIB 26
33	Plin. *HN* 2. lxxv. 183–lxxvi. 185	F 41	IIB 38
34	Plin. *HN* 2. cxii. 247–8	F 28	IIB 39
35	Plin. *HN* 6. xxxiv. 171	F 42	IIB 37
36	Plin. *HN* 12. xxx. 53	F 27	IIB 43
37	Agathem. 1. 2	F 32	IIC 1
38	Theon of Alexandria pp. 394–5	F 26	IIA 2
39	Amm. Marc. 22. 15. 31	F 43	IIB 40
40	Markian. *Peripl.* 1. 4	F 29	IIB 12

41	*Anametresis/Perimetros* 1	F 38	IIC 19
42	*Nik.*, ll. 405–12	F 146	IIIB 113
43	Caes. BGall. 6. 24	F 150	IIIB 118
44	*Vita Arati* 1	F 138	IIIB 102
45	Str. 1. 2. 20, C28	F 136	IIIB 100
46	Str. 1. 4. 9, C66	F 155	IIC 24
47	Str. 2. 1. 1–3, C67–8	F 47	IIIA 2
48	Str. 2. 1. 5, C69	F 50	IIIA 8
49	Str. 2. 1. 7, C69	F 73	IIC 21
50	Str. 2. 1. 10–11, C70–1	F 51	IIIA 11+35
51	Str. 2. 1. 16, C74	F 61	IIIA 13
52	Str. 2. 1. 19, C76	F 67	IIIA 9
52	Str. 2. 1. 20, C77	F 40	IIB 36
52	Str. 2. 1. 20, C77	F 68	IIIA 10
52	Str. 2. 1. 21, C77–8		IIB 29
52	Str. 2. 1. 22, C78	F 66	IIIB 2+5
52	Str. 2. 1. 22, C78	F 79	IIIB 19
52	Str. 2. 1. 23–6, C78–80	F 83	IIIB 25
52	Str. 2. 1. 27, C81	F 84	IIIB 26
52	Str. 2. 1. 28, C81	F 80	IIIA 30
52	Str. 2. 1. 29, C82–3	F 63	IIB 17, IIIA 31, IIIB 30
52	Str. 2. 1. 30, C83–4		
52	Str. 2. 1. 31, C84	F 49	IIIB 3+7
52	Str. 2. 1. 31, C84	F 82	
52	Str. 2. 1. 32, C85	F 92	IIIA 29
52	Str. 2. 1. 33, C85–6	F 56	IIIA 46
52	Str. 2. 1. 34, C86	F 85	IIIB 27
52	Str. 2. 1. 34, C86–7	F 64	IIIA 27, IIIB 11
52	Str. 2. 1. 35, C87–8	F 54	IIIA 15
52	Str. 2. 1. 36, C88–9	F 62	IIA 32, IIIA 28+33, IIIB 47
52	Str. 2. 1. 37, C89–90	F 55	IIIA 16
52	Str. 2. 1. 38, C90–1		
52	Str. 2. 1. 39, C91–2	F 52	IIIA 14+34, IIIB 65
52	Str. 2. 1. 40, C92	F 134	IIIB 97

52	Str. 2. 1. 40, C92–3	F 65	IIIA 40
52	Str. 2. 1. 40, C92–3	F 102	IIIB 54
52	Str. 2. 1. 41, C93–4	F 131	IIIB 66+96
53	Str. 2. 2. 2, C95	F 58	IIB 22
54	Str. 2. 4. 2, C104	F 132	IIIB 96
55	Str. 2. 4. 4, C106–7	F 133	IIIB 110+123+119
56	Str. 2. 4. 8, C108	F 135	IIIB 97
57	Str. 2. 5. 14, C118–19	F 53	IIIA 12
58	Str. 2. 5. 16, C120	F 46	IIIA 24
59	Str. 2. 5. 20, C123	F 104	IIIB 56
60	Str. 2. 5. 24, C125–6	F 128	IIB 28
61	Str. 2. 5. 35, C132–3	F 57	IIIA 17
61	Str. 2. 5. 36, C133	F 59	IIIA 18–19
61	Str. 2. 5. 38–41, C133–4	F 60	IIIA 20–2
62	Str. 3. 2. 11, C148	F 153	IIIB 122
63	Str. 3. 4. 7, C159	F 152	IIIB 120
64	Str. 3. 5. 5, C170	F 106	IIIB 58
65	Str. 5. 2. 6, C224	F 151	IIIB 116
66	Str. 8. 7. 2, C384	F 139	IIIB 103
67	Str. 8. 8. 4, C389	F 140	IIIB 105
68	Str. 10. 4. 5, C475	F 129	IIIB 94
69	Str. 11. 2. 15, C497	F 113	IIIB 73
70	Str. 11. 6. 1, C506–7	F 110	IIIB 68
71	Str. 11. 7. 3, C509	F 109	IIIB 67
72	Str. 11. 8. 8–9, C513–14	F 108	IIIB 20+63
73	Str. 11. 12. 4–5, C522	F 48	IIIA 23
74	Str. 11. 14. 7, C529	F 119	IIIB 84
74	Str. 11. 14. 8, C529	F 89	IIIB 32
75	Str. 14. 2. 29, C663–4	F 88	
76	Str. 14. 6. 4–5, C683–4	F 130	IIIB 91
77	Str. 15. 1. 10–11, C688–9	F 69	IIIB 6
78	Str. 15. 1. 13–14, C690	F 74	IIIB 12
79	Str. 15. 1. 20, C693	F 75	IIIB 17
80	Str. 15. 2. 1, C720	F 77	IIIB 22
81	Str. 15. 2. 8–9, C723–4	F 78	IIIB 20+23
82	Str. 15. 2. 14, C726	F 81	IIIB 240
83	Str. 15. 3. 1, C727	F 86	IIIB 34

84	Str. 16. 1. 12, C741	F 96	IIIB 36
85	Str. 16. 1. 15, C743	F 90	IIIB 37
86	Str. 16. 1. 21–2, C746–7	F 87	IIIB 38+31
87	Str. 16. 3. 2–6, C765–7	F 94	IIIB 39
88	Str. 16. 4. 2–4, C767–9	F 95	IIIB 48
89	Str. 17. 1. 1–2, C785–6	F 98	IIIB 51
90	Str. 17. 1. 19, C802	F 154	IB 9
91	Str. 17. 3. 1–2, C824	F 100	IIIB 59
92	Str. 17. 3. 8, C829	F 107	IIIB 60
93	Plin. *HN* 3. v. 75	F 127	IIIB 92
94	Plin. *HN* 5. vi. 39	F 101	IIIB 53
95	Plin. *HN* 5. vi. 40	F 103	IIC 20
96	Plin. *HN* 5. vii. 41–2	F 105	IIIB 57
97	Plin. *HN* 5. ix. 47	F 116	IIIB 77
98	Plin. *HN* 5. xxxiii. 127	F 126	IIIB 85
99	Plin. *HN* 6. i. 3	F 115	IIIB 78
100	Plin. *HN* 6. xv. 36	F 111	IIIB 71
101	Plin. *HN* 6. xxi. 56	F 70	IIIB 8
102	Plin. *HN* 6. xxiv. 81	F 76	IIIB 18
103	Plin. *HN* 6. xxviii. 108	F 93	IIIB 41
104	Plin. *HN* 6. xxxiii. 163	F 97	IIIB 50
105	Arr. *Anab.* 5. 6. 2–3	F 71	IIIB 9
106	Arr. *Ind.* 3. 1–5	F 72	IIIB 10
107	Amm. Marc. 22. 8. 10–13	F 114	IIIB 79
108	Σ Ap. Rhod. 2. 399–401 A	F 120	IIIB 75
109	Σ Ap. Rhod. 2. 1247 A	F 112	IIIB 72
110	Σ Ap. Rhod. 4. 131–5 B	F 121	IIIB 76
111	Σ Ap. Rhod. 4. 282–91 B	F 149	IIIB 99
112	Σ Ap. Rhod. 4. 310	F 148	IIIB 98
113	Σ Ap. Rhod. 4. 1215	F 145	IIIB 112
114	Σ Eurip. Med. 2	F 117	IIIB 80
115	Procl. *In Ti.* 1. 37b (on 22e), i. 120 Diehl	F 99	IIIB 52
116	Steph. Byz. α 44 Agraioi	F 142	IIIB 108
117	Steph. Byz. α 254 Amaxa	F 123	IIIB 87
118	Steph. Byz. α 493 Assyria	F 91	IIIB 35
119	Steph. Byz. α 547 Autariatai	F 144	IIIB 111

120	Steph. Byz. γ 8 Gangra	F 122	IIIB 86
121	Steph. Byz. δ 143 Dyrrhachion	F 143	IIIB 109
122	Steph. Byz. ι 123 Ichnai	F 137	IIIB 101
123	Steph. Byz. τ 39 Tarsos	F 124	IIIB 88
124	Steph. Byz. τ 52 Tauriskoi	F 147	IIIB 117
125	Tzetzes (Isaak/Ioannes), *On Lycophron* 1285	F 118	IIIB 82
126	Eust. *Dionys. Per.* 867	F 125	IIIB 89
127	Eust. *Il.* 2. 612	F 141	IIIB 106

13 Mnaseas of Patara (*FGrH* 2031‡)		Cappelletto (fr.)
1	Harp. s.v. Hippia Athena	2
2	Fulg. *Myth.* 2. 16	1
3	Ath. 4. 47, 158c	3
4	Ath. 7. 47, 296b–c	4
5	Ath. 12. 40, 530c	5
6	Steph. Byz. ε 6 Engelanes	6
7	Hdn. *General Prosody* 7 fr. 42 Hunger	10
8	Ael. *NA* 17. 44 (46)	7
9	Ammonius 333	8
10	Fulg. *Explanation* 2	9
11	Phot. *Lexikon* s.v. Praxidike	12
12	Σ Theoc. 1. 64 c	11
13	Zen. *Proverbs* 2. 67	29
14	Ath. 8. 3, 331d	14
15	Arnobius, *Against the Nations*, 3. 37	13
16	Steph. Byz. α 151 Akanthos	26
17	Steph. Byz. δ 146 Dodone	16
18	Steph. Byz. δ 151 Dotion	27
19	Phot. *Lexikon* s.v. Zamolxis	28
20	Epimerismi Homerici s.v. Mousa	15

21	Σ Ap. Rhod. 1. 916–18 b	17
22	Σ Ap. Rhod. 2. 675	18
23	Σ Ap. Rhod. 2. 1052–7 a	19
24	Σ Ap. Rhod. 4. 263–4 b	20
25	Σ Eur. *Phoen.* 651	21
26	Σ Eur. *Rhes.* 36	22
27	Σ Hom. *Od.* 18. 85 b	23
28	Σ Pind. *Ol.* 10. 34 g	24
29	Σ Pind. *Pyth.* 4. 106 a	25
30	Σ Ap. Rhod. 1. 1126–31 b	30
31	Ath. 8. 37, 346d–e	31
32	Joseph. *AJ* 1. 93	33
33	Joseph. *Ap.* 1. 216–17	34
34	Joseph. *Ap.* 2. 112	35
35	Zen. *Proverbs* 2. 106	42
36	Harp. s.v. Saboi	32
37	Steph. Byz. δ 18 Dardanos	41
38	Σ Ap. Rhod. 1. 131	36
39	Σ Hom. *Il.* 19. 291–2	37
40	Σ Hom. *Il.* 20. 234 d	38
41	Σ Luc. *Iupp. Trag.* 6	39
42	Σ Theoc. 13. 75c	40
43	Hsch. s.v. *Barkaiois ochois*	43
44	Plin. *HN* 37. xi. 38	44
45	Zen. *Proverbs* 3. 25	46
46	Σ Ap. Rhod. 2. 498–527 a	45
47	Phot. *Lexikon* s.v. *pythou chelidonos*	47
48	Plut. *De Is. et Os.* 37 (*Mor.* 365f)	50
49	Hdn. *General Prosody* 11 (263. 35–264. 1 Lentz)	49
50	Ath. 7. 62, 301d	48
51	Σ Aesch. *Per.* 747	51
52	Σ Dionysios Thrax 6	52
53	Σ Hom. *Il.* 15. 336 c	53

14 Skymnos of Chios		*FGrH* 2047	Gisinger
1	Hdn. *On the Unique Word* 1. 19 (Hdn. 925. 5–8 Lentz)	F 9	F 1
2	Steph. Byz. α 413 Areos nesos	F 8	F 2
3	Steph. Byz. ε 123 Hermonassa	F 6	F 4
4	Σ Ap. Rhod. 4. 277–8 A	F 7	F 3
5	Apollonius, *Mir.* 15	F 5	F 9
6	Steph. Byz. α 21 Agathe	F 1	F 8
7	Steph. Byz. π 56 Paros	F 2	F 6
8	Σ Ap. Rhod. 4. 282–91 B (1st part)	F 3	F 7
8	Σ Ap. Rhod. 4. 282–91 B (2nd part)	F 4	F 5

15 Agatharchides of Knidos (*FGrH* 2001‡)		Burstein (1989)	Müller (1855)
1	Phot. *Bibl.* cod. 250. 441b 16–445b 36		
2	Diod. 3. 11. 4–48. 5		
2	Phot. *Bibl.* cod. 250. 445b 36–460b 16		
2	Phot. *Bibl.* cod. 250. 460b 3–16 (*BNJ* 86 T 3)		
3	Str. 16. 4. 13–15, C772–4		
3	Str. 16. 4. 5, C769	fr. II.2	
3	Str. 16. 4. 7–10, C770–1	fr. II.3	
4	Plin. *HN* 8. viii. 24–5	fr. II.1	
5	Plut. *Quaest. conv.* 8. 9 (*Mor.* 733b 5–c 1)	fr. I.1	fr. 113
6	Ael. *NA* 5. 27. 6	fr. 79	fr. 79a
7	Ael. *NA* 17. 41 (43)	fr. 71b	
8	Phot. *Bibl.* cod. 213. 171a 6–b 17 (*BNJ* 86 T 2)		

16 Hipparchos of Nikaia (*FGrH* 2112‡)		Dicks (fr.)
1	Cic. *Att.* 2. 6	D
2	Str. 1. 2. 1–2, C14–15	E

3	Str. 2. 1. 41, C93–4	F
4	Str. 8. 1. 1, C332	G
5	Str. 12. 4. 9, C566	B
6	Plin. *HN* 2. ix. 53	H
7	Plin. *HN* 2. xxiv. 95	I
8	Sext. Emp. *Math.* 5	L
9	Ael. *NA* 7. 8	C
10	Cat. Cod. Astr. Gr. 5. 1, p. 205	K
11	Servius in Verg. *Geo.* 1. 137	J
12	*Suda* ι 521 Hipparchos	A
13	Str. 1. 1. 2, C2	1
14	Str. 1. 1. 9, C5–6	4
15	Str. 1. 1. 12, C7	11
16	Str. 1. 2. 3, C16	2
17	Str. 1. 2. 20, C27	3
18	Str. 1. 3. 12, C55	6
19	Str. 1. 3. 13–15, C55–7	8–10
20	Pomponius Mela 3. 7. 7	5
21	Eust. *Dionys. Per.* 473	7
22	Str. 2. 1. 4, C68–9	12
23	Str. 2. 1. 7, C69–70	13
24	Str. 2. 1. 11–12, C71	14–15
25	Str. 2. 1. 19–20, C76–7	16–17
26	Str. 2. 1. 21–2, C77–8	19
27	Str. 2. 1. 27, C80–1	21
28	Str. 2. 1. 29, C81–2	22
29	Str. 2. 1. 34–5, C86–7	23–5
30	Str. 2. 1. 36, C88–9	20, 26–7
31	Str. 2. 1. 38–40, C90–2	28–32
32	Str. 2. 1. 41, C94	33–4
33	Str. 1. 1. 21, C12	40
34	Str. 1. 4. 1, C62	35
35	Str. 1. 4. 4, C63	53
36	Str. 2. 1. 12–13, C71–2	55, 59, 44
37	Str. 2. 1. 18, C75	58, 61
38	Str. 2. 5. 7, C113	36

I. CONCORDANCE OF EXTRACTS BY CHAPTER • 1117

39	Str. 2. 5. 8, C115	54
40	Str. 2. 5. 34, C131–2	39
40	Str. 2. 5. 35, C132	43
40	Str. 2. 5. 36, C133	46–7
40	Str. 2. 5. 38, C133	48
40	Str. 2. 5. 39, C134	49–50
40	Str. 2. 5. 40, C134	51
40	Str. 2. 5. 41, C134	52, 56
40	Str. 2. 5. 42, C134–5	57
40	Str. 2. 5. 42, C135	60, 62
41	Plin. *HN* 2. cxii. 247	38
42	Ptol. *Geog.* 1. 7. 4	45
43	Ptol. *Geog.* 1. 7. 9	42
44	Ptol. *Syntaxis Mathematica* 1. 67. 22–68. 6	41
45	Σ Ptol. *Geog.* 1. 3. 3	37
46	Synesios, *Letter* 331b	63

17 *Nikomedean Periodos* ['Ps.-Skymnos']		*FGrH* 2048	Marcotte	Diller ('*Eux.*')	Diller ('*Nic.*')
fr.	lines 1–747	T 1			
1	*Eux.* 109 Podossinov	F 1	F 1	§80	748–50
2	Steph. Byz. δ 90 Dionysou *polis*	F 2a	F 2a		751–7
3	*Eux.* 107 Podossinov	F 2b	F 2b	§78	751–7
4	*Eux.* 105 Podossinov	F 3	F 3	§76	758–9
5	*Eux.* 103 Podossinov	F 4	F 4	§74	760–3
6	*Eux.* 101 Podossinov	F 5	F 5	§72	764–5
7	*Eux.* 99 Podossinov	F 6	F 6	§70	766–70
8	*Eux.* 97 Podossinov	F 7a	F 7a	§68	771–88
9	*Eux.* 94 Podossinov	F 7b	F 7b	§65	788–93
10	*Eux.* 92 Podossinov	F 8	F 8	§63	794
11	*Eux.* 91 Podossinov	F 9	F 9	§62	795–800
12	*Eux.* 88–9 Podossinov	F 10	F 10	§59–60	801–17
13	*Eux.* 87 Podossinov	F 11	F 11	§58	818–19
14	*Eux.* 82–3 Podossinov	F 12	F 12	§53–4	820–31
15	*Eux.* 80 Podossinov	F 13	F 13	§51	832–3
16	*Eux.* 79 Podossinov	F 14	F 14	§50	834–6

17	*Eux.* 78 Podossinov end	F 15a	F 15a	§49 end	837–60
18	*Eux.* 78 Podossinov beg.	F 15b	F 15b	§49 beg.	861–74
19	*Eux.* 74 Podossinov	F 16	F 16	§45	885–94
20	*Eux.* 77 Podossinov	F 17a	F 17a	§47 end	875–84
21	*Eux.* 76 Podossinov	F 17b	F 17b	§47 beg.	895–8
22	*Eux.* 66 Podossinov	F 18	F 18	§24B	899–913
23	*Eux.* 51 Podossinov	F 19	F 19	§9B	914–24
24	*Eux.* 45 Podossinov	F 20	F 20	§3B	925–37
25	*Eux.* 37	F 21	F 21		938
26	*Eux.* 35	F 22	F 22		939–49
27	*Eux.* 34	F 23	F 23		950–2
28	*Eux.* 33	F 24	F 24		953–5
29	*Eux.* 27	F 25	F 25		956–81
30	*Eux.* 25	F 26	F 26		982–5
31	*Eux.* 22	F 27	F 27		986–97
32	*Eux.* 18	F 28	F 28		998–1000
33	*Eux.* 16	F 29	F 29		1001–11
34	*Eux.* 14	F 30	F 30		1012–15
35	*Eux.* 10	F 31	F 31		1016–19
36	*Eux.* 8	F 32	F 32		1020–1
37	*Eux.* 7	F 33	F 33		1022–4
38	*Eux.* 6	F 34	F 34		1025–6

18 Artemidoros of Ephesos (***FGrH*** 2008‡)		Hoffmann	Stiehle	Schiano
1	Str. 4. 1. 4–5, C179–80			F 11
2	Str. 4. 1. 8, C183	F 1	F 22	F 15
3	Str. 4. 1. 11, C185	F 2	F 32	F 13
4	Plin. *HN* 2. cxii. 242–6	pp. 273–5	F 1	F 1a
5	Plin. *HN* 4. xxxvii. 121	*Epit.* 18	F 8	F 2a
6	Plin. *HN* 5. vi. 40	F 70	F 86	F 4a
7	Plin. *HN* 5. ix. 47	*Epit.* 17	F 81	F 3a
8	Agathem. 3. 10	p. 277		F 2b
8	Agathem. 3. 10	p. 277		F 3b
8	Agathem. 3. 10	p. 277		F 4b
8	Agathem. 4. 15–19	pp. 277–9		F 1b
8	Agathem. 5. 20	pp. 279–80		F 9b

9	P. Oxy. 24. 2694v. 18–32			F 9a
10	Markian. *Peripl.* 2. 19			F 18
11	Steph. Byz. β 148 Bounnos	p. 269	F 2	F 19
12	Steph. Byz. γ 50 Genoa	F 36	F 40	F 5
13	Steph. Byz. δ 45 Dekieton	p. 283	F 41	F 7
14	Steph. Byz. δ 58 Derton	*Epit.* 3	*Epit.* 4	F 6
15	Steph. Byz. κ 4 Kabellion	F 5	F 4	F 14
16	Steph. Byz. λ 61 Ligyres	*Epit.* 2	*Epit.* 3	F 8
17	Steph. Byz. μ 94 Mastramele	*Epit.* 1	*Epit.* 2	F 12
18	Steph. Byz. ν 13 Narbon			F 17
19	Steph. Byz. σ 116 Sekoanos	F 4	F 5	F 16
20	Steph. Byz. τ 53 Tauroëis	F 6	F 3	F 10
21	Steph. Byz. α 6 Abdera	F 17	F 15	
22	Steph. Byz. η 13 Hemeroskopeion	F 18	F 19	
23	Steph. Byz. ι 19a Iberiai	F 19	F 21	
24	Steph. Byz. κ 81 Karthaia	F 16	F 17	
25	Steph. Byz. κ 92 Karnos	p. 284	F 29	
26	Steph. Byz. μ 35 Malake	*Epit.* 4	p. 243	
27	Steph. Byz. ν 37 Nestos	p. 269	F 27	
28	Steph. Byz. τ 208 Tropis	F 22	F 30	
29	Steph. Byz. ψ 1 Psamathous	p. 284	F 28	
30	Steph. Byz. ω 16 Orisia/Oria	F 15	F 18	
31	Const. Porph. *Adm. imp.* 23	F 19	F 21–2	
32	Steph. Byz. β 62 Belitanoi	F 23	F 31	
33	Steph. Byz. κ 118 Kastalon	F 24		
34	Steph. Byz. τ 20 Tanos	F 28	F 53	
35	Steph. Byz. τ 63 Teanon	F 27	F 39	
36	Steph. Byz. τ 120 Tibyris	F 26	F 38	
37	Steph. Byz. φ 107 Phrourentanoi	F 25	F 37	
38	Porph. *De antr. Nymph.* p. 57 (§4 Davis *et al.*)	F 46	F 55	

39	Steph. Byz. φ 10 Phalakrai	p. 284	F 54
40	Steph. Byz. π 43 Parthenios	p. 285	F 68
41	Steph. Byz. ε 129 Erythra	F 54	F 71
42	Steph. Byz. ι 84 Hipponesos	F 53	F 72
43	Steph. Byz. λ 85 Lopadoussa	F 55	F 73
44a	Str. 17. 2. 1–5, C821–4		
44b	Diod. 3. 5. 1–11. 2 (*BNJ* 86 F 1 (3. 11. 1–3)		F 82 (3. 11. 1–2)
			F 92 (3. 1–11)
45	Steph. Byz. ψ 2 Psebo	p. 286	F 93
46	Steph. Byz. ψ 3 Psenako	p. 285	F 83
47	Steph. Byz. ψ 22 Psochemmis	F 62	F 84
48	Steph. Byz. δ 150 Doros	F 75	*Epit.* 15; F 111
49	Steph. Byz. τ 26 Taprobane	F 77	F 106
50	Steph. Byz. υ 51 Hysia	F 76	F 109a
51	Steph. Byz. ψ 7 Pseudokorasion	F 74	F 113
52	Ath. 8. 8, 333f–334a	F 82	F 121
53	Steph. Byz. ι 69 Ixiai	F 83	F 123
54	Steph. Byz. κ 90 Karne	p. 287	F 112
55	Steph. Byz. τ 79 Telmessos	F 81	F 120
56	Steph. Byz. κ 167 Korokondame	F 93	F 137
57	Steph. Byz. χ 18 Chalkitis	F 92	F 133
58	Str. 3. 1. 4, C137–8	F 8	F 13
59	Str. 3. 1. 5, C138	F 9	F 12
60	Str. 3. 2. 11, C148	F 10	F 11
61	Str. 3. 4. 3, C157	F 11	F 16
62	Str. 3. 4. 3, C157	F 56	F 77. 2
63	Str. 3. 4. 7, C159	F 12	F 26
64	Str. 3. 4. 17, C164	F 13	F 23

65	Str. 3. 5. 1, C167	F 20	F 25
66	Str. 3. 5. 5, C170	F 59	F 10
67	Str. 3. 5. 7, C172	F 14	F 14
68	Str. 4. 4. 6, C198	F 3	F 36
69	Str. 5. 2. 6, C224	F 34	F 48
70	Str. 5. 4. 6, C245	F 30	F 43
71	Str. 6. 1. 11, C261–2	F 31	F 44
72	Str. 6. 2. 1, C267	F 33	F 49
73	Str. 6. 3. 9–10, C283–5	incl. F 32	F 45–6
74	Str. 7, fr. 22a		F 66
75	Str. 8. 2. 1, C335	F 37	F 59
76	Str. 8. 6. 1, C367	F 39	
77	Str. 8. 8. 5, C389	F 38	F 59a
78	Str. 9. 5. 8, C433	F 42	F 63
79	Str. 9. 5. 15, C436	F 40	F 64
80	Str. 10. 2. 21, C459–60	F 41	F 57
81	Str. 10. 3. 5, C465		
82	Str. 10. 4. 3, C474–5		F 62
83	Str. 10. 5. 3, C485	F 44	F 60
84	Str. 11. 2. 14, C496–7	F 94	F 138
85	Str. 12. 7. 2, C570	F 87	F 119
86	Str. 12. 8. 1, C571	F 89	F 131
87	Str. 13. 3. 5, C622		F 129
88	Str. 14. 1. 22–3, C640–1		F 126
89	Str. 14. 1. 26, C642	F 88	F 127
90	Str. 14. 2. 10, C655		F 124
91	Str. 14. 1. 29, C663	F 84	F 125
92	Str. 14. 3. 3, C665	F 86	F 122
93	Str. 14. 5. 3, C670	F 85. 1	F 116 (?)
94	Str. 14. 5. 16, C675		F 115
95	Str. 14. 5. 22, C677		F 114
96	Str. 15. 1. 72, C719	F 79	F 109
97	Str. 16. 2. 33, C760	F 85. 2	F 116
98	Str. 16. 4. 5, C769–70	F 65	F 96
98	Str. 16. 4. 5–20, C769–79	F 65	F 96–102
98	Str. 16. 4. 15, C774–5	F 65	F 97
98	Str. 16. 4. 16, C775	F 65	F 98
98	Str. 16. 4. 17, C775–6	F 65	F 99

98	Str. 16. 4. 18, C776–8	F 65	F 100
98	Str. 16. 4. 19, C778–9	F 65	F 101
98	Str. 16. 4. 20, C779	F 65	F 102
99	Str. 17. 1. 18, C801	F 63	F 87
100	Str. 17. 1. 24, C803–4	F 64	F 88
101	Str. 17. 3. 2, C825	F 58	F 76
102	Str. 17. 3. 8, C829	F 57	F 77. 1
103	Str. 17. 3. 10, C830	F 61	F 79
104	Plin. *HN* 1. 2		
104	Plin. *HN* 1. 3		
104	Plin. *HN* 1. 4		
104	Plin. *HN* 1. 5		
104	Plin. *HN* 1. 6		
104	Plin. *HN* 1. 7		
104	Plin. *HN* 1. 36		
105	Plin. *HN* 4. xii. 77		F 70
106	Plin. *HN* 5. x. 59	F 68	
107	Plin. *HN* 5. xxxv. 129	F 91	F 117
108	Plin. *HN* 6. xv. 36–7		F 110
109	Plin. *HN* 6. xxii. 70	F 80	F 108
110	Plin. *HN* 6. xxxii. 156	F 72	
111	Plin. *HN* 6. xxxiii. 163–4	F 71	F 103
112	Plin. *HN* 6. xxxv. 183	F 69	F 94
113	Plin. *HN* 7. ii. 30	F 78	F 107
114	Plin. *HN* 36. xvii. 79	F 67	F 91
115	Ath. 3. 76, 111d (*BNJ*² 438 F 1)		
116	Harp. s.v. *Ganion kai Ganiada*		F 65
117	Hsch. s.v. *Skyria dikē*	F 43	
118	Hsch. s.v. Talantion	p. 273	F 52
119	Markian. *Epit. Men.* 3–4		
120	Markian. *Peripl.* 1. 1		FF 7, 95
121	Markian. *Peripl.* 2. 4		F 9
122	*Eux.* 92	F 95	F 67
123	Steph. Byz. α 4 Abarnos	p. 288	F 132
124	Steph. Byz. α 36 Ankon	p. 284	F 47
125	Steph. Byz. α 39 Agnotes	F 21	F 35

I. CONCORDANCE OF EXTRACTS BY CHAPTER

126	Steph. Byz. α 92 Aiga	p. 287	F 130	
127	Steph. Byz. α 239 Alonis	p. 284	F 5	
128	Steph. Byz. α 462 Artemita	p. 285	F 56	
129	Steph. Byz. α 496 Astai	p. 288	*Epit.* 10	
130	Steph. Byz. α 522 Atramitai	p. 286	F 104	
131	Steph. Byz. α 579 Apsyrtides	*Epit.* 8	*Epit.* 6	
132	Steph. Byz. β 59 Belbina	F 52		
133	Steph. Byz. β 144 Boulinoi	pp. 269–70	F 51	
134	Steph. Byz. γ 18 Gaitouloi	p. 285	F 75	
135	Steph. Byz. γ 75 Gigonos	F 50	F 78	
136	Steph. Byz. γ 119 Gynaikospolis	pp. 285–6	F 85	
137	Steph. Byz. δ 77 Didyme	p. 287	F 61	
138	Steph. Byz. ε 161 Eupalia	F 49	F 58	
				Müller
139	Steph. Byz. θ 22 Themisonion	*Epit.* 15		F 21
140	Steph. Byz. ι 115 Istros	F 90	F 62 bis	
141	Steph. Byz. κ 307 Kothon	*Epit.* 9		F 12
142	Steph. Byz. κ 234 Krya	*Epit.* 16	*Epit.* 1	
143	Steph. Byz. λ 36 Laodamanteia	*Epit.* 13		F 17
144	Steph. Byz. λ 119 Los	*Epit.* 10		F 13
145	Steph. Byz. μ 243 Myonesos	F 48	F 128	
146	Steph. Byz. μ 253 Myrmekion	F 51 + p. 288	F 69	
147	Steph. Byz. ξ 12 Xouches	*Epit.* 12		F 17
148	Steph. Byz. π 7 Paltos	*Epit.* 14	*Epit.* 16	
149	Steph. Byz. σ 242 Solkoi	*Epit.* 5	*Epit.* 5	
150	Steph. Byz. σ 263 Spina	F 35	F 42	
151	Steph. Byz. τ 66 Tegestra	*Epit.* 7	*Epit.* 8	
152	Steph. Byz. τ 159 Tourdetania	F 7	F 20	
153	Steph. Byz. τ 233 Tyros	p. 287	F 105	

154	Steph. Byz. φ 36 Pharousioi	F 60	F 74
155	Steph. Byz. φ 69 Philippoi	*Epit.* 11	*Epit.* 9
156	Steph. Byz. φ 76 Phlanon	*Epit.* 6	*Epit.* 7
157	Steph. Byz. ω 21 Ostiones	p. 282	F 34
158	Const. Porph. *Them.* 1. 42. 9		F 130
159	Tzetzes (Isaak/Ioannes), On Lycophron 633		F 24
160	*Epimerismi Homerici* s.v. *cheiros*	F 29	F 80
161	Proverbia e cod. Bodl.	F 45	
162	Σ Ap. Rhod. 2. 946–54 B		F 134
163	Σ Ap. Rhod. 2. 963–5 A		F 135
164	Σ Ap. Rhod. 3. 854–9 C	pp. 272–3	*Epit.* 18
165	Σ Ap. Rhod. 4. 257–62 B		F 136
166	Σ Dionys. Per. 14	F 47	
167	P. Artemid.		
168	Codex Monacensis 287. 161^v–162^r	F 66	F 90

19 Poseidonios of Apameia (*FGrH* 2041‡)		Kidd	*BNJ* 87
1	Str. 1. 1. 1, C1–2	T 75	—
2	Str. 2. 2. 1, C94	T 76a	T 15a
2	Str. 2. 2. 1–2. 3. 8, C94–104	F 49	T 19c
2	Str. 2. 3. 8, C104	T 76b	T 15b
2	Str. 2. 3. 8, C104	T 85	T 15b
3	Str. 2. 5. 14, C119	F 204	F 99
4	Str. 2. 5. 43, C135–6	F 208	F 76
5	Str. 8. 1. 1, C332	T 77	T 14
6	Str. 10. 3. 5, C465	T 78	T 16
7	Str. 11. 1. 5–6, C491–2	F 206	F 101a
8	Str. 17. 1. 21, C803	F 207	F 101b
9	Plin. *HN* 6. xxi. 57–8	F 212	F 100
10	Kleomedes 1. 4. 90–131 Todd (1. 6. 31–3 Ziegler)	F 210	F 78

11	Kleomedes 1. 7. 1–50 Todd (1. 10. 50–2 Ziegler)	F 202	F 97
12	Agathem. 1. 2	F 200a	F 98a
13	Achilles Tatius, *Introduction to Aratos' Phainomena*, 31	F 209	F 77
14	Solin. *Collectanea* 52. 1–2	F 213	—
15	Eust. *Il.* 7. 446	F 200b	—
16	Eust. *Dionys. Per.* 1	F 201	F 98b
17	Procl. *In Ti.* 4. 277d–e (on 40a-b), iii. 124–5 Diehl	F 205	—
18	Julian of Ascalon	F 203	—
19	Symeon Seth, *On the Usefulness of the Heavenly Bodies*, 44	F 211	—
20	Str. 1. 3. 16, C58	F 231	F 87
21	Str. 3. 2. 9, C146–7	F 239	—
22	Str. 6. 2. 3, C268–9	F 234	F 92
23	Str. 7. 5. 8, C316	F 235	F 93
24	Str. 11. 9. 1, C514	F 233	F 87a
25	Str. 13. 1. 67, C614–15	F 237	F 95
26	Str. 16. 1. 15, C743	F 236	F 94
27	Str. 16. 2. 42–3, C764	F 279	F 70
28	Str. 16. 4. 20, C779	F 238	F 96
29	Sen. *QNat.* 6. 21. 2	F 230	—
30	Sen. *QNat.* 6. 24. 6	F 232	—
31	Ath. 6. 23–5, 233d–234c	F 240a	F 48
32	Eust. *Od.* 4. 89	F 240b	—
33	Str. 1. 1. 7, C4	F 216	F 83
34	Str. 1. 1. 8–9, C5–6	F 214	F 82a
34	Str. 1. 1. 8–9, C5–6	T 79a	—
35	Str. 1. 3. 9, C53–4	F 221	F 91
36	Str. 1. 3. 12, C55	F 215	F 82b
36	Str. 1. 3. 12, C55	T 79b	—
37	Str. 3. 3. 3, C153	F 220	F 84
37	Str. 3. 3. 4, C153	F 224	F 49
38	Str. 3. 5. 7–8, C172–4	F 217	F 85

38	Str. 3. 5. 9, C174–5	F 218	F 86
39	Str. 4. 1. 7, C182–3	F 229	F 90
40	Str. 5. 1. 8, C214–15	F 225	F 89
41	Str. 6. 2. 11, C277	F 227	F 88
42	Str. 17. 1. 5, C790	F 222	F 79
43	Str. 17. 3. 10, C830	F 223	F 80
44	Sen. QNat. 2. 26. 4–7	F 228	—
45	Ath. 8. 7, 333b–d	F 226	F 29
46	Priscianus Lydus, Solutions to Chosroës, 6	F 219	—
47	Str. 3. 1. 5, C138	F 119	F 45
48	Str. 3. 4. 3, C157	F 247	F 50
49	Str. 3. 4. 15, C163	F 243	F 52
50	Str. 3. 5. 5, C169–70	F 246	F 53
51	Str. 3. 5. 10, C175	F 241	F 54
52	Str. 4. 1. 14, C188	F 248	F 34
53	Str. 6. 2. 1, C265–6	F 249	F 63
54	Str. 6. 2. 7, C273	F 250	F 64
55	Str. 16. 2. 4, C749–50	F 251	F 65
56	Str. 16. 2. 17, C755	F 244	F 66
57	Str. 17. 3. 4, C827	F 245	F 73
58	Ath. 1. 51, 28d	F 242	F 68
59	Ath. 14. 61, 649d	F 55a	F 3
60	Ath. 6. 84, 263c–d	F 60	F 8
61	Ath. 5. 46, 210e–f	F 62b	F 10
62	Ath. 4. 36–7, 151e–152f	F 67	F 15
63	Ath. 9. 8, 369c–d	F 70	F 19
64	Ath. 4. 39, 153e	F 73	F 22
65	Str. 1. 2. 34, C41–2	F 280	F 105a
66	Str. 3. 4. 13, C162–3	F 271	F 51
67	Str. 3. 4. 17, C165	F 269	F 58a
68	Str. 5. 2. 1, C218	F 268	F 57a
69	Str. 7. 2. 1–2, C292–4	F 272 (extended)	F 31
70	Str. 7. 3. 2–4, C295–7 and 7. 3. 7, C300	F 277a	F 104
71	Str. 16. 4. 27, C784–5	F 281a	F 105b
72	Ath. 2. 24, 45f	F 283	F 72

73	Eust. *Il.* 2. 782	F 281b	—
74	Eust. *Il.* 13. 6	F 277b	—
75	Σ Ap. Rhod. 2. 675	F 270	F 103

21 Menippos of Pergamon (*FGrH* 2029‡)			
1	Markian. *Epit. Men.*		
1	Markian. pref. to *Epit. Men.*		
2	*Anthologia Graeca* 9. 559 (Krinagoras)		
3	Agathem. 5. 20		
4	Steph. Byz. ε 123 Hermonassa		
5	Steph. Byz. ν 13 Narbon		
6	Steph. Byz. ν 59 Nikopolis		
7	Steph. Byz. χ 9 Chaldia		
8	Steph. Byz. χ 15 Chalkedon		
9	Const. Porph. *Them.* 10. 9		
9	Steph. Byz. σ 155 Sikelia		
10	Const. Porph. *Them.* 1. 2	*BNJ*² 709 F 13	*FGrH* 2046 T 7

before Chapter 22	
	Cicero, *De re publica*, 6. 21–2

22 Juba II of Mauretania		*BNJ*² 275
1	Plin. *HN* 6. xxx. 124	F 29
2	Ath. 3. 25, 83a–c	F 6
3	Plin. *HN* 5. i. 14–16	F 42
4	Plin. *HN* 5. x. 51–5	F 38a
5	Plin. *HN* 5. x. 59	F 39
6	Plin. *HN* 6. xxxiv. 175–xxxv. 179	F 35
7	Plin. *HN* 6. xxxvi. 201	F 43
8	Plin. *HN* 6. xxxvii. 202–5	F 44

9	Plin. *HN* 8. iv. 7	F 47a
10	Plin. *HN* 8. xlv. 107	F 57
11	Plin. *HN* 10. lxi. 126–7	F 60
12	Plin. *HN* 13. lii. 142	F 67
13	Plin. *HN* 37. xviii. 69	F 77
14	Plin. *HN* 37. xxxv. 114	F 79
15	Philostr. *VA* 2. 13	F 47b
16	Amm. Marc. 22. 15. 8	F 38b
17	Plin. *HN* 8. xiii. 35	F 58
18	Plin. *HN* 9. lvi. 115	F 71
19	Plin. *HN* 31. xv. 18	F 40–1
20	Plin. *HN* 6. xxxvi. 96–100	F 28
21	Plin. *HN* 6. xxxi. 136–41	F 1
22	Plin. *HN* 6. xxxii. 149–56	F 30–3
23	Plin. *HN* 6. xxxiii. 165–70	F 34
24	Plin. *HN* 12. xxi. 38–xxii. 39	F 62
25	Plin. *HN* 12. xxxi. 56	F 2
26	Plin. *HN* 12. xxxii. 60	F 63
27	Plin. *HN* 12. xxxiv. 67	F 64
28	Plin. *HN* 12. xxxviii. 78–xl. 80	F 65
29	Plin. *HN* 13. vii. 34	F 66
30	Plin. *HN* 15. xxviii. 99	F 68
31	Plin. *HN* 25. v. 14	F 69
32	Plin. *HN* 32. iv. 10	F 3
33	Plin. *HN* 33. xl. 118	F 72
34	Plin. *HN* 35. xxii. 39	F 74
35	Plin. *HN* 36. xlvi. 163	F 73
36	Plin. *HN* 37. ix. 24	F 76
37	Plin. *HN* 37. xviii. 73	F 78
38	Plin. *HN* 37. xxxii. 107–8	F 75
39	Ael. *NA* 15. 8	F 70
40	Hsch. s.v. Terebinthos	F 45
41	Plin. *HN* 25. xxxviii. 77–9	F 7
42	Dioskorides 3. 82. 1–2	F 8b

43	Galen, *De compositione medicamentorum secundum locos*, 9, p. 271	F 8a

23 Isidoros of Charax		**BNJ² 781**
1	*Stathmoi Parthikoi*	F 2
2	Plin. *HN* 1. 2	T 3a–b
2	Plin. *HN* 1. 3	T 3a–b
2	Plin. *HN* 1. 4	T 3a–b
2	Plin. *HN* 1. 5	T 3a–b
2	Plin. *HN* 1. 6	T 3a–b
3	Plin. *HN* 2. cxii. 242	F 6
4	Plin. *HN* 2. cxii. 245	F 7 beg.
5	Plin. *HN* 2. cxii. 246	F 7 end
6	Plin. *HN* 4. iv. 9	F 12
7	Plin. *HN* 4. xvi. 102	F 11
8	Plin. *HN* 4. xxiii. 121	F 8
9	Plin. *HN* 5. vi. 40	F 9
10	Plin. *HN* 5. ix. 47	F 10
11	Plin. *HN* 5. xxxiii. 127	F 19
12	Plin. *HN* 5. xxxv. 129	F 13
13	Plin. *HN* 5. xxxvi. 132	F 14
14	Plin. *HN* 5. xxxvii. 135	F 15
15	Plin. *HN* 5. xxxviii. 136	F 16
16	Plin. *HN* 5. xxxix. 140	F 17
17	Plin. *HN* 5. xliii. 150	F 18
18	Plin. *HN* 6. xxxi. 141	T 1
19	[Luc.] *Makrobioi*, 15 and 17	F 3–4
20	Ath. 3. 46, 93d–94b	F 1
21	Markian. *Epit. Men.* 2	T 2
22	Hsch. s.v. Dousaren	F 5

before Chapter 32		
	Seneca the Younger, *Medea*, 311–17; 364–79	

34 Markianos (*FGrH* 2027‡)	
1	*Periplous*
2	Steph. Byz. α 56 Adaroupolis
3	Steph. Byz. α 90 Aiboudai
4	Steph. Byz. α 180 Akytania
5	Steph. Byz. α 197 Albion
6	Steph. Byz. α 360 Apokopa
7	Steph. Byz. α 468 Aroma
8	Steph. Byz. α 478 Askitai
9	Steph. Byz. α 485 Aspis
10	Steph. Byz. α 499 Astarte
11	Steph. Byz. β 1 Babai
12	Steph. Byz. β 169 Brettia
13	Steph. Byz. γ 121 Gypseïs
14	Steph. Byz. ζ 5 Zadrame
15	Steph. Byz. ι 4 Iazyges
16	Const. Porph. *Adm. imp.* 23
16	Steph. Byz. ι 19a Ibēriai
17	Steph. Byz. ι 113 Istriana
18	Steph. Byz. κ 112 Kassanitai
19	Steph. Byz. κ 168 Koromane
20	Steph. Byz. κ 240 Ktesiphon
21	Steph. Byz. λ 13 Ladisakites kolpos
22	Steph. Byz. λ 72 Lindonion
23	Steph. Byz. λ 89 Lousitania
24	Steph. Byz. μ 39 Mallada
25	Steph. Byz. μ 64 Margana
26	Steph. Byz. μ 100 Mauritaniai

27	Steph. Byz. μ 152 Mesanites kolpos
28	Steph. Byz. μ 191 Minaioi
29	Steph. Byz. μ 213 Mosylon
30	Steph. Byz. μ 247 Myrike
31	Steph. Byz. ν 13 Narbon
32	Steph. Byz. ν 59 Nikopolis
33	Steph. Byz. ο 66 Homeritai
34	Steph. Byz. ο 73 Onne
35	Steph. Byz. σ 126 Siagathourgoi
36	Steph. Byz. σ 151 Sithenoi
37	Steph. Byz. σ 165 Sinai
38	Steph. Byz. τ 121 Tingis
39	Steph. Byz. χ 3 Chadramotitai
40	Steph. Byz. χ 57 Chrysē
41	Markian. pref. to *Epit. Men.*
42	Steph. Byz. α 271 Amisa
43	Synesios, *Letter* 101
44	Synesios, *Letter* 119
45	Priscianus Lydus, *Solutions to Chosroës*, 42. 8–14

after Chapter 36

Anth. Gr. 14. 121 (Metrodoros)

II. CONCORDANCE OF EXTRACTS BY SOURCE AUTHOR

Also includes authors of epigraphs, as well as authors of continuous text who are the subject of a chapter, if extracts from their text also appear as extracts of another author (*a fortiori*, this will be an earlier author). Includes sources more than once if they appear in two or more places in the volumes. Where a reference locator stands with blank cells to its left, understand the locator in the first column to be the same as in the row above (see e.g. Agathemeros 1. 1).

	GAGW ch.	*extract*
Achilles Tatius		
Introduction to the Phainomena of Aratos, 31	Poseidon.	13
Aelian, *NA*		
5. 27. 6	Agatharch.	7
7. 8	Hipparch.	9
10. 16	Eudoxos	27
15. 8	Juba	39
17. 41 (43)	Agatharch.	8
17. 44 (46)	Mnaseas	8
Aelius Aristeides		
Orat. 36. 108	Hekat.	97
Aëtios, *Placita*		
2. 20. 6	Hekat.	8
3. 17. 3	Pytheas	25
4. 1. 7	Eudoxos	23
Agatharchides of Knidos		
64	Hekat.	2
Agathemeros son of Orthon		
1. 1	Hekat.	9
	Eudoxos	3
1. 2	Eudoxos	4
	Dikaiarch.	10
	Eratosth.	37
	Poseidon.	12
1. 5	Dikaiarch.	11

	GAGW ch.	extract
2. 6–7	Timosth.	18
3. 10	Artemid.	8
4. 15–19	Artemid.	8
5. 20	Timosth.	19
	Artemid.	8
	Menipp.	3
Ammianus Marcellinus		
22. 8. 10–13	Hekat.	60
	Eratosth.	107
22. 15. 31	Eratosth.	39
22. 15. 8	Juba	16
Ammonius		
333	Mnaseas	9
Anametresis/ Perimetros		
1	Eratosth.	41
Anthologia Graeca		
7. 78 (Dionysios of Kyzikos)	epigraph to Ch. 12	
7. 256 (Plato)	before Ch. 4	
9. 144 (Anyte)	before Introduction	
9. 559 (Krinagoras)	Menipp.	2
14. 121 (Metrodoros)	after Ch. 36	
Anyte of Tegea		
Anth. Gr. 9. 144	before Introduction	
Apollonios Paradoxographos		
15	Skymnos	5
19	Herakl. Krit.	4
38	Eudoxos	55
Aristotle (*see also* Pseudo-Aristotle)		
Mete. 2. 6, 363a 21–365a 14	Timosth.	38
Mete. 2. 6, 363a 25–b 1	Introduction	§V. 3
Pol. 7. 13, 1332b 12–27	Skylax	2

	GAGW ch.	*extract*
Arnobius		
Against the Nations, 3. 37	Mnaseas	15
Arrian		
Anab. 5. 3. 1–4	Eratosth.	23
Anab. 5. 6. 2–3	Eratosth.	105
Anab. 5. 6. 5	Hekat.	92
Ind. 3. 1–5	Eratosth.	106
Ind. 43. 11–12	Hanno	7
Athenaios		
1. 51, 28d	Poseidon.	58
2. 24, 45f	Poseidon.	72
2. 82, 70a	Hekat.	87
2. 82, 70a–b	Hekat.	11
2. 82, 70a–c	Skylax	7
2. 82, 70b	Hekat.	88
	Hekat.	89
3. 25, 83a–c	Juba	2
3. 25, 83c	Hanno	8
3. 46, 93d–94b	Isidoros	20
3. 76, 111d	Artemid.	115
4. 31, 148f	Hekat.	28
4. 36–7, 151e–152f	Poseidon.	62
4. 39, 153e	Poseidon.	64
4. 47, 158c	Mnaseas	3
5. 46, 210e–f	Poseidon.	61
6. 23–5, 233d–234c	Poseidon.	31
6. 84, 263c–d	Poseidon.	60
7. 31, 288c	Eudoxos	58
7. 47, 296b–c	Mnaseas	4
7. 62, 301d	Mnaseas	50
8. 3, 331d	Mnaseas	14
8. 7, 333b–d	Poseidon.	45
8. 8, 333f–334a	Artemid.	52
8. 37, 346d–e	Mnaseas	31

II. CONCORDANCE OF EXTRACTS BY SOURCE AUTHOR

	GAGW ch.	extract
9. 8, 369c–d	Poseidon.	63
9. 47, 392d–e	Eudoxos	13
9. 79, 410e	Hekat.	12
	Hekat.	104
10. 13, 418e	Hekat.	101
10. 67, 447c	Hekat.	100
10. 67, 447d	Hekat.	47
12. 40, 530c	Mnaseas	5
14. 61, 649d	Poseidon.	59

Avienus, *Ora maritima*		
32–42	Hekat.	13
32–44	Ps.-Skyl.	4
370–4	Ps.-Skyl.	5

Caesar		
BG 6. 24	Eratosth.	43

Cat. Cod. Astr. Gr.		
5. 1, p. 205	Hipparch.	10

Cicero		
Att. 2. 6	Hipparch.	1
Att. 6. 2. 3	Dikaiarch.	1
De re publica, 6. 21–2	*before Ch. 22*	

Clement of Alexandria		
Protreptikos 5. 64. 5 (5. 56 Butterworth)	Eudoxos	36

codex Heidelbergensis 398, 55ʳ–56ʳ (Hanno)	Hanno	0

codex Monacensis 287, 161ᵛ–162ʳ	Artemid.	168

codex Parisinus graecus 571, fos. 417–30	Herakl. Krit.	2

codex Parisinus suppl. gr. 443		
pp. 62. 1–106. 11 (Ps.-Skyl.)	Ps.-Skyl.	0

	GAGW ch.	*extract*
pp. 111. 10–114. 13	Dion. Kall.	1
pp. 114. 13–121. 23	Herakl. Krit.	1
pp. 121. 24–123. 19	Herakl. Krit.	3
pp. 123. 20–124. 25	Dion. Kall.	2

Constantine Porphyrogennetos

De adm. imp. 23	Artemid.	31
	Markian.	16
Them. 1. 2	Skylax	12
	Ps.-Skyl.	7
	Menipp.	10
Them. 1. 42. 9	Artemid.	158
Them. 10. 9	Menipp.	9

Didymos

Dem. Phil. 11. 11. 28–37	Timosth.	2

Diodoros Sikeliotes

3. 5. 1–11. 2	Artemid.	44
3. 11. 4–48. 5	Agatharch.	6

Diogenes Laërtios

8. 8. 90	Eudoxos	14
9. 11. 83	Eudoxos	15

Dionysios of Halikarnassos

Thuc. 5	Hekat.	3

Dionysios of Kyzikos

Anth. Gr. 7. 78	before Ch. 12	

Dioskorides

3. 82. 1–2	Juba	42

Epimerismi Homerici

s.v. *cheiros*	Artemid.	160
s.v. *memetreatai*	Hekat.	59

	GAGW ch.	extract
s.v. Mousa	Mnaseas	20
Eustathios		
Dion. Peri. 1	Poseidon.	16
Dion. Peri. 473	Hipparch.	21
Dion. Peri. 867	Eratosth.	126
Il. 2. 612	Eratosth.	127
Il. 2. 782	Poseidon.	73
Il. 7. 446	Poseidon.	15
Il. 13. 6	Poseidon.	74
Od. 4. 89	Poseidon.	32
Eux.		
6	*Nik.*	38
7	*Nik.*	37
8	*Nik.*	36
10	*Nik.*	35
14	*Nik.*	34
16	*Nik.*	33
18	*Nik.*	32
22	*Nik.*	31
25	*Nik.*	30
27	*Nik.*	29
33	*Nik.*	28
34	*Nik.*	27
35	*Nik.*	26
37	*Nik.*	25
45	*Nik.*	24
51	*Nik.*	23
66	*Nik.*	22
74	*Nik.*	19
76	*Nik.*	21
77	*Nik.*	20
78	Hekat.	61
	Nik.	17–18
79	*Nik.*	16
80	*Nik.*	15

	GAGW ch.	*extract*
82–3	*Nik.*	14
87	*Nik.*	13
88–9	*Nik.*	12
91	*Nik.*	11
92	*Nik.*	10
	Artemid.	122
94	*Nik.*	9
97	*Nik.*	8
99	*Nik.*	7
101	*Nik.*	6
103	*Nik.*	5
105	*Nik.*	4
107	*Nik.*	3
109	*Nik.*	1

Fulgentius		
Explanation 2	Mnaseas	10
Mythologies 2. 16	Mnaseas	2

Galen		
De compositione medicamentorum secundum locos, 9, p. 271	Juba	43

Geminos		
6. 8–9	Pytheas	15
15	Eratosth.	32
17. 5	Dikaiarch.	2

Harpokration		
s.v. *eph' hieron*	Timosth.	22
s.v. *Ganion kai Ganiada*	Artemid.	116
s.v. Hippia Athena	Mnaseas	1
s.v. *hypo gēn oikountes*	Skylax	6
s.v. *kypassis*	Hekat.	84
s.v. Lipara	Eudoxos	77
s.v. *rhodōniá*	Hekat.	33
s.v. Saboi	Mnaseas	36

	GAGW ch.	*extract*
Herodian		
General Prosody 5 fr. 34 Hunger	Hekat.	49
General Prosody 7 fr. 42 Hunger	Mnaseas	7
General Prosody 11 (263. 35–264. 1 Lentz)	Mnaseas	49
On the Unique Word 1. 13. 19–20 (920. 7–8 Lentz)	Hekat.	73
On the Unique Word 1. 19	Skymnos	1
On the Unique Word 2. 31. 25–6 (937. 9–10 Lentz)	Hekat.	110
On the Unique Word 2. 31. 26 (937. 10–11 Lentz)	Hekat.	56
On the Unique Word 2. 36. 29–31 (942. 11–13 Lentz)	Hekat.	96
Herodotos		
2. 143. 1	Hekat.	1
4. 13–15	Aristeas	1
4. 16	Aristeas	1
4. 44	Skylax	1
4. 85. 2–86. 3	*Introduction*	§VI. 2. a
Hesychios		
s.v. *Barkaiois ochois*	Mnaseas	43
s.v. *bous Kyprios*	Eudoxos	79
s.v. Dousaren	Isidoros	22
s.v. *Skyria dikē*	Artemid.	117
s.v. Talantion	Artemid.	118
s.v. Terebinthos	Juba	40
Hipparchos		
Arat. 1. 4. 1	Pytheas	1
Homer		
Od. 11. 121–34	*before Prologue*	
Ioannes Lydus		
Mens. 4. 107 Wünsch	Dikaiarch.	14
Josephus		
AJ 1. 93	Mnaseas	32

	GAGW ch.	extract
Ap. 1. 216–17	Mnaseas	33
Ap. 2. 112	Mnaseas	34
Julian of Ascalon	Poseidon.	18
Kallimachos		
Epigrams, 18	before Ch. 9	
Kleomedes, Meteora		
1. 4. 90–131 Todd	Poseidon.	10
1. 4. 208–10 Todd	Pytheas	26
1. 5. 57–75 Todd	Dikaiarch.	8
1. 7. 1–50 Todd	Poseidon.	11
Kosmas Indikopleustes		
11. 80. 6–9	Pytheas	30
Krinagoras		
Anth. Gr. 9. 559	Menippos	2
Markianos of Herakleia		
Epit. Men. 2	Hanno	9
	Skylax	10
	Pytheas	31
	Timosth.	23
	Isidoros	21
Epit. Men. 3. 10–27	Timosth.	23
Epit. Men. 3–4	Artemid.	119
Epit. Men.	Menipp.	1
Peripl. 1. 1	Artemid.	120
Peripl. 1. 4	Eratosth.	40
Peripl. 2. 4	Artemid.	121
Peripl. 2. 19	Artemid.	10
pref. to Epit. Men.	Menipp.	1
	Markian.	41
pref. to Ps.-Skyl.	Skylax	9
	Ps.-Skyl.	6

	GAGW ch.	extract
Martianus Capella		
6. 590–1	Dikaiarch.	12
6. 595	Pytheas	28
6. 608–9	Pytheas	29
Maximus of Tyre		
Dissertatio 10. 2	Aristeas	3
Dissertatio 38. 3	Aristeas	4
Metrodoros		
Anth. Gr. 14. 121	after Ch. 36	
Natalis Comes		
7. 2	Hekat.	26
9. 9	Hekat.	27
Nikomedean Periodos ['Ps.-Skymnos']		
lines 109–20	Timosth.	1
lines 405–12	Eratosth.	42
P. Artemid.	Artemid.	167
P. Hawara 80–1 (Anonymus Periegetes)	Herakl. Krit.	5
P. Oxy. 24. 2694ᵛ. 18–32	Artemid.	9
Palaiphatos		
31	Hanno	1
Philostratos		
VA 2. 13	Juba	15
VA 3. 47	Skylax	8
Photios		
Bibl. cod. 72. 49b 39–50a 4 (Ktesias)	*Introduction*	§III. 3. m
Bibl. cod. 213. 171a 6–b 17	Agatharch.	1

	GAGW ch.	*extract*
Bibl. cod. 250. 441b 16–445b 36	Agatharch.	2
Bibl. cod. 250. 445b 36–460b 16	Agatharch.	6
Bibl. cod. 250. 460b 3–16	Agatharch.	6
Lexikon s.v. Haimon	Eudoxos	43
Lexikon s.v. Praxidike	Mnaseas	11
Lexikon s.v. *pythou chelidonos*	Mnaseas	47
Lexikon s.v. Zamolxis	Mnaseas	19

Plato

| *Anth. Gr.* 7. 256 | before Ch. 4 | |

Pliny the Elder

1. 2	Pytheas	16
	Dikaiarch.	6
	Artemid.	104
	Isidoros	2
1. 3	Artemid.	104
	Isidoros	2
1. 4	Hekat.	7
	Pytheas	17
	Dikaiarch.	6
	Timosth.	11
	Artemid.	104
	Isidoros	2
1. 5	Hekat.	7
	Dikaiarch.	6
	Timosth.	11
	Artemid.	104
	Isidoros	2
1. 6	Hekat.	7
	Timosth.	11
	Dikaiarch.	6
	Artemid.	104
	Isidoros	2
1. 7	Artemid.	104
1. 18	Hekat.	7
1. 36	Artemid.	104

II. CONCORDANCE OF EXTRACTS BY SOURCE AUTHOR • 1143

	GAGW ch.	extract
1. 37	Pytheas	18
2. ix. 53	Hipparch.	6
2. xxiv. 95	Hipparch.	7
2. lxv. 162	Dikaiarch.	7
2. lxvii. 169	Hanno	4
2. lxxv. 183–lxxvi. 185	Eratosth.	33
2. lxxvii. 186–7	Pytheas	19
2. xci. 217	Pytheas	20
2. cxii. 242	Isidoros	3
2. cxii. 242–6	Artemid.	4
2. cxii. 245	Isidoros	4
2. cxii. 246	Isidoros	5
2. cxii. 247	Hipparch.	41
2. cxii. 247–8	Eratosth.	34
3. v. 75	Eratosth.	93
4. iv. 9	Isidoros	6
4. xii. 77	Artemid.	105
4. xiii. 94	Hekat.	58
4. xiii. 95	Pytheas	21
4. xvi. 102	Pytheas	22
	Isidoros	7
4. xvi. 104	Pytheas	23
4. xxiii. 121	Isidoros	8
4. xxxvii. 121	Artemid.	5
5. i. 14–16	Juba	3
5. i. 8	Hanno	5
5. vi. 39	Eratosth.	94
5. vi. 40	Eratosth.	95
	Artemid.	6
	Isidoros	9
5. vii. 41–2	Eratosth.	96
5. ix. 47	Timosth.	12
	Eratosth.	97
	Artemid.	7
	Isidoros	10
5. x. 51–5	Juba	4
5. x. 59	Artemid.	106
	Juba	5

	GAGW ch.	extract
5. xxxiii. 127	Eratosth.	98
	Isidoros	11
5. xxxv. 129	Timosth.	13
	Artemid.	107
	Isidoros	12
5. xxxvi. 132	Isidoros	13
5. xxxvii. 135	Isidoros	14
5. xxxviii. 136	Isidoros	15
5. xxxix. 140	Isidoros	16
5. xliii. 150	Isidoros	17
6. i. 3	Eratosth.	99
6. v. 15	Timosth.	14
6. xv. 36	Eratosth.	100
6. xv. 36–7	Artemid.	108
6. xxi. 56	Eratosth.	101
6. xxi. 57–8	Poseidon.	9
6. xxii. 70	Artemid.	109
6. xxiv. 81	Eratosth.	102
6. xxvi. 96–100	Juba	20
6. xxviii. 108	Eratosth.	103
6. xxx. 124	Juba	1
6. xxxi. 136–41	Juba	21
6. xxxi. 141	Isidoros	18
6. xxxii. 149–56	Juba	22
6. xxxii. 156	Artemid.	110
6. xxxiii. 163	Timosth.	15
	Eratosth.	104
6. xxxiii. 163–4	Artemid.	111
6. xxxiii. 165–70	Juba	23
6. xxxiv. 171	Eratosth.	35
6. xxxiv. 175–xxxv. 179	Juba	6
6. xxxv. 183	Timosth.	16
	Artemid.	112
6. xxxvi. 198	Eudoxos	75
	Timosth.	17
6. xxxvi. 200	Hanno	6

	GAGW ch.	extract
6. xxxvi. 201	Juba	7
6. xxxvii. 202–5	Juba	8
7. ii. 24	Eudoxos	31
7. ii. 30	Artemid.	113
8. iv. 7	Juba	9
8. viii. 24–5	Agatharch.	3
8. xiii. 35	Juba	17
8. xlv. 107	Juba	10
9. lvi. 115	Juba	18
10. lxi. 126–7	Juba	11
12. xxi. 38–xxii. 39	Juba	24
12. xxx. 53	Eratosth.	36
12. xxxi. 56	Juba	25
12. xxxii. 60	Juba	26
12. xxxiv. 67	Juba	27
12. xxxviii. 78–xl. 80	Juba	28
13. vii. 34	Juba	29
13. lii. 142	Juba	12
15. xxviii. 99	Juba	30
25. v. 14	Juba	31
25. xxxviii. 77–9	Juba	41
31. ix. 13	Eudoxos	76
31. xiii. 16	Eudoxos	57
31. xv. 18	Juba	19
32. iv. 10	Juba	32
33. xl. 118	Juba	33
35. xxii. 39	Juba	34
36. xvii. 79	Artemid.	114
36. xlvi. 163	Juba	35
37. ix. 24	Juba	36
37. xi. 35–6	Pytheas	24
37. xi. 38	Mnaseas	44
37. xviii. 69	Juba	13
37. xviii. 73	Juba	37
37. xxxii. 107–8	Juba	38
37. xxxv. 114	Juba	14
37. lxxvii. 201–2	*Introduction*	§III. 3. n

	GAGW ch.	extract
Plutarch		
De Is. et Os. 6 (Mor. 353a–c)	Eudoxos	24
De Is. et Os. 21 (Mor. 359c)	Eudoxos	25
De Is. et Os. 37 (Mor. 365f)	Mnaseas	48
De Is. et Os. 64 (Mor. 377a)	Eudoxos	26
De Pyth. or. 17 (Mor. 402d)	Eudoxos	50
Non posse suaviter vivere secundum Epicurum, 10 (Mor. 1093b–c)	Eudoxos	2
Quaest. conv. 8. 9 (Mor. 733b 5–c 1)	Agatharch.	5
Polybios		
3. 39. 6–11	Introduction	§VI. 2. g
3. 47. 9	Introduction	§VI. 2. g
3. 48. 10–12	Introduction	§VI. 2. g
Pomponius Mela		
3. 7. 7	Hipparch.	20
3. 89–99	Hanno	3
Porphyrius		
De antro Nymph. p. 57 (§4 Davis et al.)	Artemid.	38
Life of Pythagoras, 7	Eudoxos	78
Priscianus Lydus		
Solutions to Chosroës, 6	Poseidon.	46
Solutions to Chosroës, 42. 8–14	Markian.	45
Proclus		
In Hes. Op. 640	Eudoxos	51
In Ti. 1. 31f (on 22b), i. 102 Diehl	Eudoxos	28
In Ti. 1. 37b (on 22e), i. 120 Diehl	Eratosth.	115
In Ti. 4. 277d–e (on 40a–b), iii. 124–5 Diehl	Poseidon.	17
Proverbia e cod. Bodl.	Artemid.	161

	GAGW ch.	extract
Ps.-Antigonos of Karystos		
123	Eudoxos	6
129	Eudoxos	32
	Eudoxos	71
138	Eudoxos	46
147	Eudoxos	33
148	Eudoxos	47
153	Eudoxos	54
161	Eudoxos	72
162	Eudoxos	7
163	Eudoxos	73
Ps.-Arist. *Mir. ausc.*		
37, 833a 9–12	Hanno	2
173, 847a 5–7	Eudoxos	8
Ps.-Longinus		
10. 4	Aristeas	2
Ps.-Lucian		
Makrobioi, 15 and 17	Isidoros	19
Ptolemy of Alexandria		
Geog. 1. 15. 3	Timosth.	20
Geog. 1. 15. 5	Timosth.	21
Geog. 1. 7. 4	Hipparch.	42
Geog. 1. 7. 9	Hipparch.	43
Geog. 3. 17. 1–2	Introduction	§VI. 1. e
Synt. Math. 1. 67. 22–68. 6	Hipparch.	44
scholia to Aeschylus		
Per. 303	Timosth.	29
Per. 747	Mnaseas	51
scholia to Ap. Rhod.		
1. 131	Mnaseas	38
1. 551 A	Hekat.	16
1. 916–18 B	Mnaseas	21

	GAGW ch.	extract
1. 922	Eudoxos	44
1. 1126–31 B	Mnaseas	30
1. 1177–8 A	Ps.-Skyl.	2
2. 296–7 B	Timosth.	31
2. 399–401 A	Eratosth.	108
2. 498–527 A	Mnaseas	46
2. 498–527 Q	Timosth.	32
2. 498–527 V	Timosth.	33
2. 531–2	Timosth.	34
2. 675	Mnaseas	22
	Poseidon.	75
2. 946–54 B	Artemid.	162
2. 946–54 C	Hekat.	29
2. 963–5 A	Artemid.	163
2. 998–1000	Hekat.	23
2. 1052–7 A	Mnaseas	23
2. 1247 A	Eratosth.	109
3. 846–7 A	Timosth.	35
3. 854–9 C	Artemid.	164
4. 131–5 B	Eratosth.	110
4. 257–62 B	Hekat.	17
	Artemid.	165
4. 263–4 B	Mnaseas	24
4. 263–4 B	Eudoxos	69
4. 277–8 A	Skymnos	4
4. 282–91 B	Hekat.	18
	Eratosth.	111
	Skymnos	8
4. 310	Eratosth.	112
4. 761–5 A	Pytheas	27
4. 1215	Ps.-Skyl.	3
	Eratosth.	113
4. 1712	Timosth.	36

scholia to Dionysios Periegetes		
p. 428, col. i. 7–9	Hekat.	10
l. 14	Artemid.	166

	GAGW ch.	extract
scholia to Dionysios Thrax		
6	Mnaseas	52
scholia to Euripides		
Med. 2	Eratosth.	114
Phoen. 651	Mnaseas	25
Rhes. 36	Mnaseas	26
Tro. 221	Eudoxos	70
scholia to Homer		
Il. 15. 336 C	Mnaseas	53
Il. 19. 291–2	Mnaseas	39
Il. 20. 234 D	Mnaseas	40
Od. 4. 477 EPQHT	Eudoxos	30
Od. 10. 139	Hekat.	15
Od. 11. 239 HQT	Eudoxos	45
Od. 18. 85 B	Mnaseas	27
scholia to Lucan		
9. 411	Timosth.	37
scholia to Lucian		
Iuppiter Tragoedus 6	Mnaseas	41
scholia to Pindar		
Ol. 10. 34 g	Mnaseas	28
Pyth. 4. 106 A	Mnaseas	29
scholia to Ptolemy		
Geog. 1. 3. 3	Hipparch.	45
scholia to Theokritos		
1. 64 C	Mnaseas	12
13. 22–3 AB	Timosth.	30
13. 75 C	Mnaseas	42

	GAGW ch.	extract
Seneca the Younger		
Medea 311–17; 364–79	before Ch. 32	
NQ 2. 26. 4–7	Poseidon.	44
NQ 6. 21. 2	Poseidon.	29
NQ 6. 24. 6	Poseidon.	30
Servius		
In Verg. Geo. 1. 137	Hipparch.	11
Sextus Empiricus		
Against the Professors, 5. 1	Hipparch.	8
Pyrrh. hypot. 1. 152	Eudoxos	12
Solinus		
Collectanea 52. 1–2	Poseidon.	14
Stephanos of Byzantion		
α 4 Abarnos	Hekat.	68
	Artemid.	123
α 6 Abdera	Artemid.	21
	Eudoxos	37
α 21 Agathe	Eudoxos	59
	Timosth.	24
	Skymnos	6
α 36 Ankon	Artemid.	124
α 39 Agnotes	Artemid.	125
α 44 Agraioi	Eratosth.	116
α 56 Adaroupolis	Markian.	2
α 65 Adria	Hekat.	37
α 71 Azania	Eudoxos	60
α 79 Atharrhabis	Hekat.	94
α 90 Aiboudai	Markian.	3
α 92 Aiga	Artemid.	126
α 108 Aigion	Eudoxos	61
α 151 Akanthos	Mnaseas	16
α 180 Akytania	Markian.	4
α 197 Albion	Markian.	5

	GAGW ch.	extract
α 200 Alexandreiai	Timosth.	25
α 239 Alonis	Artemid.	127
α 245 Amazoneion	Hekat.	70
α 254 Amaxa	Eratosth.	117
α 271 Amisa	Markian.	42
α 288 Amphanai	Hekat.	19
α 357 Apia	Timosth.	26
α 360 Apokopa	Markian.	6
α 413 Areos nesos	Skymnos	2
α 437 Armenia	Eudoxos	16
α 457 Artake	Timosth.	27
α 462 Artemita	Artemid.	128
α 468 Aroma	Markian.	7
α 472 Asdynis	Eudoxos	29
α 475 Asine	Eudoxos	62
α 476 Askalon	Eudoxos	17
α 478 Askitai	Markian.	8
α 485 Aspis	Markian.	9
α 493 Assyria	Eratosth.	118
α 496 Astai	Artemid.	129
α 499 Astarte	Markian.	10
α 522 Atramitai	Artemid.	130
α 547 Autariatai	Eratosth.	119
α 579 Apsyrtides	Artemid.	131
β 1 Babai	Markian.	11
β 59 Belbina	Artemid.	132
β 62 Belitanoi	Artemid.	32
β 144 Boulinoi	Artemid.	133
β 148 Bounnos	Artemid.	11
β 169 Brettia	Markian.	12
γ 8 Gangra	Eratosth.	120
γ 18 Gaitouloi	Artemid.	134
γ 31 Gandarai	Hekat.	90
γ 50 Genoa	Artemid.	12
γ 68 Gephyra	Hekat.	45
γ 75 Gigonos	Artemid.	135
γ 119 Gynaikospolis	Artemid.	136

	GAGW ch.	extract
γ 121 Gypseïs	Markian.	13
δ 18 Dardanos	Mnaseas	37
δ 45 Dekieton	Artemid.	13
δ 52 Dexaroi	Hekat.	40
δ 58 Derton	Artemid.	14
δ 77 Didyme	Artemid.	137
δ 90 Dionysou polis	*Nik.*	2
δ 143 Dyrrhachion	Eratosth.	121
δ 146 Dodone	Mnaseas	17
δ 150 Doros	Hekat.	81
	Artemid.	48
δ 151 Dotion	Mnaseas	18
ε 6 Engelanes	Mnaseas	6
ε 43 Heleneios	Hekat.	98
ε 55 Elibyrge	Hekat.	34
ε 123 Hermonassa	Hekat.	62
	Skymnos	3
	Menipp.	4
ε 129 Erythra	Artemid.	41
ε 161 Eupalia	Artemid.	138
ε 179 Ephesos	Hekat.	99
ζ 5 Zadrame	Markian.	14
ζ 30 Zygantis	Eudoxos	63
η 13 Hemeroskopeion	Artemid.	22
θ 22 Themisonion	Artemid.	139
θ 60 Thrinke	Hekat.	109
ι 4 Iazyges	Markian.	15
ι 19a Iberiai	Artemid.	23
	Markian.	16
ι 29 Idyros	Hekat.	76
ι 69 Ixiai	Artemid.	53
ι 84 Hipponesos	Artemid.	42
ι 113 Istriana	Markian.	17
ι 115 Istros	Artemid.	140
ι 123 Ichnai	Eratosth.	122
κ 4 Kabellion	Artemid.	15
κ 26 Kale Akte	Eudoxos	38

	GAGW ch.	*extract*
κ 81 Karthaia	Artemid.	24
κ 90 Karne	Artemid.	54
κ 92 Karnos	Artemid.	25
κ 102 Karyanda	Skylax	11
κ 112 Kassanitai	Markian.	18
κ 118 Kastalon	Artemid.	33
κ 119 Kastanaia	Eudoxos	52
κ 138 Kaulonia	Hekat.	36
κ 167 Korokondame	Artemid.	56
κ 168 Koromane	Markian.	19
κ 211 Kremmyon	Eudoxos	64
κ 234 Krya	Artemid.	142
κ 240 Ktesiphon	Markian.	20
κ 246 Kybos	Hekat.	108
κ 287 Kyre	Hekat.	82
κ 307 Kothon	Artemid.	141
κ 313 Korykos	Hekat.	71
	Hekat.	80
λ 13 Ladisakites kolpos	Markian.	21
λ 36 Laodamanteia	Artemid.	143
λ 46 Lemnos	Hekat.	52
λ 61 Ligyres	Artemid.	16
λ 72 Lindonion	Markian.	22
λ 85 Lopadoussa	Artemid.	43
λ 89 Lousitania	Markian.	23
λ 119 Los	Artemid.	144
μ 35 Malake	Artemid.	26
μ 39 Mallada	Markian.	24
μ 64 Margana	Markian.	25
μ 81 Maroneia	Hekat.	50
μ 86 Maskotos	Hekat.	105
μ 94 Mastramele	Artemid.	17
μ 100 Mauritaniai	Markian.	26
μ 108 Megasa	Hekat.	107
μ 119 Melanchlainoi	Hekat.	57
μ 125 Meleteios kolpos	Hekat.	72
μ 126 Melia	Hekat.	30

	GAGW ch.	extract
μ 131 Melissa	Hekat.	111
μ 152 Mesanites kolpos	Markian.	27
μ 191 Minaioi	Markian.	28
μ 212 Mossynoikoi	Eudoxos	18
μ 213 Mosylon	Markian.	29
μ 227 Mygissos	Hekat.	31
μ 232 Mykoi	Hekat.	86
μ 243 Myonesos	Artemid.	145
μ 247 Myrike	Markian.	30
μ 249 Myrikous	Hekat.	69
μ 253 Myrmekion	Artemid.	146
μ 262 Mytilene	Hekat.	54
ν 3 Nagidos	Hekat.	77
ν 13 Narbon	Artemid.	18
	Menipp.	5
	Markian.	31
ν 37 Nestos	Artemid.	27
ν 59 Nikopolis	Menipp.	6
	Markian.	32
ξ 2 Xanthos	Hekat.	75
ξ 12 Xouches	Artemid.	147
ο 25 Oine	Hekat.	20
ο 66 Homeritai	Markian.	33
ο 73 Onne	Markian.	34
ο 79 Opikoi	Eudoxos	65
π 7 Paltos	Artemid.	148
π 43 Parthenios	Artemid.	40
π 49 Parikane	Hekat.	83
π 56 Paros	Skymnos	7
π 176 Plataiai	Eudoxos	53
σ 116 Sekoanos	Artemid.	19
σ 126 Siagathourgoi	Markian.	35
σ 143 Side	Hekat.	78
σ 151 Sithenoi	Markian.	36
σ 155 Sikelia	Menipp.	9
σ 165 Sinai	Markian.	37
σ 174 Sintia	Eudoxos	39

	GAGW ch.	extract
σ 204 Skiapodes	Hekat.	103
σ 227 Skylletion	Eudoxos	66
σ 229 Skymniadai	Eudoxos	40
σ 237 Syrmatai	Eudoxos	19
σ 242 Solkoi	Artemid.	149
σ 263 Spina	Eudoxos	67
	Artemid.	150
τ 20 Tanos	Artemid.	34
τ 26 Taprobane	Artemid.	49
τ 39 Tarsos	Eratosth.	123
τ 52 Tauriskoi	Eratosth.	124
τ 53 Tauroëis	Artemid.	20
τ 63 Teanon	Artemid.	35
τ 66 Tegestra	Artemid.	151
τ 79 Telmessos	Artemid.	55
τ 91 Tenedos	Hekat.	53
τ 120 Tibyris	Artemid.	36
τ 121 Tingis	Markian.	38
τ 159 Tourdetania	Artemid.	152
τ 178 Tremile	Hekat.	32
τ 208 Tropis	Artemid.	28
τ 233 Tyros	Artemid.	153
υ 30 Hyops	Hekat.	35
υ 49 Hysaeïs	Hekat.	102
υ 51 Hysia	Artemid.	50
υ 57 Hyope	Hekat.	85
φ 8 Phakousa	Hekat.	93
φ 10 Phalakrai	Artemid.	39
φ 12 Phalanna	Hekat.	21
φ 36 Pharousioi	Artemid.	154
φ 46 Phelessaioi	Eudoxos	68
φ 69 Philippoi	Artemid.	155
φ 76 Phlanon	Artemid.	156
φ 77 Phlegra	Eudoxos	41
φ 86 Phoinikoussai	Hekat.	106
φ 107 Phrourentanoi	Artemid.	37
χ 1 Chabarenoi	Eudoxos	20

	GAGW ch.	extract
χ 2 Chadisia	Hekat.	24
χ 3 Chadramotitai	Markian.	39
χ 6 Chaironeia	Hekat.	44
χ 7 Chalaion	Hekat.	43
χ 8 Chalastra	Hekat.	48
χ 9 Chaldia	Menipp.	7
χ 13 Chalkeia	Timosth.	28
χ 15 Chalkedon	Menipp.	8
χ 17 Chalkis	Hekat.	46
	Eudoxos	42
χ 18 Chalkitis	Artemid.	57
χ 19 Chalybes	Hekat.	65
	Eudoxos	21
χ 22 Chaonia	Hekat.	39
χ 24 Charadros	Hekat.	79
χ 39 Chemmis	Hekat.	95
χ 40 Cherronesos	Hekat.	51
χ 44 Chios	Hekat.	55
χ 47 Choi	Hekat.	63
χ 48 Choirades	Hekat.	64
χ 57 Chrysē	Markian.	40
ψ 1 Psamathous	Artemid.	29
ψ 2 Psebo	Artemid.	45
ψ 3 Psenako	Artemid.	46
ψ 7 Pseudokorasion	Artemid.	51
ψ 21 Psophis	Hekat.	25
ψ 22 Psochemmis	Artemid.	47
ω 13 Opiai	Hekat.	91
ω 15 Orikos	Hekat.	41
ω 16 Orisia/Oria	Artemid.	30
ω 21 Ostiones	Pytheas	32
	Artemid.	157

Stobaios

Anth. 1. 38. 2	Dikaiarch.	13

	GAGW ch.	*extract*
Strabo		
1. 1. 1	Eudoxos	1
1. 1. 1, C1	Hekat.	4
1. 1. 1, C1–2	Dikaiarch.	3
	Eratosth.	1
	Poseidon.	1
1. 1. 2, C2	Hipparch.	13
1. 1. 7, C4	Poseidon.	33
1. 1. 8–9, C5–6	Eratosth.	24
	Poseidon.	34
1. 1. 9, C5–6	Hipparch.	14
1. 1. 11, C7	Hekat.	5
	Eratosth.	2
1. 1. 12, C7	Hipparch.	15
1. 1. 21, C12	Hipparch.	33
1. 2. 1–2, C14–15	Hipparch.	2
1. 2. 3, C15–17	Eratosth.	3
1. 2. 3, C16	Hipparch.	16
1. 2. 7, C18	Eratosth.	4
1. 2. 11–14, C21–3	Eratosth.	5
1. 2. 15, C24	Eratosth.	6
1. 2. 17, C25	Eratosth.	7
1. 2. 18–19, C26	Eratosth.	8
1. 2. 20, C27	Hipparch.	17
1. 2. 20, C28	Eratosth.	45
1. 2. 20–4, C28–30	Eratosth.	9
1. 2. 21, C29	Timosth.	3
1. 2. 28, C34 (Ephoros)	*Introduction*	§VI. 2. e
1. 2. 31, C38	Eratosth.	10
1. 2. 34, C41–2	Poseidon.	65
1. 2. 37, C44	Eratosth.	11
1. 3. 1–2, C47–8	Eratosth.	12
1. 3. 3–4, C48–50	Eratosth.	13
1. 3. 9, C53–4	Poseidon.	35
1. 3. 11–15, C54–7	Eratosth.	14
1. 3. 12, C55	Hipparch.	18
	Poseidon.	36
1. 3. 13–15, C55–7	Hipparch.	19

	GAGW ch.	extract
1. 3. 16, C58	Poseidon.	20
1. 3. 22, C61–2	Eratosth.	15
1. 3. 23–1. 4. 1, C62	Eratosth.	16
1. 4. 1, C62	Hipparch.	34
1. 4. 1–2, C62–3	Pytheas	2
	Eratosth.	25
1. 4. 3, C63	Pytheas	2
	Hipparch.	35
1. 4. 4, C63–4	Pytheas	2
1. 4. 5, C64	Pytheas	2
1. 4. 6–8, C64–6	Eratosth.	26
1. 4. 9, C66	Eratosth.	46
2. 1. 1–3, C67–8	Eratosth.	47
2. 1. 4, C68–9	Hipparch.	22
2. 1. 5, C69	Eratosth.	48
2. 1. 7, C69	Eratosth.	49
2. 1. 7, C69–70	Hipparch.	23
2. 1. 9, C70	Eratosth.	17
2. 1. 10–11, C70–1	Eratosth.	50
2. 1. 11–12, C71	Hipparch.	24
2. 1. 12, C71–2	Pytheas	3
2. 1. 12–13, C71–2	Hipparch.	36
2. 1. 16, C74	Eratosth.	51
2. 1. 18, C75	Pytheas	4
	Hipparch.	37
2. 1. 19, C76	Eratosth.	52
2. 1. 19–20, C76–7	Hipparch.	25
2. 1. 20, C77	Eratosth.	27
	Eratosth.	52
2. 1. 21, C77–8	Eratosth.	52
2. 1. 21–2, C77–8	Hipparch.	26
2. 1. 22, C78	Eratosth.	52
2. 1. 23–6, C78–80	Eratosth.	52
2. 1. 27, C80–1	Hipparch.	27
2. 1. 27, C81	Eratosth.	52
2. 1. 28, C81	Eratosth.	52
2. 1. 29, C81–2	Hipparch.	28

	GAGW ch.	extract
2. 1. 29, C82–3	Eratosth.	52
2. 1. 30, C83–4	Eratosth.	52
2. 1. 31, C84	Eratosth.	52
2. 1. 32, C85	Eratosth.	52
2. 1. 33, C85–6	Eratosth.	52
2. 1. 34, C86	Eratosth.	52
2. 1. 34, C86–7	Eratosth.	52
2. 1. 34–5, C86–7	Hipparch.	29
2. 1. 35, C87–8	Eratosth.	52
2. 1. 36, C88–9	Eratosth.	52
	Hipparch.	30
2. 1. 37, C89–90	Eratosth.	52
2. 1. 38, C90–1	Eratosth.	52
2. 1. 38–40, C90–2	Hipparch.	31
2. 1. 39, C91–2	Eratosth.	52
2. 1. 40, C92	Timosth.	4
2. 1. 40, C92–3	Eratosth.	52
2. 1. 41, C93	Timosth.	5
2. 1. 41, C93–4	Eratosth.	52
	Hipparch.	3
2. 1. 41, C94	Timosth.	6
2. 2. 1–2. 3. 8, C94–104	Poseidon.	2
2. 2. 2, C95	Eratosth.	53
2. 3. 2, C97	Eratosth.	28
2. 3. 5, C102	Pytheas	5
2. 4. 1–2, C104	Pytheas	6
	Eratosth.	18
2. 4. 1–3, C104–5	Dikaiarch.	4
2. 4. 2, C104	Eratosth.	54
2. 4. 4, C106–7	Eratosth.	55
2. 4. 8, C108	Eratosth.	56
2. 5. 5–9, C112–16	Eratosth.	29
2. 5. 7, C113	Hipparch.	38
2. 5. 7–8, C114–15	Pytheas	7
2. 5. 8, C115	Hipparch.	39
2. 5. 13, C118	Eratosth.	30
2. 5. 14, C118–19	Eratosth.	57

	GAGW ch.	extract
2. 5. 14, C119	Poseidon.	3
2. 5. 16, C120	Eratosth.	58
2. 5. 20, C123	Eratosth.	59
2. 5. 24, C125–6	Eratosth.	60
2. 5. 34, C131–2	Hipparch.	40
2. 5. 35, C132	Hipparch.	40
2. 5. 35, C132–3	Eratosth.	61
2. 5. 36, C133	Eratosth.	61
	Hipparch.	40
2. 5. 38–41, C133–4	Eratosth.	61
2. 5. 39, C134	Hipparch.	40
2. 5. 40, C134	Hipparch.	40
2. 5. 41, C134	Hipparch.	40
2. 5. 42, C134–5	Hipparch.	40
2. 5. 42, C135	Eratosth.	31
	Hipparch.	40
2. 5. 43, C135	Hipparch.	40
2. 5. 43, C135–6	Poseidon.	4
2. 5. 43, C136	Pytheas	8
3. 1. 4, C137–8	Artemid.	58
3. 1. 5, C138	Artemid.	59
	Poseidon.	47
3. 1. 7, C139–40	Timosth.	7
3. 2. 9, C146–7	Poseidon.	21
3. 2. 11, C148	Pytheas	9
	Eratosth.	62
	Artemid.	60
3. 3. 3–4, C153	Poseidon.	37
3. 4. 3, C157	Artemid.	61
	Artemid.	62
	Poseidon.	48
3. 4. 4, C157–8	Pytheas	10
3. 4. 7, C159	Eratosth.	63
	Artemid.	63
3. 4. 13, C162–3	Poseidon.	66
3. 4. 15, C163	Poseidon.	49
3. 4. 17, C164	Artemid.	64

	GAGW ch.	extract
3. 4. 17, C165	Poseidon.	67
3. 5. 1, C167	Artemid.	65
3. 5. 5, C169–70	Poseidon.	50
3. 5. 5, C170	Dikaiarch.	5
	Eratosth.	64
	Artemid.	66
3. 5. 7, C172	Artemid.	67
3. 5. 7–9, C172–5	Poseidon.	38
3. 5. 10, C175	Poseidon.	51
4. 1. 4–5, C179–80	Artemid.	1
4. 1. 7, C182–3	Poseidon.	39
4. 1. 8, C183	Artemid.	2
4. 1. 11, C185	Artemid.	3
4. 1. 14, C188	Poseidon.	52
4. 2. 1, C190	Pytheas	11
4. 4. 1, C195	Pytheas	12
4. 4. 6, C198	Artemid.	68
4. 5. 5, C201	Pytheas	13
5. 1. 8, C214–15	Poseidon.	40
5. 2. 1, C218	Poseidon.	68
5. 2. 6, C224	Eratosth.	65
	Artemid.	69
5. 4. 6, C245	Artemid.	70
6. 1. 11, C261–2	Artemid.	71
6. 2. 1, C265–6	Poseidon.	53
6. 2. 1, C267	Artemid.	72
6. 2. 3, C268–9	Poseidon.	22
6. 2. 4, C271	Hekat.	42
6. 2. 7, C273	Poseidon.	54
6. 2. 11, C277	Poseidon.	41
6. 3. 9–10, C283–5	Artemid.	73
7. 2. 1–2, C292–4	Poseidon.	69
7. 3. 1, C295	Pytheas	14
7. 3. 2–4, C295–7	Poseidon.	70
7. 3. 6, C298–9	Hekat.	6
7. 3. 6–7, C298–300	Eratosth.	19
7. 3. 7, C300	Poseidon.	70

	GAGW ch.	extract
7. 5. 8, C316	Hekat.	38
	Poseidon.	23
7, fr. 21a	Eudoxos	34
7. fr. 22a	Artemid.	74
8. 1. 1, C332	Hipparch.	4
	Poseidon.	5
8. 2. 1, C335	Artemid.	75
8. 3. 9, C341	Hekat.	22
8. 6. 1, C367	Artemid.	76
8. 6. 21, C378–9	Eudoxos	56
8. 7. 2, C384	Eratosth.	66
8. 8. 4, C389	Eratosth.	67
8. 8. 5, C389	Artemid.	77
9. 1. 1, C390–1	Eudoxos	48
9. 2. 35, C413	Eudoxos	49
9. 3. 10, C421–2	Timosth.	8
9. 5. 8, C433	Artemid.	78
9. 5. 15, C436	Artemid.	79
10. 2. 21, C459–60	Artemid.	80
10. 3. 5, C465	Artemid.	81
	Poseidon.	6
10. 4. 2, C474	Eudoxos	74
10. 4. 3, C474–5	Artemid.	82
10. 4. 5, C475	Eratosth.	68
10. 5. 3, C485	Artemid.	83
11. 1. 5–6, C491–2	Poseidon.	7
11. 2. 14, C496–7	Artemid.	84
11. 2. 15, C497	Eratosth.	69
11. 6. 1, C506–7	Eratosth.	70
11. 7. 3, C509	Eratosth.	71
11. 7. 4, C509–10	Eratosth.	20
11. 7. 5, C510	Eudoxos	22
11. 8. 8–9, C513–14	Eratosth.	72
11. 9. 1, C514	Poseidon.	24
11. 12. 4–5, C522	Eratosth.	73
11. 14. 7, C529	Eratosth.	74
11. 14. 8, C529	Eratosth.	74

	GAGW ch.	extract
12. 3. 21, C550	Eudoxos	35
12. 3. 22, C550–1	Hekat.	67
12. 3. 25, C552–3	Hekat.	66
12. 3. 42, C562–3	Eudoxos	9
12. 4. 8, C566	Skylax	3
12. 4. 9, C566	Hipparch.	5
12. 7. 2, C570	Artemid.	85
12. 8. 1, C571	Artemid.	86
13. 1. 4, C582	Eudoxos	10
13. 1. 4, C583	Skylax	4
	Ps.-Skyl.	1
13. 1. 36, C599 (Hestiaia)	*Introduction*	§VI. 4. c
13. 1. 67, C614–15	Poseidon.	25
13. 2. 5, C618	Timosth.	9
13. 3. 5, C622	Artemid.	87
14. 1. 8, C635	Hekat.	74
14. 1. 22–3, C640–1	Artemid.	88
14. 1. 26, C642	Artemid.	89
14. 1. 29, C663	Artemid.	91
14. 2. 10, C655	Artemid.	90
14. 2. 20, C658	Skylax	5
14. 2. 29, C663–4	Eratosth.	75
14. 3. 3, C665	Artemid.	92
14. 5. 3, C670	Artemid.	93
14. 5. 16, C675	Artemid.	94
14. 5. 22, C677	Artemid.	95
14. 6. 4–5, C683–4	Eratosth.	76
15. 1. 7, C687	Eratosth.	21
15. 1. 10–11, C688–9	Eratosth.	77
15. 1. 13–14, C690	Eratosth.	78
15. 1. 20, C693	Eratosth.	79
15. 1. 72, C719	Artemid.	96
15. 2. 1, C720	Eratosth.	80
15. 2. 8–9, C723–4	Eratosth.	81
15. 2. 14, C726	Eratosth.	82
15. 3. 1, C727	Eratosth.	83
16. 1. 12, C741	Eratosth.	84

	GAGW ch.	extract
16. 1. 15, C743	Eratosth.	85
	Poseidon.	26
16. 1. 21–2, C746–7	Eratosth.	86
16. 2. 4, C749–50	Poseidon.	55
16. 2. 17, C755	Poseidon.	56
16. 2. 33, C760	Artemid.	97
16. 2. 42–3, C764	Poseidon.	27
16. 2. 44, C764	Eratosth.	22
16. 3. 2–6, C765–7	Eratosth.	87
16. 4. 2–4, C767–9	Eratosth.	88
16. 4. 5, C769	Agatharch.	4
16. 4. 5, C769–70	Artemid.	98
16. 4. 5–20, C769–79	Artemid.	98
16. 4. 7–10, C770–1	Agatharch.	4
16. 4. 13–15, C772–4	Agatharch.	4
16. 4. 15, C774–5	Artemid.	98
16. 4. 16, C775	Artemid.	98
16. 4. 17, C775–6	Artemid.	98
16. 4. 18, C776–8	Artemid.	98
16. 4. 19, C778–9	Artemid.	98
16. 4. 20, C779	Artemid.	98
	Poseidon.	28
16. 4. 27, C784–5	Poseidon.	71
17. 1. 1–2, C785–6	Eratosth.	89
17. 1. 5, C790	Poseidon.	42
17. 1. 18, C801	Artemid.	99
17. 1. 19, C802	Eratosth.	90
17. 1. 21, C803	Poseidon.	8
17. 1. 24, C803–4	Artemid.	100
17. 2. 1–5, C821–4	Artemid.	44
17. 3. 1–2, C824	Eratosth.	91
17. 3. 2, C825	Artemid.	101
17. 3. 4, C827	Poseidon.	57
17. 3. 6, C827	Timosth.	10
17. 3. 8, C829	Eratosth.	92
	Artemid.	102
17. 3. 10, C830	Artemid.	103
	Poseidon.	43

	GAGW ch.	extract
Suda		
α 3900 Aristeas	Aristeas	5
δ 1062 Dikaiarchos	Dikaiarch.	15
ε 360 Hekataios	Hekat.	14
ι 521 Hipparchos	Hipparch.	12
σ 710 Skylax of Karyanda	Skylax	13
Symeon Seth		
On the Usefulness of the Heavenly Bodies, 44	Poseidon.	19
Synesios		
Letter 101	Markian.	43
Letter 119	Markian.	44
Epist. ad Paeonium 331b	Hipparch.	46
Theon of Alexandria		
pp. 394–5	Eratosth.	38
Theon of Smyrna		
3. 3	Dikaiarch.	9
Theophrastos		
On Winds, 62	Timosth.	Intr.
Tzetzes (Ioannes), *Chiliades*		
7. 621–36	Skylax	14
7. 633–8	Eudoxos	5
7. 678–84	Aristeas	6
7. 678–9	Aristeas	6
7. 680–2	Aristeas	6
7. 683–4	Aristeas	6
Tzetzes (Isaak/ Ioannes), *On Lykophron*		
633	Artemid.	159
1285	Eratosth.	125

	GAGW ch.	*extract*
Vita Arati		
1	Eratosth.	44
Xenophon		
Anab. 4. 4. 1–13	Introduction	§VI. 2. c
Anab. 4. 8. 1	Introduction	§VI. 2. c
Zenobios, *Proverbs*		
2. 67	Mnaseas	13
2. 106	Mnaseas	35
3. 25	Mnaseas	45
5. 56	Eudoxos	11

Selective Index

D. Graham J. Shipley

Space forbids a complete name index, which would multiply the length of this one many times over. There are entries corresponding to most extracts ('fragments') and to most sections of continuous texts, but only a smaller proportion of the briefest entries are indexed (e.g. quotations from Stephanos of Byzantion). Some ethnic group names and place-names (especially of regions) may be combined in one form or another. Topics covered in chapter introductions are not normally indexed if they are already indexed from the translated texts.

Locators referring to texts rather than subjects are normally grouped at the start of an entry (or sub-entry) in date order (e.g. CS, then ArP, then SK, etc.).

Subsections (but not line numbers of verse) are in subscript type.

A locator giving an extent (e.g. 2–4) does not necessarily mean continuous discussion across the locations to which it refers.

§ marks a section of the Introduction to the book, 'intr.' the introduction to a specific chapter. In citations of the main Introduction, spaces are closed up here (e.g. §VI.2.a), unlike in the rest of the book.

Special abbreviations are used for the chapter texts:

Agc = Agatharchides
Agm = Agathemeros
ArP = Aristeas of Prokonnesos
Arr = Arrian, *Periplous*
Art = Artemidoros
Avi = Avienus, *OM*
AWP = *Airs, Water, & Places*
CS = Catalogue of Ships
DB = Dionysios of Byzantion
Dik = Dikaiarchos
DK = Dionysios s. Kalliphon
DM = Ps.-Aristotle, *De mundo*
DP = Dionysios Periegetes
Era = Eratosthenes
Eud = Eudoxos of Knidos
Eux = Ps.-Arrian, *Euxine*
Exp = *Expositio*
Han = Hanno
Hek = Hekataios

Hip = Hipparchos
HK = Herakleides Kritikos
Hyp = *Hypotyposis*
Isi = Isidoros
Jub = Juba
Mkn = Markianos
Mna = Mnaseas
Mnp = Menippos
Nik = *Nikomedean Periodos* (*vulgo* 'Ps.-Skymnos')
PME = *Periplus maris Erythraei*
Pos = Poseidonios
PS = Ps.-Skylax
PsP = Ps.-Plutarch
Pyt = Pytheas
SC = Skymnos of Chios
SK = Skylax of Karyanda
Sta = *Stadiasmos*
Tim = Timosthenes

Abdera (in Iberia), Art 21, 61
Achaia (Peloponnese), PS 42
Achaia Phthiotis, PS 63
Achaians (Black Sea), *Eux* 66
Achale I., Avi 184
Acheloös, R., origin of name, PsP 22
Achilles: Art 117; patron of sailors, Arr 23_{1-2}
Achilles' I. (Leuke I.): PS 68_4, *Nik* B 9, Arr 21–3, DP 543–8, *Eux* 93–5, 97
Achilles' Racetrack: Arr 21_1, *Eux* 87 bis, 116
Achilles' Village, *Eux* 121
acrostics: DK 1–23, DP 109–34, 307–11, 513–32, 681–5, & endnote; on translating, §X.4
Adouli: port, *PME* 4; village, *PME* 4
Adriatic: Hek 37, PS 15–27, *Nik* 369–414, DP 481–97; E side, DP 384–97; islands, *Nik* 426–33; Agm 23; peoples, Era 113
advancement of knowledge, §II.1
Adyrmachidai, PS 107_1
Aegean sea (*see also under* islands): dimensions, *Hyp* 50; distances, PS 113; islands, CS 653–80, Hek 51–4, PS 48, 58, Tim 9, 36, *Nik* 550–8, 579–86, 643–5, 659–63, 679–95, Agm 25, 26
Aelanites gulf (*see* Ailanites g.; Laeanitae g.)
Aeschylus: on marvels, §III.3.m; quoted, Pos 39, Arr 19_2, *Eux* 71
aether, $DM\ 2_3$
Aetheria (or Egeria), §VI.1.f
Aethiopia, *see* Aithiopia
Africa (*see also* Libyē): circumnavigation, Pos 2_{3-4}; length: Art 6
Africa (province): *Exp* 61
Agatharchides of Knidos: Ch. 15; literary style, Agc B 8; on his own work, Agc 65, 112; source for Artemidoros, Art 98_{20}; style, Agc 63; transmission, §VIII.3; writings, Agc B 8
Agathemeros son of Orthon, Ch. 29
Agrioi, Agc 61, Art 98_{10}
Agrippa, M. Vipsanius, §VI.1.f, §V.4
Ailanites gulf (*see also* Laeanitae g.), Agc 90, Art 110, Mkn B 1_9
Aiolian Is., Pyt 27, *Nik* 257–63
Aiolis, PS 96, Art 87
airs: nature of, $DM\ 2_5$; variation, Agc 66
Airs, Waters, & Places, Ch. 5
Aischines, praised, Agc 21
Aithiopes: at war, Agc 19–20, Art $44b_{8,10}$; blackness not frightening, Agc 16; customs,
Art $44a_{1-3}$; in Morocco, PS 112_{5-12}; peoples, Art $44b_8$, Jub 6_{176-9}; southern, *Hyp* 18; western, Han 7, *Nik* 157, *Hyp* 18
Aithiopia: emeralds, Jub 13; mantichoras, Jub 10
'Aithiopian' (fish), Agc 111
Aitolia, CS 638–44, PS 35, *Nik* 473–9, DK 57–63
Akarnania: DK 47–57; places in, Art 25
Akathartos gulf, Agc 84, Art 98_5
Akridophagoi, Agc 59, Art 98_{12}
Akytania: coastal distances, Mkn B 2_{21-3}; defined, Mkn B 2_{20}
Albion, Avi 112, Mkn B 2_{44}
Alexander the Great: Era 20, 23, *PME* 41, 47; and Arabia, Agc 105; and limits of world, §III.3.k; and progress of geography, §II.1; and Thebes, Agc 21; meets heffalump, PsP 1_5; successors, *PME* 47
Alexandria: DP 254–9; distance from Kyrene, Era 94; economy & society, *Exp* 35–7
Alexis, on islands, $DM\ 3_3$ n.
alluviation: §III.4.d, PS 34_3, DB 23; of Tigris, Jub 21
aloe, traded, *PME* 28
Alpheios: 'loveliest of rivers', DP 410; origin of name, PsP 19
Alps, Avi 637
altars: in Bosporos, DB 8, 16, 24, 28, 46, 71, 74, 86; to Hadrian, Arr 1_2
Amantia, PS 26_{1-2}
Amastris, Arr 14_1, *Eux* 15
Amazons, Hek 29
amber, Pyt 18, 24, Mna 44, *Nik* 391–7
Ambrakia, PS 33_1, PS 34, DK 24, 32, 40
Amisos, Arr 15_3, *Eux* 26
Anacharsis, §VI.4.a
analogies, and divine power, $DM\ 6_{3-13}$
Anametresis of the Pontos, ch. 36 appendix
Anaximandros, §V.2
anchor, of *Argo*, Arr 9_2
anchorages, §X.3.a
animals (*see also* wild a.): Arabian gulf, Agc 68–71, Art 98_{15-16}; Trogodytike, Agc 73–7
Annales history, §II.1
Anonymi Cosmographia, §VI.1.f
anonymous texts, §VII.4
Anthedon, HK 1_{23-4}
anti-clockwise organization (*see also* clockwise o.), §VI.1.b
Antinoös, implicit tribute, Arr 23_4
Antiochos III, Jub 21

Antonine Itinerary, §VI.1.f
Anyte of Tegea, epigraph before Introduction
Aornis, DP 1151
Apameia, Isi A 1_1
apes, in N. Africa, Pos 57
Aphrodites Hormos, Agc 83, Art 98_5
Apollodoros of Athens: §VI.4.c, *Nik* intr.; unnamed, *Nik* 19–46
Apollodotos (king), *PME* 47
Apollonia (Sozopolis), *Eux* 114
Apollonios of Rhodes; §VI.3; and Timosthenes, Tim intr.
Apsaros, Arr 6_{1-3}, 7_4, *Eux* 40, 53
Apsyrtos, Arr 6_3, *Eux* 40
Apulia, Art 73
Aqaba, gulf of: *see* Ailanites g.; Laeanitae g.
Aquitania, *see* Akytania
Arabes: Jub 6_{176-8}; customs, Art 98_{18}
Arabia: PS 105, *PME* 20, DP 923–61, *Exp* 38; aromatics, Jub 25–9; described, Era 88, Art 98_{18}, Jub $22_{149-52, 154-6}$; islands, Jub 22; peoples, Agc 90–2, 94–8, Mkn B 1_{17}; size, Agm 14; structure, Mkn B 1_{15}
Arabia Eudaimon, Agc 99
Arabian gulf (*see also* Red Sea): *PME* 7; animals, Agc 68–71; colour, *Hyp* 36; dimensions, Era 104, Art 111, Agm 14, *Hyp* 44; E side, Agc 87–112; entrance, *PME* 25; form, Agc 81, Agm 14; islands, Agc 93; peoples, Agc 30–9; sailing conditions, Agc 84–5; W side, Agc 81–6
Arachosia, Isi A 1_{19}
Arar, origin of name, PsP 6
Arausio Cadaster, §V.4
Araxes, origin of name, PsP 23
archaeology, of gold mines, Agc 29
archaic period, geographers, §VI.4.a
archery (*see also* bows): Kynegetai, Agc 53; Skythia, *AWP* 20; Trogodytike, Art $98_{9, 10}$
arctic circles, local, Hip 40_{35-6}
Argo: anchor, Arr 9_2; ship, Hek 16–18
Argolis, CS 559–80, PS 49–54
Argonauts (*see also* Jason): Hek 21, Tim 34, DB 24, 46, *Eux* 119; route, Hek 17–18, SC 8, Art 165
Ariake, *PME* 41
Ariane, form, Era 52_{22}, 28–9, 31, Era 80–1
Arimaspians, ArP 1
Aristagoras of Miletos, §V.2
Aristeas of Prokonnesos, Ch. 1
Aristophanes, *Clouds*, on maps, §V.2

Aristotle (*see also* Pseudo-Aristotle): ***Meteorologika***, 2. 6, Ch. 10 appendix, *see also* §VI.2.f; on diagrams, §V.3
Arkadia: CS 603–14, Eud 57, 60, 69, PS 44, Dik 1, *Nik* 525–34; diet, Hek 28; headgear, Era 127; legends, Hek 25; mythology, Mna 23–4; rivers, Era 67, Mna 14
Arkadians, older than Moon, Mna 24
Armenia: Eud 16; in Xenophon, §VI.2.c
Armenia, Lesser, *Exp* 43
army, Roman, in Black Sea, Arr 3_1, 6_2, 9_{3-5}, 10_3
aromatic plants, Agc 99, 101, 103
aromatics, traded, *PME* 7–8, 10, 12–13
Arrian of Nikomedeia (*see also* Pseudo-Arrian bis): §VI.2.h; ***Periplous of the Euxine***, Ch. 27; his geographical corpus, §VIII.2.a
Artemidoros of Ephesos: Ch. 18 (*see also* next entry): career, Art 119–20; commended, Mkn C 3 *bis*; criticized, Art 102; diplomatic role, Art 89; work described, Mkn C 3
Artemidoros Papyrus, Art 167
Artemis (*see also* next entry), at Ephesos, Art 1, 88
Artemis Diktynna, DB 56
artichokes, SK 7, Hek 87–9
Asia (*see also* Western A.): PS 70–106, Mna 30–42, DP 620–1165; and Europe, *AWP* 12, 16, 23; as ideal, §III.3.n *bis*, *AWP* 12_{2-6}; coastal length, Agm 10, Mkn B 1_{50-2}; dimensions, PS 106_4, Art 7; divisions, Era 105–6; eastern, DP 1080–127; extent, Era 97; form, DP 620–6, 887–96; gulfs, DP 630–5; peoples, DP 650–1165, *Hyp* 19–24 (former p., Isi B 11)
Asia Minor: Hek 63–80, PS 93–102, Art 85–95; coasts, DP 799–880; distances, Art 91, *Sta* 154–254; isthmus, *Nik* B 25, 29, Art 95, DP 861–5, *Eux* 27–8; N part, DP 783–6; regions, *Exp* 39–47; S coast, DP 839–80; W coast, DP 799–838
Asians, majority unmanly, *AWP* 16
asphalt, Era 85, Pos 27
Assyria (in Asia Minor), DP 970–5
Assyria (in Black Sea), PS 89, Art 162
astrology, and astronomy, Hip 8, 10
astronomy: and astrology, Hip 8, 10; and geography, Hip 33, 40, 42–3
Athenai (Black Sea), Arr 3_4–4_2, *Eux* 39
Athenai (Euboia), Era 44
Athenaion Limen (Black Sea), *Eux* 81
Athenians, self-image, *AWP* intr.

Athens: CS 546-56, HK 1_{1-7}, *Nik* 559-66, *Exp* 52; as ideal, §III.3.n
Atlantic: Pyt 9-10, Era 12, 24, Avi (55), 82-4, 114-29, 398, 403-15; and Mediterranean, §III.4.c; and Nile, Dik 14; beginning, Jub 6; two parts, Era 24_8
Atlas, Mt., Jub 2
atlases, modern, §XI.4
Attica: CS 546-58, PS 57; topography, Tim 29
Aualites gulf, *PME* 7
Augustus (*see also* Octavian): and progress of geography, §II.1; expedition to East, Jub 21, Isi B 18
Ausonia, synonym for Italy, DP 333, 339, 383
Avien(i)us, *Ora maritima*, Ch. 32
Azania, *PME* 15-18
Azov, Sea of, *see* Maiotis

baboons, Agc 75
Babylon, DP 1005-13
Bacchus, *see* Bakchos
Baitike: Mkn B 2_4; breadth, Mkn B 2_{10}; coastal distances, Mkn B 2_{9-11}; defined, Mkn B 2_8; temple in, Pos 48
Bakare, *PME* 55-6
Bakchos (*see also* Dionysos), in India, DP 1152-65
Balearic Is., Art 65, Avi 471
Baltic, Pyt 21
Barake gulf, *PME* 40
barbarians: Era 46; in Black Sea, DB 2
Barbarikon (city), *PME* 38-9
Barbaroi, beyond Egypt, *PME* 2
Barygaza, *PME* 40-6, 50-2, 57, 64
Bathykolpos, DB 71
Batmizomaneis, territory of, Agc 92
beacons, §III.3.j
beer, Hek 47
Belgike: coastal distances, Mkn B 2_{29-30}; defined, Mkn B 2_{27}
Belitanoi, Art 32
bematists, §IV.1, PS intr.
Berenike (city), Jub 23, *PME* 2-4
Berytus, *Exp* 25
birds: in Egypt, Art $44a_4$; of Diomedes, Jub 11; on Achilles' I. (Leuke), *Nik* B 9, Arr 21_{3-4}, *Eux* 94
Bithynia: SK 3, PS 92_1, *Exp* 49; distances, Mnp A 8
bitumen, Eud 32, Pos 23
black (skin colour), not frightening, Agc 16

Black Sea: PS 67_9-68_5, 70-92, SC 2-4, *Nik* 718-47, B 1-34; Bithynian coast, Arr 12-13, *Eux* 3-13; circumference, Era 99-100, 107, Agm 11, *Eux* 121; dimensions, §VI.2.a, Hek 59-61, *Hyp* 41-53; distances, Art 105, 122, Mnp A 8-10 (interim summations, *Eux* 11, 69, 79, 85, 92, 120-1); E limit, Arr 11_4; E part, Tim 14; N coast, Arr 20 (?); NW coast, *Eux* 78-119; NE coast, Arr 17_2-20, *Eux* 37-77; W coast, Arr 24-5; form, DP 146-69, DB 2; in Europe, Hek 56-7; Kappadokian coast, Arr 1-12; limit, *Eux* 53; limit of Roman control, *Eux* 54; names, Era 19_{6-7}; nations, DB 2; Paphlagonian coast, Arr 14-17$_1$, *Eux* 13-23; peoples, Hek 57, 63-5, Eud 12, 15, 18, 20-1, PS 70-92, Era 19_7, *Nik* B 17-20, Art 84, Arr 11, DP 652-786, *Eux* 22, 35, 50-3, 66, 74, 76, 78, 82; Thracian coast, *Eux* 97-118
boats, sewn, *PME* 14-15, 36
bodies of water, technical terms, §X.3.a
Boïdion (concubine), DB 110
Boiotia: CS 494-516, Hek 44-5, Eud 49, 51, 53, PS 38, 59, HK 1_{8-25}, *Nik* 488-501, Art 50, DK 82-107; extent, DK 102-4
Bordeaux Itinerary, §VI.1.f
Borysthenes, R., *Nik* B 12, *Eux* 87-9
Bosporios, C., origin of name, DB 7
Bosporos, Kimmerian, *see* Kimmerian B.
Bosporos, Thracian (*see also under* currents): Tim 22, 30, Hip 18, 21, *Eux* 2; character, DB 1; width, Agm 11, DB 4; *Hyp* 51
boundaries: of continents (*see also* 'divisions' *under* continents): Tim 12, Era 20, 26_7, *Nik* B 16, Arr 19_2, Agm 3, Avi 331-2, 693-7, *Hyp* 3, 46; local, Era 26_8
Bous, C. (in Bosporos), DB 110
bows, Skythian, Black Sea resembles: Hek 60, Era 107, DP 157-62, *Hyp* 53
Bracheia sea: *Hyp* 33; dimensions, *Hyp* 43
brass, traded, *PME* 6
Braudel, F., §II.1
Braxmani, *Exp* 8
bread, Ionian, Art 115
Brettanike (*see also* Britain), Pyt 2_2, 6
bricks, Pos 25
bridges, of Darius, DB 57
Britain (*see also* Albion): Pyt 22, 24; circumference, SC 5, Isi B 7; flora, SC 5; size, Era 18
Britannia, *Exp* 67
British Library MS Add. 19391, §VIII.2.a

Brittany, Pyt 2_5, 12, 32
buffaloes (?), Agc 77
bulls, flesh-eating, Agc 77, Art 98_{16}
burial customs: Agc 45, 64; Aithiopian, Art $44b_{9.3}$, Trogodytai, Art 98_{17}
Bythmaneis, their fauna, Agc 91
Byzantion: *Eux* 119; character, DB 7–16; foundation, DB 8–9, 23, 24, 34, 49, 53; origin of name, DB 24; situation, DB 6; war v. Philip (V?), DB 65
Byzas, DB 24

Caesar, Julius, *PME* 26
Caesarea (in Syria), *Exp* 26
calendar, Egyptian, Eud 28
Camarini, way of life, *Exp* 4–7, 12
camelopards, Art 98_{16}
Campanians, PS 10, Art 70
canals: §III.4.c; Era 14_{11}; Ptolemy II's, Jub 23
Canaria I., Jub 205
cannibals, alleged, *PME* 62
canoes, *PME* 15, 60
Canopus: elevation, Pos 17; observed at Gadeira, Pos 3
Cape of Spices, *PME* 12
capital punishment, in Aithiopia, Art $44b_5$
Cappadocia, DP 970–4, *Exp* 40
cardoons, *see* artichokes
Caria, *Exp* 47
carrots, in Dalmatia, Pos 63
Carthage: PS 111_1, *Exp* 61; islands, Hek 106; territory, PS 110_1–111_9
Carthaginian explorers, *see* Hanno; Himilco
cartographic perspective, §V.7–8
cartography, modern, §XI.4
Caspian sea: Era 70, Art 164, DP 706–25; caves, Eud 22; dimensions, Art 108, Agm 13, *Hyp* 42; peoples beyond, DP 726–61
Cassiterides Is., *see* Oestrymnides, *and next entry*
Cassius (Mt), and tin, Avi 259–61
Catalogue of Ships, *see* Prologue (preceding Ch. 1)
Cataracts, of Nile, Jub 4_{54}
cattle, white, Agc 105
Caucasus: Era 109, Arr 11_5, *Eux* 53; implied as continental boundary, DP 20–2; location adjusted, Era 23; name, Era 69; origin of name, $PsP 5_3$; peoples, DP 680–91, 695–705
cavalry, Roman, $Arr 3_1$
caves (*see also* sea-caves), Eud 6, 22

Celtiberians, *see* Keltiberians
Celts, *see* Keltoi
central Greece, CS 494–558, 638–44, 681–760, PS 34–9, 56–65, HK 1–3, *Nik* 439–63, 473–510, 559–66, 587–617, Art 78–80, DK 57–107, DP 423–7, 430–46
central parallel, of *oikoumene*, Era 52_{33}, 58, 75, DP 10–11
central position, as ideal: §III.3.n; of Asia, AWP 12_{2-6}; of Earth, $DM 2_1$ of Hellas, Dik 10, Agm 2; of *oikoumenē*, $DM 3_1$
Chalkidike, Hek 49
Chalkis (Aitolian), Art 80
Chalkis (Euboia), HK 1_{26-30}
Chalkis (singer), DB 42
change (*see also under* land): and permanence, $DM 5_{4-5}$; geographical response to, §III.4; geological, Era 13_3, 22; in seas, Era 10, 14, 13_4
channels, manmade, PS 34_1
Chaones, PS 28
Charakene, Jub 21_{136-7}
Charax Spaosinou, Jub 21_{138-41}
Chares of Athens, DB 110
Charmo(u)thas (harbour), Agc 95, Art 98_{18}
Chelonophagoi, Agc 47b, Art 98_{14}
Cherson, *Eux* 85–6
China, Mkn nn. 14, 39–40, 82; *Hyp* n. 9; *see also* Seres; Sinai; Thina; Thinai
chlamys, form of *oikoumenē*, Era 29_6, 57
chōrographia, §III.1.d
Christian periods, geographers, §VI.1.f
Chryseia (Chryse), DP 589–90
Chrysopolis, DB 109
Cicero, epigraph before Ch. 22
Cilicia, *see* Kilikia
Cimbrian migrations, Pos $2_{3.6}$
cinnabar, Jub 33, *PME* 30
Cinnamon-bearing Land, Era 25, 57, 61
circumcision: Agc 62; Arabia, Agc B 3_5, Art 98_5; Egypt, Art $44a_5$; Trogodytike, Art $98_{9,17}$
circumference, of Earth, Era 34–5, 40–1, Hip 34, 38, 40_{34}, 41, 45
circumpolar stars, Pyt 26, 30, Era 61_{36}, 38, Agc 106, Hip 25, 40_{35-6}, Jub 20_{98}
cities: layouts, HK $1_{1, 12, 23, 27-8}$; orientation, AWP 3–6
citron, Jub 2
Clashing Rocks, *see* Kyaneai, Symplegadai
Classical period: geographers, §VI.4.b; maps, §V.3

client kings, *Eux* 52, 58, Arr 11$_{2-3}$, 17$_3$, 18$_3$
climate: and physiology, *AWP passim*; extremes, Agc 66-7; instability, §III.4.e; seasonal, Eud 23
climatic zones, §III.3.f
cloak, form of *oikoumene*, Era 29$_6$, 57
clockwise organization (*see also* anti-clockwise o.), Hek intr., §VI.1.d, §III.1.a, §III.3.g
coastal description, §III.1.b
coastal sailing, Mkn B 1$_2$
codices: **A**, §VIII.2.a; **B**, §VIII.2.a; **D**, §VIII.2.b
coins: old, in market, *PME* 47; traded, *PME* 6, 8, 24, 28, 39, 56, 63
colonies: Aithiopian, *Nik* 150-8; beyond continuous Hellas, *Nik* 628-742 *passim*; Black Sea, DB 2; Carthaginian, Han 2, 5, B 5, *Nik* 159-62, 196-8, 298-9; Greek, ArP intr., (in West) *Nik* 147-9, 201-63 *passim*, 303-40 *passim*, 407-14, 435-43, 453-63 *passim*, (in Sicily, *Nik* 270-99 *passim*); in Black Sea, *Nik* B 1-38 *passim*; in Greece, DK 25, 114-15; Paphlagonian, in Italy, *Nik* 387-90; Phoenician, in Morocco, Era 92; within Greece, *Nik* 474-617 *passim*
Columns, *see* Pillars of Herakles
comedies, quoted, HK 1$_{5-6, 11, 22, 25, 30}$, 3$_7$
comets, *DM* 2$_5$
commerce (*see also* trade), as motivation towards geography, §II.1
common sense geography, §III.2.c
conjonctures, §II.1
Constantine VII Porphyrogennetos: §VI.1.f; and Steph. Byz., §VI.2.j; consults MS D, §VIII.2.b
Constantinople: *Exp* 50; Markianos lectures at, Mkn F 43
constellations (*see also* stars, circumpolar): and seasons, Agc 106, Hip 40, 43; catalogued, Hip 7, 11
continents (*see also* Asia; boundaries; Europe; Libyē): Era 91, *Nik* 76-7, DP 7-9; coastal lengths, Mkn B 1$_5$; divisions, §III.3.g, *AWP* 13, Era 26$_7$, Pos 2$_{3,7}$, Mnp A 6, *DM* 3$_6$, DP 10-26, Mkn B 1$_4$, Mkn C 6, *Eux* 71, 72; number, Tim 37, Hyp 3; origin, *DM* 3$_1$; origins of names, Agm 4; ranked, Hyp 26-31; relative positions, Hyp 4; sizes, Mkn B 1$_6$
continuous Hellas, PS 33$_2$, 65$_2$, *Nik* 470-2, DK 24, 31-8
continuous texts, §VIII.1, §IX
copper, *Nik* 166, *PME* 6, 24, 28, 36, 49, 56

coral, *PME* 28
Corinth: PS 40, 55, *Exp* 52; topography, Eud 56, 64
corpora, of geographical texts, §VIII.2
Corsica (*see also* Kyrnos), PS 6
cosmology, early, §VII.1.b
cosmos (*see also* kosmos): *DM* 2$_{1-2}$, 6$_1$; composed of opposites, *DM* 5$_{1-3}$
courage, *AWP* 16
Crete: CS 645-52, PS 47, *Nik* 535-49, DK 110-29, *Exp* 64; circumference, Art 82; coastal distances, Sta 318-55; dimensions, Agm 26; extent, DK 111-15; in Ptolemy, §VI.1.e; mythology, Mna 30; peoples, DK 114-18; places in, Art 34
criticism, textual, §VII.2
crocodiles: Eud 33; hunted, *PME* 15; in Caesarea, Jub 4$_{51}$
cultural prestige, and geographical writing, §VII.1.e
currents: changing, Era 14$_{12}$; in Bosporos, DB 1, 3-6, 49, 53, 57-8
Cyaneae (*see also* Kyaneai), DB 87, 89
Cyclades: PS 48, 58$_{1-2}$, DK 130-44, 146-8, *Exp* 63; listed, Art 83
Cynetae, Avi 200-6
Cyprus: PS 103, Era 76, *Exp* 63; circumference, Isi B 12; coastal distances, Sta 297-315; crossings from Asia Minor, Sta 178, 186, 197, 204, 233, 316-17; diet (?), Eud 79; dimensions, Tim 13, Art 107, Agm 26
Cyrenaica: *Exp* 62; distance from Peloponnese, Era 69; distances, Sta 53-84

Dachinabades, region, *PME* 50-1
Dalmatia, crops, Pos 63
Damascus, vines, Pos 58
Damastes of Sigeion, §VI.4.b
Damirica, *see* Limyrike
Danapris (*see also* Borysthenes), *Eux* 87
Danube, *see* Istros
Danubian provinces, *Exp* 57, Hyp 11-12
Darius I: SK 1; bridges Bosporos, DB 57
data, treatment by geographers, §IV.c
dates (fruit), traded, *PME* 36-7
Daunitai, PS 15
day-marks, in navigation, §III.3.j
days: and nights, Pyt 4, 19, 23, 28; length, Pyt 15-16, 19, 28, Era 61$_{36, 38-41}$, Hip 24, 37, 40$_{36-42}$, Art 59, Avi 651-73; of sailing, Mkn C 5

Dead Sea, asphalt, Pos 27
death, of Aithiopian kings, Art 44b$_6$
Debai, Agc 97, Art 98$_{18}$
declinations, of stars, Hip 42
dedications: to Achilles & Patroklos, Arr 21$_{2-3}$, 22$_{1-2}$; to Achilles, *Eux* 94
deforestation, Era 76
degrees (divisions of circle), Hip 40$_{34}$
Deimachos, errors of, Era 52$_{19}$
Delos, distances from, *Sta* 284
Delphi: Eud 50, DP 441–6; and Timosthenes, Tim 8; centre of Greece, Agm 2
Delta (Nile): Hek 96; topography, Art 99–100
Demetrius, general of Philip (V?), DB 65
dēmos, translation of, §X.3.c
Demosthenes (orator), praised, Agc 21 *bis*
'descriptive geography', §II.2
deserts, of N. Africa, *Exp* 62
Diagnosis of Geography, §VIII.2.a
diagrams, in text, §V.3
diaplous, PME intr.
Dicaea, C., DB 70
Dicks, D. R., quoted, §IV
didactic geography, §VII.1.d
diet: Aithiopia, Art 44a$_2$; Aithiopia, Art 44b$_{8,6}$; Arkadia, Hek 28; Cyprus (?), Eud 79; Egypt, Hek 100–1; Egypt, Art 44a$_5$; Germans, Pos 64; Ichthyophagoi, Agc 38, 40; Trogodytai, Art 98$_{17}$
Dikaiarchos of Messana: Ch. 9: and Ps.-Skylax, PS intr., Dik intr.; appraised, Dik 4; writings, Dik 15
dimensions, *see under oikoumenē*
Diomedean birds, Jub 11
Diomedes' I., DP 483
Dionysios of Byzantion, Ch. 30
Dionysios of Kyzikos, epigraph to Ch. 12
Dionysios Periegetes, Ch. 28
Dionysios son of Kalliphon: Ch. 20; Athenian (?), DK intr.
Dionysodoros, on size of Earth, Era 34
Dionysos, DP 939–49, 1152–65
dioptras, Dik 9, Era 37, 52
Dioskourias: Arr 10$_4$, 11$_5$, 17$_{1-2}$, 18$_1$, *Eux* 48, 55; limit of Roman control, *Eux* 54; population, Tim 14
Dioskourides' I., PME 30–1
directions, translation of, §X.3.b
discovery (*see also* exploration), as geographical ambition, §III.2.c

diseases (*see also* plagues), AWP *passim*
distances: across Mediterranean, Tim 20–1; in Iberia, Art 167; long, Dik 4, Era 25–6, Art 74, Isi B 5, 8–10, 17, Pyt 2, 6; measurement of, §IV, Mkn C 5
divers (birds), Jub 11
diversity: of geographical writing, §III.2.b; of *oikoumene*, Agc 66–7
divine, the, DM 6
divine power, DM 6$_2$
dogheads, Agc 75, Art 98$_{16}$
Dog-milkers, Agc 61, Art 98$_{10}$
dogs, giant, Jub 8
dolphins, musical, DB 42
domestic animals, Egypt, Eud 27
Dorians, *Nik* 592–6
Doros, Art 48
dress: Aithiopian, Art 44b$_{8,5}$; Egyptian (?), Hek 104; Keltiberian, Art 64; Persian, Hek 84
Dromos Achilleos, Arr 21$_1$, *Eux*$_{87}$ *bis*, 116
Duo Korakes, Art 68
dwellings, of Fish-eaters, Agc 43–4
dyes, traded, *PME* 39
Dyrrachion, Era 121

Earth: as geographical topic, §III.3.a; centrality, DM 2$_1$; circumference, §III.3.a, Era 34–5, 40–1, Hip 34, 38, 40$_{34}$, 41, 45, Pos 11, Mkn B 1$_4$, *Hyp* 1; dimensions, Dik 8; form, Era 13–14, DP 170–4; sphericity (*see also* spherical Earth), Dik 12
earthquakes, §III.4.b, Pos 20, 29, DM 4$_9$
ebony, traded, *PME* 36
economic change, §III.4.f
eels, Eud 58
Egeria, pilgrim, §VI.1.f
Egypt: Hek 89–104, AWP 12$_7$, Eud 24–30, PS 106$_{1-5}$; as continent, Tim 37; authors' treatment, Art 44b$_{11}$; boundaries, Agc 10, *PME* 1; culture, *Exp* 34; customs, Art 44a$_3$; details, Art 45–7; diet, Hek 100–1; distances, W of Alexandria, *Sta* 1–52; economy & society, *Exp* 34–7; exports, *PME* 6; extent, Tim 16; fauna & flora, Art 44a$_4$; nomes, Agc 22; southern tribes, Agc 30
Egyptians: DP 232–68; fighting Aithiopes, Art 44b$_{102-3}$; inhospitable, Era 90
Eirinon gulf, *PME* 40
Elephant-eaters, Agc 54–6, Art 98$_{10}$
elephant-hunting (*see also* Ptolemaïs Theron): Agc B 3$_{5-14}$ *passim*, Art 98$_{5-15}$ *passim*;

Aithiopes, Agc 54–6; Ptolemaic, Agc 1, 57, B 4; a thing of the past, Era 61_{35}
Elephantophagoi, Agc 54–6, Art 98_{10}
elephants: Aithiopia, Art $44b_{102-6}$; behaviour, Agc B 3_{14}, Art 98_{14}; distribution, Agc 9; NW Africa, Jub 3; on ships, Agc 84, 85; oracular, PsP 1_5; tusks, Jub 9, 15
Elephas (Mt), Agc B 3_{14}, Art 98_{14}
Elis, CS 591–2 (?), 615–24, PS 43
elites, and geography, §II.2
emeralds, Jub 13, 37
Empedokles, quoted, $DM\ 6_{10}$
Encheleis, PS 25
Enetoi (Veneti), PS 19
entertainment, and geographical writing, §VII.1.e, §III.2.b
environment: and lifestyle, Pos 61; and physiology, AWP passim
Epeiros, Hek 39–40, Nik 444–52
Ephesos: Art 88; and Romans, Art 89; Artemidoros and, Art 1
Ephoros of Kyme: §VI.2.e; quoted, Eux 74, 78 bis
epigrams, quoted, Era 51
epigraphy, see inscriptions
Epirus, Exp 53
epitaphs, cited, DB 110 & n.
epitomes, construction of, Mnp A 4, Mkn C 4
equatorial zone, breadth, Hip 44
equilibrium, in cosmos, DM 5
Eratosthenes of Cyrene: Ch. 12; and Pytheas, Era 18; criticized, Era 3, 5–10, 12, 26, 52_{29-31}, $_{33-41}$, 54–5, 65, Mkn C 3; mistrust of myths, Era 21; quoted (?), Pos $2_{3.5}$
Erembians, Pos 65, 71, 73, DP 963–8
Eretrians, epigraph before Ch. 4
erosion, coastal, DB 19, 49
Erytheia: Avi 309; as Fortunate Island, Pyt 9, Era 62, Art 60
Erythra (C.), Art 41
Erythraian sea: PME 1, Hyp 35; dimensions, Agm 13–14; divisions, Era 103; level, Hip 19; name, Agc 2–5, Art 98_{20}; peoples, Agc 30–49
Etesian winds, Tim 33
ethnika, defined, §VI.2.j
ethnography: in geographical writing, §VII.1.e; of S. Egypt, Agc 30–48
ethnos, translation of, §X.3.c
Etna, Pos 22
Etruscans (see also Tuscia; Tyrrhenoi), PS 5, 17

etymology, see names; words
Euboia, CS 536–45, Hek 46, Era 44, Nik 566–78
Eudaimon Arabia: Agc 99, PME 26, Mkn B 1_{15}, B 1_{17}; circuit, Mkn B 1_{19}, B 1_{21}; structure, Mkn B 1_{19}
Eudoxos of Knidos: Ch. 6; and Pytheas, Pyt intr.; reliable, Eud 5; writings, Eud 3
Eudoxos of Kyzikos, §VI.4.c, Pos $2_{3.4-5}$
Euesperides, PS 108_2
Eumedes (explorer), Art 98_7, Agc B 3_7
euphorbia: discovery, Jub 41–3; processing, Jub 41–2
Euphrates: DP 976–82; origin of name, PsP 20
Euripides, quoted, HK 3_3
Europe: Hek 33–57, Mna 1–29, DP 270–619; and Asia, AWP 12, 16, 23–4; as ideal land, §III.3.n bis; Black Sea coast, Eux 78–119; boundary with Libya, Avi 331–2, 693–7; breadth, Art 5; coastal length, Agm 10; dimensions, PS 69; eastern peoples, DP 330–4; form, Era 56, DP 270–80; islands, Hyp 13; length, Art 8_{10}, Isi B 8; long distances, Art 74; northern peoples, DP 302–29; peoples, DP 281–446; provinces, Hyp 6–8, 10–12; rivers, Hyp 9–10; the far NE, Hek 23; western coastal length, Mkn B 2_1, B 2_{46}; western peoples, DP 281–301
Europeans, variable character, AWP 23_1–24_6
Eurotas, origin of name, PsP 17
Eusebios of Caesarea, §VI.1.f
euthanasia, Agc 64
Euthymenes of Massalia, §VI.4.a, Pyt intr.
Eux., Ch. 36
Euxeinos Pontos (see also Black Sea), form, DB 2
événements, §II.1
experience, underlying geography, §II.2
exploration (see also discovery *and next entry*): §VII.1.a; by Ptolemies, Agc 41b; of world limits, §III.3.k
'exploratory geography' (see also preceding entry), §II.2
exports, from Egypt to Berbers, PME 6
Expositio totius mundi . . ., Ch. 33
extant works, §VIII.1
extremities, of world, §III.3.k

Fanum (see also Hieron), on E side of Bosporos, DB 92–3
fate, $DM\ 7_5$

fathoms, §IV.2
fauna, Iberia, Pos 49
feasting, in E. Africa, Agc 38
feminization, of men, Agc 103
fennel, Jub 8
fish (see 'Aithiopian'; oysters): Bosporos, (abundance) DB 1, 5-6, 16-17, 21, 28, 50, 60, 68, 76, 97-8, (dearth) DB 3, 30, (migration) DB 5, 18, 30, 71, 102, Lykia, Art 52, Nile, Art 44a$_{4,5}$; not to be eaten, Agc 111
Fish-eaters, see Ichthyophagoi
fishers, in E. Indian Ocean, Agc 50
fishing: Barygaza, PME 44; Bosporos, DB 5, 16-17, 21, 23, 30, 50, 60, 68; dangers, DB 50; Erythraian sea, Agc 32-5; Menuthias, PME 15; Red Sea, Art 98$_{13}$
flat Earth theory, §VI.1.f, §III.3.a
floods, §III.4.b
foreign parts, in geographical writing, §III.3k-l
foreign peoples, §III.2.c
forests, in Gaul, Era 43
Forma Urbis Romae, §V.4
fortifications, Arr 9$_{3-5}$
Fortunate Island(s), Pyt 9, Era 62, Art 60, Jub 8
fragmentary sources: §VI.4, §VIII.1, §VIII.3; defined, §VII.3; presentation, §IX
frankincense: Jub 25-6, 28, PME 8, 10-12, 27-30, 32, 36, 39; harvesting, PME 29
Frankincense-bearing Land, Art 98$_{14}$, Agc B 3$_{14}$, PME 27, 29, 31
fresh water, AWP 7
friends, of Aithiopian kings, Art 44b$_7$
frigid zones, Pyt 8, Era 32$_1$, Hip 40$_{43}$
frogs, plagues of, PS 22. 2, Agc 60
Frozen Sea, Pyt 23, DP 32, 316, Hyp 45
fully reasoned geography, §III.2.c
functional purposes, and geographical writing, §II.2

Gadeira (see also next 2 entries): Art 59-60, 67, Pos 50; and Seleukos of Babylon, Pos 38; wells, Pos 38
Gades, Avi 85, 269
Gadir, name, Avi 267
Gaius Caesar, Jub 32
Galatia, Exp 41
Gallipoli peninsula, see Thracian Chersonese
Ganges: Era 78, Art 96, PME 63, Mkn B 1$_{37}$, B 1$_{39}$; origin of name, PsP 4
Gangetic gulf, Mkn B 1$_{37-9}$

Garden of the Hesperides, PS 108$_4$
Garindaneis, at war, Agc 90$_{1-2}$
Gasandoi, land of, Agc 98b
Gaul (see also Keltike): PS 3-4, Pyt 11-12, Era 43, Art 2-3, Avi 565-713, Exp 58; isthmus, Pos 52
gazetteers, Hip 23
Gedrosia, Mkn B 1$_{31-3}$
gemstones (see also precious stones), of India, DP 1118-22
generic composition, §III.2.a
genos, translation of, §X.3.c
genre: and periploi, §III.1.b; in Classical literature, §III.2.a
geographers, early, Hek 2, 4-6
geōgraphia, definition, §II.1
geographical writing: classification, §III.1; motives, §II.2, §III.2.c; social settings, §II.2; topics, §III.3
geography (see also under Homer): ancient, (classification) §II.2, (development of tradition), §II.2; and historiography, §II.2; benefits, Nik 92-102; 'common sense', §III.2.c; definitions, §II.1; 'descriptive', §II.2 init., §III.2 init.; development, §VII.1, Mkn C 3; early, Eud 1, Era 1-3; 'exploratory', §II.2 init., §III.2 init.; history of, Mkn C 2; human v. environmental, Pos 2$_{3.7-8}$; humanistic, §II.1; in general, Pos 34; manipulation, Era 20, 23; 'mathematical', §II.2 init., §III.2 init.; Mediterranean, modern writings, §XI.3; modern editions, §XI.2; modern overviews, §XI.1; nature of, Pos 1; of Pos, scientific not descriptive, Pos 5; progress of, Art 81; progressive correction, Pos 6; theory and practice, Art 167
geometrical forms: and India, Era 77; as descriptors, §V.7; criticized, Era 52$_{30}$; use, Era 52$_{31}$
geometry, spherical, Hip 45
Germania (see also next 2 entries), Era 43
Germania, Great: coastal distances, Mkn B 2$_{32-6}$; defined, Mkn B 2$_{31}$; dimensions, Mkn B 2$_{36}$
Germaniai: Hyp 7; coastal distances, Mkn B 2$_{29-30}$; defined, Mkn B 2$_{27-8}$
Germans: diet, Pos 64; habits, Pos 74
Geron Halios, DB 49
Gerrhaioi, Agc 89, 104
gēs periodos: as form of writing, §III.1.a, §III.2.a

ghee, traded, *PME* 14, 41
Gibraltar, *see* Pillars of Herakles; strait of Gibraltar
giraffes, Agc 73, Art 98$_{16}$
glass, traded, *PME* 6–7, 17, 39, 49, 56
gnomons: Pos 4; their shadows, Hip 40$_{38, 41}$
god, the: and cosmos, *DM* 6; names, *DM* 7$_{1-3}$; powers, *DM* 7$_{4-5}$; unity, *DM* 7$_6$
gods, created the lands, *DP* 1168–79
gold (*see also next entry*): corrupting effect, Pos 31–2; fluvial, PsP 7$_3$; in Arabia, Agc 104; mining, Agc 24–9, DP 1114–17; processing, Agc 26–8; sand similar to, DB 76; trade, *Nik* 166, *PME* 6, 8, 24, 36, 49, 63
gold-dust, Arabia, Agc 97, 98
Gorgades Is. (*see also next 2 entries*), Han B 3$_{99}$, B 6
Gorgons (?) (*see also* gorillas), Han 18
gorillas (?) (*see also preceding 2 entries*), Han 18, B 3$_{93}$, B 6
Gracchus, Ti. Sempronius, §V.4
grain, traded, *PME* 7, 14, 17, 24, 31–2, 41, 56
Great Britain, *see* Britain
Great Sea: divisions, *Hyp* 32–6; names, *Hyp* 45
Greece: as ideal land, §III.3.n; central, DK 57–107; length, Art 77; mainland, Hek 38–45; southern, *Exp* 52 west-central, DK 24–57
Greek culture, and Roman, §III.1 init.
Greeks, in Black Sea, DB 2
guinea fowl, PS 112$_1$, Mna 44, Agc 83, Art 98$_5$
guinea worms, Agc 59, B 5
gulf of *Aqaba, see* Ailanites g.; Laeanitae g.
gulf of Corinth, *Nik* 508–10
gulf of Sinai, Mkn B 1$_{46-8}$
Gymnesiai Is., Art 63, 65, 159
Gynaikospolis, Art 136

Hadrian, Arr 1–2, *Eux* 1
Haimos, Mt: *Eux* 110; origin of name, PsP 11$_3$
Hair of Isis (plant), Jub 12
Halymdessos (Sal-), *Eux* 117
Halys, R., *Eux* 24, *Nik* B 30, Arr 14$_5$–15$_1$
Hannibal, route, §VI.2.g
Hanno of Carthage: Ch. 4, Jub 2; and Polybios, §VI.2.g
harbours: Tim intr.; built, Arr 16$_6$; 'closed', PS §29 & n.; technical terms, §X.3.a
harmony, in cosmos, *DM* 6$_{10-11}$
hats, Arkadian, Era 127
health, and environment, *AWP passim*

Hebros, origin of name, PsP 3
Hegesias, criticized, Agc 21
Heidelberg codex, §VIII.2.a
Hekataios of Miletos: Ch. 3: alleged shortcomings, Hek 67; cosmology, Hek 8; life, Hek 14; travels, Hek 1; use of maps, §V.2; writings, Hek 11–12
Heleioi, Art 98$_9$
heliacal settings and risings, Agc 106
Helike, disappearance, §III.4.b, Era 66
Hellas (Greece): DP 398–446; as ideal land, §III.3.n; continuous, PS 33$_2$, 65$_2$, *Nik* 470–2, DK 24, 31–8; extent, HK 3$_{1, 6-8}$
Hellas (region of Thessaly), HK 3$_6$
hellebore, PS 37
Hellenes: manly, AWP 16$_5$; v.barbarians, Era 46
Hellenistic period: geographers, §VI.4.c; maps, §V.3
Hellespont: Hek 68, Tim 34, Art 123; continental boundary, DP 17; region, *Exp* 48; width, *Hyp* 50
Hemeroskopeion, Art 22
hemispheres, of Earth: N, Era 29$_5$; S, Era 15
Heniochoi, *Eux* 51
Heracleots, subjection, Pos 60
Herakleia Pontike, Arr 12$_3$, *Eux* 9–11
Herakleides Kritikos, Ch. 11
Herakleides Lembos, Agc B 8
Herakles: Eud 11, 13, Mna 8, 29; labours, Hek 22, 24–5, 27
Hermes, statue of, Arr 2$_{1-2}$
Hermesianax (of Kolophon?), criticized, Agc 21
Hermolaos, epitomator of Steph. Byz., §VI.2.j
Herodotos of Halikarnassos: §VI.2.a; on Black Sea, §VI.1.a; on Egypt, Art 44a$_5$; on sailing times, §IV.b
Heroes' I., *see* Achilles' I.
Hesperides (Euesperides, city), PS 108$_2$
Hesperides (Garden of), PS 108$_4$
Hesperou Keras, Han 14
Hestiai, in Bosporos, DB 53
Hestiaia, female geographer, §VI.4.c
Hiberi, Avi 250, 472, 552
Hiberia, Avi 253, 613
Hiberni, *see* Hierni
Hibernia (*see also* Ierne), Mkn B 2$_{42-3}$
Hiberus (river), Avi 248, 503
hides, traded, *PME* 39
Hierni, Avi 108–12
Hierokles, §VI.1.f

Hieron (Iberian cape), Art 58–9, Avi 333–4
Hieron of Zeus Ourios (Bosporos): Tim 22, 30, DB 75, Arr 12$_2$, 25, Mkn C 6, *Eux* 1–3, 11, 69, 119–20; as 'Fanum', DB 75; departure point, Mnp A 7
Himilco of Carthage, §VI.4.a, Avi 117–19, 380, 412
Hippalos (pilot), discoveries, §VI.4.c, *PME* 57
Hipparchos of Nikaia: Ch. 16: and Pytheas, Hip 37; criticized, Hip 24–31; criticizes Eratosthenes, Hip 25–32; on maps, §V.3
Hippokrates of Kos (?), *Airs, Waters, & Places*, Ch. 5
Hispania (*see also* Hispaniai; Spania): defined, Mkn B 2$_{6-7}$; size, Art 4
Hispaniai, *Hyp* 7
historians, *see* style
historical geography, §II.1
historiography (*see also* style), and geography, §II.2
history: of geography, §II.1; and myth, Agc 7–8
hodological space, §V.8
homeland, in geographical writing, §III.3.n, §II.1
Homer (*see also* next entry): and geography, §VI.3, Hek 4–5, Era 1–9, 11, 19, Hip 16–17; and Mysians, Pos 70; and Okeanos, Pos 33; and tides, Pos 33; emendations, Eud 35; quoted, *DM* 6$_{11}$ *bis*, Arr 8$_2$, and epigraph before Prologue
Homeric *Catalogue of Ships*, *see* prologue (preceding Ch. 1)
honey: Eud 55, 63; in myth, Mna 29
Horden, J. N. P. B., §II.1
Horn of the South (Trogodytike), Art 98$_{14}$, Agc B 3$_{14, 15}$
Horn of the South (West Africa), Han 17
Horn of the West, Han 14
horses, traded, *PME* 24
human geography, §II.1
humanistic geography, §II.1
humour, and geographical writing, §VII.1.e, §III.2.b
Hunter Folk, Agc 53
hunting (*see also* elephant-h.; h.-stations), Aithiopian, Art 44b$_{10}$
hunting-stations (*see also* elephant-hunting), Agc B 3$_{8-10, 14}$, Art 98$_{8-10, 14}$
Hydaspes, origin of name, PsP 1
hyenas (?), Agc 78, Art 98$_{16}$

Hylloi, Era 42
Hylophagoi, Agc 52
Hyperboreans, ArP 1, 4–5, Mna 22, Pos 75
hyphormoi, *see* minor anchorages
Hypotyposis of Geography, Ch. 35
Hyrkania, rivers, Era 71
Hyrkanian sea, *see* Caspian s.
Hyssou Limen, Arr 3$_1$, *Eux* 38

Iambics to King Nikomedes, Ch. 17
Iapyges, PS 14
Iberes, PS 2–3, Avi 98–109, 480
Iberia: Hek 34–5, PS 1–2, Pyt 9, Era 62–3, *Nik* 139–66, Art 10, 24, 63, Avi 85–713 *passim*; defined, Mkn B 2$_{6-7}$; dimensions, Era 55; divisions, Art 23; fauna, Pos 49; in Artemidoros Papyrus, Art 167; places in, Art 21–2, 24, 26, 30–2; places in, Art 26; provinces, Art 31
Iberians, *see* Iberes
Ichthyophagoi: Agc 84, Art 98$_7$; 3rd group, Agc 43; 4th group, Agc 44–7; 5th group, Agc 48; beyond Red Sea, Agc 40–2; happy, Agc 49; in Red Sea, Agc 31–9
Ida, origin of name, PsP 13$_3$
Ierne (*see also* Hierni), Pyt 7$_8$, Era 29$_8$
illiteracy, Agc 41a
Illyria (*see also* next entry): PS B 3, Mna 6, 17, *Nik* 415–25; places in, Art 11, 28
Illyrioi, PS 22–6
immigration, at Dioskourias, Tim 14
Imperial Roman period, geographers, §VI.1.f
inaccessible peoples, Agc 46
Inachos, origin of name, PsP 18
incense, traded, *PME* 9–12
incest, PsP 1$_1$, 3$_1$, 7$_1$, 14$_1$, 17$_1$, 21$_1$, 22$_1$
increase of knowledge, §II.1
India (*see also* Indike): SK 1–2, 7 (?), DP 1107–65; climate, Pos 9, 14; dimensions, Era 52$_{19}$, 101, Hip 23, Art 109; exports, *PME* 6; fertility, Era 78$_{13}$, 79; flora, Hek 89; form, Era 48, 52$_{22}$, 77, Hip 29, DP 1127–34; Greater, *Exp* 16; latitude, Era 52$_{20-1}$, Hip 25, 27; Lesser, *Exp* 17–18; location, Era 47, 52$_{19-22}$; orientation, Pos 9, 14; peoples, Hek 90–1; rivers, Era 78, DP 1137–48; size, Era 106
Indian Ocean: eastern (*see also* next entry), Agc 50; western, *see* Erythraian sea
Indian sea: Mkn B 1$_{16}$; divisions, Mkn B 1$_{13}$, B 1$_{16}$; form, Mkn B 1$_{12}$; peoples, Mkn B 1$_{12}$

1178 • SELECTIVE INDEX

Indike (*see also* India): outside Ganges, Mkn B $1_{16, 40-2}$; within Ganges, Mkn B $1_{16, 34, 38-9}$
Indikon Pelagos, *Hyp* 34
Indos, R.: SK 1, Era 78, DP 1088–94, 1132, 1137; mouths, *PME* 38; origin of name, PsP 25
infertility, Skythian, *AWP* 22_{1-11}
Insana Laurus, DB 95
inscriptions: Hip 19; 'barbarian', Agc 93b; cited, Hip 19_{15}, DB 110 & n.; Greek & Latin, on Leuke I., *Eux* 95, Arr 21_{2-3}; to Hadrian, Arr 1_2
'insensitive' Fish-eaters, Agc 41
intellectual culture, §II.2
intuitive geography, §III.2.c
inundations, §III.4.b
Io, DB 7, 24
Ionia: DP 821–38; as ideal land, §III.3.n; coastal length, Art 91; distances, Sta 293–6
Ionian islands, CS 625–37, *Nik* 446, 464–9, Art 38, DK 48–52, Agm 23
Ionian Renaissance, Hek intr.
Ionians, etymology, Hek 33
Iouernia, *see* Ierne
Ireland, *see* Ierne
iron, traded, *PME* 6, 8, 10
Isauria, Art 51, *Exp* 45
Isidoros of Charax, Ch. 23
Isis' hair (sea plant), Agc 110, Jub 12
islands (*see also* Ionian i.; *see also under* Aegean): Eud 71–5, *Nik* 87–8, 372–3; Adriatic, *Nik* 426–33; Aithiopian, Hek 102; Arabian gulf, Agc 93; Black Sea, Sk 2, DP 541–53; Bosporos, DB 86; catalogued, Avi 51–6; Europe, *Hyp* 13–14; Greece, DP 498–505, 511–38; in *oikoumenē*, DP 447–619; in Red Sea, Art 98_{14}, Jub 23; Indian Ocean, Tim 17; Mediterranean, DP 447–553, *Exp* 63–6; Nile, Hek 99; Ocean, *DM* 3_5, DP 554–611; off Carthage, Hek 106; off Etruria, Art 159; off Iberia, Art 63, 65; off Libyē, Era 96; off Massalia, Art 9; sizes, Tim 19, Art 8_{20}, *DM* 3_3 & n., (circumferences) Isi B 7, 12–16, Agm 20–3, (greatest) PS 114, Mkn 1_8, (ranked) *Hyp* 27
Ismenos, origin of name, PsP 2
isolation, of Fish-eaters, Agc 46
Issedones (Issedoi), ArP 1, 6
isthmuses: Pos 7–8; of Asia Minor, PS 102; of Asia Minor, *Nik* B 29, Art 95; of continents, DP 20–5; of Gaul, Pos 52

Istroi, PS 20
Istros (city), *Nik* B 7–8, *Eux* 98
Istros (river): *Nik* B 7–8, *Eux* 92–3, 96–9; course, SC 8, *Hyp* 9; island within, Era 111–12; mouths, Arr 20_3, 24_1, *Eux* 96–7; sources, Hip 19, *Nik* 194–5
Italia (Magna Graecia), *Nik* 300–60
Italy: Hek 36–7, Eud 65–8, PS 5–12, 14–19, DP 98–102, *Exp* 53–6, *Hyp* 8; as ideal land, §III.3.n *ter*; form, DP 339–44; peoples, DP 345–83; places in, Art 13; topography, Art 73
Itanos (?), Art 34
Ithaca, Art 38
itineraria, §VI.1.f
Itinerarium Burdigalense, §VI.1.f
Ityke (Utica), PS 111_5
Iunior Philosophus, Ch. 33
ivory, traded, *PME* 4, 6–7, 10, 16–17, 49, 56

Jacoby, F.: project, §VII.3; continuation, §VII.3, §II.2
Jason, Arr 9_2, 25_3, DB 24, 46, 49, 75, *Eux* 51, 119
jewels: in Arabia, Agc 104; traded, *PME* 56
Jews, Mna 34–5
Juba II of Mauretania, Ch. 22
Julian of Ascalon, on distances, §IV.c
Junior Philosophus, *see* Iunior P.

Kaikos, origin of name, PsP 21
Kalatis (Kallatis), *Eux* 102
Kallimachos, epigraph before Ch. 9
Kalpes Limen, Arr 12_{4-5}, *Eux* 5
Kampanoi (Campanians), PS 10
Kanobos, continental boundary, DP 11–13
Kappadokia, DP 970–4
Karambis, C., Arr 14_3, *Eux* 17
Karandas (dolphin-killer), DB 42
Karia: PS 99_{1-2}; coastal length, Art 91; distances, Sta 255–92; places in, Art 55
Karmania, Era 82, Pos 72, Jub 20_{98}, 22, 25, 33, Mkn B 1_{26-30}
Kartago, *see* Carthage
Karyanda, SK 5, 11
Kasandreis, land of, Agc 98a
Kassiterides, Pyt intr.
Kassopia, PS 31
kēboi (or *kēpoi*, a quadruped), Agc 74a, 76, Art 98_{16}
Keltiberians, Art 64, Pos 66

Keltike (*see also* Gaul): *Nik* 167–94, *Art* 17–18, 20; access to, *Art* 60; places, *Art* 127
Keltogalatia: *Art* 10; defined, Mkn B 2_{19}
Keltoi: SC 6; ethnography, Pos 62; Hellenic customs, *Nik* 183–5; in Italy, PS 18
Kephallenia, *Art* 38
Kepos, in Bosporos, DB 18
Keras, of Bosporos, DB 5, 6, 32
Kerkyra, *Art* 39
Kerne, Han 8–10, B 1, PS 112_{5-7}
Keys, of Pontos, DB 69
Kilikia: PS 102, *Exp* 39, 45; distances, *Sta* 154–83; places, *Art* 93–4
Kimbric peninsula (*Jutland*?), Mkn B 2_{33-4}
Kimmerian Bosporos: Hek 62, Mnp B 4, Arr 19_1, *Eux* 54, 68, 79; king, Arr 17_3; places in, *Art* 57
kings (*see also* client k.; kingship): Indian, SK 2, of Mosynoikoi, *Eux* 35, of Sabaioi, Agc 102
kingship (*see also* preceding entry): Aithiopian, *Art* $44a_2$, $44b_{5-7,9}$; Persian, *DM* 6_{3-5}; principles, Agc 11–18
Kithairon (Mt), origin of name, PsP 2_{2-3}
Kleides (Kleithra) of Pontos, DB 69
kleistos, PS §29 & n.
klimata (*see also* zones of latitude), §III.3.f, Pos 4
knowledge: advancement of, §II.1; systematization of, Hek intr.
Koile Syria, monsters, Pos 56
Kolchians, PS 81, Era 50_{11}, 108, Mna 42, SC 2, 4, *NP* 24, Arr 7_1, 11_1, DP 489, 689, 762–3, 1029–38, *Eux* 38, 50
Kolchis, Era 47_3, 48, 52_{39}, Hip 32_{39}, Pos 7, Arr 25_3, *Hyp* 20
Koloboi, *Art* $98_{10, 13}$, Agc B $3_{10, 13}$
Korkyra (Corfù), PS 29
Kosmos Indikopleustes, §VI.1.f
kosmos (*see also* cosmos): *DM* 2_{1-2}; as good order, *DM* 5_4
Kossinoi (Ostiones), *Art* 157
Kotys (king), Arr 17_3, *Eux* 54
Kreophagoi, *Art* $98_{9,13,14}$ = Agc B $3_{9,13,14}$
Krinagoras, epigram, Mnp B 2
Kriou Metopon (Black Sea), PS 68_{2-4}, *Nik* B 32, *Art* 84, Mnp A 9, PsP 14_4, *Hyp* 51, *Eux* 18, 81, 84
Kriou Metopon (Crete), PS $47_{1,3}$, Era 68, *Sta* 334–5, *Hyp* 47
kroko(u)ttai, Agc 78, *Art* 98_{16}

Ktesias of Knidos: §VI.2.d; on marvels, §III.3.m
Kyaneai (*see also* Cyaneae): Tim 30, *Eux* 119
Kyllene (Mt.), measured, Dik 2
Kynamolgoi, Agc 61, *Art* 98_{10}
kynara, SK 7, Hek 87–9
Kynegetai, or Kynegoi, Agc 53
kynokephaloi, *Art* 98_{16}
Kyrene: PS 108_3; distance from Alexandria, Era 94
Kyrnos: PS 6; visibility, Era 65, *Art* 69

Laconia (*see also* Lakedaimon; Lakonike): *Exp* 52; cities, *Art* 76
Lactantius, §VI.1.f
Laeanitae/Laeanites gulf (*see also* Ailanites), Agc 90_4, *Art* 110, Jub 22_{156}
Lakedaimon (*see also* Laconia), CS 581–90, PS 46
lakes: Arabia, Era 84; marvellous, Eud 54, 57, Jub 19
Lakonike (*see also* Laconia), places in, *Art* 29
land: distances, measurement of, §IV.a; that was formerly sea, §III.4.d, Eud 9, Era 13_4, $14_{13, 15}$, Hip 19
landscape, political interpretation, §III.2.b
Laodicia, *Exp* 27
Laon (comic poet), quoted, HK 1_{22}
late antique period: geographers, §VI.1.f; maps, §V.5
late Roman period, *see preceding entry*
Latinoi, PS 8
latitude: §VI.1.e, §III.3.c, Pyt 2–4, 7, Era 27–8; accuracy, Era 50–1; beginnings, Eud 48; difficulties, Era $52_{33, 35, 37-9}$; measurement, Hip 24–31, 34–6, 39, 45; of stars, Hip 42
Laurel, Manic, DB 95
lead, traded, *PME* 49, 56
leadership, and cosmos, *DM* 6_{3-5}
leopards, Agc B 7, Agc 71
Lepreon, Dik 1
Leptiminus, PS 110_{7-8}
Lesbos, PS 97
Leukanoi, PS 12
Leuke (Achilles' I.; *Zmiinyi*), PS 68_4, Arr 21–3, DP 543–8, *Eux* 93
Leuke Akte (Egypt), *Sta* 14
Leukosyroi, *Art* 162–3
levels, of Earth, changes, Pos $2_{3.6}$
Libya (province), *Exp* 62
Libyans, eastern limit, *Art* $44a_3$

Libyē (*see also* Africa): *AWP* 12₇, *Eud* 55, 63, PS 107–11, Tim 28, Mna 43–6; boundary with Europe, Avi 331–2, 693–7; beyond Pillars, Hek 110; coastal length, Agm 10; described, Era 91; dimensions, PS 111₈; eastern, peoples, Mkn B 1; except Egypt, Hek 105–11; form, Era 89, 91, DP 174–5; length, Isi B 9; nations, *Hyp* 16–18; outside Pillars, Han 1, PS 112; peoples, DP 176–269; places in, Art 41–3, 143, 147, 154; provinces, *Hyp* 15; rivers, Pos 43; structure, Mkn B 1; western, Tim 10
Libyrnoi, PS 21
lice, or guinea worm, Agc 59
lighthouses: §III.3.j; in Bosporos, DB 78
Liguria: PS 3–4, Tim 24, SC 6, Pos 67–8, Avi 129–45, 628–30; places in, Art 12, 14, 16
Ligy(r)es, *see* Liguria
limits, of *oikoumene*, §III.3.k
Limyrike, *PME* 31–2, 47, 51, 53, 56–7, 60, 64
lions, Agc 51, 69–70
literary writing, §VII.5, §VII.1.e, §III.1.b
Lixos (city), PS 112₃, Era 92, Art 101–2
Lixos (river), Han 6, Lixos (river), PS 112₃
lizards, Jub 8, *PME* 30
Locust-eaters, Agc 59, Art 98
locusts, Agc 59, Art 98
Lokris, CS 527–35, Hek 43, PS 36, 60, *Nik* 480–4, 587–91, DK 64–71
London manuscript, §VIII.2.a
longitude: §VI.1.e, §III.3.d; accuracy, Era 50; difficulties, Era 52₃₇₋₉, 58; measurement, Hip 27–31, 34, 36
long-term change, §III.4.d
longue durée, §II.1, §III.4.d
Lopadoussa, Art 43
lost works: *see* fragments; quotations
Lotophagoi, PS 110₁
Lotus-eaters, Art 62, Art 102, DP 205–6
Lougdounesia: coastal distances, Mkn B 2₂₅₋₆, defined, Mkn B 2
Lougdounon (*Lyon*), origin of name, PsP 6₄
Lousitania: Art 32, Pos 37; coastal distances, Mkn B 2₁₃₋₁₅, defined, Mkn B 2
Lycia, *see* Lykia
Lydia: PS 98, DP 837–46; history, Mna 31
Lykia: Hek 32, PS 100, *Exp* 46; cities, Art 92; distances, Sta 233–54; places in, Art 55; springs, 52
Lykormas, origin of name, PsP 8
Lyon, *see* Lougdounon

Lysippos (comic poet), quoted, HK 1₅
Lysitania, *see* Lousitania

Macedonia: PS 66, *Nik* 618–42, 646–58, DP 427, *Exp* 51; whether in Hellas, DK 35–8
machaira (stone), Eud 8
Madagascar, *see* Menouthias
Maeander, origin of name, PsP 9
Maeotis, *see* Maiotis
Magi, *Exp* 3
Magna Graecia, *Nik* 300–60
Maiotis (Lake): circumference, PS 68₂, Hek 61, Era 20, *Nik* B 15b–16, Avi 32–6, *Eux* 49, 69–74, 75, 78; and Tanaïs, Arr 19₁; boundary of Europe & Asia, *AWP* 13₁; circumference, Arr 19₃, *Hyp* 53, *Eux* 121; connected to Ocean, *PME* 64; connected to R. Phasis, PsP 5₂; continental division, PS 92₂; described, DB 2; dimensions, Pyt 7; latitude, Hip 40₄₂, Pos 7₅; limit of known lands, *DM* 3₅; misunderstood, Era 20; 'Mother of the Pontos', DP 163–8, DB 2; N limit of *oikoumene*, Agc 67; peoples, DP 652–60; size, *Eux* 73
Makai (people), PS 109₂₋₃
Makrokephaloi, *AWP* 14
Malaca, Avi 181
Malaca, R., Avi 426
Malaō, *PME* 8
Maleai (C.), Art 77
Malieis, PS 62₂
Manic Laurel, DB 95
manliness, *see* masculinity
mantichora, Jub 10
manuscripts: principal geographical corpora, §VIII.2.a–b; tradition, §VII.2
maps: Hek 9–10; accuracy, Era 50₁₁; Classical period, §V.3; display pieces, §V.6; Hellenistic period, §V.3; invention, §V.2; late antique, §V.5; limits of use, §V.6; modern, §XI.4; Roman period, §V.4; use of, §V.1
Maranitai, at war, Agc 90₁₋₂
marble: green (?), Jub 37; traded, *PME* 24
Mare Concretum, Pyt 23
Mariandynians, subjection, Pos 60
Marinos of Tyre, §VI.1.e
maritime space, control, §III.3.j
Markianos of Herakleia: Ch. 34; preface to *Epit. Men.*, Mnp A 3–6 (part), Mkn C 41 (whole); his geographical corpus, §VIII.2.b; lectures at Constantinople (?), Mkn F 43; on

sea distances, §IV.c; provincial governor (?), Mkn F 44; research methods, Mkn C 1–2
Marmaridai, PS 108$_1$
Marmarike, distances, Sta 34–52
marshes, AWP 7
Marsh-folk, Art 98$_9$
Marsyas, origin of name, PsP 10
marvels: Eud 6–8, 22, 31–2, 46–7, 54–5, 60, 71–3, 76, Era 16–17, 19, Mna 14; bizarre peoples, SK 8, 14; in geographical writing, §III.3.m
masculinity, AWP 16, 21$_1$, 22$_{1-11}$, Agc 103
Massagetai, DP 740–5
Massalia, Art 1, 15, Avi 560, 704
'Massaliote *periplous*', §VI.4.a, Pyt intr., Avi intr.
Massilia, *see* Massalia
'mathematical geography', §II.2
Mauretania: Exp 60; islands, Hub 7
measurement (*see also* observational data): in geography, §III.3.e; of distance, §IV
measuring instruments, Dik 9, Era 37, 52, Hip 7, 24, 45–6
Meat-eaters, Art 98$_{9, 13, 14}$, Agc B 3$_{9, 13, 14}$
Medea, DP 1021–8, DB 51, 68, 88
Medes, DP 1016–19
Media, Isi A 1$_{4-7}$
medicine, *see* euphorbia; health; hellebore; plants
Mediterranean: and Atlantic, Mkn B 1$_3$; breadth, Hyp 48; central parts, DP 92–111; coastal length, Mkn B 1$_5$; divisions, Era 93, DM 3$_4$, DP 69–94, 104–37, Agm 9, Hyp 48–50; E parts, DP 112–45; extent, Mkn B 1$_3$; filling of, §III.4.c; length, Era 95, Hyp 40, Hyp 47; level, Hip 19; W parts, DP 69–91
Megara, Nik 502–7
Megarid, PS 39, 56, DK 108a–109b
Mela, Pomponius, §VI.1.b
Meleagrid birds (guinea fowl), PS 112$_1$, Mna 44, Agc 83, Art 98$_5$
Melieis, PS 62$_1$
Mellapokopsas, C., DB 20
men, *see* masculinity
Menace (Mainake?), Avi 427, 431
Menandros (king), PME 47
Menippos of Pergamon: Ch. 21: commended, Mkn C 3; *Epitome* (by Markianos), Mnp A 7–10; his geographical corpus, §VIII.2.b; Markianos' appraisal, Mnp A 3–6 (part), Mkn C 41 (whole); structure of work, Mkn C 6; transmission, Mnp B 9–10
Menouthias, PME 15
mental mapping, §V.8
merides, of *oikoumenē*, Hip 27, 30
meridians (*see also* parallels; prime m.), Era 25
Meroë: Era 53, Agc B 3$_8$, Art 98$_8$, PME 2; described, Era 89, Art 44a$_2$; kingship, Art 44b$_{5-7, 9}$; latitude, Era 28, 33, 53, 61, Hip 25; location, Art 112; peoples, Agc 51
Mesopotamia: DP 992–1015, Exp 22; distances, Isi A 1$_1$, Jub 1; form, Era 52$_{23-7}$, 34, 86
Messene (region), PS 45
Messenia (unnamed), CS 591–602
metals: from India, PME 6, in Spain, Pos 21
meteors, DM 2, 4
Metrodoros, epigraph after Ch. 36
Midakritos, explorer, Pyt intr.
migration (*see also* colonies; immigration), Cimbrian, Pos 2$_{3,6}$, Pos 69
minerals (*see also* precious stones), in Egypt, Agc 23
mining (*see also* gold m.), techniques, Agc 25–6
minium, Jub 33
Mnaseas of Patara, Ch. 13
models, *see* genre
Molottia, PS 32, Nik 447–52
monsters (*see also* sea-m.), in Koile Syria, Pos 56
Moon: DM 2$_4$; and tides, Pyt 25
Moscha, PME 32
mosquitoes, Agc 51
Mosyllon, PME 10
Mosynoikoi, Nik B 26, Eux 35
motivations, in geographical writing, §II.2, 3.c
Moundou, PME 9
mountains (*see also* Pelion): Eud 42; heights, Dik 2, 7, 9, Era 37; in cult, HK 2$_8$; in navigation, Tim 27, 31; names, PsP *passim*; ranked, Hyp 28; red, Agc 83
Mouza, PME 7, 16–17, 21, 24
mules, traded, PME 24
Muses, Mna 20
music, by Timosthenes, Tim 8
mussels, in Arabia, Jub 32
Mutilated (people), Art 98$_{10, 13}$ = Agc B 3$_{10, 13}$
Mykenai (Mt), origin of name, PsP 18$_6$
Myos Hormos, Agc 83, Art 98$_5$, PME 1, 19
myrrh: Jub 27; traded, PME 7–8, 10, 24

Mysia, PS 93, B 2, Art 86
Mysians, and the *Iliad*, Pos 70
mythical peoples, SK 14, Hek 100
mythology: Mna 1–4, 11–12, 15, 20, 23–30, 34–40, 46, 48, 50, 52–3; falsity, Agc 7–8

Nabataeans, Art 98$_{18}$, *PME* 19
names: Mna 9, SC 1; of mountains & rivers, PsP *passim*; rendering, §X.2
naphtha, Era 85, Pos 26
Narbōn, Art 18
Narbonese Gaul, Art 10
nard, traded, *PME* 39, 48–9, 56, 63
Naro, i.e. Narbo, Avi 587
Nasamones, PS 109$_2$, DP 208–9
nations (*see also* peoples; races), ranked, *Hyp* 26
Nature, violence of, §III.4.b
navigation: aids, §III.3.j, using mountains, Tim 27, 31, using stars (?), Tim 32
navy, Roman, in Black Sea, Arr 5$_{1-2}$, 6$_2$, 9$_5$
Nearchos, voyage, Jub 20$_{96}$
Nelkynda, *PME* 54–6
Nicaea (in Bithynia), *Exp* 49
Nicomedia (in Bithynia), *Exp* 49
nights (*see also under* days), length, Pyt 15, 19, 23, 28, 30
Nikomedean Periodos, Ch. 17
Nikomedes, king of Pergamon, *Nik* 2
Nile: Hek 92, Art 168, Pos 42, DP 220–31, *Exp* 34, 36; as boundary, DP 230–1; cataracts, Jub 4$_{54}$; cause of its rise, Eud 30, Dik 14, Era 115; course, Agc 23, Jub 4$_{52-4}$, 16$_{9-10}$; Delta, Hek 96; described, Era 89; distances, Art 106; names, Jub 4$_{53-4}$; origin of name, PsP 16; search for source, §III.3.k; sources, Jub 4$_{51}$, 16$_8$; tributaries, Agc B 3$_8$, Art 98$_8$
nilios, Jub 14
Nomades (*see also* nomads), AWP 18$_{2-4}$, Agc 62b$_1$, Art 98$_7$
nomads (*see also* Nomades): in E. Africa, Agc 37; Trogodytai, Art 98$_{17}$
non-violence, among Fish-eaters, Agc 41
North Africa, apes, Pos 57
North Pole, Pyt 1
northern hemisphere, Era 29$_5$
North-west Greece, PS 28–33
Notitiae, various, §VI.1.f n.
Notitia Urbis Constantinopolitanae, §VI.1.f n., DB intr.

Notou Keras (or Keros), Han 17, Agc B 3$_{14, 15}$, Art 98$_{14}$
novas, Hip 7
Nubia, and Ptolemy (II?), Agc 11–18
numbers, treatment by geographers, §IV.c

observational data (*see also* measurement), in geography, §II.2
observational geography, §VII.1.c
obsidian, *PME* 5
Ocean (*see also* Atlantic; Indian Ocean; seas): Pyt 14, Era 24, Avi 82–4, 102, 204, 390–5, 402; a waste, *Exp* 59; and Mediterranean §III.4.c; divisions, Avi 396–401; in geographical writing, §III.3.h; scope of Poseidonios' work, Pos 2$_{2.1}$, 3$_{.8}$; variation within, Hip 14
ochre, Jub 34
Octavian (*see also* Augustus), Avi 279
Oestrymnic gulf, Avi 95
Oestrymnici, Avi 155
Oestrymnides (islands), Avi 96, 130
Oestrymnides (people; *see also* Ostidiaioi), Avi 113
Oestrymnis (Portugal?), Avi 91, 154–7
oikoumenē: breadth, Era 47–8, 53, Hip 22, Art 4$_{245-6}$, 7, 8$_{18-19}$, Agm 2, 18–19, Mkn B 1$_6$, *Hyp* 39; centrality, DM 3$_1$; coastal length, Agm 10; created by gods, DP 1168–79; dimensions, PS 113, Pyt 2–3, Dik 4, 10, 11, Era 25–6, 29$_{8-9}$, 31, 37, 41, Isi B 3–4, Mkn B 1$_4$, *Hyp* 1–2; diversity, Agc 66–7; divisions, Hip 26–31; extent, Era 15, 24, 26, 29, 31, 41; form, §III.3.b, Eud 4, Era 29$_{5-7}$, 30, 38, 47, 57–8, DP 4–7, Agm 2; length, Art 4$_{242-4}$, 8$_{15-17}$, Pos 2$_{3.6}$, Agm 2, 15–17, Mkn B 1$_6$, *Hyp* 39; N–S extent, Agc 67; W limit, *Exp* 59
Okeanos: DM 3$_4$, DP 3–4; and Homer, Pos 33; by Asia, DP 628–35; divisions, DM 3$_5$, DP 26–57; N parts, *Hyp* 45; S parts, *Hyp* 45; western, Mkn B 2$_{2-3}$
Okelis, *PME* 7, 25–6
Olbia, *Eux* 89
Old Man of the Sea, DB 49
olive oil, traded, *PME* 6, 32
olives, traded, *PME* 7
olive-trees, and tides, Agc 110
Olynthos, and Philip II, Agc 21
Ombrikoi (Umbrians), PS 16
Onesikritos, voyage, Jub 20$_{96}$

Ophiodes I., Agc 84, Art 98$_6$
Ophiussa, Avi 148, 152, 172, 196
Opone, *PME* 13
opposites, and similars, *DM* 5$_{1-3}$
oppression, by Ptolemaic empire, §III.4.f
oracles: of Achilles, Arr 22$_3$; quoted, DB 23 & n.
orientation, of cities, *AWP* 3–6
origins, of river & mountain names, PsP *passim*
Orikoi, PS 27
Oropos, HK 1$_{6-7}$
Orosius, §VI.1.f
orpiment, traded, *PME* 56
Osdroena, *Exp* 22
Osismioi, Pyt 12
Ostidiaioi (*see also* Oestrymnides), Pyt 2$_5$, 12
Ostiones, Art 157
Ostrich-eaters, Agc 58, Art 98$_{11}$
ostriches, Agc 58
Other, the: ancient response, §III.2.c; not frightening, Agc 16; tolerance of, Era 46
Outer sea, western, Mkn B 2$_{2-3}$
Ouxisame (*Ushant*), Pyt 2$_5$
oysters, in Bosporos, DB 37
Ozene, *PME* 48–9

Pagasai, gulf of, Art 79
Paionia, Hek 47
Paktolos, origin of name, PsP 7
Palaisimoundou, *PME* 61
Palatinus Heidelbergensis 398, §VIII.2.a
palm fruits, Jub 29
Pamphylia: PS 101; distances, *Sta* 214–32
Pangaios, origin of name, PsP 3$_4$
Pannonia, *Exp* 57
Pantikapaion, *Eux* 67, 78 *bis*
Paphlagonia: PS 90, *Exp* 44; distances, Mnp A 9; Markianos as governor, Mkn F 44
papyrus, from Alexandria, *Exp* 36
parallels: dividing *oikoumenē*, Agm 5; through Mediterranean, Dik 11, Era 47, 50, Hip 24; beginnings, Eud 48; of latitude, Era 26, 29, 61; of longitude, Pyt 2, 7
paraplous, as form of writing, §III.1.b
parasangs, Pos 18
Parisinus supplément grec 443, §VIII.2.b
Parisinus supplément grec 443a, §VIII.2.a
Parthians, DP 1039–52
past, the, in geographical writing, §II.2

Patrokles, criticized, Era 48–9, Hip 23
Patroklos: patron of sailors, Arr 23$_3$; votives to, Arr 21$_3$
patronage, and geographical writing, §VII.1.e, §II.2, *Nik* 1–64, 103–8
Paulinus (Suetonius), expedition, Jub 3
Pausanias of Antioch, §VI.4.c, *Nik* intr.
Pausanias of Damascus, §VI.4.c, *Nik* intr.
Pausanias of Magnesia, §VI.1.d
pearl-fishing, Isi B 20, *PME* 35
pearls: Jub 18, 39; traded, *PME* 56, 59, 61, 63
Pelion (Mt), HK 2$_{1-11}$, 4
Peloponnese: CS 559–624, Eud 55–8, 60–2, 64, PS 40–6, 49–55, Dik 1, *Nik* 511–34, DP 403–22, *Exp* 52; beginning of Hellas, HK 3$_2$; circumference, Art 75, Isi B 6; dimensions, Agm 24, Avi 152–4; distance to Africa, Era 69
Peneios, R., DK 33
peninsulas, largest, Mkn B 1$_8$
peoples (*see also* nations; races): bizarre, SK 8, 14, Hek 103, Eud 31; disappearing, Isi B 11; extinct, Era 98; foreign, §III.2.c; in geographical writing, §III.3.l; mythical, SK 14, Hek 100, Era 17, 19$_6$; on Earth, DP 1166–79
pepper, traded, *PME* 49, 56
peraia, of Rhodes, Art 91
perfumes, in Arabia, Agc 99, 101, 103
Pergamon, kings, *Nik* 2, 16–18, 48–64
periēgēsis: as form of writing, §III.1.c, §III.2.a; defined, §III.1
Perimetros of the Pontos, ch. 36 appendix
periodos, defined, §III.1
periodos gēs, as form of writing, §III.1.a, §III.2.a
'periplographic genre', §II3.a
periploi: as group of texts, Mnp A 3, Mkn C 2–3; functional, §III.1.b; literary, §III.1.b; variable quality, Mkn C 1–2
periplous: as form of writing, §III.1.b, §III.2.a; defined, §III.1; structure, Mkn B 1$_{10}$
Periplous of the Euxine, *see* Arrian; Pseudo-Arrian
Periplus maris Erythraei, Ch. 25
permanence (*see also* change): *DM* 5$_{4-5}$; divine basis, *DM* 6
Perse, wife of Helios, Hek 15
Persia, DP 1053–79
Persian empire: Hek 81–8, *DM* 6; and progress of geography, §II.1

Persian gulf: *PME* 35–6, Mkn B 1$_{15}$, *Hyp* 35; described, Era 87; rivers, Jub 20$_{99}$; size, Agm 12
Persian kings, exploration under, §III.3.k
Persian sea, *see* Persian gulf
Persians: as Other (?), *AWP* intr.; customs, *Exp* 19; name, Agc 6–7
Persis, Era 83, Mkn B 1$_{23-5}$
Peutinger Map, §VI.1.f
Pharmacias, DB 68
Pharo, in Bosporos, DB 78
Phasis (city), Arr 9
Phasis (region), *AWP* 15
Phasis (river): PS 81, Era 108, *Nik* B 24, Art 165, DP 691–4, *Eux* 44–7; as boundary, Arr 19$_2$, *Eux* 72; origin of name, PsP 5; properties of water, Arr 8
Pherekrates (comic poet), quoted, HK 1$_{25}$
Phidalia, DB 59
Philae, location, Jub 5
Philainou Bomoi, PS 109$_3$
Phileas of Athens: §VI.4.b; on Macedonia & Hellas, DK 35–8
Philesios, statue of, Arr 2$_{1-2}$
Philip II of Macedonia: Art 161, DB 27, 65; and Olynthos, Agc 21
Philip V of Macedonia, war v. Byzantion, DB 65
Philiskos (comic poet), quoted, HK 1$_{30}$
philosophy: and geographical writing, §VII.1.e; early, ArP intr., Eud 37
Phoenicia: PS 104$_{2-3}$; distances, Art 97; places in, Art 54
Phoenicians: DP 905–22; at Kerne, PS 112$_{7-11}$; in W. Libyē, Era 92
Phoinikōn, in Arabia, Agc 87–8
Phokaians, and Massalia, Art 1
Phokis, CS 517–26, PS 37, 61, *Nik* 485–7, DK 72–81
Photios I: *Bibliotheke*, §VI.2.k; on Ktesias, §III.3.m
Phrourentanoi, Art 37
Phrygia, PS 94, Tim 27, *Exp* 42
phylon, translation of, §X.3.c
physical geography, §II.1
pigs, horned, Agc B 6
Pillars of Herakles (*see also* strait of Gibraltar): PS 111$_6$, 112$_1$, B 5, Tim 7, Era 10, Art 66, Pos 50, *DM* 3$_4$, DP 64–8, 72–3, 335–6, Avi 86–9, 341–74, 417–18, Mkn B 1$_3$; location, Dik 5, Era 64, Art 121, Mkn B 2$_4$

Piraeus: HK, appendix; anonymous description, §VI.4.c
pirates, Jub 6, 38, *PME* 16, 20, 53
Pisidia, Art 85
pistachios, Pos 59
pitch, Eud 54
place, sense of, DB 1
place-names (*see also under* names), origins, DM 3, PsP *passim*, Agm 4, DB 7, 24, 60
plagues: of animals, Agc 60, 91; of insects, Agc 51, 60
plains, stony, Pos 39
planets, *DM* 2$_{3-4}$
plants, medicinal/magical, HK 2$_{3-6}$, 4, Jub 31, PsP 1, 3–5, 7–8, 10, 13–14, 17–25
Plataiai, HK 1$_{11}$
Plato, epigraph before Ch. 4
Pliny the Elder: §VI.1.c; as source, §VIII.3
PME, Ch. 25
poetic genres, §III.2.a
poetry: §VII.5.b, §VI.3; quoted (*see also under* Empedokles; epigrams; Homer; tragedies; Xenon), HK 1$_{5-6, 11, 17, 22, 25, 30}$, 3$_{3,7}$, Era 51, DB 23 & n.
poles, Pyt 1, Hip 40, 42, *DM* 2$_1$
political change, §III.4.f
Polybios of Megalopolis: as geographer, §VI.2.g; and Hanno's text, Han intr.; on Eratosthenes, Era 6, 55; on Hannibal's route, §VI.2.g; on Pytheas, Pyt 6, 11, Era 18
Pomponius Mela, §VI.1.b
Ponērōn Polis, Art 161
Pontos Euxeinos (*see also* Black Sea): circumference, Agm 11; dimensions, *Hyp* 41, 51–3; form, DB 2
Pontus (provinces), *Eux* 23
Pontus (region), *Exp* 44
'popular' geography, §II.2
Portus Mulierum, origin of name, DB 60
Poseidippos (comic poet), quoted, HK 1$_{11}$, 3$_7$
Poseidon, temple, DB 9
Poseidonios of Apameia, Ch. 19
power, of the god, *DM* 6$_2$
precious stones: *PME* 10, DP 1075–7, 1102–7, 1118–22; traded, *PME* 56, 61
precipitation: causes, *DM* 4$_3$; varieties, *DM* 4$_2$
preservation, of geographical writings, §VII.2, §VIII
Prettanikai Is., Mkn B 2$_{41-9}$
priests, Aithiopian, Art 44a$_3$ fin.
prime meridian, Era 53, 58, 61

printed editions, early, §VIII.2.a
professions, and geographical writing, §II.2
progress, in geography, relation to empires, §II.1
Prometheus, Era 23, Mna 52, Pos 39, PsP 5$_3$, Arr 11$_5$, 19$_2$, Eux 53, 71
Propontis: Nik 713–16; dimensions, Hyp 51; distances, Art 74
prose genres, §III.2.a
prose writing, §VII.5.a, §VI.1
prosperity, of Sabaioi & Gerrhaioi, Agc 104
Provence, cities, Art 2
proverbs, explained, Mna 13, 47
Pseudo-, meaning, §VII.4
Pseudo-Aristotle, *De mundo*, Ch. 24
Pseudo-Arrian, *Periplous of the Erythraian sea (PME)*, Ch. 25
Pseudo-Arrian, *Periplous of the Euxine (Eux.)*, Ch. 36
Pseudo-Hippolytos (?), *Stadiasmos*, Ch. 31
pseudonymous texts, §VII.4
Pseudo-Plutarch, *On Rivers . . .*, Ch. 26
Pseudo-Skylax: Ch. 7; as source, PS B 4, 7
'Pseudo-Skymnos', Ch. 17
Psophis, foundation, Hek 25
Ptolemaic empire, oppressive, §III.4.c
Ptolemaïs Theron, Agc 86, B 3$_7$, Art 98$_7$, PME 3
Ptolemy II Philadelphos: Agc 1, 20, B 3$_{5,7}$, Art 98$_{5,7}$; and a snake, Agc 80b; and elephant-hunting (?), Agc 57; temple, DB 41; urged to attack Nubia (?), Agc 11–18
Ptolemy III Euergetes, Agc 41b
Ptolemy of Alexandria: §VI.1.e; on Crete, §VI.1.e
Punica, distances in, Sta 113–24
punishment, capital, in Aithiopia, Art 44b$_5$
Purcell, N., §II.1
purple, in islands, Jub 7
Purpurarii Is., Jub 8
Pygmaioi, invented, Art 44a$_1$
Pyramids, Art 114
Pyrene/Pyrenees, Avi 473, 533, 555, 559, 562, 565
Pyrrhias Cyon, DB 57
Pythagoras, Eud 78
Pythagoreanism, ArP intr.
Pytheas of Massalia: Ch. 8: and Eratosthenes, Era 18; and Eudoxos, Pyt intr.; and Hipparchos, Hip 37; denounced by Polybios, §VI.2.g; impugned, Pyt 2, 5–6, 7$_8$, 9–11, 14

Pythian Melody, Tim 8
pythons, Agc 80, Art 98$_{16}$

quotations: of lost works, §VIII.3; of verse, *see under* Ephoros; Eratosthenes; poetry

races (*see also* nations; peoples), on Earth, DP 1166–79
rainbows, DM 4$_7$
rainwater, AWP 8–9
rape, PsP 3$_1$, 4$_1$, 7$_1$, 8$_1$, 17$_1$, 18$_1$, 20$_1$, 1$_1$, 24$_1$, 25 *bis*, Exp 20
Ravenna Cosmography, §VI.1.f
ravens, Art 68
realgar, Jub 34
Red Sea (*see also* Arabian gulf; Erythraian s.), Pos 46, Tim 15; islands, Art 98$_{14}$, Jub 23; W coast, Jub 23
regions, in geographical writing, §III.3.l
religion: Aithiopian, Art 44a$_3$, 44b$_{9.1-2}$; Brettanic, Art 68; Egypt, Eud 24–6, Exp 34, 35; in early Greece, ArP intr.; in Etruria, Exp 56; at Rome, Exp 55
revolutions, of heavenly bodies, DM 6$_7$
Rhagai, Pos 24
Rhapta, PME 16
rhinoceroses: Agc 72, Art 98$_{15}$, PME 4; horn, traded, PME 6, 17
Rhizophagoi, Agc 51, Art 98$_9$
Rhodanus (*Rhône*): Avi 626–8, 631–50, 674–88, 691–7; not boundary of Europe & Libya, Avi 693–7
Rhodes: CS 653–70, PS 99$_3$, Exp 63; circumference, Art 90, Isi B 13; distances from, Sta 272; etymology, Hek 33; in Eratosthenes, Era 60; peraia, Art 53
Rhodope (Mt), origin of name, PsP 11$_3$
Rhône, Art 2
rice, traded, PME 14, 31, 37, 41
rivers: Hek 38, 42, 49, Eud 45; Arkadia, Mna 14; Black Sea, Nik B 7–8, 11–12, 24, 30, 34, 36–7; greatest in Europe, PS 69; Hyrkania, Era 71; India, Era 78, DP 1137–48; Libyē, Art 103, Pos 43; mythology, Hek 26; names, SC 1, PsP *passim*; Persian gulf, Jub 20$_{99}$; ranked, Hyp 29–31; underground, Era 67; variation, Agc 66; western Asia, Era 71, 74
roadsteads: Levant, Sta 128; N. Africa, Sta 3, 7, 9, 30, 51, 99, 126
rock crystal, Jub 35–6
rock pythons, Agc 80

Rogues' City, Art 161
Roman culture, and Greek, §III.1 init.
Roman empire, and progress of geography, §II.1
Rome: PS 5, *Exp* 55; as ideal land, §III.3.n
Root-eaters, Agc 51, Art 98_9
roses, and etymology, Hek 33
rounding, of numbers, §IV.c
Rutilius Namatianus, §VI.1.f

Sabaioi: Art 98_{19}; kings, Agc 102; land, Agc 99, 102–4
Sabaites *ethnos*, PME 23
Sacred Aithiopes (or Western?), PS 112_{5-12}
sacrifices, to Achilles, Arr 22_{2-4}
saffron, traded, *PME* 24
Sagaris, origin of name, PsP 12
sailing seasons, PME 14, 24
sailing times, §IV.b
Salamis, CS 557–8
Salike, Art 49, Mkn B 1_8, 1_{35}, *Hyp* 25, 27; see also Taprobane
Salmydessos, *Eux* 117
saloi, see roadsteads
salt, aromatic, Pos 28
Samnites, PS 11
Samothrake, *Nik* 679–95
sanctuaries (*see also* altars; temples): Asia Minor, *Sta* 154; Bosporos, DB 12–13, 26, 34, 36, 52, 56, 75; Crete, *Sta* 318, 336, 338; Cyprus, *Sta* 297, 307; N. Africa, *Sta* 4, 14, 38, 49
sandarach, Jub 34
Sannoi, *Eux* 50
Saône, Art 19
Sapra Thalassa, DB 23
Sarapis's I., *PME* 33
Sardinia, *see* Sardo
Sardinian sea: Pos 35; coasts, *Nik* 196–263
Sardo (Sardinia): PS 7; visibility, Era 65, Art 69
Sarmatia (*see also* Sauromatai), Mkn B 2_{38-40}, *Hyp* 10, *Eux* 74
Sarraceni, *Exp* 20
Satyros (explorer), Agc B 3_5, Art 98_5
Saubatha, *PME* 27
Saunitai (Samnites), PS 11
Sauromatai (*see also* Sarmatia; Syrmatai): AWP 17, *Eux* 74
schoinoi: Art 100; distances in, Isi A 1; length, Era 36
scholarship, modern, §XI.1–3

science, evolution of, §VII.1.b
scientific aims, §III.1.b
scorpions, Agc 60
sea, the (*see also* Ocean; seas): in geographical writing, §III.3.j; changed into land, §III.4.d
sea-caves, Agc 95
sea distances: SK 10; Aegean, PS 113; Black Sea, Hek 59–60; measurement, §IV.b
sea levels, §III.4.c, Era 14, Hip 19
seals: coexisting with people, Agc 42; in Red Sea, Agc 89b
sealstones, Eratosthenes' theory, Era 52_{22-9}, 31–2, 34–6, Hip 26–8
'sea lung', Pyt 6
sea-monsters, Agc 85, Jub 20_{99}, Jub 32, DP 596–602
Sea of Azov, *see* Maiotis
seas: connexions, Hip 19; depth, §III.3.f, Era 13_4, Pos 35; dimensions, Era 12–14, Agm 8, Mkn B 1_7, *Hyp* 40–4; individual, in geographical writing, §III.3.l
seasons: and climate, Eud 23; and health, AWP 10–11, 13, 24
seaweed, Agc 85, *Hyp* 32
Sebastopolis (*see also* Dioskourias), Arr 10_{3-4}, 17_1, *Eux* 48, 55
Second Sophistic, §VI.1.d
Seed-eaters, Agc 52, Art 98_9
Sekoanos, Art 19
Seleucia, *Exp* 28
Seleukis, organization, Pos 55
Seleukos of Babylon, Pos 38
semi-precious stones, traded, *PME* 39, 48–9, 56
Semos of Delos, *Nik* intr.
Semystra (nymph), DB 24
Seneca the Younger, epigraph before Ch. 32
sense of place, DB 1
Seres (*see also* next entry), Jub 24, DP 752–7, Mkn B 1_{44}
Serike, end of known world, *Hyp* 19
sesame oil, traded, *PME* 14, 41
Sesatai, *PME* 65
shamanism, possible, ArP intr.
shape of *oikoumenē*, Pos 12, 15–16
shells: Jub 18; traded, *PME* 17
ships, speed, Mkn C 5
shipwrecks: Agc 84–5; at Barygaza, *PME* 46; in Black Sea, Arr 5_{1-2}
Sicily: PS 7, 13, *Nik* 264–82, DP 467–76, *Exp* 65; dimensions, Tim 19; distances from, Art

72; form, Pos 53; legends, Mnp B 9; mythology, Mna 27; strongholds, Pos 54
sickness, *see* health
Sidon, Pos 30
Sikyon, PS 41
silk (*see also* Seres): from Tylos, Jub 24; traded, *PME* 56, 64
silphium, PS 108$_2$
silver: corrupting effect, Pos 31–2; in Arabia, Agc 104; traded, *PME* 6, 8, 10, 24, 28, 49
similars, and opposites, *DM* 5$_{1-3}$
similes, and divine power, *DM* 6$_{3-13}$
Simmias, Ptolemaic explorer, Agc 41b
Simoi, Agc 58, Art 98$_{11}$
Simounda (*see also* Taprobane), *Hyp* 25
Sinai (people) (*see also* gulf of Sinai): Mkn B 1$_{12, 16, 43-4}$, *Hyp* 24; territory, Mkn B 1$_{47}$
Sinope, *Nik* B 31, Arr 14$_5$, DP 775–9, *Eux* 21
Sipylon, origin of name, PsP 9$_4$
Sirius, rising, Hip 43
Skamandros, origin of name, PsP 13
Skandiai Is., Mkn B 2$_{34}$
Skylax of Karyanda: Ch. 2 (*see also* Pseudo-Skylax): identity, SK 9; scope, SK 12; voyage, SK 1; writings, SK 13
Skymnos of Chios, Ch. 14
Skyros, Art 117
Skythia: Hek 58, PS 68$_{1-3}$, *Nik* B 15a; Black Sea coast, *Eux* 89–116
Skythian bows, *see* bows
Skythians (*see also* Sauromatai): ArP 1, AWP 17–22, Era 19$_7$; customs, Eud 36
Skythike, *see* Skythia
slaves: in Skythia, AWP 21$_3$; traded, *PME* 8, 13, 31 (female), 36, 49 (m. and f.)
snakes (*see also* guinea worms): Agc 84, Art 98$_{6,16}$, *PME* 38, 40, 55; Aithiopia, Art 44b$_{105-6}$; crested, Jub 17; giant, Agc 80, Jub 17, 19; in Iberia, Avi 156–7; poisonous, Agc 100
Snub-nosed (people), Agc 58, Art 98$_{11}$
social change, §III.4.f
solstices: Hip 40; summer, Era 33, 35
Sophokles, quoted, HK 1$_{17}$
Sousiane, Mkn B 1$_{20-2}$
southern hemisphere, Era 15
Sozopolis (Apollonia), *Eux* 114
space: in geographical writing, §VI.2 init.; maritime, control of, §III.3.j
Spain (*see also* Hispania; Iberia): Pos 37, *Exp* 59; flora, Pos 51; metals, Pos 21

Spania, *Exp* 59
Spate, O. H. K., quoted, before §I
Spermatophagoi, Agc 52, Art 98$_9$
spherical Earth, §III.3.a, Dik 12, Era 29$_5$
spherical geometry, Hip 45
sphinxes, Agc 74
sphragides, *see* sealstones
spices: Agc 89, 99, 103; traded, *PME* 10
spiders, Agc 60
spindle whorl, form of *oikoumenē*, Era 29$_6$, 30
spondylos, *see* spindle whorl
Sporades, *Nik* 579–86, DK 144–50
springs: AWP 7; at Gadeira, Art 67; hot, Agc 82, Art 98$_5$; magical, Eud 46–7, 60, 71–2, 76
Sri Lanka, *see* Salike; Taprobane
stade: as unit of distance, §IV.a; disagreements over, Mkn B 1$_2$; length, Era 36; problems of, Mnp A 5, Mkn B 2$_5$, C 5
Stadiasmos (Pseudo-Hippolytos?), Ch. 31
stagnant water, AWP 7
stars: catalogued, Hip 11; circumpolar, Pyt 26, 30; fixed, *DM* 2$_3$; for navigation, Tim 32 (?), Agc 106; new, Hip 7
statues: of boy, in Bosporos, DB 93; of Hadrian, Arr 1$_2$; traded, *PME* 28
Stephanos of Byzantion: §VI.2.j; as source, §VIII.3; translation of, §X.1
Stoma, *see* Bosporos
stones, magical, Eud 8, PsP 1, 6–7, 9–14, 17–25
storms, Black Sea, Arr 3$_{3-4}$, 4$_{3-4}$
Strabo: §VI.1.a; as source, §VIII.3; as universal geographer, §II.1; commended, Mkn C 3
strait of Gibraltar (*see also* Pillars of Herakles): PS B 5, Tim 7, *Nik* 139–47; length, *Hyp* 48
Straton, on depths of seas, Era 13$_4$
Strouthophagoi, Agc 58, Art 98$_{11}$
Strymon, origin of name, PsP 11
style, literary: ArP 5, Hek 3, Eud 2, Agc 21, B 8, *Nik* 33–44; of Ps.-Skylax, PS B 6
subterranean people, SK 6
Suda, §VI.2.l
Suetonius Paulinus, expedition, Jub 3
sufferings, of gold-miners, Agc 24
sugar (cane), traded, *PME* 14
suicide, PsP 1–9, 11–14, 16–23, 25
Suidas, *see* Suda
Sun: *DM* 2$_4$; and tides, Pyt 20, Dik 13; appearance in tropics, Agc 107; maximum elevation, Pyt 3; where it sleeps, Pyt 15, 30
sunsets: at Gadeira, Art 59; at sea, Pos 47
surveyors, §IV.a

surviving works, §VIII.1
Syagros, *PME* 30
Sybaris, fate of, *Nik* 337–60
Syene: Era 53, Art 106; latitude, Era 29, 33, 35 (?), 39, 53, 61; location, Art 112, Jub 5
Symplegadai (-es) (*see also* Kyaneai), Era 114, 125, DB 3
Syria: Eud 17, PS 104$_1$, Pos 45, DP 897–926; cities, *Exp* 23–33; distances, *Sta* 128–53; economy & society, *Exp* 31
Syrians, lifestyle, Pos 61
Syrmatai (*see also* Sauromatai), Eud 19, PS 68.5
Syrteis: *DM* 3$_4$, Era 59, DP 104–8, 198–203, 477–80
Syrtis Major: PS 109; distances, *Sta* 85–99
Syrtis Minor: PS 110$_8$; distances, *Sta* 100–12
systematization of knowledge, Hek intr.

Tabula Peutingeriana, §VI.1.f
Tanagra, HK 1$_{8-10}$, 1$_{25}$
Tanaïs: DP 659–79; and Maiotis, Arr 19$_1$, *Eux* 78; as boundary, Arr 19$_1$, DP 14–17, 661–3, DB 2, *Eux* 70–1, 74; mouths, Art 166; origin of name, PsP 14
Tanos (Itanos?), Art 34
Taprobane (*see also* Palaisimoundou; Salike; Simounda): Era 78$_{14}$, Hip 20, Art 49, DP 591–6, Mkn B 1$_{35-6}$; location, Era 57; people, Art 113; size, Era 102
Taras, gulf of, Art 71
Tarrakōn (Tarraco), Art 63, Avi 519
Tarrakonesia: coastal distances, Mkn B 2$_{18}$; defined, Mkn B 2$_{16}$; dimensions, Mkn B 2$_{17}$
Tartessians, Avi 113–14, 179, 254, 423–4, 428, 463
Tartessiorum Mons, Avi 308
Tartessos (-is, -us): Pyt 9, Era 62, *Nik* 161–3, 198–9, Art 60, DP 337, Avi 54, 85, 223, 269; end of Libya, Avi 331–2; gulf of, Avi 265; river, Avi 225, 284
Taulantioi, PS 26$_1$
Taurike Chersonesos, *Nik* B 14
Taurike, *Eux* 81–5
Tauroëis, Art 20
Tauroi (mountains in Red Sea), Art 98$_7$
Tauros (range in Asia), DP 638–49
Taÿgetos (Mt), origin of name, PsP 17$_3$
teak, traded, *PME* 36
technical terms, translation of, §X.3
Telmessos, Art 55

temperate zones: *AWP* 12, Dik 11, Era 28, 32$_{2,4}$, Hip 36
temples (*see also* altars; sanctuaries): of Achilles, Arr 21; of Artemis, at Ephesos, Art 88; to Achilles, *Eux* 95; in Bosporos, DB 9, 14, 41, 56–7, 62–3, 75, 92; to Hadrian, Arr 2$_2$
testimonia: defined, §VII.3; presentation, §IX
textiles, *PME* 6–8, 14, 24, 28, 31–2, 36, 39, 41, 48–50, 56, 61, 63–4, *Exp* 31
textual criticism, §VII.2
Thapsakos, Era 52$_{29}$, 36
Thebes (Boiotia): HK 1$_{12-22}$; and Alexander, Agc 21; mythology, Mna 25
Theodosius (pilgrim), §VI.1.f
theology, and geographical writing, §VII.1.e
Theon Ochema, Han 16
Theophanes of Hermopolis, §VI.1.f
Theriodes gulf, Mkn B 1$_{45}$
Thermodon: DP 772–82; origin of name, PsP 15
Thespiai, HK 1$_{25}$
Thesprotoi, PS 30
Thessaly: CS 681–759 (unnamed), PS 64–5, HK 2$_1$, Mna 17–18, *Nik* 592–617, DK 40, *Exp* 52; relationship to Hellas, HK 3$_1$, 3$_{6-8}$
Theudosia, *Eux* 80
Thina, *PME* 64–5
Thinai, Mkn B 1$_{16}$, *Hyp* 24
Thoule (*see also* Thyle): Pyt 2$_2$, 6–7, 13, 23, 26, 29, Era 29, Isi B 5, DP 580–6, *Hyp* 13; search for, §III.3.k
Thrace: Hek 48, 50–1, PS 67, Era 45, Mna 16, *Nik* 664–78, 696–712, 729, DP 429–30, *Exp* 50; Black Sea coast, *Eux* 97–118; places, Art 116
Thracian Bosporos, *see* Bosporos
Thracian Chersonese, PS 67$_{5-6}$, *Nik* 698–712
Thracians: Era 19$_2$; of Bithynia, Arr 12$_5$
Thucydides of Athens, §VI.2.b
thunderstorms, *DM* 4$_6$
Thyle (*see also* Thoule), Art 4
tides: §III.4.e, Pyt 16, Era 14$_{11}$, Art 60, Pos 34, 36, *DM* 4$_{10}$; and Homer, Pos 33; and Moon, Pyt 25; and Sun, Pyt 20, Dik 13; at Barygaza, *PME* 45–6; ebb and flow, Pos 36; in Bracheia sea, *Hyp* 33; in geographical writing, §III.3.h; in India, *PME* 45; in Indian Ocean, Agc 50; theories of, Agc 109–10
Tigris: DP 983–91; alluviation, Jub 21; origin of name, PsP 24
Timaea (tower), DB 77

SELECTIVE INDEX • 1189

Timagetos, on harbours, Tim intr.
Timavus, R., Pos 40
timber, traded, *PME* 36
time: in geographical writing, §VI.2 init.; influence of, Agc 67
Timosthenes of Rhodes: Ch. 10; criticized, Tim 4–6, 23, Mkn C 3
tin: Avi 98, 259–61, 293, 296; deposits, *Nik* 399–400; trade, *Nik* 165; and Mt Cassius, Avi 259–61; traded, *PME* 7, 28, 49, 56
Tmolos (Mt), origin of name, PsP 7_5
Tomeas (Tomis), *Eux* 100–1
tools, traded, *PME* 6, 17
topaz, Agc 84, Art 98_6, Jub 36, 38
torrid zones, Era 32_3, Hip 36, Pos 10, 19
tortoises, *PME* 3, 30
tortoiseshell, *PME* 4, 7, 10, 13, 16–17, 30–1, 33, 56, 61, 63
towers (*see also* lighthouses; Timaea): Asia Minor, Sta 185, 237–8; Black Sea, *Nik* B 26, *Eux* 35; Bosporos, DB 12, 77, 88; Crete, Sta 345, 349; Iberia, Art 167_{iv}; N. Africa, Sta 13, 38, 41, 78, 96, 100–2, 124
town planning, HK $1_{1, 12, 23, 27-8}$
trade: Arabia, *Exp* 38; as motivation towards geography, §II.1; Asia Minor, *Exp* 39–42, 45, 47–9; at Kerne, PS 112_7; Crete, *Exp* 63; Cyprus, *Exp* 63; Danube lands, *Exp* 57; Egypt, *Exp* 35–6; Gaul, *Exp* 58; Italy, *Exp* 53–5; North Africa, *Exp* 60–1; Sicily, *Exp* 63; Spain, *Exp* 59; Syria, *Exp* 24, 27–33 *passim*; Thrace, *Exp* 50–3
tragedies, quoted (*see also under* Aeschylus), HK 1_{17}, 3_3
translations, presentation, §X
transliteration, of Greek, §X.1
transmission: of geographical writings, §VII.2, §VIII
Trapezous, Arr 1_1, *Eux* 36
trees, in Spain, Pos 51
tribute, paid to Rome, Arr 11_2
trigonometry, spherical, Hip 45
Trinakria, name for Sicily, DP 467
Troad, SK 4, Hek 69, Eud 10, PS 95, PS B 1, Tim 25–6, Mna 41
Trogodytai: SK 6, Han 7, Jub 6; customs, Agc 62–4, 66–7, 84, Art 98_{17}; pirates, Jub 38
Trogodytes' Is., Jub 12
Trogodytike: Agc 86b, B 3_5, Art 98_{5-14}, Jub 19, 23; animals, Agc 73–7
Trojan war, Hek 66, Mna 41

tropics, distance between, Hip 44
Troy, plain of, §VI.4.c fin.
tsunamis, §III.4.b, DM 4_{10} (?)
Tuan, Y.-F., §II.1
turnips, in Dalmatia, Pos 63
Turtle-eaters, Agc 47b, Art 98_{14}
turtle-hunting, Agc 47
Tuscia, *Exp* 56
Two Ravens (harbour), Art 68
Tylos, Jub 24
Tyras (river), *Nik* B 11, *Eux* 90–2
Tyre, *Exp* 24
Tyrrhenoi (Etruscans), PS 5, 17

Umbrians, PS 16
underground people, SK 6
unedo (fruit), Jub 30
unguents, traded, *PME* 24, 49
units of measurement, §IV
unknown lands: Mkn B $1_{12, 16, 43-4, 46}$; beyond Azania, *PME* 18; of Thinai, *PME* 66
Utica, PS 111_5

Varro, on maps, §V.4
Vatopedinus 655, §VIII.2.a
Veneti, PS 19
verse writing, §VII.5.b, §VI.3
vessels (utensils), traded, *PME* 6, 8
Vicarello cups, §VI.1.f
vines, at Damascus, Pos 58
violets, and etymology, Hek 33
visibility, at sea, Art 69
volcanoes, §III.4.b, Han 14 n., 15–16, B 2, B 3_{95}, B 7, Pyt 27, *Nik* 257–61, Pos 41, 44, DM 4_8
Volsci, PS 9
votives, on Achilles' I., Arr 21_{2-3}, 22_{1-2}, *Eux* 95
vulcanism, §III.4.b

waters: AWP 7–9, 19_4; variation, Agc 66
wealth: of Sabaioi, Art 98_{19}; of Sabaioi & Gerrhaioi, Agc 104
weapons: Aithiopian, Art $44b_{84}$; traded, *PME* 17; fire-hardened, PS 112_9, Agc $53b_2$
weather: causes, Tim $38_{364b\,21-365a\,5}$, DM 2_6, $4_{1,11}$; forecasting, Hip 9; violent, §III.4.b
wells: Eud 7, Era 33_{183}; at Gadeira, Pos 38
Western Aithiopes, PS 112_{5-12}, *Nik* 157
Western Asia: Isi B 10, Hek 81–8; distances, Era 72_9, Hip 31–2, Isi A 1; peoples, Era 72,

81, 83, *Exp* 3–15; regions, Era 73, 75, 82, 83, DP 897–1079; rivers, Era 71, 74
western central Greece, DK 24–57
Western Sea (Ocean), DP 58–68
wild animals, *PME* 38, 40, 50, 55
Wild Men, Agc 61, Art 98_{10}
wind rose: monumentalized (?), Tim intr.; of eight, Agm 6; of twelve, Agm 7
winds: *AWP* 3–6, 19_2, Tim 18, 33, 38, Era 9; Aristotle on, ch. 10 app.; causes, *DM* 4_3; dangers, Arr 3_2–5_3; in Black Sea, *Eux* 39, 93; in tropics, Agc 107b–108; morning, *Eux* 44; names, Tim 3, 18, *DM* 4_4, Arr 4_{2-3}, 6_1, 21, Agm 6–7, *Hyp* 37–8; offshore in morning, Arr 3_2; peoples in direction of each, Agm 7; seasonal, *DM* 4_5; translation of names, §X.3.b; violent, *DM* 4_6
wine, traded, *PME* 6–7, 17, 24, 36–7, 39, 49, 56
Woman's City, Art 136
women: Aithiopian, Art $44a_3$; at Thebes, HK 1_{17-19}; dress, Art 64; health, *AWP* 3_3, 4_4, 7_6, 8, $10_{3-6, 12}$; geographers, §VI.4.c fin.; in gold mines, Agc 26; of Heliopolis (Syria), *Exp* 30; of Hellespont, *Exp* 48; of Nomades, *AWP* 18_4; of Paphlagonia & Pontus, *Exp* 44; of Sauromatai, *AWP* 17_{2-3}; rulers, Agc B 3_8, Art 98_8, *Exp* 20; Skythian, *AWP* 20_2, 21_{2-3}; see also Portus Mulierum
wonders, in geographical writing, §III.3.m
Wood-eaters, Agc 52
words (*see also* etymology), notable, Mna 10

Xenon (unknown poet), quoted, HK 1_6
Xenophon of Athens: §VI.2.c, Arr 1_1, 2_3, 12_2, *Eux* 5, 32, 50, 117; cited, Arr 12_2, 16_3; expedition, Arr 12_5

Zeugma, Isi A 1_1
Zeus: titles, *DM* 7_{1-3}; *see also* god, the; *and next entry*
Zeus Ourios (Hieron), Arr 12_2, 25, *Eux* 1–3, 119–21
Zmiinyi I., *see* Leuke
zodiac, *DM* 2_{3-4}
zones, of latitude: §III.3.f, Era 28–9, 32, Hip 15, 136, 44, Pos $2_{2.1-3.4}$, 4, *Hyp* 2; number, Pos 13; *see also* frigid z.; temperate z.; torrid z.